Using the Biological Literature

BOOKS IN LIBRARY AND INFORMATION SCIENCE

A Series of Monographs and Textbooks

FOUNDING EDITOR

Allen Kent

School of Library and Information Science
University of Pittsburgh
Pittsburgh, Pennsylvania

1. Classified Library of Congress Subject Headings: Volume 1, Classified List, *edited by James G. Williams, Martha L. Manheimer, and Jay E. Daily*
2. Classified Library of Congress Subject Headings: Volume 2, Alphabetic List, *edited by James G. Williams, Martha L. Manheimer, and Jay E. Daily*
3. Organizing Nonprint Materials, *Jay E. Daily*
4. Computer-Based Chemical Information, *edited by Edward McC. Arnett and Allen Kent*
5. Style Manual: A Guide for the Preparation of Reports and Dissertations, *Martha L. Manheimer*
6. The Anatomy of Censorship, *Jay E. Daily*
7. Information Science: Search for Identity, *edited by Anthony Debons*
8. Resource Sharing in Libraries: Why · How · When · Next Action Steps, *edited by Allen Kent*
9. Reading the Russian Language: A Guide for Librarians and Other Professionals, *Rosalind Kent*
10. Statewide Computing Systems: Coordinating Academic Computer Planning, *edited by Charles Mosmann*
11. Using the Chemical Literature: A Practical Guide, *Henry M. Woodburn*
12. Cataloging and Classification: A Workbook, *Martha L. Manheimer*
13. Multi-media Indexes, Lists, and Review Sources: A Bibliographic Guide, *Thomas L. Hart, Mary Alice Hunt, and Blanche Woolls*
14. Document Retrieval Systems: Factors Affecting Search Time, *K. Leon Montgomery*
15. Library Automation Systems, *Stephen R. Salmon*
16. Black Literature Resources: Analysis and Organization, *Doris H. Clack*
17. Copyright–Information Technology–Public Policy: Part I–Copyright–Public Policies; Part II–Public Policies–Information Technology, *Nicholas Henry*
18. Crisis in Copyright, *William Z. Nasri*
19. Mental Health Information Systems: Design and Implementation, *David J. Kupfer, Michael S. Levine, and John A. Nelson*

ADDITIONAL VOLUMES IN PREPARATION

Using the Biological Literature: A Practical Guide

Third Edition, Revised and Expanded

Diane Schmidt and Elisabeth B. Davis
University of Illinois at Urbana-Champaign
Urbana, Illinois

Pamela F. Jacobs
University of Guelph
Guelph, Ontario, Canada

MARCEL DEKKER, INC.   NEW YORK · BASEL

ISBN: 0-8247-0667-6

The second edition was published as *Using the Biological Literature: A Practical Guide, Second Edition, Revised and Expanded*, by Elisabeth B. Davis and Diane Schmidt.

This book is printed on acid-free paper.

Headquarters
Marcel Dekker, Inc.
270 Madison Avenue, New York, NY 10016
tel: 212-696-9000; fax: 212-685-4540

Eastern Hemisphere Distribution
Marcel Dekker AG
Hutgasse 4, Postfach 812, CH-4001 Basel, Switzerland
tel: 41-61-261-8482; fax: 41-61-261-8896

World Wide Web
http://www.dekker.com

The publisher offers discounts on this book when ordered in bulk quantities. For more information, write to Special Sales/Professional Marketing at the headquarters address above.

Current printing (last digit):
10 9 8 7 6 5 4 3 2 1

PRINTED IN THE UNITED STATES OF AMERICA

Preface

This book grew out of a series of handouts prepared for students using the Biology Library at the University of Illinois at Urbana-Champaign. Its purpose is to acquaint students new to the literature of biology with important primary and secondary resources of the field. Aimed toward undergraduate and graduate biology students, it is also appropriate for anyone interested in searching the biological literature and keeping up with its bibliography.

This guide to the literature of the biological sciences presents a comprehensive list of important sources that may be found in large research libraries, with an emphasis on current materials in the English language. Retrospective reference works have been selected for historical perspective and to provide access to the taxonomic literature. All the main fields of the biological sciences are covered; applied areas such as medicine, clinical psychology, veterinary medicine, agriculture, horticulture, nutrition, and the teaching of biology are not included.

The entries are grouped by subject area, into chapters, which are subdivided by form of material. Entries are annotated only once according to their primary focus, although some are cross-referenced elsewhere. Every textbook listed is recommended, although not all of them are annotated. A certain knowledge of scientific literature is assumed, and there is minimal explanation of the definitions, uses, or importance of primary and secondary literature. A very brief discussion of searching strategies and indexing policies is included in Chapter 2, but it is assumed that more detailed information on how to search for information in the biological sciences is available elsewhere. Periodical editorial policy and subject scope have been included with journal annotations as an aid to the student looking for publication possibilities. Unless otherwise cited, quotations in the body of an annotation are taken from prefatory material of the item under consideration. Finally, annotations in this edition have been expanded to compare the use of similar resources.

The second edition of *Using the Biological Literature* was published just

as the development of Web browsers such as Mosaic and the subsequent explo-
sion of Web-accessible resources changed information-seeking behavior. The
third edition features greatly expanded coverage of Web information, although
most standard, authoritative resources are still to be found in the print format.
Electronic journals have also become much more common since the second edition was published, and a discussion of their complicated subscription and access
methods is included in Chapter 1. An associated Web page at www.library.uiuc.
edu/bix/biologicalliterature/ has been created, with links to all the major resources discussed in this edition.

This book could not have been written without assistance. We would like
to acknowledge the Research and Publication Committee of the University of
Illinois at Urbana-Champaign Library, which provided support for the completion
of this research. We would also like to thank Susan K. Kendall for her assistance
in editing the manuscript and suggesting titles to be added. In addition, we would
like to express our appreciation for the cooperation of the other life sciences
librarians and staff at the University of Illinois. In particular, the assistance of
the Biology Library staff and graduate assistants has been invaluable. And finally,
this book could not have been written without the excellent collections of the
University of Illinois Library.

Diane Schmidt
Elisabeth B. Davis
Pamela F. Jacobs

Contents

1

Introduction

The start of a new millennium is an auspicious time to review the sweep of events in the history of the biological sciences. The changes that have taken place over the last millennium have been nothing less than astounding. If Gutenberg's printing revolution 500 years ago was arguably the most influential event of the millennium, it is clear that the rise of the biological sciences and the transformation of information dissemination during the same period were astonishing. In a similar mode, the emerging dominance of the Internet in the worldwide distribution system for goods, services, and information has had an enormous impact on biological research and literature retrieval in the five years since the last edition of this book was published.

During this half decade, science has continued to expand in complexity and technical sophistication while the amount of science being published has increased at a breathless pace. The end result is a biological literature that is sorely pressed to respond to problems of accuracy in content, technical errors in execution, inferiority in production, and rise in cost. Big science, identified with the physical sciences forty years ago, has given way to big biology, shown by the swing of the pendulum as funds are diverted by U.S. politicians away from particle accelerators to research investigating the human genome, for example. Similarly, characteristics of big science have changed since physics was in the forefront: large experimental facilities as the centerpiece of a few major collaborative research programs have evolved into multiple user, multiexperimental facilities not dominated by any one scientific discipline. There is growing partnership and cooperation between separate scientific disciplines with the emergence of truly interdisciplinary approaches to scientific problems—big science coming of age, if you will. This initiative is reflected in bioscience education by the rearrangement of academic departments along the lines of the emerging emphasis on interdisciplinary research. Funding for research is available from a growing number of private philanthropic foundations, such as the Alfred P. Sloan Foundation, the Andrew W. Mellon Foundation, the Bill and Melinda Gates Foundation, the Howard Hughes Medical Research Institute, the M. J. Murdock Charitable Trust, and the Whitehead Institute for Biomedical Research, just to name a few of the more prominent contributors.

Scientific agenda in relation to ethical issues is becoming ever more consequential in the public dialogue of national advisory bodies, professional societies, religious institutions, and local governments. Recurring themes of biotechnology safety; Internet security; genetic engineering; patenting of living organisms; animal rights; redefinition of copyright law with regard to the digital revolution; and other fundamental ethical, moral, and legal questions are of intense concern and global significance to both the biologist and the informed layperson. There is legitimate apprehension that the establishment of information and knowledge elites will lead to a class struggle between the haves and have-nots, as those who possess scientific and technical expertise come to dominate input and outcome of economic, political, legal, and societal actions in the present information revolution.

The history of biological literature reflects the evolution of biology the discipline, and in this context it is interesting to review the progress of biology as a science to gain perspective into the development of its literature. The following description of biology's milestones will be brief with the understanding that the names, experiments, and publications singled out are representative, not enumerative of the biological advances made over the centuries.

EARLY HISTORY

The word *biology* was first used by Jean Baptiste Lamarck and Gottfried Treviranus in the early nineteenth century, but the study of living things began long before that. The ancient Greeks, and Aristotle in particular, are credited with "inventing" natural science. Although there was neither a social organization for science nor a self-perpetuating scientific community, knowledge was valued for its own sake as well as for the understanding of nature. There were few attempts to manipulate nature or apply scientific knowledge systematically. The important goal was the use of rational, general, and logical explanations—in other words, Greek culture valued a new way of looking at the natural world.

Aristotle has had an immense influence on the history of biology, evoking overall a high evaluation of his biological observations. His biology was intimately linked to experience and his theories relied on his astute observations of animal structure and human anatomy. Aristotle developed a comprehensive philosophy with the major premise being that everything in nature has a purpose. Although this concept of teleology was discarded at the time of Charles Darwin, this idea of final causes was valuable to the progress of biology. For example, William Harvey's discovery of how blood circulates was based on productive, biologically useful Aristotelian questions about the purposes of the veins.

Science in the Middle Ages was basically located in three centers: the Latin West, the Latin East, and Islamic countries. In the Latin West fragments of Greek science were passed on by the scholastics in monasteries. Although basic knowledge was preserved, nothing new was added. Pliny's encyclopedic *Natural History* represented all that was known of natural history in the West. Byzantium was able to preserve more than its Western counterpart but the outcome was the same: preservation was the mode during the Dark Ages. Islamic countries, as the third center, made more rapid progress in spreading Greek science. The Arabs' political expansion and assimilation were expeditious in using Greek knowledge and promoting support for medical, astrological, and mathematical study. Islam not only preserved Greek science, it added to it. Galen, the most important ancient physician and teacher other than Hippocrates, was almost unknown outside of Islam. His work, translated into Arabic and then again into Latin, remained the authority for medical students for hundreds of years despite its many inaccuracies. In fact, Galen's work was virtually unquestioned until the sixteenth century when Vesalius' willingness to dissect and to experiment raised scientific investigation to a new level signaling the beginnings of modern science.

Until the sixteenth century, scientific writings were preserved in manuscript and copies of books were rare, expensive to own and to duplicate. Descriptive writing, commentary, and herbals represent the incunabula left to posterity. Not until the invention of the printing press in the sixteenth century was scientific writing available to the common person.

SEVENTEENTH CENTURY

Some of the scientists important to seventeenth-century biology were William Harvey, Rene Descartes, Frances Bacon, Marcello Malpighi, and Antonie van Leeuwenhoek. Harvey epitomized experimentation in biology in contrast with Descartes, whose theories reduced everything to mechanical explanations, a point of view that ultimately failed. The name Francis Bacon is linked to the scientific revolution and to the inspiration of the Royal Society of London. Although he made no discoveries himself, he was a reformer who advocated observation, collection, and organization of data. Bacon, who had a great impact on science, promoted experimentation, emphasized systematic investigation, and encouraged publication of results. He believed science to be utilitarian, and that knowledge leads to the relief of humanity's estate.

The seventeenth century saw the spread of the printed word and the organization of learned societies to disseminate information about scientific investigations. The first journal serving scientists, the *Philosophical Transactions of the Royal Society of London*, was begun in 1665 (and is still being published), and by 1880 there were 100 journals serving scientific purposes. The mid-seventeenth century saw a new value system for science based on the beliefs that science was communal and that knowledge was secular and apolitical and should be shared. There was high interest in experimentation and the mode of science was mathematical and utilitarian. In England, France, and Italy learned societies were the major transmitters of scientific values and were instrumental in the systematic communication of scientific results.

The microscope was discovered in the seventeenth century by Dutch lensmakers but its use, for the most part, passed into the hands of amateurs. Antonie van Leeuwenhoek was not a trained or educated person and his observations on microscopic life allowed no biological generalizations. Robert Hooke described "cells" in cork; even so, the microscope as a scientific instrument did not demonstrate its power until the problems of light source and spherical and chromatic aberrations were resolved in the nineteenth century. The Italians put the microscope to the most use; for example, Marcello Malpighi used the instrument in his embryological investigations to contribute to the studies of preformation, epigenesis, ovism, and spontaneous generation that were of interest to seventeenth-century biologists. Unfortunately, difficulties of generation and development were too complicated and complex to reduce to simple chemical or mechanical analogies.

John Ray, the seventeenth-century botanist, gave the first modern description of species based on morphological, structural, and biological information. Classification attempts such as his were somewhat more successful in terms of organization but there were serious problems with extant and fossil species that were for the time being insoluble. In summary, problems in biology yielded only sparingly to the various attacks of the seventeenth century, and there were very few lasting achievements.

EIGHTEENTH CENTURY

The eighteenth century may be characterized as an energetic age of exploration, collection, and organization. As an example of this activity, the number of described plant species is relevant: in 1700, 6,000 species were ascertained; by 1800, there were 50,000. J. J. Dillenius was employed by William Sherard of England to be, probably, the first person in history paid as a full-time taxonomist.

Carolinus Linnaeus was the dominant figure of the eighteenth century. To this day, he reigns supreme as a classifier and inventor of the binomial system of classification. He was a prodigious writer, an indefatigable worker, and an amazing teacher whose inspired disciples explored the world proselytizing botanists to the Linnean system, providing descriptive standards and stimulating research. Linnaeus' most important rival was the Comte de Buffon, an extraordinary writer and the author of a great natural history for the layperson.

In the New World most of the biological work was carried on by naturalists, college professors, and physicians trained as botanists. Science was a transplant with a great dependence on Mother England, with the result that much of the biological literature was transmitted to England for publication in the *Philosophical Transactions of the Royal Society of London*. American biologists and botanists operated on personal funds with extremely limited facilities and with little formal training or education. Americans were busy being pioneers and science was limited to natural history, practically the only way that untrained amateurs could compete. Men such as John and William Bartram, John Bannister, and Thomas Jefferson all made contributions to biological knowledge, overcoming arduous conditions and difficulties that made science a dangerous and uncertain undertaking. The most famous early American scientist was, of course, Benjamin Franklin, whose discoveries, inventions, experiments, and commentaries are well chronicled.

Biology was in a transitional phase during the eighteenth century, compelled to wait on the chemical revolution begun by Lavoisier in the late 1780s before it could fully develop as a scientific discipline. By the end of the eighteenth century the characteristics of the industrial revolution became the characteristics of science: it was middle class, nonestablishment, provincial, nonconformist, and applied to industrial use.

New forms of communication and new specialized societies were established in the eighteenth century. Itinerant lecturers published their lectures as scientific texts, and the appearance of greatly ambitious encyclopedias, such as Diderot's *Encyclopedie* in 1751, represented intellectually significant achievements. Numerous societies continued to publish their members' scientific papers, allowing biological events to be recorded and disseminated. There was a maturity in the development of science around 1800 as a consensus of scientific identity and method emerged. The appearance of social institutions and the gathering of a broader base of social support and interest permitted science to rise as an authority, to challenge traditional influences, and to stand on its own as an independent source of knowledge. The number of scientific journals grew from 100 in 1800 to 10,000 in 1900, an incredible increase that forced the development of the great abstracting and indexing tools of the nineteenth century because biologists could no longer depend on their own reading to cover the scientific literature. Botanists relied on *Botanisches Centralblatt*, *Just's Botanischer Jahresbericht*, and *Zeitschrift für Pflanzenkrankheiten*; zoologists trusted *Zoologischer Bericht*, *Berichte über Wissenschaftliche Biologie*, and *Zoological Record*; bacteriologists used *Zentralblatt für Bakteriologie*.

NINETEENTH CENTURY

Biology in the nineteenth century made quite striking advances based on the consolidating concepts of evolution, cellular organization, and the germ theory of disease. Rigorous methodology had developed, and biology was recognized as a unified discipline focusing on the processes of life and the functions of the organism. Natural history was discarded as physical and chemical terms were used to explain physiological processes.

The many unanswered questions emanating from the multitude of biological explanations of the eighteenth century culminated in making evolution the major concept of the nineteenth century. The works of Buffon, Erasmus, Darwin, and Lamarck were precursors of evolutionary thought that set the stage for Charles Darwin's revolutionary work, *On the Evolution of Species by Means of Natural Selection*, published in 1859. Darwin's theory achieved eventual acceptance based on massive evidence and a selective mechanism for evolution. Not until the turn of the century, when Gregor Mendel's work in genetics was rediscovered, was Darwin's mechanism of evolution comprehensively explained.

After the American Revolution, America's scientific connections with England and the Royal Society were largely cut off and scientists traveled to France and then to Germany for their scientific training and education. During this period the United States had few really prominent natural historians. Science was still empirical, based on fieldwork, and not theoretical. Conflict between science and religion was fairly widespread in America. Most of the few American colleges were tiny, sectarian institutions organized to teach classical subjects and produce people of high moral character rather than to conduct research for the advancement of knowledge. It was only after the Civil War that American education was renovated, that scientific societies flourished, that Harvard was brought to scientific prominence, and that Johns Hopkins University was founded on the German laboratory and university model. By the end of the nineteenth century America had scientific eminence, scientific journals, academic scientists, educational institutions, and scientific societies with social approval.

TWENTIETH CENTURY

Mendelian genetics had an important effect on many naturalists, statisticians, and experimentalists in the United States who became involved in the modern theory of evolution. By 1911 the United States was leading the world in genetic research as money poured into land grant institutions, research careers had become a reality for biologists, and interest in agriculture had become popular. Thomas Hunt Morgan with his research on the genetics of the fruit fly *Drosophila melanogaster* became the first American to win a Nobel Prize. By the 1930s the scientific forces of paleontology, geology, genetics, and natural history were all contributing to the broad assumptions of evolution.

Probably the second most important biological event after Darwin occurred in 1953 when James D. Watson and Francis Crick published the results of their research on DNA. This revolution in molecular biology was vastly different from that of classical genetics almost a century earlier. The roots of molecular biology were founded in physical, biochemical, and structural research totally unlike the evidence collected by Charles Darwin and Alfred Wallace. Unlike the nineteenth century, scholarly competition was fierce. There was a huge amount of scientific information swirling around the participants, team research was in vogue, and massive funding was available. Watson and Crick rushed to publication, unlike Darwin, who waited 20 years to publish his theory after developing it.

The spectacular events popularized by *The Double Helix: A Personal Account of the Discovery of the Structure of DNA* epitomize the significant occurrences in biological literature during this period. Specialist literature abounded; big science begat big scientific publishing programs; academic science libraries became decentralized; and library collections experienced a remarkable growth rate. The need to collect both descriptive and functional literature put an unbelievable strain on biology library budgets. Not only was it necessary to provide the voluminous cumulative literature of a discipline based on rare and costly titles, complete runs of periodicals, and a large core of reference books, but it was also necessary to purchase new journal subscriptions and the latest editions of monographs in order to have available all the latest information.

TWENTY-FIRST CENTURY

While it is too early to say for certain what biological research will be like in the twenty-first century, the trends begun in the last half of the twentieth century will undoubtably continue to influence activities well into the future. Molecular biology, genomics, biotechnology, and related fields will continue to expand and produce major new discoveries and products. However, plain old taxonomy and other basic organismal sciences are experiencing a resurgence and this will continue. The current emphasis on biodiversity and conservation has produced an interest in at least identifying the world's living organisms before they become extinct.

The publication of the results of the Human Genome Project provide a good preview of what will likely be the future of the literature of Big Science. Two groups raced to be the first to create a draft, a public project titled the International Human Genome Sequencing Consortium (IHGSC) and a private company called Celera Genomics. While the results were published in mid-February 2001 in special issues of *Science* and *Nature*, the most traditional of formats, the sequence itself is nearly unusable in print format. It was made available at a Web site hosted by the University of California at Santa Cruz (http://genome. cse.ucsc.edu/) and individual gene sequences continue to be submitted to public databases such as GenBank, DDBJ, and EMBL (see Chapter 6, ''Molecular and Cellular Biology,'' for further discussion of these databases). The journal issues were made freely available on the Web at http://www.nature.com/genomics/ (*Nature*) and http://www.sciencemag.org/content/vol291/issue5507/ (*Science*). The tensions between the public and private ventures were widely reported and are almost certainly a sign of a continuing trend as commercial interests and basic research converge.

The growth and expansion of the scientific literature is another continuing trend. Almost every biology library currently faces a crisis due to the cost of serial publications. More and more journals are published each year, and established journals regularly increase their frequency or page count and with that, their price. In the early 1990s, it was not unusual for journal prices to go up 20% in a single year. Clearly, library budgets cannot hope to keep up with these increases, and thus since the mid-1980s, almost every library has been forced to cancel journals, many of them forced into an annual ritual of cancellation.

There are many causes for this budget crisis, including the publish-or-perish dilemma of untenured faculty and the ever-increasing amount of research being done. For example, in 1999 the life sciences accounted for more than 50% of U.S. federal investment in basic research, a great change from funding for basic research that took place from World War II through the 1990s and focused basically on physical sciences and engineering. The attendant proliferation of specialist biology journals and the effect of the changing strength of the dollar on titles published elsewhere also had major impact. The scientists are frequently well aware of the problem, having seen journals of importance for their own research get canceled. Various remedies have been proposed, including efforts to get promotion and tenure decisions based on quality of research rather than quantity (thus avoiding the ''salami syndrome'' in which a project is sliced into many small articles rather than one major one).

Another source of journal price increase comes from the dawning of the electronic age in publishing. Publishers are trying numerous experiments in electronic publishing, often passing their start-up costs along to libraries. They also fear the loss of revenue from individual subscribers canceling personal subscriptions if they are available for free in libraries. Both of these pressures have led to an increased cost of serials.

The crisis in library funding has been a long time in the making, and efforts are underway to relieve the strain. Libraries have joined together in regional and national consortia to serve larger groups of users with interlibrary loan and access to Internet-based electronic resources. Academic faculty, professional associations, and governmental bodies are looking at ways to subsidize scholarly communications, streamline journal production, and centralize report distribution using both print and electronic means. Probably the best hope for access to the scientific literature lies in some combination of solutions, but this transition is a timc-consuming one and its results may not be clearly evident until well into the future.

CHARACTERISTICS OF BIOLOGICAL LITERATURE

Characteristics of the biological literature are typical of other scientific disciplines. Bonn and Smith report an estimated 55,000 sci/tech titles worldwide, with about 9,500 titles from the United States. About 95% of the cited literature in the sciences is published in serials. Thus, biological literature is international in scope; dependent on serial publications for dissemination; interdisciplinary, and overlapping; and complex in origin, with the primary periodical as the most important source of new information. Biological literature is distinguished by its broad spectrum, its volume, its generator who is also its user, and its appeal to the public interest.

In general, the number of scientific, scholarly periodicals has doubled every 10- to 15-year interval during the twentieth century. Since World War II, however, there has been logarithmic growth of serial publications and the growth of biological journals has paralleled this burst. The increase during the last decade has been especially explosive for the life sciences, making it one of the fastest growing disciplines.

The source of all this activity can be attributed to learned societies, commercial publishers, and university presses. Types of literature issued from points of origin are primary, secondary, and tertiary publications. Primary publications report original research, the first published record of scientific investigations, and are represented by periodicals, preprints, research reports, patents, dissertations, and trade technical bulletins. Secondary literature publications are reference works that derive from primary sources. Examples are encyclopedias, handbooks, treatises, bibliographies, reviews, abstracting and indexing serials, and translations. Tertiary sources, which discuss science rather than contribute to it, are textbooks, directories, and guides to the literature.

The geographic origin of biological literature may be fairly described using the information provided by BIOSIS, publisher of *Biological Abstracts*, the largest, most comprehensive biological abstracting service in the English language. Surveys of the literature sources monitored by BIOSIS in 2000 report that about 52% were from Europe and the Middle East, 31% from North America, 14% from Australia and Asia, 2% from Central and South America, and 1% from Africa. Growth in biological literature since World War II has been particularly great from Japan, Russia, and from Spanish-Portuguese publications.

In 1962 Bourne reported that English was the dominant language of scientific literature, and this is still true today, as more and more journals are being published in, or being translated into, English. Garfield and Welljams-Dorof reported in 1992 that 95% of the microbiology articles indexed in *Science Citation*

Index in 1991 were in English, with Russian the next most frequent at a mere 5%. The results are similar in other indexes.

The most popular frequency of biological serials is irregular, followed by quarterly, monthly, and annual publications in decreasing order. Subject coverage and emphasis of biological literature are on basic and applied research that is interdisciplinary. The biological literature is scattered, fragmented, and dispersed with 65 to 68% of cited articles appearing in less than 20% of the biological journals. Over the last decade the interfacing, overlap, and integration of disciplines have been typical of biology with tremendous growth especially in areas relevant to endocrinology, immunology, and the neurosciences. Biological investigations often have more immediate, apparent impact on society, and because of this characteristic research in the life sciences is heavily reported and critiqued in the popular press. The power of the biological revolution is visible through articles on biotechnology, aging, molecular genetics and the genetics of diseases such as breast cancer, and computational aspects of various disciplines, just to name a few topics of wide interest.

ELECTRONIC BIOLOGICAL LITERATURE

The vast proliferation of the biological literature has made the computer an indispensable part of any biologist's toolkit. Abstracts and indexes have been computerized since the early 1970s and were originally searched by trained intermediaries such as librarians and information specialists. Beginning in the mid-1980s, CD-ROMs (Compact Disk-Read Only Memory) have widened the access of electronic databases beyond the expert searcher and have allowed the end-user (the person actually using the information) to perform his or her own searches. In addition, many libraries offer locally mounted or Web-accessible databases for their patrons. These databases are available with many different search engines, some easier to use than others but all intended for untrained users.

The early wave of computerization made secondary tools such as abstracts and indexes more widely available and more easily used. The next wave, which is still in progress, is to improve access to the primary literature, particularly journal articles. Electronic journals have become commonplace today; only a few years ago they were a novelty, eliciting a great deal of discussion concerning utility, availability, cost, archival storage, ownership, intellectual property rights, peer review, and copyright compliance. These controversial issues are still relevant, but publishers are moving rapidly into the electronic age. All of the major commercial publishers and most of the major association publishers currently make their journals available electronically, and there are several initiatives in the biological sciences to aid smaller society publishers move to full text. Stanford University Library has been offering electronic publishing assistance since 1995 through its HighWire Press (http://www.highwire.org). They currently provide access to nearly 200 journals published by societies and university presses. A more recent initiative made by the Scholarly Publishing and Academic Resources Coalition (SPARC), called BioOne (http://www.bioone.org), will create a single database containing articles from journals published by member societies from the American Institute of Biological Sciences (AIBS). It was launched in April 2001 with about 30 journals participating, with more to come.

Almost all of the e-journals presently available are electronic versions of existing print journals. In the heady early days of electronic publishing a number of new paradigms were envisioned, including abolishing or drastically modifying the present system of peer review. Preprint archives such as Paul Ginsparg's Los Alamos physics service (http://xxx.lanl.gov) were seen as a way of providing speedy access to research. In fact, the physics preprint server has become one of the primary communications channels among high-energy physicists since its inception in 1991. Its very success has lead to a need for quality control, so arrangements were made with several major physics journals to provide a peer-reviewed ''stamp of approval'' for some of the submissions. A proposal for a similar preprint archive for the life sciences, made as part of National Institute of Health's (NIH's) PubMed Central initiative, was scrapped after protests from life sciences researchers who were concerned about the lack of quality control.

In some electronic publishing models, readers would post comments about the articles so that an article would be rated according to consensus among the community of like-minded researchers rather than by a just a few gatekeepers. In less radical models, new journals would be published in electronic format only, without a print equivalent but after undergoing the usual peer review process. The acceptance of even these more traditional new journals has been slow, however. The first well-funded online journal in the life sciences was the *Online Journal of Current Clinical Trials (OJCCT)*, which was founded in July 1992. Despite extensive efforts, it was initially difficult to find authors willing to publish in the journal, even after 1994, when it gained an official stamp of approval by becoming the first online journal indexed in *Index Medicus*.

One problem that a number of Web-savvy users have identified is the lack of links between citations in indexing databases such as Biological Abstracts to the actual full-text article. This should be a simple matter in the Web environment, and in fact standards exist to allow this cross-linking. The difficulty lies more in persuading publishers to cooperate with existing indexes rather than creating their own proprietary search engines. However, many databases have begun to link citations and full-text journals, though libraries may not have implemented these links due to licensing or other issues. PubMed, the free search engine for the Medline database (http://www.nlm.nih.gov/databases/freemedl.html), has offered direct links to full-text articles since 1999. Users can access full-text articles from journals for which their institution has subscriptions.

Another series of initiatives will create comprehensive full-text databases such as the NIH's PubMed Central (http://www.pubmedcentral.nih.gov/). This initiative is controversial and shows quite clearly how difficult it can be to make major changes in the realm of scientific publishing and dissemination. The original PubMed Central proposal, first publicized in March 1999, was for a single all-inclusive database containing biomedical research papers from traditional journals as well as preprints. The articles and preprints would be accessible at no cost to users. Both parts of the proposal proved to be controversial, and when the PubMed Central project went online in February of 2000, it was with a far more limited scope than originally planned. As of February 2001, only about 10 journals were available on PubMed Central. Traditional publishers who objected to aspects of the original proposal got together in November 1999 and came up with a plan of their own to create the Publisher's Reference Service, which cross-links references in full-text articles to articles from different publishers.

An equally controversial plan, developed and advanced by scientists, was proposed in the fall of 2000. The Public Library of Science proposal (available at http://www.publiclibraryofscience.org/) built upon the PubMed Central initiative. Scientists were asked to sign an open letter that urged publishers to allow the content of their journals to be freely available in central archives, or what the letter called an "an international online public library." The signers of the letter also pledged that they would not edit, publish in, or subscribe to journals that did not follow this policy. Both parts of the proposal were controversial. A number of scientific societies as well as commercial science publishers came out against the proposal, but it succeeded in generating a great deal of discussion and may result in more open access to older journal literature. Regardless of the direct results of the Public Library of Science proposal, this will certainly not be the last attempt to change scholarly communication as we know it.

Publishers, librarians, and scientists are uncertain about what to expect in the new world of electronic publishing. There are a number of models for electronic subscriptions, many of them not favoring libraries or users. A few years ago, the most common subscription format was to bundle the print and electronic subscriptions together at a single fee, with no choice about whether to subscribe to the electronic or print formats alone (the "free with print" model). Some publishers offer electronic subscriptions for an additional 20 to 30% of the print subscription fee, as long as the print subscription is continued. Others permit electronic-only subscriptions to their journals, usually at about 90% of the equivalent print subscription. Several publishers offer package deals, forcing libraries to subscribe to all of the publisher's electronic journals. Another trend is to allow only site licensing, where the cost of the subscription depends on the number of potential users. A growing number of journals offer free access to older articles, usually after one year. HighWire Press's site currently offers the largest number of free back issues. All of these subscription models may or may not include a choice of HTML or PDF formats. In some cases, institutions can not access PDF files (which are scanned images of journal pages), though individual subscribers can. Or perhaps the PDF files are only available for older articles, usually after one year. The variety of subscription models is nearly endless.

When computer networks burst upon the scene in the early 1990s, they profoundly changed the way in which researchers communicated. In many ways, the Internet is used as an expansion of the eternal invisible college. It makes networking and brainstorming with colleagues from distant areas a daily occurrence, rather than something that only happens at conferences or symposia. In addition to using e-mail, many researchers subscribe to one or more discussion groups such as USENET groups, listservs, or bulletin boards. These discussion groups make it convenient and easy to communicate with other experts and to tap into vast amounts of data, whether it is *Arabidopsis* genetics or molecular sequences.

While there is still a great deal of uncontrolled or unofficially sanctioned data available through the World Wide Web (WWW), the Web also houses an enormous data treasure trove of use to biologists. There are encyclopedias, dictionaries, nomenclatures, herbaria listings, museum holdings, historically important materials, and the roster goes on and on. Many of the authoritative resources developed by traditional publishers are only available by subscription, though limited sections of the resource may be freely accessible as a draw to the site. Of the free information, some of what is available is noncopyrighted, unreviewed information posted by volunteers or is rather narrow in scope. However, much of what is left is extremely valuable. Scientific associations and governmental agencies often have excellent Web sites that are full of data, for instance.

Researchers in the biological sciences create massive amounts of data that must be accessible to be useful. The data may include ecological data from long-term studies, the holdings of museum collections, or molecular or genetic sequences. Formerly, the data were published in articles or books and rarely updated, but with the development of the Internet, this material is far more accessible and easier to manipulate. Molecular biology is a good example of a discipline that uses electronic publishing to share new data with a multidisciplinary research community through electronic productions like GenBank, PDB (the Protein Data Bank), the Human Genome Project, and the like. What is unique about these databases is that data is accepted before being published in the journal literature, and in fact most journals require that sequences be added to GenBank prior to their publication in print.

The sudden appearance and exponential growth of the huge and complex Web has made it a victim of its own success in some ways. Information on the Web is linked in complex and arbitrary ways and its accessibility is often severely compromised by erratic indexing. According to Lawrence and Giles, writing in *Nature*, there is no single search engine that indexes more than 16% of the Web, and only 6% of Web servers have scientific or educational contents. All servers are significantly biased toward indexing the popular and well-linked pages, while new unlinked pages can take up to six months before appearing on search engine listings. Obviously, this situation can delay or prevent widespread usability of new high-quality information. The difficulty in keeping up with the ever-changing electronic world has also created a level of anxiety among users. A survey done by the Higher Education Research Institute at the University of California, Los Angeles found that keeping up with information technology beat out teaching loads and publication pressures as a source of stress (see http://www.gseis. ucla.edu/heri/cirp.htm). Keeping up with changing URLs is a problem that even search engines have not been able to completely solve. In recognition of the problem, all of the URLs for sites mentioned in this book will be collected together in a Web site and kept up-to-date for an extended period of time. You can find this page at http://www.library.uiuc.edu/bix/biologicalliterature/.

While the basic strategies and tactics of scientific research remain the same, electronic resources and the WWW are changing the medium in which biological information is exchanged and distributed. Internet-accessible sources are certainly enhancing and expanding, if not completely replacing, the authoritative print resources annotated in this book. As cyberspace becomes more transparent to the casual user and as authoritative, older materials are electronically converted to the Internet, its dependability and usefulness will increase. For now the Internet acts as a complement and/or a supplement—most people agree that printed materials have a higher comfort level and are handier to consult than the computer screen for most purposes. On the other hand, who's to say what the future will hold?

BIBLIOGRAPHY

Allen, D. E. *The Naturalist in Britain: A Social History*. London: Allen Lane, 1976.

The American College Teacher: National Norms for the1998–99 HERI Faculty Survey. Linda J. Sax et al. Los Angeles, CA: Higher Education Research Institute, University of California, Los Angeles, 1999. (Also available at http://www.gseis.ucla.edu/ heri/cirp.htm; accessed March 16, 2000.)

Arber, A. *Herbals: Their Origin and Evolution*. New, enl. ed. Cambridge, England: Cambridge University Press, 1938.

Bonn, George S. and Linda C. Smith. Review of scientific literature, sources, types, information science and the role of libraries and information technology. *McGraw-Hill Encyclopedia of Science and Technology*, 8th ed., v. 10. New York: McGraw-Hill, 1997, pp. 139–45.

Bourne, C. P. The world's technical journal literature: An estimate of volume, origin, language, field, indexing and abstracting. *American Documentation* 13:159–68, 1962.

Butler, Declan. The writing is on the web for science journals in print. *Nature* 397(6716): 195–200, 1999.

Drucker, P. F. Beyond the information revolution. *Atlantic Monthly* 284(4): 47–57, 1999.

Garfield, E. Has scientific communication changed in 300 years? *Current Contents/Life Sciences* 23(8): 5–11, 1980.

Garfield, E. and A. Welljams-Dorof. The microbiology literature: Language of publication and their relative citation impact. *FEMS Microbiology Letters* 100(1): 33–38, 1992.

Gribskov, M. The new biological literature. Editorial: *Bioinformatics* 15(5): 347, 1999.

The Human Genome (Special Issue). *Nature* 409(6822), 2001.

The Human Genome (Special Issue). *Science* 291(5507), 2001.

Jasanoff, Sheila. Knowledge elites and class war; would life be better if we left the difficult decisions to experts alone? *Nature* 401(6753): 531, 1999.

Kronick, D.A. The scientific journal: Devant le deluge. *Current Contents/Agriculture, Biology, and Environmental Sciences* 23(27): 6–10, 1992.

Lawrence, S. and C. L. Giles. Accessibility of information on the web. *Nature* 400(6740): 107–9, 1999.

Robbins, R. J. Biological databases: a new scientific literature. *Publishing Research Quarterly* 10(1): 3–27, 1994.

Siegfried, T. Science's century: a quantum leap in knowledge defined an era. *The Dallas Morning News*, October 19: 1F, 1998.

Steere, W. C. *Biological Abstracts/BIOSIS: The First Fifty Years. The Evolution of a Major Science Information Service*. New York: Plenum, 1976.

Thompson, K. S. Scientific publishing: An embarrassment of riches. *American Scientist* 82(6): 508–11, 1994.

2

Subject Access to Biological Information

INTRODUCTION

Unless a researcher is already completely familiar with all books and articles in a particular subject (and who is?), it is necessary to do subject searches. Finding material on a particular subject is often more complicated than it seems. However, whether searchers are looking for books or articles, and whether they are looking in a paper card catalog or index, or in a computer public terminal or database, some basics stay the same. Using the right terms to look up a subject is one of the most critical steps in finding useful material, along with looking in the right places. Naturally, there are many aids to help researchers find the material they are looking for. The vocabulary used by the people who classify books and create article indexes is one important aid.

This chapter will deal with some topics that are important when doing subject searches in the biological sciences. While knowing about Boolean logic, truncation symbols, and other database searching strategies is of critical importance in performing a complete and well-focused database or Web search, these topics will not be discussed here because there are many other places where searchers can find useful tips. Each database or Web search engine has help screens, for instance, though some of them are more useful than others.

DEFINITIONS

Controlled vocabulary describes any terms that are decided upon by indexers or catalogers and used to describe the subject of a book or article. These terms may or may not be the same words that an author uses to describe his or her writings. The form of controlled vocabulary that is most familiar to biologists is the use of scientific or Latin names. *Felis concolor* is the "controlled vocabulary" term for the animal that may be called puma, cougar, mountain lion, panther, painter, screamer, catamount, or lion.

Subject heading is the traditional way of describing the subject of a book. Anyone who has looked up a subject in a card catalog has used subject headings. They may consist of a main heading and one or more subheadings, such as "Flowers—North America—Identification." Usually, only a few subject headings are used to describe the entire book. The most commonly used subject headings at large libraries are the Library of Congress Subject Headings (LCSH). Smaller libraries may use the *Sears List of Subject Headings*, which is similar but less detailed.

While subject headings are usually used to describe whole books, *descriptor* is used to identify individual concepts covered in an article or, sometimes, a book. Descriptors usually define much narrower topics than subject headings do, and many more are used to describe the article, often up to 15 or 20. These descriptors are usually added to a record by indexers, who decide which words are used as descriptors.

The opposite of controlled vocabulary is *natural language* or *free text*, in which no attempt is made to standardize subject terms, and the author's own words are used to describe the subject. Searching for either puma or cougar in an index is an example of free-text searching.

One term that is often used to describe words used for natural language searching is *keyword*, which is usually just a term used to search for a topic anywhere in a record, including title, subject headings, abstract, and so on. Unfortunately, sometimes keyword is also used as a synonym for descriptor.

ADVANTAGES AND DISADVANTAGES

Controlled vocabulary terms offer many advantages when doing searches, but there are also disadvantages. Scientific names are an example of the advantages of using controlled subject terms to pull together all possible synonyms of a term. One does not need to think of all possible ways in which an author might name *Felis concolor*. Controlled terms also usually control for the use of plurals and alternate spellings. Searching for "puma" may miss items in which the word "pumas" is used. Controlled terms added to a record can also eliminate ambiguity in an author's selection of words. Is the cat in a title such as *The Ghost Cat of the Rockies* a cougar, a tabby cat, or just a figment of the author's imagination?

Controlled vocabulary terms may also be more specific than the associated natural-language terms. Stress, for instance, means one thing to a psychologist, another to an ecologist, and still another to a civil engineer. Using a subject heading such as "Stress, psychological" would eliminate those articles dealing with metal fatigue, and thus reduce the stress on the searcher.

Of course, there are disadvantages to using controlled vocabulary terms as well. One problem that is familiar to users of the LCSH system is matching your idea of the subject with LCSH's idea of the subject. It is not intuitively obvious, for instance, that "Motion pictures" is the proper term for movies and film, while videos are under "Video recordings." Under previous editions, the proper heading for beehives was "Honeybee—Housing," though "Beehives" is now correct. For books on wolverine behavior, is the proper heading "Wolverine—Behavior" or "Animal behavior—Wolverines"?

Another disadvantage to controlled vocabulary is that subject headings change slowly, if at all, so that hot new fields may be poorly covered. For instance, the field of bioinformatics is not indexed in LCSH as such. Books and journals are given subject headings such as "Computational biology" or "Molecular biology—data processing," among others. In addition, card catalogs and online systems may not be updated every time a change occurs, so unless cross references are included (and used), searchers may not find materials indexed under previous or subsequent headings.

Yet another serious problem is that different systems use different terms. The LCSH system uses "Tumors" while *Index Medicus* uses "Neoplasms," and either term will work in *Biological Abstracts*. Indexes such as the *Biology and Agriculture Index* and the *Reader's Guide to Periodical Literature* use subject headings that are similar, but not identical, to the headings used by the Library of Congress. For instance, these indexes use "Tumors" rather than "Neoplasms," as does LCSH, but they use "Cancer–Therapy" whereas LCSH uses "Cancer–Treatment." Each time a researcher uses a new system or index, he or she must figure out which of several possible terms is the "proper" one.

One way to avoid the problems involved with choosing the correct controlled vocabulary term is to do a search first using whatever terms seem appropriate, then examine the records that you find for terms that indexers or catalogers have used to describe the article or book. To find books on bioinformatics, for instance, do a keyword search on "bioinformatics" and then look at the subject terms for books that look interesting. Select subject headings that seem appropriate, such as "Computational Biology," "Genes—Analysis—Data processing," or "Amino acid sequence—Databases" and redo your search using one or more of these terms.

IMPORTANT INDEXING SYSTEMS FOR BIOLOGY

While it is entirely possible to do good searches without ever using controlled vocabulary, it is still useful to at least be aware of the main indexing systems. The three most important indexing systems for biologists are the LCSH system, Biological Abstracts Relational Indexing, and the Medical Subject Headings (MeSH) system. LCSH is used to find books, the Biological Abstracts codes are used to find articles in the print or computer versions of *Biological Abstracts*, and MeSH is used to locate either books or articles in medical areas, including the most important medical index, *Index Medicus*. For a more detailed description of *Biological Abstracts* and *Index Medicus* and their computer versions, see the chapter on abstracting and indexing tools. An additional important indexing scheme that deserves mention is that used by *Chemical Abstracts*.

Library of Congress Subject Headings

LCSH is published annually and has been in use since 1897. The most recent edition is the twenty-fourth, which was published in 2001. LCSH subdivides subject headings in several ways, including topical (such as "Flowers—Identification"), form of publication (such as "Flowers—Bibliography"), chronological period (such as "Flowers—Pre-Linnean works"), and geographical location (such as "Flowers—North America"). Several subheadings may be strung together, as in the earlier example of "Flowers—North America—Identification." In previous editions, and to some extent in the present edition, subject headings were often in inverted form. Thus, extinct birds were formerly listed under "Birds—Extinct," but are now listed as "Extinct Birds." Each edition of LCSH is published by the Library of Congress in the form of a thesaurus of headings. Currently there are five volumes of headings. There are many cross-references in these big, red subject-heading lists, including pointers leading to correct subject headings, as well as to broader, narrower, and related terms. The subject heading lists also include selected subheadings, although not all possible subheadings will be listed for each main heading. It is very helpful to consult the subject heading lists to find the proper heading or for suggestions for further searches for books.

LCSH is used in computer catalogs as well as in card catalogs. Some online systems have extensive cross-references leading to the proper LCSH term, while others do not. Where these cross-references are included, searching for material is made much easier. Whether searched in paper or on computer, however, using the correct LCSH will greatly improve the retrieval of useful materials.

Biological Abstracts

Biological Abstracts, the most important index for biologists, has some very useful and advanced subject indexing in its computerized version, which is known as BIOSIS Previews. Prior to 1998, BIOSIS used both keywords (natural language) and concept codes (controlled vocabulary). After 1998, they switched to using keywords and Relational Indexing, which is intended to preserve the relationship between search terms. Keywords are taken from the language used by authors, and are listed in the *BIOSIS Previews Search Guide*. The keywords listcd in the search guide are intended to give searchers search hints, but any term may be used as a keyword.

The Concept Codes used before 1998 were numeric codes for broad subject categories such as pollution or limnology. After 1998, these broad categories were searchable as phrases in the new Major Concept field. Several new fields have been developed in Relational Indexing, such as the PS field for parts or structures of organisms (the digestive system, for instance). There are now separate fields for diseases, chemicals, gene or protein sequences, methods, geopolitical locations, geological time periods, brand names, and several others. A new field, Alternate Indexing, has been developed that contains MeSH disease terminology (see following text). Other forms of indexing may be added to this field in the future.

BIOSIS also has several fields for searching for organisms. These fields include Super Taxa (for broad categories such as Mammalia), Organisms (for scientific or common names of species), and Taxa Notes (for common names of species and broader groups such as insects). An article on red wolves, for instance, would also be indexed in the Super Taxa group as Canidae, in the Organisms field as *Canis rufus*, and in the Taxa Notes field as Nonhuman mammal. The Super Taxa and Taxa Notes fields list taxonomic groups hierarchically, so our red wolves would be found listed as carnivores, nonhuman mammals, mammals, nonhuman vertebrates, vertebrates, and animals.

Medical Subject Headings

MeSH are the subject headings created by the National Library of Medicine (NLM) for use in medical library card and online catalogs, the print index *Index Medicus*, and the database MEDLINE, as well as the other publications of NLM. MeSH listings are updated every year, and are absolutely essential when using these sources.

The MeSH for use with the printed *Index Medicus* are published each year as Volume 1 of the *Cumulated Index Medicus*. A much more detailed listing for users of the online database MEDLINE is also published each year. The online aids consist of three separate volumes, of which the *Medical Subject Headings: Annotated Alphabetic List* is the most frequently used. This document lists all of the subject headings, as well as the allowable subheadings. This list is designed for the use of indexers, but it includes many notes that are equally useful for interested searchers.

Another MeSH listing is the *Permuted Medical Subject Headings*. This volume takes each significant word from the MeSH terms and lists all the MeSH, including cross-references, in which that term is used. Thus, under ''lobe'' the list includes ''Epilepsy, frontal lobe,'' ''Epilepsy, temporal lobe,'' ''Frontal lobe,'' ''Middle lobe syndrome,'' ''Occipital lobe,'' ''Optic lobe,'' ''Parietal lobe,'' and

''Temporal lobe.'' Users of PubMed can also use the MeSH Browser at http://www.ncbi.nlm.nih.gov:80/entrez/meshbrowser.cgi. This is a searchable database providing all of the detailed information found in the print *Medical Subject Headings* volumes.

MeSH divides up medical subjects very narrowly, while listing only broad subject headings for related but nonmedical subjects. As well as the main subject headings, MeSH also includes subheadings of various types, including publication types, geographic subheadings, and common descriptors that are added to every article to which they apply. These common descriptors (or ''check tags'') include terms such as ''animal'' (for animal studies), ''female,'' and ''in vitro.'' There are also topical subheadings, which further describe the subject heading. These subheadings include terms such as ''adverse effects'' and ''diagnostic use.''

A related medical subject classification used in MEDLINE is the tree structure, which is listed in *Medical Subject Headings: Tree Structures*. The tree structure is a hierarchical arrangement of the MeSHs, so that narrower subjects can be combined and searched using broader categories. Thus, A is anatomy, C is diseases, C4 is neoplasms, C4.557.337 is leukemia, C4.557.337.428 is lymphocytic leukemia, and C4.557.337.428.511 is acute lymphocytic leukemia. It is possible to search a broad subject by truncating the tree number (known as ''exploding'' the tree). Exploding C4.557.337 will retrieve all forms of leukemia. The help screens for the PubMed search engine at http://www.ncbi.nlm.nih.gov:80/entrez/query/static/help/pmhelp.html are extensive and contain much more information on searching the database. Also see Katcher's *MEDLINE: A Guide to Effective Searching*.

In addition to the PubMed MeSH Browser mentioned previously, users of PubMed have another useful aid. The database includes automatic term mapping. This means that terms that are not proper MeSH terms are matched against the MeSH Translation Table and other lists, and if an appropriate match is found the MeSH term will automatically be searched as well as the keyword. If the term is mapped to the right MeSH term, this can greatly improve search results, though it can also result in some odd or undesirable hits.

Chemical Abstracts

Chemical Abstracts does not use the same names for biologically or medically important chemicals as the other biological or medical indexes, which can have a significant impact on subject searches. Guanine, for instance, is accepted by *Index Medicus* and *Biological Abstracts*, but not by *Chemical Abstracts*. The *Chemical Abstracts Index Guide*, which is updated each year and with each *Cumulative Index*, lists the proper headings used in *Chemical Abstracts* for chemical compounds, classes of substances, applications, properties, and other subjects.

The *Index Guide* also lists the CAS (Chemical Abstracts Service) Registry Number for chemicals. These registry numbers are useful because they are often less complicated than their related chemical names and pull together all synonyms of a particular chemical. They are also used in many other databases, including all other CAS databases; MEDLINE and other medical databases and indexes; and BIOSIS Previews. An example of an *Index Guide* entry is the one for guanine, in which a searcher is directed to see 6H-Purin-6-one,2-amino-1,7-dihydro- or the Registry Number 73–40–5.

OTHER IMPORTANT SYSTEMS

While the previously discussed indexing systems are the most important for the field of biology, there are several others that merit mention. Each scientific index has its own subject headings list, with the exception of the *Science Citation Index*, which uses only author-provided keywords or keywords generated from the titles of cited articles. To use the other indexes to their fullest, it is useful to find the subject listing, often called a thesaurus, and give it some study. Indexes such as the *Bibliography of Agriculture* and *CAB (Commonwealth Agriculture Bureau) Abstracts* (which both use the *CAB Thesaurus*), the *CSA Biological Sciences Database*, *Psychological Abstracts*, and *Zoological Record* all have subject listings of varying importance. These thesauri, like the LCSH and MeSH lists, usually provide the approved subject terms as well as broader, narrower, and/or related terms.

INTERNET RESOURCES

Unlike library materials, which generally have good subject access, information available through the WWW is in a state of chaos. At present, there is little subject indexing, although this situation is improving. In this section, we will discuss general strategies for finding useful information. The situation is constantly changing, so the information provided here should be taken as only a general guide.

There are literally thousands of discussion groups, which have been created to allow like-minded enthusiasts to talk to each other. Topics range from *Chlamydomonas* research to women in biology. Many, though not all, are Usenet groups. Go to http://www.usenet.org/ for more information about Usenet groups. Most Usenet groups regularly post Frequently Asked Questions (FAQs) and often have good pointers to other sources of information. For instance, the BIOSCI/ bionet Frequently Asked Questions FAQ at ftp://rtfm.mit.edu/pub/usenet/bionet. announce/BIOSCI_bionet_Frequently_Asked_Questions is general in nature and provides information on a variety of discussion groups for biologists. In addition to the Usenet groups, there are over 30,000 LISTSERV mailing lists. Information about these LISTSERV lists can be obtained at the CataList Web site at http://www.lsoft.com/lists/listref.html.

The WWW now has about 800 million pages of poorly indexed but potentially valuable information. There are two basic strategies for finding Web resources on a topic of interest. One strategy is to use one of the many search engines such as Google or a meta-search engine such as metaCrawler. There are two problems with this strategy. The first is that no single search engine indexes more than a third of the Web, so you may miss many good sites. The second problem is that you may not be able to narrow your search down so that you find only relevant sites. Searching for ''wolf'' will get you information on both the Wolf Trap Foundation for the Performing Arts and the mammal (not to mention everyone named Wolf) unless your search is very carefully constructed. Searching for such a common word can bring up hundreds of thousands of pages, most of them completely irrelevant. All of the good search engines allow Boolean searching, which can help narrow your search, but unfortunately each search engine works in a slightly different way and help screens can be difficult to locate. It is very easy to do a bad search of the Web; doing a good one takes more effort.

The other strategy for finding useful Web pages is to use a directory of Web links. Yahoo (http://www.yahoo.com) is one of the first Web directories, though there are many others. More specialized directories include the Infomine collection from the University of California, Riverside (http://infomine.ucr.edu/Main.html), which seeks out resources of interest to academics or the Internet Public Library (http://www.ipl.org/index.text.html), which does the same for more general-interest material. These directories provide access to selected Web pages arranged in a subject hierarchy, and may also provide descriptions and evaluations of the Web sites. Several of the more useful of these general directories are listed in Chapter 3, ''General Sources.'' Many individuals and institutions have created more specialized directories of links. Most associations include lists of useful Web links on their home pages, for instance. These collections can be very narrowly focused and comprehensive, or general and superficial. The Web pages created by individuals are especially likely to become outdated, though of course any collection of links is vulnerable to obsolescence. The most extensive or valuable of these subject-specific directories are listed in each of the following subject chapters. In recognition of the fact that collections of URLs become outdated quickly, the URLs for resources listed in this book have been gathered together at http://www.library.uiuc.edu/bix/biologicalliterature/ and will be kept up to date.

BIBLIOGRAPHY

BIOSIS Previews Search Guide. 1977– . Philadelphia, PA: Biological Abstracts. Updated annually.

CAB Thesaurus. 1999 ed. Wallingford, England: CAB International, 1999. 2 v. ISBN 0851993664. Updated irregularly.

Chemical Abstracts Index Guide. v. 69– , 1968– . Columbus, OH: American Chemical Society. ISSN 0009-2258. Updated annually.

Katcher, Brian S. *MEDLINE: A Guide to Effective Searching*. San Francisco, CA: Ashbury Press, 1999. 149 p. ISBN 096734459X, 0967344506 (pa).

Life Sciences Thesaurus. 4th ed. Bethesda, MD: Cambridge Scientific Abstracts, 1998. ISBN 0942189477. Updated irregularly.

Library of Congress Subject Headings. 16th ed. Washington, DC: Cataloging Distribution Service, Library of Congress, 1993. 4 v. ISSN 1048-9711. Updated irregularly.

Medical Subject Headings: Annotated Alphabetic List. 1975– . Bethesda, MD: Medical Subject Headings Section, Library Operations, National Library of Medicine. ISSN 0147-5711. Updated annually.

Medical Subject Headings: Tree Structures. 1972– . Bethesda, MD: Medical Subject Headings Section, Library Operations, National Library of Medicine. ISSN 0147-099X. Updated annually.

Permuted Medical Subject Headings. 1976– . Bethesda, MD: Medical Subject Headings Section, Library Operations, National Library of Medicine. ISSN 1045-2338. Updated annually.

Sears List of Subject Headings. 16th ed. New York: Wilson, 1997. 786 p. ISBN 0824209206. Updated irregularly.

Thesaurus of Psychological Index Terms. 6th ed. Arlington, VA: American Psychological Association, 1991. ISBN 1557981116. Updated irregularly.

Zoological Record Search Guide. 1985– . Philadelphia, PA: BioSciences Information Service. Updated irregularly.

3

General Sources

This chapter describes selected sources that are relevant to biology in general, with no attempt to be comprehensive. These titles were chosen as especially appropriate for undergraduates needing an introduction to the field, or for anyone requiring sources covering the broad spectrum of the biological sciences. In addition, we have added a number of resources that are useful for new graduate students, including books on how to fit in to a lab, how to publish a paper, and so on. Knowledge of most of the publications annotated in this chapter is helpful in effectively utilizing the more specialized chapters that follow. Arrangement is by topic, presenting publications that acquaint readers to the field of biology from the viewpoint of the history of the life sciences, mathematical and statistical sources, and pertinent techniques, just to name a few of the sections that follow. These general sources may be used as a base upon which to expand or define more specific subjects, to open up the literature as a beginning, not an end.

ASSOCIATIONS

American Association for the Advancement of Science (AAAS). 1200 New York Ave., NW, Washington, DC 20005. URL: http://www.aaas.org. Founded 1848. This is the largest general scientific organization representing all fields of science. Membership includes 143,000 individuals and 296 scientific societies, professional organizations, and state and city academies. Objectives are to further the work of scientists to facilitate cooperation among them, to foster scientific freedom and responsibility, to improve the effectiveness of science in the promotion of human welfare, to advance education in science, and to increase public understanding and appreciation of the importance and promise of the methods of science in human progress. Publications include *Science*, *Science Books and Films*, *Science Education News*, symposium volumes, and general reference works. The

Web site provides information about AAAS, news about science and society, science education, careers, media, awards, science books and films, and more.

American Institute of Biological Sciences (AIBS). 1444 I St. NW, Ste. 200, Washington, DC 20005–2210. URL: http://www.aibs.org. Founded 1947. 6,000 members. This is a professional member organization and federation of biological associations, laboratories and museums whose members have an interest in the life sciences. Publications: *BioScience*, brochures, and a membership directory. The Web site includes information about AIBS, publications, an online membership directory, classified ads and employment, outreach and education, and online registration for meetings. AIBS member societies are participating in the electronic publishing venture, BioOne (see Chapter 1).

Association for Tropical Biology (ATB). c/o W. John Kress, Exec. Dir., Department of Botany, MRC-166, National Museum of Natural History, Smithsonian Institution, Washington, DC 20560. URL: http://atb.botany.ufl.edu/atb/. Founded 1963. 1,350 members. An international organization of persons who are interested in tropical biology, seeking to coordinate existing information and provide new information about the plants and animals (including humans) of the tropics. Affiliated with AIBS. Publications: *Biotropica; Tropinet.* The Web page provides links to both of these publications, and information about meetings, membership directory, staff, etc.

Association of Applied Biologists (AAB). Wellesbourne, Warwickshire CV35 9EF, England. URL: http://www.aab.org/uk. Founded 1904. 1,200 members. Research scientists in private and state applied biology institutes and universities in 60 countries interested in furthering development in the field of applied biology. Publications: *Annals of Applied Biology.*

Association of Systematics Collections (ASC).1725 St. NW, Ste. 601, Washington, DC 20006-1401. URL: http://www.ascoll.org/. Founded 1972. 125 members. Educational institutions, museums, and government agencies (which maintain permanent collections in systematics biology) aim to foster the care, management, preservation, and improvement of systematics collections and to facilitate their use in science and society. Publishes *ASC Newsletter.* The Web page contains information about ASC and its resources; news of special interests to members.

Canadian Federation of Biological Societies (CFBS); Federation Canadienne des Societes de Biologie (FCSB). 750 Courtwood Crescent, Ste. 215, Ottawa, ON, Canada K2C 2B5. URL: http://www.cfbs.org. Founded 1957. 12 members. Biological societies representing 3,000 biologists and professionals in related fields. Promotes the advancement of the biological sciences and biology education; seeks to insure the development of a forward-looking science and technology policy for Canada. Publications: *CFBS Newsletter*; membership directory. The Web page links to information about the society, members, grants and awards, publications, the annual meeting, and so forth.

Council of Biology Editors (CBE). c/o Drohan Management Group, 11250 Roger Bacon Dr., Ste.8, Reston, VA 20190-5202. Phone: (703) 437-4377. Founded 1957. 1,289 members. Active and former editors of primary and secondary journals in the life sciences and those in scientific publishing and editing consider all aspects of communication in the life sciences with emphasis on publication, especially in primary journals and retrieval in secondary media. Publications: *CBE Views*, membership directory, *Scientific Style and Format*, and assorted brochures and pamphlets.

Federation of American Societies for Experimental Biology (FASEB). 9650 Rockville Pike, Bethesda, MD 20814–3998. URL: http://www.faseb.org. Founded 1912. 40,000 members in 10 member societies. Member societies include American Physiological Society, American Society for Biochemistry and Molecular Biology, American Society for Pharmacology and Experimental Therapeutics, American Society for Investigative Pathology, American Society for Nutritional Sciences, American Association of Immunologists, American Society for Cell Biology, Biophysical Society, American Association of Anatomists, and The Protein Society. Publishes the *FASEB Journal*, a directory of members, and a newsletter. The Web page has links to the member societies, public affairs, career resources, meetings and conferences, membership directories, publications, and employment opportunities.

Institute of Biology (IOB). 20 Queensberry Place, London, Greater London SW7 2DZ, England. URL: http://www.iob.org. Founded 1950. 17,000 members. The purpose of this group is to advance education and research in biology. Conducts educational programs and presents awards. Publications: *Biologist*, the *Journal of Biological Education*, and occasional publications. The Web page provides links to information about IOB, education and training, news, publications, the IOB shop, membership, affiliated societies, and U.K. branches.

International Union of Biological Sciences (IUBS); Union Internationale des Sciences Biologiques. c/o Dr. Talal Younes, 51 Blvd. de Montmorency, F-75016 Paris, France. URL: http://www.iubs.org. Founded 1919. 117 member societies. This is an organization of national societies and international associations and commissions engaged in the study of biological sciences. Their aims are to promote the study of biological sciences; to initiate, facilitate, and coordinate research and other scientific activities; to ensure the discussion and dissemination of the results of cooperative research; to promote the organization of international conferences; and to assist in the publication of their reports. Publications: *Biology International*; the proceedings of the IUBS General Assembly; a directory. The

Web page links to IUBS information about programs, biodiversity data, young scientists, women in biology, and developing countries.

Marine Biological Association of the United Kingdom (MBAUK). The Laboratory, Citadel Hill, Plymouth, Devon PL1 1PB, England. URL: http://www.mba. ac.uk. Founded 1884. 1,500 members. Marine biologists, botanists, and scientists encourage cooperation among members; disseminates information on latest research; studies living resources of the seas. Publications: *Journal of the Marine Biological Association.* The Web page provides access to MBA information, research, biodiversity initiative, education, communication, membership, and other sites of interest.

National Academy of Sciences (NAS). 2101 Constitution Ave. NW, Washington, DC 20418. Phone: (202) 334–2000, Fax: (202) 334-2158. URL: http://www. nas.edu. Founded 1741. 1,600 members. Honorary organization dedicated to the furtherance of science and engineering. Members are elected in recognition of their distinguished and continuing contributions. Founded by an act of Congress to serve as official adviser to the federal government on scientific and technical matters. Publishes *Proceedings of the National Academy of Sciences of the United States of America* and *Biographical Memoirs.* The very extensive Web site provides information on the Academy, news bulletins, numerous online reports created by the Academy, and links to the National Academy Press. Nearly 2,000 books published by the press can be viewed for free on their Web site.

Society for Experimental Biology (SEB); Societe de Biologie Experimentale (SBE). Burlington House, Piccadilly, London, Greater London W1V 0lQ, England. URL: http://www.sebiology.com. Founded 1923. 2,150 members. Experimental biologists, students, universities, and scientific institutions involved in disseminating information on recent advances in experimental biological research. Publications: *Journal of Experimental Botany; The Plant Journal*; proceedings of symposia. The Web page provides information about the society, their membership, publications, meetings, education, travel grants, news, jobs, and online access to *B.U.G.S.: Biology Undergraduate Stuff*, which is basically a news site about careers, learning resources, competitions, societies, etc.

Society for Experimental Biology and Medicine (SEBM). 195 W. Spring Valley Ave., Maywood, NJ 07607. URL: http://www.sebm.org. Founded 1903. 1,500 members and 3 regional groups actively engaged in research in experimental biology and experimental medicine. Publication: *Experimental Biology and Medicine* (formerly *Proceedings of the Society of Experimental Biology and Medicine*). The Web site links to SEBM governance, meetings, chapters, membership, and travel grants.

Society of Systematic Biologists (SSB). EEB U-3043, University of Connecticut, Storrs, CT 06269-3043. URL: http://www.utexas.edu/depts/systbiol/. Founded 1948. The society represents 1,550 scientists interested in classification of animals or other aspects of taxonomy or systematics. They promote the study of animals, invertebrate and vertebrate, living and fossilized, and all aspects of systematic zoology. The society publishes *Systematic Biology*. The Web page provides information about the society, their journal, and announcements.

Tropical Biology Association. c/o Ms. Rosie Trevelyan, Dept. of Zoology, University of Cambridge, Downing St. Cambridge CB1 3EJ, England. Phone: 44 1223336619. URL: http://www.zoo.cam.ac.uk/tba/. Founded 1994. 37 members. The association aims to meet the challenge of biodiversity conservation by establishing an informed, well-motivated community of tropical biologists based both in Europe and in tropical countries.

AUDIOVISUAL MATERIALS AND SOURCES

Science Books and Films. See complete annotation in the Bibliographies section.

The Software Encyclopedia. 1985/86– . New York: Bowker. Annual. $285.00. ISSN 0000-006X. Contains fully annotated listings for more than 32,400 new and established programs in all areas and in all formats, from statistical packages to desktop publishing. Also available online.

The Video Librarian. v. 1– , 1986– . Bremerton, WA: Randy Pitman. Monthly. $47.00. ISSN 0887-6851. This review periodical provides evaluative, dependable reviews for video recordings. It is indexed in *Library Literature*.

The Video Source Book. 1st– ed, 1979– . Syosset, NY: National Video Clearinghouse. Annual. $345.00. ISSN 0748-0881. This comprehensive catalog to documentaries, theatrical releases, television programs, training programs and other resources is arranged by title with subject access. Major producers and distributors are included with indexes for alternate title, credits, special formats, awards, and distributors. Complete bibliographic information is provided for each title.

BIBLIOGRAPHIES

The following bibliographies, catalogs, and book review indexes may be used to verify book titles, to update and evaluate editions, and to provide purchasing and availability information for books, microforms, serials, and other materials. General bibliographies for current and retrospective journal articles are discussed in the chapter on abstracts and indexes.

AcqWeb. Vanderbilt University. URL: http://acqweb.library.vanderbilt.edu/. AcqWeb is a major source of publisher information. It is designed for librarians, but contains vast numbers of links that would be of interest to other people, such as their lists of Web book reviews, out-of-print book sellers, and reference resources.

BIOSIS Serial Sources. 1995– . Philadelphia, PA: BIOSIS. Annual. $140.00 (paper). ISSN 1086-2951.   This highly useful directory lists 5,100 current titles, as well as 13,000 archival titles indexed by *Biological Abstracts* and *Biological Abstracts/RRM*. It includes publisher information, ISSN, CODEN, abbreviation, and publication frequency for each title. The *Serial Sources* is useful for confirming the title or abbreviation for a journal. It is also available on CD-ROM. Formerly: *Serial Sources for the BIOSIS Previews Database.*

Book Review Index (BRI). 1969– . Detroit, MI: Gale Research Inc. Bimonthly. ISSN 0524-0581.   Available in print and online from DIALOG. *BRI* contains references to more than two million reviews of approximately one million books and periodical titles, scanning more than 500 magazines and newspapers.

Books in Print. 1948– . New York: Bowker. Annual. $550.00. ISSN 0068-0214. Available electronically.   This is the major source of bibliographic information on books currently published and in print in the United States Scientific, technical, medical, scholarly, and popular works, as well as children's books, are included. Also, see *Scientific and Technical Books & Serials in Print*, annotated later in this section. The database is available online, on CD-ROM, and on the Web at http://www.booksinprint.com/bip/. Some sections of the Web version are available at no charge, such as publisher's homepages and publisher highlights. The main database is only available on a subscription basis.

CAB International Serials Checklist. 1995 ed. New York: CAB International. 483 p. $85.00 (paper). ISBN 0851989713 (paper).   This list contains references to over 11,000 journals, annual reports, technical reports, working papers, and newsletters regularly screened for *CAB Abstracts*. While not updated very often (the previous edition was done in 1988), this is the best directory for information on agricultural journals.

Chemical Abstracts Service Source Index: 1907–1999 Cumulative (CASSI). Columbus, OH: Chemical Abstracts Service, 2000. 3 v. $1,395.00.   This serial list for the *Chemical Abstracts* database has about 155,000 entries covering over 80,000 scientific journals and nonserial publications. CASSI cumulates every five years and is also available as quarterly updates, on microfiche, and on CD-ROM. CASSI is particularly useful because it covers a vast number of journals in all fields of science and technology back to 1907 and is thus valuable for its coverage of obscure foreign journals or journals that have ceased publication.

Clewis, Beth. *Index to Illustrations of Animals and Plants.* New York: Neal-Schuman, 1991. 217 p. ISBN 1555700721.   This is useful as a supplement to both Munz and Thompson (see following text), and it follows a similar format. Clewis covers books published in the 1980s and lists 62,000 entries for access to 142 books with illustrations for plants and animals from around the world. The book is arranged by common name with indexes for scientific name and book title.

Guide to Microforms in Print. 1975–   . Germany: K. Saur. *Author/Title.* Annual. $430.00. ISSN 0164-0747. *Subject.* Annual. $430.00. ISSN 0163-8386. *Supplement.* 1979–   . ISSN 0164-0739.   Includes books, journals, and other materials in microform with the exception of dissertations and theses.

Journal Citation Reports (JCR). 1975–   . Philadelphia: Institute for Scientific Information. Annual. Price varies.   JCR is a useful source of evaluation information on over 8,000 journals worldwide. It accompanies the *Science Citation Index* and its sibling indexes (see following text), and has been published annually since 1975, first in print, then on microfilm, and now on CD-ROM or on the Web. The JCR helps users evaluate and compare journals, providing information such as the Impact Factor (a measure of the frequency with which the ''average article'' in a journal has been cited in a particular year), the Immediacy Index (a measure of how quickly the ''average article'' in a journal is cited), and the Citing Half-Life (used for evaluating the age of the majority of articles cited in a journal). The JCR also lists journals by subject, which is useful for suggesting journals to submit papers to.

Library of Congress Online Catalog. Washington, DC: Library of Congress. URL: http://lcweb.loc.gov/catalog/.   A database of approximately 12 million records representing books, serials, computer files, manuscripts, cartographic materials, music, sound recordings, and visual materials in the library's collections. The WorldCat database, annotated in the following text, covers more books and other materials but is available only by subscription, so searching the Library of Congress or a major university catalog is a good alternative for finding books about a subject or confirming bibliographic details if WorldCat is not available.

List of Journals Indexed in Index Medicus. 1960–   . Bethesda, MD: U.S. Dept. of Health, Education, and Welfare, Public Health Service, National Institutes of Health, National Library of Medicine. Annual. $38.00. ISSN 0093-3821.   This serials list provides information on the 3,419 journals indexed in the print *Index Medicus.* It is also available in PDF format from NLM at http://www.nlm.nih.gov/tsd/serials/lji.html.

List of Serials Indexed for Online Users. 2000–   . Bethesda, MD: The National Library of Medicine (NLM). Annual. URL: http://www.nlm.nih.gov/tsd/serials/

lsiou.html. This serials list has long been a popular reference tool. It covers 9,334 serial titles, including 4,302 titles currently indexed for MEDLINE. It was published in print format from 1983 to 1999, but is now available only in PDF format from the NLM site. The *List of Journals Indexed in Index Medicus*, previous, covers only journals indexed in the print title, so the online version covers a broader range of serial types and subjects.

Meisel, Max. *A Bibliography of American Natural History: The Pioneer Century, 1769–1865 . . . The Role Played by the Scientific Societies; Scientific Journals; Natural History Museums and Botanical Gardens; State Geological and Natural History Surveys; Federal Exploring Expeditions in the Rise and Progress of American Botany, Geology, Mineralogy, Paleontology, and Zoology.* Mansfield, CT: Maurizio Martino, 1994. 3 v. $195.00. ISBN 0945345704. A reprint of the work originally published in 1924.

Munz, Lucile Thompson and Nedra G. Slauson. *Index to Illustrations of Living Things Outside North America; Where to Find Pictures of Flora and Fauna.* Hamden, CT: Archon Books, 1981. 441 p. ISBN 0208018573. A companion volume to John W. Thompson's *Index to Illustrations.* Arrangement is by common name to illustrations of plants, birds, and animals. There is a scientific name index and a bibliography of sources. Updated by Clewis (see page 33).

National Union Catalog. Washington, DC: U.S. Library of Congress. Complete bibliographic records for books, manuscripts, audiovisual and cartographic materials, etc., cataloged at the Library of Congress, and other U.S. libraries. Records are available since the late eighteen hundreds, issued in various sections, in hundreds of volumes. In essence, this is the U.S. national bibliography emanating from the national library. Although not specifically cited here, other countries maintain their own national bibliographies, available in print in larger public and university libraries. WorldCat, listed in the following text, is essentially NUC's successor.

Plant, Animal & Anatomical Illustration in Art & Science: A Bibliographical Guide from the 16th Century to the Present Day. Compiled by Gavin D. R. Bridson and James J. White. Detroit: Omnigraphics, 1990. 450 p. ISBN 0906795818. This very complete guide covers illustrations for natural history, medicine, botany, and zoology. Historical bibliography is well-served in this volume to include sources important since antiquity. Also, see Clewis, Munz, and Thompson.

Science Books and Films. v. 1– , 1965– . Washington, DC: American Association for the Advancement of Science. Bimonthly. $40.00. ISSN 0098–342X. Available electronically. Includes reviews of new science books, software, and

# #

AV materials, providing more comprehensive coverage of science and technology than any other review publication.

Smit, Pieter. *History of the Life Sciences.* See this entry in the Histories section for complete information.

Thompson, John W. *Index to Illustrations of the Natural World. Where to Find Pictures of the Living Things of North America.* Hamden, CT: Shoe String Press, 1983 reprint of the 1977 ed. 265 p. ISBN 0208020381. This book indexes illustrations to more than 9,000 species of animals and plants from 206 books. Arrangement is by common name with a scientific name index. Companion to Munz, and updated by Clewis.

Ulrich's International Periodicals Directory. 1932– . 5 v. New Providence, NJ: R. R. Bowker. Annual. $649.00. ISSN 0000-0175. A classified list of serials covering periodicals and annuals published worldwide, U.S. newspapers, refereed serials, serials available electronically or on CD-ROM, vendor lists, cessations, and indexes to publications of international organizations, ISSN, and titles. *Ulrich's* provides complete bibliographic information including beginning date, frequency, price, publisher and address, ISSN, circulation, and brief description when available. Available on CD-ROM, online, and on the Web.

Whitaker's Books in Print. 1988– . London: J. Whitaker & Sons. Annual. $813.00. ISSN 0953–0398. This resource provides comprehensive indexing of books published in the U.K. as well as those published throughout the world that are printed in the English language and are available within the U.K. Formerly *British Books in Print.* Available on CD-ROM, online, and on the Web.

WorldCat. Dublin, OH: OCLC Online Computer Library Center. URL: http://www.oclc.org. Offers over 41 million records for books, journals, and other materials cataloged by member libraries in the United States and around the world. This database is available by subscription only, but is the most comprehensive catalog of library materials available anywhere. The WorldCat database lists which participating libraries own each item, and there are records for a number of Web resources that have been deemed valuable enough to catalog. Essentially the successor to the *National Union Catalog*, previous.

Zoological Record Serial Sources. 1988– . Philadelphia, PA: BIOSIS. Annual. $70.00 (paper). ISSN 1041-4657. This journal list is similar to the *BIOSIS Serial Sources*, previous, and is equally useful for verifying journals. It covers 4,500 current titles and 5,500 archival titles. The list of current titles is also available at http://www.biosis.org/training_support/documentation/ZR_journals.html.

CLASSIFICATION, NOMENCLATURE, AND SYSTEMATICS

The sources in this section provide general information for classification schemes for living organisms. For more specific details consult individual chapters on botany, entomology, microbiology, or zoology.

BIOSIS Previews Search Guide. See the discussion in Chapter 2. This essential guide for online searchers provides a taxonomic overview of the hierarchical structure used for microorganisms, plants, and animals.

Cladistics: The International Journal of the Willi Hennig Society. v. 1– , 1985– . London: Academic Press. Quarterly. $289.00. ISSN 0748-3007. Available electronically. The journal's scope is "wide, covering theory, method, the philosophical aspects of systematics, and the role of systematic and evolutionary studies in the investigation of biogeographical and other general biological phenomena."

The Diversity of Living Organisms. R. S. K. Barnes, ed. Malden, MA: Blackwell Science, 1998. 345 p. $29.95 (paper). ISBN 0632049170. "This text is a profusely illustrated, quick reference guide to all types of living organism from the single-celled prokaryotes and eukaryotes to the multicellular fungi, plants, and animals." (from the publisher) The book is particularly useful for the small, obscure groups of organisms, because it examines organisms only to the level of the class (so mammals only get a page of description and illustration, the same as the planktonic Heliozoa).

Enzyme Nomenclature. International Union of Biochemistry and Molecular Biology Nomenclature Committee. URL: http://www.chem.qmw.ac.uk/iubmb/enzyme/. The Web version of *Enzyme Nomenclature 1992*, including all of the supplements (see following text). The Web site provides general information on enzyme nomenclature, links to information about pathways, and suggestions on how to propose new enzymes and changes in the nomenclature.

Enzyme Nomenclature 1992: Recommendations of the Nomenclature Committee of the International Union of Biochemistry and Molecular Biology on the Nomenclature and Classification of Enzymes. Edwin C. Webb, ed. San Diego: Academic Press, 1992. 862 p. $128.00, $73.00 (paper). ISBN 0122271645, 0122271653 (paper). 3,196 enzymes are listed with their recommended name, their EC number, type reaction, and the systematic name based on the classification of the enzyme. Nonrecommended names are included as are comments and references to justify each entry. A glossary, abbreviations, and an index are also provided. Annual supplements were published in *European Journal of Biochemistry* from 1993 to 1999.

Index to Organism Names. Philadelphia, PA: BIOSIS. URL: http://www. biosis.org/free_resources/ion.html. Provides basic information on nomenclature and hierarchy for plant and animal names. Currently, the database includes bacteria, algae, mosses, fungi, and animals.

Jeffrey, Charles. *Biological Nomenclature*. 3rd ed. London: Edward Arnold, 1989. 86 p. ISBN 0713129832 (paper). While out of print, this slim volume is available at many libraries and provides a good introduction to nomenclature. While the various codes of nomenclature should be examined for details, this book will help explain the system.

Kitching, Ian J., et al. *Cladistics: The Theory and Practice of Parsimony Analysis.* 2nd ed. New York: Oxford University Press, 1998. 228 p. (Systematics Association Publications, 11). $75.00, $29.95 (paper). ISBN 0198501390, 0198501382 (paper). Designed as an integrated overview of the techniques and methods of modern cladistics. An updated version of *Cladistics: A Practical Course in Systematics*, by Peter Forey, et al.

Maddison, D. R. and W. P. Maddison. 1998. *The Tree of Life: A Multi-Authored, Distributed Internet Project Containing Information About Phylogeny and Biodiversity*. URL: http://phylogeny.arizona.edu/tree/phylogeny.html. Intended to provide a means for finding information on all taxa of living organisms. The project is unfinished, of course, but provides a good starting point for exploring the natural world.

Margulis, Lynn and Karlene V. Schwartz. *The Five Kingdoms: An Illustrated Guide to the Phyla of Life on Earth*. 3rd ed. New York: W.H. Freeman, 1998. 520 p. $29.95 (paper). ISBN 071673026X , 0716730278 (paper). Arranged by the five kingdoms of Monera, Protoctista, Fungi, Animalia, and Plantae this reference discusses classification schemes, the general features of each kingdom, an illustrative phylogeny, and a bibliography of suggested reading for selected members of each phylum. An appendix lists genera, including genus, phylum, and common name for each. There is a glossary. Also available on CD-ROM.

Minelli, Alessandro. *Biological Systematics: The State of the Art*. New York: Chapman & Hall, 1993. 387 p. $69.00. ISBN 0412364409. A comprehensive essay on modern biological systematics. The book includes history, molecular methods, theory and practice, methodology of phylogenetic reconstruction, and discussion of cladistics and computers. There are 23 appendices providing various important classification schedules, an extensive bibliography, and references.

Molecular Systematics. David M. Hillis, Craig Moritz and Barbara K. Mable, eds. 2nd ed. Sunderland, MA: Sinauer, 1996. 655 p. ISBN 0878932828 (paper). Overview of molecular systematics.

NCBI Taxonomy Homepage. Bethseda, MD: NCBI, 2000– . URL: http:// www.ncbi.nlm.nih.gov/Taxonomy/taxonomyhome.html/. As of January 1, 2001, 87,994 species were represented in the GenBank database of gene sequences. This page was created to make public the names of organisms with sequences in GenBank and is not a taxonomic authority. However, it is a useful guide to best practice and contains many links to other taxonomic resources.

Panchen, Alex L. *Classification, Evolution, and the Nature of Biology*. New York: Cambridge University Press, 1992. 403 p. $39.95 (paper). ISBN 0521305829, 0521315786 (paper). A historical treatise on the relationships between classifications and patterns of phylogeny.

Quicke, D. L. J. *Principles and Techniques of Contemporary Taxonomy*. London: Chapman & Hall, 1993. 200 p. $151.00, $77.50 (paper). ISBN 075140019X, 0751400203 (paper). A survey of the arguments and techniques of systematics as they are applied to all groups of organisms, including principles of nomenclature and classification, and the practice of cladistics.

Schuh, Randall T. *Biological Systematics: Principles and Applications*. Ithaca, NY: Cornell University Press, 2000. 236 p. $45.00. ISBN 0801436753. A textbook covering the background, methods, and applications of cladistics.

Species 2000. International Union of Biological Sciences. URL: http:// www.sp2000.org/default.html. ''Species 2000 has the objective of enumerating all known species of plants, animals, fungi and microbes on Earth as the baseline dataset for studies of global biodiversity.'' Eighteen organizations have formed a federation to combine existing taxonomic databases.

Synopsis and Classification of Living Organisms. Sybil P. Parker, Editor in Chief. New York: McGraw-Hill, 1982. 2 v. ISBN 0070790310 (set). Treats higher-level taxonomy. The systematic positions and affinities of all living organisms are presented in synoptic articles for all taxa down to the family level. Linnaean classifications and citations are included as a guide to the specialized literature. An appendix discusses the history and role of nomenclature in the taxonomy and classification of organisms, and provides classification tables.

A Synoptic Classification of Living Organisms. R. S. K. Barnes, ed. Oxford, England: Blackwell Scientific Publications, 1984. 273 p. ISBN 0632011459. A dictionary/mini-encyclopedia of classification and diversity that presents an outline, synoptic account of the classification of living organisms from prokaryotic bacteria, through protists, to the multicellular fungi, plants, and animals. There are references and suggestions for further reading, and an index to taxa is provided.

Systematic Biology. v. 41– , 1992– . London: Taylor and Francis. Quarterly. $109.00. ISSN 1063–5157. Available electronically. ''Papers for the journal are original contributions to the theory, principles, and methods of systematics as well as phylogeny, evolution, morphology, biogeography, paleontology, genetics, and the classification of all living things.''

Tudge, Colin. *The Variety of Life: A Survey and a Celebration of All the Creatures that Have Ever Lived*. New York: Oxford University Press, 2000. 684 p. $49.95. ISBN 0198503113. An overview of living organisms. Unlike *The Diversity of Living Organisms*, previous, Tudge discusses general topics in taxonomy as well as surveying organisms. "Popular" groups such as reptiles and mammals get more room here, and microorganisms and plants are covered in less detail.

Winston, Judith E. *Describing Species: Practical Taxonomic Procedure for Biologists*. New York: Columbia University Press, 1999. 518 p. $65.00, $35.00 (paper). ISBN 0231068247, 0231068255 (paper). "This book is intended to introduce students and professional scientists to basic taxonomic procedure and enable them to carry out whatever taxonomic writing they need in their studies or careers.''

DICTIONARIES AND ENCYCLOPEDIAS

Acronyms, Initialisms, and Abbreviations Dictionary. 1976– . Annual edition or supplement. Detroit, MI: Gale Research Co. 4 v. $929.00/set. ISBN 078763381X. The 28th edition (2000) contains more than 495,000 definitions to make it the ultimate authority for all subjects including biology. Also by the same company, see *International Acronyms, Initialisms & Abbreviations Dictionary*, 5th ed., 2000, $264.00, ISBN 0810377977; *Reverse Acronyms Initialisms & Abbreviations Dictionary*, 28th ed, 2000, $445.00, ISBN 0787633860; and *Reverse International Acronyms, Initialisms & Abbreviations Dictionary*, 5th ed., 2000, $225.00, ISBN 0787642762.

Blinderman, Charles. *Biolexicon: A Guide to the Language of Biology*. Springfield, IL: Thomas, 1990. 363 p. $48.95. ISBN 0398056714. This guide to the vocabulary of biology and medicine helps students decipher the language by providing insights into philosophy, religion, history, mythology, theories of evolution, Renaissance anatomy, and spooky obsessions. The book is arranged by broad topic rather than by presenting lists of terms.

Borror, Donald Joyce. *Dictionary of Word Roots and Combining Forms Compiled from the Greek, Latin, and Other Languages, with Special Reference to Biological Terms and Scientific Names*. Mountain View, CA: Mayfield, 1960. 134 p. $9.65 (paper). ISBN 0874840538 (paper). This is of particular value to the beginning student or taxonomist.

Cambridge Illustrated Dictionary of Natural History. R. J. Lincoln and G. A. Boxshall, eds. Cambridge, MA: Cambridge University Press, 1987. 413 p. $28.95 (paper). ISBN 0521305519 (paper). Content reflects the popular image of natural history: life on Earth. Over 700 line drawings supplement the definitions.

Concise Dictionary of Biomedicine and Molecular Biology. Juo, Pei-Show, ed. Boca Raton, FL: CRC Press, 1996. 992 p. $85.00, $129.00 (CD-ROM). ISBN 0849324602, 0849321751 (CD-ROM). Over 23,000 entries cover the fields of cell biology, biochemistry, and biomedicine, including 4,000 chemical structures and their functions, and 1,100 equations of enzymatic reactions.

The Concise Encyclopedia of the Ethics of New Technologies. Ruth Chadwick, ed. San Diego: Academic Press, 2001. 404 p. $79.95. ISBN 0121663558. Most of the new technologies discussed in this book are biomedical, such as brain death, genetic screening, or xenotransplantation.

Dictionary of Chemical Names and Synonyms. For a complete annotation, see Chapter 5, "Biochemistry and Biophysics."

Dictionary of Light Microscopy, compiled by the Nomenclature Committee of the Royal Microscopical Society (RMS). (Microscopy handbooks, 15). Oxford, England: Oxford University Press for the RMS, 1989. 139 p. $18.95. ISBN 019856421X. Over 1,250 terms were chosen to conform to current usage, international standards, and the word's origin and meaning. Incorrect, obsolete, and inconsistent terms are indicated. RMS hopes that the recommended terms will be used by manufacturers, for teaching purposes, and for scientific papers. Appendixes include figures and tables, and English-French-German equivalent terms. Cover title: *RMS Dictionary of Light Microscopy.*

Dictionary of Natural Products. For a complete annotation, see Chapter 5, "Biochemistry and Biophysics."

Dictionary of the History of Science. Annotated in the Histories section of this chapter.

Dictionary of Theoretical Concepts in Biology. Keith E. Roe and Richard G. Frederick, eds. Metuchen, NJ: Scarecrow Press, 1981. 267 p. $40.00. ISBN 081081353X. Provides access to the literature through 1979 on 1,166 named theoretical concepts by citing original sources and reviews illuminating those concepts. Both plant and animal biology are represented.

Dorland's Illustrated Medical Dictionary. 29th ed. London: W.B. Saunders, 2000. 2,087 p. ISBN 0721662544. A standard biomedical dictionary, with numerous illustrations.

Elsevier's Dictionary of Biology. Rauno Tirri, et al., eds. New York: Elsevier,

1998. 757 p. $201.00. ISBN 0444825258. Covers about 10,000 terms in all areas of biology and allied fields. Intended for students and teachers.

Elsevier's Dictionary of Microscopes and Microtechniques: In English, French, and German. Robert Serre, ed. New York: Elsevier, 1993. 286 p. $144.50, $160.00 (CD-ROM). ISBN 0444889736, 0444501398 (CD-ROM). A trilingual dictiona:y covering 1,827 terms found in contemporary microscope and micro-techniques publications. Definitions, synonyms, cross-references, and a complete bibliography to sources are provided.

Encyclopedia of Bioethics. Rev. ed. Warren T. Reich, editor-in-chief. New York: Macmillan Reference, 1994. 5 v. $550.00 (set). ISBN 0028973550 (set). A complete revision of the award-winning encyclopedia, this set contains 460 authoritative, original articles, extensive bibliographies, and a comprehensive index. Coverage: ethical and moral dimensions of scientific and technological innovations; basic concepts of life, death, health, etc.; principles and virtues used as guides for human behavior; ethical theories; the changing nature of ethics; worldwide religious traditions; history of medical ethics; and disciplines contributing to bioethics from anthropology to the sociology of science.

Encyclopedia of Biostatistics. Peter Armitage and Theodore Colton, eds. New York: J. Wiley, 1998. 6 v. $2,750.00 (set). ISBN 0471975761 (set). Contains over 1,200 articles written by more than 800 contributors. Covers statistical methods in health sciences such as epidemiology and public health and in biological sciences such as genetics and bacterial growth. There are also numerous articles covering standard statistical methods. The emphasis is on statistics in the health sciences.

Encyclopedia of Ethical, Legal and Policy Issues in Biotechnology. Thomas H. Murray and Maxwell J. Mehlman, eds. New York: Wiley, 2000. 2 vol. $695.00. ISBN 0471176125. This authoritative compendium for scientists, academics, legal consultants, and government agencies offers comprehensive coverage of technical details and the regulatory policy aspects of various topics including human subject research, gene therapy, cloning, the Human Genome Project, and animal and medical biotechnology.

Encyclopedia of Human Biology. Renato Dulbecco, ed. San Diego, CA: Academic, 1997. 9 v. $2,205.00 (set). ISBN 0122269705 (set). Over 673 articles, each averaging about ten pages, provides authoritative, up-to-date information on human biology, covering anthropology, behavior, biochemistry, biophysics, cytology, ecology, evolution, genetics, immunology, neurosciences, pharmacology, physiology, toxicology, etc. There are over 3,000 illustrations; 50 color plates; 200 tables; 5,500 bibliographic entries; and 4,000 glossary entries. The advisory board reads like the who's who of the scientific world to include 11 Nobel Laureates.

Encyclopedia of Life Sciences. New York: Nature Publishing Group, 2001. 20 v. $3,200.00. ISBN 1561592749.   This is billed by the publisher as "the most ambitious single reference source ever published in the biological sciences." Over 5,000 of the world's leading experts will contribute 4,000 articles across the complete field of the life sciences. Also available online (by subscription only), the continuously updated *ELS Online* will provide various methods of accessing the data and will offer direct links from references to primary literature and other resources. A major new encyclopedia.

Encyclopedia of Toxicology. Philip Wexler, ed. San Diego, CA: Academic Press, 1998. 3 v. $525.00 (set). ISBN 012227220X (set).   This encyclopedia covers basic, critical, and controversial elements in toxicology, including key concepts: dose response, mechanisms of action, testing procedures, endpoint responses, target sites, individual chemicals, and classes of chemicals. There is also information on radiation and noise, history, laws, regulation, education, organizations, and databases. Volume 3 includes an index.

The Facts on File Dictionary of Biology. 3rd ed. Robert Hine, ed. New York: Facts On File, 1999. 361 p. $40.00, $17.95 (pa). ISBN 0816039070, 0816039089 (pa).   Contains 3,300 entries covering all aspects of biology, defining the most commonly used biological terms. Includes an appendix with charts of the animal and plant kingdoms and amino-acid structures. Aimed at a high-school audience.

Henderson, Isabella Ferguson. *Henderson's Dictionary of Biological Terms.* Eleanor Lawrence, ed. 12th ed. London: Prentice Hall, 2000. 719 p. $12.50 (paper). ISBN 0582414989 (paper).   Provides definitions of over 23,000 terms in biology, botany, zoology, anatomy, cytology, genetics, embryology, and physiology. Appendices cover outlines of the plant, fungi, protoctista, and animal kingdoms and the bacteria and archaea domains, plus virus families and the etymological origin of common word elements.

International Dictionary of Medicine and Biology. Sidney I. Landau, ed. New York: Wiley, 1986. 3 v. $495.00. ISBN 047101849X.   This unabridged dictionary of 159,000 definitions covers the fields of the traditional basic and clinical medical sciences, technological specialties, and the delivery of health care.

Jaeger, Edmund C. *A Source-Book of Biological Names and Terms.* 3rd ed. Springfield, IL: Thomas, 1978. 360 p. $61.95. ISBN 0398009163.   The classic guide to the vocabulary of biology.

McGraw-Hill Dictionary of Bioscience. Sybil P. Parker, editor-in-chief. New York: McGraw-Hill, 1996. 448 p. $24.95. ISBN 0070524300 (paper).   This comprehensive reference defines nearly 16,000 major terms in the biosciences culled from the *McGraw-Hill Dictionary of Scientific and Technical Terms*. An excellent dictionary for all levels of biologists.

McGraw-Hill Encyclopedia of Science and Technology, 8th ed. Sybil P. Parker, editor-in-chief. New York: McGraw-Hill, 1997. 20 v. $1,995.00 (set). ISBN 0079115047 (set). A preeminent, comprehensive science and technology encyclopedia that deserves its continued excellent reputation. Available on the Web (by subscription only) as AccessScience@McGraw-Hill, continuously updated. Also available on CD-ROM as the *Multimedia Encyclopedia of Science and Technology* ($1,295.00; ISBN 0071341730).

Medawar, Peter Brian and J. S. Medawar. *Aristotle to Zoos: A Philosophical Dictionary of Biology*. Cambridge, MA: Harvard University Press, 1983. 305 p. ISBN 0674045351. Confined to biological topics, this book is not a dictionary in the usual sense. It is arranged alphabetically, but in its authors' words, it is for browsing and reflection among theoretical concepts and ideas. The entries range from several lines to several pages. There is an index.

The Merck Index: An Encyclopedia of Chemicals, Drugs, and Biologicals, 12th ed. Rahway, NJ: Merck, 1996. 1 v. $45.00. ISBN 0911910123. This is an invaluable encyclopedia of more than 10,000 significant drugs, chemicals, and biologicals, including concise information for each substance: chemical, common and generic names; trademarks and their associated companies; Chemical Abstracts Service (CAS) Registry Numbers; molecular formulae and weights; physical and toxicity data; therapeutic and commercial uses; citations to the literature; and chemical structures. Available online and on CD-ROM from several vendors.

Multilingual Illustrated Dictionary of Aquatic Animals and Plants. Commission of the European Communities. Oxford, England: Fishing News Books, 1993. 900 p. ISBN 0852382065. Scientific name, family name, and name in each of nine languages for over 1,400 species of fish, crustaceans, molluscs, seaweeds, and other fishery products landed for commercial purposes.

Oxford Dictionary of Biology. 4th ed. Oxford, England: Oxford University Press, 2000. 640 p. $14.95 (paper). ISBN 0192801023 (paper). This encyclopedia covers over 4,000 entries in all areas of biology. There are numerous illustrations, and appendices covering simplified classification of plants and animals and a geological time chart. A useful dictionary for beginners.

Science and Technology Encyclopedia. Chicago, IL: University of Chicago Press, 2000. 572 p. $22.50 (paper). ISBN 0226742679 (paper). Includes over 6,500 alphabetical entries covering all the sciences. Designed for nonmajor college and high-school students, but also useful for anyone looking for definitions in areas outside their field of expertise. Originally published in the U.K. as *Philip's Science and Technology Encyclopedia*.

Stedman's Medical Dictionary. 27th ed. Philadelphia, PA: Lippincott Williams & Wilkins, 2000. 2,098 p. $49.95, $29.95 (paper), $59.95 (book and CD-ROM). ISBN 068340007X, 0683400193 (paper), 0781727278 (book and CD-ROM). This volume (or *Dorland's Illustrated Medical Dictionary*) is an excellent source for medical terminology useful to biological scientists.

Tsur, Samuel A. *Elsevier's Dictionary of the Genera of Life*. New York: Elsevier, 1999. 556 p. $152.00. ISBN 0444829059. An alphabetical listing of about 5,300 genera of bacteria, fungi, plants, and animals. Each entry includes the genus, Latin, and common names of the family or order, and information about one or more sample species. There is a distinct medical orientation to the entries, because most of the sample species are of medicinal or disease-carrying importance.

USP Dictionary of USAN and International Drug Names. 2000 ed. Rockville, MD: United States Pharmacopeia, 2000. 1,115 p. $249.00. ISBN 1889788074. The annual authorized list of established names for drugs in the United States, published in accordance with the directions of the Nomenclature Committee of the USP Committee of Revision, with the cooperation of the United States Adopted Names Council. This essential, quick reference format lists U.S. adopted name, molecular formula, chemical name, registry number, pharmacologic and/or therapeutic activity, brand name, manufacturer, code designation, and graphic formula.

Van Nostrand's Scientific Encyclopedia. 8th ed. Douglas M. Considine and Glenn D. Considine, eds. New York: Van Nostrand Reinhold, 1995. 2 v. $299.00 (set), $295.00 (CD-ROM). ISBN 0442018649 (set), 0471293237 (CD-ROM). A highly respected science encyclopedia, with coverage of the life and environmental sciences.

World of Biology. Kimberley A. McGrath, ed. Detroit, MI: Gale Group, 1999. 942 p. $130.75. ISBN 0787630446. This single-volume encyclopedia contains 1,340 entries covering all areas of biology. In addition to the subject entries, there are a number of biographies of famous biologists. The encyclopedia also has a chronology of the history of biology. Each entry includes extensive lists for further reading, and there are numerous illustrations. A good choice for undergraduates or high-school students.

DIRECTORIES

For more information about specific societies, consult the Associations section of this chapter and the multivolume *Encyclopedia of Associations*. Also, check out specific societies or subjects on the Web. Many associations include membership directories on their Web sites.

Agricultural Information Resource Centers: A World Directory 2000. 3rd ed. Jane S. Johnson, et al., eds. Twin Falls, ID: IAALD, 2000. 718 p. $181.50. ISBN 0962405221. A directory to over 2,000 agricultural information resource centers from around the world. There are institution and subject indexes.

American Library Directory. 1923– . 2 v. New York: R. R. Bowker. Annual. $299.00. ISSN 0065–910X. Covers over 30,000 public, academic, special and government libraries, and library-related organizations in the United States and Canada. Provides detailed listings of contact information, statistics such as expenditures and collection size, collection strengths, and key personnel.

American Type Culture Collection. For information, see the Classification section in Chapter 8, "Microbiology and Immunology."

Directory of Research Grants. 1975– . Phoenix, AZ: Oryx Press. Annual. $135.00. ISSN 0146–7336. Includes over 6,200 sources for research grants and scholarships in the United States offered by federal, state, and local governments; commercial organizations; associations; and private foundations. Also available online as GRANTS database, on CD-ROM, and on the Web as GrantSelect.

Directory of Scholarly Electronic Journals and Academic Discussion Lists. Washington, DC: Association of Research Libraries, Office of Scholarly Communication, 2000– . Irregular. $95.00. ISSN 1524-2439. Lists over 3,900 peer-reviewed journal titles available electronically, and over 4,600 e-conferences. Available online with print subscription, or with online-only subscription. Back issues are freely available at http://www.arl.org/scomm/edir/archive.html. Formerly *Directory of Electronic Journals, Newsletters, and Academic Discussion Lists.*

Encyclopedia of Associations. 1st– ed. Detroit, MI: Gale Research Co., 1956– . 36th ed.: 3 v. $1,085/set. Provides detailed entries for over 22,000 associations, organization, clubs, and other nonprofit membership groups in all fields in the United States. Vol. 1, in 3 parts: *National Organizations of the U.S.* ISBN 0787631132 $520.00; Vol. 2: *Geographic and Executive Indexes.* ISBN 0787631124 $400.00; Vol. 3: *Supplement.* ISBN 0787631116. $430.00. Vol. 4: *International Organizations,* 29th ed.; 2 v. plus supplement. ISBN 0787648159, $545.00. Also available online, on CD-ROM, and on the Web as Associations Unlimited (by subscription only).

Field Station Directory. Organization of Biological Field Stations. URL: http://www.obfs.org/Table_1_Links/stat_all.html. Lists about 180 biological field stations in North and Central America, Mexico, and the Caribbean, including location, environment, facilities, and ongoing research and educational programs.

Foundation Directory. 1st ed.– . 1960– . New York: The Foundation Center. Annual. $215.00. ISSN 0071–8092. Comprehensive directory of 35,000 of the largest active grant funding foundations, community foundations, operating foundations, and corporate grant makers. *Foundation Directory, Part 2* ($185.00) covers midsized foundations, and an annual *Supplement* ($125.00) updates the main volumes. Available online, on CD-ROM, and on the Web.

Fulltext Sources Online. 1989– . Medford, NJ: Information Today. Semiannual. $198.00. ISSN 1040–8258. Available electronically. Lists over 11,000 newspapers, journals, and magazines available online in full text. Covers the major aggregators such as DIALOG, Questel, and Westlaw and publications with Web sites. The directory is also available on the Web as *Fulltext Sources Online Private Zone* (subscription required). Formerly: *BiblioData Fulltext Sources Online.*

International Research Centers Directory. 1982– . Detroit, MI: Gale. Annual. $515.00. ISSN 0278–2731. Covers more than 8,700 government, university, and independent nonprofit and commercial research and development organizations around the world, excluding the United States. Available online and on the Web.

Linscott's Directory of Immunological and Biological Reagents. See the annotation in the Chapter 8, "Microbiology and Immunology" for the "world's resource for locating immunological and biological reagents."

National Faculty Directory. 32nd ed. Detroit, MI: Gale Group, 2001. 3 v. $780.00. ISBN 0787633755 (set). A directory listing over 730,000 faculty members at junior colleges, colleges, and universities in the United States and Canada.

Peterson's Guide to Graduate Programs in the Biological Sciences. 1966– . Princeton, NJ: Peterson's Guides. Annual. $49.95. ISSN 0894–9360. Comprehensive guide to over 3,800 postbaccalaureate programs in the United States and Canada. Available online, on CD-ROM, and on the Web.

Research Centers Directory. 1st– . 1960– . Detroit, MI: Gale. Irregular. $595.00 (2 v.) ISSN 0080–1518. The 2001 edition covers more than 14,200 university related, independent, and nonprofit research centers in the United States and Canada. This comprehensive guide encompasses life sciences, physical sciences and engineering, private and public policy affairs, sociology and cultural studies, multidisciplinary and research coordinating centers. Arrangement is by subject with indexes for alphabetized associations and keywords, geographic locations, and subjects. Also available online and on the Web.

World Guide to Libraries. 9th ed.– , 1989– . New York: K. G. Saur. Irregular. $330.00. ISSN 0936–0085. This two-volume directory covers over 42,500 national libraries, general research libraries, academic and professional school libraries, school libraries, public libraries, ecclesiastical libraries, corporate libraries, special libraries maintained by other institutions, and government libraries from 200 countries. Available on CD-ROM.

World Guide to Scientific Associations and Learned Societies. 7th ed. New Providence, NJ: K. G. Saur, 1998. 529 p. $396.00. ISBN 3598205813. All areas of academic study, culture, and technology are covered in this directory of 17,000 national and international societies. The arrangement is alphabetical by country, then by association name. Listings include association name, address, telephone, telefax, e-mail address, year founded, number of members, president, general secretary, focus area, and periodical publications. There are indexes for name, subject, publications, and German-English concordance to areas of specialization.

World Guide to Special Libraries. 4th ed. New York: K. G. Saur, 1998. 2 v. $873.00. ISBN 3598222491. Covers over 39,900 libraries in 192 countries, including private and public research libraries, school libraries, university libraries, and company libraries. Arranged by subject, with an alphabetical index.

FIELD GUIDES

There are a large number of excellent field guides available. Rather than providing a comprehensive list, this section annotates some of the more popular field guide series. For more information, consult specific chapters depending on subject matter, in other words, see Chapter 10, ''Plant Biology,'' for botanical identification manuals.

Schmidt, Diane. *A Guide to Field Guides: Identifying the Natural History of North America.* Englewood, CO: Libraries Unlimited, 1999. 304 p. ISBN 1563087073. Describes over 1,300 field guides to all kinds of organisms from North America. Most are in print, though a few classics are also included.

Schmidt, Diane. *International Field Guides.* Urbana, IL: University of Illinois, 1999– . URL: http://www.library.uiuc.edu/bix/fieldguides/main.htm. Companion to the print guide to North American field guides listed previously. Over 1,500 field guides from all parts of the world are described. Most are in English, though some are in other languages.

Series

Audubon Society Field Guides. Published by Knopf in New York, this well-known series presents color photographs rather than drawings. In addition to guides to single groups of organisms (birds, flowers, etc.), a new series, the National Audubon Society Regional Field Guide series, covers all of the major groups of organisms, plus geology, weather, and general natural history for particular regions such as the Pacific Northwest or the Mid-Atlantic.

Golden Field Guides. Published in New York by Golden Press, these field guides cover all of North America rather than isolated sections of the United States. These guides are particularly convenient to use because they provide descriptions, illustrations, and maps of each bird or tree on the same two-page spread. Most of the guides in this series have not been updated recently, so they are beginning to be out of date.

HarperCollins is the best-known publisher of field guides internationally. There are a number of subseries, and many of the major U.S. guides are co-published by HarperCollins (formerly Collins, and many of the series titles are still listed as Collins).

Peterson Field Guide Series. Published by Houghton Mifflin in Boston, this famous series covers almost every group of plants and animals in almost every part of North America. The guides use drawings rather than photographs, though some of the more recently revised field guides include photographs as well as drawings.

Pictured Key Series. This series includes more esoteric groups of organisms than most field guides and is designed for the use of students or researchers. Each volume consists of a book-length dichotomous key, and contains extensive introductory material, black and white illustrations, and glossary. There are guides to trematodes and freshwater algae along with more familiar subjects such as birds and flowers. Some of the guides cover organisms worldwide, though most are restricted to North America.

GENERAL WORKS

Bloom, Dale F., Jonathan D. Karp, and Nicholas Cohen. *The Ph.D. Process: A Student's Guide to Graduate School in the Sciences.* New York: Oxford University Press, 1999. 272 p. $16.95 (paper). ISBN 0195119002 (paper). A comprehensive, detailed, and practical guide to how to survive and thrive in grad school.

Brown, Andrew. *The Darwin Wars: How Stupid Genes Became Selfish Gods.* London: Simon & Schuster, 1999. 241 p. $21.00. ISBN 068485144X. The author discusses beliefs about evolution from the viewpoints of science and religion and their contending theories. Sources and further reading are provided.

Janovy, John. Jr. *On Becoming a Biologist.* Lincoln, NE: University of Nebraska Press, 1996. 160 p. $10.00. ISBN 0803275862 (paper). This very readable book presents a view of what life would be like as a biologist. Janovy comments on careers, ethics, what biologists do and how they do it, with the message that it's not only exciting to be a biologist, but fun, too.

Mayr, Ernst. *The Growth of Biological Thought: Diversity, Evolution, and Inheritance*. Cambridge, MA: Belknap Press, 1982. 974 p. $24.95 (paper). ISBN 0674364457 (paper). A broad survey of biology and its dominant concepts by one of the eminent players.

Mayr, Ernst. *Toward a New Philosophy of Biology; Observations of an Evolutionist*. Cambridge, MA: Belknap Press of Harvard University Press, 1988. 564 p. $20.50 (paper). ISBN 0674896661 (paper). Written to strengthen the bridge between biology and philosophy, pointing to the direction in which a new philosophy of biology will move.

Ruse, Michael. *Philosophy of Biology Today*. Albany, NY: State University of New York Press, 1988. 155 p. $16.95. ISBN 088706910X. The author views this book as a handbook to the philosophy of biology with the aim of introducing newcomers to the field. There is a 52-page bibliography of references.

Slack, J. M. W. *Egg & Ego: An Almost True Story of Life in the Biology Lab*. New York: Springer-Verlag, 1998. 192 p. $26.95. ISBN 0387985603 (paper). This book presents a lighthearted look at the nature of academic science, intended especially for biology students who expect to pursue a life at the bench. The "Egg" in the title refers to the science of developmental biology, the author's specialty; the "Ego" pertains to the vanity of the scientists who must persuade themselves and others of their scientific worth vis à vis research funding, publishing in highly rated journals, and working in prestigious institutions.

Sober, Elliott. *Philosophy of Biology*. 2nd ed. Boulder, CO: Westview Press, 2000. 236 p. (Dimensions of philosophy series). $27.00 (paper). ISBN 0813391261 (paper). The author aims to provide a firm grasp of the structure of evolutionary biology, the evidence for it, and the scope of its explanatory significance.

Sterelny, Kim and Paul E. Griffiths. *Sex and Death: An Introduction to Philosophy of Biology*. Chicago, IL: University of Chicago Press, 1999. 440 p. (Science and its conceptual foundations). $60.00, $22.00 (paper). ISBN 0226773035, 0226773043 (paper). A general survey of the philosophy of biology, with emphasis on evolutionary biology. The authors also discuss genetics, developmental biology, and behavior (especially human behavior).

Thompson, D'Arcy Wentworth. *On Growth and Form*. New York: Dover, 1992. 1,116 p. $26.95 (paper). ISBN 0486671356 (paper). A classic in the literature of biology, first published in 1917, this book is still in print and still read by biologists. The author discusses the role of mathematics and physics in the form and growth of living organisms, covering everything from variations in the shapes of seashells to the arrangement of florets in a complex flower. Also available in an abridged edition from Cambridge University Press, ISBN 0521437768 ($14.95).

GUIDES TO INTERNET RESOURCES

The Internet is a superstore of information, from directories to genetic sequence databases. There are electronic catalogs, newsgroups, mailing lists, and electronic journals, just to name a few categories that biologists will find interesting. There are innumerable yellow pages–type print directories to Web resources, which of course are out-of-date by the time they are typeset. Check your local bookstore or library to find one that suits your needs. Following is a list of directories to use as starting points for exploring the rapidly evolving, ever-growing electronic information highway.

AltWeb: Alternatives to Animal Testing. Johns Hopkins University. URL: http://altweb.jhsph.edu/. Designed to foster the replacement of animal testing with other, more acceptable methods. A collaboration of a number of research organizations, developed by the Center for Alternatives to Animal Testing at Johns Hopkins. Provides links to resources in three broad categories, Science and Regulation, Educational Resources, and General Information.

Argus Clearinghouse. Argus Associates, Inc. URL: http://www.clearinghouse. net. Contains annotated links to many Web resources for the biological sciences. This site does not index as many Web sites as other directories such as the WWW Virtual Library, but each entry has been judged on such criteria as design and organization.

Bioethics.net: Where the World Finds Bioethics. Philadelphia, PA: Center for Bioethics, University of Pennsylvania, 2000–   . URL: http://www.bioethics. net/. Contains a wide variety of material on bioethics issues, for both beginners and more advanced users. There are lists of conferences, news items, homework help, and many links arranged by subject.

BioMedNet. Elsevier Science. URL: http://www.bmn.com/. This site requires free registration to access many of its features. It includes several free databases (including MEDLINE, SwissProt, and a Mouse Knockout database), the science news magazine *HMS Beagle*, and an annotated list of Web Links.

BioScience Research Tool. Durham, NH: Biochemie.net. URL: http://www. biochemie.net/. ''This web site provides you with hundreds of advanced online tools and resources, selected by BioScientists for BioScientists.'' It is arranged by subject, and includes journals, societies, databases, and much more.

Directory of Scholarly Electronic Journals, Newsletters, and Academic Discussion Lists. Look at the Directories section for information.

Humphries, Julian. Biodiversity and Biological Collections Web Server. New Orleans, LA: University of New Orleans, 1995– . URL: http://biodiversity. bio.uno.edu/. "Devoted to information of interest to systematists and other biologists of the organismic kind." Covers everything from microorganisms to plants to animals, and includes links to societies, directories, journals, and other Web sites.

INFOMINE: Biological, Agricultural, and Medical Sciences. Riverside, CA: University of California-Riverside. URL: http://infomine.ucr.edu/search/bioagsearch.phtml. INFOMINE is a scholarly Internet resource collection. It provides links to resources such as online subject guides, databases, and textbooks, as well as newsgroups, directories, archives, and indexes. Some resources, such as electronic journals, are only available for UC-Riverside affiliates, but most are universally available.

Online Ethics Center for Engineering and Science. Cleveland, OH: Case Western Reserve University, 1995– . URL: http://onlineethics.org/. Provides links to a number of useful resources dealing with ethical issues in science. The biology links include material on the use of animals in research, laboratory safety, and more general ethical issues.

Open Directory Project, 1998– . URL: http//dmoz.org/Science/Biology/. A Netscape/AOL project. This well-known directory uses volunteer editors to create its extensive collection of links, with peer review as a quality check. There were over 18,000 biology sites in May 2001, most of them well chosen. ODP data is used by other Web directories, including Google, Lycos, and many specialized directories.

UniGuide: Academic Guide to the Internet. Aldea Communications, 1998– . URL: http://www.aldea.com/guides/ag/attframes2.html. "Academic Guide to the Internet," from Aldea Communications. This directory is arranged by broad categories. Lists conferences, directories, grants, libraries, newsgroups, video conferences, and Web databases, journals, and software. Each guide is reviewed by librarians and content experts. Formerly: InterNIC Academic Guide to the Internet.

WWW Virtual Library: Bioscience. WWW Virtual Library, 1994– . URL: http://www.vlib.org/Biosciences.html. Arranged by subject category, this venerable guide has been around since the dawn of the Web and is supported by a number of societies. The subject categories may be very narrow (plant parasitic nematodes) or broad (cell biology), and vary in quality, currency, and size. This is a good starting point for almost any subject.

yourDictionary.com. yourDictionary.com, Inc., 2001. URL: http://www. yourdictionary.com/diction4.html. This site lists specialized Web dictionaries and encyclopedias, including dictionaries covering subjects such as anatomy, dinosaurs, carnivorous plants, and medicinal herbs.

GUIDES TO THE LITERATURE

BIOSIS Previews Search Guide. For more information, see Chapter 2, "Subject Access."

Hurt, Charlie Deuel. *Information Sources in Science and Technology.* 3rd ed. Englewood, CO: Libraries Unlimited, 1998. 346 p. (Library and information science text series). $45.00 (paper). ISBN 1563085283, 1563085313 (paper). A standard guide to major sources in science and technology, with over 1,500 annotations covering all areas from biology to engineering, including agriculture and health sciences.

Information Sources in the Life Sciences. 4th rev. ed. H. V. Wyatt, ed. New Providence, NJ: Bowker/Saur, 1997. (Guides to Information Sources). 264 p. $95.00. ISBN 1857390709. This guide is designed to help students learn about the scientific literature. There are chapters discussing various types of resources, from newsletters and invisible colleges to databases and other indexes. In addition, there are chapters broken down by subject that discuss the literature of that specific subject.

Introduction to Reference Sources in the Health Sciences. 3rd ed. Fred W. Roper and Jo Anne Boorkman, eds. Metuchen, NJ: Scarecrow Press, 1994. 301 p. $37.00. ISBN 0810828898. Designed for library school students who are interested in the medical sciences. The list of reference sources is useful for everyone.

Malinowsky, H. Robert. *Reference Sources in Science, Engineering, Medicine, and Agriculture.* Phoenix, AZ: Oryx, 1994. 328 p. $49.95. ISBN 0897747453 (paper). More than 2,400 bibliographic entries covering science, engineering, medicine, and agriculture provide complete descriptions of important reference materials for the student and/or librarian.

Morehead, Joe and Mary Fetzer. *Introduction to United States Government Information Sources.* 6th ed. Englewood Cliffs, CO: Libraries Unlimited, 1999. 446 p. $47.50. ISBN 1563083359 (paper). This classic textbook serves as a guide to sources of government publications in print, nonprint, and electronic format.

Stern, David. *Guide to Information Sources in the Physical Sciences.* (Reference Sources in Science and Technology Series) Littleton, CO: Libraries Unlimited, 2000. 222 p. $65.00 ISBN 1563087510. This guide provides a basic overview of current trends, and the most important paper and electronic information resources in the field of physics. Information on grants, personal bibliographic database tools, document delivery, copyright, and class reserves is also presented.

Walford's Guide to Reference Material: Science and Technology. 8th ed. A. J. Walford, Marilyn Mullay, and Priscilla Schlicke, eds. London: Library Association, 1999. v. 1. $269.00 (v. 1). ISBN 185604341X (v. 1). A standard guide to reference sources.

Wiggins, Gary. *Chemical Information Sources.* New York: McGraw-Hill, 1991. 352 p. (McGraw-Hill series in advanced chemistry). $84.50. ISBN 0079099394. A well-known comprehensive guide to the literature of chemistry, covering both print and online resources. Updated on the Web at the Cheminfo site at http://indiana.edu/cheminfo/index.html (see Chapter 5, "Biochemistry and Biophysics," for details).

HANDBOOKS

The ACS Style Guide: A Manual for Authors and Editors. 2nd ed. Janet S. Dodd, ed. Washington, DC: American Chemical Society, 1997. 460 p. $26.95 (paper). ISBN 0841234612, 0841234620 (paper). Covers all the usual topics for scientific style manuals, including formats, grammar and style, preparing illustrations, copyright law, and preparing talks and poster sessions. Also discusses conventions used in presenting chemical information.

Ambrose, Harrison W. and Katharine Peckham Ambrose. *A Handbook of Biological Investigation.* 6th ed. Winston-Salem, NC: Hunter Textbooks, 2001. 220 p. $24.95 (paper). ISBN 0887252664 (paper). A guide to doing biological research for undergraduates. It covers deciding on a project, statistical methods, doing literature searches, and how to write and illustrate a scientific paper.

Barker, K. *At the Bench: A Laboratory Navigator.* New York: Cold Spring Harbor Laboratory Press, 1998. 460 p. $47.00. ISBN 0879695234. A humorous guide to life in the laboratory, covering both social and technical aspects. The reader will learn everything from how to get along with co-workers, how to use common equipment, and how to perform first aid on a computer keyboard after a soft-drink spill.

Biomass Handbook. Osamu Kitani and Carl W. Hall, eds. New York: Gordon and Breach, 1989. 963 p. $744.00. ISBN 2881242693. Aim is to provide comprehensive knowledge of biomass and related systems, including recent technological developments in biotechnology, production, conversion, transportation, and utilization. Contains numerous tables, charts, graphs, and statistics plus author and subject indexes.

The Chicago Manual of Style. 14th ed. Chicago: University of Chicago Press, 1993. 921 p. $36.00. ISBN 0226103897.   One of the standard style manuals. Most of the advice in this manual is aimed at authors in the humanities and social sciences, though the manual provides information on scientific citation style.

CRC Handbook of Chemistry and Physics. 81st ed. Boca Raton, FL: CRC Press, 2000. 2,556 p. $129.95, $195.00 (CD-ROM). ISBN 0849304814, 849308798 (CD-ROM).   Indispensable, reliable source for chemical, physical, and engineering data including mathematical tables, elements and inorganic compounds, general chemical tables, physical constants, etc. Also available on the Web ($1,295).

CRC Handbook of Laboratory Safety. 5th ed. Boca Raton, FL: CRC Press, 2000. 808 p. $149.99. ISBN 0849325234.   Authoritative reference providing information on OSHA safety regulations, protective equipment, chemical reactions, hazards of ventilation, fire, toxic substances, radiation, infection, microbiological techniques, etc.

Day, Robert A. *How to Write and Publish a Scientific Paper.* 5th ed. Phoenix, AZ: Oryx, 1998. 296 p. $34.95, $24.50 (paper). ISBN 1573561649, 1573561657 (paper).   A highly regarded guide to organizing, writing, and submitting scientific research for publication. The latest edition includes information on electronic publishing formats such newsgroups, electronic journals, and the Web.

Electronic Reference Formats Recommended by the American Psychological Association. American Psychological Association, 1999. URL: http://www.apastyle. org/elecref.html.   Covers citing e-mail communications, Web sites and specific Web documents, and electronic documents retrieved from an electronic database or full-text resource. The APA style is similar to most scientific styles and provides good guidelines for citing electronic resources.

The Facts on File Biology Handbook. New York: Facts on File, 2000. 223 p. (Facts on File science library). $35.00. ISBN 0816040796.   A general handbook for high school students and undergraduates, in four sections: an illustrated glossary, brief biographies of scientists, chronologies of events, and essential charts and tables.

Gad, Shayne C. and Stephanie M. Taulbee. *Handbook of Data Recording, Maintenance, and Management for the Biomedical Sciences.* Boca Raton, FL: CRC Press, 1996. 85 p. $54.95. ISBN 0849301378.   "Explains how to maintain a scientific log that will withstand peer, federal, and other reviewing agencies' scrutiny . . . . It covers data monitoring, recording and maintenance; quality assurance; and printed forms, and the laws and regulations that impact their design and use."

Geigy Scientific Tables. 8th rev. ed. West Caldwell, NJ: Ciba-Geigy Corp. 6 v. 1981–1992. ISBN 0914168509. Tables for units of measurement, body fluids, nutrition, statistics, mathematical formulae, physical chemistry, blood, somatometric data, biochemistry, inborn error of metabolism, pharmacogenetics and ecogenetics, heart and circulation, and bacteria and protozoa. Although these volumes are now out of print, they are still extremely useful.

Genetics and Cell Biology on File. New York: Facts On File, 1997. 1 v. $165.00 (binder), $165 (CD-ROM). ISBN 0816035725 (binder), 0816024128 (CD-ROM). A series of noncopyright illustrations for classroom use. Divided into Techniques, Cell Types and Evolution, Cell Biology, Cell Division, Classical Genetics, Molecular Genetics, and Population Genetics and Evolution.

Hailman, J. P. and K. B. Strier. *Planning, Proposing, and Presenting Science Effectively: A Guide for Graduate Students and Researchers in the Behavioral Sciences and Biology.* New York: Cambridge University Press, 1997. 182 p. $49.95, $17.95 (paper). ISBN 0521560233, 0521568757 (paper). This guide was written specifically for students in biology and behavioral sciences and offers practical guidelines on the process from writing proposals to presenting results. Includes a list of criteria for evaluating research proposals.

Handbooks and Tables in Science and Technology. 3rd ed. Russell H. Powell, ed. Phoenix, AZ: Oryx, 1994. 359 p. $95.00. ISBN 0897745345. Compilation of over 3,600 handbooks and tables in science, technology, and medicine, completely indexed by subject, keyword, author/editor, and title. The main section is arranged alphabetically by title and includes complete bibliographic information, and a brief annotation. Popular "how to" handbooks, dictionaries, encyclopedias, field guides, maps, directories, biographical sources, indexing, abstracting, and current awareness sources are generally excluded.

The Handbooks of Aging: Consisting of Three Volumes: Critical Comprehensive Reviews of Research Knowledge, Theories, Concepts, and Issues. 4th ed. James E. Birren, ed. San Diego, CA: Academic Press, 1996. 3 v. $69.95 (v. 1), $54.95 (v. 2), $54.95 (v. 3). ISBN 0126278733 (v. 1, paper), 0121012603 (v.2, paper), 0120991934 (v.3, paper). V. 1: *Handbook of the Biology of Aging*; V. 2: *Handbook of the Psychology of Aging*; V. 3: *Handbook of Aging and the Social Sciences.*

Illustrating Science: Standards for Publication. Bethesda, MD: Council of Biology Editors, 1988. 296 p. $49.95. ISBN 0914340050. Purpose of the book is to develop specific standards and guidelines for publication of illustrated scientific material. The Association of Medical Illustrators, the Guild of Natural Science Illustrators, the Biological Photographic Association, and the Graphic Artists Guild collaborated on this project. Also, refer to Zweifel later in this section.

Knowing How to Practice Safe Science. Chevy Chase, MD: Howard Hughes Medical Institute, 1998. URL: http://www.practicingsafescience.org/. This free online course provides information on laboratory safety. A final exam is available if the entire course is completed. The site also offers links to other laboratory safety resources.

Kotyk, Arnošt. *Quantities, Symbols, Units, and Abbreviations in the Life Sciences: A Guide for Authors and Editors.* Totowa, NJ: Humana Press, 1999. 130 p. $39.50, $15.60 (paper). ISBN 0896036162, 0896036499 (paper). Provides guidelines for the use of terms in the biological sciences, based on recommendations from the member societies of the International Council of Scientific Unions (ICSU). The guide includes information from mathematics, statistics, physics, chemistry, the health sciences, paleontology, and psychology as well as biology.

Lee, R. U. *How to Find Information: Medicine and Biology.* London: British Library, Science Reference and Information Service, 1996. 20 p. ISBN 0712308377 (paper). This slim little booklet provides information on how to do literature searches in the life sciences. While the author is British and the details of search systems are dated, the booklet is still useful for finding general tips and search strategies.

Lewis, Richard J., Sr. *Hazardous Chemicals Desk Reference.* 4th ed. New York: John Wiley, 1997. 1,644 p. $149.00. ISBN 0471287792. Provides information on over 6,000 common compounds used in laboratories and in manufacturing. Each chemical has an Essential Data Profile with information on its potential as a poison, irritant, corrosive, explosive, and carcinogen along with synonyms, usage, and other data.

Life Sciences on File. Rev. ed. New York: Facts On File, 1999. 1 v. $165.00 (binder), $165.00 (CD-ROM). ISBN 0816038724 (binder), 0816042160 (CD-ROM). Contains reproducible diagrams and drawings covering life sciences topics. In six sections (unity of life, continuity, maintenance, human biology, and ecology). A very useful supplement to textbooks and classroom exercises. Also available online.

McMillan, Victoria E. *Writing Papers in the Biological Sciences.* 2nd ed. Boston, MA: St. Martin's Press, 1997. 197 p. $24.85. ISBN 0312115040. The second edition of this well-reviewed book covers important topics like locating and using the biological literature, handling data, using tales and figures, writing research and review papers, documentation, preparing the final draft, using writing to prepare exams, and other forms of biological writing. Additional readings are suggested.

The Nature Yearbook of Science and Technology 2001. Declan Butler, ed. London: Macmillan Reference, 2001. 1,500 p. $80.00. ISBN 0333945743. Includes articles, facts and figures on science research, top science institutes and leading scientists, annual prizes, and much more.

Pechenik, Jan A. *A Short Guide to Writing About Biology*. 4th ed. New York: Longman, 2001. 318 p. $25.00. ISBN 0321078438.   This book, aimed at college students and teachers, covers aspects of biology writing and related topics such as laboratory reports, term papers, preparing research proposals, letters of application and resumes, and giving oral presentations. Both content and style of writing are covered.

Ramamoorthy, S. and E.G. Baddaloo. *Handbook of Chemical Toxicity Profiles of Biological Species*. Boca Raton, FL: Lewis, 1995. 2 v. ISBN 1566700132 (v. 1), 1566700140 (v. 2).   Each volume includes an index to the chemicals covered and a list of toxicity data by species. Volume 1 covers aquatic species and volume 2 covers avian and mammalian species (mostly standard laboratory animals).

Scientific Style and Format: The CBE Manual for Authors, Editors, and Publishers. 6th ed. New York: Cambridge University Press, 1994. 825 p. $39.95. ISBN 0521471540.   This manual covers publication style guidelines (i.e., how publications should be styled and formatted) for all of the scientific disciplines. There are specific guidelines for scientific conventions in such areas as chemical names, cells and genes, and astronomical objects. There are also sections on formatting for books, journals, and other publication types, and information on the publishing process.

Shields, Nancy E. and Mary E. Uhle. *Where Credit Is Due: A Guide to Proper Citing of Sources, Print and Nonprint*. 2nd ed. Lanham, MD: Scarecrow Press, 1997. 208 p. $32.50. ISBN 0819832119.   This standard guide provides a step-by-step approach, with the second edition including electronic source material.

Smith, Robert V. *Graduate Research: A Guide for Students in the Sciences*. 3rd ed. Seattle, WA: University of Washington Press, 1998. 192 p. $15.00 (paper). ISBN 0295977051 (paper).   Problems of developing and improving research skills and preparing for professional careers are addressed in this step-by-step, detailed guide. Topics range from ''Getting Started'' to ''Getting a Job,'' with chapters on ethics; time management; library work; choosing an advisor, a research problem, and role models, just to mention a few topics discussed in this highly recommended and very useful guide.

Valiela, Ivan. *Doing Science: Design, Analysis, and Communication of Scientific Research*. New York: Oxford University Press, 2001. 294 p. $75.00, $39.50 (paper). ISBN 0195079620, 0195134133 (paper).   A graduate student's guide to research, from formulating questions to presenting the results. The author, a researcher at the Woods Hole Marine Biology Laboratory, discusses writing papers and presenting data in detail, from writing clear, direct prose to presenting data in an understandable manner. There are also chapters on the public perception of science and the future of science.

Walker, Janice R. and Todd W. Taylor. *The Columbia Guide to Online Style.* New York: Columbia University Press, 1998. 218 p. $37.00, $18.50 (paper). ISBN 0231107889, 0231107897 (paper).   A very highly regarded guide to citing e-mail and discussion group messages, Web pages, and numerous other electronic sources. Much of the information in the guide is also freely available on the Web at http://www.columbia.edu/cu/cup/cgos/idx_basic.html.

Winter, Charles A. and Kathleen Solikoff. *Opportunities in Biological Science Careers.* Rev. ed. Lincolnwood, IL: VGM Career Horizons, 1998. 149 p. $14.95. ISBN 084422300X.   The aim of this book is to provide information on career guidance, potential employers, and job hunting.

Zweifel, Frances W. *A Handbook of Biological Illustration.* 2nd ed. Chicago, IL: University of Chicago Press, 1988. 160 p. (Chicago Guides to Writing, Editing, & Publishing). $14.00. ISBN 0226997014 (paper).   The objective is to assist the nonartist biologist in producing useful, and even aesthetically pleasing, illustrations. Written by a well-known freelance biological illustrator. See, also, *Illustrating Science* annotated earlier in this section.

HISTORIES

The American Development of Biology. Ronald Rainger, et al., eds. New Brunswick, NJ: Rutgers University Press, 1991. 380 p. $20.00 (paper). ISBN 0813517028 (paper).   This book, like *The Expansion of American Biology* (see following text), was commissioned by the American Society of Zoologists to celebrate its centennial (1889–1989).

American Men and Women of Science: A Biographical Directory of Today's Leaders in Physical, Biological and Related Science. 21st ed. New York: Bowker, 2001. 8 v. $1,150.00 (set). ISBN 0835243443 (set).   Information includes birthplace and date, spouse and children's names, scientific field, education, honors and awards, experience, research focus, professional membership, e-mail, fax, and mailing address.

Appel, Toby A. *Shaping Biology: The National Science Foundation and American Biological Research, 1945–1975.* Baltimore, MD: Johns Hopkins University Press, 2000. 393 p. $42.50. ISBN 080186321X.   A historical account of biological research support from the National Science Foundation during a thirty-year period. This history gives a picture of policy decisions and actions that helped shape the field of biology.

Archives of Natural History. v. 1– , 1981– . London: Natural History Museum. Three issues per year. ISSN 0260–9541.   Published by the Society for the History of Natural History and is devoted to publishing papers within the broad field of the interest of the Society. Supersedes the *Journal of the Society for the Bibliography of Natural History*.

Asimov, Isaac. *Asimov's Biographical Encyclopedia of Science and Technology: The Lives and Achievements of 1,510 Great Scientists from Ancient Times to the Present Chronologically Arranged*. 2nd rev. ed. Garden City, NY: Doubleday, 1982. 941 p. ISBN 0385177712.   Biographical guide to the history of science concentrating chiefly on the last two centuries.

Asimov, Isaac. *A Short History of Biology*. Westport, CT: Greenwood Press, 1980. 189 p. $47.50. ISBN 0313225834.   This brief history is by one of the most prolific and well-known popular science writers. Originally published in 1964.

Bailey, Martha J. *American Women in Science 1950 to the Present: A Biographical Dictionary*. Santa Barbara, CA: ABC-CLIO: 1998. 455 p. $75.00. ISBN 0874369215.   Three hundred biographical entries provide information on the female scientist's background, employment history, honors, publications, and scientific and social impact. For a broader scope from antiquity to the mid-twentieth century, see *Biographical Dictionary of Women in Science* in the following text.

The Biographical Dictionary of Scientists. 3rd ed. Roy Porter and Marilyn Bailey Ogilvie, eds. New York: Oxford University Press, 2000. 6 vol. $125.00. ISBN 0195216636.   Contains biographical information for over 1,200 scientists from astronomy, chemistry, physics, biology, mathematics, engineering, technology, and geology. Seven chronological reviews of significant developments in various scientific areas, an extensive glossary, a list of Nobel laureates, and a comprehensive index are included.

Biographical Dictionary of Women in Science: Pioneering Lives from Ancient Times to the Mid-20th Century. Marilyn Bailey Ogilvie and Joy Dorothy Harvey, eds. New York: Routledge, 2000. 1,500 p. $195.00. ISBN 0415920388.   Analyses of nearly 3,000 scientists' lives, works, and accomplishments; may be updated by Bailey's *American Women in Science 1950 to the Present*, previous.

Biographical Encyclopedia of Scientists. 2nd ed. John Daintith, et al., eds. Philadelphia, PA: Institute of Physics, 1994. 2 v. $220.00. ISBN 0750302879 (set).   Contains a biography section of over short 2,000 entries. Name and subject indexes.

Bonta, Marcia Myers. *Women in the Field: America's Pioneering Women Naturalists*. College Station, TX: Texas A & M University Press, 1991. 229 p. $16.95

(paper). ISBN 089096467X, 0890964890 (paper). Biographies of 25 women
naturalists, from colonial time to the present. A companion book *American
Women Afield*, reprints material written by many of these women. Both provide
an interesting window into the history of women naturalists.

Cambridge Dictionary of Scientists. David Millar, et al., eds. New York: Cambridge University Press, 1996. 387 p. $23.75. ISBN 0521567181. This diction-
ary profiles a limited number (1,300) of leading scientists from early to modern
times across the range of scientific disciplines. Appropriate for secondary and
college collections.

Concise Dictionary of Scientific Biography. 2nd ed. New York: Charles Scribners,
2000. 1,097 p. $156.25. ISBN 0684806312. Published under the auspices of
the American Council of Learned Societies, this is an abridgement of the authoritative and comprehensive *Dictionary of Scientific Biography* (see following text),
complete through Supplement 11, and includes an index.

Conn, Steven. *Museums and American Intellectual Life, 1876–1926*. Chicago,
IL: University of Chicago Press, 1998. 293 p. $32.50. ISBN 0226114929. This
study of American museums between 1876 and 1926 uses case studies to describe
how museums of that period functioned as places of intellectual and scientific
work. Chapters range from natural history to commercial to ethnological to art
museums, and explain how museums of this period gradually passed their intellectual and scientific role to other institutions.

The Correspondence of Charles Darwin. Frederick Burkhardt and Sydney Smith
eds. New York: Cambridge University Press, 1985– . Price varies. A monumental work of scholarship that includes a host of famous biologist/scientist cor-
respondents. Currently up to volume 11, covering the year 1863.

Dictionary of the History of Science. W. F. Bynum et al., eds. Princeton, NJ:
Princeton University Press, 1985 reprint. 494 p. $31.95 (paper). ISBN
0691023840 (paper). Seven hundred signed articles discuss the key ideas and
core features of recent Western science in all fields. A useful briefly annotated
bibliography and biographical index are included.

Dictionary of Scientific Biography. Charles Coulston Gillispie, ed. New York:
Scribner, 1981. 9 v. $1,650.00 (set). ISBN 068480588X (set). "Published under
the auspices of the American Council of Learned Societies." Covers all areas
of science with over 5,000 lengthy, detailed entries and citations to portraits for
the most famous scientists. Includes bibliographies and index. For the abridged
edition, see *Concise Dictionary of Scientific Biography*, previous.

The Expansion of American Biology. Keith R. Benson et al., eds. New Brunswick,
NJ: Rutgers University Press, 1991. 357 p. $45.00. ISBN 0813516501. This is

the second in the two-part series commissioned by the American Society of Zoologists of original, unpublished articles discussing twentieth-century American biology. (Also, see *The American Development of Biology*, previous.)

Farber, Paul Lawrence. *Finding Order in Nature: The Naturalist Tradition from Linnaeus to E. O. Wilson*. Baltimore, MD: Johns Hopkins University Press, 2000. 136 p. (Johns Hopkins introductory studies in the history of science). $39.95. ISBN 0801863899, 0801863902 (paper). This history, first in a series of introductory studies, surveys the past 300 or so years of natural history, providing beginning naturalists an orientation to their field.

Ford, Brian J. *Images of Science: A History of Scientific Illustration*. New York: Oxford University Press, 1993. 208 p. ISBN 0195209834. The author chronicles the importance of the role of illustration in spreading scientific information (and error), and in establishing the origin and development of ideas.

Fry, Iris. *Emergence of Life on Earth, a History and Scientific Overview*. New Brunswick, NJ: Rutgers University Press, 2000. 327 p. $55.00, $24.00 (paper). ISBN 0813527392, 0813527406 (paper). This is a review of the main ideas on the origin of life from antiquity until the twentieth century. Fry examines contemporary theories and major debates from the historical, scientific, and philosophical points of view.

Himmelfarb, Gertrude. *Darwin and the Darwinian Revolution*. Chicago, IL: Ivan R. Dee, 1996. 510 p. $18.95 (paper). ISBN 1566631068 (paper). This classic historical study reports the impact of Darwinism on the intellectual climate of the nineteenth century as it challenges the conventional view of Darwin's greatness.

Historical Studies in the Physical and Biological Sciences. v. 16– , 1986– . Berkeley: University of California Press. Semiannual. $71.00. ISSN 0890–9997. Continues *Historical Studies in the Physical Sciences* and covers history of physics, biology, and other sciences.

Hughes, Arthur Frederick William. *The American Biologist Through Four Centuries*. Springfield, IL: Thomas, 1982. 386 p. ISBN 0398045984 (paper). Biographies of American biologists.

Irmscher, Christoph. *The Poetics of Natural History: From John Bartram to William James*. New Brunswick, NJ: Rutgers University Press, 1999. 320 p. $42.00. ISBN 0813526159. Accounts of lives, attitudes, and collections of early North American naturalists deliver an interesting addition to the natural history of colonial America.

Isis: An International Review Devoted to the History of Science and its Cultural Influences. v. 1– . 1913– . Chicago, IL: University of Chicago Press for the History of Science Society. Quarterly. $178.00. ISSN 0021–1753. Provides review articles, research notes, documents, discussions, news, and critical bibliographies of the history of science and its cultural influences. An excellent source for keeping up with the historical literature of the biological sciences.

Jardine, Lisa. *Ingenious Pursuits; Building the Scientific Revolution.* New York: Nan A. Talese, 1999. 464 p. $35.00 ISBN 0385493258. This introductory text for nonhistorians takes a revisionist approach to the scientific revolution, with emphasis on natural history.

Journal of the History of Biology. v. 1– 1968– . Norwell, MA: Kluwer. Triennial. $270.00. ISSN 0022–5010. Available electronically. "Devoted to the history of the biological sciences, with additional interest and concern in philosophical and social issues confronting biology. While all historical epochs are welcome, particular attention has been paid in recent years to developments during the nineteenth and twentieth centuries."

Kronick, David A. *Scientific and Technical Periodicals of the Seventeenth and Eighteenth Centuries: A Guide.* Metuchen, NJ: Scarecrow, 1991. 332 p. $48.00. ISBN 0810824922. A list of 1,851 early European and American periodicals from 1665 to 1800.

Lahav, Noam. *Biogenesis: Theories of Life's Origin.* New York: Oxford University Press, 1999. 349 p. $65.00. ISBN 0195117549. An up-to-date discussion of the interdisciplinary study of the origin of life, delving into history, experimental strategies, theories, models, and controversies.

Magner, Lois N. *A History of Medicine.* New York: Dekker, 1992. 393 p. $59.95. ISBN 0824786734. A concise account of medical history from paleopathology to the practices of modern medicine.

Magner, Lois N. *A History of the Life Sciences,* 2nd ed. New York: Dekker, 1994. 496 p. $39.95. ISBN 0824789423. Introduction to the main themes of biology through the post Watson-Crick period.

Maienschein, Jane. *Transforming Traditions in American Biology 1880–1915.* Baltimore, MD: Johns Hopkins University Press, 1991. 288 p. $50.00. ISBN 0801841267. A snapshot of the history of the development of the biological sciences in the United States, focusing on Edmund Beecher Wilson, Thomas Hunt Morgan, Edwin Grant Conklin, and Ross Granville Harrison.

Mayr, Ernst. *This Is Biology: The Science of the Living World.* Cambridge, MA: Belknap Press, 1998. 352 p. $16.95. ISBN 0674884698. An active participant and an eloquent standard bearer of the theory of evolution, Mayer traces the development of biology from ancient Greeks to the arrival of modern molecular techniques.

Moore, John Alexander. *Science as a Way of Knowing: The Foundations of Modern Biology*. Cambridge, MA: Harvard University Press, 1999. 530 p. $18.95 (paper). ISBN 0674794826 (paper). "The story of the development of concepts in the biological sciences" told in four parts: Understanding Nature, Growth of Evolutionary Thought, Classical Genetics, and the Enigma of Development.

Nobel e-Museum. Stockholm: The Nobel Foundation, 2000. URL: http://www.nobel.se/medicine/index.html. This is the official site of the Nobel Foundation, and includes lists of all Nobel laureates, with biographical information, press releases, and discussion of the importance of the laureates' work.

Notable Women in the Life Sciences: A Biographical Dictionary. Benjamin F. Shearer and Barbara Smith Shearer, eds. Westport, CT: Greenwood, 1996. 440 p. $52.50. ISBN 0313293023. Includes 97 women from North America and the world. The scientists range from historical figures such as Hildegard of Bingen to modern women such as Barbara McClintock. The subjects were chosen because they were well known and/or were winners of major prizes. Each entry includes biographical information and an explanation of the importance of the subject's research, and many include interviews.

The Origins of Natural Science in America: The Essays of George Brown Goode. Sally Gregory Kohlstedt, ed. Washington, DC: Smithsonian Institution Press, 1991. 432 p. ISBN 1560980982. A reprint of five essays by the American naturalist, curator, and museum administrator George Brown Good (1851–1896). Originally published in 1901.

Overmier, Judith A. *The History of Biology: A Selected, Annotated Bibliography*. New York: Garland, 1989. (Bibliographies of the History of Science and Technology, vol. 15). 157 p. ISBN 0824091183. This award-winning bibliography includes 619 annotated entries providing access to the history of biology. There are 17 pages of author and subject indexes that are especially useful for the beginning historian of science.

The Philosophy of Biology. David L. Hull and Michael Ruse, eds. (Oxford Readings in Philosophy). New York: Oxford University Press, 1998. 630 p. $24.95 (paper). ISBN 0198752121 (paper). This volume combines articles from the philosophy, history, and sociology of science, considering such issues as evolutionary theory, biology and ethics, the challenge from religion, and the social implications of contemporary biology.

Singer, Charles. *A History of Biology to about the Year 1900: A General Introduction to the Study of Living Things*. Rev. ed. Ames, IA: Iowa State University Press, 1989. (History of science and technology reprint series). 616 p. ISBN 0813809371. A classic history, originally published in 1959.

Smit, Pieter. *History of the Life Sciences; An Annotated Bibliography*. New York: Hafner Press, 1974. 1,071 p. ISBN 0028525108.   This historical bibliography contains more than 4,000 entries with full bibliographical information plus a summary review of the work cited. The work is divided into general references and tools; historiography of the life and medical sciences; a selected list of biographies, bibliographies, etc., of famous biologists, and medical men; and an index of personal names.

Watson, James D. *The Double Helix: A Personal Account of the Discovery of the Structure of DNA*. For a complete annotation, see the History section in Chapter 6, "Molecular and Cellular Biology."

MATHEMATICS AND STATISTICS

This array of resources was selected to give choices to the beginning student and the more experienced researcher.

Bailey, Norman T. J. *Statistical Methods in Biology*. 3rd ed. New York: Cambridge University Press, 1995. 255 p. $20.95 (paper). ISBN 0521470323, 052146983X (paper).   A basic statistics "cookbook." Includes a summary of statistical formulae, and appendixes of abridged statistical tables.

Biomathematics. v. 1–   . 1970–   . New York: Springer-Verlag. Irregular. Price varies. ISSN 0067–8821.   Volume 24, *Molecular Evolution* by Vadim Ratner is the most recent. The series provides a tool kit of modeling techniques with examples from population ecology, reaction kinetics, biological oscillators, developmental biology, evolution, and other areas, with emphasis on practical applications.

Biometrics: Journal of the Biometric Society. v. 3– , 1947– . Alexandria, VA: Biometric Society. Quarterly. $110.00. ISSN 0006–341X.   The objectives "are to promote and extend the use of mathematical and statistical methods in the various subject-matter disciplines, by describing and exemplifying developments in these methods and their application in a form readily assimilable by experimenters and those concerned primarily with analysis of data." Formerly: *Biometrics Bulletin*.

Brown, David and P. Rothery. *Models in Biology: Mathematics, Statistics and Computing*. New York: Wiley, 1993. 688 p. $84.95. ISBN 0471933228.   An introduction to the use of mathematical models in biology, statistical techniques for fitting and testing them, and associated computing methods.

Bulletin of Mathematical Biology. v. 35– , 1973– . New York: Academic Press. Bimonthly. $741.00. ISSN 0092–8240. Available electronically.   "Devoted to research at the junction of computational, theoretical and experimental biology.'' Formerly: *Bulletin of Mathematical Biophysics.*

CRC Standard Mathematical Tables and Formulae. 30th ed. Daniel Zwillinger, ed. Boca Raton, FL: CRC, 1999. 812 p. $49.95. ISBN 0849324793. Covers constants and conversion factors; algebra; combinatorial analysis; geometry; trigonometry; logarithmic, exponential, and hyperbolic functions; analytic geometry; calculus; differential equations; linear algebra; special functions; numerical methods; probability and statistics; and financial tables.

Clarke, Geoffrey M. *Statistics and Experimental Design: An Introduction for Biologists and Biochemists.* 3rd ed. New York: Wiley, 1994. 160 p. $35.00 (paper). ISBN 0340593245 (paper). Describes how to use statistical methods, interpret the results, and illustrate reports with suitable graphics. Numerous examples and exercises.

Elston, Robert C. and William D. Johnson. *Essentials of Biostatistics.* 2nd ed. Philadelphia, PA: F. A. Davis, 1994. 328 p. $33.95 (paper). ISBN 0803631235 (paper). An overview of statistical principles, with emphasis on concepts rather than computations.

Fowler, Jim, Louis Cohen, and Phil Jarvis. *Practical Statistics for Field Biology.* 2nd ed. New York: Wiley, 1998. 259 p. $44.95 (paper). ISBN 0471982954, 0471982962 (paper). Not just another statistics text, the authors promise that this book is written specifically to serve field biologists ''whose data are often non-standard and frequently 'messy.' ''

Fry, J. C. *Biological Data Analysis: A Practical Approach.* Oxford, England: IRL Press at Oxford University Press, 1993. 418 p. $65.00. ISBN 0199633401. Aimed at advanced undergraduates as well as professional biologists, this book shows how to analyze biological data with commonly available software packages. There are appendices containing software packages and statistical tables.

Gonick, Larry and Woollcott Smith. *The Cartoon Guide to Statistics.* New York: HarperPerennial, 1993. 230 p. $16.00 (paper). ISBN 0062731025 (paper). A good starting place for those who suffer from fear of statistics to find help in overcoming their fears and gaining a basic understanding of the use and abuse of statistics and probability. Gonick has created other cartoon guides, including a guide to genetics (annotated in Chapter 7, ''Genetics, Biotechnology, and Developmental Biology'').

IMA Journal of Mathematics Applied in Medicine and Biology. v. 1– . 1984– . Oxford, England: Oxford University Press. Quarterly. $335.00. ISSN 0265–0746. Available electronically. ''This journal includes leading edge contributions in pedigree analysis in genetics, the immunology and epidemiology of infectious diseases including AIDS, and many other areas in mathematical biology and biomedicine.'' A publication of the Institute of Mathematics and its Applications.

Journal of Mathematical Biology. v. 1– . 1974– . New York: Springer-Verlag. Monthly. $1,113.00. ISSN 0303–6812. Available electronically. The journal ''focuses on mathematical biology—work that uses mathematical approaches to gain biological understanding or explain biological phenomena.''

Manly, Bryan F. J. *The Design and Analysis of Research Studies.* New York: Cambridge University Press, 1992. 353 p. $39.95 (paper). ISBN 0521425808 (paper). A practical guide on how to design research studies, analyze quantitative data, and interpret the results.

Milton, J. Susan. *Statistical Methods in the Biological and Health Sciences.* 3rd ed. New York: McGraw-Hill, 1998. 600 p. $88.44. ISBN 0072901489. Intended for a first course in statistical methods, or for those with little experience with statistical methods. Emphasis is on understanding the principles as well as practicing them. Specifically chosen for biology and health sciences, knowledge of calculus is not assumed.

Roberts, E. A. *Sequential Data in Biological Experiments: An Introduction for Research Workers.* London: Chapman & Hall, 1992. 240 p. $101.50. ISBN 0412414104. The aim is ''to provide research workers with methods of analyzing data from comparative experiments with sequential observations and to demonstrate special features of the design of such experiments.''

Rohlf, F. James and Robert R. Sokal. *Statistical Tables.* 3rd ed. San Francisco, CA: Freeman, 1994. 220 p. $27.55 (paper). ISBN 071672412X (paper). Ancillary text to Sokal and Rohlf's *Biometry*, providing statistical tables for the biological sciences.

Sokal, Robert R. and F. James Rohlf. *Biometry: The Principles and Practice of Statistics in Biological Research.* 3rd ed. San Francisco, CA: Freeman, 1994. 880 p. ISBN 0716724111. Companion to Rohlf and Sokal's *Statistical Tables. Biometry* emphasizes practical applications of science, from physical and life science examples.

Wardlaw, A. C. *Practical Statistics for Experimental Biologists.* 2nd ed. New York: Wiley, 2000. 249 p. $95.00, $40.00 (paper). ISBN 0471988219, 0471988227 (paper). A user-friendly handbook describing basic statistical methods and software packages.

Zar, Jerrold H. *Biostatistical Analysis.* 3rd ed. Upper Saddle River, NJ: Prentice Hall, 1996. 1 v. $79.00. ISBN 0130845426. A standard textbook/reference covering a wide variety of techniques. Includes examples and problems, with answers.

Zwillinger, Daniel and Stephen Kokoska. *CRC Standard Probability and Statistics Tables and Formulae.* Boca Raton, FL: Chapman & Hall/CRC, 2000. 554 p. $49.95. ISBN 1584880597. Provides standard statistical tables, with descriptions of each test and examples.

METHODS AND TECHNIQUES

Arnold, Zach M. *A Technical Manual for the Biologist: A Guide to the Construction and Use of Numerous Tools of Value to the Economy-Minded Student of Microscopic and Small Macroscopic Free-Living Organisms.* Pacific Grove, CA: Boxwood Press, 1993. $24.95. ISBN 0940168243. This manual is based on marine protozoological techniques, tools, and apparatus that were developed for marine geobiology. More general discussions demonstrate its wider potential: field and laboratory procedures and equipment, pedagogical methods, working with plastics, safety, and references to the original literature.

Bradbury, Savile and Brian Bracegirdle. *Introduction to Light Microscopy.* 2nd ed. (Microscopy Handbooks, No. 42). New York: Springer-Verlag, 1998. 144 p. $32.95. ISBN 038791515X (paper). Introduction to the light microscope in the outstanding series from the Royal Microscopical Society; includes a glossary and a list for further reading.

Carter, David J. and Annette K. Walker. *Care and Conservation of Natural History Collections.* Boston, MA: Butterworth-Heinemann, 1999. 226 p. (Butterworth-Heinemann series in conservation and museology). $99.95. ISBN 0750609613. Arranged by type of organism. Lists and describes specific methods for preserving specimens and general issues such as pest management and proper documentation. Both modern and classic methods are described and evaluated for utility and safety.

Cleveland, William S. *Visualizing Data.* Summit, NJ: Hobart Press, 1993. 360 p. $45.00. ISBN 0963488406. The central theme of this book is that visualization is critical to data analysis. Cleveland illustrates how graphing data and fitting mathematical functions to the data can illuminate information and reveal unexpected patterns.

Dykstra, Michael J. *A Manual of Applied Techniques for Biological Electron Microscopy.* New York: Plenum Press, 1993. 252 p. $39.50. ISBN 0306444496. Laboratory procedures for preparation of biological samples for scanning and transmission electron microscopy. Principles for preserving specimen integrity, tips for formulating solutions, procedures for preparation, sectioning techniques, post-staining procedures, and basic approaches are all included.

Electron Microscopy in Biology: A Practical Approach. (Practical Approach Series). Robin Harris, ed. New York: IRL Press, 1991. 308 p. $49.95 (paper). ISBN 0199632197, 0199632154 (paper). Still useful, this volume describes detailed protocols for a wide range of procedures relating to the electron microscopy of tissues, cells, and their components. Included are fundamental methods for specimen preparation, tissue fixation, embedding, sectioning, freeze-substitution, immunogold labeling, autoradiography, and enzyme histochemistry.

Fluorescent and Luminescent Probes. 2nd ed. Mason, W. T., ed. San Diego, CA: Academic Press, 1999. 647 p. $79.95. ISBN 0124478360, spiral bound. With comprehensive treatment of all the major areas of the field, this useful guide provides explanations of underlying theories and a great deal of practical information.

Glasbey, C. A. and G. W. Horgan. *Image Analysis for the Biological Sciences.* New York: J. Wiley, 1995. 218 p. (Statistics in practice). $99.95. ISBN 0471937266. Shows how to analyze a variety of image types, from photomicrographs to satellite images. The appendix provides information on selecting hardware and software for particular applications.

Glauert, Audrey M. and Peter R. Lewis. *Biological Specimen Preparation for Transmission Electron Microscopy.* Princeton, NJ: Princeton University Press, 1998. 316 p. $165.00. ISBN 0691007497. An essential guide to all the latest and reliable methods, aimed at both beginners and experts.

Goldstein, Joseph I., et al. *Scanning Electron Microscopy and X-Ray Microanalysis: A Text for Biologists, Materials Scientists, and Geologists.* 2nd ed. New York: Plenum, 1992. 820 p. $78.00. ISBN 0306441756. This is a text with emphasis on the practical aspects of technique, the basics of operation, image formation, sample preparation, and usage in particular fields.

Gu, Min. *Principles of Three-Dimensional Imaging in Confocal Microscopes.* River Edge, NJ: World Scientific, 1996. 337 p. $60.00. ISBN 9810225504. A systematic introduction and discussion of the various principles and methodology in confocal scanning microscopy, a useful tool in many fields including biological studies and industrial inspection.

Häder, Donat-Peter. *Image Analysis: Methods and Applications.* 2nd ed. Boca Raton, FL: CRC Press, 2001. 463 p. $129.95. ISBN 0849302390. Covers both microscopic and macroscopic image analysis in biology. Revised edition of *Image Analysis in Biology.*

Hangay, George and Michael Dingley. *Biological Museum Methods.* Orlando, FL: Academic Press, 1985. 2 v. $149.00. ISBN 0123233011 (v. 1); 012323302X (v. 2). This set tries to ''highlight the main aspects of the preparator's work, describe as many techniques as practical, and guide the reader to the relevant literature.'' Volume 1 covers vertebrates, while volume 2 covers plants and invertebrates.

Hayat, M. A. *Stains and Cytochemical Methods.* New York: Plenum Press, 1993. 474 p. $125.50. ISBN 0306442949. Considers both theoretical aspects and practical details of cytochemical stains as applied to the detection of macromolecules and heavy metals. Includes staining methods for high-resolution and high-voltage electron microscopy; procedures for staining thin cryosections; step-by-step procedures for staining lipids, nucleic acids, proteins, glycogen, cartilage, muscle, and nervous tissue; preservation of samples; and subcellular localization of metals.

Hunter, Elaine, et al. *Practical Electron Microscopy; A Beginner's Illustrated Guide.* 2nd spiral ed. New York: Cambridge University Press, 1993. 192 p. $36.95. ISBN 0521385393. Extensively illustrated laboratory manual of transmission electron microscopy techniques.

Knoche, Herman W. *Radioisotopic Methods for Biological and Medical Research.* New York: Oxford University Press, 1991. 432 p. $62.00. ISBN 0195058062. This book presents theoretical aspects of radioisotopic methods. Particular attention is given to (1) principles and practices of radiation protection; (2) radioactivity measurement, standardization and monitoring techniques, and instruments; (3) mathematics and calculations basic to the use and measurement of radioactivity; and (4) biological effects of radiation.

Malaro, Marie C. *A Legal Primer on Managing Museum Collections.* 2nd ed. Washington, DC: Smithsonian Institution Press, 1998. 507 p. $60.00, $31.95 (paper). ISBN 1560987626, 1560987871 (paper). Covers a range of topics in managing all kinds of museum collections, such as what is a museum and legal issues in appraisals, acquisitions, loans, and others.

Methods. For a complete annotation, see Chapter 6, ''Molecular and Cellular Biology.''

MethodsFinder 2.0 (BIOSIS). See Chapter 6, ''Molecular and Cellular Biology'' for more information about this Web database for laboratory methods and procedures.

Methods in Enzymology. See Chapter 6, ''Molecular and Cellular Biology'' for a complete annotation.

Optical Microscopy; Emerging Methods and Applications. Brian Herman and John J. Lemasters, eds. New York: Academic Press, 1997. 441 p. $103.00. ISBN 0123420601. A synopsis of the most recent and comprehensive descriptions of new techniques, with emphasis on the life sciences.

Principles and Techniques of Electron Microscopy: Biological Applications. 4th ed. M.A. Hayat, ed. New York: Cambridge University Press, 2000. 543 p. $100.00. ISBN 0521632870. Provides practical instructions on how to process biological specimens and a detailed discussion on the principles underlying the various processes.

Procedures in Electron Microscopy, A. W. Robards and A. J. Wilson, eds. New York: Wiley, 1994. (Wiley Looseleaf Publications). Variously paged. 700 p. $1,475.00. ISBN 0471928534. A comprehensive, updateable lab manual that includes tested techniques and preparation methods, descriptions of expected results, troubleshooting tips, safety notes, special equipment, interpretation of methods, and references. The price includes updates.

Scanning and Transmission Electron Microscopy: An Introduction. Stanley L. Flegler, et al. New York: Oxford University Press, 1995. 225 p. $47.95. ISBN 0195107519. This authoritative introduction to practical and theoretical fundamentals of electron microscopy discusses essentials, including operation, image production, analytical techniques, and potential applications.

Science of Biological Specimen Preparation for Microscopy. Marek Malecki and Godreid M. Roomans, eds. Chicago, IL: Scanning Microscopy International, 1996. 476 p. (Scanning microscopy, Supplement 10). $95.00. ISBN 0931288495. This and earlier editions record the proceedings of the Pfefferkorn Conferences on the Science of Biological Specimen Preparation for Microscopy and Microanalysis.

Smith, Robert F. *Microscopy and Photomicrography; A Working Manual*, 2nd ed. Boca Raton, FL: CRC, 1994. 162 p. $62.95. ISBN 0849386829 (spiral bound). This manual is intended for students in the life sciences, medical technologists, histologists, and pathologists, with the aim of providing practical working information without complicated mathematics. There are numerous illustrations and photographs to assist the readers in obtaining maximum performance and image quality from their optical systems. Lists of sources and references are included.

Technical Tips Online. Cambridge, England: Elsevier Trends Journals, 1995– . URL: http://research.bmn.com/tto. Provides ''peer-reviewed Technical Tips (novel methods or significant improvements on existing methods), Core Protocols (invited from experienced laboratories) and Application Notes (information from Companies about specific products).'' Accessible from BioMedNet, which requires free registration.

Three-Dimensional Confocal Microscopy: Volume Investigation of Biological Specimens. John K. Stevens, Linda R. Mills, Judy E. Trogadis, eds. San Diego, CA: Academic Press, 1994. 507 p. $115.00. ISBN0126683301. ''The goal of this book is to familiarize the reader with these new technologies and to demonstrate their applicability to a wide range of biological and clinical problems.''

Visualization of Receptors: Methods in Light and Electron Microscopy. Gerald Morel, ed. Boca Raton, FL: CRC, 1999. 435 p. $125.00. ISBN 0849326443. Techniques cover immunocytology, radioautography, *in situ* hybridization, reverse transcriptase *in vitro* polymer chain reaction (PCR), and X-ray crystal structure analysis. Details of protocols with illustrations of results and commentaries are included.

X-Ray Microanalysis in Biology: Experimental Techniques and Applications. David C. Sigee et al., eds. New York: Cambridge University Press, 1993. 337 p. $90.00. ISBN 0521415306. An up-to-date look at the use of X-ray microanalysis in biology. There are four main themes: detection and quantification of X-rays, associated techniques, specimen preparation, and applications for many different areas of biology, including animal and plant cell physiology, medicine, pathology and studies on environmental pollution.

TEXTBOOKS AND TREATISES

Alexander, R. McNeill. *The Human Machine.* New York: Columbia University Press, 1992. 176 p. $43.50. ISBN 0231080662. This book is about how the human body works, with emphasis on the various athletic movements such as running, swimming, or jumping.

Cain, Michael L., et al. *Discover Biology.* Sunderland, MA: Sinauer, 2000. 675 p. $67.00. ISBN 0393973778, 039310334X (CD-ROM). For single-semester nonmajor introductory biology courses.

Campbell, Neil A., Lawrence G. Mitchell, and Jane B. Reece. *Biology: Concepts and Connections.* 3rd ed. San Francisco, CA: Benjamin/Cummings, 2000. 809 p. $84.70. ISBN 0805365850. For undergraduate biology courses.

Gould, James L. and William T. Keeton, with Carol Grant Gould. *Biological Science.* 6th ed. New York: Norton, 1996. 2 v. $207.00, $65.00 (paper). ISBN 0393969207, 0393969487 (paper). A very successful general biology text.

Lewis, Ricki, et al. *Life.* 3rd ed. Boston, MA: McGraw-Hill, 1998. 976 p. $44.00 (paper). ISBN 0697285634, 0072283068 (paper). The fourth edition of this popular undergraduate text is due out in 2002.

Lewis, Ricki A. *Discovery: Windows on the Life Sciences.* Malden, MA: Blackwell Science, 2001. 235 p. $32.95 (paper). ISBN 0632044527 (paper). This best-selling author provides an enjoyable, useful insight into life science topics that dominate today's headlines, such as stem cells, prions, and cloning. Appropriate for undergraduate students enrolled in introductory biology or nonmajor courses.

Mader, Sylvia S. *Human Biology.* 6th ed. Boston, MA: McGraw-Hill, 2000. 514 p. ISBN: 0072905840, 0072289244 (CD-ROM). A general textbook for nonmajor courses, covering everything from the chemistry of life to sexually transmitted diseases. The seventh edition is due out in 2002.

McFadden, Carol H. and William T. Keeton. *Biology: An Exploration of Life.* New York: Norton, 1995. 996 p. ISBN 0393957160.

Minkoff, Eli C. and Pamela J. Baker. *Biology Today: An Issues Approach.* 2nd ed. New York: Garland, 2001. 718 p. $65.00 (paper). ISBN 0815327609 (paper). An undergraduate text that covers the issues raised by biological knowledge as well as the science itself.

Morphogenesis: An Analysis of the Development of Biological Form. Edward F. Rossomando and Stephen Alexander, eds. New York: Marcel Dekker, 1992. 449 p. $199.00. ISBN 082478667X. The aim of this review of several representative systems is to unite work on morphogenesis and focus on future research efforts.

Panchen, Alec L. *Classification, Evolution, and the Nature of Biology.* New York: Cambridge University Press, 1992. 403 p. $39.95 (paper). ISBN 0521305829, 0521315786 (paper). This book addresses the philosophical and historical relationship between patterns of classification and patterns of phylogeny.

Perry, James W. and David Morton. *Photo Atlas for Biology.* Belmont, CA: Wadsworth, 1996. 144 p. $20.95 (paper). ISBN 0534235565 (paper). Six hundred photos in full color in this visually oriented reference manual guide the novice through laboratory work in biology, botany, and zoology. Arranged by taxonomy and subject, in other words, microscopy, cell structure, plant structure, fungi, and so forth. Useful for understanding and reviewing lab work and specimens. It is also a good source of illustrations.

Purves, William K., et al. *Life: The Science of Biology.* 6th ed. Sunderland, MA: Sinauer, 2001. 1,044 p. $105.00. ISBN 0716738732, 0716738759 (book plus CD-ROM), 0716738740 (CD-ROM). Introductory college text presenting biological data and ideas, accompanied by beautiful art work. Also available as a split edition, in three volumes.

Raven, Peter and George Johnson. *Biology.* 6th ed. Dubuque, IA: McGraw-Hill, 2001. ISBN 0073031208. A comprehensive account of all aspects and principles of biology.

Starr, Cecie and Ralph Taggart. *Biology: The Unity and Diversity of Life.* 9th ed. Pacific Grove, CA: Brooks/Cole, 2001. 942 p. $93.95. ISBN 0534377955 (book plus CD-ROM). Comprehensive introductory biology text suitable for college-level courses.

PERIODICALS

This section lists journals and accompanying serials that are of use to the general biologist. For general subject specific periodicals, see the section to which they pertain (i.e., *Biomathematics* is included in the Mathematics and Statistics section of this chapter). For subject specific journals, refer to the particular subject chapter.

Some of the most valuable aids in verifying or identifying serial titles are the lists of serials indexed by database publishers. Annotations for the most important serials lists, corresponding to the most prominent databases for biologists, (*Biological Abstracts*, *Chemical Abstracts*, and MEDLINE) may be found in the Bibliographies section.

American Scientist. v. 1– . 1913– . New Haven, CT: Sigma Xi, The Scientific Research Society of North America. Bimonthly. $50.00. ISSN 0003–0996. Available electronically. Articles of interest to a wide range of scientists; it also provides a very comprehensive book review section. Sigma Xi, the society that publishes the journal, was founded in 1886 as an honor society for scientists and engineers.

Bioinformatics. v. 14– , 1998– . Oxford, England: Oxford University Press. Ten issues yearly. $640.00. ISSN 1367–4803. Available electronically. Publishes "original scientific papers and excellent review articles in the fields of computational molecular biology, biological databases and genome bioinformatics." Formerly *Computer Applications in the Biosciences*.

Biological Reviews of the Cambridge Philosophical Society. v. 1– , 1923– . London: Cambridge University Press. $184.00. ISSN 0006–3231. Available electronically. This journal "covers the entire range of the biological sciences, presenting three or four review articles per issue. Although scholarly and with extensive bibliographies, the articles are aimed at non-specialist biologists as well as researchers in the field."

The Biologist. v. 16– , 1969– . London: Institute of Biology. Bimonthly. $70.00. ISSN 0006–3347. Available electronically. This journal presents overview articles, news, and reviews for professional biologists in the areas of biomedical, environmental, agricultural, and educational sciences. Continues the *Institute of Biology Journal*.

BioScience. v. 14– . 1964– . Washington, DC: American Institute of Biological Sciences. Monthly. $225.00. ISSN 0006–3568. Available electronically. This official publication of the American Institute of Biological Sciences contains research articles, news and reports from the Institute, information about people, places, new products, books, and professional opportunities. Continues the *AIBS Bulletin*.

Computers in Biology and Medicine; An International Journal. v. 1– , 1971– . Oxford, England: Elsevier. Bimonthly. $1,154.00. ISSN 0010–4825. Communication of the revolutionary advances being made in the applications of the computer to the fields of biomedical engineering and medical informatics.

Current Biology. v. 1– , 1991– . London: Cell Press. Semimonthly. $173.00. ISSN 0960–9822. Available electronically. High-impact journal with news and reviews from the frontiers of biology.

Frontiers in Bioscience: A World Wide Journal and Virtual Library. v. 1– , 1996– . Tampa, FL: Frontiers in Bioscience Publications. Annual. Free. ISSN 1093–9946. Available electronically at http://www.bioscience.org/. *Frontiers in Bioscience* is a nonprofit organization created by scientists for scientists for fostering international scientific communication and for providing scientists, physicians, and patients with a diverse array of information, tools, and techniques. The primary site is located in the United States with mirror sites in Israel, France, and China. It is dedicated to fostering science, education and peer-reviewed research in biochemistry, microbiology, parasitology, virology, immunology, biotechnology, and bioinformatics.

Journal of Biomedical Informatics. 2001– . San Diego, CA: Academic Press, Bimonthly. $455.00. ISSN 1532–0464. Available electronically. Endorsed by the American Medical Informatics Association, and the American College of Medical Informatics, this journal issues original reports in all areas in which computers and biomedicine intersect, automated classification of single and multidimensional patterns, computer applications and methods for biomedical research, mathematical models of biological systems, physiological data acquisition, and use of computers for automated control of biomedical environments. Formerly *Computers and Biomedical Research*.

The Journal of Experimental Biology. v. 7– , 1930– . London: Company of Biologists. Monthly. $1,825.00. ISSN 0022–0949. Available electronically. The journal "publishes papers on the form and function of living organisms at all levels of biological organisation, from the molecular and subcellular to the integrated whole animal. Our authors and readers reflect a broad interdisciplinary group of scientists who study molecular, cellular and organismal physiology in an evolutionarily and environmentally based context." Formerly *British Journal of Experimental Biology*.

Journal of Theoretical Biology. v. 1– , 1961– . London: Academic Press. Semimonthly. $3,030.00. ISSN 0022–5193. Available electronically. Publishes "theoretical papers that give insight into biological processes. It covers a very wide range of topics and is of interest to biologists in many areas of research. Many of the papers make use of mathematics, and an effort is made to make the papers intelligible to biologists as a whole."

Micron: The International Research and Review Journal for Microscopy. v. 24– , 1993– . New York: Elsevier. Bimonthly. $1,106.00. ISSN 0968–4328. Available electronically. Covers original and review articles for all work involving design, application, practice or theory of microscopy and microanalysis in biology, medicine, agriculture, metallurgy, materials sciences, and physical sciences. Incorporates *Micro and Microscopica Acta* and *Electron Microscopy Reviews.*

Nature. v. 1– , 1869– . New York: Nature America. Weekly. $835.00. ISSN 0028–0836. Available electronically. One of the highest-ranking general scientific journals, *Nature* reports a large component of current biological research. Recently broken into several additional subject-specific journals, it accepts research articles, review articles, and brief reports of research. It also summarizes news and comment of interest for a wide scholarly audience; reviews of significant books are included. Highlights from the print journal are available at the *Nature* Web site, http://www.nature.com/nature/.

New Scientist. v. 52– , 1971– . London: New Science Publications. Weekly. $145.00. ISSN 0262–4079. Available electronically. General science, British periodical publishing science and technology news, commentary, feature articles, and book reviews. Selected news and feature articles are available for free at the magazine's Web site at http://www.newscientist.com/. Formerly *New Scientist and Science Journal.*

Philosophical Transactions of the Royal Society of London: Series B (Biological Sciences). v. 178– . 1887– . London: Royal Society. Monthly. $1,600.00. ISSN 0080–4622. Available electronically. A multidisciplinary journal in the biological sciences publishing fundamental, classic papers for leading scientists in the world's longest-running scientific journal. The *Philosophical Transactions* were first published in 1665.

Proceedings of the National Academy of Sciences of the United States of America (PNAS). v. 1– , 1915– . Semimonthly. $886.00. ISSN 0027–8424. Available electronically. A leading scientific journal of great import to the biological sciences with papers that are contributed by, or communicated to, a member of the Academy for transmittal in the *Proceedings.* Papers are accepted in all areas of science and must report theoretical or experimental research of "exceptional importance or novelty."

Science. v. 1– , 1880– . Washington, DC: American Association for the Advancement of Science. Weekly. $340.00. ISSN 0036-8075. Available electronically. Prestigious general scientific journal with a majority of biological articles reporting original research, news, comments, book reviews, and special sections for grants, laboratory aids, etc. At http://www.scienceonline.org there is access to content highlights; at http://www.sciencenow.org you can find daily coverage of science and science policy by the *Science* news team.

Science News. v. 89– , 1966– . Washington, DC: Science Service. Weekly. $54.00. ISSN 0036–8423. Available electronically. A weekly news magazine that covers the entire spectrum of sciences. Selected articles are available for free at http://www.sciencenews.org/. Formerly: *Science News Letter.*

The Sciences. v. 1– , 1961– . New York: New York Academy of Sciences. Monthly. $21.00. ISSN 0036–861X. Called "the cultural magazine of science. It combines the literary and aesthetic values of a fine consumer magazine with the authority of a scholarly journal to lead the reader in an enlightening exploration of the world of science."

The Scientist: The News Journal for the Life Scientists. v. 1– . 1986– . Philadelphia, PA: The Scientist. Biweekly (except in August and December). $64.00. ISSN 0890–3670. Available electronically. This publication reports relevant and timely information and analysis of general sciences news, controversial topics, information on new tools and technology, details of interest to the profession, and brief notes for career opportunities, equipment, letters, obituaries, etc. It provides a forum for discussion of issues in research, technology, employment, and funding opportunities. Available at no charge on the Web at http://www. the-scientist.com.

REVIEWS OF THE LITERATURE

Advances in Experimental Medicine and Biology. 1967– . New York: Plenum. Irregular. ISSN 0065–2598. Individually priced. This is an important monographic series with each volume organized around a distinctive topic relevant to experimental medicine and biology. Vol. 471, 1999: *Oxygen Transport to Tissue XXI.* "Proceedings of the 26th Annual Meeting of the International Society on Oxygen Transport to Tissue, held Aug. 23–28, 1998 in Budapest, Hungary."

Advances in Marine Biology. v. 1– . 1963– . Orlando, FL: Academic Press. Irregular. Individually priced. ISSN 0065–2881. A high-quality review series dealing with various aspects of marine biology.

Annals of the New York Academy of Sciences. v. 1– , 1877– . New York: New York Academy of Sciences. Irregular. Price varies. ISSN 0077–8923. The series "provides multidisciplinary perspectives on research in fields of current scientific interest." Each volume is on a specific topic, such as Alzheimer's Disease or cell death. About 30 volumes are published per year, and can be purchased individually or as a series.

Annual Review of Biomedical Engineering. v. 1– , 1999– . Palo Alto, CA: Annual Reviews. Annual. ISSN 1523–9829. Available electronically. A new addition to the highly regarded *Annual Reviews* series, this title covers review articles on topics such as prostheses, simulation of movement, and stem cell bioengineering.

Annual Review of Medicine. v. 1– , 1950– . Palo Alto, CA: Annual Reviews. Annual. ISSN 0066–4219. Available electronically. Another of the *Annual Reviews* series that provides reviews of important areas in medicine.

BioEssays. v. 1– , 1984– . New York: Wiley. Monthly. $545.00. ISSN 0265–9247. Available electronically. A review-and-discussion journal publishing news, reviews, and commentaries in contemporary biology that have a molecular, genetic, cellular, or physiological dimension.

Cold Spring Harbor Symposia on Quantitative Biology. v. 1– , 1933– . Cold Spring Harbor, NY: Cold Spring Harbor Laboratory. Annual. $205.00. ISSN 0091–7451. Excellent review papers from symposia, each on a particular biological topic. Vol. 62, 1998: *Pattern Formation During Development*.

Index to Scientific Reviews. For complete annotation, see Chapter 4, "Abstracts and Indexes."

Perspectives in Biology and Medicine. v. 1– , 1957– . Baltimore, MD: Johns Hopkins University Press. Quarterly. $81.00. ISSN 0031–5982. Available electronically. This excellent review journal serves as a vehicle for interpretive and innovative essays, new hypotheses, biomedical history, and humorous pieces.

Quarterly Review of Biology. v. 1– , 1926– . Chicago, IL: University of Chicago Press. Quarterly. $148.00. ISSN 0033-5770. "Critical reviews of recent research in the biological sciences." At least half of each issue is devoted to book reviews of interest to life scientists; new biological software is also reviewed. Full text of back issues is available from JSTOR.

Scientific American. v. 1– , 1845– . New York: Scientific American. Monthly. $39.95. ISSN 0036–8733. Available electronically. Scholarly review articles written for the educated layperson; also includes news, comments, games, and book reviews. Selected articles and news items are available for free at http://www.sciam.com/.

4

Abstracts and Indexes

INTRODUCTION

This chapter can be seen as a companion to Chapter 2, "Subject Access to Biological Information." Abstracts and indexes are used to locate articles, proceedings, and occasionally books and book chapters in various subjects. Because the literature of biology is so vast, it should come as no surprise to find that there are many indexes offering access to that literature. This chapter annotates the major indexes and abstracts that cover general science and/or multiple subjects in biology. Those indexes that deal with narrower fields, such as entomology or plant taxonomy, will be covered in the appropriate subject chapter.

Most abstracts and indexes are available electronically, often in multiple formats. The most common access methods are online, on CD-ROM or diskette, and on the Web. Online access has been available since the late 1960s. This is a pay-as-you-go method of access, and is usually provided as mediated searches done by a librarian or other expert searcher. Online searches are often charged back to the requester. Most online databases do not go back farther than about 1970. For older material you usually have to search through the old paper indexes. The major databases are available from multiple vendors. Companies such as DIALOG, Ovid, and STN provide access to dozens or hundreds of specialized databases. If your library does not subscribe to an index in one of the other formats, online may be the only way to gain access to the data.

CD-ROMs have been around since the early 1980s, and represented a big step forward for individual researchers. They provided local access to databases and were intended for the use of researchers, not librarians. Because they are usually purchased on a subscription basis, it does not matter how many people use the database, or for how long. Major CD-ROM providers include Ovid and SilverPlatter, among others. The CD-ROM databases may be provided as stand-alone workstations, or the CDs may be mounted on a local hard drive and accessed through a local area network. Again, most databases are available from multiple vendors and subscriptions are available for varying lengths of time, usually back to around 1980. A very few databases are available on diskette. These are usually either very small, specialized databases or databases with frequent updates such as *Current Contents*, which is updated weekly.

The latest system of data delivery is the Web, of course. Most of the major online and CD-ROM vendors provide some sort of Web-accessible database searching. Your library has to subscribe to the service and to individual databases, however. Only a very few biological or scientific databases are searchable for free on the Web, primarily databases published by the National Library of Medicine such as MEDLINE or TOXLINE. An advantage of searching over the Web rather than a locally mounted database is that the individual library is spared the cost of maintaining servers. Because Web databases are mounted on the publisher's site, they can also be updated more quickly than locally mounted databases. One problem with this access method is that the speed of searching is dependent on Internet traffic, and may slow down drastically at busy times. Cambridge Scientific Abstracts (CSA), Ovid, and SilverPlatter offer Web-accessible databases. Many individual publishers such as ISI (*Science Citation Index*) also provide access to their own databases over the Web. Dates available vary, but databases are usually available back to the 1980s. Again, this depends on what your library has chosen to subscribe to.

A few companies are preparing databases consisting of Web resources. Naturally, these databases contain only a few hundreds or thousands of the millions of Web pages but they are carefully selected and cataloged. It may be easier to find authoritative, reliable resources from one of these Web databases than by poking about in a Web search engine. OCLC, ISI, and CSA have all created their own databases of Web resources.

The search engines for these access methods are usually similar. All allow searchers to use Boolean logic, though there are differences in the details of truncation symbols, phrase searching, and the like. Most of the access methods allow users to download or print their results in several different formats, some of which may be more easily imported into citation management programs such as ProCite or EndNote. Most of the databases consist of only citations and abstracts, not the full text of articles. Increasingly, the Web-accessible systems are adding functionality such as providing full text of articles (if your institution subscribes to the journal), interlinking references so you can go from the bibliography of an article to the articles it cites, and allowing simultaneous searching of Web pages and articles. Many systems allow the creation of saved searches (also known as Selective Dissemination of Information or Current Awareness searches). Individuals create a search strategy (also known as a profile) that is then performed regularly and the results sent to the researcher, usually by e-mail. Saved searches can be created for subject searches, or depending on the database, for tables of contents. Most publishers also provide free automatic table of contents searches, the results often arriving long before the print journal.

Electronic versions of print indexes often have different titles depending on their format. The information provided for computer databases in this chapter includes these titles and formats (online, CD-ROM, or Web). Prices are listed for print indexes, but because the price for electronic versions often vary widely with the format of the database and the type of institution subscribing, no prices are given for databases. In addition, because the situation is very fluid and some databases are available from many vendors (at least nine in the United States alone for BIOSIS Previews), specific vendors and dates covered are not listed. The information given in this chapter is likely to become outdated rapidly because changes occur on an almost daily basis.

CURRENT AWARENESS

AGRICOLA (**AGRIC**ultural **O**n**L**ine **A**ccess).   From the National Agriculture Library, it covers the worldwide literature of agriculture, including journal articles, monographs, government documents, technical reports, and proceedings. Since 1985, the *CAB Thesaurus* has been used to create subject headings. This database is valuable for life-sciences students and researchers who are interested in plants or animals of economic importance. Available online, on CD-ROM, and through the Web. Print version: *Bibliography of Agriculture*. v. 1– , 1942– . Phoenix, AZ: Oryx. $1,275. ISSN 0006-1530. The database contains more material than the print index. AGRICOLA is available on the Web at no charge at http://www.nalusda.gov.

Bibliography of Bioethics. v. 1– , 1975– . Detroit, MI: Kennedy Institute of Ethics. Annual. $60.00. ISSN 0363-0161.   Annual publication identifying central issues of bioethics. Covers articles, monographs, essays, laws, court decisions, audiovisual materials, and unpublished documents. Each volume provides introduction, list of journals cited, thesaurus, subject entry section, title, and author indexes.

BIOBUSINESS. 1985–98. Philadelphia, PA: BIOSIS.   Database indexing approximately 1,100 technical and business journals, magazines, proceedings, patents, and books covering all areas of the business applications of biological research. Topics covered include agriculture, biotechnology, genetic engineering, medicine, and pollution. Ceased publication in 1998.

BIOETHICSLINE. 1973– . Bethesda, MD: National Library of Medicine. Bimonthly.   Database containing references to ethical issues in health care and biomedicine, including topics such as genetic engineering, AIDS, and patient rights. Covers books, book chapters, journal articles, newspaper articles, court decisions, laws, and other documents. Available online, on CD-ROM, and through the Web as part of the PubMed database (see following text). It was formerly a separate database available for free using Internet Grateful Med, but this service was retired in the spring of 2001.

Biological Abstracts. v. 1– , 1926– . Philadelphia, PA: BIOSIS. Biweekly. $8,400.00 (main series), $3470.00 (cumulative indexes). ISSN 0006-3169. The most comprehensive biological abstracting service in the English language in the world. Over 9,000 journals reporting original research are scanned. The index covers all subjects in biology and biomedicine, and is always a good place to start researching a topic in almost any area. However, try one of the more general indexes such as *Biological and Agricultural Index* or *Biology Digest* (both annotated in the following text) for topics such as animal rights or for biographical information. *Biological Abstracts* covers only articles reporting original research, and does not include items such as book reviews or letters to the editor. Review articles, proceedings, and similar items are indexed in *Biological Abstracts/RRM* (see following). Abstracts are arranged by subject with author, biosystematic, generic, and subject indexes. Biweekly with six-month cumulative indexes, which are a separate subscription. Five-year microfilm cumulations, 1959–1989. Available online as part of BIOSIS Previews (see following). Also available on CD-ROM as BA on CD. For information on searching *Biological Abstracts*, see Chapter 2, ''Subject Access to Biological Information,'' and for a complete listing of publications scanned for *Biological Abstracts*, see *BIOSIS Serial Sources* (''General Sources,'' Chapter 3).

Biological Abstracts/RRM (Reports, Reviews, Meetings). v. 18– , 1980– . Philadelphia, PA: BIOSIS. Monthly. $4,100.00. ISSN 0192-6985. Companion to *Biological Abstracts*, cumulated every six months. Worldwide coverage of material not covered in *Biological Abstracts* such as editorials, reports, bibliographies, proceedings, symposia, books, chapters, review journals, translated journals, nomenclature rules, etc. Successor to *Bioresearch Index* (1967–1979). Arranged like *Biological Abstracts* in broad subject categories with five indexes. Available online as part of BIOSIS Previews (see following text) and on CD-ROM as BA/RRM on CD.

Biological and Agricultural Index. v. 1– , 1916/18– . New York: Wilson. Monthly. Price varies. ISSN 0006-3177. Appropriate for beginning students and the public. Covers 225 journals and is complementary to *General Science Index* (see following text). A good source for information on topics such as animal rights that are not covered by *Biological Abstracts*. It also covers items such as book reviews and letters to the editor that are not included in *Biological Abstracts*. Alphabetical subject and author index. Available online, on CD-ROM, and on the Web.

Biology Digest. v. 1– , 1974– . Medford, NJ: Plexus. Monthly. $139.00. ISSN 0095-2958. This digest covers around 300 biological journals. The level is appropriate for undergraduates and the general public. Unlike *Biological and Agricultural Index, Biology Digest* includes abstracts, which are arranged by subject. There are author and key word indexes in each issue that are cumulated annually, as well as a monthly feature article. Available online, on CD-ROM, and on the Web.

BIOSIS Previews. See also *Biological Abstracts* and *Biological Abstracts/ RRM*. This database is a combination of the print *Biological Abstracts* and *Biological Abstracts/RRM*, which are both available as separate databases. Many libraries have canceled the print *Biological Abstracts* and are using the database as the version of record, and the pricing policies adopted by the publisher have encouraged this trend. Available online and on CD-ROM from several vendors. In addition, OCLC's FirstSearch system offers a student version titled BasicBIOSIS. This database consists of a four- to five-year rolling file indexing about 360 major journals. The BIOSIS site at http://www.biosis.org/ provides a number of useful free resources for biologists, in particular resources for taxonomy.

CAB Abstracts. 1973– . Wallingford, England: CAB International. This database consists of records from the nearly 50 CABI (Commonwealth Agricultural Bureaux International) abstract journals. Covers over 10,000 journals, books, technical reports, theses, proceedings, patents, and other document types. Has truly international coverage; important for applied research in plant biology and zoology. Topics covered include agriculture, forestry, veterinary medicine, nutrition, leisure, and Third World issues. Available online in various sections (as CABA), and on CD-ROM (as CABCD) for the full database; also available on CD-ROM in sections dealing with particular subjects.

Chemical Abstracts. v. 1– , 1907– . Columbus, OH: Chemical Abstracts Service. Weekly. $21,600.00 (discount available for academic institutions). ISSN 0009-2258. Covers over 8,000 journals, making it the most important English-language index in chemistry. Scans scientific and engineering journals, patents, conference proceedings, reports, and monographs. Essential source for biological topics with chemical facets. Available online (as CA or CA SEARCH). STN also offers the online database CAOLD, which consists of *Chemical Abstracts* records from 1907–66, and there are several Web access methods such as SciFinder and SciFinder Scholar (for academic institutions, provides simultaneous searching of *Chemical Abstracts* and MEDLINE. Also available on CD-ROM as CA on CD from Chemical Abstracts (1997 to date), updated monthly. The 10th–13th Cumulative Indexes are also available on CD-ROM, covering 1977–96; the 14th Cumulative Index will be available in 2002. OCLC FirstSearch also provides a limited edition of the database aimed at students, called the CA Student Edition (1967 to date). For a complete list of journals scanned for *Chemical Abstracts,* see annotation for *Chemical Abstracts Service Source Index* in "General Sources," Chapter 3. Searching *Chemical Abstracts* is discussed in "Subject Access to Biological Information," Chapter 2.

Conference Papers Index (CPI). 1–   , 1972–   . Bethesda, MD: Cambridge Scientific Abstracts. 22/yr. $1280.00. ISBN 0162-704X.   Indexes papers presented at scientific conferences including international, national, and regional meetings; scans final programs, abstracts booklets, and published proceedings. Includes information on publications resulting from meetings. Covers life and physical sciences and engineering. Available online and on the Web.

CSA Biological Sciences Collection. 1980–   . Bethesda, MD: Cambridge Scientific Abstracts.   This computerized index is the combination of 21 abstracting journals from Cambridge Scientific Abstracts, including *Animal Behavior Abstracts, Biochemistry Abstracts* (three sections), *Biotechnology Research Abstracts* (four sections), *Calcified Tissues Abstracts, Chemoreception Abstracts, Entomology Abstracts, Genetics Abstracts, Human Genome Abstracts, Immunology Abstracts, Microbiology Abstracts* (three sections), *Neurosciences Abstracts, Oncogenes and Growth Factors Abstracts, Toxicology Abstracts,* and *Virology and AIDS Abstracts.* Available online, on CD-ROM, and on the Web.

Current Awareness in Biological Sciences. v. 1–   , 1954–   . Amsterdam: Elsevier. 144/yr. $7,824.00. ISSN 0733-4443.   Consists of 12 print sections of the *Current Advances* series, also available individually. Includes sections on biochemistry, biotechnology, cell and developmental biology, ecology, genetics, neuroscience, physiology, plant biology, others. Covers about 1,700 international journals. Until 1983, called *International Abstracts of Biological Sciences.* Available online as Elsevier BIOBASE, which also includes material not found in the print version.

Current Contents/Agriculture, Biology, and Environmental Sciences (CC/ABES). v. 1–   , 1970–   . Philadelphia, PA: Institute for Scientific Information (ISI). Weekly. $655.00. ISSN 0011-3379.   Compilation of tables of contents of over 900 major journals as well as major series. Arranged by subject. There is also a title-word subject index and author index, as well as publisher address listing in each issue. Subjects covered in *CC/ABES* include agriculture, botany, entomology, ecology, mycology, ornithology, veterinary medicine, and wildlife management. The most current listing of journal contents available; much more timely than most indexes. Available online, on CD-ROM as Current Contents Search (available in several combinations of sections), on the Web, and on weekly diskettes from ISI.

Current Contents/Life Sciences. v. 1– , 1958– . Philadelphia, PA: Institute for Scientific Information. $655.00. ISSN 0011–3409.   Companion to *CC/ABES*, covering topics such as biochemistry, biomedical research, biophysics, endocrinology, genetics, immunology, microbiology, neurosciences, and pharmacology. Available in 1,200- and 600-title versions. Also available on the Web, online, on CD-ROM and on diskette (see previous).

Dissertation Abstracts International, Section B: Physical Sciences and Engineering. v. 1– , 1938– . Ann Arbor, MI: Bell and Howell. Monthly. $475.00. ISSN 0419–4217.   Covers mostly U.S. academic institutions, though many Canadian institutions are covered. British and European dissertations and U.S. master's theses are included from 1988 on, and abstracts are available from 1980 on. This resource is an essential tool for students looking for a thesis or dissertation topic, and is also useful as an additional source of information on any subject because many dissertations are not published in any other format. There are projects being discussed that would make the full text of dissertations available electronically, but these have had only limited success to date. *Dissertation Abstracts* is available online, on CD-ROM, and on the Web. The electronic version goes back to 1861.

EventLine. 1989– . Amsterdam: Elsevier. Monthly.   Database listing information on past and future conventions, symposia, exhibitions, and sporting events. Covers all the sciences and business. Includes information on events up to the year 2015. Available online, on CD-ROM, and on the Web.

Excerpta Medica. v. 1– , 1947– . Amsterdam: Excerpta Medica Foundation; New York: Elsevier. Frequency varies. Price varies.   Abstracting journals issued in over 50 sections by topic. Covers over 3,600 journals published in 70 countries. Entries are in classed arrangement with author and subject indexes for each issue. Annual index cumulations. Abstracts are written for readers using English as a second language so the summaries are usually concise and easy to understand. Although coverage is worldwide, it is not as comprehensive as either *Biological Abstracts* or *Index Medicus*. Suitable for use in basic biological sciences although published for use by medical researchers and/or physicians. Available online as EMBASE and on CD-ROM. The database includes EMTREE, a hierarchically ordered controlled thesaurus, which contains 38,000 preferred terms and more than 150,000 synonyms.

General Science Index. v. 1– , 1978– . New York: Wilson. Monthly. Price varies. ISSN 0162-1963.   Annual cumulation. Suitable for undergraduates and public libraries. Covers 167 magazines and journals in all sciences, including biological; no abstracts. For nonspecialists only, although it does index magazines and journals more completely than most indexes; includes book reviews, editorials and other short reports. A companion to *Biological and Agricultural Index*. Available online, on CD-ROM, and on the Web. Also available as the General Science Abstracts, which includes abstracts from 1993 to date, and General Science Full Text, which includes indexing and abstracts for all 167 titles and the full text of 39 journals from 1995 to date.

Geobase. 1980– . Amsterdam: Elsevier. Monthly. Covers geography, earth and environmental sciences, and ecology. Fully indexes 2,000 journals and partially indexes another 3,000 books, journals, and proceedings. Available online, on CD-ROM, and on the Web. Corresponds to the print abstracting journals *Geographical Abstracts: Physical Geography, Geographical Abstracts: Human Geography, Ecological Abstracts, International Development Abstracts, Oceanographic Literature Review*, and *Geomechanics Abstracts*.

Index Medicus. New series, v. 1– , 1960– . Washington, DC: National Library of Medicine. Monthly. $522.00. ISSN 0019-3879. Comprehensive, worldwide indexing service for the biomedical sciences. Indispensable for medically related subjects and for the basic medical sciences. Uses medical subject headings (MeSH). Supersedes *Current List of Medical Literature* (1941–59), *Quarterly Cumulative Index Medicus* (1927–56), *Quarterly Cumulative Index to Current Medical Literature* (1917–27), and *Index Medicus, or Quarterly Classified Record of the Current Medical Literature of the World* (1903–27). Up to 1997, it was also available as *Abridged Index Medicus*. Available electronically as MEDLINE and PubMed (see entries below). For more information on using the MeSHs, see Chapter 2.

Index to Scientific Reviews. v. 1– , 1974– . Philadelphia, PA: Institute for Scientific Information. Semiannual. $1,565.00 ISSN 0360-0661. Scans journals and books for review articles. Multidisciplinary. Citation, subject, corporate, and source indexes to the volumes cumulated annually. Available on CD-ROM.

Index to Scientific and Technical Proceedings. v. 1– , 1978– . Philadelphia, PA: Institute for Scientific Information. Monthly. $2,440.00. ISSN 0149-8088. Appropriate for retrospective and current searches, bibliographic verification, and acquisition of the published conference literature, although *Biological Abstracts/RRM* (see previous) covers the biological sciences more completely. Conferences and individual papers are indexed. Cumulated semiannually.

INPADOC. 1968– . Vienna: European Patent Office. Weekly. Database containing listings of patents from 56 countries. Includes title, inventor, assignee, and information on country, patent family, and some legal status information. Also available on microfiche and online.

Internet Grateful Med. See MEDLINE.

MEDLINE. The electronic version of *Index Medicus*. The database includes material that is not covered in the print index, including dental and nursing journals. Since 2000, the coverage of basic life sciences has increased as well. Available online, on CD-ROM, and on the Web from many sources, some dating back to 1958. The MEDLINE database is available for free from the National Library of Medicine's NLM Gateway site (URL: http://gateway.nlm.nih.gov/). This site allows users to search across multiple NLM databases such as AIDSLINE, MEDLINE, and MEDLINE*plus* (which provides consumer health information), and is aimed at unsophisticated Internet users, from physicians to patients and students. This site also provides access to OldMEDLINE, which covers medical journals from 1958–65. The Gateway site replaces the old Internet Grateful Med system, which was retired in the spring of 2001. A version of MEDLINE is also available for free on the Web as PubMed (see following text). This version is aimed at researchers.

Monthly Catalog of United States Government Publications. v. 1– , 1895– . Washington, DC: Government Printing Office. Monthly. $229. ISSN 0362-6830. Essential for locating government documents. List of government publications arranged by department. There are author, title, subject, and series/report indexes in each issue. Complete bibliographic information is supplied for each entry including price and ordering directions. Available online, on CD-ROM, and on the Web. Many online government publications are available from the FirstGov site at http://firstgov.gov/. This site is designed as to provide the public with easy access to all online U.S. Federal Government resources.

National Technical Information Service (NTIS). Lists technical reports available from the NTIS, including research supported by federal grants and some state and local governments. Some international agencies are also represented. Available online, on CD-ROM, and on the Web. Material published after 1990 is freely searchable at NTIS's Web site, http://www.ntis.gov/search.htm. Print version: *Government Reports Announcements and Index*, v. 75–96, 1975–96. Formerly *U.S. Government Research and Development Reports* and *Government Reports Announcement*.

Official Gazette of the United States Patent and Trademark Office. Patents. v. 1– , 1872– . Washington, DC: Government Printing Office. Weekly. $2,708.00. ISSN 0098-1133. Listing of patents; includes abstract and sketches. PatentsPatentee, classification, and geographical indexes. Available online as CLAIMS/U.S. PATENT ABSTRACTS and on CD-ROM as CASSIS/BIB. Also available from the U.S. Patents and Trademark Office (USPTO) at http://www.uspto.gov. The USPTO site includes a searchable database containing the full text of all U.S. patents issued since January 1, 1976, and full-page images of each page of every U.S. patent issued since 1790.

PASCAL. 1973– . Paris: Institut de l'Information Scientifique & Technique. This database consists of records from the 79 print *PASCAL* (Programme Applique a la Selection et a la Compilation Automatiques de la Literature) indexes, which are the major French indexes. In French and English. International coverage of all science and technical areas, including biology. Formerly (to 1984) *Bulletin Signaletique*. Available online and on CD-ROM as Pascal Biomed, indexing 6,500 journals from 1987 to date.

Pollution Abstracts. v. 1– , 1970– . Bethesda, MD: Cambridge Scientific Abstracts. Bimonthly. $1,245.00. ISSN 0032-3624. Has annual index. Covers air, water, soil, and noise pollution as well as sewage and solid waste management, toxicology, and environmental action. Scans articles and documents. Available online, on CD-ROM as part of the CSA Biological Sciences Collection (see previous) and on the Web.

Psychological Abstracts. v. 1– , 1927– . Washington, DC: American Psychological Association. Monthly. $1,075.00. ISSN 0033–2887. The most important psychology index. It covers animal behavior and neurobiology, among other subjects of interest to biologists. Has author and subject indexes. Starting in 1980, the database contains citations that do not appear in the print version. Available online as PsycINFO from 1967 to the present. Two versions are available on CD-ROM: PsycINFO (the full database; 1967 to date), and PsycLIT (containing only articles, books, and book chapters from 1887 to date). The PsycINFO Historical File contains citations from 1887 to 1966 and is available on CD-ROM. Also available on the Web.

PubMed. PubMed is another version of the MEDLINE database and offers a number of useful services aimed at the biological research community. It is available for free at the National Center for Biotechnology Information's site at http://www.ncbi.nlm.nih.gov/entrez/query.fcgi. The PubMed database indexes articles that are not included in the main MEDLINE database, including all articles from journals that are indexed selectively in MEDLINE. Citations show up earlier in PubMed than in MEDLINE as well. PubMed also provides links to articles from over 700 full text journals and to the molecular biology databases of DNA/protein sequences and 3D structure data that have been developed by the National Center for Biotechnology Information (NCBI). Researchers can set up Current Awareness searches through the "Cubby" feature. There are also a number of other useful services such as browseable databases for journal titles and MeSH, and citation matching services.

Referativnyi Zhurnal. v. 1– , 1958– . Moscow: Vsesoyuznyi Institut Nauchno-Tekhnicheskoi Informatsii (VINITI). Monthly. Price varies. Monthly. Major, comprehensive abstracting service in Russian; in 64 sections. In subject categories, with annual author and scientific name indexes.

Science Citation Index. v. 1– , 1961– . Philadelphia, PA: Institute for Scientific Information (ISI). Bimonthly. $11,730.00. ISSN 0036-827X. Multidisciplinary index to international science literature. Citation, source, corporate, and subject (keyword) indexes. The citation index groups all articles that have referenced the same earlier work and so provides a different sort of access to the literature than is usually found. Covers about 4,500 journals. Available online as SCISEARCH and on CD-ROM (as Science Citation Index Compact Disk Edition) from ISI, 1980 to date. Also available on the Web as Web of Science from ISI. There are two sibling publications, the *Social Sciences Citation Index* and the *Arts and Humanities Citation Index.* See also the Journal Citation Reports in the Bibliographies section of Chapter 3, "General Sources."

Toxicology Abstracts. v. 1– , 1978– . Bethesda, MD: Cambridge Scientific Abstracts. Monthly. $750.00. ISSN 0140-5365. Covers all forms of toxicology, including pharmaceuticals, agrochemicals, cosmetics, drug abuse, radiation, and legislation. Includes author and subject indexes. Also available online and on CD-ROM as part of the CSA Biological Sciences Collection (see previous).

TOXLINE. 1965– . Bethesda, MD: National Library of Medicine. Monthly. This database consists of records from a number of sources dealing with toxicology. Most of the records are from MEDLINE, but a number are from BIOSIS Previews and *International Pharmaceutical Abstracts.* Also included are files from a number of other sources, including information from various Federal agencies, *Pesticides Abstracts,* the *Poisonous Plants Bibliography, Toxicity Bibliography,* and a number of other sources. Dates included vary; some of the files go back to 1950. Sections of the full database are available online and on CD-ROM. Also available on the Web at no charge as part of the National Library of Medicine's TOXNET service at http://toxnet.nlm.nih.gov/.

Web of Science. See *Science Citation Index.*

World Translation Index. v. 1– , 1978–97. Delft, Netherlands: International Translations Centre. Monthly. ISSN 0259-8264. Annual cumulation. Formerly (until 1987) *World Transindex*; formed by merger of several other translations indexes. Provides bibliographic and availability information on existing translations of material dealing with science and technology. Available online from 1979 to 1997. Ceased publication in 1997.

Zoological Record. v. 1– , 1864– . Philadelphia, PA: BIOSIS. Annual. $4,100.00 (all 20 sections). ISSN 0144-3607. The most comprehensive zoological index in the world. Includes books, proceedings, and over 6,500 periodicals.

Covers worldwide literature of the year to which it refers. Exhaustive coverage for systematic zoology. Annual publication means that the print *Zoological Record* is basically a retrospective tool. Complete bibliographic information provided in author index. Other indexes in each issue are subject, geographic, paleontological, and systematic. Issued in 20 sections relating to a phylum or class of the animal kingdom. Individual sections available separately. List of references used as classification and nomenclature authorities also included. Available online and on CD-ROM. The *Zoological Record Search Guide* (see "Subject Access to the Biological Literature," Chapter 2) and the *Zoological Record Serial Sources* (see "General Sources," Chapter 3) are helpful aids.

RETROSPECTIVE TOOLS

The indexes listed in the following text are essential tools for locating articles published in the nineteenth and early twentieth centuries. *Biological Abstracts, Index Medicus,* and *Zoological Record* all go back to the late nineteenth and early twentieth centuries and are also valuable retrospective indexes. For more specialized early indexes, see the individual subject chapters.

Berichte Biochemie und Biologie: Referierendes Organ der Deutschen Botanischen Gesellschaft und der Deutschen Zoologischen Gesellschaft. v. 1–521, 1926–80. New York: Springer-Verlag.   Abstracting periodical in German of the Deutschen Botanische Gesellschaft. Entries are arranged by subject. Cumulative author and subject indexes.

Index-catalogue of the Library of the Surgeon-General's Office. 1st–5th series, 1880–1961. Washington, DC: G.P.O.   This series indexes the publications held in the library of the Army's Surgeon-General and predates *Index Medicus*. The articles and transactions are indexed in a mixed author and subject list, and while the emphasis is naturally on the U.S. medical literature, other biological subjects from around the world are included.

International Catalogue of Scientific Literature. 1st–14th annual issues. 1901–14. London: Published for the International Council by the Royal Society of London.   Outgrowth of the *Catalogue of Scientific Papers* (see following). Covers the years 1901–14. Author and subject catalogue. Divided into sections, for example, section M is devoted to botany, section L to general biology. Journal lists with abbreviated titles are provided.

Royal Society of London. *Catalogue of Scientific Papers, 1800–1900.* London, Royal Society of London, 1867–1902.   "Index to the Titles and Dates of Scientific Papers contained in the Transactions of Societies, Journals, and other Periodical Works. . . ." An essential retrospective source. Entries are arranged by author's name. Abbreviations used are explained and are particularly helpful in locating titles of ceased periodicals.

5

Biochemistry and Biophysics

Biochemistry and biophysics have been grouped together in this chapter. Biochemistry is "the study of the chemistry of living organisms, especially the structure and function of their chemical components," while biophysics is "the study of physical aspects of biology" (*Oxford Dictionary of Biology*, 4th ed., 2000). Both are integral parts of biology, and their interdisciplinary relationship with basic biological sciences often blurs subject area lines. Frequently, the materials and literature for one discipline will satisfy the demands or questions posed by the other.

There will be substantial overlap, also, between biochemistry and biophysics with molecular and cellular biology, which are listed in Chapter 6.

ABSTRACTS AND INDEXES

Current Advances in Protein Biochemistry. v. 9– , 1992– . Amsterdam: Elsevier. Monthly. $1,154.00. ISSN 0965-0504. A current awareness service with citations arranged in subject classification; also contains comprehensive listing of review articles. Formerly: *Current Advances in Biochemistry*. Available online, on CD-ROM, and on the Web as part of Current Awareness in Biological Sciences (CABS) (see Chapter 4).

Current Contents/Physical, Chemical and Earth Sciences. v. 1– , 1961– . Philadelphia, PA: Institute for Scientific Information. Weekly. $760.00. ISSN 0163-2574. Provides tables of contents from the major journals in the area. Covers biochemistry and biophysics. See also *Current Contents/Life Sciences* in Chapter 4. Available online and on CD-ROM as part of Science Citation Index.

Current Physics Index. v. 1– , 1975– . Melville, NY: American Institute of Physics. Quarterly. $1,495.00. ISSN 0098-9819. "Each quarterly issue contains the approximately 11,000 abstracts of articles published in the primary journals of one quarter, classified by subject." The index covers only 54 journals. Also available online and on the Web as part of the SPIN (Searchable Physics Information Notices) database (see following text).

Nucleic Acids Abstracts. See the complete annotation in Chapter 6, "Molecular and Cellular Biology."

Physics Abstracts. v. 1– , 1969– . London: Institution of Electrical Engineers. Semimonthly. $4,600.00. ISSN 0036-8091. The most important abstracting service in physics; in subject order, with author indexes. Also available online using INSPEC, a database produced by the Institution of Electrical Engineers. Formerly: *Science Abstracts, Part A: Physics Abstracts.*

SPIN Database. Melville, NY: American Institute of Physics. URL: http://ojps.aip.org/spinweb/. A searchable database covering journals of the American Institute of Physics and several member and affiliated societies, except the American Physical Society. The SPIN database is updated regularly and covers nearly one million research records in the physical sciences from 1975 to the present. Available using SPIN Web, an online journal publishing service of AIP, this service also provides advance SPIN abstracts and links to *Physical Review Abstracts.*

Toxicology Abstracts. v. 1– , 1978– . Bethesda, MD: Cambridge Scientific Abstracts. Monthly. $1,150.00. ISSN 0140-5365. Covers all areas of toxicology. Available online, on CD-ROM, and on the Web as part of PolTox I and the Biological Sciences Collection.

See also *Biological Abstracts, Biology Digest, Chemical Abstracts*, and *Current Contents* in Chapter 4, "Abstracts and Indexes."

ASSOCIATIONS

American Chemical Society (ACS). 1155 16th St. NW, Washington, DC 20036. Phone: (202) 872-4600, Fax: (202) 872-4615. E-mail: meminfo@acs.org. URL: http://www.acs.org. Founded 1876. 151,000 members. Scientific and educational society of chemists and chemical engineers. Computerized services include the database Chemical Journals of the ACS Online, which contains full text of 23 ACS journals and online services (CAS—Chemical Abstract Service Online), an interactive chemical information search service, and STN International, a scientific and technical information network. Publishes 23 journals including *Analytical Chemistry, Biochemistry, Chemical Abstracts, Chemical and Engineering News, Journal of Agricultural and Food Chemistry, Journal of Chemical Education, Journal of the American Chemical Society, Journal of Physical and Chemi-*

cal Reference Data, etc. The ACS Web site is a major source of information for chemists.

American Institute of Chemists (AIC). 515 King St., Ste. 420, Alexandria, VA 22314. Phone: (703) 836-2090, Fax: (703) 684-6048, E-mail: sdobson@clarionmr. com. URL: http://www.theaic.org. Founded 1923. 4,000 members. Chemists and chemical engineers. Promotes advancement of chemical professions in the United States; protects public welfare by establishing and enforcing high practice standards; represents professional interests of chemists and chemical engineers. Publishes annual *Professional Directory* and *The Chemist*. The Web site is primarily for membership information.

American Institute of Physics (AIP). 1 Physics Ellipse, College Park, MD 20740-3843. Phone: (301) 209-3100, Fax: (301) 209-0843, URL: http://www.aip. org. Founded 1931. Ten national member societies, including 100,000 members in the fields of physics, astronomy, and related disciplines. Seeks to assist in the advancement and diffusion of the knowledge of physics and its application to human welfare. Publishes several scientific journals. Web site contains extensive information for physicists.

American Society for Biochemistry and Molecular Biology (ASBMB). 9650 Rockville Pike, Bethesda, MD 20814. Phone: (301) 530-7145, Fax: (301) 571-1824, E-mail: asbmb@asbmb.faseb.org. URL: http://www.faseb.org/asbmb. Founded 1906. 9,300 members. Biochemists and molecular biologists who have conducted and published original investigations in biological chemistry and/or molecular biology. Publishes *Journal of Biological Chemistry*. Formerly American Society of Biological Chemists. Web site primarily for society information.

Biochemical Society (BS). 59 Portland Pl., London W1N 3AJ, England. Phone: 44 171 5805530, Fax: 44 171 6377626, E-mail: genadmin@biochemsoc.org. uk. URL: http://www.biochemistry.org. Founded 1911. 9,000 members. Objectives are to promote biochemistry and to provide a forum for information exchange and discussion of various aspects of teaching and research in biochemistry. Publishes *Biochemical Journal, Biochemical Society Transactions, Essays in Biochemistry*, etc. Web site contains membership information, some links of interest to biochemists.

Biophysical Society (BPS). c/o Rosalba Kampman, 9650 Rockville Pike, Bethesda, MD 20814. Phone: (301) 530-7114, Fax: (301) 530-7133, E-mail: society @biophysics.faseb.org. URL: http://www.biophysics.org/biophys/. Founded 1957. 5,600 members. Biophysicists, physical biochemists, and physical and biological scientists interested in the application of physical laws and techniques to the analysis of biological or living phenomena. Publishes *Annual Meeting Abstracts Journal, Biophysical Journal, Biophysical Society Directory*, and *Bio-*

physical Society Newsletter. Web site provides career information, membership information, and a buyer's guide.

Biophysical Society of Canada (BSC). 435 Ellice Ave., Winnipeg, MB, Canada R3B 1Y6. Phone: (204) 984-5146; Fax: (204) 984-6978; E-mail: henry.mantsch @nrc.ca. URL: http://www.ibd.nrc.ca/bsc. Founded 1985. 80 members. Biophysicists and other scientists working in related fields. Promotes biophysical research and education; gathers and disseminates information among members and other scientific organizations. Publishes newsletter, directory. Web site provides membership information, access to newsletter, and links to other biophysical associations.

Canadian Society for Chemistry (CSC). 130 Slater St., Ste. 550, Ottawa, ON, Canada K1P 6E2. Phone: (613) 232-6252; Fax: (613) 2232-5862. E-mail: cic_adm@fox.nstn.ca. URL: http://www.cheminst.ca/chemistry/. Founded 1985. 3,500 members. Scientific association of chemists in education, government, and industry. Covers chemical research, development, management, and education. Publishes *Canadian Chemical News.* Web site primarily for society information, but has links to other chemical resources.

Federation of European Biochemical Societies (FEBS). c/o Prof. Julio E. Celis, Gen. Sec., Department of Medical Biochemistry and Danish Centre for Human Genome Research, Bldg. 170, Ole Worms Alle, DK-8000 Aarhus, Denmark. Phone: 45 89422880, Fax: 45 86120090, E-mail: febs@biokemi.au.dk. URL: http://www.febs.unibe.ch. Founded 1964. 39,000 members. Purpose is to further research and education in the field of biochemistry and to disseminate research findings. Publishes *European Journal of Biochemistry* and *FEBS Letters.* Web site primarily for society information.

International Union of Biochemistry and Molecular Biology (IUBMB). 18 Leyden Crescent, Saskatoon, Saskatchewan, Canada S7J 2S4. Phone: (306) 374-1304, Fax: (306) 955-1314, E-mail: fvella@sk.sympatico.ca. URL: http://www. iubmb.unibe.ch. Founded 1955. 65 members. National academies, research councils, or biochemical societies; associated bodies represent national biochemical and molecular biology societies; special members are organizations representing industrial and other groups. Publishes *Biochemical Education, Biochemical Nomenclature and Related Documents, BioFactors, Journal of Biotechnology and Applied Biochemistry,* and *Trends in Biochemical Sciences.* Web site primarily for society information.

International Union of Pure and Applied Biophysics (IUPAB). Department of Biochemistry and Molecular Biology, University of Leeds, Leeds LS2 9JT, England. Phone: 44 113 2333023, Fax: 44 113 1333167, E-mail: a.c.t.north@

leeds.ac.uk. URL: http://bmbsgi11.leeds.ac.uk/iupab. Founded 1966. National committees appointed by academies and research councils representing 50 countries. Purposes are to organize international cooperation in biophysics and to promote communication between the various branches of biophysics and allied subjects; to encourage cooperation between the societies that represent the interests of biophysics; and to contribute to the advancement of biophysics. Publishes *Quarterly Reviews of Biophysics* and *IUPAB News*. Web site primarily for members.

Pan-American Association of Biochemistry and Molecular Biology (PABMB). c/o Dr. Jack Preiss, Michigan State University, Dept. of Biochemistry, East Lansing, MI 48824-1319. Phone: (517) 353-3137, Fax: (517) 353-9334, E-mail: preiss@pilot.msu.edu. URL: http://www.bch.msu.edu/preiss/pabmb/PABMBHome.html. Founded 1969. 12 members. Societies of professional biochemists in the Americas and culturally related European Countries. Promotes the sciences of biochemistry by disseminating information and encouraging contacts between its members. Publishes *Symposium Proceedings*. Formerly: Pan-American Association of Biochemical Societies. Web site primarily for members.

Protein Society. c/o R.W. Newburgh, Ph.D., 9650 Rockville Pike, Bethesda, MD 20814. Phone: (301) 571-0662, Fax (301) 571-0666, E-mail: newburgh@protein.faseb.org. URL: http://www.faseb.org/protein/. Founded 1986. To promote international interactions among investigators in order to explore all aspects of the "building blocks of life: protein molecules." Membership is open to scholars and researchers interested in the analysis, chemistry, folding, structure, function, and regulation of proteins. Publishes *Protein Science*. Web site provides membership information and a nice list of "Resources for Protein Scientists."

DICTIONARIES AND ENCYCLOPEDIAS

Biochemical Nomenclature and Related Documents: A Compendium. 2nd ed. C. Liebecq, ed. Brookfield, VT: Portland Press, 1992. 350 p. $36.00. ISBN 1855780054. This is an essential reference containing current recommendations on nomenclature issued by the nomenclature committees of the International Union of Biochemistry. It also includes text from, and references to, other important nomenclature documents.

The Cassell Dictionary of Physics. Percy Harrison, ed. London: Cassell Academic, 1998. 216 p. $27.95. ISBN 0304350346. Various appendices provide information on SI units, prefixes, and conversion factors; common measures; fundamental constants; electromagnetic spectrum; periodic table of the elements; elementary particles; the solar system; common differential coefficients and integrals; and the Greek alphabet.

Compendium of Chemical Terminology: IUPAC Recommendations. 2nd ed. Alan D. McNaught and Andrew Wilkinson, eds. (IUPAC Chemical Nomenclature Series). Oxford, England: Blackwell, 1997. $49.50 (paper). ISBN 0865426848 (paper). Commonly referred to as the "Gold Book." Alphabetical listing of nearly 7,000 terms recommended by the International Union of Pure and Applied Chemistry (IUPAC) with authoritative definitions, spanning the whole range of chemistry. The online version is titled IUPAC Compendium of Chemical Terminology, (URL: http://www.chemsoc.org/chembytes/goldbook/ index.htm) and corresponds to the second printed edition and includes a few minor corrections.

Concise Encyclopedia of Biochemistry and Molecular Biology. 3rd rev. ed.   See Chapter 6, "Molecular and Cellular Biology," for full annotation.

Dictionary of Chemical Names and Synonyms. Philip Howard and Michael Neal, eds. Boca Raton, FL: Lewis/CRC Press, 1992. 1,800 p. $178.95. ISBN 0873713966. Finding-aid for approximately 20,000 chemicals by names and synonyms, Chemical Abstracts Services registry numbers, chemical formulae, and structure.

Dictionary of Chemical Names and Synonyms Electronic Edition. Philip Howard and Michael Neal, eds. Endicott, NY: Synapse Information Resources, 1998. $195.00 (CD-ROM). ISBN 189059508X. This new edition provides valuable ease of use for 25,000 chemical with 150,000 synonyms.

Dictionary of Chemistry. 3rd ed. John Daintith, ed. (Oxford Paperback Reference), New York: Oxford University Press, 1996. $13.95 (paper). ISBN 0192800310 (paper). Revised with 1,000 new entries, this authoritative edition covers terms in chemistry, physical chemistry, and biochemistry. Laboratory techniques, chemical engineering, and environmental issues are discussed, including a table of elements and their properties.

Dictionary of Chemistry. Andrew Hunt, ed. Chicago, IL: Fitzroy Dearborn, 1999. $45.00. ISBN 1579581404. Full explanations, brief definitions of terms, and instructions on how to work calculations are provided for entries of practical and applied chemistry, analytical chemistry, and organic preparations. Some specialist areas like spectroscopy, environmental chemistry, and biochemistry are included.

Dictionary of Natural Products. v. 1–7 plus supplements, 1993–   . New York: Chapman & Hall/CRC Press. $5244.95 (set, v. 1–7). ISBN 0412466201 (set, v. 1–7). Updated regularly. Also available as a subscription on CD-ROM, updated every six months ($6,600.00, ISBN 0412491508). An authoritative, comprehensive source of information for 100,000 natural products and related compounds containing chemical, structural, and bibliographic data. There are extensive indexes, including a Species Index, and a Type of Compound Index. Currently up to Supplement 4, published in 1997 ($624.00). Chapman & Hall also publishes other major chemical dictionaries that are in print or on CD-ROM: *Dictionary of Organic Compounds, Dictionary of Inorganic Compounds, Dictionary of Alkaloids, Dictionary of Analytical Reagents,* and *Dictionary of Steroids.*

Dictionary of Physics. Michael Chapple, ed. Chicago, IL: Fitzroy Dearborn, 1999. 264 p. $45.00. ISBN 15795881293. ''This edition based on *The Complete A-Z Physics Handbook,* first published in the United Kingdom by Hodder and Stoughton Educational, 1997.'' Useful especially for students, this dictionary is formatted like the Fitzroy Dearborn–published *Dictionary of Chemistry* (see previous), with brief definitions of terms, followed by a fuller analysis, and worked examples of problems.

Dictionary of Physics. 4th ed. Alan Isaacs, ed. (Oxford Paperback Reference). New York: Oxford University Press, 2000. 500 p. $14.95. ISBN 0192801031. This well-respected dictionary covers terms and concepts in physics, mathematics, astrophysics, metallurgy, electronics, and physical chemistry. One thousand new entries discuss particle physics, cosmology, Higgs field, anthropic principle, nanotubes, and nanotechnology. Like the Oxford *Dictionary of Chemistry,* this reference is an excellent value.

Dictionary of Steroids: Chemical Data, Structures, and Bibliographies. R. A. Hill et al., eds. Boca Raton, FL: CRC Press, 1991. 2 v. $1.044.95 (set). ISBN 0412270609 (set). This unique synthesis provides bibliographic, structural, and chemical data for over 10,000 steroids, aiming to document all known naturally occurring steroids of plant and animal origin plus the most important synthetic steroids.

Enzyme Nomenclature 1992: Recommendations of the Nomenclature Committee of the International Union of Biochemistry and Molecular Biology on the Nomenclature and Classification of Enzymes. See Chapter 3, ''General Sources,'' for full annotation.

Facts on File Dictionary of Chemistry. 3rd ed. John Daintith, ed. New York: Facts on File, 1999. 272 p. $40.00. ISBN 0816039097. Over 3,000 entries explaining the most important and commonly used chemical terms, techniques, materials, and applications.

Facts on File Dictionary of Physics. 3rd ed. John Daintith et al., eds. New York: Facts on File, 1999. 256 p. ISBN 0816039119. $40.00. Updated and containing 22,400 entries for commonly used terms in modern physics. Two hundred new entries present developments in particle physics, cosmology, low-temperature physics, and quantum theory, appropriate at the student level.

Glick, David M. *Glossary of Biochemistry and Molecular Biology*. rev. ed.   See Chapter 6, "Molecular & Cellular Biology," for full annotation.

Hawley's Condensed Chemical Dictionary. 13th ed. Richard J. Lewis, ed. New York: John Wiley, 1997. 1,248 p. $138.00. ISBN 0471292052.   The most widely recognized dictionary of industrial chemicals, terms, processes, reactions, and related terminology. This new edition adds new products as well as toxicity evaluation and reactivity/flammability data. CAS numbers, chemical synonyms, process and instrumentation information, and definitions are thoroughly updated. An excellent reference work for practical chemists, researchers, and students.

IUBMB Recommendations on Biochemical & Organic Nomenclature, Symbols & Terminology etc. International Union of Biochemistry and Molecular Biology. URL: http://www.chem.qmw.ac.uk/iubmb/index.html.   This Web site provides links to numerous IUBMB and IUPAC recommendations on biochemical terminology, including enzymes, nucleic acids, steroids, vitamins, and other chemicals.

Kirk-Othmer Encyclopedia of Chemical Technology. 4th ed. Jacqueline I. Kroschwitz and Michalina Bickford, eds. New York: Wiley, 1999. 1,500 p. $350.00. ISBN 0471296988.   Condenses the fourth edition of the revered 27-volume encyclopedia, which provides expert and comprehensive coverage of the field of chemical technology.

McGraw-Hill Dictionary of Chemistry. Sybil P. Parker, ed. New York: McGraw-Hill, 1996. 352 p. $16.95 (paper). ISBN 0070524289 (paper).   Created from the *McGraw-Hill Dictionary of Scientific and Technical Terms*, this comprehensive, portable reference defines more than 6,000 chemical terms in organic and inorganic chemistry, physical chemistry, biochemistry, and chemical engineering.

McGraw-Hill Dictionary of Physics. 2nd ed. Sybil P. Parker, ed. New York: McGraw Hill, 1996. 416 p. $24.95 (paper). ISBN 0070524297 (paper).   Exhaustive, authoritative coverage (almost 8,000 terms) of terms from every major discipline of physics. Appropriate for professionals, students, writers, or the general reader with scientific interests.

The Merck Index: An Encyclopedia of Chemicals, Drugs, and Biologicals.   See Chapter 3, "General Sources," for full annotation.

Oxford Dictionary of Biochemistry and Molecular Biology. Anthony Smith, ed.   See Chapter 6, "Molecular & Cellular Biology," for full annotation.

DIRECTORIES

ACS Directory of Graduate Research. Washington, DC: American Chemical Society, 1999. $70.00. ISSN 0193-5011.   The most comprehensive source of information on chemical research and researchers at universities in the United States and Canada. It lists faculties, academic research, publications, doctoral and master's theses in departments or divisions of chemistry, chemical engineering, biochemistry, medical/pharmaceutical chemistry, clinical chemistry, polymer science, food science, and environmental science. It contains information on degrees offered, areas of specialization, interdisciplinary programs, faculty biographical information, titles of papers published within the last two years. Also available as DGRWeb at http://www.pubs.acs.org/dgrweb. DGRWeb contains all the information in the *ACS Directory of Graduate Research* and is easily searchable online.

Chemical Research Faculties: An International Directory. Washington, DC: American Chemical Society, 1996. $199.95. ISBN 0841233012. International directory listing academic research institutions and chemical societies in chemistry, chemical engineering, biochemistry, and medical/pharmaceutical chemistry, enabling researchers to locate colleagues by country, academic institution, or by name.

Chemical Sciences Graduate School Finder. 1997–98. Washington, DC: American Chemical Society, 1997. $21.95. ISBN 0841235120. List of graduate schools with complete information on admissions, fields of study (including biochemistry), and a geographic index.

Chemcyclopedia. v. 1– , 1983– . Washington, DC: American Chemical Society. Annual. ISSN 0736-6019. Available in print as an annual supplement to *Chemical and Engineering News*, the complete guide is accessible on the Web at http://pubs.acs.org/chemcy/. This online guide provides detailed information about chemical products and companies. It is searchable by chemical name, CAS registry number, and category.

College Chemistry Faculties 1996 Directories. Washington, DC: American Chemical Society, 1996. $94.95. ISBN 0841233004. Comprehensive directory of U.S. and Canadian chemistry, biochemistry, and chemical engineering teachers in universities, two- and four-year colleges.

Directory of Physics, Astronomy and Geophysics Staff, 1997 Biennial Edition. College Park, MD: American Institute of Physics, 1997. Biennial. 500 p. $65.00 (paper). ISBN 1563966654 (paper). This is billed as the definitive source for access to the global physics community, a veritable *Who's Who* in the physical sciences. It contains information on more than 30,000 scientific staff members at institutions and organizations worldwide. The AIP also maintains directories of AIP members and affiliated societies at their home page although access to them may require authentication as an OJPS (Online Journal Publishing Service) or SPIN (Searchable Physics Information Notices) Web subscriber, or as a society member.

2000 Graduate Programs in Physics, Astronomy and Related Fields. College Park, MD: American Institute of Physics, 1999. Annual. 964 p. $50.00 (paper). ISBN 1563968878 (paper). Information on graduate programs in North America. Includes general information for specific universities, number of faculty, admission and graduate requirements, and enrollment. Faculty and research specialties are listed.

GUIDES TO INTERNET RESOURCES

The American Institute of Physics (AIP) is the largest organization of physicists in North America, located at College Park, MD. Their home page at http://www.aip.org is relevant because of its huge amount of valuable information for the physical sciences per se and for access to sources on the Internet such as details about AIP and its member societies, public information, meetings and conferences, online journal publishing service, AIP journals, *Physics Today*, magazines, books, proceedings, publishing services, education and student services, science policy, its history center, and working at AIP.

The American Chemical Society (ACS), Washington, DC, is an organization of over 150,000 members that provides similar services for the chemical sciences at its home page http://www.acs.org including services of interest to chemists, information about educational scholarships and grants, awards administered by ACS, ACS Library, various member benefits, meetings, ACS periodicals, career services, etc. Various databases are searchable (CAS, patents, abstracts, LabGuide Online, Chemcylopedia Online).

Other Chemistry Web Sites

BMRB BioMagResBank. Dept. of Biochemistry, University of Wisconsin–Madison. URL: http://www.bmrb.wisc.edu. A repository for data from NMR spectroscopy (an indispensable part of the biochemists toolkit) on proteins, peptides, and nucleic acids. The July 31, 1995 release of the database contains over 94,000 unique chemical shifts including more than 6,000 13C shifts and 4,000 15N shifts. Topics covered are biological macromolecules, NMR spectral parameters, kinetics, thermodynamics, and structure. The present form of the database is described in the publication "A Relational Database for Sequence-Specific Protein NMR Data" by B. R. Seavey, et al., in *Journal of Biomolecular NMR* 1: 217–36, 1991. Work is in progress to enlarge the scope of the database.

Chembytes Infozone. URL: http://www.chemsoc.org/chembytes/home.htm. Provides information from the ACS and the Royal Society of Chemistry on projects, online chemical magazine, access to some journals and major reference publications, news, products, the online version of the *IUPAC Compendium of Chemical Technology*, patents, funding opportunities, library and information sources from the Royal Society library, etc.

Chemfinder. Cambridge, MA: CambridgeSoft. URL: http://www.chemfinder. com. This Web site provides free information and access to National Cancer Institute databases, reference services, reagents, subscriptions, software, lab equipment, etc. It can be described as a "virtual handbook."

Chemical Industry Search Engine. URL: http://www.chemindustry.com/. A worldwide search engine of the chemical industry that provides access to industry centers, equipment and software, chemical resources, news, organizations, services, career and community information, chemical technology, events, and academic institutions.

Chemical Information Page. Bethesda, MD: Specialized Information Services (SIS), National Library of Medicine. URL: http://sis.nlm.nih.gov/Chem/ ChemMain.html. Provides information on drugs, pesticides, environmental pollution, and other potential toxins. The Specialized Information Services division maintains a site for access to the structures of chemical substances, searchable by chemical structure and identifier. SIS provides a primary chemical dictionary (ChemID) that is accessible free using Internet Grateful Med (IGM) (See "Abstracts and Indexes," Chapter 4).

Linstrom, Peter J. and W. G. Mallard. NIST Chemistry WebBook. Washington, DC: National Institute of Standards and Technology. NIST Standard Reference Database Number 69, February 2000 Release. URL: http://webbook.nist.gov/ chemistry/. Provides access to thermochemical, thermophysical, and ion energetics data, compiled by the National Institute of Standards and Technology (NIST). Search options include formula, name, CAS registry number, author, structure, physical properties, special data sets, 3D structures, citation guide, and species list (a list of all of the chemical species). The documentation is authoritative. The chemistry that you need all in one place.

Wiggins, Gary. Cheminfo: Chemical Information Sources from Indiana University. Bloomington, IN: Indiana University. URL: http://www.indiana.edu/ %7Echeminfo/. This is a guide to chemical literature and information sources on the Web and elsewhere.

Winter, Mark. Chemdex. Sheffield, England: University of Sheffield. URL: http://www.shef.ac.uk/chemistry/chemdex/welcome.html. Chemdex has been on the Web since 1993, maintaining a directory of chemical sites on the Internet. It is possible to search on chemistry, universities and other institutions, government organizations, companies, communication sources, databases, societies, software, etc.

GUIDES TO THE LITERATURE

Maizell, Robert E. *How to Find Chemical Information: A Guide for Practicing Chemists, Educators, and Students.* 3rd ed. New York: Wiley-Interscience, 1998. 523 p. $69.95 ISBN 0471125792. This best-selling guide covers chemical information search strategies; resources; communication patterns; access to articles, patents, translations, and specifications; the Chemical Abstracts Service as well as other abstracting and indexing services; U.S. government information centers, online systems, the Internet, and CD-ROMs; reviews, journals, encyclopedias, and other major reference works. Highly recommended by the American Chemical Society.

Stern, David. *Guide to Information Sources in the Physical Sciences.* See "General Sources," Chapter 3, for full annotation. Includes material on biophysics.

Wiggins, Gary. *Chemical Information Sources.* See "General Sources," Chapter 3, for full annotation. This guide is updated regularly on the Web site Cheminfo (see "Guides to Internet Resources," previous).

HANDBOOKS

This section includes both print and electronic formats. Rather than duplicate the discussion on computer-based and electronic databases that appears in Chapter 6, refer to the fully annotated Databases section in Chapter 6, "Molecular and Cellular Biology."

There is a great deal of overlap that occurs between biochemistry and other biological disciplines. For example, databanks for protein and enzyme sequences are annotated in "Molecular and Cellular Biology," Chapter 6, and gene sequence databases are discussed in "Genetics, Biotechnology, and Developmental Biology," Chapter 7.

ACS Style Guide: A Manual for Authors and Editors. 2nd ed. Washington, DC: American Chemical Society, 1998. 260 p. $26.95. ISBN 0841234620. Covers American Chemical Society style conventions, plus newly emerging technology and concepts. There are sections on format, grammar, and usage, as well as the use and preparation of illustrations, chemical structures, and tables in scientific papers. There are discussions of copyright law as it relates to publishing, and the basics of planning and preparing poster and oral presentations. Other issues presented include numbers and math, references, chemical compounds, conventions in chemistry, and the peer-review process.

AIP Style Manual. Prepared under the direction of the AIP Publication Board, 4th ed. Melville, NY: American Institute of Physics, 1990. 66 p. $10.00 (paper). ISBN 088318642X (paper). "For guidance in writing, editing, and preparing physics manuscripts for publication."

Biochemical Pathways: An Atlas of Biochemistry and Molecular Biology. Gerhard Michal, ed. New York: Wiley, 1998. 277 p. $115.00. ISBN 0471331309. This book provides concise information on the metabolic sequences in the pathways, the chemistry and enzymology of conversions, the regulation of turnover, and the effect of disorders. Detailed, color-coded charts are provided to explain metabolic pathways and their relation to regulation pathways.

Biochemistry Labfax. J. A. A. Chambers and David Rickwood, eds. San Diego, CA: Academic Press, 1994. 356 p. $74.00 (spiral). ISBN 0121673405 (spiral). Designed for practicing scientists, this reference contains information on radioisotopes, enzymes, proteins, nucleic acids, lipids, and selected techniques such as chromatography, electrophoresis, etc. Databases, suppliers, chemical and mathematical formulas, and references are provided.

Comprehensive Biological Catalysis. Michael Sinnott, ed. San Diego, CA: Academic Press, 1998. 4 v. $899.00 (set). ISBN 0126468605 (set). This work provides a comprehensive review of enzyme catalysis from a chemical perspective, including background chemistry. The fourth volume consists of a "Chemical Lexicon" with explanations of alphabetically arranged terms and concepts.

CRC Handbook of Chemistry and Physics. Indispensable. See "General Sources," Chapter 3, for full annotation.

Dawson, R. M. C., et al. *Data for Biochemical Research*. 3rd ed. Oxford, England: Clarendon Press, 1989. 580 p. (Oxford Science publications). ISBN 0198552998 (paper). Supplies data on the range of compounds used by biochemists.

Enzyme Handbook. D. Schomburg and D. Stephan, eds. New York: Springer-Verlag, 1990– . v. Each volume priced separately. An impressive compendium covering over 3,000 enzymes for the practicing enzymologist. Entries will be updated as necessary by added supplemental volumes. Currently up to v. 17, published in 1998.

Handbook of Proteolytic Enzymes. Alan J. Barrett, Neil D. Rawlings, and J. Fred Woessner, eds. Orlando, FL: Academic Press, 1998. 1,666 p. $299.95 (book plus CD-ROM). ISBN 0120793709 (book plus CD-ROM). Excellent, comprehensive reference book that provides information on the chemical and biological properties of proteases. Also comes as CD-ROM edition alone.

Hardy, James K. Hazardous Chemical Database. Akron, OH: University of Akron, 1996– . URL: http://ull.chemistry.uakron.edu/erd/. Another database of interest in this area is the one compiled by Dr. Hardy and his research group at the University of Akron. This collection provides information for 2,662 hazardous chemicals; keywords include names, formulas, and registry numbers. Also, consult Lewis's printed desk reference and the Hazardous Substances Data Bank, see following text.

Hazardous Substances Data Bank (HSDB). Bethesda, MD: National Library of Medicine. URL: http://www.toxnet.nlm.nih.gov/cgi-bin/sis/htmlgen?HSDB. This data bank covers the broad scope of hazardous substances for human and animal toxicity, safety and handling, environmental fate, etc. It is scientifically peer reviewed. Also accessible using Chemical Information Page (see Guides to Internet Resources, previous).

Indiana University Molecular Structure Center. Bloomington, IN: Indiana University Department of Chemistry. URL: http://www.iumsc.indiana.edu. This home page provides links to information about the center, molecular structures, and crystallographic links. It is possible to download X-ray crystallographic data on the structure of organic and inorganic molecules and even find 3D models of almost 300 molecules in a section titled "Common Molecule Pages."

The Ion Channel Factsbook. Edward C. Conley and William J. Brammar, eds. v. 1– , 1995–2001. 4 v. Orlando, FL: Academic Press. $56.00 (v. 1), $58.00 (v. 2), $42.00 (v. 3), $69.00 (v. 4). ISBN 0121844501 (v. 1), 012184451X (v. 2), 0121844528 (v. 3), 0121844536 (v. 4). These *Factsbook*s provide a comprehensive summary of molecular properties for all known types of ion channel proteins in a cross-reference and computer updatable format. Identifies similarities and differences between ion channel types. V. 1: *Extracellular Ligand-Gated Channels*, v. 2: *Intracellular Ligand-Gated Channels*, v.3: *Inward Rectifier and Intercellular Channels*, and v. 4: *Voltage-Gated Channels*.

Isacke, Clare and Michael Horton. *The Adhesion Molecule Factsbook.* 2nd ed. San Diego, CA: Academic Press, 2000. (Factsbook series). 288 p. $59.95 (paper). ISBN 0123565057 (paper). Concise information on structure, function, and biology of cell adhesion molecules in an accessible format, including key references.

Journal of Physical and Chemical Reference Data. v. 1– , 1972– . Melville, NY: American Institute of Physics for the National Institute of Standards and Technology. Bimonthly. $728.00. ISSN 0047-2689. Available electronically. Data compilation and reviews produced under the National Standard Reference Data System provides reliable up-to-date reference data for atomic and molecular science, chemical kinetics, spectroscopy, thermodynamics, transport phenomena, crystallography, materials science, etc.

Lange's Handbook of Chemistry. 15th ed. John A. Dean, ed. New York: McGraw-Hill, 1998. 1,424 p. $120.00. ISBN 0070163847. Highly regarded one-volume source book of factual information for chemists to satisfy general information needs. This excellent time-saver provides data on organic compounds, conversion tables, mathematics, inorganic chemistry, properties of atoms, physical properties, thermodynamic properties, spectroscopy, electrolytes, electromotive forces, chemical equilibrium, physicochemical properties, polymers, and practical laboratory information.

Lewis, Richard J. *Hazardous Chemicals Desk Reference.* 4th ed. New York: Wiley, 1996. 1,680 p. $149.00. ISBN 0471287792. This authoritative, handy reference offers immediate access to vital, detailed hazard information on more than 6,000 compounds commonly used in industry, manufacturing, labs, and the workplace. It presents new or updated Essential Safety Profiles for each chemical, assessing their hazardous potential as poisons, irritants, corrosives, explosives, and carcinogens. For updating Lewis, also see the online Hazardous Substances Data Bank (HSDB) annotated in this section.

Maynard, John T. and Howard M. Peters. *Understanding Chemical Patents: A Guide for the Inventor.* 2nd ed. Washington, DC: American Chemical Society, 1991. 183 p. $41.95. ISBN 0841219974. Description of the patent system from understanding the terminology, to working with patent attorneys, agents, and technical liaison personnel.

A Physicist's Desk Reference. 3rd ed. Richard E. Cohen, ed. Melville, NY: American Institute of Physics, 2000. 600 p. $64.95. ISBN 0387989730. This valuable handbook ''presents the essence of concepts and numerical data contained primarily in archival journals in which physicists and astronomers publish.'' There are reports on physical constants, acoustics, astronomy and astrophysics, and medical physics.

Purich, Daniel L. and R. Donald Allison. *Handbook of Biochemical Kinetics.* Orlando, FL: Academic Press, 1999. 816 p. $150.00. ISBN 0125680481. The authoritative handbook presents the logic for kinetic approaches to distinguish rival models or mechanisms, with comments on techniques and their limitations and pitfalls. Also included are over 1,500 definitions of kinetic and mechanistic terminology, with key references; over 1,000 enzymes, complete with Enzyme Commission numbers, reactions catalyzed, and reference to reviews and/or assay methods; and over 5,000 selected references to kinetic methods appearing in the *Methods in Enzymology* series (see entry in Chapter 6, ''Molecular & Cellular Biology'').

Watson, Steve and Steve Arkinstall. *The G-Protein Linked Receptor Factsbook.* San Diego, CA: Academic Press, 1994. (Factsbook series). 427 p. $29.95. ISBN 0127384405. Similar to the other titles in the Factsbooks series, this compilation provides a catalog of over 50 entries on all members of the seven-transmembrane family of cell surface receptors and their associated G-proteins and effectors, including acetylcholine, adrenaline, dopamine, glutamine, 5-HT, G-proteins, phospholipase, adenylyl cyclase. There is information on structure, molecular weights, and glycosylation sites; distribution; receptors; pharmacology; effector pathways; amino acid sequence; PIR, SWISSPROT, and EMBL/GenBank accession numbers; gene structure and organization; and key references.

White, John Stephen and Dorothy Chong White. *Source Book of Enzymes.* Boca Raton, FL: CRC Press, 1997. $95.00. ISBN 0849394708. This encyclopedic handbook presents tabular data on the biological source, specific activity, concentration or volume activity, unit definition, preparation form or reaction buffer, etc., for over 7,000 commercially available enzymes, restriction endonucleases, DNA methyltransferases and enzyme mixtures, blends, and complexes. There is a worldwide listing of almost 100 enzyme suppliers, including local brokers and distributors, plus complete indexes of Enzyme Commission numbers.

HISTORIES

Several entries in this section are out of print, but have been included with the expectation that they have kept their historical value and are available in libraries that collect in the history of science, biochemistry, or biophysics.

The American Institute of Physics maintains the Center for History of Physics (http://www.aip.org/history) for information about the history of physics in relation to education, exhibits, the library, visual archives, oral histories, publications, and grants.

Biographical Dictionary of Scientists: Physicists. David Abbott, ed. New York: Peter Bedrick Books, 1984. 212 p. ISBN 0911745793. Historical introduction to physics. Alphabetical biographical entries of several paragraph's length include important physicist's dates and major works. This book and its companion *Biographical Dictionary of Scientists: Chemists,* also by David Abbott, are both out of print although they may be available for use in large public or college libraries.

Brock, William H. *The Norton History of Chemistry.* New York: Norton, 1993. (History of Science). 744 p. $19.95 (paper). ISBN 0393310434 (paper). For the general reader as well as the chemistry student, this history surveys chemistry from its early beginnings through the twentieth century. Each chapter is devoted to a significant development in chemical history.

Brush, Stephen G. and Lanfranco Belloni. *The History of Modern Physics: An International Bibliography.* New York: Garland, 1983. 334 p. ISBN 0824091175. Guidance for novices, including specific information about the subject in brief annotations. *Modern physics* is defined as beginning with the discovery of X-rays in 1895.

Chemistry of Life: Eight Lectures on the History of Biochemistry. J. Needham, ed. New York: Cambridge University Press, 1970. ISBN 0521073790. This collection is part of a series of lectures given by Cambridge University biochemists under the aegis of the history of Science Committee and Department. Topics addressed by important figures in the field include photosynthesis, biological oxidations, microbiology, neurology, animal hormones, vitamins, foundations of modern biochemistry, and pioneers of biochemistry in the nineteenth century.

Contrasts in Scientific Style; Research Groups in the Chemical and Biochemical Sciences. Philadelphia, PA: American Philosophical Society, 1990. 473 p. (Memoirs series, v. 191) $20.00. ISBN 0871691914. Sequel to *Molecules and Life* (see following) discussing the emergence of large research groups during the nineteenth century.

Foundations of Modern Biochemistry: Early Adventures in Biochemistry. Margery G. Ord and Lloyd A. Stocken, eds. Greenwich, CT: JAI Press, 1995–98. 4 v. $128.50 each. ISBN 1559389605 (v. 1). Aimed at students of biochemistry, biology, and medicine, this set traces the development of biochemistry from 1900 on, including a chapter discussing progress in previous centuries. There may be more volumes in the planning stages.

Fruton, Joseph S. *A Bio-Bibliography for the History of the Biochemical Sciences since 1800.* Philadelphia, PA: American Philosophical Society, 1982. $20.00. ISBN 0871699834. *A Supplement to a Bio-Bibliography for the History of the Biochemical Sciences since 1800.* Philadelphia, PA: American Philosophical Society, 1986. 262 p. ISBN 087169980X. Data on the lives and work of people who participated in providing chemical explanations of biological phenomena. Each of the entries includes reference to biographical or bibliographical reference works or citations of books and articles in serial publications.

Heilbron, J. L. and Bruce R. Wheaton. *Literature on the History of Physics in the 20th Century.* Berkeley, CA: Office for History of Science and Technology, University of California, 1981. (Berkeley papers in history of science, 5). 485 p. $20.00. ISBN 0918102057. Survey of sources gleaned from *Isis, Dictionary of Scientific Biography*, Poggendorff's *Handworterbuch*, etc., for twentieth-century physicists. Entries are coded for category, classifier (person, institution, field), and subject breakdown. *An Inventory of Published Letters* is a companion volume; see the annotation under its author listing (Wheaton and Heilbron).

Home, R. W. *The History of Classical Physics: A Selected, Annotated Bibliography*. (Bibliographies of the History of Science and Technology, v. 11). New York: Garland, 1984. 324 p. ISBN 0824090675.   Classical physics embraces the years between 1700–1900. This annotated bibliography is arranged in broad topics for general bibliographical works, individual biographies, collected works, general histories, eighteenth century physics, physics in transition, nineteenth century physics.

Kevles, Daniel J. *The Physicists: The History of a Scientific Community in Modern America*. New York: Harvard University Press, 1995. Reprint ed. $17.95. ISBN 0674666569 (paper).

The Life and Times of Modern Physics; History of Physics II. Melba Phillips, ed. (Readings from *Physics Today*, no. 5). New York: Springer-Verlag, 1993. 300 p. $44.95. ISBN 0883188465.   Recent articles from *Physics Today* chronicles the people and events shaping modern science and society. Includes profiles, personal memoirs, and histories of important institutions and organizations.

Molecules and Life; Historical Essays on the Interplay of Chemistry and Biology. New York: Wiley-Interscience, 1972. 579 p. ISBN 0471284483.   Covers the period from 1800–1950 discussing "Ferments to Enzymes," "Nature of Proteins," "Nuclein to the Double Helix," "Intracellular Respiration," and "Pathways of Biochemical Change."

Nobel Prize Winners: Chemistry. Frank N. Magill, ed. Pasadena, CA: Salem Press, 1990. 3 v. $210.00 (set). ISBN 089356561X (set).   The three volumes cover the years 1901–89. There are descriptions of the laureate's life, work and scientific career, speeches and critical commentary, most significant experiments, theories, and publications. Comprehensive index of nationality, important people, key terms, theories, labs, institutions, and area of concentration. History and overview of the prize in chemistry, and a portrait of each laureate are included.

Nobel Prize Winners: Physics. Frank N. Magill, ed. Pasadena, CA: Salem Press, 1989. 3 v. ISBN 0893565571 (set).   Arranged in an identical manner to *Nobel Prize Winners: Chemistry* (previous).

Nye, Mary Jo. *Before Big Science: the Pursuit of Modern Chemistry and Physics, 1800–1940*. New York: Harvard University Press, 1999. Reprint ed. 304 p. $16.95 (paper). ISBN 0674063821 (paper).   This is the first of a series aiming to present a comprehensive survey of Western science, from the Greeks to the present, for students and lay readers.

Pais, Abraham. *The Genius of Science: A Portrait Gallery of Twentieth-Century Physicists*. New York: Oxford University Press, 2000. 356 p. $30.00 ISBN.   Sixteen thumbnail sketches of seventeen figures from twentieth-century physics.

The Physical Review: The First Hundred Years; A Selection of Seminal Papers and Commentaries. H. Henry Stroke, ed. New York: Springer-Verlag, 1995. 1,400 p. $100.00 (paper). ISBN 1563961881 (paper). This set contains select seminal papers published in the first 100 years of *The Physical Review*, including commentaries from many eminent physicists. This is a valuable collection for the serious student of physics. The book is packaged with a CD-ROM that contains over 6,000 additional pages of text.

Resources for the History of Physics: I. Guide to Books and Audiovisual Materials. II. Guide to Original Works of Historical Importance and Their Translations into Other Languages. Stephen G. Brush, ed. Hanover, NH: University Press of New England. 1972. 176 p. ISBN 087451066X. Resources for physics teachers, arranged by topic or format. Entries are evaluated for age group with subject and institution codes.

Selected Topics in the History of Biochemistry, Personal Recollections, VI. G. Semenza and Rainer Jaenicke, eds. Amsterdam: Elsevier, 2000. 768 p. (Comprehensive biochemistry, Section VI; History of biochemistry, v. 41). $196.50. ISBN 0444505474. This volume covers fourteen biochemists, covering a wide range of topics. See the series title *Comprehensive Biochemistry* in the Textbooks and Treatises section for full annotation.

Slater, Edward Charles. *Biochimica et Biophysica Acta: The Story of a Biochemical Journal.* New York: Elsevier, 1986. 122 p. ISBN 0444807691. Interesting history of one of the most important biochemical/biophysical journals in the world.

Solomon, A. K. "A Short History of the Foundation of the International Union for Pure and Applied Biophysics," *Quarterly Review of Biophysics* 1: 107–24 (1968).

Teich, Mikulas and Dorothy M. Needham. *A Documentary History of Biochemistry 1770–1940.* Rutherford, NJ: Fairleigh Dickinson University Press, 1992. $85.00. ISBN 0838634877. Selected collection of reprints, over half of them translated into English for the first time, on the evolution of the study of the chemistry of life into modern biochemistry.

Twentieth Century Physics. Laurie M. Brown, Abraham Pais, and A. B. Pippard, eds. Philadelphia, PA: Institute of Physics, 1995. 3 v. $395.00. ISBN 1563963140. Excellent source of references to twentieth-century physics with subject and name indexes; a combination reference and history book.

Wheaton, Bruce R. and J. L. Heilbron. *An Inventory of Published Letters to and from Physicists, 1900–1950.* Berkeley, CA: UC Regents, Office for History of Science and Technology, University of California, Berkeley, 1982. (Berkeley papers in history of science, 6), $20.00. ISBN 0918102065. Contains quotations from the correspondence of almost 6,000 physicists, active from 1895–1955, that appear in printed books and articles in *Literature on the History of Physics in the 20th Century* listed under Heilbron in this section.

METHODS AND TECHNIQUES

Consult the Handbooks section for practical laboratory information, and don't forget to check out the Methods section in Chapter 6, "Molecular and Cellular Biology."

Bollag, Daniel M. *Protein Methods*. New York: Wiley-Liss, 1996. 415 p. $59.99. ISBN 0471118370 (spiral bound).   Well-reviewed collection of methods.

Current Chemical Reactions. v. 1– , 1979– . Philadelphia, PA: Institute for Scientific Information. Monthly. ISSN 0163-6278.   Guide to revised and newly modified reactions and syntheses reported in 100 current source journals. Each entry includes complete bibliographic information, description of the reaction, flow chart, and notice of explosive reactions. Author, journal, corporate, and permuted subject indexes are provided. Also produced as annual Current Chemical Reactions Database (available on magnetic tape or by FTP from ISI).

Current Protocols in Protein Science. 1995– . New York: Wiley. Two volume looseleaf manual with quarterly updates. $495.00 (looseleaf), $495.00 (CD-ROM). ISBN 0471111848 (looseleaf), 0471140988 (CD-ROM).   This volume in the Current Protocols series covers both basic and advanced methods used in protein purification, characterization, and analysis as well as post-translational modification and structural analysis. More than 800 basic, support, and alternate protocols are included.

Extracellular Matrix Protocols. Charles H. Streuli and Michael E. Grant, eds. (Methods in Molecular Biology, v. 139). Towota, NJ: Humana Press, 2000. $89.50. ISBN 0896036243.   Readily reproducible methods to investigate the extracellular matrix and the altered cell-ECM interactions playing a role in human health and disease.

Freifelder, David Michael. *Physical Biochemistry: Applications to Biochemistry and Molecular Biology*. 2nd ed. New York: W. H. Freeman, 1982. 761 p. $67.95. ISBN 071673152.   Techniques are arranged in sections reviewing direct observation, general laboratory methods, separation and identification, hydrodynamic methods, spectroscopic methods, and miscellaneous techniques. See David Sheehan, in the following text, for more current information.

Glycoanalysis Protocols. Elizabeth F. Hounsell, ed. (Methods in Molecular Biology, v. 76). Towota, NJ: Humana Press, 1998. 272 p. $79.50. ISBN 0896033554.   Proven analytical methods covering glycoprotein macromolecular structural analysis, oligosaccharide profiling, lipid conjugate characterization, microorganism structure determination, and proteoglycan function.

Graham, Richard C. *Data Analysis for the Chemical Sciences: A Guide to Statistical Techniques.* New York: VCH, 1993. 536 p. $99.95. ISBN 0471187909. Statistical methods and bibliographical references for statistical data analysis tools. Includes many examples for problem solving and extensive statistical tables.

Journal of Biochemical and Biophysical Methods. v. 1– , 1979– . Amsterdam: Elsevier Science. Monthly. $1,146.00 ISSN 0165-022X. Available electronically. Deals with all methodological aspects of biochemistry, biophysics, and molecular biology. Accepts original papers and short notes; includes book reviews.

Laboratory Techniques in Biochemistry and Molecular Biology, v. 1– , 1969– . P. C. van der Vliet, ed. Amsterdam: Elsevier. Irregular. Price varies. ISSN 0075-7535. Well-established technique review series. Vol. 28: *Synthetic Peptides as Antigens,* by M. V. H. Van Regenmortel and S. Muller, 1999. 398 p. $76.00. ISBN 0444821767 (paper). Gives current state-of-the-art use of synthetic peptides in molecular biology and practical protocols on how to conjugate peptides, immunize animals with peptides, and monitor immune responses to peptides in vitro.

Meier, Peter C. and Richard E. Zund. *Statistical Methods in Analytical Chemistry,* 2nd ed. (Chemical Analysis, v. 153). New York: Wiley, 2000. 608 p. $94.95. ISBN 0471293636. This volume is part of a best-selling and well-received series of monographs on analytical chemistry and its applications. The authors intend to convey, in a very practical manner, an appreciation of the importance of statistics to analytical chemistry. The use of computers and computerized graphics are included.

Methods. v. 1– , 1990– . See full annotation in Chapter 6, "Molecular and Cellular Biology."

Methods in Enzymology. v. 1– , 1955– . See full annotation in Chapter 6, "Molecular and Cellular Biology."

Methods of Biochemical Analysis. v. 1– , 1954– . New York: Wiley. Irregular. Price varies. ISSN 0076-6941. Each volume deals with biochemical methods and techniques used in different areas of science. Vol. 38: *HPLC in Enzymatic Analysis* edited by Edward F. Rossomando, 1998, 451 p.

Principles and Techniques of Practical Biochemistry. 5th ed. Keith Wilson and John M. Walker, eds. New York: Cambridge University Press, 2000. 784 p. $49.95 (paper). ISBN 052165873X (paper). The updated edition of a very popular text introduces basic experimental techniques routinely used in practical biochemistry today.

Protein Protocols Handbook. John M.Walker, ed. Towota, NJ: Humana Press, 1996. 809 p. $94.00 (spiral bound). ISBN 0896033392 (spiral bound).   Laboratory manual of commonly used analytical techniques for proteins and peptides for chemists and researchers. Presents alternatives to standard techniques and identifies the strengths and weaknesses of each procedure.

Protein Purification Protocols. Shawn Doonan, ed. Towota, NJ: Humana, 1996. (Methods in molecular biology, v. 59). 405 p. $74.50 (spiral bound). ISBN 0896033368 (spiral bound).   Laboratory methods on protein isolation for students or researchers new to the technique. Includes a chapter on chromatography.

Proteins: Analysis and Design. Ruth Hogue Angeletti, ed. Orlando, FL: Academic Press, 1998. 550 p. $99.95. ISBN 0120587858.   A guide to analyzing details of protein structure and function relationships and their life cycles within the cell. Designed for researchers new to this technology.

Proteolytic Enzymes: Tools and Targets. Erwin E. Sterchi and Walter Stocker, eds. (Springer Lab Manual). New York: Springer-Verlag, 1999. 366 p. $82.00. ISBN 3540612335.   Contents provide a variety of laboratory methods.

Proteome and Protein Analysis. R. M. Kamp, D. Kyriakidis, and Th. Choli-Papadopoulou. New York: Springer-Verlag, 1999. 372p. $125.00. ISBN 3540658912.   Selected papers presented at XIIth International Conference on Methods in Protein Structure Analysis, in 1998. Covers new, sensitive and rapid methods for analysis of proteins, with special emphasis placed on the total cell protein, the proteome.

Sheehan, David. *Physical Biochemistry: Principles and Applications*. New York: John Wiley, 2000. 360 p. $65.00 (paper). ISBN 0471986631 (paper).   This book involves the measurement of physical properties of biomolecules or the use of physical techniques in the study of biochemical processes. It may be used to update the classic Freifelder, see previous.

TEXTBOOKS AND TREATISES

Aidley, David J. *The Physiology of Excitable Cells*. 4th ed. New York: Cambridge University Press, 1998. 550 p. $47.95 (paper). ISBN 0521574218 (paper).

Alpen, Edward L. *Radiation Biophysics*. 2nd ed. San Diego, CA: Academic Press. 1998. 484 p. $74.00. ISBN 0120530856.

Austin, R.H. and S. Chan. *Biophysics for Physicists*. River Edge, NJ: World Scientific, 2001. $78.00, $37.00 (paper). ISBN 9810205007, 9810205015 (paper).

Bergethon, Peter R. *The Physical Basis of Biochemistry*. New York: Springer-Verlag, 1998. 650 p. $69.95. ISBN 0387982620.

Bloomfield, Molly M. *Chemistry and the Living Organism*. 6th ed. New York: Wiley, 1996. 672 p. $89.95. ISBN 0471107778.

Bogdanov, Konstantin Yu. *Biology in Physics: Is Life Matter?* (Polymers, Interfaces, and Biomaterials Series). San Diego, CA: Academic Press, 1999. 237 p. $69.96. ISBN 0121098400. This book explores the concepts and techniques of biophysics and illustrates the latest advances in understanding many of the specific mechanisms used by living organisms. This interdisciplinary exchange of scientific information explains how physics can be used when biology is studied.

Branden, Carl-Ivar and John Tooze. *Introduction to Protein Structure*. 2nd ed. New York: Garland Pubs, 1999. 410 p. $47.95 (paper). ISBN 0815323050 (paper).

Campbell, Gaylon S. and John M. Norman. *An Introduction to Environmental Biophysics*. 2nd ed. New York: Springer-Verlag, 1998. 286 p. $44.95 (paper). ISBN 0387949372 (paper).

Comprehensive Biochemistry. G. Semenza, ed. v. 1– , 1962– . Amsterdam: Elsevier. Irregular. Price varies. ISSN 0069-8032. "An advanced treatise in biochemistry which assembles the principle areas of the subject in a single set of books." In six sections: organic and physicochemical concepts (Section I, Volumes 1–4), chemistry of the major constituents of living material (Section II, Volumes 5–11), enzymology (Section III, Volumes 12–16), metabolism (Section IV, Volumes 17–21), and the molecular basis of biological concepts (Section V, Volumes 22–29), and history of biochemistry (Section VI, Volumes 30–40). See *New Comprehensive Biochemistry*, in the following text, for an update.

Daune, Michel. *Molecular Biophysics: Structures in Motion*. New York: Oxford University Press, 1999. 499 p. $52.95 (paper). ISBN 0198577826 (paper).

Essentials of Glycobiology. Ajit Varki, et al., eds. Cold Spring Harbor, NY: Cold Spring Harbor Laboratory Press, 1999. 653 p. $95.00 (paper). ISBN 0879695609 (paper).

Fersht, Alan. *Structure and Mechanism in Protein Science: A Guide to Enzyme Catalysis and Protein Folding*. New York: W. H. Freeman, 1999. 614 p. $84.95. ISBN 0716732688.

Grimnes, Sverre and Orjan Martinsen. *Bioimpedance and Bioelectricity Basics*. San Diego, CA: Academic, 2000. 374 p. $99.00. ISBN 0123032601.

Hammes, Gordon G. *Thermodynamics and Kinetics for the Biological Sciences*. New York: Wiley-Interscience, 2000. 163 p. ISBN 0471374911 (paper). Presents a basic introduction to thermodynamics and kinetics for molecular biologists and others who need to understand molecular phenomena. The book uses a minimum of mathematics and covers a wide range of topics. There are numerous examples from the biological sciences. Each chapter includes problems for students to work, though not the answers.

Koch, Christof. *Biophysics of Computation: Information Processing in Single Neurons*. (Computational Neuroscience). New York: Oxford University Press, 1998. $562 p. $67.95. ISBN 0195104919.

Koolman, Jan and Klaus-Heinrich Rohm. *Color Atlas of Biochemistry*. New York: Thieme Medical, 1996. 435 p. $32.00 (paper). ISBN 0865775842 (paper).

Lehninger Principles of Biochemistry. 3rd ed. David L. Nelson and Michael M. Cox. New York: Worth Publishing, 2000. $116.45. ISBN 1572591536; 0716738678 (CD-ROM); 1572599316 (book and CD-ROM).

Lesk, Arthur M. *Introduction to Protein Architecture: The Structural Biology of Proteins*. New York: Oxford University Press, 2001. 347 p. $45.00 (paper). ISBN 0198504748 (paper).   For upperclass undergraduates and beginning graduate students.

Matthews, Harry R. *Biochemistry: A Short Course*. New York: John Wiley, 1997. 505 p. $62.95 (paper). ISBN 0471022055 (paper).

Miller, James and Jane Miller. *Statistics for Analytical Chemistry*. 3rd ed. New York: Prentice-Hall, 1993. 256 p. $82.50 (paper). ISBN 0130309907 (paper).

Otto, Matthias. *Chemometrics: Statistics and Computer Application in Analytical Chemistry*. New York: John Wiley, 1999. 314 p. $79.95 (paper). ISBN 352729628X (paper).

Pokorny, Jiri and Tsu-Ming Wu. *Biophysical Aspects of Coherence and Biological Order*. New York: Springer-Verlag, 1998. 240 p. $109.00. ISBN 3540646516.

Price, Nicholas C. and Lewis Stevens. *Fundamentals of Enzymology: The Cell and Molecular Biology of Catalytic Proteins*. 3rd ed. New York: Oxford University Press, 1999. 478 p. $110.00, $50.00 (paper). ISBN 0198502303, 019850229X (paper).   An all-around view of the field.

Stryer, Lubert. *Biochemistry*. 4th ed. New York: W. H. Freeman, 1995. 1,064 p. $107.95. ISBN 071673687X (Book and CD-ROM edition).

Van Holde, Kensal E. *Principles of Physical Biochemistry*. New York: Prentice Hall, 1998. 657 p. $81.00. ISBN 0137204590.

Voet, Donald and Judith G. Voet. *Biochemistry*. 2nd ed. New York: Wiley, 1995.

1,361 p. $120.95. ISBN 047158651X.   Kept up-to-date by supplements. 1998 supplement: 91 p., ISBN 047132213X, $21.95.

PERIODICALS

Journals are selected that are key to the dissemination of original research in the areas of biochemistry and biophysics. Increasingly, journals are available in both in-print and electronic formats. The transition from print to electronic availability is a gradual and steady development, and one that should not be overlooked when searching for current journals.

Analytical Biochemistry. v. 1– , 1960– . San Diego, CA: Academic Press. Monthly. $3,095.00. ISSN 0003-2697. Available electronically.   Publishes original research on methods and methodology of interest to the biological sciences and all fields that impinge on biochemical investigations.

Archives of Biochemistry and Biophysics. v. 1– , 1942– . San Diego, CA: Academic Press. Monthly. $3,495.00. ISSN 0003-9861. Available electronically.   An international journal dedicated to the dissemination of fundamental knowledge in all areas of biochemistry and biophysics.

Biochemical and Biophysical Research Communications. v. 1– , 1959– . San Diego, CA: Academic Press. Semimonthly. $3,495.00. ISSN 0006-291X. Available electronically.   Devoted to the rapid dissemination of timely and significant observations in the diverse fields of modern experimental biology.

Biochemical Journal. v. 1– , 1906– . Colchester, England: Portland Press. Semimonthly. Price varies. ISSN 0264-6021. Available electronically.   Journal published on behalf of the Biochemical Society, London. Includes high-quality research papers from all fields of biochemistry discussing new results, new interpretations, or new experimental methods.

Biochemical Pharmacology. v. 1– , 1958– . New York: Elsevier. Semimonthly. $5,074.00. ISSN 0006-2952. Available electronically.   International journal reporting research in pharmacology from investigations in biochemistry, biophysics, molecular biology, genetics, structural biology, computer models, and physiology. Studies with intact animals, organs, cells, subcellular components, enzymes or other cellular molecules and model systems are acceptable if they define mechanisms of drug action.

Biochemistry (U.S.). v. 1– , 1962– . Washington, DC: American Chemical Society. Weekly. $2,351.00. ISSN 0006-2960. Available electronically.   Publishes experimental results on all areas of biochemistry, "Perspectives in Biochemistry," and concise reviews on topics of timely interest.

Biochemistry and Cell Biology/Biochimie et Biologie Cellulaire. v. 64– ,
1986– . Ottawa, Canada: National Research Council of Canada. Monthly.
$375.00. ISSN 0829-8211. Available electronically.   Selected by the Canadian
Biochemical Society and the Canadian Society for Cellular and Molecular Biology as their recommended medium for the publication of scientific papers. Formerly: *Canadian Biochemistry and Cell Biology.*

Biochimica et Biophysica Acta. v. 1– , 1947– . Amsterdam: Elsevier Science.
Frequency varies. Price varies. ISSN varies by section. Available electronically.   International journal of biochemistry and biophysics published in nine sections: bioenergetics, biomembranes, general subjects, protein structure and molecular enzymology, lipids and lipid metabolism, gene structure and expression,
molecular cell research, molecular basis of disease, and review sections.

Bioelectromagnetics. v. 1– , 1980– . New York: Wiley. Bimonthly. ISSN
0197-8462. Available electronically.   Published for the Bioelectromagnetics Society, and devoted to research on biological systems as they are influenced by
natural or manufactured electric and/or magnetic fields at frequencies from DC
to visible light.

Biological Chemistry. v. 378– , 1996– . Berlin, Germany: Walter de Gruyter.
Monthly. $850.00. ISSN 1431-6730. Available electronically.   For rapid publi-
cation of reports on molecular studies of exceptional biological interest. Formerly: *Biological Chemistry Hoppe-Seyler.*

Biophysical Chemistry. v. 1– , 1973– . Amsterdam: Elsevier Science.
Monthly. $2,751.00. ISSN 0301-4622. Available electronically.   "International
journal devoted to the physics and chemistry of biological phenomena."

Biophysical Journal. v. 1– , 1960– . New York: Rockefeller University Press.
Monthly. $857.00. ISSN 0006-3495. Available electronically.   This publication,
edited by the Biophysical Society in cooperation with the Division of Biological
Physics of the American Physical Society, is a leading journal for original research in molecular and cellular biophysics. It features full-length original research papers, brief communications on topics of special interest, reviews of important topics, brief discussions of recent work, overviews of curricular design,
book and software reviews, calendar, and employment opportunities.

*Chemico-Biological Interactions; A Journal of Molecular and Biochemical Toxi-
cology.* v. 1– , 1969– . Amsterdam, Netherlands: Elsevier. Monthly.
$2,154.00. ISSN 0009-2797. Available electronically.   Devoted to the mecha-
nisms by which exogenous chemicals produce changes in biological systems.

Chemistry and Biology. v. 1– , 1994– . New York: Elsevier. Monthly.

$1,097.00. ISSN 1074-5521. Available electronically. Publishes research articles in biochemistry, biology, and chemistry.

European Biophysics Journal. v. 11– , 1984– . New York: Springer-Verlag. Bimonthly. $938.00. ISSN 0175-7571. Available electronically. Publishes papers reporting research in the study of biological phenomena by using physical methods and concepts. Formerly: *Biophysics of Structure and Function.*

European Journal of Biochemistry. v. 1– , 1967– . Oxford, England: Blackwell Science. Frequency varies. $2,812.00. ISSN 0014-2956. Available electronically. Published for the Federation of European Biochemical Societies. This journal covers research on molecular biology, nucleic acids, biochemistry, and biophysics.

Glycobiology. v. 1– , 1990– . New York: Oxford University Press. Bimonthly. $710.00. ISSN 0959-6658. Available electronically. A unique forum for research into structure and function of glycoconjugates or on any aspect of proteins that specifically interact with glycoconjugates. For researchers in biomedicine, biosciences, and the biotechnology industries.

International Journal of Biochemistry and Cell Biology. v. 1– , 1970– . New York: Elsevier. Monthly. $2,207.00. ISSN 1357-2725. Available electronically. Publishes papers on research in all areas of contemporary biochemistry, highlighting up-to-date reviews on major developments in modern biochemistry and cell biology.

Journal of Biochemistry (Tokyo). v. 1– , 1922– . Tokyo: Japanese Biochemical Society. Monthly. $240.00. ISSN 0021-924X. Global electronic access provided free by the publisher. In English. Publishes original research and communications requiring prompt publication.

Journal of Bioenergetics and Biomembranes. v. 1– , 1970– . New York: Kluwer. Bimonthly. $500.00. ISSN 0145-479X. Available electronically. Devoted to publication of original research that contributes to fundamental knowledge in the areas of bioenergetics, membranes, and transport.

Journal of Biological Chemistry. v. 1– , 1905– . Baltimore, MD: Williams & Wilkins for the American Society for Biochemistry and Molecular Biology. Weekly. $1,600.00. ISSN 0021-9258. Available electronically. A leading journal that publishes papers on a broad range of topics of interest to biochemists.

Journal of Lipid Research. v. 1– , 1959– . Bethesda, MD: Lipid Research. Frequency varies. $366.00. ISSN 0022-2275. Available electronically. Promotes basic research in the lipid field. Invited reviews.

Journal of Membrane Biology. v. 1– , 1969– . New York: Springer-Verlag.

Semimonthly. $1,720.00. ISSN 0022-2631. Available electronically. Original articles and reviews in broadly defined areas of the biology of lipids involved in problems of biochemistry, molecular biology, structural biology, cell biology, molecular biology, and metabolism. The major criteria for inclusion: new insights into mechanisms of lipid function and metabolism and/or genetic regulation of lipid metabolism.

Journal of Photochemistry and Photobiology. A, Chemistry. v. 40– , 1987– . Lausanne, Switzerland: Elsevier. Semimonthly. $3970.00. ISSN 1010-6030. Available electronically. Continues in part, *Journal of Photochemistry*, and is concerned with quantitative or qualitative aspects of photochemistry, including papers on applied photochemistry.

Journal of Photochemistry and Photobiology. B, Biology. v. 1– , 1987– . Lausanne, Switzerland: Elsevier. Quarterly. $2,497.00. ISSN 1011-1344. Available electronically. Official journal of the European Society for Photobiology. Accepts research papers on light and its interactions with the processes of life; also includes news on technological developments, forthcoming events, and conference reports.

Photochemistry and Photobiology. v. 1– , 1962– . Lawrence, KS: Allen Press for the American Society for Photobiology. Monthly. $581.00. ISSN 0031-8655. Official organ of the American Society for Photobiology. Publishes papers on all aspects of photochemistry and photobiology although it is primarily concerned with articles having current or foreseeable biological relevance.

Protein Engineering. v. 1– , 1986– . New York: Oxford University Press. Monthly. $775.00. ISSN 0269-2139. Available electronically. Application of specific theoretical and experimental disciplines promoting understanding of the structural and biochemical basis of protein function.

Protein Science: A Publication of the Protein Society. v. 1– , 1992– . New York: Cambridge University Press. Monthly. $967.00. ISSN 0961-8368. Available electronically. This journal is dedicated to the exploration of all scientific aspects of the building blocks of life: protein molecules. It presents advances to the understanding of proteins in their broadest sense, that is, in their discovery, isolation, function, and molecular structure. The Protein Society also publishes presentations of their symposia (e.g., *Techniques in Protein Chemistry VIII*, the Tenth Symposium, published in 1997 by Academic Press, ISBN 0124735576).

Radiation and Environmental Biophysics. v. 11– , 1974– . New York: Springer-Verlag. Quarterly. ISSN 0301-634X. Available electronically. Devoted to fundamentals and applications of biophysics of ionizing and nonionizing radiation; biological effects of physical factors such as temperature, pressure, gravitational forces, electricity, and magnetism; and biophysical aspects of environmental and space influence. Formerly: *Biophysik.*

REVIEWS OF THE LITERATURE

Advances in Biophysics. v. 1– , 1970– . Limerick, Ireland: Elsevier Scientific and Japan Scientific Societies Press for the Biophysical Society of Japan. Annual. $328.00. ISSN 0065-227X. Annual survey of biophysical research in English.

Advances in Enzyme Regulation. v. 1– , 1963– . New York: Elsevier. Annual. $738.00. ISSN 0065-2571. Annual survey of research developments in enzyme regulation.

Advances in Enzymology and Related Areas of Molecular Biology. v. 1– , 1941– . Chichester, England: John Wiley. Irregular. ISSN 0065-258X. Reviews selected areas.

Advances in Protein Chemistry. v. 1– , 1944– . Orlando, FL: Academic Press. Irregular. Price varies. ISSN 0065-3233. Monographic review series.

Annual Review of Biochemistry. v. 1– , 1932– . Palo Alto, CA: Annual Reviews. Annual. $136.00. ISSN 0066-4154. Available electronically. The leading review serial in biochemistry. The table of contents includes citations to related articles in other *Annual Reviews*, for example, *Biophysics and Biophysical Structure, Cell Biology, Genetics, Immunology, Medicine, Microbiology, Neuroscience, Nutrition, Physiology, Plant Physiology and Molecular Biology.*

Annual Review of Biophysics and Biomolecular Structure. v. 21– , 1992– . Palo Alto, CA: Annual Reviews. Annual. $140.00. ISSN 1056-8700. Available electronically. This series reviewing biophysics began in 1972 and has held an important place in the science literature ever since. Like the *Annual Review of Biochemistry, Biophysics* includes references to related articles in other *Annual Reviews.* Formerly: *Annual Review of Biophysics and Bioengineering.*

Current Opinion in Chemical Biology. v. 1– , 1997– . London: Elsevier. Bimonthly. $884.00. ISSN 1367-5931. Available electronically. Reviews developments in bioorganic chemistry and biology. Each issue covers a particular theme such as biopolymers or analytical techniques.

Current Opinion in Lipidology. v. 1– , 1990– . Hagerstown, MD: Lippincott, Williams, and Wilkins. Bimonthly. $616.00. ISBN 0957-9672. Available electronically. Review of the literature in lipidology.

Current Opinion in Structural Biology. v. 1– , 1991– . London: Elsevier. Bimonthly. $1,056.00. ISSN 0959-440X. Available electronically. Similar in format to *Current Opinion in Chemical Biology*, previuos. Sections include nucleic acids, folding and binding, and macromolecular assemblages.

Critical Reviews in Biochemistry and Molecular Biology. v. 24– , 1989– . Boca Raton, FL: CRC. Bimonthly. $461.00. ISSN 1040-9238. Available electronically. Includes critical surveys of specific topics of current interest selected on the advice of the Editorial Board. Formerly: *Critical Reviews in Biochemistry.*

Essays in Biochemistry. v. 1– , 1965– . London: Portland Press. Annual. $29.95. ISSN 0071-1365. Covers rapidly developing areas of biochemistry and molecular and cellular biology that are of particular interest to students and their teachers.

Life Chemistry Report: International Journal of Chronobiology. v. 1– , 1982– . New York: Gordon and Breach. Irregular. $766.00. ISSN 0278-6281. Available electronically. Overview of advances in the fields of biochemistry, molecular biology, pharmacology, and medicine. This review journal publishes the latest developments in chemistry as they relate to the life sciences.

New Comprehensive Biochemistry. A. Neuberger and L. L. M. van Dennen, eds. v. 1– , 1981– . Amsterdam: Elsevier. Irregular. Price varies. ISSN 0167-7306. Review series designed to keep scientists up-to-date and informed of developments in the biochemical sciences. Each volume has a distinctive title (e.g.), vol. 34, *Biological Complexity and the Dynamics of Life Processes*, 1999).

Progress in Biophysics and Molecular Biology. v. 1– , 1950– . New York: Elsevier. Bimonthly. $1,524.00. ISSN 0079-6107. Available electronically. International review journal covering the ground between the physical and biological sciences.

Progress in Lipid Research. v. 1– , 1981– . New York: Elsevier. Quarterly. $1,042.00. ISSN 0163-7827. Available electronically. International review journal in the chemistry of lipids.

Quarterly Reviews of Biophysics. v. 1– , 1968– . New York: Cambridge University Press. Quarterly. $304.00. ISSN 0033-5835. Available electronically. Official journal of the International Union for Pure and Applied Biophysics. This publication provides a forum for general and specialized communication between biophysicists working in different areas.

Trends in Biochemical Sciences. v. 1– , 1976– . Amsterdam: Elsevier. Monthly. $1,308.00. ISSN 0376-5067. Available electronically. Reviews of the literature plus research news, perspectives, techniques, letters to the editor, book reviews, job trends, and calendar.

6

Molecular and Cellular Biology

Molecular biology is defined as "the study of the structure and function of large molecules associated with living organisms, in particular proteins and the nucleic acids DNA and RNA" (*Oxford Dictionary of Biology*, 4th ed., 2000), while cellular biology is the study of cells, "the structural and functional unit of most living organisms" (*Oxford Dictionary of Biology*, 4th ed., 2000). Molecular biology is among the most rapidly growing fields within biology with recent success stories such as the sequencing of the entire human genome (reported in *Science* and *Nature*).

Molecular biology is unusual in that the major information source for molecular biologists is not journal articles, but public databases such as GenBank, PDB, and DDBJ (annotated in the following database section). This is one reason why there are relatively fewer handbooks and treatises for molecular biology than there are for other biological subjects.

There is a natural affinity between this chapter and the ones discussing reference materials for biochemistry (Chapter 5) and genetics (Chapter 7). Given this very substantial overlap, it is essential to review the sources annotated in these chapters for a more complete understanding of the literature of molecular biology.

ABSTRACTS AND INDEXES

Current Advances in Cell and Developmental Biology, v. 1– , 1984– . Amsterdam: Elsevier Science. Monthly. $1,508.00. ISSN 0741-1626. Specialized current awareness service for cell and developmental biology; one of a series of similar Elsevier titles.

Current Advances in Genetics and Molecular Biology. v. 1– , 1984– . Amsterdam: Elsevier Science. Monthly. $2,241. ISSN 0741-1642.   Current awareness service for genetics and molecular biology.

Nucleic Acids Abstracts. v. 1– , 1970–   . Bethesda, MD: Cambridge Scientific Abstracts. Monthly. $885.00. ISSN 1070-2466.   Covers RNA, DNA, and enzyme research. Available electronically.

PubMed. URL: http://www.ncbi.nlm.nih.gov/entrez/query.fcgi.   PubMed is the most important index for molecular biology. See the entry in Chapter 4, "Abstracts and Indexes," for full annotation.

ASSOCIATIONS

American Society for Biochemistry and Molecular Biology (ASBMB).   See Chapter 5, "Biochemistry and Biophysics," for full annotation.

American Society for Cell Biology (ASCB). 8120 Woodmont Ave., Suite 750, Bethesda, MD 20814-2755. Phone: (301) 347-9300. Fax: (301) 347-9310. E-mail: ascbinfo@ascb.org. URL: http://www.ascb.org.   Founded in 1960. 9,000 members. Includes scientists with educational or research experience in cell biology or an allied field. Placement service is offered. Publications: *ASCB Newsletter, Molecular Biology of the Cell.* Web site provides membership information and access to the society's products and services, meetings, news, publications, public policy, and careers.

European Molecular Biology Laboratory (EMBL). Meyerhofstr. 1, D-69117 Heidelberg, Germany. Phone: 49 6221 3870. Fax: 49 6221 387306. URL: http://www.embl.org.   Founded 1975. 16 member countries. Conducts molecular biological research in the following areas: cellular biology, differentiation, biological structures, genetics, biochemical instrumentation, and biocomputing. Their Web site lists their outstation locations and provides access to information about each site.

European Molecular Biology Organization (EMBO). Postfach 10 22 40, 69012 Heidelberg, Germany. Phone: 49 6221 383031. Fax: 49 6221 384879. E-mail: embo@embl-heidelberg.de. URL: http://www.embo.org.   Promotes the advancement of molecular biology in Europe and neighboring countries, administers programs funded by the European Molecular Biology Conference consisting of fellowships and courses. The organization holds courses and workshops, and presents an annual award. Publications: *EMBO Journal* and *EMBO Reports.* They hold periodic general assemblies and an annual symposium. Their Web site provides links to other European organizations, members' home pages, international university addresses, etc.

International Cell Research Organization (ICRO). Organisation Internationale de Recherche sur la Cellule. c/o UNESCO-House, SC/LSC, 1 rue Miollis, F-75732 Paris, France. Phone: 33 45688378. Fax: 33 45685818. E-mail: icro@unesco.org. URL: http://www.unesco.org/icro/. Founded 1962. 400 members. Scientists, researchers, and laboratories in 75 countries encourage and facilitate the exchange of information on basic cell biology research. The organization organizes international training courses in microbiology, biotechnology, and cell and molecular biology; they compile statistics. Web site provides information on training courses and has a limited number of other useful links.

International Federation of Cell Biology (IFCB). c/o Dept. of Cellular and Structural Biology, University of Texas Health Science Center, 7703 Floyd Curl Dr., San Antonio, TX 78229. Phone: (210) 567-3817. Fax: (210) 567-3803. URL: http://www.loncstar.texas.net/~icameron/organize.html Founded 1972. 21 member associations. National and regional associations of cell biologists promoting international cooperation among scientists working in cell biology and related fields, and contributing to the advancement of cell biology in all of its branches. Publishes *Cell Biology International*. Formerly: International Society for Cell Biology and International Society for Experimental Cytology.

International Union of Biochemistry and Molecular Biology (IUBMB). Annotated in Chapter 5, "Biochemistry and Biophysics."

RNA Society (RNAS). 9650 Rockville Pike, Bethesda, MD 20814-3998. Phone: (301) 530-7120. Fax: (301) 530-7049. E-mail: rna@faseb.org. URL: http://www.pitt.edu/~rna1/. Founded 1993. 800 members. Professionals working in molecular, evolutionary, and structural biology, biochemistry, biomedical sciences, chemistry, genetics, virology, and related disciplines with an interest in the structure and functions of ribonucleic acid (RNA). Publishes *RNA*. Web site provides membership and conference information, and a limited list of related links.

Society for In Vitro Biology (SIVB). 9315 Largo Dr., Ste. 255, Largo, MD 20774. Phone: (301) 324-5054. Fax: (301) 324-5057. E-mail: sivb@sivb.org. URL: http://www.sivb.org. Founded 1946. 2,500 members. Professional society of individuals using mammalian, invertebrate, plant cell tissue, and organ cultures as research tools in chemistry, physics, radiation, medicine, physiology, nutrition, and cytogenetics. Publishes *In Vitro-Animal* and *In Vitro-Plant*. Their Web site provides access to society information and links to the full text of society publications.

DATABASES

Molecular biology information is available extensively on the World Wide Web. Many of the databases discussed here provide access to gene or protein sequences. Each time a researcher sequences a gene or protein, he or she is expected not only to publish the sequence in a research journal, but also to submit the sequence to a sequence database. Sometimes journals will not accept articles until the sequences have appeared in a database, which is one of the few cases in which journals will accept data previously published elsewhere. The annual *Nucleic Acids Research* database issue is the best source for information on the major databases. The 2001 database issue (v. 29, issue 1 or http://nar. oupjournals.org/content/vol29/issue1/) lists 95 databases, and there are many others as well.

DDBJ (DNA Data Bank of Japan). Mishima, Japan: National Institute of Genetics. 1986– . URL: http://www.ddbj.nig.ac.jp/. Collaborates with GenBank and EMBL to collect nucleotide sequences.

EMBL (European Molecular Biology Laboratory). 1980– . Heidelberg, Germany: EMBL Data Library. URL: http://www.embl.org/Services/index.html. A nucleotide sequence database, created in collaboration with GenBank and DDBJ.

Entrez. URL: http://www.ncbi.nlm.nih.gov/Database/index.html. Entrez "is a search and retrieval system that integrates information from databases at NCBI. These databases include nucleotide sequences, protein sequences, macromolecular structures, whole genomes, and MEDLINE, through PubMed."

GenBank. 1982– . Bethesda, MD: National Center for Biotechnology Information. URL: http://www.ncbi.nlm.nih.gov/Genbank/index.html. NIH's "annotated collection of all publicly available DNA sequences." Contained over seven million sequence records from 47,000 species in June 2000.

Protein Data Bank (PDB). 1993– . Research Collaboratory for Structural Bioinformatics (RCSB). URL: http://www.rcsb.org/pdb/. "The single international repository for the processing and distribution of 3-D macromolecular structure data primarily determined experimentally by X-ray crystallography and NMR." It was established at Brookhaven National Laboratories in 1971 and contained just seven structures; by June 2000, there were over 12,500 structures. The PDB Web site provides links to many molecular biology databases and other resources.

DICTIONARIES AND ENCYCLOPEDIAS

Concise Encyclopedia of Biochemistry and Molecular Biology. 3rd rev. ed. Berlin: Walter De Gruyter, 1996. $99.95. ISBN 3110145359. Contains 4,500 entries and about 1,000 figures, formulas, and tables, with citations to recent literature.

Dictionary of Cell and Molecular Biology. 3rd ed. J. M. Lackie and J. A. T. Dow, eds. San Diego, CA: Academic Press, 1999. 512 p. $39.95. ISBN 0124325653 (paper).   This excellent dictionary will be valuable for both libraries and laboratories for many years. This new edition provides over 7,000 definitions of term useful for students as well as professional biologists.

Encyclopedia of Cell Technology. Raymond E. Spier, ed. New York: John Wiley, 2000. 2 v. $750.00. ISBN 0471161233.   Comprised of over 110 articles written and reviewed by internationally recognized experts, this reference work provides complete coverage of all aspects of both animal and plant cultures, including ethical and regulatory issues; the basic science of cells and cell culture, techniques and equipment used in growing cultures and harvesting product; product development and classification; licensing and patenting; and the history of cell technology.

Encyclopedia of Molecular Biology. Thomas Creighton, ed. New York: John Wiley, 1999. 4 v. (Wiley Biotechnology Encyclopedias). $1,500.00 (set). ISBN 0471153028 (set).   This encyclopedia focuses on the fundamentals of molecular biology and encompasses all aspects of the expression of genetic information. It has value as a first point of reference for both newcomers to the field and established professionals.

Encyclopedia of Molecular Biology and Molecular Medicine. Robert A. Meyers, ed. New York: John Wiley, 1997. 6 v. $2,760.00 (set). ISBN 3527284788 (set).   This comprehensive, detailed treatment of molecular biology and molecular medicine provides a single source library of molecular genetics and the molecular basis of life with focus on molecular medicine. Articles are designed as self-contained treatments including appropriate figures, tables and drawings, definitions, and references to the literature.

Glick, David M. *Glossary of Biochemistry and Molecular Biology*, rev. ed. Miami, FL: Portland Press, 1996. 214 p. $28.00. ISBN 1855780887.   Three thousand definitions of contemporary nomenclature useful for people peripheral to academe or involved in its development: administrators, secretaries, and teachers.

Oxford Dictionary of Biochemistry and Molecular Biology. Anthony Smith, ed. Rev. ed. New York: Oxford University Press, 2000. $65.00. ISBN 0198506732.   This comprehensive work of over 17,000 uniformly concise entries covers substances and the processes in which they are involved; methods and concepts; meanings of symbols and abbreviations; structures and activities of chemical compounds; proteins and enzymes with their functions or reactions and codes to help locate them in sequential databases; and biographical sketches of Nobel Laureates in the represented disciplines. There are more than 800 diagrams of chemical structures.

GENERAL WORKS

Cantor, Charles R. and Cassandra L. Smith. *Genomics: The Science and Technology Behind the Human Genome Project*. New York: John Wiley and Sons, 1999. 596 p. $125.00. ISBN 0471599085. Designed to provide workers in genome projects and other interested parties with an overview of the techniques used in DNA sequencing chapters. The final chapter discusses the results and implications of genome projects, and there is a chapter listing the major DNA, RNA, and protein sequence databases.

Jacob, François. *Of Flies, Mice, and Men*. Cambridge, MA: Harvard University Press, 1998. 158 p. $14.95 (paper). ISBN 0674631110, 0674005384 (paper). Jacob, who shared the 1965 Nobel Prize in Medicine, presents seven essays covering the history, philosophy, and future of molecular biology in an informal yet erudite work.

Kolata, Gina. *Clone: The Road to Dolly, and the Path Ahead*. New York: William Morrow, 1998. 276 p. $23.00, $14.00 (paper). ISBN 0688156924, 0688166342 (paper). A fascinating account of the personalities and scientific discoveries leading to the cloning of Dolly the sheep by Ian Wilmut and his team in 1997. The author, a *New York Times* reporter, takes a journalist's view of the events. Includes discussion of the ethical issues involved in cloning adult mammals.

Rensberger, Boyce. *Life Itself: Exploring the Realm of the Living Cell*. New York: Oxford University Press, 1996. 290 p. $15.95 (paper). ISBN 0195108744 (paper). Interesting introduction, written for the popular market.

Thomas, Lewis. *Lives of a Cell: Notes of a Biology Watcher*. New York: Penguin, 1995 reissue edition. 154 p. $11.95 (paper). ISBN 0140047433 (paper). A biology classic.

GUIDES TO INTERNET RESOURCES

Gannon, Pamela M. Cell and Molecular Biology Online: An Informational Resource for Cell and Molecular Biologists. URL: http://www.cellbio.com/index.html. There are links to sites for research, communication, perspectives on careers, educational resources, and various other items for information.

European Bioinformatics Institute (EBI). URL: http://www.ebi.ac.uk. This center for research and services in bioinformatics manages databases of biological data including nucleic acids, protein sequences and macromolecular structures, with access to databases such as SRS, EMBL, SWISS-PROT, InterPro, etc.

Genomics: A Global Resource. URL: http://genomics.phrma.org. Presented by the Pharmaceutical Research and Manufacturers of America and cosponsored by the American Institute of Biological Sciences (AIBS). This site offers access to links for genome news, legislation, regulation, issues, bioinformatics databases, and much more. There is also a Genomics Lexicon. While the site is sponsored by a manufacturer's association, there is no detectable "spin" on the information presented. The site would be most useful for researchers and students, but there are a number of resources that would be of interest to the general public.

Human Genome Project. The Department of Energy. URL: http://www.ornl.gov/ hgmis/. A great deal of information on the Human Genome Project, including educational materials; information on genetics and medicine; and a collection of ethical, legal, and social issues.

LiMB (Listing of Molecular Biology Databases). URL: gopher://gopher.nih.gov/ 77/gopherlib/indices/limb/index. LiMB contains information about the contents and details of maintenance of databases related to molecular biology.

Molecular Biologist Toolkit. URL: http://healthlinks.washington.edu/basic_ sciences/molbio/. Links to sites for bioinformatics resources, nucleic acid analysis, protein analysis, genomics, software, educational resources, laboratory resources, protocols and methods, reference tools, and supplies are listed.

Molecular Biology Info and Search Engines. CMS Molecular Biology Resource. URL: http://restools.sdsc.edu/biotools/biotools20.html. Index of resources include Molecular Biology-Biotechnology Specific Search Servers, Biotechnology Searching Users Guides, Other Molecular Biology Compiled Internet Resources such as the List of WWW Biological Servers and the Molecular Biology Databases on the Internet.

National Biotechnology Information Facility (NBIF). URL: http://www. nbif.org/. This Web site is divided into three main sections: Educational Resources, Internet Resources, and Products and Services. The Internet Resources list a wide assortment of compendiums and resource links for grant information; biotechnology products, careers and training; biotechnology-related science and resources; gene browser, other biotech centers; a database for standards and recommendations for naming and measuring in chemistry; Molecular Biology Gateway and other molecular biology links; and National Library of Medicine, to name a few.

The National Center for Biotechnology Information (NCBI). URL: http:// www.ncbi.nlm.nih.gov/. The place to go for information on molecular biology, genomics, and biotechnology. This Web site provides links to information for researchers, ranging from news briefs and online tutorials to information on the latest tools for data mining. The site also includes links to the numerous federally funded genomics projects, GenBank, and other molecular biology databases, and much more.

The National Human Genome Research Institute (NHGRI). URL: http://
www.nhgri.nih.gov/. A division of the National Institute of Health that is
charged with directing the Human Genome Project. Its Web site contains a wealth
of information on genetics and genome projects, including links to other sites,
the Glossary of Genetic Terms (see Chapter 7, "Genetics, Biotechnology, and
Developmental Biology"), downloadable handouts dealing with genetics and
techniques used in the Human Genome Project, and news about the project.

Research Collaboratory for Structural Bioinformatics (RCSB). URL: http://
www.rcsb.org/index.html. This is a nonprofit consortium dedicated to improving our understanding of the function of biological systems through the study of
the 3D structure of biological macromolecules. This group from Rutgers, the San
Diego Supercomputer Center, and the Biotechnology Division of the National
Institutes of Standards and Technology provide databases, software and software
standards, education, and community service.

The Sanger Centre. URL: http://www.sanger.ac.uk. There are links to several
model organism Web sites, concentrating on genome and genetics databases for
Dictyostelium, zebrafish, and livestock genomes. This guide is less comprehensive than the WWW Virtual Library Model Organisms guide.

Smith, Christopher M. CMS Molecular Biology Resource. San Diego, CA: Computational Biology Group, San Diego Supercomputer Center. URL: http://
www.sdsc.edu/projects/ResTools/cmshp.html. "A compendium of electronic
and Internet-accessible tools and resources for Molecular Biology, Biotechnology, Molecular Evolution, Biochemistry, and Molecular Modeling." It is organized by function.

UK Human Genome Mapping Project Resource Centre (HGMP-RC). URL:
http://www.hgmp.mrc.ac.uk. This site provides access to all the latest databases and bioinformatics tools for genetic and genomic research. Registration for
use of these tools is free for academics.

HANDBOOKS

Attwood, Teresa K. and David J. Parry-Smith. *Introduction to Bioinformatics.*
Essex, England: Longman, 1999. (Cell and Molecular Biology in Action Series).
218 p. ISBN 0582327881. This text on bioinformatics discusses the application
of computers in biological science and the analysis of biological sequence data,
which are essential tools in molecular biology. It is linked to a Web site and
introduces key databases, tools and resources, and outlines pitfalls of methods.

Bioinformatics: A Practical Guide to the Analysis of Genes and Proteins. Andreas D. Baxevanis and B. F. Francis Ouellette, eds. (Methods of Biochemical Analysis, v. 39). New York: Wiley, 1998. $172.00. ISBN 0471324418. Fourteen chapters discuss tools and databases used in bioinformatics.

Cell Biology LABFAX. G. B. Dealtry and D. Rickwood, eds. San Diego, CA: Academic Press, 1992. 254 p. $49.95. ISBN 012207890X. Covers formulation of salt solutions; subcellular fractionation techniques and characteristics of electron microscopy; DNA content of cells; membrane composition; properties and receptors; metabolic inhibitors; cyclic nucleotides; steroid and peptide hormones; growth regulators; and cell cycle oncogenes.

Cell Culture Labfax. M. Butler and M. Dawson, eds. San Diego, CA: Academic Press, 1997, first published jointly in the UK, by Bios Science Publishing and Academic Press, 1992. (Labfax Series) 247 p. $78.00. ISBN 0121480607. This convenient lab reference guide supports the needs of the laboratory scientist and the process engineer who grow cells in culture. It is aimed at both beginners and experienced researcher who need ready access to information.

Cross, Patricia C. and K. Lynne Mercer. *Cell and Tissue Ultrastructure: A Functional Perspective.* 2nd ed. New York: W. H. Freeman, 1995. 420 p. $52.75. ISBN 0716770334. This collection of electron micrographs provides a complete up-to-date introduction to cell ultrastructure, with emphasis on cell anatomy and physiology. The volume is arranged with the right-hand pages presenting micrographs, or portraits of cells from major organs in every organ system. The left-hand pages describe the basic structure and function of the cell in the micrograph on the opposite page. Accompanying line drawings and diagrams place the micrographs in context with surrounding tissue.

The Cytokine Handbook. 3rd ed. Angus Thomson, ed. San Diego, CA: Academic Press, 1998. 1,017 p. $125.00 ISBN 012896623. Comprehensive source of information of the haemopoietic growth factors and the interleukin and interferon families of molecules, cytokine by cytokine.

Cytokine Reference: A Compendium of Cytokines and Other Mediators of Host Defense. Joost J. Oppenheim and Marc Feldmann, eds. San Diego, CA: Academic Press, 2000. Online database and 2 vol. set. $695.00. ISBN 0122526732 (set). This encyclopedic handbook is written by a group of experts to provide essential and comprehensive information on all known cytokines, including chemokines, growth factors and neuropeptides, and hundreds of entries with detailed descriptions of cytokine genes, proteins, cell sources, activities, receptors, receptor signal transduction, gene activation, pathophysiology, therapeutics, and techniques. Also available as an online database (by subscription only). The database is regularly updated and includes full-color diagrams and sequences plus links to other databases, including MEDLINE, PDB, SWISS-PRO, and GenBank. It is billed by the publisher as the "most complete on-line work for anyone interested in the role of cytokines in host defense processes."

Enzymes in Molecular Biology: Essential Data. C. J. McDonald, ed. New York: John Wiley, 1997. 144 p. $40.00 (paper). ISBN 047194842X (paper). This pocket-sized volume is a useful source for the most commonly used enzymes for the manipulation of DNA, RNA, and proteins. Each enzyme entry lists properties, applications, problems, and much more.

The Extracellular Matrix Factsbook. 2nd ed. Shirley Ayad, Ray Boot-Handford, and Martin Humphries, eds. San Diego, CA: Academic Press, 1998. 301 p. $53.00 (paper). ISBN 0120689111 (paper). Completely revised, updated, and expanded by over 50%, this handbook contains over 85 entries on the diverse group of macromolecules that assemble to form the extracellular matrix, by providing information on molecular structure, isolation, primary structure, structural and functional sites, gene structure, database accession numbers, and entry-specific references.

Genetics and Cell Biology on File.   For a complete annotation, see Chapter 3, "General Sources."

Guidebook to the Cytoskeletal and Motor Proteins. 2nd ed. Thomas Kreis and Ronald Vale, eds. New York: Oxford University Press, 1999. $60.00 (paper). ISBN 0198599560 (paper). Covers actin and its associated proteins, microtubule proteins, as well as motor proteins. Useful reference and study guide.

Guidebook to the Extracellular Matrix, Anchor, and Adhesion Proteins. 2nd ed. Thomas Kreis and Ronald Vale, eds. New York: Oxford University Press, 1999. 568 p. (Guidebook Series). $150.00, $70.00 (paper). ISBN 0198599595, 0198599587 (paper). Up-to-date information on protein purification, activities, antibodies, and genes for proteins found in the extracellular matrix and those known to be involved in cell-to-cell contact and adhesion.

Ibelgaufts, Horst. COPE: Cytokines Online Pathfinder Encyclopaedia. Version 4.0 (August 1999). URL: http://www.copewithcytokines.de. This online handbook was composed by a researcher at the University of Munich in an effort to help people cope with the number and actions of various cytokines. Arranged alphabetically, each cytokine is defined by function. There are over 6,650 hyperlinked entries. This site appears to be more comprehensive than the *Cytokine Handbook* although it has not received editorial review.

Molecular Biology and Biotechnology: A Comprehensive Desk Reference. Robert A. Meyers, ed. New York: VCH, 1995. 1,034 p. $235.00, $99.95 (paper). ISBN 047118571X, 0471186341 (paper). Two hundred and fifty articles provide self-contained treatments of topics involved in understanding the molecular basis of life and the application of that knowledge in genetics, medicine, and agriculture. Appropriate mathematics and references are included. There are over 120 tables and 500 illustrations, and a glossary of basic terms.

Molecular Biology Labfax. 2nd ed. T. A. Brown, ed. San Diego, CA: Academic, 1998. 2 v. (Labfax series). ISBN 0121360555 (v. 1). Volume 1, *Recombinant DNA*, covers basic data relevant to research on bacteria and bacteriophages; restriction and methylation; DNA and RNA modifying enzymes; genomes; and cloning vectors. Volume 2, *Gene Analysis*, covers general topics such as chemicals and reagents and lab safety in addition to more specific techniques relating to gene analysis (PCR, blotting, sequencing, etc.).

Morlcy, Bernard J. and Mark J. Walport. *The Complement Factsbook.* San Diego, CA: Academic Press, 2000. 228 p. $49.95 (paper). ISBN 0127333606 (paper). Comprehensive and concise biochemical information about proteins of the complement system, including C1q collections, C3 family proteins, serine proteases, regulators of complement activation, cell surface receptors, and terminal pathway proteins. The focus is on the human system; key references included.

Oxford Handbook of Nucleic Acid Structure. Stephen Neidle, ed. Oxford, England: Oxford University Press, 1999. 662 p. $140.00. ISBN 0198500386. Comprehensive reference text on all aspects of nucleic acid structure with particular emphasis placed on results from X-ray crystallography and NMR studies. Nineteen chapters describe in detail the variety of DNA and RNA structural types discovered to date.

Practical Handbook of Biochemistry and Molecular Biology. Gerald D. Fasman, ed. Boca Raton, FL: CRC Press, 1989. 601 p. $115.95.ISBN 0849337054. Contains methodologies and data relating to biochemistry and molecular biology. Material is derived and updated from the multivolume *CRC Handbook of Biochemistry and Molecular Biology.*

Rickwood, David, D. B. Hames, and Dipak Patel. *Cell and Molecular Biology: Essential Data.* New York: John Wiley, 1995. 224 p. $39.95 (paper). ISBN 047195568X (paper). Pocket-sized, quick reference of core data for workers in cell and molecular biology.

Twyman, R. M. *Advanced Molecular Biology: A Concise Reference.* New York: Springer-Verlag, 1999. 499 p. $39.95 (paper). ISBN 0387915982 (paper). This well-reviewed text also provides in-depth coverage of 30 essential topics in molecular biology with focus on genetic information and its expression. This book is aimed at undergraduates, graduate students, academics new to the area.

HISTORIES

Cook-Deegan, Robert. *The Gene Wars: Science, Politics, and the Human Genome*. New York: Norton, 1993. 416 p. $25.00. ISBN 0393035727.   A history of the early years of the Human Genome Project, covering events and personalities both in the United States and abroad, written by an author who was witness to much of the events described. The first four chapters offer a discussion of the science involved in the Human Genome Project at a level suitable for the general public.

Davies, Kevin. *Cracking the Genome: Inside the Race to Unlock Human DNA*. New York: Free Press, 2001. 320 p. $25.00. ISBN 0743204794.   This history of the effort to sequence the human genome concentrates on recent developments, especially the race between Craig Venter's Celera company and the international Human Genome Project, but also discusses events that took place leading up to the project.

Edsall, J. T. and D. Bearman. Survey of sources for the history of biochemistry and molecular biology. *Federation Proceedings* 36 (8): 2069-2073, July 1977.   This paper describes the effort to collect and preserve sources for the study of the history of biochemistry and molecular biology. Thirteen histories are cited in the references. The "Survey of sources . . ." is "the first major undertaking in this field, for the biological sciences, in the 20th century."

Fruton, Joseph S. *Proteins, Enzymes, Genes: The Interplay of Chemistry and Biology*. New Haven, CT: Yale University Press, 1999. 784 p. $45.00. ISBN 0300076088.   Authoritative survey of the history of biochemistry and molecular biology during the past 200 years by an eminent historian of science and the former head of the department of biochemistry at Yale. This history provides a treasury of references.

Harris, Henry. *The Birth of the Cell*. New Haven, CT: Yale University Press reprint, 2000. 256 p. $17.00 (paper). ISBN 0300082959 (paper).   This classic by Henry Harris, an excellent historian and distinguished medical scientist, focuses on the scientific aspects of the cell theory. The book covers the seventeenth, eighteenth, and nineteenth centuries, is well-referenced, and beautifully illustrated.

Hunter, Graeme K. *Vital Forces: The Discovery of the Molecular Basis of Life*. San Diego, CA: Academic Press, 2000. 364 p. $29.95 (paper). ISBN 0123618118 (paper).   This new history tells the story of the biochemical revolution by combining science and biographies of the scientists involved, including Louis Pasteur, Gregor Mendel, Linus Pauling, and Francis Crick.

Judson, Horace Freeland. *Eighth Day of Creation: Makers of the Revolution in Biology.* Cold Spring Harbor, NY: Cold Spring Harbor Laboratory Press, 1996. 714 p. $39.00 (paper). ISBN 0879694785 (paper). A revised and expanded edition of Judson's 1978 history of the human and scientific origins of molecular biology. It includes a preface by Sir John Maddox, a new foreword, and an epilogue on the further development of molecular biology into the era of recombinant DNA.

Landmark Papers in Cell Biology: Selected Research Articles Celebrating Forty Years of the American Society for Cell Biology. Joseph G. Gall and J. Richard McIntosh, eds. Cold Spring Harbor, NY: Cold Spring Harbor Laboratory Press, 2001. 532 p. $45.00. ISBN 0879696028. A collection of 42 important papers on eukaryotic research from the last 40 years.

Mazzarello, Paolo. A Unifying Concept: The History of Cell Biology. *Nature: Cell Biology* 1 (1): E13–E15, May, 1999. A brief history of cell biology.

Morange, Michel. *A History of Molecular Biology.* Cambridge, MA: Harvard University Press, 2000. 352 p. $19.95 (paper). ISBN 0674001699 (paper). This account traces the history of molecular biology from the turn of the century convergence of genetics and biochemistry to gene splicing and cloning techniques of the 1980's, describing major discoveries along the way.

Olby, R. C. *The Path to the Double Helix: The Discovery of DNA.* New York: Dover, 1994. 522 p. $14.95 (paper). ISBN 0486681173 (paper). This book retains its value by presenting a comprehensive account of the origins of molecular biology.

Phage and the Origins of Molecular Biology. John Cairns, Gunther S. Stent, and James D. Watson, eds. Cold Spring Harbor, NY: Cold Spring Harbor Laboratory Press, 2000. 366 p. $29.00 (paper). ISBN 0879695951 (paper). Published on the occasion of the sixtieth birthday of Max Delbruck. Expanded edition of the 1966 collection of 35 essays by pioneers of molecular biology.

Schrodinger, Erwin. *What is Life?: The Physical Aspect of the Living Cell with Mind and Matter and Autobiographical Sketches.* New York: Cambridge University Press reprint edition, 1992. 200 p. $12.95 (paper). ISBN 0521427088 (paper). The reviewer, Adam S. Wilkins, writing in *Bioessays* (15 (11): 767–9, Nov. 1993) commented that Schrodinger's book was a "milestone in conceptual development of modern biology, and specifically of molecular biology."

Summers, William C. *Felix D'Herelle and the Origins of Molecular Biology.* New Haven, CT: Yale University Press, 1999. 230 p. $30.00. ISBN 0300071272. This history is the first full-length biography of D'Herelle, a significant figure in the history of molecular biology and the first to show the use of bacteria for biological control of insect pests.

Watson, James D. *Double Helix: Being a Personal Account of the Discovery of the Structure of DNA.* New York: Atheneum, 1980. 226 p. $11.95 (paper). ISBN 0689706022 (paper).   The exciting story behind the author's account of the discovery of the structure of DNA has a little bit of everything: suspense, adventure, melodrama, and humor.

METHODS AND TECHNIQUES

There are innumerable excellent books, series, and Web sites containing information on protocols for molecular biology. This selected list contains a great deal of redundancy in order to provide access to various levels and currency of techniques. It may be necessary and most effective to peruse several examples, concluding with protocols that have been updated in an online database. Also, refer to Chapter 5, "Biochemistry and Biophysics," and Chapter 7, "Genetics, Biotechnology, and Developmental Biology," and see the section "Methods, Protocols and Software" listed in the WWW Virtual Library of Cell Biology at http://vl.bwh.harvard.edu/.

Bioinformatics Methods and Protocols. Stephen Misener and Stephen A. Krawetz, eds. Totowa, NJ: Humana, 2000. 500 p. (Methods in molecular biology). ISBN 0896037320.   Includes information on sequence analysis packages, molecular biology software, Web-based resources, and the present limits of computer analysis. The editors also include a section on teaching bioinformatics, which includes basic information on searching MEDLINE and Science Citation Index, plus information on electronic journals and finding funding sources on the Web.

Bioinformatics: Sequence, Structure and Databanks: A Practical Approach. Des Higgins and Willie Taylor, eds. (The Practical Approach Series, 236) New York: Oxford University Press, 2000. 249 p. $55.00. ISBN 0199637903.   Covers practical important topics in the analysis of protein sequences and structures. It includes comparing amino acid sequences to structures, comparing structures to each other, searching information on entire protein families as well as searching with single sequences, how to use the Internet and how to set up and use the SRS molecular biology database management system.

Biological Procedures Online (BPO). Faculty of Science, University of Waterloo, 1998–   . ISSN 1480-9222. URL: http://www.science.uwaterloo.ca/mwreimer/bpo.htm.   Science Med Central publishes four, peer-reviewed electronic technique journals at this site: medicine, biology, chemistry, and physics. Archival issues of BPO are available on CD-ROM.

Calcium Signaling. James W. Putney, Jr., ed. Boca Raton, FL: CRC Press, 1999. (Methods in Signal Transduction). 400 p. $129.00. ISBN 0849333865.   Spans all conceptual and technical areas of molecular and cell biology, and touches on key methodological approaches useful for students and senior faculty investigating calcium function and regulation, biological processes and systems; and cellular and molecular basis of disease. Step-by-step techniques address problems associated with calcium sequence systems. There are detailed illustrations.

Cell Biology: A Laboratory Handbook. 2nd ed. Julio E. Celis, ed. San Diego, CA: Academic Press, 1998. 4 v. $179.95. ISBN 0121647250 (spiral).   Comprehensive laboratory manual compiling current and classic protocols for cell biology that have stood the test of time. The first volume deals with tissue culture and associated techniques and discusses viruses. The second volume covers organelles and cellular structures, assays, antibodies, immunocytochemistry, vital staining of cells, and Internet resources. The third volume presents light microscopy and contrast generation, electron microscopy, intracellular measurements, cytogenetics and hybridization, and transgenics and gene knockouts. The fourth volume completes the set, discussing topics such as transfer of macromolecules, expression systems, differential gene expression, and proteins.

Cell Biology: Essential Techniques. David Rickwood and James R. Harris, eds. (Essential Techniques Series). New York: John Wiley, 1997. 192 p. $49.94 (paper). ISBN 0471963151 (paper).   Quick and easy access to key protocols in cell biology contained in a pocket-sized manual.

Cell Separation Methods and Applications. Diether Recktenwald and Andreas Radbruch, eds. New York: Dekker, 1998. 331 p. $155.00 ISBN 0824798643.   This work provides basic methods for the analytical and preparative isolation of specific populations of biological cells and includes an appendix of cell properties for cell separations and CD antigens.

Cell and Tissue Culture: Laboratory Procedures. A. Doyle, J. B. Griffiths, and D. G. Newell, eds. New York: Wiley, 1998. 252 p. $125.00 (spiral). ISBN 0471982555 (spiral).   Comprehensive collection of cell and tissue culture *in vitro* techniques, describing key cells, core techniques, regulatory aspects, and how to scale up the culture for commercial production. Alternative procedures, background information, and references supplement the main procedures described by the editors.

Computational Methods in Molecular Biology. Steven L. Salzberg, David B. Searls, and Simon Kasif, eds. New York: Elsevier, 1998. (New Comprehensive Biochemistry, vol. 32). 371 p. $59.00 (paper). ISBN 0444828753, 0444502041 (paper).   This is a clearly written, excellent description of the latest computer technology for analyzing DNA, RNA, and protein sequences for the noncomputer scientist. It is valuable in assisting biologists in making better choices of algorithms to use.

Current Protocols in Cell Biology. 1998–   . Juan S. Bonifacino et al., eds. New York: John Wiley. Looseleaf manual with quarterly updates. $395.00 (looseleaf), ISBN 0471241083 (looseleaf), 0471241059 (CD-ROM).   This looseleaf series contains protocols for the basic culture and fractionation of cells; microscopic localization and tracking; and analysis of biosynthesis, modification, and transport of specific molecules as well as more complex protocols. See *Current Protocols in Molecular Biology* for more details on this series.

Current Protocols in Cytometry. 1997–   . J. Paul Robinson et al., eds. New York: Wiley. Looseleaf manual with quarterly updates. $395.00 (looseleaf), $450.00 (CD-ROM). ISBN 0471161314 (looseleaf), 0471161322 (CD-ROM).   Provides flow and image cytometry methods, plus coverage of cytometry instrumentation, safety and quality control, and data processing and analysis. Published in affiliation with the International Society for Analytical Cytology. See *Current Protocols in Molecular Biology*, for more details on this series.

Current Protocols in Molecular Biology. 1988–   . New York: Wiley. Looseleaf manual with quarterly updates. $635.00 (looseleaf), $635.00 (CD-ROM). ISBN 047150338X (looseleaf), 0471306614 (CD-ROM).   Designed for maximum ease of use in a laboratory setting, this loose-leaf publication covers a wide range of techniques in molecular biology. Protocols, background information, and a guide to the choice of methods are provided, often with extensive troubleshooting guides. This review of molecular biology techniques may be updated, in the loose-leaf format, by supplements, corrections, and improved protocols. Also available on CD-ROM, with quarterly updates and on the Web (for institutional subscribers only, price varies). See also *Short Protocols in Molecular Biology*.

Darbre, Philippa D. *Basic Molecular Biology: Essential Techniques*. New York: John Wiley, 1999. 208 p. $44.95. ISBN 0471977055 (spiral).   This introduction provides an overview of the basic methods and focuses on simple step-by-step protocols of core techniques. Aimed at novices in the field.

Davis, Leonard G., et al. *Basic Methods in Molecular Biology*. 4th ed. New York: McGraw-Hill, 1995. 455 p. $75.00. ISBN 838506429 (spiral).   This established, successful methods book emphasizes how to select one procedure over another.

DNA Sequencing Protocols. 2nd ed. Colin A. Graham et al., eds. Totowa, NJ: Humana Press, 2001. (Methods in Molecular Biology, vol. 167). 200 p. $99.50. ISBN 0896037169.   Although the second edition was not available at this writing, the first edition was a comprehensive guide to over 38 DNA sequencing methods and techniques. It included cycle sequencing, sequencing PCR products, sequencing lambola and cosmids, multiplex sequencing, direct blotting electrophoresis, sequencing by chemiluminescence, and automated sequencing.

DoubleTwist: Protocol Online—Your Lab's Reference Book. DoubleTwist, Inc., 1999– . URL: http://www.protocol-online.net. This keyword-searchable site provides protocols and discussion forums for molecular biology, cell biology, and immunology; a BioMail News Group; and BioResearch Chat. The "Quick Access Table" organizes the protocols by discipline and topic, aiding retrieval.

Electron Microscopy Methods and Protocols. M. A. Nasser Hajibagheri, ed. Totowa, NJ: Humana Press, 1999. 283 p. $89.50 (spiral). ISBN 0896036405 (spiral). The 15 contributions describe key electron microscopy techniques for examining cells, tissues, biological macromolecules, molecular structure, and their intcractions. For new and experienced researchers.

Emerging Tools for Single-Cell Analysis: Advances in Optical Measurement Technologies. Gary Durack and J. Paul Robinson, eds. New York: Wiley-Liss, 2000. (Cytometric Cellular Analysis) 359 p. $129.95. ISBN 0471315753. This book's goal is to re-evaluate current technology in single-cell properties using optically based measurement systems. Integrating engineering and biology, this book discusses sorting, confocal microscopy, and color scanning microscopy.

Essential Molecular Biology: A Practical Approach. 2nd ed. T. A. Brown, ed. New York: Oxford University Press, 2000. 2 v. (The Practical approach series). $93.75 (v. 1), $43.00 (v. 1, paper). ISBN 0199636435 (v. 1), 0199636427 (v. 1, paper). This example of the highly regarded Practical Approach series covers the fundamental techniques of gene cloning. The second edition of volume 2 is forthcoming.

Farrell, Robert E., Jr. *RNA Methodologies: A Laboratory Guide for Isolation and Characterization.* 2nd ed. San Diego, CA: Academic Press, 1998. 533 p. $59.95 (spiral). ISBN 0122496957 (spiral). This book presents mammalian RNA isolation strategies and a collection of tested and optimized protocols for basic, as well as for more sophisticated, procedures. There are 11 appendices containing flow charts, tables, graphs to aid explanation and learning, and a glossary.

Flow Cytometry Applications in Cell Culture. Mohamed Al-Rubeai and A. Nicholas Emery, eds. New York: Dekker, 1996. 331 p. $150.00. ISBN 0824796144. This useful resource presents practical biotechnological applications of flow cytometry techniques for the study of animal, plant, and microbial cells explaining methodologies for sample preparation, staining, and analysis.

Flow Cytometry and Cell Sorting. 2nd ed. A. Radbruch, ed. New York: Springer-Verlag, 2000. (Springer Lab Manual). 223 p. $89.95 (paper). ISBN 354065308 (paper). This introduction for beginners describes cellular fluorescence techniques as well as fluorescence-activated or magnetic cell-sorting technologies useful for molecular and cellular biology.

Flow Cytometry Protocols. Mark J. Jaroszeski and Richard Heller, eds. Totowa, NJ: Humana Press, 1998. 274 p. $74.50 (paper). ISBN 0896035387 (paper). Twenty-two papers describe the fundamentals of flow cytometry, its instrumentation and analysis, including well-tested protocols.

Freshney, R. Ian. *Culture of Animal Cells*, 4th ed. New York: John Wiley, 2000. 600 p. $79.95. ISBN 0471348899.   Updated training manual suitable for class work, with detailed instructions for proven, fundamental principles and techniques of animal cell culture. Includes resources for specialized equipment and supplies.

Gannon, Pamela. Cell and Molecular Biology Online. Concord, MA: Cell Biology Online, 1996– . URL: http://www.cellbio.com/protocols.html.   The Methods and Protocols section of this directory lists various online resources, primarily from specific research laboratories, for cell and molecular biology research protocols. Some of topics addressed are antibody design, cell biology, DNA sequencing, microscopy, molecular biology, PCR Jump Station, and vector database.

Invertebrate Cell Culture: Novel Directions and Biotechnology Applications. Karl Maramorosch and Jun Mitsuhashi, eds. Enfield, NH: Science Publishers, 1997. 296 p. $109.00. ISBN 1578080118.   Current research describes the methods and diverse biotechnological applications of invertebrate cell culture worldwide.

Mather, Jennie P. and Penelope E. Roberts. *Introduction to Cell and Tissue Culture: Theory and Technique*. New York: Plenum, 1998. (Introductory Cell and Molecular Biology Techniques). 226 p. $29.50 (paper). ISBN 0306458594 (paper).   This is for both novices and experts, and includes modern tissue culture methods for cell biology, genetics, nutrition, endocrinology, and physiology. It provides technical cell-culture information, and theoretical perspective for problems, exercises, and techniques. Contains useful appendices of other aspects of cell and tissue culture.

Methods. v. 1– , 1990– . San Diego, CA: Academic Press. Bimonthly. Price varies. ISSN 1046-2023. Available electronically.   A companion journal to *Methods in Enzymology* focusing on rapidly developing techniques. Each topical issue is organized by an editor expert in the area, and includes specific technical approaches with detailed protocols.

Methods in Cell Biology. v. 1– , 1964– . Orlando, FL: Academic Press. Irregular. Price varies. ISSN 0091-679X.   This book series publishes protocols in a wide range of areas. Each chapter presents a detailed background of the described method, its theoretical foundations, and its applicability to different biomedical material. Recent titles include *Cytometry, Part A* and *Part B*; *Mitosis and Meiosis*, and *The Zebrafish: Genetics and Genomics*.

Methods in Cell Science. v. 17– , 1995– . Dordrecht, Netherlands: Kluwer. Quarterly. $250.00. ISSN 1381-5741. Available electronically. This journal lists specific directions for cell, tissue, and organ culture procedures. Formerly: *Journal of Tissue Culture Methods*, and before that, *TCA Manual*.

Methods in Enzymology. v. 1– , 1955– . Orlando, FL: Academic Press. Irregular. Price varies. ISSN 0076-6879. This series has been one of the standard sources for methods and protocols since its inception. There are over 300 volumes to date, 10 to 20 per year, and all of them are still in print. Each volume covers a single topic such as hyperthermophilic enzymes or branched chain amino acids. There are two CD-ROMs as well, one providing full text of 30 volumes on recombinant DNA and the other consisting of the index of volumes 1–275.

MethodsFinder 2.0. 1998– . Philadelphia, PA: BIOSIS. URL: http://www. methodsfinder.org. Weekly updates. Price varies. The MethodsFinder database is a rapid way to find methods information, all in one place. Methods are aggregated from journal articles, methods books, full-text Web sites from companies and researchers, and full-text meetings presentations. It is searchable with a browsable index compiled by experienced life science professionals. Information includes method name, reagents and equipment used. The site allows submission of protocols and provides methods news and other biology links of interest. This commercial site gives a free trial of its contents. Additional information about BIOSIS services may be found in Chapter 2, ''Subject Access to Biological Information.''

Methods in Molecular Biology. v. 1– , 1984– . Clifton, NJ: Humana Press. Irregular. Price varies. ISSN 1064-3745. Practical, hands-on laboratory protocols for a wide range of basic and advanced techniques in all areas of experimental biology and medicine. About 50 volumes are published per year in this book series. Recent volumes include *Afinity Chromatography: Methods and Protocols*; *DNA Sequencing Protocols*, 2nd ed.; *Glycoanalysis Protocols*, 2nd ed.; and *Mass Spectrometry of Proteins and Peptides*. A sister series, *Methods in Molecular Medicine*, includes several titles that might also be of interest to molecular biologists.

Molecular Biomethods Handbook. Ralph Rapley and John M. Walker, eds. Totowa, NJ: Humana Press, 1998. 728 p. $89.50. ISBN 0896035018. An authoritative group of scientists provide a wide-ranging collection of bioanalytical techniques used in their laboratories and throughout the world. Theory, application, key techniques, and extensive references are included.

Nei, Masatoshi and Sudhir Kumar. *Molecular Evolution and Phylogenetics*. New York: Oxford University Press, 2000. 333 p. $50.00 (paper). ISBN 0195135857 (paper).   This text is an excellent reference for statistical methods that are appropriate in the study of molecular evolution by illustrating how the methods are used in actual data analysis.

Nucleic Acids Protocols Handbook. Ralph Rapley, ed. Totowa, NJ: Humana Press, 2000. 1,072 p. $149.50. ISBN 0896034593.   This is a treasury of all the key molecular biology methods used in the modern laboratory. It describes theory, instructions, and a listing of materials required.

Nucleic Acids Research Methods. Oxford, England: Oxford Journals Online, 2000– . URL: http://www3.oup.co.uk/nar/methods.   This online journal is only available on the Web and contains papers not published in the print *Nucleic Acids Research* (*NAR*), although such papers are listed in the print version. Access to the methods section is included with subscription to the print *NAR*.

PCR. M. J. McPherson, et al., eds. New York: Springer-Verlag, 2000. (The Basics series). 120 p. $35.95 (paper). ISBN 0387916008 (paper).   A practical introduction to PCR practices in the lab. The book offers basic theory, background material, and suggestions for suitable protocols for novices or experienced researchers.

PCR Applications; Protocols for Functional Genomics. Michael A. Innis, David H. Gelfand, and John J. Sninsky. San Diego, CA: Academic Press, 1999. 566 p. $59.95 (spiral). ISBN 0123721857 (spiral).   This sourcebook delivers expert advice with contemporary protocols and some personal opinions. The emphasis is on supplying both a reference and a practical tool for a wide range of research applications.

PCR in Bioanalysis. Stephen J. Meltzer, ed. Totowa, NJ: Humana Press, 1998. 292 p. $89.50. ISBN 0896034976.   Covers the use of the polymerase chain reaction in the diagnosis of infectious disease: detection of amplified or deleted DNA sequences and circulating tumor cells, the quantitative measurement of mRNA expression; the identification and cloning of differentially expressed genes; and the process of screening for chain-terminating mutations.

Peruski, Leonard F. and Anne Harwood Peruski. *The Internet and The New Biology: Tools for Genomic and Molecular Research*. Washington, DC: ASM Press, 1997. 314 p. $34.95 (paper). ISBN 1555811191 (paper).   This book "explores and explains some of the computational biology tools found on the Internet and how they can be applied to problems in genomic and molecular biology." The authors discuss general tips on using the Internet as well as all of the major molecular biology databases. Their discussion of using the databases focus on four areas: how to submit sequences to public databases, how to search the databases for sequences, how to search for sequence motifs, and how to retrieve sequences from the databases.

Pevzner, Pavel A. *Computational Molecular Biology; An Algorithmic Approach.* Cambridge, MA: MIT Press, 2000. (Computational Molecular Biology) 314 p. $44.95. ISBN 0262161974. This major text covers a broad range of algorithmic and combinatorial topics, connecting them to molecular biology and to biotechnology, aimed at both biologists and computer scientists with limited background in computational biology. The author combines computational, statistical, experimental, and technological methods in fundamental areas of computational molecular biology.

Practical Approach on CD-ROM/2. Version 2.0. Oxford, England: Oxford University Press, 1999. 1 CD-ROM disk. $360.00. This CD-ROM product includes the full text of 83 of the volumes from the Practical Approach series, and is available in Windows and Macintosh versions. The CD-ROM includes protocols from *Animal Cell Culture*, *Antisense Technology*, *In Situ Hybridization*, *Protein Targeting*, and many more.

Ream, Walt and Katharine G. Field. *Molecular Biology Techniques: An Intensive Laboratory Course.* San Diego, CA: Academic Press, 1998. 228 p. $39.95 (paper). ISBN 0125839901 (paper). This is an intensive introduction to basic methods using well-tested protocols for cloning, PCR, Southern (DNA) blotting, Western blotting, DNA sequencing, oligo-directed mutagenesis, and protein expression.

Sambrook, Joseph and David W. Russell. *Molecular Cloning: A Laboratory Manual.* 3rd ed. Cold Spring Harbor, NY: Cold Spring Harbor Laboratory Press, 2001. 3 v. $295.00, $195.00 (paper). ISBN 0879695765, 0879695773 (paper). This handbook has long been a mainstay in molecular biology laboratories. The third edition has been completely revised. It contains both basic and more specialized techniques, plus appendices listing supplies and suppliers, electronic resources, and other essential information. New for this edition is a companion Web site, http://www.MolecularCloning.com. The site will provide updated protocols, searching and printing of the protocols, a discussion board, and links to other Web resources.

Short Protocols in Molecular Biology: A Compendium of Methods from Current Protocols in Molecular Biology. 4th ed. Frederick M. Ausubel, et al., eds. New York: John Wiley, 1999. 1,056 p. $120.00. ISBN 047132938X. Selected protocols from the standard in the field. These shortened versions are designed for use at the lab bench by researchers who are already familiar with the methods.

Spector, David L., Robert D. Goldman, and Leslie A. Leinwand. *Cells: A Laboratory Manual*. Cold Spring Harbor, NY: Cold Spring Harbor Laboratory Press, 1997. 3 v. $255.00 (set). ISBN 0879695218 (spiral).   Tested protocols arranged in three volumes addressing three main areas: culture and biochemical analysis of cells, light microscopy and cell structure, and subcellular localization of genes and their products.

Strom, Mark. Molecular Biology Protocols. U.S. Dept. of Commerce (NOAA, NMFS, NWFSC). URL: http://www.nwfsc.noaa.gov/protocols.html.   This Web site provides access to molecular biology protocols such as DNA Purification Techniques, DNA Transformation/Library Preparation, Southern/Northern Blotting, DNA Sequencing, Oligonucleotides, PCR and Related Methods, RNA Methods, Protein Electrophoresis, Protein Purification, Autoradiography Tips, Safety, and other references.

Technical Tips Online.   See Chapter 3, "General Sources," for full annotation.

TEXTBOOKS AND TREATISES

Alberts, Bruce, et al. *Essential Cell Biology: An Introduction to the Molecular Biology of the Cell*. New York: Garland Publishers, 1997. 650 p. $72.95. ISBN 0815320450 (book and CD-ROM).   An introductory text by the same highly regarded authors as *Molecular Biology of the Cell*.

Alberts, Bruce et al. *Molecular Biology of the Cell*. 3rd ed. New York: Garland, 1994. 1,294 p. $80.95. ISBN 0815316194.   This landmark textbook has all-star team of authors.

Brown, T. A. *Genomes*. New York: Wiley-Liss, 1999. 472 p. $69.95 (paper). ISBN 0471316180 (paper).   Undergraduate molecular biology textbook that takes a new tack, emphasizing the role of genomes rather than genes. In three parts: how genomes are studied, how genomes function, and how genomes replicate and evolve.

Calladine, C.R. and Horace R. Drew. *Understanding DNA: The Molecule and How It Works*. 2nd ed. San Diego, CA: Academic Press, 1997. 283 p. $59.95, $39.00 (paper).   ISBN 0121550877, 0121550885 (paper).   Designed as a very basic textbook for undergraduates or the general public. While some very complex issues are discussed, they are covered in a conversational style and technical terms are avoided (i.e., the illustrations of the nucleus show that the nuclear membrane has "little holes").

Cell Polarity. David G. Drubin, ed. (Frontiers in Molecular Biology, v. 28) New York: Oxford University Press, 2000. 320 p. $55.00 (paper). ISBN 0199638020 (paper).   Principles of cell polarity development in a wide variety of cell types.

Cooper, Geoffrey. *The Cell: A Molecular Approach.* Sunderland, MA: Sinauer, 2000. 689 p. $85.95. ISBN 0878931066. Also available in CD-ROM ed. Textbook designed for one-semester introductory cell biology courses.

Cross, Patricia C. and K. Lynn Mercer. *Cell and Tissue Ultrastructure; A Functional Perspective.* 2ⁿᵈ ed. See the Handbooks section for full annotation.

Elastic Filaments of the Cell. Henk L. Granzier and Gerald H. Pollack, eds. (Advances in Experimental Medicine and Biology, v. 481). New York: Plenum, 2000. 425 p. $179.50. ISBN 0306464101. For researchers in this rapidly developing area.

Elliott, William H. and Daphne C. Elliott. *Biochemistry and Molecular Biology.* 2ⁿᵈ ed. New York: Oxford University Press, 2000. 437 p. $91.00. ISBN 019857794X, 0198700458 (paper). An introductory text covering molecular biology and biological aspects of biochemistry.

Essentials of Molecular Biology. 3ʳᵈ ed. David Freifelder; George M. Malacinski, ed. Boston, MA: Jones and Bartlett, 1998. 532 p. $65.95 (paper). ISBN 0867208600 (paper). Introductory text for first- and second-year undergraduates.

From Genes to Cells. Stephen R. Bolsover, et al., eds. New York: Wiley-Liss, 1997. 424 p. $59.95 (paper). ISBN 0471597929 (paper). Undergraduate text covering cell biology, genetics, molecular biology, metabolism, and neurobiology.

Goodsell, David S. *The Machinery of Life.* New York: Copernius Books, 1998 reprint ed. 156 p. $19.50 (paper). ISBN 0387982736 (paper). Presents scale-model images of life including macromolecules, substrates, and large assemblies. Excellent drawings explain the mechanisms of life. Written for the nonspecialist but also of use to the biochemist. Divided into three sections: molecules and life, molecules into cells, and cells in health and disease.

Introduction to Computational Molecular Biology. Joao Carlos Setubal, ed. Boston, MA: PWS, 1997. 320 p. $72.95. ISBN 0534952623. Well-received text.

Karp, Gerald. *Cell and Molecular Biology: Concepts and Experiments.* 2ⁿᵈ ed. New York: John Wiley, 1999. 816 p. $97.95. ISBN 0471192791. Well-rounded text containing glossary and index.

Lauffenburger, Douglas A. and Jennifer J. Linderman. *Receptors: Models for Binding, Trafficking, and Signalling.* New York: Oxford University Press, 1996 reprint ed. 365 p. $50.00. ISBN 0195106636. Bridges the gap between chemical engineering and cell biology with a mathematical modeling approach to quantitative experiments for enhanced understanding of cell phenomena. The book includes the entire spectrum of receptor processes.

Li, Wen-Hsiung. *Molecular Evolution*. Sunderland, MA: Sinauer, 1997. 487 p. $64.95. ISBN 08789346634.   A synthesis of the developments in molecular evolution during the last two decades.

Lodish, Harvey, et al. *Molecular Cell Biology*. 4th ed. New York: Freeman, 2000. 1,084 p. $98.00. ISBN 0716731363.   Revised and updated edition of rigorous undergraduate text, with CD-ROM.

Margulis, Lynn. *Symbiosis in Cell Evolution: Microbial Communities in the Archean and Proterozoic Eons*. 2nd ed. New York: Freeman, 1993. 452 p. $66.50. ISBN: 0716770288, 0716770296 (paper).   Margulis's once-controversial theory that modern eukaryotic organisms are the result of the symbiotic combination of multiple prokaryotic organisms is now widely accepted. This is a fascinating exploration of the role of symbiogenesis in the evolution of life on earth.

Mitochondria and Cell Death. G. C. Brown, D. G. Nicholls, and C. E. Cooper, eds. Princeton, NJ: Princeton University Press, 1999. 225 p. (Biochemical Society Symposia, no.66). $75.00. ISBN 0691050260.   Overview of an active research area on the involvement of mitochondria in cell death and disease.

Mount, David W. *Bioinformatics: Sequence and Genome Analysis*. Cold Spring Harbor, NY: Cold Spring Harbor Laboratory Press, 2001. 560 p. $150.00, $95.00 (paper). ISBN 0879695978, 0879696087 (paper).   This guide is a comprehensive introduction to bioinformatics at both the undergraduate and graduate level. There is a related Web site at http://www.bioinformaticsonline.org (accessible to purchasers of the book) that provides links to the Web resources discussed in the book.

Proteomics: From Protein Sequence to Function. S. R. Pennington and Michael J. Dunn. New York: Springer-Verlag, 2001. 313 p. $44.95. ISBN 03879-15893.   Reviews recent developments and standard methods in proteomics.

The RNA World: The Nature of Modern RNA Suggests a Prebiotic RNA. 2nd ed. Raymond F. Gesteland, Thomas R. Cech, and John F. Atkins, eds. Cold Spring Harbor, NY: Cold Spring Harbor Laboratory Press, 1999. 709 p. (Cold Spring Harbor monograph series, 37). $65.00 (paper). ISBN 0879695617 (paper); 0879695269.   According to the publisher, this interesting book "offers a completely current perspective on the modern world of RNA and the light it sheds on a prebiotic era perhaps dominated by this extraordinarily versatile molecule."

Visualizing Biological Information. Clifford A. Pickover, ed. River Edge, NJ: World Scientific, 1995. 186 p. $74.00. ISBN 9810214278.   The emphasis in this book is the development of graphic representation of information-containing sequences such as DNA and amino acid sequences in order to help analyze the data for biologically relevant patterns. Contributors have used some unusual techniques to attempt to present biological data, such as developing musical scores from DNA sequences.

PERIODICALS

In addition to the leading biological journals (*American Journal of Physiology*, *Journal of Biological Chemistry*, *Nature*, *Proceedings of the National Academy of Sciences of the United States of America*, and *Science*, annotated elsewhere in the book) refer to the periodicals listed in the following text and in Chapter 5, "Biochemistry and Biophysics," and Chapter 7, "Genetics, Biotechnology, and Developmental Biology." All of these journals have been chosen because of their recognized importance and impact.

BioScience Reports. v. 1– , 1981– . Dordrecht, Netherlands: Kluwer. Published for the Biochemical Society. Bimonthly. $596.49. ISSN 0144-8463. Available electronically. For the rapid publication of research papers in all areas related to cell surface function, and the molecular and cellular biology of the cell surface. Available electronically.

Cell. v. 1– , 1974– . Cambridge, MA: Cell Press. Biweekly. $755.00. ISSN 0092-8674. Available electronically. *The* leading journal in the field with the highest journal impact factor in the world.

Cell and Tissue Research, v. 1– , 1924– . New York: Springer-Verlag. Monthly. $3,909.55. ISSN 0302-766X. Available electronically. Vertebrate and invertebrate structural biology and functional microanatomy, emphasizing neurocytology, neuroendocrinology, endocrinology, reproductive biology, morphogenesis, immune cells and systems, immunocytology, and molecular cell structure.

Cell Growth and Differentiation. v. 1– , 1990– . Philadelphia, PA: American Association for Cancer Research. Monthly. $385.00. ISSN 1044-9523. Available electronically. This journal is a source for *in vitro* and *in vivo* studies of both normal and abnormal cellular processes. It covers all aspects of cell behavior and cell growth control, and the molecular biology of cancer.

Cell Motility and the Cytoskeleton. v. 6– , 1986– . New York: Wiley-Liss. Monthly. ISSN 0886-1544. Available electronically. Publishes articles concerning all phenomena related to cell motility, including structural, biochemical, biophysical, and theoretical approaches. Also publishes review articles, brief communications, and book reviews. Formerly: *Cell Motility*.

Cellular and Molecular Life Sciences. v. 53– , 1997– . Basel: Birkhauser. Monthly. $1,522.00. ISSN 1420-682X. Available electronically. Publishes "contributions focusing on molecular and cellular aspects of biomedicine, cell biology, immunology, molecular genetics, neuroscience, biochemistry, pharmacology and physiology related to pharmacology." Formerly: *Experientia.*

Cellular Signalling. v. 1– , 1989– . New York: Elsevier. Monthly. $1,295.00. ISSN 0898-6568. Available electronically. Publishes original papers in all aspects of mechanisms, actions, and structural components of cellular signalling systems.

Chromosoma. v. 1– , 1939– . Heidelberg, Germany: Springer-Verlag. Monthly. $1,235.00. ISSN 0009-5931. Available electronically. Covers eukaryotic chromosome structure and function, nuclear organization and function, molecular biology of eukaryotic genomes, and reviews.

Chromosome Research. v. 1– , 1993– . Dordrecht, Netherlands: Kluwer. $969.00. Semiquarterly. ISSN 0967-3849. Available electronically. "*Chromosome Research* provides for the rapid publication of high quality research papers covering a wide field of investigation into the molecular, supramolecular, evolutionary and dynamic aspects of chromosome and nuclear biology."

Cytometry, v. 1- , 1983- . New York: Wiley-Liss. 9 times/yr. $900.00. ISSN 0196-4763. Available electronically. The journal of the International Society for Analytical Cytology. All aspects of analytical cytology, which is defined broadly as characterization and measurement of cells and cellular constituents for biological, diagnostic, and therapeutic purposes. Covers cytochemistry, cytophysics, cell biology, molecular biology, statistics, instrumentation, clinical laboratory practice, and other relevant subjects.

DNA and Cell Biology. v. 9– , 1990– . New York: Mary Ann Liebert. Monthly. $989.00. ISSN 1044-5498. Available electronically. Publishes papers, short communications, reviews, laboratory methods, and editorials on any subject dealing with eukaryotic or prokaryotic gene structure, organization, expression, or evolution. Formerly: *DNA.*

EMBO Journal, v. 1- , 1982- . New York: Oxford University Press. Biweekly. $1,290.00. ISSN 0261-4189. Available electronically. Published for the European Molecular Biology Organization. Rapid publication of full-length papers describing original research of general rather than specialist interest in molecular biology and related areas.

EMBO Reports. v. 1– , 2000– . Oxford, England: Oxford University Press. Monthly. ISSN 1469-221X. Available electronically. This companion to *EMBO Journal* publishes scientific reports, reviews, and commentaries on science and society relating to molecular biology.

European Journal of Cell Biology. v. 19– , 1979– . Jena, Germany: Urban und Fischer Verlag. Monthly. $259.81. ISSN 0171-9335. Available electronically.   Under the auspices of the European Cell Biology Organization, this journal publishes papers on the structure, function, and macromolecular organization of cells and cell components. Aspects of cellular dynamics, differentiation, biochemistry, immunology, and molecular biology in relation to structural data are preferred fields. Formerly: *Cytobiologie.*

Experimental Cell Research. v. 1–   , 1950–   . San Diego, CA: Academic Press. 16/yr. $3,690.00. ISSN 0014-4827. Available electronically.   The chief purpose of this journal is to promote the understanding of cell biology by publishing experimental studies on the general organization and activity of cells. The scope includes all aspects of cell biology.

FASEB Journal. v. 1–   , 1987–   . Bethesda, MD: Federation of the American Society for Experimental Biology. Monthly. $425.00. ISSN 0892-6638. Available electronically.   A research publication that integrates one or more disciplines, preferably those that apply molecular and biological methods, along with functional studies, to the study of biological questions that bear on developmental biology, pathophysiology, or molecular biology. Formerly: *Federation of American Societies for Experimental Biology. Federation Proceedings (United States).*

FEBS Letters. v. 1–   , 1968–   . Amsterdam: Elsevier Science on the behalf of the Federation of European Biochemical Societies. Weekly. $3,778.00. ISSN 0014-5793. Available electronically.   "An international journal for the rapid publication of short reports in biochemistry, biophysics and molecular cell biology."

Genome Research. v. 5–   , 1995–   . Cold Spring Harbor, NY: Cold Spring Harbor Laboratory Press. Monthly. $781.00. ISSN 1088-9051. Available electronically.   The journal focuses on genome studies in all species, and presents research that provides or aids in genome-based analyses of biological processes. Complete data sets are published as online supplements on the journal's Web server. Incorporates *PCR Methods and Application.*

Journal of Cell Biology. v. 1–   , 1955–   . New York: Rockefeller University Press. Biweekly. $780.00. ISSN 0021-9525. Available electronically.   Edited in cooperation with the American Society for Cell Biology. Reports substantial and original findings on the structure and function of cells, organelles, and macromolecules. Includes mini-reviews and commentaries offering a personalized perspective or synthesis of information on a topic of interest to the general readership.

Journal of Cell Science. v. 1–   , 1966–   . Cambridge, England: Company of Biologists Ltd. Biweekly. $2,034.00. ISSN 0021-9533. Available electronically.   Critical work over the full range of cell biology. Scientific excellence is the single most important criterion for acceptance. Formerly: *Quarterly Journal of Microscopical Science.*

Journal of Cellular Biochemistry, v. 18– , 1982– . New York: Wiley-Liss. 18/yr. $4,155.00. ISSN 0730-2312. Available electronically. Description of original research in which complex cellular, pathologic, clinical, or animal model systems are studied by molecular biological, biochemical, quantitative ultrastructural or immunological approaches. Formerly: *Journal of Supramolecular Structure and Cellular Biochemistry* and *Journal of Supramolecular Structure.*

Journal of Membrane Biology. v. 1– , 1969– . New York: Springer-Verlag. 18/yr. $ 1,839.00. ISSN 0022-2631. Available electronically. An international journal for studies on the structure, function, and genesis of biomembranes.

Journal of Molecular Biology, v. 1– , 1959– . San Diego, CA: Academic Press. Weekly. $4,699.37. ISSN 0022-2836. Available electronically. Studies of living organisms or their components at the molecular level. Suitable subject areas: proteins, nucleic acids, genes, viruses and bacteriophages, and cells.

Journal of Structural Biology. v. 1– , 1957– . Orlando, FL: Academic Press. Monthly. $770.00. ISSN 1047-8477. Available electronically. This journal publishes papers dealing with the structural analysis of biological matter at all levels of organization by means of light and electron microscopy, X-ray differentiation, nuclear magnetic resonance, and other imaging techniques yielding structural information. Formerly: *Journal of Ultrastructure and Molecular Structure* and *Journal of Ultrastructure Research.*

Matrix Biology. v. 14– , 1994– . New York: Elsevier. 8 issues per year. $584.00. ISSN 0945-053X. Available electronically. The journal publishes articles utilizing most scientific technologies including molecular biology, cell biology, immunochemistry, structural biology, computational biology, theoretical biology, and macromolecular chemistry where the subject is extracellular matrix or is substantially related to matrix and its biological role. The official journal of the International Society for Matrix Biology. Formerly: *Matrix.*

Molecular Biology of the Cell. v. 1– , 1990– . Bethesda, MD: American Society for Cell Biology. Monthly. $525.00. ISSN 1059-1524. Available electronically. Papers describe and interpret results of original research concerning molecular aspects of cell structure and function. The journal encourages papers with scope bridging several areas of biology, for example, cell biology and genetics.

Molecular Biology Reports: An International Journal on Molecular and Cellular Biology. v. 1– , 1973– . Dordrecht, Netherlands: Kluwer. Quarterly. $365.00. ISSN 0301-4851. Available electronically. Publishes original research and mini-reviews in areas such as DNA replication and transcription, RNA processing, intracellular transport, and related subjects.

Molecular Cell. v. 1– , 1997– . Cambridge, MA: Cell Press. Monthly. $544.00. ISSN 1097-4164. Available electronically. This companion to *Cell* defines the field of molecular biology from structure to human diseases, concentrating on molecular analyses.

Molecular and Cellular Biology, v. 1– , 1981– . Washington, DC: American Society for Microbiology. Biweekly. $644.00. ISSN 0270-7306. Available electronically. Devoted to the advancement and dissemination of fundamental knowledge concerning the molecular biology of eukaryotic cells of both microbial and higher organisms.

Molecular Membrane Biology. v. 11– , 1994– . Washington, DC: Taylor & Francis. Quarterly. $389.00. ISSN 0968-7688. Publishes articles in all molecular aspects of membrane structure and function. Formerly: *Membrane Biochemistry*.

Nature: Cell Biology. v. 1– , 1999– . New York: Nature America. Monthly. $650.00. ISSN 1465-7392. Available electronically. A sister journal to *Nature* with an interdisciplinary forum for exchange of ideas between all areas of cell biology.

Nature: Structural Biology. v. 1– , 1994– . New York: MacMillan Press. Monthly. $975.00. ISSN 1072-8368. Available electronically. A sister journal to *Nature* for "molecular form and function." This international journal publishes original research on all fields relating to cell function of biological macromolecules as analyzed by the full range of molecular, biological, biophysical, and biochemical techniques.

Nucleic Acids Research. v. 1– , 1974– . Oxford, England: Oxford University Press. Semimonthly. $1,970.00. ISSN 0305-1048. Available electronically. Rapid publication for papers on physical, chemical, biochemical, and biological aspects of nucleic acids and proteins involved in nucleic acid metabolism and/or interactions. The first issue of the year is known as the "Database Issue," because it provides information on nearly 300 molecular, genetic, and bioinformatics resources, most of them available on the Web. The 2001 database issue is available at http://nar.oupjournals.org/content/vol29/issue1/.

Proteins: Structure, Function, and Genetics. v. 1– , 1987– . New York: Wiley-Interscience. Monthly. $1,860.00. ISSN 08873585. Available electronically. Concentrates on advances in all areas of protein research: structure, function, genetics, computation, and design.

Proteome. v. 1– , 2001– . Berlin: Springer-Verlag. Quarterly. $243.00. ISSN 1439-7277. Available electronically. Publishes articles dealing with functional, spatial and temporal aspects of protein function in normal and/or disease states.

Steroids. v. 1– , 1963– . New York: Elsevier. Monthly. $1,003.00. ISSN 0039-128X. Available electronically. Publishes articles dealing with original research on all aspects of steroids, including molecular biology, biosynthesis, endocrinology, and metabolism. The official publication of the International Study Group for Steroid Hormones.

Structure with Folding and Design. v. 7– , 1999– . New York: Elsevier. Monthly. $1,148.00. ISSN 0969-2126. Available electronically. This high-impact journal labels itself "form and function in molecular biology." Formerly: *Structure* from 1993–9.

REVIEWS OF THE LITERATURE

Advances in Enzymology and Related Areas of Molecular Biology, v. 1– , 1941– . New York: Wiley. Irregular. Price varies. ISSN 0065-258X. Review of literature in designated areas. Formerly: *Advances in Enzymology and Related Subjects of Biochemistry.*

Advances in Molecular and Cell Biology. v. 4– , 1992– . Greenwich, CT: JAI Press. Irregular. Price varies. ISSN 0898-8455. Publication reviewing research in molecular and cell biology, each volume has a distinctive title. Formerly: *Advances in Cell Biology*, 3 v., 1987–90.

Advances in Structural Biology, v. 1– , 1992– . Greenwich, CT: JAI Press. Annual. Price varies. ISSN 1064-6000. "A research annual" for cytology and molecular structure.

Annual Review of Cell and Developmental Biology, v. 10– , 1994– . Palo Alto, CA: Annual Reviews, Inc. Annual. $128.00. ISSN 1081-0706. Available electronically. Reflects current state of scientific research in cellular and molecular biology. Besides review articles in this very active and intense area, the volumes also list other reviews of interest to cell biologists from other *Annual Review* publications. Formerly: *Annual Review of Cell Biology.*

BioEssays: Advances in Molecular, Cellular and Developmental Biology. v. 1– , 1984– . Cambridge, England: Wiley. Monthly. $625.00. ISSN 0265-9247. Reviews articles, features, book reviews, forthcoming events.

Cell Immortalization. Alvaro MacIeira-Coelho, ed. New York: Springer-Verlag, 1999. 207 p. $125.00. ISBN 3540656189. This review describes the most outstanding theoretical hypotheses explaining the infinite proliferative potential of a cell population, called cell immortalization.

Cold Spring Harbor Symposia on Quantitative Biology, 1933– . Cold Spring Harbor, NY: Cold Spring Harbor Laboratory Press. Annual. Price varies. ISSN

0091-7451. Distinguished annual proceedings series, each volume reviewing a particular topic in detail. This is an important reference for molecular biologists as well as biochemists. V. 62: *Pattern Formation During Development.*

Current Opinion in Cell Biology, v. 1– , 1989– . Cambridge, England: Elsevier Science. Bimonthly. $944.00. ISSN 0955-0674. Available electronically. Reviews all advances, evaluates key references, and provides a comprehensive listing of papers. Issues of the *Current Opinion* titles contain ''Web Alerts'' that are discussion on various Web pages that are relevant to the papers published in that issue.

Current Opinion in Structural Biology, v. 1– , 1991– . Cambridge, England: Elsevier Science. Bimonthly. $1,056.00. ISSN 0959-440X. Available electronically. Similar in format and content to other *Current Opinion* journals: reviewing advances, and providing a bibliography of current world literature.

International Review of Cytology: A Survey of Cell Biology. v. 1– , 1952– . San Diego, CA: Academic Press. Irregular. Price varies. ISSN 0074-7696. A leading series presenting current advances and comprehensive reviews in cell biology, both plant and animal.

Molecular Basis of Cell Cycle and Growth Control. Gary S. Stein et al., eds. New York: John Wiley, 1999. 389 p. $89.95. ISBN 0471157066. A well-rated book for graduate and medical students reporting on current understanding in cell growth and regulation from conceptual, experimental, and clinical perspectives.

NATO ASI Series H: Cell Biology. 1986– . New York: Springer-Verlag. Series covers current advances in molecular biology, biochemistry, genetics, and microbiology. V. 106: *Lipid and Protein Traffic: Pathways and Molecular Mechanisms.*

Nature Reviews: Molecular Cell Biology. v. 1– , 2000– . London: Nature. Monthly. $904.00. ISSN 1471-0072. Available electronically. This review journal provides reviews and perspectives articles on a range of topics in molecular cell biology such as chromosome biology, programmed cell death, and bioenergetics.

Nucleic Acids and Molecular Biology. v. 1– , 1987– . New York: Springer-Verlag. Irregular. Price varies. ISSN 0933-1891. Review of nucleic acids and their structure, function, and interaction with proteins.

Progress in Cell Cycle Research. v. 1– , 1995– . Dordrecht, Netherlands: Kluwer. Annual. Price varies. ISSN 1087-2957. Book series of reviews covering firmly established facts, rather than conflicting or unconfirmed results, providing broad reviews of an area or a particular topic, gene family, or phase-specific event.

Progress in Nucleic Acid Research and Molecular Biology. v. 1–   , 1963–   . San Diego, CA: Academic Press. Irregular. Price varies. ISSN 0079-6603.   A forum for discussion of new discoveries, approaches, and ideas in molecular biology, including contributions from leaders in their fields.

Seminars in Cell and Developmental Biology. v. 7–   , 1996–   . London: Academic Press. Bimonthly. $418.67. ISSN 1084-9521. Available electronically. Each issue is devoted to a topical, important subject in cell biology, edited by an international authority. Formed by the merger of *Seminars in Cell Biology* and *Seminars in Developmental Biology.*

Trends in Cell Biology. v. 1–   , 1991–   . Cambridge, England: Elsevier Trends Journals. Monthly. $969.00. ISSN 0962-8924.   This highly regarded journal covers all aspects of current research in cell biology.

7

Genetics, Biotechnology, and Developmental Biology

Genetics is "the branch of biology concerned with the study of heredity and variation." Biotechnology is "the development of techniques for the application of biological processes to the production of materials of use in medicine and industry." Development is "the complex process of growth and maturation that occurs in living organisms" (*Oxford Dictionary of Biology*, 4th ed., 2000). The more applied aspects of biotechnology and genetics such as plant or animal breeding and industrial biotechnology are not included.

All of the subjects covered in this chapter overlap with other chapters. For instance, molecular biologists study DNA while geneticists study genes so Chapter 6, "Molecular and Cellular Biology," should also be checked for information sources. Research in development may be done by geneticists, cell biologists, or physiologists, so other related resources are found in Chapter 6 and Chapter 11, "Anatomy and Physiology."

ABSTRACTS AND INDEXES

Agricultural and Environmental Biotechnology. v. 1– , 1993– . Bethesda, MD: Cambridge Scientific Abstracts. Quarterly. $455.00. ISSN 1063-1151. Covers biotechnology in food science, agriculture, and the environment. Plant genome studies are also covered, as well as topics such as bioremediation, transgenic plants and animals, water treatment, etc. Available online as part of Biotechnology and Bioengineering Abstracts and the Biological Sciences Collection on CD-ROM, and on the Web. Print version comes with free Web access to current year and one-year backfile.

ASFA Marine Biotechnology Abstracts. v. 1– , 1989- . Bethesda, MD: Cambridge Scientific Abstracts. Quarterly. $425.00. ISSN 1043-8971. Covers marine biotechnology, including aquaculture, biofouling, chemical products, etc. Formerly: *Marine Biotechnology Abstracts*. Available online as part of Aquatic Sciences and Fisheries, Biotechnology and Bioengineering Abstracts, and the Biological Sciences Collection on CD-ROM and on the Web. Print version comes with free Web access to current year and one-year backfile.

Biotechnology and Bioengineering Abstracts. 1982– . Bethesda, MD: CSA. Monthly. "This database provides bibliographic coverage of ground-breaking research, applications, regulatory developments and new patents across all areas of biotechnology and bioengineering, including medical, pharmaceutical, agricultural, environmental and marine biology." Consists of the print indexes *Agricultural and Environmental Biotechnology Abstracts, ASFA Marine Biotechnology Abstracts, Biotechnology Research Abstracts, Genetics Abstracts, Medical and Pharmaceutical Biotechnology Abstracts*, and *Microbiology Abstracts Section A: Industrial and Applied Microbiology.* Available through CSA's Internet Database Service and on CD-ROM.

Biotechnology Citation Index. 1991– . Philadelphia, PA: Institute for Scientific Information. Bimonthly. A subsection of *Science Citation Index* dealing with biotechnology. Only available on CD-ROM.

Current Advances in Genetics and Molecular Biology. v. 1– , 1984– . New York: Elsevier. Monthly. $2,056.00. ISSN 0741-1642. Current awareness service for genetics and molecular biology. Also available as part of Current Awareness in Biological Sciences (see Chapter 4, "Abstracts and Indexes").

Current Biotechnology. v. 1– , 1983- . Cambridge, England: Royal Society of Chemistry. Monthly. $1,229.00. ISBN 0264-3391. Formerly: *Current Biotechnology Abstracts*. Covers all aspects of biotechnology including news items, patents, general information such as forthcoming events, and article citations. About 200 journals and newsletters are scanned. A list of source items is listed with each issue. Available online as Current Biotechnology Abstracts.

Derwent Biotechnology Abstracts. v. 1– , 1982– . London: Derwent Publications. Bimonthly. ISSN 0262-5318. Scans over 1,300 journals as well as proceedings and patents in all areas of biotechnology. Available online and on CD-ROM.

Excerpta Medica. Section 22: Human Genetics. v. 1– , 1963– . Amsterdam: Excerpta Medica. $2,932.00. Biweekly. ISSN 0014-4266. Continues *Human Genetics Abstracts*. Available online and on CD-ROM as part of the complete EMBASE database (see Chapter 4, "Abstracts and Indexes").

Genetics Abstracts. v. 1– , 1968– . Bethesda, MD: Cambridge Scientific Abstracts. Monthly. $1,295.00. ISSN 0016-674X. Covers all areas of genetics, including biotechnology and basic genetic research. Available online as part of Biotechnology and Bioengineering Abstracts and the Biological Sciences Collection on CD-ROM and on the Web. Print version comes with free Web access to current year and one-year backfile.

Medical and Pharmaceutical Biotechnology. v. 1– , 1993– . Bethesda, MD: Cambridge Scientific Abstracts. Bi-Monthly. $195.00. ISSN 1063-1178. Covers genetically engineered drug delivery systems, including bioreactors, vaccines, cell culture, etc. Formerly: *Biotechnology Research Abstracts.* Available online as part of Biotechnology and Bioengineering Abstracts and the Biological Sciences Collection on CD-ROM and on the Web. Print version comes with free Web access to current year and one-year backfile.

Plant Genetic Resources Abstracts. v. 1– , 1992– . Wallingford, UK: CAB International. Quarterly. $460.00. ISSN 0966-0100. Covers plant genetic resources for plants of economic importance, including scientific, legal, economic, and agricultural aspects. Available on CD-ROM as PlantGeneCD; also available on CD-ROM and online as part of CAB Abstracts.

See also *Biological Abstracts*, *Biological Abstracts/RRM*, *Index Medicus*, *Chemical Abstracts*, and *Current Contents/Life Sciences* described in Chapter 4, "Abstracts and Indexes."

ASSOCIATIONS

American Genetic Association (AGA). P.O. Box 257, Buckeystown, MD 21717-0257. Phone: (301) 695–9292. Fax: (301) 695-9292. E-mail: agajoh@mail. ncifcrf.gov. URL: http://lifesciences.asu.edu/aga/. Founded in 1903. 750 members. Emphasis on applied areas. Publishes *Journal of Heredity*. Formerly: American Breeders Association.

American Society of Human Genetics (ASHG). 9650 Rockville Pike, Bethesda, MD 20814-3998. Phone: (301) 571-1825. Fax: (301) 530-7079. E-mail: society @genetics.faseb.org. URL: http://www.faseb.org/genetics/ashg/ashgmenu.htm. Founded in 1948. 6,361 members in 1999. Physicians, genetic counselors, researchers interested in human genetics. Publishes *American Journal of Human Genetics*. Web site primarily for society information.

British Society for Developmental Biology. MRC Brain Development Programme, Centre for Developmental Neurobiology, King's College London, New Hunt's House (4th Floor), Grey's Hospital Campus, London SE1 9RT. URL: http://www.ana.ed.ac.uk/BSDB. Aims "to represent developmental biology to external organizations in the UK and Europe." Organizes meetings and publishes newsletter.

European Society of Human Genetics. Clinical Genetics Unit, Birmingham Women's Hospital, Birmingham B152TG UK. Phone: 44 121 623 6830. E-mail: eshg@eshg.org. URL: http://www.eshg.org. Founded 1967. "Promotes research in basic and applied human and medical genetics and facilitates contact between all persons who share these aims." Publishes *European Journal of Human Genetics*.

The Genetical Society. Roslin Institute, Roslin, Midlothian EH24 9PS Scotland. E-mail: mail@genetics.org.uk. URL: http://www.genetics.org.uk. Founded in 1919. Approximately 2,000 members. The "world's first society devoted to the study of mechanisms of inheritance." For all active geneticists in the UK interested in research or teaching. Publishes *Heredity* and *Genes and Development*.

Genetics Society of America (GSA). 9650 Rockville Pike, Bethesda, MD 20814–3998. Phone: (301) 571-1825. Fax: (301) 530-7079. E-mail: estrass@genetics. faseb.org. URL: http://www.faseb.org/genetics/gsa/gsamenu.htm. Founded in 1931. 4,100 members. All areas of genetics. Publishes *Genetics*. Awards GSA medal and Thomas Hunt Morgan Medal. Annual conference. Web site primarily for society information.

Genetics Society of Canada, La Société de Génétique du Canada. #1112, 141 Laurier Ave. W., Ottawa, Ontario, K1P 5J3 Canada. URL: http://gsc.rsvs.ulaval. ca. Society for professional geneticists in Canada. Publishes quarterly *Bulletin* and acts with the National Research Council to publish *Genome*. Holds annual meeting.

International Society of Developmental Biologists (ISDB). Hubrecht Laboratory, Netherlands Institute for Developmental Biology, Uppsalalaan 8, NL-3584 CT Utrecht, Netherlands. Phone: 31 30 2510211. Fax: 31 30 2516464. E-mail: postmaster@niob.knaw.nl. URL: http://www.elsevier.com/inca/homepage/sah/ isdb/menu.htm. Founded 1911. 900 members, both individual and corporate. Scientists from 31 countries. Promotes the study of developmental biology by encouraging research and communication in the field. Organizes conferences and workshops. Absorbed the Developmental Biology Section, International Union of Biological Sciences. Publishes *Mechanisms of Development* and *Developmental Biology and Teratology*. Web site hosted by Elsevier, primarily for membership information. Formerly: International Institute of Embryology.

Japanese Society of Developmental Biologists (JSDB). Laboratory of Developmental Programs, Department of Biology, Tokyo Metropolitan University, 1–1, Minamiohsawa, Hachiohji, Tokyo, 192–0397, Japan. Phone 81 426 77 2572. Fax: 81 426 77 2559. E-mail: jsdb@comp.metro-u.ac.jp. URL: http://www. bcasj.or.jp/jsdb/e_index.html. Founded in 1968. 1,300 members. Professional society for developmental biologists, researchers and educators. Publishes *Development, Growth and Differentiation*. Web site primarily for membership information.

Society for Developmental Biology (SDB). 9650 Rockville Pike, Bethesda, MD 20814–3998. Phone: (301) 571-0647. E-mail: sdb@faseb.org. URL: http://www.sdbonline.org. Founded 1939. 2,100 members. Professional society of biologists interested in problems of development and growth of organisms. Publishes *Developmental Biology*. Web site contains membership information and conference information, links to developmental biology sites, and the "Developmental Biology Cinema," which links to several online video sequences of developing organisms. Formerly: Society for the Study of Development and Growth.

ATLASES

The Atlas of Chick Development. Ruth Bellairs and Mark Osmond, eds. San Diego, CA: Academic Press, 1997. 323 p. $116.00. ISBN 0120847906. Textual description of the anatomical development of organ systems, plus about 100 chiefly black-and-white plates depicting chick embryo development sequentially.

Atlas of Xenopus *Development*. G. Bernardini et al., eds. New York: Springer-Verlag, 1999. 93 p. $92.00. ISBN 884700036X. For researchers and students new to the study of the *Xenopus* embryo. Full-color photographs and micrographs as well as scanning electron micrographs.

Conn, David Bruce. *Atlas of Invertebrate Reproduction and Development*, 2nd ed. New York: Wiley-Liss, 2000. 300 p. ISBN 0471237965. Black-and-white micrographs depict the morphological development of all the major phyla of invertebrates, including molluscs, arthropods, chordates, nematodes, and others.

The Early Development of Xenopus Laevis*: An Atlas of the Histology*. Peter Hausen and Metta Riebesell, eds. New York: Springer-Verlag, 1991. $189.00. ISBN 0387537406. With 42 plates of micrographs and drawings as illustration, describes the morphological and histological stages of development of this key model organism.

Jiràsek, Jan.E., J.E. Jiràsek, and Louis G. Keith. *An Atlas of the Human Embryo and Fetus: A Photographic Review of Human Prenatal Development*. New York: Parthenon, 2001. (The Encyclopedia of Visual Medicine Series). 144 p. $99.00. ISBN 185070659X. An atlas and textbook on human development with color photographs, useful for both experienced embryologists and for students.

Kaufman, M.H. *The Atlas of Mouse Development*. San Diego, CA: Academic Press, 1992. 512 p. $172.00. ISBN 0124020356. Includes over 180 plates and numerous photographs, micrographs, and electron micrographs covering the development of the mouse from preimplantation to term. See companion book, *The Anatomical Basis of Mouse Development*, in the Textbooks and Treatises section.

Hartenstein, Volker. *Atlas of* Drosophila *Development*. Cold Spring Harbor, NY: Cold Spring Harbor Laboratory Press, 1993. 57 p. $39.00. Schematic color drawings of all the stages in *Drosophila* development, plus textual description of the events at each stage.

Matthews, Willis W. and Gary C. Schoenwolf. *Atlas of Descriptive Embryology*. 5th ed. Upper Saddle River, NJ: Prentis-Hall, 1997. 266 p. $52.00. ISBN 013593740X. Mainly photomicrographs and line drawings, covers comparative embryology in human, other mammals, frog, chick, insects, and invertebrates.

DATABASES

See also the sequence databases listed in Chapter 6, "Molecular and Cellular Biology," and the Guides to Internet Resources Section in both this chapter and Chapter 6.

Caenorhabditis elegans WWW Server. URL: http://elegans.swmed.edu/. Provides access to all the most important information on the Web for researchers who study this roundworm, a model organism for developmental genetics. This Web site provides access to WormBase, a "repository of mapping, sequencing and phenotypic information, information about labs and announcements of conferences," and the electronic *Worm Breeder's Gazette*.

FlyBase. URL: http://flybase.bio.indiana.edu:82/. "FlyBase is a comprehensive database for information on the genetics and molecular biology of *Drosophila*. It includes data from the *Drosophila* Genome Projects and data curated from the literature. FlyBase is a joint project with the Berkeley and European *Drosophila* Genome Projects." Includes a tremendous amount of information, such as a bibliography of *Drosophila* citations, a directory of researchers, descriptions of chromosomal aberrations, lists of *Drosophila* stocks, genome project data, *Drosophila* images, and much more.

FlyView. URL: http://pbio07.uni-muenster.de/. An image database of *Drosophila* developmental genetics including gene expression patterns in mutants, wild-type, and enhancer-trap lines. Text descriptions of the images allow searching.

GenBank. See Chapter 6, "Molecular and Cellular Biology," for full annotation.

The Mouse Atlas and Gene Expression Database. URL: http://genex.hgu.mrc. ac.uk. Copyright 1994– . The Medical Research Council and the University of Edinburgh, UK. Available on CD-ROM for $48.00 (see Web site). An ongoing project to eventually become a complete source for 3D-image information on morphology, gene expression, and mutant phenotypes in mouse development. It currently provides a controlled anatomical vocabulary for each stage of development and the initial series of digital 3D embryos. The vocabulary is linked to the images so that queries of the database can be performed. This resource will allow developmental geneticists to synthesize information from a wide variety of sources. On the Web for free, but the CD-ROM will probably work faster.

Mouse Genome Informatics. URL: http://www.informatics.jax.org/mgihome/. Copyright 2000, the Jackson Laboratory, Bar Harbor, ME. Maintained by the Jackson Laboratory, a major mouse mutant repository and center for mouse research, this site "provides integrated access to data on the genetics, genomics and biology of the laboratory mouse" including genetic maps, phenotypes, gene expression data, and sequence information. Includes the Mouse Genome Database, the Gene Expression Database and the Mouse Genome Sequence projects.

TBASE (The Transgenic/Targeted Mutation Database). URL: http://tbase.jax. org. Maintained by the Jackson Laboratory, Bar Harbor, ME. Attempts to organize all the information about transgenic animals and targeted mutation lines generated worldwide. One can search by species, technique, DNA construct, phenotype, lab, etc., and also submit information on a new mutant line. Selected data from TBASE is highlighted every few months in *Trends in Genetics* (see the Periodicals section). The "Knockout Model of the Month" features an especially interesting new animal model, and a useful glossary of terms is included.

Xenbase: A Xenopus Web Resource. URL: http://www.xenbase.org. A "database of information pertaining to the cell and developmental biology of the frog, *Xenopus*." Also contains genetic and genomic information, as well as directories, methods, links to databases and electronic journals, announcements of conferences, and more.

The Zebrafish Information Network Database. URL: http://zfin.org/index.html. Eugene, OR: Zebrafish International Resource Center. Provides access to a wealth of information for researchers on this fish, which is a major model organism for developmental studies. Database includes developmental atlases and dictionaries, genetic mutants and maps, nomenclature, publications, resources, conference information, and directories of people in the field. Also contains link to the NIH Zebrafish Genome Initiative.

DICTIONARIES AND ENCYCLOPEDIAS

Babel, W., M. Hagemann, and W. Hohne. *Dictionary of Biotechnology: English-German*. New York: Elsevier, 1989. 113 p. $150.00. ISBN 0444989005. Translates over 7,000 terms in English to German. Includes an appendix listing some biotechnologically important micro-organisms.

Bains, W. *Biotechnology from A to Z*. New York: Oxford University Press, 1998. 2nd ed. 411 p. $27.95. ISBN 0199636931 (paper). An "extended glossary" of over 1,000 terms in biotechnology, defined in 350 short entries. Designed to provide an introduction to the concepts discussed, rather than to simply define them.

BioTech's Life Sciences Dictionary. Bloomington, IN: Indiana University, 1996. URL: http://biotech.icmb.utexas.edu/search/dict-search.html. Contains over 8,300 terms dealing with biochemistry, biotechnology, botany, cell biology, and genetics. The database was formerly hosted at Indiana University, but is now on a University of Texas server. The definitions are generally brief and fairly technical; they would be most useful for undergraduates and up.

The Encyclopedia of Bioprocess Technology: Fermentation, Biocatalysis, and Bioseparation. Michael C. Flickinger and Stephen W. Drew, eds. New York: John Wiley, 1999. 5 v. (Wiley biotechnology encyclopedias). $1,750.00. ISBN 0471138223 (set). Presents the "applications and established theories in biotechnology—focusing on industrial applications of fermentation, biocatalysis and bioseparation."

Encyclopedia of Cell Technology. R. E. Spier, ed. New York: Wiley, 2000. 2 v. (Wiley biotechnology encyclopedias). $750.00 (set). ISBN 0471161233 (set), 047116643X (v. 1), 0471166235 (v. 2). Designed to improve the "facilitation and encouragement of the transference of ideas and practical processes between animal and plant cell techologies." Articles cover both basic cell science and technical large- and small-scale bioreactor procedures.

Encyclopedia of Ethical, Legal, and Policy Issues in Biotechnology. Murray, Thomas H. and Maxwell J. Mehlman, eds. 3 v. New York: John Wiley & Sons, 2000. $695.00. ISBN 0471176125. Focuses on all aspects of ethics, law, and policy dealing with biotechnology.

Encyclopedia of Genetics. Sydney Brenner, et al., eds. San Diego, CA: Academic Press, 2001. 2,800 p. $899.00. ISBN 0122270800. The most comprehensive encyclopedia covering genetics.

Encyclopedia of Genetics. Jeffrey A. Knight, ed. Pasadena, CA: Salem Press, 1999. 2 v. $250.00 (set). ISBN 089356978X (set). Designed for general readers. Contains 172 entries of varying lengths but standard format: summary of topic, subdiscipline, significance of topic, key terms, main body, and references. Appendices include a timeline, biographical dictionary of 75 geneticists, and a 350-term glossary. The entries are appropriate for their intended audience.

Encyclopedia of Reproduction. Ernst Knobil and Jimmy D. Neill, eds. San Diego, CA: Academic Press, 1998. 4 v. $630.00. ISBN: 0122270207. Excellent reference resource. All aspects of reproduction and reproductive technologies, including cloning and transgenics, and a little bit of development are covered in all kinds of animal species. Entries assume background knowledge of biology.

Glossary of Genetic Terms. Bethesda, MD: National Human Genome Research Institute (NHGRI), Division of Intramural Research, 1998– . URL: http://www.nhgri.nih.gov/DIR/VIP/Glossary. A small (150-term) glossary of genetic terms. The terms are selected from those commonly found in news reports on the Human Genome Project and are aimed at the general public. There is a pronunciation guide, brief definition, and related terms for each term. In addition, the glossary includes a lengthy audio explanation of the term, read by well-known scientists. The audio portion requires RealAudio Player software, which can be downloaded from the NHGRI site.

Kahl, Günter. *Dictionary of Gene Technology*. New York: VCH, 1995. 550 p. $150.00. ISBN 3527300058. Covers 4,000 terms. Aimed at students in molecular biology and scientists in other fields, plus journalists and politicians, according to the preface. The definitions are quite technical, so the dictionary is really not useful for the general public. However, the numerous illustrations and definitions of acronyms make it quite valuable for students and researchers.

King, Robert C. and William D. Stansfield. *A Dictionary of Genetics*. 5th ed. New York: Oxford University Press, 1997. 439 p. $39.95 (paper). ISBN 0195094417, 0195094425 (paper). Over 6,600 definitions. Includes nongenetic terms often encountered in genetics literature. Also has appendices on the classification of organisms, major domesticated species, a chronology of genetics with an index of major events and geneticists covered in the chronology, a list of genetics periodicals, and a brief list of genetic databases. This classic dictionary is designed for the use of beginning genetics students and scientists from other disciplines, so the definitions are fairly technical.

Kirk-Othmer Encyclopedia of Chemical Technology. Jacqueline I. Kroschwitz, executive ed. New York: John Wiley and Sons, 1993– . 27 v. $320.00 per v. ISBN (set) 0471527041. Includes articles of interest to biotechnology, including biosensors, genetic engineering, and biotechnology.

Nill, Kimball R. *Glossary of Biotechnology Terms*. 2nd ed. Lancaster, PA: Technomic, 1998. 264 p. $54.95. ISBN 1566765803. This glossary started life as an in-house glossary for a biotech firm, and it shows its parentage. Scientific, pharmaceutical, and agricultural biotechnology terms are found here, plus terms and acronyms relating to governing bodies both in the United States and abroad that deal with patenting and drug approval.

Rédei, G. P. *Genetics Manual: Current Theory, Concepts, Terms*. Singapore: World Scientific, 1998. 1,142 p. $78.00. ISBN 9810227809.   Provides concise technical information on diseases, techniques, and other concepts.

Rieger, R., A. Michaelis, and M. M. Green. *Glossary of Genetics: Classical and Molecular*. 5th ed. New York: Springer-Verlag, 1991. 553 p. $69.95, $39.00 (paper). ISBN 0387520546, 0387520546 (paper).   Some definitions consist of a short essay, though most are brief. Citations to original publications are included for many terms. Includes genetic-engineering terms.

Schmid, Rolf and Saburo Fukui. *Dictionary of Biotechnology in English-Japanese-German*. New York: Springer-Verlag, 1986. 1324 p. $392.00. ISBN 038715566X.   Includes over 6,000 terms in three main sections, one translating English terms into Japanese and German, one translating Japanese terms into English and German, and one translating German terms into English.

Steinberg, Mark L. and Sharon D. Cosloy. *Facts on File Dictionary of Biotechnology and Genetic Engineering*. New York: Facts on File, 2000. 2nd ed. 240 p. $29.95, $17.95 (paper). ISBN 0816042756, 0816042756 (paper).   Comprehensive dictionary intended primarily for undergraduates and laypeople.

Walker, John M. and Michael Cox. *The Language of Biotechnology: A Dictionary of Terms*. Washington, DC: ACS Professional Reference Book, 1995. 255 p. $55.00, $31.95 (paper). ISBN 0841229570, 0841229821 (paper).   Attempts to "define routinely used specialized language in the various areas of biotechnology." As might be expected from a chemical publisher, there are more definitions of chemical laws and apparatus than in the other dictionaries. Includes illustrations.

DIRECTORIES

BioScan: The Worldwide Biotech Industry Reporting Service. v. 1–   , 1986–   . Atlanta, GA: American Health Consultants, Inc. Bimonthly. $1,395.00. ISSN 0887-6207.   Directory of 1,500 international biotechnology companies. Entries include strategic alliances, mergers, product acquisitions, new products, licensing and research and development agreements, principal investors, financial information, and key personnel. Also available on CD-ROM (Windows only) for the same price as print.

Biotechnology Guide USA: Companies, Data and Analysis. Mark D. Dibner, ed. 4th ed. New York: Grove's Dictionaries, 1999. 710 p. $295.00 (paper). ISBN 1561592552 (paper).   Covers 1,500 U.S. companies. Includes basic company information such as revenue, number of patents received, number of employees, etc. Also includes industry analysis.

Coombs, J. and Y. R. Alston. *The Biotechnology Directory: Products, Companies, Research and Organizations.* New York: Grove's Dictionaries, 2000. 950 p. $295.00. ISBN 1561592501. Profiles over 9,000 commercial and noncommercial biotechnology organizations. Includes information sources, international societies, university departments, government institutes, and a buyer's guide to products and services.

Directory of Biotechnology Companies. 1999– . Larchmont, NY: Mary Ann Liebert, Inc. Annual. $588.00. ISBN 0913113816. Lists over 4,000 biotechnology companies in 14 separate directories. Each entry provides information such as address, contacts, number of employees, focus, funding, markets, and products under development. Formerly: *Genetic Engineering News Directory of Biotechnology.* Also available on CD-ROM as GEN Directory of Biotechnology Companies ($778.00).

National Biotech Register. v. 1– , 1992– . Wilmington, MA: Barry. Annual. $79.95. ISSN 1074-9942. Consists of three sections, including about 3,500 brief company profiles, a subject listing of companies by research area, and a listing of trademarks. Freely available on the Web at http://www.biotech-register.com/ (company address and phone numbers only).

Virtual Library—Developmental Biology. URL: http://sdb.bio.purdue.edu/Other/VL_DB.html. Maintained by the Society for Developmental Biology. More directory than "virtual library," this site contains links organized by subject or organism to various developmental biology labs with a description of ongoing research. Also indexes departments, programs, institutes, societies, and organizations in the field of developmental biology.

GENERAL WORKS

Aldridge, Susan. *The Thread of Life: The Story of Genes and Genetic Engineering.* Cambridge, England: Cambridge University Press, 1996. 258 p. $29.95, $12.95 (paper). ISBN 0521465427, 0521625092 (paper). In four parts: the discovery of DNA and genetics, genetic engineering, biotechnology, and some related areas such as the selfish gene theory and genes and the environment. A readable discussion of genetic engineering for the educated layperson.

Coen, Enrico. *The Art of Genes: How Organisms Make Themselves.* Oxford, England: Oxford University Press, 1999. 386 p. $35.00. ISBN: 0198503431. A good nontechnical book uses metaphors from art to describe the development of plants, animals and humans and the role of genes in that process.

Pollack, Robert. *Signs of Life: The Language and Meanings of DNA.* Boston, MA: Houghton Mifflin, 1994. 212 p. $19.95. ISBN 0395644984. An introduction to modern genetics written for nonscientists, based on the extended metaphor of the genome as book, with chapter headings such as "The Molecular Word Processor." Very well written and easily understood, covering both scientific and ethical aspects of genetics.

Rifkin, Jeremy. *The Biotech Century: Harnessing the Gene and Remaking the World*. New York: Tarcher/Putnam, 1998. $24.95, $13.95 (paper). ISBN 087477909X, 0874779537 (paper). Rifkin raises a number of issues and potential dangers inherent in the new biotechnology techniques and world view.

GUIDES TO INTERNET RESOURCES

The Internet is particularly useful for geneticists and developmental biologists, due to the large number of publicly accessible genome and mutant databases that are accessible through the Internet (see Databases section, this chapter and in Chapter 6). In addition, many genome projects are accessible through the Web, including genomes for the dog, *C. elegans*, forest trees, *Arabidopsis*, zebrafish, the mouse, maize, *Mycoplasma capricolum*, *Saccaromyces*, and *E. coli*, just to name a few.

Bill Wasserman's Developmental Biology Page. Chicago, IL: Loyola University. URL: http://www.luc.edu/depts/biology/dev.htm. This excellent site provides links to Web sites for human development and for all the common model organisms used in developmental research: *Drosophila*, *Xenopus*, zebrafish, *C. elegans*, sea urchin, mouse, and *Arabidopsis*. There are also links to journals and several movies of developmental processes.

Biotechnology Information Directory Section—the World Wide Web Virtual Library. URL: http://www.cato.com/biotech. Directory to numerous Web sites containing biotechnology information indexed by subject categories. Includes links to companies, products and services, databases, and software.

Bishop, M. J. *Genetics Databases*. Academic Press, 1999. 320 p. $49.95. ISBN 0121016250. A guide for genetics researchers to all the Web sites and databases available for finding and analyzing DNA, RNA, protein sequences, and other genetic data.

The DNA Learning Center at Cold Spring Harbor Laboratory. URL: http://vector.cshl.org/. This Web site provides a wide variety of information on genetics, molecular genetics, and genome projects. It includes the free, highly regarded *DNA from the Beginning* program, "an animated primer on the basics of DNA, genes, and heredity." Also includes numerous links to other genetics and genome sites.

The *Drosophila* Virtual Library. URL: http://www.ceolas.org/fly. Links to databases, protocols, *Drosophila* labs, commercial suppliers, and other Web resources of interest to *Drosophila* researchers.

ICRF Handbook of Genome Analysis. See the Handbooks section for full annotation. Includes an extensive list of databases and genome resource centers plus basic information on using Internet resources, from e-mail to the Web. There is even a "UNIX System Survivor's Guide."

Links to the Genetics World. URL: http://www.ornl.gov/hgmis/links.html. Part of the Human Genome Project Information site, provides links to sites about the Human Genome Project, other genetics and life sciences sites, protein research information, transgenic animal sites; and to many centers doing genetics research.

National Center for Biotechnology Information (NCBI). URL: http://www.ncbi.nlm.nih.gov/. See annotation in Chapter 6 for more information on this center, which is one of the most important resources for molecular biologists and geneticists.

GUIDES TO THE LITERATURE

Biotechnology Information Resources: North and South America. Barbara A. Rapp, ed. Medford, NJ: Learned Information, 1994. 144 p. $32.50 (paper). ISBN 0938734814 (paper). Lists and annotates information sources by type, such as primary research databases, indexes, journals, patents, Internet resources, and organizations.

Coombs, J. and Y. R. Alston. *The Biotechnology Directory: Products, Companies, Research and Organizations.* See the Directories section for full annotation. Includes sections on biotechnology information sources.

LeVine, Harry III. *Genetic Engineering: A Reference Handbook.* See the Handbooks section for full annotation. Includes directory of organizations and extensive annotated listing of print and nonprint resources for the informed layperson.

HANDBOOKS

Ashburner, Michael. Drosophila: *A Laboratory Handbook.* Cold Spring Harbor, NY: Cold Spring Harbor Press, 1989. 1331 p. ISBN 0879693215. A summary of *Drosophila* biology, including chromosomes, taxonomy, and developmental and molecular biology. Designed for rapid reference. This book is now out of print, but see Ashburner's new *Drosophila Protocols* in the Methods section.

Atkinson, Bernard and Ferda Mavituna. *Biochemical Engineering and Biotech-*

nology Handbook. New York: Stockton, 1991. 1271 p. ISBN 1561590126. Includes information on a wide variety of biotechnological topics, including properties of important microorganisms, microbial metabolism, product information, reactors, downstream processing, and so on.

Biomass Handbook. Osamu Kitani and Carl W. Hall, eds. New York: Gordon and Breach, 1989. 963 p. $676.00. ISBN 2881242693. Covers all forms of biomass, plant and animal, and includes information on biomass production, conversion, and utilization. Also includes information on biotechnology for biomass production and utilization and statistics and properties of biomass.

Biotechnology Handbooks. Tony Atkinson and Roger F. Sherwood, series eds. New York: Plenum, 1987– . Price varies. ISSN 1052-6153. This series covers various microorganisms of interest to biotechnology. Ten volumes have been published to date, including topics such as *Penicillum and Acremonium, Clostridia, Photosynthetic Prokaryotes*, and others. Each volume includes taxonomic information and more specific chapters written by experts on various basic and applied areas such as genetics, bioconversions, and solvent production.

Brown, T. A., ed. *Molecular Biology Labfax.* 2nd ed. See Chapter 6, "Molecular and Cellular Biology", for full annotation. Both volumes of this two volume set include information of interest to molecular geneticists.

Crawley, Jacqueline N. *What's Wrong with my Mouse? Behavioral Phenotyping of Transgenic and Knockout Mice.* New York: Wiley-Liss, 2000. 368 p. $79.95. ISBN: 0471316393. A handbook for molecular geneticists to learn how to study behavioral neuroscience problems exhibited in their gene-knockout mice. Also useful for behavioral neuroscientists new to the mouse as a model organism.

Handbook of Statistical Genetics. D. J. Balding, M. Bishop, and C. Cannings, eds. New York: John Wiley, 2000. (Wiley series in probability and statistics). 1000 p. $235.00. ISBN 0471860948. Intended for both statisticians and geneticists, this handbook includes numerous samples and further references.

ICRF Handbook of Genome Analysis. Nigel K. Spurr, Bryan D. Young, and Stephen P. Bryant, eds. Malden, MA: Blackwell Science, 1998. 2 v. $295.00. ISBN 0632037288. Contains 123 protocols in several areas of human genome analysis, including genetic mapping, physical mapping, and DNA sequencing. Volume 2 covers other model systems such as mice, *Drosophila, C. elegans*, yeast, and plants. There is also an extended section on Internet resources.

King, Robert C. *Handbook of Genetics.* New York: Plenum, 1974– . 5 v. (v. 1 *Bacteria, Bacteriophages, and Fungi*; v. 2 *Plants, Plant Viruses and Protists*; v. 3 *Invertebrates of Genetic Interest*; v. 4 *Vertebrates of Genetic Interest*;

and v. 5 *Molecular Genetics*).   While some of the information in these volumes has become dated, there is still no single source to replace them.

LeVine, Harry III. *Genetic Engineering: A Reference Handbook*. Santa Barbara, CA: ABC-CLIO, 1999. 264 p. (Contemporary World Issues). $45.00. ISBN 0874369622.   "The purpose of this book is to provide sufficient background on the issues involved with the application of genetic engineering to allow concerned citizens to participate in the decisions that must be made. . . ." Includes chronology; overview of the issues in several areas; biographical sketches of 20 public figures and scientists; a section on "Facts, Data and Opinion," selected references to books, audiovisual materials, and databases; and a glossary.

Lindsley, Dan L. and Georgianna G. Zimm. *The Genome of* Drosophila melanogaster. San Diego, CA: Academic Press, 1992. 1,133 p. $121.00. ISBN 0124509908.   A compendium of information about the genetics and chromosomes of the fruit fly. An update of Lindsley and Grell's *Genetic Variations of* Drosophila melanogaster, published in 1968. Also includes chromosome maps, which are available separately ($19.95, ISBN 0124509916). A standard, also known as the "Red Book." Updated information can be found in the FlyBase database, see the Databases section.

Liu, Ben Hui. *Statistical Genomics: Linkage, Mapping, and QTL Analysis*. Boca Raton, FL: CRC, 1997. 611 p. $79.95. ISBN 0849331668.   Covers basic biology and statistics for genome studies, then covers statistical methods and computer tools for all areas of genomics, such as Quantitative Trait Loci mapping, screening genetic markers, and many others. Designed for use either as a handbook or textbook.

McKusick, V.A. *Mendelian Inheritance in Man: Catalogs of Human Genes and Genetic Disorders*. 12th ed. Baltimore, MD: Johns Hopkins University Press, 1998. 3 v. $195.00. ISBN 0801857422.   This handbook catalogs hereditary diseases in humans; it is useful for genetic counseling. All known genetic disorders are described, along with their loci, if known, and references to the literature. The catalog is also freely available through the Web as OMIM (Online Mendelian Inheritance in Man) at NCBI (URL: http://www.ncbi.nlm.nih.gov/omim/).

O'Brien, Stephen J., ed. *Genetic Maps: Locus Maps of Complex Genomes*. 6th ed. Cold Spring Harbor, NY: Cold Spring Harbor Press, 1993. $195.00. ISBN 0879694149.   Provides information on the genetic organization of different species; the only comprehensive source for genetic maps. The comprehensive reference volume is still in print, but the six individual paperback volumes (viruses, bacteria, lower eukaryotes, nonhuman vertebrates, humans, and plants) are not.

Sukatsch, Dieter A. and Alexander Dziengel. *Biotechnology: A Handbook of Practical Formulae*. New York: Wiley, 1987. 160 p. ISBN 0470207299 (paper). A "summary of current nomenclature, definitions and associated equations currently in use in the field of biotechnology." The handbook has separate chapters on microbiology, biochemistry, physical chemistry, biochemical engineering, and an appendix providing physical constants, symbols, coefficients, and other useful data.

Westerfield, Monte. *The Zebrafish Book: A Guide for the Laboratory Use of Zebrafish* Danio (Brachydanio) rerio. 4ᵗʰ ed. Eugene, OR: University of Oregon Press, 2000. $17.00. No ISBN.   Contains information about all areas of zebrafish laboratory breeding, cell culture, molecular, genetic, and histological methods. The full text of the third edition is available at http://zfin.org/zf_info/zbook/zfbk.html.

HISTORIES

Bowler, Peter J. *The Mendelian Revolution: The Emergence of Hereditarian Concepts in Modern Science and Society*. Baltimore, MD: Johns Hopkins University Press, 1989. 207 p. ISBN 0801838886.   An account of the major changes in thinking about heredity and reproduction made in the last two centuries, with emphasis on the emergence of genetics in the early twentieth century.

Evolutionary Genetics: From Molecules to Morphology. Rama S. Singh and Costas B. Krimbas, eds. Cambridge, England: Cambridge University Press, 2000. 702 p. $95.00. ISBN 0521571235.   This collection in tribute to population geneticist Richard C. Lewontin covers the history and current research of population genetics.

The Founders of Evolutionary Genetics: A Centenary Reappraisal. Sahotra Sarkar, ed.. Boston, MA: Kluwer Academic, 1992. 300 p. $141.50, $55.50 (paper). ISBN 0792317777, 0792333926 (paper).   Discusses the role of four geneticists, R.A. Fischer, J.B.S. Haldane, H.J. Muller, and S. Wright in founding what the editor calls "evolutionary genetics." Several chapters were written by students or coworkers of the subjects.

Gehring, Walter J. and Frank Ruddle. *Master Control Genes in Development and Evolution: The Homeobox Story (Terry Lectures)*. New Haven, CT: Yale University Press, 1998. 296 p. $45.00. ISBN 0300074093.   An eminent developmental biologist describes the work done in his laboratory since the late 1970s on homeobox genes, a key family of genes involved in developmental patterning and found in all higher organisms from *Drosophila* to humans.

Harwood, Jonathan. *Styles of Scientific Thought: The German Genetics Community 1900–1933*. Chicago, IL: University of Chicago Press, 1993. 423 p. $65.00. ISBN 0226318818.   Discusses the German geneticists of the early part of the twentieth century, who were more interested in development and evolution than in the gene concept studied by American geneticists.

Jacob, Francois. *The Logic of Life: A History of Genetics*. New York: Viking Penguin, 1989. ISBN 0140552421. A history of genetics written by one of the great geneticists of the 1950s.

Kay, Lily E. *Who Wrote the Book of Life?: A History of the Genetic Code*. Stanford, CA: Stanford University Press, 2000. 441 p. (Writing science). $60.00, $24.95 (paper). ISBN 0804733848, 0804734178 (paper). A poststructuralist analysis of the history of molecular genetics, focusing on the ways in which the metaphors used to think about genetics have shaped research and the public understanding of how DNA works.

Keller, Evelyn Fox. *The Century of the Gene*. Cambridge, MA: Harvard University Press, 2000. 186 p. $22.95. ISBN 0674003721. "The aim of this book is to celebrate the surprising effects that the successes of this project [the Human Genome Project] have had on biological thought." The author reviews four major threads in our understanding of molecular genetics: the role of the gene in providing both genetic stability and variation, the meaning of gene function, the contrasts between a genetic program and a developmental program, and the importance of resiliency in the development of organisms.

Kohler, Robert E. *Lords of the Fly*: Drosophila *Genetics and the Experimental Life*. Chicago, IL: University of Chicago Press, 1994. 321 p. $45.00, $17.95 (paper). ISBN 0226450627, 0226450635 (paper). "This book is about the material culture and way of life of experimental scientists. It is also about a particular and familiar community of experimental biology, the *Drosophila* geneticists, and their no less familiar co-worker, the fruit fly."

Medvedev, Zhores A. *The Rise and Fall of T.D. Lysenko*. New York: Columbia University Press, 1969. 284 p. Presents a first-hand account of this "bizarre chapter" in the history of Soviet genetics from 1937 to 1964.

Milestones in Biotechnology: Classic Papers on Genetic Engineering. Julian Davies and William S. Reznikoff, eds. Boston, MA: Butterworth-Heinemann, 1992. 570 p. ISBN 0750692510. Provides the full text of major papers in the history of genetic engineering and biotechnology.

Perspectives on Genetics: Anecdotal, Historical, and Critical Commentaries, 1987–1998. James F. Crow and William F. Dove, eds. Madison, WI: University of Wisconsin Press, 2000. 723 p. $19.95. ISBN 029916604X (paper). Reprint of the first 12 years of the Perspectives columns from the journal *Genetics*. Includes obituaries, commentaries, histories, mini-reviews, and brief memoirs on a variety of topics in genetics.

Sturtevant, A.H. *A History of Genetics*. Cold Spring Harbor, NY: Cold Spring Harbor Laboratory Press, 2001 (reprint of 1965 edition). 174 p. $19.00. ISBN

0879696079. A classic work on the early history of genetics. This new reprint edition has a Web site at http://www.esp.org/books/sturt/history.

Tiley, N.A. *Discovering DNA: Meditations on Genetics and a History of the Science*. New York: Van Nostrand Reinhold, 1983. 288 p. ISBN 044226204. A philosophical discussion of the history of genetics, from ancient times to genetic engineering, including ethical aspects. Has appendices containing the full text of the original Watson-Crick articles and other important works.

Wallace, Bruce. *The Search for the Gene*. Ithaca, NY: Cornell University Press, 1992. 224 p. $39.95, $16.95 (paper). ISBN 0801426804, 0801499674 (paper). A discussion of "how we have gotten where we are" in our understanding of genetics. It is written for the general public, with good explanations of even the more esoteric theories and results. There are also amusing tidbits of information about the personalities of the scientists involved.

Wallace, Bruce and Joseph O. Falkingham III. *The Study of Gene Action*. Ithaca, NY: Cornell University Press, 1997. 260 p. $45.00, $16.95 (paper). ISBN 0801432650, 0801483409 (paper). A companion volume to *The Search for the Gene*. The authors cover the progress in understanding the action of genes (molecular genetics) since Mendel's work was rediscovered, discussing the importance of major studies and the changes in technology that made them possible.

Watson, James D. *Double Helix*. See Chapter 6, "Molecular and Cellular Biology" for full annotation.

METHODS AND TECHNIQUES

Animal Cell Biotechnology. v. 1–   , 1985–   . Orlando, FL: Academic Press. Intended to provide both state-of-the-art reviews of animal cell biotechnology for experts and methods for culturing animal cells.

Chromosome Structural Analysis: A Practical Approach. Wendy Bickmore, ed. Oxford, England: Oxford University Press, 1999. 234 p. (A Practical Approach Series, 200). $115.00, $55.00 (paper). ISBN 0199636990, 0199636982 (paper). Guide to laboratory methods for studying and manipulating chromosomes, especially fluorescence *in situ* hybridization and immunofluorescence.

Current Protocols in Human Genetics. Nicholas C. Dracopoli et al., eds. New York: John Wiley & Sons, 1994–   . 3 v. Quarterly. $575.00 (looseleaf), $595.00 (CD-ROM). ISBN 0471034207, 0471057223 (CD-ROM). Part of the Current Protocols series. Covers topics ranging from collecting family histories and pedigrees, to molecular genetics, physical mapping, and cytogenetics. Available in looseleaf, CDROM, and intranet versions.

Developmental Biology Protocols. Rocky S. Tuan and Cecilia W. Lo, eds. 3 v. Totowa, NJ: Humana Press, 2000. 571 p. (Methods in Molecular Biology, v. 135–7). $350.00 (set). ISBN 0896038556 (set), 0896035786 (set, paper). All of the latest protocols used in developmental biology research from cell lineage analysis, chimera production, laser ablation, and microscopy techniques to genetic, transgenic, and molecular biological techniques.

Drosophila *Protocols.* William Sullivan, Michael Ashburner, and R. Scott Hawley, eds. Cold Spring Harbor, NY: Cold Spring Harbor Press, 2000. $115.00. 728 p. ISBN 0879695862. "Describes thirty-seven procedures most likely to be used in the next decade for molecular, biochemical, and cellular studies on *Drosophila....*" This is an update and "evolution" of Ashburner's Drosophila: *A Laboratory Manual.* See the Handbooks section.

Freshney, R. Ian. *Culture of Animal Cells.* 3rd ed. New York: Wiley-Liss, 1993. 496 p. $69.95. ISBN 0471589667. For both novices and experienced researchers. Classic work covering all aspects of cell culture, from setting up a laboratory to advanced techniques.

Gene Targeting: A Practical Approach. Alexandra L. Joyner, ed. 2nd ed. New York: Oxford University Press, 2000. (The Practical Approach Series, 212). 293 p. $110.00. $55.00 (paper). ISBN 0199637938 019963792X (paper). An introduction and reference for creating mutations in the mouse genome through homologous recombination and gene targeting in embryonic stem cells, updated and revised with the latest techniques.

Genome Analysis. Kay E. Davies and Shirley M. Tilghman, series ed. v. 1– , 1990– . Cold Spring Harbor, NY: Cold Spring Harbor Laboratory Press. Price varies. ISSN 1050-8430. "*Genome Analysis* is a series of short, single-theme books that review the data, methods, and ideas emerging from the study of genetic information in humans and other species." Volumes to date include *Genetic and Physical Mapping, Gene Expression and its Control, Genes and Phenotypes, Strategies for Physical Mapping,* and *Regional Physical Mapping.*

Genome Analysis: A Laboratory Manual. Cold Spring Harbor, NY: Cold Spring Harbor Press, 1997–9. 4 v. $230 per volume, $140 per volume (comb). ISBN 0879694955 (v. 1), 0876964963 (v. 1, comb), 0879695102 (v. 2), 0879695110 (v. 2, comb), 0879695129 (v. 3), 0879695137 (v. 3, comb), 0879695145 (v. 4), 0879695153 (v. 4, comb). A standard manual. The four volumes are *Analyzing DNA, Detecting Genes, Cloning Systems,* and *Mapping Genomes.* The protocols were written by experts at Cold Spring Harbor Laboratory and assume only a basic knowledge of molecular biology.

Greenspan, Ralph J. *Fly Pushing: The Theory and Practice of* Drosophila *Genetics.* Cold Spring Harbor, NY: Cold Spring Harbor, 1997. 155 p. $30.00. ISBN

0879694920. Designed as "a bridge to that folklore [i.e., tools for studying *Drosophila*] for the uninitiated." Covers the basic information needed to work with this common organism, written in an informal manner (as in the discussion of "coddling" sickly stocks). Each section includes problems to test the novice's understanding of the material. A companion to Ashburner's Drosophila: *A Laboratory Handbook* (see the Handbooks section).

Hogan, Brigid, et al. *Manipulating the Mouse Embryo: A Laboratory Manual.* 2nd ed. Cold Spring Harbor, NY: Cold Spring Harbor Press, 1994. 497 p. $105.00 (spiral). ISBN 0879693843 (spiral).   An update of a classical lab manual dealing with recombinant DNA and its use in studying mammalian embryonic development. A "bible" for those who want to produce transgenic, gene-knockout, or chimeric mice.

In Situ Hybridization: A Practical Approach. 2nd ed. D.G. Wilkinson, ed. New York: Oxford University Press, 1999. 224 p. (Practical Approach Series, 196). $55.00 (paper). ISBN 0199636583.   Update of a guide to *in situ* hybridization in chromosomes or in tissues for genetic or developmental studies.

Jowett, Trevor. *Tissue In Situ Hybridization: Methods in Animal Development* (An EMBO Practical Course). New York: Wiley, 1997. 128 p. $65.00. ISBN 0471164038.   New and established techniques for *in situ* hybridization in whole mount embryos or in tissue sections. From the European Molecular Biology Organization Practical Course for Scientists.

Manual of Industrial Microbiology and Biotechnology. Arnold L. Demain and Julian E. Davies, eds. Washington, DC: American Society for Microbiology, 1999. 830 p. $93.95. ISBN 1555811280.   The purpose of this manual is to "bring together in one place the biological and engineering methodology required to develop a successful industrial process from the isolation of the culture to the isolation of the product." A greatly expanded update of a classical manual.

Methods in Biotechnology. v. 1– , 1997– . Totowa, NJ: Humana. Price varies.   A new series, companion to *Methods in Molecular Biology*, see following text. Volumes include v. 1, *Immobilization of Enzymes and Cells* and v. 8, *Animal Cell Biotechnology: Methods and Protocols.*

Methods in Enzymology. v. 1– , 1955– . San Diego, CA: Academic Press.   See Chapter 3, "General Sources" for full annotation. Includes many volumes of methods relating to genetics and biotechnology.

Methods in Molecular Biology. v. 1– , 1984– . Totowa, NJ: Humana. Price varies.   See Chapter 6, "Molecular and Cellular Biology" for full annotation. Several of these volumes refer to molecular genetics, developmental genetics, and biotechnology, such as v. 62, *Recombinant Gene Expression Protocols*; v.

68, *Gene Isolation and Mapping Protocols*; and v. 123, In Situ *Hybridization Protocols*.

Methods in Molecular Genetics. v. 1– , 1993– . San Diego, CA: Academic Press. Price varies. "A new series, *Methods in Molecular Genetics*, provides practical experimental procedures for use in the laboratory." Volumes to date include *Gene and Chromosome Analysis, Parts A, B, and C*; *Molecular Microbiology*; *Molecular Virology*; and *Microbial Gene Techniques*.

Miesfeld, Roger L. *Applied Molecular Genetics*. New York: Wiley-Liss, 1999. 293 p. $49.95. ISBN 0471156760. A book about methods that explains the science behind those methods. Good for students and beginning researchers.

Molecular Embryology: Methods and Protocols. Paul T. Sharpe and Ivor Mason, eds. Humana Press, 1999. 756 p. $145.00. ISBN: 0896033872.

Molecular Genetics of Early Human Development. Tom Strachan, S. Lindsay, and D. I. Wilson, eds. Academic Press, 1997. $111.00. ISBN: 0122204425. Scientists in the field discuss molecular genetic approaches to researching human development and include ethical considerations and clinical relevance.

Mouse Genetics and Transgenics: A Practical Approach. Ian Jackson and Catherine Abbott, eds. Oxford, England: Oxford University Press, 1999. (A Practical Approach Series, 217). $110.00, $55.00 (paper). ISBN 0199637091 0199637083 (paper). State-of-the-art protocols and techniques for studying the genetics and genomics of the laboratory mouse, by experts in the field.

Miller, Jeffrey H. *A Short Course in Bacterial Genetics*. See Chapter 8, "Microbiology and Immunology" for full annotation.

Sive, Hazel L., Robert M. Grainger, and Richard M. Harland. *Early Development of* Xenopus laevis: *A Laboratory Manual*. Cold Spring Harbor, NY: Cold Spring Harbor Laboratory Press, 1999. 338 p. $93.00. ISBN 0879695048. Protocols for researchers interested in the developmental and cell biology of early *Xenopus* embryos. Techniques are described by experts in the field.

Wu, William et al. *Methods in Gene Biotechnology*. Boca Raton, FL: CRC Press, 1997. 406 p. $99.95. ISBN 0849326591 (paper). Designed for the use of molecular biology researchers in general, but especially graduate students in need of help in designing experiments and in selecting research topics. Begins with a chapter on novel research projects for graduate students and researchers seeking ways to increase their chances of obtaining funding. Subsequent chapters describe the major techniques used in genetic biotechnology.

The Zebrafish: Genetics and Genomics. H.W. Detrich III, M Westerfield, and L.I. Zon, eds. San Diego, CA: Academic Press, 1999. 396 p. (Methods in Cell

Biology, v. 60). $64.95. ISBN 0122121724 (spiral). Complete reference for protocols used in genetic studies of the zebrafish, provided by researchers who developed the techniques. Part of a two-volume set with *The Zebrafish: Biology* (Methods in Cell Biology, v. 59, $64.95 ISBN 0122121708 [spiral]).

TEXTBOOKS AND TREATISES

Berg, Paul and Maxine Singer. *Dealing with Genes: The Language of Heredity.* Mill Valley, CA: University Science Books, 1992. 288 p. $38.00. ISBN 0935702695.

Bier, Ethan. *The Coiled Spring: How Life Begins.* Cold Spring Harbor, NY: Cold Spring Harbor Laboratory Press, 2000. 252 p. $59.00, $39.00 (paper). ISBN 0-87969-562-5, 0879695633 (paper). For the undergraduate or general science reader, a textbook of developmental biology that discusses basic developmental principles, classic and recent experiments, and key researchers in the field, along with social and ethical implications of current findings.

Biotechnology: A Multi-Volume Comprehensive Treatise. H.-J. Rehm and G. Reed, eds. 2nd, completely rev. ed. New York: VCH, 1991– . $365.00 per volume. ISBN 1560816023 (set). This massive work covers all areas in biotechnology. Twelve volumes are planned, with volumes covering topics including biochemical and biological fundamentals, products of primary and secondary metabolism, biotransformations, legal and social issues, and many others. Volumes are published out of sequence.

Browder, Leon W., William R. Jefferey, and Carol A. Erickson. *Developmental Biology.* 3rd ed. Philadelphia, PA: Saunders, 1991. $89.75. ISBN 0030135141.

Carlson, Bruce. *Human Embryology and Developmental Biology.* 2nd ed. St. Louis, MO: Mosby, 1999. 494 p. $49.00. ISBN: 0815114583. This textbook incorporates genetics, cell biology, endocrinology, and anatomy into the study of human development.

C. elegans *II.* Donald L. Riddle, ed. Cold Spring Harbor, NY: Cold Spring Harbor Laboratory Press, 1997. 1,222 p. (Cold Spring Harbor monograph series, no. 33). $175.00, $71.00 (paper). ISBN 0879694882, 0879695323 (paper). The latest knowledge about the genetics, anatomy, and development of this important model organism, the nematode worm, *C. elegans.* An important reference for *C. elegans* researchers, but also for others interested in cell or developmental biology. An update of W. B. Wood's classic *The Nematode* Caenorhabditis elegans.

Cruz, Yolanda P. *Laboratory Exercises in Developmental Biology.* San Diego, CA: Academic Press, 1993. 241 p. $34.95. ISBN 0121983900 (spiral). Laboratory exercises suitable for college classes using live organisms such as sea urchins, frogs, chicks, mice, and fruit flies. Questions following each exercise and brief references to the literature are provided.

Drlica, K. *Understanding DNA and Gene Cloning*. 3rd ed. New York: Wiley, 1997. 329 p. $34.95 (paper). ISBN 047113774X (paper).   Textbook for undergraduates and nonscientists.

Falconer, D. S. *Introduction to Quantitative Genetics*. 4th ed. New York: Longman Scientific and Technical, 1996. 438 p. $64.00. ISBN 0582243025. Provides ''the basis for understanding the genetic principles behind quantitative differences in phenotypes and how they apply to animal and plant improvement, and evolution.'' Each chapter includes a set of problems and solutions.

Gilbert, Scott F. *Developmental Biology*. 6th ed. Sunderland, MA: Sinauer, 2000. 749 p. $92.95. ISBN 0878932437.   A highly successful developmental text. The Web site Zygote (URL: http://zygote.swarthmore.edu) contains material supplementary to the book, including updates, experimental details, photos, interviews, and philosophical discussions of new technologies.

Glick, Bernard R. and Jack J. Pasternak. *Molecular Biotechnology: Principles and Applications of Recombinant DNA*. 2nd ed. Washington, DC: ASM Press, 1998. 708 p. $56.95 (paper). ISBN 1555811361 (paper).   Advanced undergraduate and graduate text, covering both scientific principles and applications of biotechnology.

Gonick, Larry and Mark Wheelis. *The Cartoon Guide to Genetics*. Updated ed. New York: Harper Perennial, 1991. 215 p. $12.00. ISBN 0062730991 (paper). Certainly one of the most unusual genetics texts; has understandable and scientifically accurate information in cartoon format.

Griffiths, A.J.F., et al. *An Introduction to Genetic Analysis*. 7th ed. W.H. Freeman, 2000. 900 p. ISBN 071673771X.   The latest edition of the popular undergraduate textbook originally by David Suzuki.

Hartl, Daniel L. *Primer of Population Genetics*. 3rd ed. Sunderland, MA: Sinauer, 2000. 221 p. $23.95 (paper). ISBN 0878933042 (paper).   Designed as a text for students and workers in areas such as wildlife management or anthropology who need a basic understanding of the principles of population genetics. Not intended as a text for use in population genetics courses. See Hartl and Clark in the following text for a population genetics text.

Hartl, Daniel L. and Andrew G. Clark. *Principles of Population Genetics*. 3rd ed. Sunderland, MA: Sinauer, 1997. 542 p. $46.50. ISBN 0878933069.

Hawley, R. Scott and Catherine A. Mori. *The Human Genome: A User's Guide*. San Diego, CA: Academic Press, 1999. 415 p. $39.95 (paper). ISBN 0123334608 (paper).   Text on human genetics for undergraduates or non-scientists. Discusses all the latest topics that have been in the news.

Joset, F., J. Guespin-Michel, and L. Butler. *Prokaryotic Genetics: Genome Organization, Transfer and Plasticity*. Oxford, England, 1993. 464 p. $54.95. ISBN 0632027282.

Kaufman, Matthew H. and Jonathan B. L. Bard. *The Anatomical Basis of Mouse Development*. San Diego, CA: Academic Press, 1999. 304 p. $99.95. ISBN: 0124020607.   A companion text to Kaufman's *Atlas of Mouse Development* (see the Atlases section), this detailed reference book provides discussion of all areas of mouse development from early embryo to organ systems, along with line drawing illustrations.

Lange, Kenneth. *Mathematical and Statistical Methods for Genetic Analysis*. New York: Springer, 1997. 265 p. ISBN 0387949097.   For students who already have a basic understanding of statistics and genetics. Covers general statistical methods then delves into tools for establishing identity coefficients, Mendelian likelihoods, evolutionary trees, and other genetic analyses.

Lewin, Benjamin. *Genes VII*. New York: Oxford University Press, 2000. 990 p. $79.95. ISBN 019879276X. Popular graduate and undergraduate textbook with a major reorganization from previous editions.

Lynch, Michael and Bruce Walsh. *Genetics and Analysis of Quantitative Traits*. Sunderland, MA: Sinauer, 1998. 980 p. $69.95. ISBN 0878934812. A textbook/reference assuming basic knowledge of statistics and genetics. It focuses on basic biology and methods of analysis of quantitative traits. Several appendices cover statistical methods. A companion book entitled *Evolution and Selection of Quantitative Traits* is planned.

Mange, Arthur P. and Elaine Johansen Mange. *Basic Human Genetics*. 2nd ed. Sunderland, MA: Sinauer, 1998. 456 p. $76.95. ISBN 0878934979.   Covers basic genetics as well as human genetics.

Miesfeld, Roger L. *Applied Molecular Genetics*. New York: Wiley-Liss, 1999. 293 p. $49.95 (paper). ISBN 0471156760 (paper).   Designed to help students understand "*how* various molecular genetic techniques are combined to accomplish a research goal." Includes several appendices listing properties of various important molecules; also includes a list of useful Internet resources.

Modern Microbial Genetics. U.N. Streips and R.E. Yasbin, eds. New York: Wiley, 1991. 548 p. $152.50. ISBN 0471568457.   Graduate-level textbook.

Molecular Systematics. 2nd ed. David M. Hillis, Craig Moritz, and Barbara K. Mable, eds. Sunderland, MA: Sinauer, 1996. 655 p. $64.95. ISBN: 0878932828 (paper). Arranged in three parts: sampling, molecular techniques, and analysis. Includes numerous protocols and statistical methods. Designed as both a textbook and resource for researchers.

Moo-Young, Murray. *Comprehensive Biotechnology: The Principles, Applications and Regulations of Biotechnology in Industry, Agriculture and Medicine*. New York: Pergamon Press, 1985. 4 v. $1,940.00 (set). ISBN 008026204X (set). This is ''intended to be the standard reference work in the field.'' It attempts to draw together information from the entire range of fields that make up biotechnology.

Nei, Masatoshi. *Molecular Evolutionary Genetics*. New York: Columbia University Press, 1987. 512 p. $105.50, $38.50 (paper). ISBN 0231063202, 0231063210 (paper). Covers statistical methods for analyzing many types of genetic data.

Nicholl, Desmond S.T. *An Introduction to Genetic Engineering*. New York: Cambridge University Press, 1994. (Studies in biology). 168 p. $20.95 (paper). ISBN 0521430542, 0521436346 (paper). Introductory text, suitable for undergraduates and high-school students.

Old, R.W. *Principles of Gene Manipulation: An Introduction to Genetic Engineering*. 5th ed. Boston, MA: Blackwell Scientific, 1994. 474 p. $54.95. ISBN 0632037121. For advanced undergraduates and graduate students.

Pattern Formation During Development. Cold Spring Harbor, NY: Cold Spring Harbor Laboratory Press, 1997. 570 p. (Cold Spring Harbor Symposia on Quantitative Biology LXII). $105.00 (paper). ISBN 0879695366 (paper). The published proceedings of this 1997 symposium present the latest findings in the developmental studies of patterning, signaling, axis formation, tissue specification, neural induction and more.

Silver, Lee. *Mouse Genetics: Concepts and Applications*. New York: Oxford University Press, 1995. 362 p. $65.00. ISBN 0195075544.

Silvers, Willys Kent. *The Coat Colors of Mice: A Model for Mammalian Gene Action and Interaction*. New York: Springer-Verlag, 1979. 379 p. ISBN 0387903674. Presents all the classical mouse coat-color mutation phenotypes, illustrated with color plates. Many of the genes responsible for these mutations have since been cloned and have turned out to be quite interesting and important.

Snustad, D. Peter and Michael J. Simmons. *Principles of Genetics*. 2nd ed. New York: Wiley, 1999. 876 p. $96.95. ISBN 047129800X. Introductory textbook in genetics for undergraduates.

Spiess, E. B. *Genes in Populations*. 2nd ed. New York: John Wiley and Sons, 1990. 790 p. $95.00. ISBN 0471849731. For advanced undergraduate and graduate courses.

Strachan, T. and Andrew P. Read. *Human Molecular Genetics*. 2nd ed. New York: Wiley-Liss, 1999. 576 p. $94.95, $59.95 (paper). ISBN 0471384151, 0471330612 (paper). Covers basic molecular genetics, gene therapy, genetic manipulation of animals, and issues specific to human genetics such as genetic testing, human disease genes, and cancer genetics. Also includes general overview of Internet resources.

Translational Control of Gene Expression. 2nd ed. Nahum Sonenberg, John W.B. Hershey, and Michael Matthews, eds. Cold Spring Harbor, NY: Cold Spring Harbor Laboratory Press, 2000. 1020 p. $115.00. ISBN 0879695684. For researchers interested in RNA and gene expression. Contributions are by experts in the field of protein systhesis.

Wagner, Robert P., Marjorie P. Maguire, and Raymond L. Stallings. *Chromosomes: A Synthesis*. New York: Wiley-Liss, 1993. 458 p. $104.00 ISBN 047156124X. For upper-level undergraduates and graduate students.

Watson, James D., et al. *Molecular Biology of the Gene*. 5th ed. Menlo Park, CA: Benjamin/Cummings, 2000. $110.00. ISBN 0805316434. Volume 1 covers general principles (history, DNA structure and replication, regulation, etc.); volume 2 covers specialized aspects (gene function in specialized systems, cancer, evolution of the gene). Designed as an undergraduate text and reference.

Weir, Bruce S. *Genetic Data Analysis II: Methods for Discrete Population Genetic Data*. 2nd ed. Sunderland, MA: Sinauer, 1996. 377 p. $42.95 (paper). ISBN 0878939024 (paper). The book's primary role is of ''describing the basic analyses of discrete genetic data, with an emphasis on making inferences about associations between alleles and about population structure.''

Wolpert, L., et al. *Principles of Development*. New York: Current Biology, 1998. 484 p. ISBN 019850263X. Undergraduate textbook written by some of the most important and influential developmental biologists alive today.

PERIODICALS

American Journal of Human Genetics (AJHG). v. 1– , 1948– . Chicago, IL: University of Chicago Press. Monthly. $525.00. ISSN 0002-9297. Available electronically. ''Since its inception in 1948, AJHG has provided a record of research and review relating to heredity in man and to the application of genetic principles in medicine, psychology, anthropology, and social services, as well as in related areas of molecular and cell biology.'' The journal of the American Society of Human Genetics.

Animal Biotechnology. v. 1– , 1990– . New York: Marcel Dekker. $525.00. Semiannual. ISSN 1049-5398. Available electronically. ''*Animal Biotechnology* is the first journal to cover the identification and manipulation of genes and their products, stressing applications in domesticated animals. The journal publishes full-length articles, short research communications, as well as appropriate reviews. The journal also provides a forum for regulatory or scientific issues related to cell and molecular biology, immunogenetics, transgenic animals, and microbiology.''

Animal Genetics. v. 1– , 1970– . Osney Mead, UK: Blackwell Scientific. Bimonthly. $472.00. ISSN 0268-9146. Available electronically. ''*Animal Genetics* reports frontline reseach on the immunogenetics, biochemical genetics and molecular genetics of economically important and domestic animals. It reports current research on genetic variation at the level of single genes, their products and functions in economically important and domestic species of animals.'' The official journal of the International Society for Animal Genetics.

Annals of Human Genetics. v. 1– , 1925– . London: Cambridge University Press. Bimonthly. $272.00. ISSN 0003-4800. Available electronically. ''Presents the results of original research directly concerned with human genetics or the application of scientific principles and techniques to any aspect of human inheritance.'' Published for the Galton Laboratory.

Applied Biochemistry and Biotechnology Part A: Enzyme Engineering and Biotechnology. v. 1– , 1976– . Clifton, NJ: Humana Press. Semimonthly. $1,025.00. ISSN 0273-2289. ''A journal devoted to publishing the highest quality innovative papers in the fields of biochemistry and biotechnology. Though the typical focus of the journal is to report applications of novel scientific and technological breakthroughs, quality papers on technological subjects that are still in the proof-of-concept stage will also be considered. In addition, *Applied Biochemistry and Biotechnology* will provide a forum for practical concepts of biotechnology utilization, including controls, statistical data analysis, problem descriptions unique to a particular application, and bioprocess economic analyses.'' Includes reviews, lists of patents, and news items as well.

Applied Microbiology and Biotechnology. v. 1– , 1975– . Berlin: Springer-Verlag. Monthly. $2,933.00. ISSN 0175-7598. Available electronically. Publishes papers in the areas of biochemical and process engineering, applied genetics and molecular biotechnology, applied microbial and cell physiology, and environmental biotechnology. Theoretical papers are excluded.

Behavior Genetics. v. 1– , 1970– . New York: Kluwer Academic/Plenum. Bimonthly. $595.00. ISSN 0001-8244. Available electronically. "Disseminates the most current original research on the inheritance and evolution of behavioral characteristics in man and other species. Contributions from eminent international researchers focus on both the application of various genetic perspectives to the study of behavioral characteristics and the influence of behavioral differences on genetic structure of populations." Published in cooperation with the Behavior Genetics Association.

Biochemical Genetics. v. 1– , 1967– . New York: Kluwer Academic/Plenum. Monthly. $760.00. ISSN 0006-2928. Available electronically. Publishes "original papers on fundamental experimental and theoretical research in the biochemical genetics of all organisms, from viruses to man. Contributions deal with the molecular aspects of genetic variation and evolution, mutation, gene action and regulation, immunogenetics, somatic cell genetics, and nucleic acid function in heredity and development, and with the biochemical aspects of genetic defects."

Biomolecular Engineering. v. 16– , 1999– . Amsterdam: Elsevier. Bimonthly. $412.00. ISSN 1389-0344. Available electronically. "*Biomolecular Engineering* publishes articles in the rapidly evolving research field developing from the fusion of molecular and cellular science with engineering. This includes the development and application of novel molecular tools including regulatory pathways, materials and approaches that are the focus of applied and basic research within industry, academia and medicine." Formerly: *Genetic Analysis, Biomolecular Engineering; Genetic Analysis, Techniques and Applications*; and *Genetic Analysis Techniques.*

Biotechnology and Applied Biochemistry. v. 1– , 1979. London: Portland Press. Bimonthly. $250.00. ISSN 0885-4513. Available electronically. "The focus of the journal is directed towards the publication of original articles and reviews concerning the expression, purification, characterization and application of biological macromolecules in therapeutics and diagnostics." Published for the International Union of Biochemistry and Molecular Biology (IUBMB).

Biotechnology and Bioengineering. v. 1– , 1958– . New York: John Wiley and Sons. Semimonthly. $3,495.00 ISSN 0006-3592. Available electronically. Covers "original articles, reviews, and mini-reviews that deal with all aspects of applied biotechnology."

Biotechnology Letters. v. 1– , 1979– . Dordrecht, Netherlands: Kluwer. Bimonthly. $1762.00. ISSN 0141-5492. Available electronically. A "rapid-publication primary journal dedicated to biotechnology as a whole—that is to topics relating to actual or potential applications of biological reactions affected by microbial, plant or animal cells and biocatalysts derived from them." Incorporates *Biotechnology Techniques*.

Biotechnology Progress. v. 1– , 1985– . Washington, DC: American Chemical Society. Bimonthly. $596.00. ISSN 8756–7938. Available electronically. "Topical areas of interest include application of chemical and engineering principles in fields such as kinetics, transport phenomena, control theory, modeling, and material science to phenomena in areas such as molecular biology, genetics, biochemistry, cellular biology, physiology, applied microbiology, and food science." Also includes short reviews.

Comparative and Functional Genomics. v. 17– , 2000– . Chichester, UK: John Wiley and Sons. Quarterly. $240.00. ISSN 0749-503X. Available electronically. "*Comparative and Functional Genomics* is a journal section, in print and electronic formats, which contains original research articles and long and short reviews that deal with the post-sequencing phases of genome analysis. The journal will provide a broad forum, covering studies of complex and model organisms. Research exploiting model organisms with fully sequenced genomes to understand gene function in more complex organisms will also fall under the remit of this journal." A section of the journal *Yeast*; comes with a subscription to *Yeast*.

Current Genetics. v. 1– , 1980– . Berlin: Springer-Verlag. Monthly. $1,550.00. ISSN 0172-8083. Available electronically. "Devoted to the rapid publication of original articles of immediate importance on genetics of eukaryotes, with emphasis on yeasts, other fungi, protists and cell organelles."

Cytogenetics and Cell Genetics. v. 12– , 1973– . Basel: S. Karger AG. Monthly. $1,034.00. ISSN 0301-0171. Available electronically. "Original research reports in mammalian cytogenetics, molecular genetics including gene cloning and sequencing, gene mapping, cancer genetics, comparative genetics, gene linkage, and related areas." Formerly: *Cytogenetics*.

Development. v. 99– , 1987– . Cambridge, England: Company of Biologists. Semimonthly. $2,250.00. ISSN 0950-1991. Available electronically. Publishes articles dealing with the mechanisms of development in both plants and animals. Formerly: *Journal of Embryology and Experimental Morphology*.

Developmental Biology. v. 1– , 1959– . San Diego, CA: Academic Press. Monthly. $4,100.00. Monthly. ISSN 0012-1606. Available electronically. "Publishes original research on mechanisms of development, differentiation, and growth in animals and plants at the molecular, cellular, and genetic levels."

Developmental Dynamics. v. 193– , 1992– . New York: Wiley. Monthly. $2,595.00. ISSN 1058-8388. Available electronically. "Provides a focus for communication among developmental biologists who study the emergence of form during animal development." Formerly: *American Journal of Anatomy.*

Development Genes and Evolution. v. 206– , 1996- . Berlin: Springer-Verlag. Monthly. $785.00. ISSN 0949-944X. Available electronically. The journal reports on "experimental work at the systemic, cellular, and molecular levels in the field of animal and plant systems." Formerly: *Roux's Archives of Developmental Biology.*

Development Growth and Differentiation. v. 11– , 1969– . Melbourne: Blackwell. Bimonthly. $625.00. ISSN 0012-1592. Available electronically.— "Publishes original papers dealing with all aspects of developmental phenomena in all kinds of organisms, including plants and micro-organisms." The official journal of the Japanese Society of Developmental Biologists. Formerly: *Nihon Hassei Scibutsu Gakkei.*

Differentiation. v. 1– , 1973– . Berlin: Blackwell Wissenschafts-Verlag. Ten issues per year. $986.00. ISSN 0301-4681. Available electronically. "A multi-disciplinary journal dealing with all the problems relating to cell differentiation, development, cellular structure and function, and cancer. Differentiation of eukaryotes at the molecular level and the use of transgenic and targeted mutagenesis approaches to problems of differentiation are of particular interest to the journal." The official journal of the International Society for Differentiation.

Environmental and Molecular Mutagenesis. v. 1– , 1979– . New York: Wiley-Liss. Bimonthly. $260.00. ISSN 0893-6692. Available electronically. "Publishes original research articles on environmental mutagenesis. It will publish manuscripts in the six general areas of mechanisms of mutagenesis; genomics; DNA damage; replication, recombination, and repair; public health; and DNA technology." The journal of the Environmental Mutagen Society.

Enzyme and Microbial Technology: Biotechnology Research and Reviews. v. 1– , 1979– . Amsterdam: Elsevier. Bimonthly. $1,832.00. ISSN 0141-0229. Available electronically. "Covers both basic and applied aspects in the use of enzymes, microbes and cells of mammalian or plant origin." Also includes economic, regulatory, and legal issues.

European Journal of Human Genetics. v. 1– , 1993– . Nature Publishing Group. Eight issues per year. $1,060.00. ISSN 1018-4813. Available electronically. "Contains information on the development of research, education and medical application in the field of human genetics." The official journal of the European Society of Human Genetics.

Gene. v. 1– , 1977– . Amsterdam: Elsevier/North Holland. Biweekly. $6,974.00. ISSN 0378-1119. Available electronically. "The journal publishes papers on all structural, functional, and evolutionary aspects of genes, chromatin, chromosomes and genomes."

Gene Expression. v. 1– , 1991– . Elmsford, NY: Cognizant Communication Corp. $495.00. Bimonthly. ISSN 1052-2166. Publishes papers in "all aspects of the gene including its structure, functions, and regulation in prokaryotes, eukaryotes, and viruses; molecular and cell biological aspects of cell growth and development, chromatin structure and function. These include topics such as DNA replication, DNA repair, gene transcription, transcriptional control, RNA processing, posttranscriptional control, oncogenes, molecular mechanisms of action of hormones, molecular mechanism of cellular differentiation, growth and development, protein synthesis, and posttranslational control."

Genes and Development. v. 1– , 1987– . Cold Spring Harbor, NY: Cold Spring Harbor Laboratory Press. Bimonthly. $795.00. ISSN 0890-9369. Available electronically. Publishes research articles in molecular biology, molecular genetics, and related areas. Published in association with the Genetical Society of Great Britain. Includes online supplements.

Genesis: The Journal of Genetics and Development. v 26– , 2000– . New York, NY: Wiley-Liss. Monthly. $1,395.00 ISSN 1526-954X. Available electronically. "Publishes original research devoted to explorations of gene function and gene regulation during biological development." Formerly: *Developmental Genetics*.

Genetica. v. 1– , 1919– . Dordrecht, Netherlands: Kluwer. Bimonthly. $1329.00. ISSN 0016-6707. Available electronically. "Rapid publication of full-length papers and short communications describing the results of original research in genetics and related scientific disciplines." Occasionally publishes special issues based on a particular theme.

Genetical Research. v. 1– , 1960– . Cambridge, England: Cambridge University Press. Bimonthly. $345.00. ISSN 0016-6723. Available electronically. "Major areas of research covered include population and quantitative genetics (both theoretical and applied), QTL mapping, molecular and developmental genetics of eukaryotes."

Genetics. v. 1– , 1916– . Bethesda, MD: Genetics Society of America. Monthly. $580.00. ISSN 0016-6731. Available electronically. "Accepts contributions that present the results of original research in genetics and related scientific disciplines." The official journal of the Genetics Society of America.

Genetics, Selection, Evolution. v. 1– , 1969– . Paris: Elsevier. Bimonthly.

$417.00. ISSN 0999-193X. Available electronically. "Open to original research papers in fields of animal and evolutionary genetics. Areas of interest include cytogenetics, biochemistry and factorial genetics, genetic analysis of natural or experimental populations, quantitative genetics and animal breeding."

Genome. v. 29– , 1987– . Ottawa, Canada: National Research Council Canada. $403.00. Bimonthly. ISSN 0831-2796. Available electronically. "Publishes reports in the fields of population, evolutionary and developmental genetics, mutagenesis, genetics and cytogenetics of animals, plants and fungi." Formerly: *Canadian Journal of Genetics and Cytology.*

Genome Research. v. 1– , 1995– . Cold Spring Harbor, NY: Cold Spring Harbor Press. Monthly. $788.00. ISSN 1088-9051. Available electronically. "The journal focuses on genome studies in all species, and presents research that provides or aids in genome-based analyses of biological processes." Complete data sets are published as online supplements on the journal's Web server.

Genomics. v. 1– , 1987– . San Diego, CA: Academic. Semimonthly. $1,495.00. ISSN 0888-7543. Available electronically. "The goal of *Genomics* is the promotion of all facets of human/mouse genetic analysis. The scope of the journal is broad, and studies of other species that provide important insights into gene function in mouse/human will be considered. . . . Papers in the areas of functional genomics, linkage and identification of genes involved in disease and complex traits, novel gene discovery, higher order genome organization, chromosome structure, and functional genetic bases for human diversity are suitable."

Hereditas. v. 1– , 1920– . Lund, Sweden: Mendelian Society of Lund. Bimonthly. $255.00. ISSN 0018-0661. "*Hereditas* is a journal for the publication of original research in genetics." Most contributors are European. Published for the Scandinavian Association of Genetics.

Heredity. v. 1– , 1947– . Oxford, England: Blackwell Scientific. Monthly. $553.00. ISSN 0018-067X. Available electronically. "Publishes articles in all areas of genetics, focusing on the genetics of eukaryotes. The traditional strengths of the journal lie in the fields of ecological and population genetics; biometrical and statistical genetics; animal and plant breeding; and cytogenetics." Published for the Genetical Society of Great Britain.

Human Genetics. v. 1– , 1964– . New York: Springer-Verlag. Monthly. $3,469.00. ISSN 0340–6717. Available electronically. "The Journal welcomes articles in the areas of Gene structure and organization, Gene expression, Mutation detection and analysis, Linkage analysis and genetic mapping, Physical mapping, Cytogenetics and Genomic Imaging, Genome structure and organisation, Disease association studies, Molecular diagnostics, Genetic epidemiology, Evolutionary genetics, Developmental genetics, Genotype-phenotype relationships,

Molecular genetics of tumorigenesis, Genetics of complex diseases and epistatic interactions, and Bioinformatics. Articles reporting animal models relevant to human biology or disease are also welcome. Preference will be given to those articles which address clinically relevant questions or which provide new insights into human biology.''

Human Heredity: International Journal of Human and Medical Genetics. v. 19– , 1969– . Basel: S. Karger. Quarterly. $295.00. ISSN 0001-5652. Available electronically. ''Devoted to methodological and applied research on the genetics of human populations, linkage analysis, and the genetic mechanisms of disease. The increasing possibilities for prenatal diagnosis also receive special attention, as do papers on new serological, biochemical and statistical methods.'' Formerly: *Acta Genetica et Statistica Medica.*

Human Molecular Genetics. v. 1– , 1992– . Oxford, England: Oxford University Press. $1,030.00. Monthly. ISSN 1043-0342. Available electronically. ''*Human Molecular Genetics* concentrates on full-length research papers covering a wide range of topics in all aspects of human molecular genetics. . . . In addition, the journal also publishes research on other model systems for the analysis of genes, especially when there is an obvious relevance to human genetics.''

Immunogenetics. v. 1– , 1974– . New York: Springer Verlag. $1,579.00. Monthly. ISSN 0093-7711. Available electronically. ''*Immunogenetics* publishes original full-length articles, brief communications, and reviews on research in the following areas: immunogenetics of cell interaction, immunogenetics of tissue differentiation and development, phylogeny of alloantigens and of immune response, genetic control of immune response and disease susceptibility, and genetics and biochemistry of alloantigens.''

International Biodeterioration and Biodegradation. v. 1– , 1965– . Barking, UK: Elsevier. Monthly. $951.00. ISSN 0964-8305. Available electronically. ''Original research papers and reviews on biological causes of deterioration or degradation.'' The official journal of the Biodeterioration Society and groups affiliated to the International Biodeterioration Association.

Journal of Applied Microbiology. v. 82– , 1997– . Oxford, England: Blackwell Scientific. Monthly. $1,448.00. ISSN 1364-5072. Available electronically. Covers ''all aspects of applied microbiology; including environmental, food, agricultural, medical, pharmaceutical, veterinary, taxonomy, soil, systematics, water and biodeterioration.'' The journal of the Society for Applied Microbiology. Subscription includes *Letters in Applied Microbiology* and Annual Symposium volumes. Formerly: *Journal of Applied Bacteriology.*

Journal of Biotechnology. v. 1– , 1984– . Amsterdam: Elsevier. 21/year. $2584.00. ISSN 0168–1656. Available electronically.   "The Journal will accept papers ranging from genetic or molecular biological positions to those covering biochemical, chemical or bioprocess engineering aspects as well as computer application of new software concepts, provided that in each case the material is directly relevant to biotechnological systems. Papers presenting information of a multidisciplinary nature that would not be suitable for publication in a journal devoted to a single discipline, are particularly welcome." Available only as a combined subscription with *Reviews in Molecular Biotechnology.*

Journal of Chemical Technology and Biotechnology. v. 1– , 1951– . Chichester, UK: John Wiley and Sons. Monthly. $1,275.00 ISSN 0268-2575. Available electronically.   "Covers a broad remit across the fields of chemical technology and biotechnology and focuses especially on those aspects where the two fields interact, particularly involving process technologies, environmental remediation and cleaner technologies." The official journal of the Society of Chemical Industry.

Journal of Heredity. v. 1– , 1910– . New York: Oxford University Press. Bimonthly. $198.00. ISSN 0022-1503. Available electronically.   "Articles discuss gene action, regulation, and transmission in both plant and animal species, including the genetic aspects of botany, cytogenetics and evolution, zoology, and molecular and developmental biology." The official journal of the American Genetic Association.

Journal of Medical Genetics. v. 1– , 1964– . London: BMJ Publishing Group. Monthly. $455.00. ISSN 0022-2593. Available electronically.   "Publishes original research on all areas of medical genetics, along with reviews, annotations, and editorials on important and topical subjects." The audience includes clinical geneticists and researchers in a variety of basic genetical disciplines.

Journal of Neurogenetics. v. 1– , 1983– . New York: Gordon and Breach. Bimonthly. $618.00 ISSN 0167-7063. Available electronically.   "The *Journal of Neurogenetics* publishes papers involving genetic and molecular neurobiology. This covers studies of genes and genetic variants that influence neural development (pattern formation and cell differentiation) and function (physiology, neurochemistry, and behavior). We encourage submission of neurogenetic investigations performed on organisms ranging from microbes (such as bacteria and paramecia) to metazoans."

Letters in Applied Microbiology. v. 1– , 1985– . Oxford, England: Blackwell Scientific Publications. Monthly. Free. ISSN 0266-8254. Available electronically.   "A journal for the rapid publication of short papers (up to six typed pages) of high scientific standard in the broad field of applied microbiology . . . . Advances in rapid methodology will be a particular feature." A free companion publication to the *Journal of Applied Microbiology*; only available with a subscription to that journal.

Mammalian Genome: Official Journal of the International Mammalian Genome Society. v. 1– , 1991– . New York: Springer Verlag. Quarterly. $723.00. ISSN 0938.8990. Available electronically. "*Mammalian Genome* focuses on the experimental, theoretical, and technical aspects of genomics and genetics in mouse, human, and other species, particularly those aspects bearing on studies of gene function. The journal aims to publish high quality original papers that present novel findings in all areas of mammalian genetic research as well as reviews on areas of topical interest." Incorporates *Mouse Genome*.

Marine Biotechnology: An International Journal on the Molecular and Cellular Biology of Marine Life and Its Technology Applications. v. 1– , 1999– . New York: Springer Verlag. Bimonthly. $323.00. ISSN 1436-2228. Available electronically. "Articles describing the molecular biology, genetics, cell biology, and biochemistry of any aquatic prokaryote or eukaryote will be considered. Papers on biotechnological applications should address fundamental questions or demonstrate novel technical developments." Formed by the merger of *Journal of Marine Biotechnology* and *Molecular Marine Biology and Biotechnology*.

Mechanisms of Development. v. 1– , 1972– . Shannon, Ireland: Elsevier. 20/ yr. $2,849.00. ISSN 0925-4773. Available electronically. "Disseminates research in developmental biology, with emphasis on the characterization of molecular mechanisms underlying the development." Publication of the International Society of Developmental Biologists.

Molecular Biotechnology: The Journal of Molecular Biology Research, Protocols, Reviews, and Applications. v. 1– , 1994– . Totowa, NJ: Humana Press. Bimonthly. $420.00. ISSN 1073-6085. "This practical periodical is devoted to the rapid issuance of essential step-by-step laboratory protocols for molecular biology techniques (both protein and nucleic acid based), and publishes review articles and original papers on the application of these techniques in both basic and applied biotechnology. The protocols follow the highly successful format used in Humana's Methods in Molecular Biology series."

Molecular and General Genetics (MGG). v. 1– , 1908– . Berlin: Springer-Verlag. Monthly. $3,378.00. ISSN 0026-8925. Available electronically. "Provides publication in all areas of general and molecular genetics—developmental genetics, somatic cell genetics, and genetic engineering—irrespective of the organism." "The first journal on genetics." Continues *Zeitschrift fur Vererbungslehre*.

Molecular Reproduction and Development. v. 1– , 1988– . New York:

Wiley-Liss. Monthly. $3,525.00. ISSN 1040-452X. Available electronically. Publishes articles dealing with the "molecular biology of reproductive and related developmental processes in humans, multi-cellular animals, and plants." Formerly: *Gamete Research.*

Mutagenesis. v. 1– , 1986– . Oxford, England: Oxford University Press. $510.00. Bimonthly. ISSN 0267-8357. Available electronically. "*Mutagenesis* is an international multi-disciplinary journal designed to bring together research aimed at the identification, characterization and elucidation of the mechanisms of action of physical, chemical and biological agents capable of producing genetic change in living organisms and the study of the consequences of such changes."

Mutation Research. Amsterdam: Elsevier. $8,371.00 ISSN 0921-8262. Available electronically. In five parts, each of which is available separately or as part of the whole. The sections are (1) *DNA Repair.* $1,071.00 Monthly. ISSN 0921-8777; (2) *Fundamental and Molecular Mechanisms of Mutagenesis.* ISSN 0027-5107. Only available as part of a full set. (3) *Genetic Toxicology and Environmental Mutagenesis.* $3315.00. Bimonthly. ISSN 1383-5718.; (4) *Mutation Research Genomics.* $357.00. Quarterly. ISSN 1383-5726; and (5) *Reviews in Mutation Research.* $714.00. Bimonthly. ISSN 1383-5742.

Nature Biotechnology. v. 14– , 1996– . New York: Nature Publishing. $650.00. Monthly. ISSN 1087-0156. Available electronically. "The primary function of *Nature Biotechnology* is to publish novel biological research papers that demonstrate the possibility of significant commercial application in the pharmaceutical, medical, agricultural, and environmental sciences." Also includes commentaries on research, regulatory, and business aspects of biotechnology. Formerly: *Bio/technology.*

Nature Genetics. v. 1– , 1992– . New York: Nature Publishing. Monthly. $650.00. ISSN 1061-4036. Available electronically. Covers "research in genetics, with particular emphasis on genetic mechanism through studies on human traits and model organisms (including mouse, yeast, *C. elegans, Drosophila*, and zebrafish)."

Neurogenetics. v. 1– , 1997– . Berlin: Springer Verlag. $399.00. Quarterly. ISSN 1364-6745. Available electronically. "*Neurogenetics* publishes findings that contribute to a better understanding of the genetic basis of normal and abnormal function of the nervous system. Neurogenetic disorders is the main focus of the journal."

Nucleic Acids Research. v. 1– , 1974– Oxford, England: Oxford University Press. Biweekly. $1,845.00. ISSN 0305-1048. Available electronically. "Publishes the results of leading edge research into physical, chemical, biochemical, and biological aspects of nucleic acids, and proteins involved in nucleic acid metabolism and/or interactions.'' The first issue each year covers genetic, protein, and genome databases and is freely available on the Web at http://nar.oupjournals.org/. A separate section, NAR Methods Online, is available only online but contents are listed in each print issue.

Oncogene: An International Journal. v. 1– , 1987– . Basingstoke, England: Macmillan Publishers. Weekly. $3,314.00. ISSN 0950-9232. Available electronically. ''*Oncogene* covers all aspects of the structure and function of oncogenes, especially: cellular oncogenes and their mechanism of activation; structure and function of their encoded proteins; oncogenes of the DNA and RNA tumour viruses; the molecular oncology of human tumours; tumour suppressor genes; growth regulatory genes; cell cycle control; growth factors and receptors; and apoptosis.'' Subscription includes *Oncogene Reviews*.

Plant Cell, Tissue and Organ Culture: An International Journal on the Cell Biology of Higher Plants. v. 1– , 1981– . Dordrecht, Netherlands: Kluwer Academic. Monthly. $1310.00. ISSN 0167-6857. Available electronically. ''Publishes original results of fundamental studies on the behavior of plant cells, tissues and organs in vitro'' including biotechnology and genetics.

Plasmid. v. 1– , 1977– . New York: Academic Press. $450.00. Bimonthly. ISSN 0147-619X. Available electronically. ''The journal focuses on the biology of extrachromosomal genetic elements in both prokaryotic and eukaryotic systems, including their biological behavior, molecular structure, genetic function, gene products, and use as genetic tools. The journal features original research reports on movable genetic elements in prokaryotes and in eukaryotes, and publishes minireviews on various aspects of extrachromosomal gene systems and molecular microbiology.''

Somatic Cell and Molecular Genetics. v. 10– , 1975– . New York: Kluwer Academic/Plenum. Bimonthly. $700.00. ISSN 0740-7750. Available electronically. Publishes in ''cellular and molecular genetics of higher eukaryotic systems. The primary emphasis is on studies with animal or plant cells in the following areas: gene expression and regulation, gene transfer into cultured cells or embryos, gene isolation, gene mapping, gene therapy, molecular biology of inherited diseases, recombination, mutation, chromosome replication, and the genetics of subcellular organelles.'' Formerly: *Somatic Cell Genetics*.

Stem Cells. v. 11– , 1993– . Dayton, OH: Alphamed. $195.00. Bimonthly. ISSN 1066-5099. Available electronically. ''*Stem Cells* publishes peer-reviewed original investigative papers and concise reviews. We welcome manuscripts reporting significant new information on normal and neoplastic stem and progenitor cell biology and molecular biology, clinical applications of gene manipulation, growth factors and cytokines, peripheral blood stem cell mobilization and transplantation, and tumor cell purging.'' Formerly: *International Journal of Cell Cloning*.

Teratogenesis, Carcinogenesis, and Mutagenesis. v. 1– , 1980– . New York: Wiley-Liss. Bimonthly. $980.00. ISSN 0270-3211. Available electronically. ''Publishes original research on the evaluation and characterization of teratogens, carcinogens, or mutagens.'' Also includes review articles.

Theoretical and Applied Genetics (TAG). v. 38– , 1968– . Berlin: Springer-Verlag. Monthly. $3,927.00. ISSN 0040-5752. Available electronically. ''TAG will publish original articles in the following areas: genetic and physiological fundamentals of plant breeding, applications of plant biotechnology, and theoretical considerations in combination with experimental data.'' Formerly: *Der Züchter*.

Transgenics: Biological Analysis Through DNA Transfer. v. 1– , 1994– . Grey, Switzerland: Harwood Academic. Bimonthly. ISSN 1023-6171. Available electronically. ''*Transgenics* is an international journal dedicated to original reports of biological analysis through DNA transfer in vivo and in vitro. *Transgenics* covers not only information related to animal models of disease, but also the use of gene transfer in tumor research, developmental biology, immunology (including immunologic tolerance), transplantation (including HLA transfectants), reproductive endocrinology, and gene therapy, among other specialties.'' Formerly: *Transgene*.

Transgenic Research. v. 1– , 1991– . Dordrecht: Kluwer. Bimonthly. $583.00. ISSN 0962-8819. Available electronically. ''*Transgenic Research* is a bimonthly international journal dedicated to the rapid publication of research in transgenic higher organisms including their production, properties resulting from the transgenic state, use as experimental tools, exploitation and application, and environmental impact. The journal aims to bridge the gap between fundamental and applied science in molecular biology and biotechnology.''

Virus Genes. v. 1– , 1987– . Dordrecht, Netherlands: Kluwer. $488.00. Bimonthly. ISSN 0920-8569. Available electronically. ''*Virus Genes* is dedicated to the publication of studies on the structure and function of virus genes, providing a forum for the dissemination of data as well as for the analysis of developments in the field.'' Covers all virus genera and families.

NEWSLETTERS

The National Agriculture Library's Biotechnology Information Center has a useful list of newsletters at http://www.nal.usda.gov/bic/Misc_pubs/newsltrs.html.

While the emphasis is on agricultural biotechnology, many general biotech newsletters are listed, along with description, price, and contact information.

Biotechnology News. v. 1– , 1981– . Maplewood, NJ: CTB International Publishers. 30/yr. $564.00. ISSN 0273-3226. Covers the biotechnology industry, including company news, regulations, trends, etc. Also includes articles on economic and social issues.

Genetic Engineering News. v. 1– , 1981– . New York: Mary Ann Liebert. $364.00. Monthly. ISSN 0270-6377. Available electronically. "Provides major coverage of significant issues, regulatory and scale-up guidelines, R&D, financial news (including public offerings, mergers, and venture capital), funding and government news, corporate profiles, university news, meeting reports, foreign reports, new product and literature information, and critical in-depth articles relating to the production of biotechnology products." Has associated Web site at http://www.genwire.com/.

Genetic Technology News. v. 1– , 1981– . New York: Technical Insights/John Wiley & Sons. Weekly. $885.00. ISSN 0272-9032. Available electronically. "*Genetic Technology News* presents the latest R&D developments and advances with an emphasis on opportunities to profit in the explosive field of genetic technology through technology transfer, joint ventures, and acquisitions. The complete gamut of genetic technology applications is covered. . . ."

Human Genome News (HGN). v. 2– , 1990– . Oak Ridge, TN: Oak Ridge National Laboratory. Quarterly. Free. ISSN 1050-6101. Available electronically at http://www.ornl.gov/TechResources/Human_Genome/publicat/hgn/hgn. html. "*Human Genome News* is a newsletter of the U.S. Human Genome Project sponsored by the genome program of the Department of Energy Office of Environmental Research. HGN is intended to facilitate communication among genome researchers and to inform persons interested in genome research." Formerly: *Human Genome Quarterly*.

REVIEWS OF THE LITERATURE

Advances in Applied Microbiology. v. 1– , 1959– . New York: Academic Press. Annual. Price varies. ISSN 0065-2164. See Chapter 8, "Microbiology and Immunology," for full annotation.

Advances in Biochemical Engineering/Biotechnology. v. 26– , 1983– . New York: Springer-Verlag. Irregular. Price varies. ISSN 0724-6145. Each volume has review articles on a particular topic in biotechnology. Recent topics include bioseparation, modern biochemical engineering, and applied molecular genetics. Formerly: *Advances in Biochemical Engineering*.

Advances in Biotechnological Processes. v. 1– , 1983– . New York: Wiley-Liss. Irregular. Price varies. ISSN 0736-2293. Review articles covering areas in biotechnology, such as upstream and downstream processes, monoclonal antibodies, waste treatment, and bacterial vaccines.

Advances in Genetics. v. 1– , 1947– . New York: Academic Press. Annual. Price varies. ISSN 0065-2660. A series of review articles presenting critical summaries of outstanding genetic problems, both theoretical and practical.

Advances in Human Genetics. v. 1– , 1970– . New York: Plenum. Irregular. Price varies. ISSN 0065-275X. A series of critical reviews covering methodologies and results from various disciplines that relate to human genetics.

Annual Review of Genetics. v. 1– , 1967– . Palo Alto, CA: Annual Reviews. Annual. $127.00. ISSN 0066-4197. Available electronically. Qualified authors are invited to contribute "critical articles reviewing significant developments" in genetics.

Annual Review of Genomics and Human Genetics. v. 1– , 2000– . Palo Alto, CA: Annual Reviews. Annual. $140.00. ISSN 1527-8204. Available electronically. Subjects covered include the human genome, genetics and disease, history of genomics, bioinformatics, genetic diseases, gene mapping, and human evolution.

Biotechnology Advances. v. 1– , 1983– . New York: Pergamon. Bimonthly. $1,106.00. ISSN 0734-9750. Available electronically. "The primary purpose is to provide regular, rapid but authoritative reviews of important advances in this field for students, researchers, managers and others in industry, government and academia. A timely series of research review papers, patent abstracts and summaries of special government reports on the principles and practices of biotechnology are covered quarterly."

Biotechnology Annual Review. v. 1– , 1995- . Amsterdam: Elsevier. Annual. $204.00. This series provides reviews in different aspects of biotechnology, including applications in medicine, agriculture and industry, plus more research-oriented reviews.

Biotechnology and Genetic Engineering Reviews. v. 1– , 1984– . Newcastle-upon-Tyne, UK: Intercept. Annual. $160.00. ISSN 0264-8725. Contains original review articles covering industrial, agricultural, and medical biotechnology, especially genetic engineering.

Critical Reviews in Biotechnology. v. 1– , 1983– . Boca Raton, FL: CRC Press. Quarterly. $455.00. ISSN 0738-8551. Available electronically. "Provides a forum of critical evaluation of recent and current publications and, periodically, for state-of-the-art reports from various geographic areas around the world." Covers biotechnological techniques for all areas, including academe and industry.

Critical Reviews in Eukaryotic Gene Expression. v. 1– , 1990- . New York: Begell House. Quarterly. $411.00. ISSN 1045-4403. "Presents timely concepts and experimental approaches that are contributing to rapid advances in our understanding of gene regulation, organization, and structure. Provides detailed critical reviews of the current literature."

Current Opinion in Biotechnology. v. 1– , 1990– . Oxford, England: Elsevier Science. Bimonthly. $1,166.00. ISSN 0958-1669. Available electronically. Each issue covers a particular topic such as analytical biotechnology or protein engineering.

Current Opinion in Genetics and Development. v. 1– , 1989– . Oxford, England: Elsevier Science. Bimonthly. $884.00. ISSN 0958-1669. Available electronically. A companion to *Current Opinion in Biotechnology*, above. Topics covered include genomes and evolution, viral genetics, and pattern formation.

Current Topics in Developmental Biology. v. 1– , 1966– . Orlando, FL: Academic Press. Annual. Price varies. ISSN 0070-2153. This important review series presents reviews and discussions on topics of interest and import at the cellular, biochemical, and morphogenetic levels.

Nature Reviews Genetics. v. 1– , 2000– . New York: Nature Publishing. Monthly. $905.00. Available electronically. *"Nature Reviews Genetics* will cover the full scientific breadth of modern genetics, capturing its excitement, diversity and implications."

Progress in Nucleic Acid Research and Molecular Biology. v. 1– , 1963– . San Diego, CA: Academic Press. Irregular. Price varies. ISSN 0079-6603. Contains review articles covering a variety of topics.

Reviews in Molecular Biotechnology. v. 74– , 1999– . Amsterdam: Elsevier. Quarterly. $364.00. ISSN 1389-0352. Available electronically. "Each themed issue publishes comprehensive review articles on "state-of-the-art" technologies, including their relevance to current and future application areas and future potential developments, in a particular subject area."

Seminars in Cell and Developmental Biology. v. 7– , 1996– . London: Academic Press. imonthly. $411.00. ISSN 1084-9521. Available electronically. Each issue is devoted to a state-of-the-art review of a selected topic, edited by a guest editor. Formed by the merger of *Seminars in Developmental Biology* and *Seminars in Cell Biology*.

Trends in Biotechnology. v. 1– , 1983– . Cambridge, England: Elsevier.

Monthly. $907.00. ISSN 0167–7799. Available electronically. "One of the most widely cited journals in biotechnology . . . focuses on innovative biotechnology R&D, identifying and reviewing key trends in a lively and readable style." Also includes upcoming meetings.

Trends in Genetics. v. 1–   , 1985–   . Cambridge, England: Elsevier. Monthly. $907.00. ISBN 0168-9525. Available electronically. Publishes review articles in areas of genetics and developmental biology of current interest; also includes upcoming meetings.

8

Microbiology and Immunology

This chapter includes reference sources useful for microbiology and immunology. Microbiology is "the scientific study of microorganisms (e.g., bacteria, viruses and fungi)." For purposes of this discussion, however, fungi such as yeasts are included with plant biology in Chapter 10, "Plant Biology." Immunology is the study of immunity, "the state of relative insusceptibility of an animal to infection by disease-producing organisms." (*Oxford Dictionary of Biology*, 4th ed, 2000) Because microbial systems are convenient and effective for studying a whole range of life processes, there is a significant overlap between this chapter and Chapters 5 through 7, covering biochemistry and biophysics, molecular and cell biology, and genetics, respectively. Although medical microbiology and immunology are not comprehensively discussed in this chapter, some basic materials are included that pertain to the study of pathogenic microbiology and diagnostic immunology.

ABSTRACTS AND INDEXES

Abstracting and indexing serials are annotated in Chapter 4 and general sources useful for both microbiologists and immunologists are annotated in Chapter 3. Basically, the three great abstracting/indexing serials for microbiology and immunology are *Biological Abstracts*, *Chemical Abstracts*, and *Index Medicus*.

Immunology Abstracts. v. 1– , 1967– . Bethesda, MD: Cambridge Scientific Abstracts. Monthly. $1,265.00. ISSN 0307-112X. Available electronically. Covers studies in humans and animals, including molecular immunology, tumor immunology, histocompatability, and disorders of the immune system. See *Virology and AIDS Abstracts* following text for more extensive coverage of AIDS. Available online, on CD-ROM and on the Web as part of the Biological Sciences Collection. Also available as a separate database.

Microbiology Abstracts, Section B: Bacteriology. v. 1– . 1966– . Bethesda, MD: Cambridge Scientific Abstracts. Monthly. ISSN 0300-8398. Available electronically. This abstracting journal covers all areas of bacteriology, including taxonomy, genetics, medical and veterinary bacteriology, antimicrobials, and others. Available online, on CD-ROM and on the Web as part of the Biological Sciences Collection. Also available as a separate database.

Microbiology Abstracts, Section C: Algology, Mycology, and Protozoology. v. 1– , 1972– . Bethesda, MD: Cambridge Scientific Abstracts. Monthly. $1,195.00. ISSN 0301-2328. Available electronically. Covers all aspects of the study of algae, fungi, protozoa, and lichens. Available online, on CD-ROM and on the Web as part of the Biological Sciences Collection. Also available as a separate database.

Virology and AIDS Abstracts. v. 1– , 1967– . Bethesda, MD: Cambridge Scientific Abstracts. Monthly. $1,195.00. Available online. ISSN 0896-5919. Covers all aspects of virology, including studies on plants, animals, and humans. Also has comprehensive coverage of AIDS, including drug tests, transmission, molecular aspects, and immunology. Available online, on CD-ROM, and on the Web as part of the Biological Sciences Collection. Also available as a separate database.

ASSOCIATIONS

American Academy of Microbiology (AAM). 1751 N. St. NW, Washington, DC 20036. Phone: (202) 942-9226. Fax: (202) 942-9380. E-mail: academy@ asmusa.org. URL: http://www.asmusa.org/acasrc/academy.htm. Founded in 1955. 1,500 members. Honorific leadership component of American Society for Microbiology concerned with microscopic and submicroscopic organisms. Encourages exchange of information among members. Publishes *Academy News & Views*. Web site primarily for membership information.

American Association of Immunologists (AAI). 9650 Rockville Pike, Bethesda, MD 20814-3994. Phone: (301) 530-7178. Fax: (301) 571-1816. E-mail: infoaai @aai.faseb.org. URL: http://12.17.12.70/aai/default.asp. Founded 1913. 5,500 members. Scientists engaged in immunological research including aspects of virology, bacteriology, biochemistry, genetics, and related disciplines. Goals are to advance knowledge of immunology and related disciplines and to facilitate the interchange of information among investigators in various fields. Promotes interaction between laboratory investigators and clinicians; conducts training courses, symposia, workshops, and lectures; bestows awards; and compiles statistics. Publishes quarterly *AAI Newsletter*; periodic *Directory*; and the *Journal of*

Immunology. Web site contains membership information, and extensive educational material for students and the general public.

American Society for Microbiology (ASM). 1752 N. Street, N. W., Washington, DC 20036 Phone: (202) 737-3600. Fax: (202) 942-8341. URL: http://www. asmusa.org. Founded in 1899. 42,000 members with 36 local groups. Scientific society of microbiologists promoting advancement of scientific knowledge in order to improve education in microbiology. Encourages the highest professional and ethical standards and the adoption of sound legislative and regulatory policies affecting the discipline of microbiology at all levels. Affiliated with the International Union of Microbiological Societies. Publishes over 20 scientific journals available in alternate formats; other professional pamphlets. Formerly: the Society of American Bacteriologists. Web site includes membership information, news, and educational materials for students.

American Type Culture Collection (ATCC). 10801 University Blvd., Manassas, VA 20110-2209. Phone: (703) 365-2700. Fax: (703) 365-2750. URL: http:// www.atcc.org. Founded 1925. 225 staff. A private organization seeking to collect, propagate, preserve, and distribute authentic cultures of microorganisms and genetic materials for reference purposes for use in educational, research, and other scientific and industrial activities. Conducts research, maintains depository for cultures, aids in processing and packaging biohazardous materials, and identifies cultures. Publishes *ATCC Connections*; *ATCC Quality Control Methods for Cell Lines*, brochures, catalogs (both in print and on the Web), and manuals. Web site provides access to catalogs, news, and information about the ATCC.

Association on Food Microbiology and Hygiene (ICFMH). c/o Institute of Hygiene and Toxicology, Federal Research Centre for Nutrition, Had-und-Neu Strasse 9, D-76131 Karlsruhe, Germany. Phone: 49 721 66250. Fax: 49 721 6625111. E-mail: wh@wood.nka.de. Founded 1953. 2,900 members. Seeks to advance the study, teaching, and practice of food microbiology and hygiene. Publishes *International Journal of Food Microbiology*.

Canadian Society for Immunology (CSI); Societe Canadienne d'Immunologie (SCI). 795 McDermot Ave., Winnipeg, MB, Canada R3E 0W3. Phone: (204) 789-3316. Fax: (204) 789-3921. E-mail: donna_chow@umanitoba.ca. URL: http://www.csi.ucalgary.ca/index.html. Immunologists and other health care professionals and scientists with an interest in immunology. Seeks to advance immunological study, research, and practice. Promotes ongoing professional development of members. Serves as a network linking members; sponsors research and educational programs. Web site contains membership information, links to other societies.

Committee on the Status of Women in Microbiology (CSWM). c/o Dr. Sara Rothman, WRAIR, Washington, DC 20307-5100. Phone: (301) 319-9940. Fax: (301) 319-9961. E-mail: sara.rothman@na.amedd.army.mil. URL: http:// www.asmusa.org/pasrc/women.htm. Founded in 1972. A committee of the American Society for Microbiology who investigate the status of women in microbiology in relation to their male counterparts in the work place and within their professional society. Reports findings and conducts seminars at the annual meeting of ASM. Works toward full and equal opportunity for educational, career, and personal development for male and female microbiologists. Affiliated with the Federation of Organizations for Professional Women. Publishes *The Communicator*. Web site provides access to *The Communicator*.

European Culture Collection Organization (ECCO). c/o Dr. Maija-liisa Suikho, VTT Biotechnology, P.O. Box 1500, FIN-02044 Espoo, Finland. Phone: 358 9 4565133. Fax: 358 9 4552103. E-mail: maija-liisa.suihko@vtt.fi. URL: http:// www.eccosite.org/. Founded 1981. 61 members. Members of European organizations in 22 countries participating in the maintenance of biological material. Encourages communication and collaborative research among members. Informs members of current developments concerning taxonomy, culture identification, and patent information. Information services: Microbial Information Network Europe (MINE). Publishes *European Culture Collections* (in English). Web site has limited information.

European Federation of Immunological Societies. Inserm U255, Institut Curie, 26, rue d'Ulm, F-75231 Paris Cedex 05, France. Phone: 33 1 44324223. Fax: 33140510420. E-mail: marc.daeron@curie.fr. URL: http://www.efis.org. Founded 1975. 16,000 members. Immunological societies from around the world focusing on Europe. Promotes the advancement of research and education in immunology. Web site includes links to databases and organizations of interest to immunologists.

The International Society for Microbial Ecology. c/o Center for Microbial Ecology, Michigan State University, East Lansing, MI 48824. Phone: (517) 353-9021. Fax: (517) 353-2917. E-mail: ISME@pilot.msu.edu. URL: http://www. microbes.org/index.htm. Founded 1998. Professional organization dedicated to the exchange of scientific information on microbial ecology. Publishes *Microbial Ecology* and *Advances in Microbial Ecology*. Web site contains membership information and microbial ecology links including a Microbe of the Month site.

International Committee on Systematic Bacteriology (ICSB). c/o Dr. E. Stackenbrandt, DSMZ GmbH, Mascheroder Weg 1b, D-38124 Braunschweig, Germany. Phone: 49 531 2626418. Founded 1930. 140 members. Multinational. A committee of the International Union of Microbiological Societies. Sponsors international collaboration and research in systematic bacteriology. Publishes quarterly *International Journal of Systematic and Evolutionary Microbiology*; *International Code of Nomenclature of Bacteria*.

International Committee on Taxonomy of Viruses (ICTV). Dept. of Biological Sciences, University of Warwick, Coventry, W. Midlands CV4 7AL, England. Phone: 44 203 523565. Fax: 44 203 523568. E-mail: iltab@scripps.edu. URL: http://www.ncbi.nlm.nih.gov/ICTV. Founded 1966. 120 members. Multinational. A committee of the Virology Division of the International Union of Microbiological Societies. Seeks to develop a standard, internationally accepted system of virus classification and nomenclature. Publishes triennial *ICTV Reports*. Web site provides extensive information on viral taxonomy.

International Union of Immunological Societies (IUIS). c/o Dr. Anne Kelso, Queensland Institute of Medical Research, Post Office Road Brisbane Hospital, Queensland 4029, Australia. Phone: 61 73362 0382. Fax: 61 73362 0105. E-mail: iuis_secgen@quir.edu.au. URL: http://www.qimr.edu.au/iuis/. Founded 1969. 51 members. National professional societies of basic and applied immunologists. Encourages the orderly development and utilization of the science of immunology; promotes the application of new developments to clinical and veterinary problems and standardizes reagents and nomenclature; and conducts educational symposia and scientific meetings. Publishes *The Immunologist*. Web site for membership information.

International Union of Microbiological Societies (IUMS); Union Internationale des Sociétés de Microbiologie. Institut de Biologie Moleculaire er Cellulaire de CNRS, 15 Rue Descartes, F-67000 Strasbourg, France. Phone: 33 3 88417022. Fax: 33 3 88610680. E-mail: vanregen@ibmcu-strasbg.fr. URL: http://www. iums.org. Founded 1930. 106 members. Multinational. National microbiological societies in 62 countries representing 100,000 microbiologists. Publishes five scientific journals and *IUMS Directory*. Web site lists affiliated groups.

Japan Collection of Microorganisms (JCM). RIKEN (The Institute of Physical and Chemical Research), 2-1 Hirosawa, Wako, Saitama 351–0198, Japan. Phone: +81 48 67 9560. Fax: +81 48 462 4617. E-mail: curator@jcm.riken.go.jp. URL: http://www.jcm.riken.go.jp. A semigovernmental research institute supported by the Science and Technology Agency of Japan. It serves as a culture collection of microorganisms and contributes to domestic, regional, and global improvements of conservation of microbiological resources in cooperation with other culture collections and institutions. Web site provides access to culture catalogs, extensive links.

Society for Applied Microbiology (SFAM). c/o Dr. Ann Baillie, The Blore Tower, Harpur Centre, Bedford, Beds. MK40 1TQ, England. Phone: 44 1234 3226661. Fax: 44 1234 326678. E-mail: info@sfam.org.uk. URL: http:// www.sfam.org.uk. Founded 1931, 1,800 members. Multinational. Individuals involved in the study of microbiology whose purpose is to promote and advance the study of microbiology, particularly bacteriology, in its application to agriculture, industry, and the environment. Publishes *Journal of Applied Microbiology*, *Letters in Applied Microbiology*, and *Environmental Microbiology*, annual symposium series, and a technical series. Holds three meetings each year. Formerly: Society for Applied Bacteriology. Web site has a particularly nice collection of other links.

Society for General Microbiology (SGM). Marlborough House, Basingstoke Rd., Spencers Wood, Reading, Berks. RG7 1AE, England. Phone: 44 1189 881800. Fax: 44 1189 885656. E-mail: admin@soc.genmicrobiol.org.uk. URL: http:// www.socgenmicrobiol.org.uk. Founded 1945. 5,500 members. Multinational. Works to advance the study of general microbiology. Bestows awards and grants. Affiliated with the International Union of Microbiological Societies, and the Federation of the European Microbiological Societies. Publishes *International Journal of Systematic and Evolutionary Microbiology*, *Journal of General Virology*, *Micrbiology*, and an annual symposium series. Web site contains membership information, news, and links.

Society for Industrial Microbiology (SIM). 3929 Old Lee Hwy., Ste. 92A, Fairfax, VA 22030-2421. Phone: (703) 691-3357. Fax: (703) 691-7991. E-mail: info@simhq.org. URL: http://www.simhq.org/. Founded 1948. 2,122 members and 2 local groups. Mycologists, bacteriologists, biologists, chemists, engineers, zoologists, and others interested in biological processes as applied to industrial materials and processes of microorganisms. Affiliated with the American Institute of Biological Sciences. Publishes *Journal of Industrial Microbiology and Biotechnology*, *Membership Directory*, and *SIM News*. Web site includes "Kids' Zone," Web picks from *SIM News*, and career information.

CLASSIFICATION, NOMENCLATURE, AND SYSTEMATICS

For more information concerning online nomenclature access sites, check the Databases section later in this chapter. There is also overlap in the Methods section for techniques relevant to classification and systematics.

Ackermann, Hans-W, Laurent Berthiaume, and Michel Tremblay. *Virus Life in Diagrams*. Boca Raton, FL: CRC Press, 1998. 221 p. $74.95. ISBN 0849331269. This atlas presents 233 virus diagrams from English, French, and German scientific literature selected for scientific content, clarity, originality, and historic, didactic, and aesthetic value. Vertebrate, invertebrate, plant, bacterial, fungal, and protozoal viruses, as well as virods and prions are covered. Entries for families or a single genus provide key words, descriptions of taxonomic status, particle morphology, host range, and major physiological features. The first four chapters present an introduction to the field, summary of virus classification, replication cycle, and comparative diagrams. There is an extensive glossary for virological and molecular terms.

American Type Culture Collection.   This nonprofit repository collects, propagates, preserves, and distributes microorganisms, cell lines, and molecular biological materials all over the world. ATCC's catalogs of strains and materials are accessible online at the ATCC home page (URL: http://www.atcc.org). The catalogs can serve as a convenient information resource on nomenclature and classification. See full annotation in the Associations section.

Approved Lists of Bacterial Names. V. B. D. Skerman et al., eds. on behalf of the Ad Hoc Committee of the Judicial Commission of the International Committee on Systematic Bacteriology. Amended ed. Washington, DC: American Society for Microbiology, 1989. 188 p. $55.00 ISBN 1555810144.   Reprinted from *International Journal of Systematic Bacteriology*, v. 30, 1980, with corrections. Moore and Moore, later in this chapter, report on name changes made from 1989–91. Also, see Euzéby, in the following text for Internet access.

Bergey's Manual of Determinative Bacteriology. 9th ed. John G. Holt, ed. Baltimore, MD: Lippincott, Williams & Wilkins, 1994. 787 p. $65.00 ISBN 0683006037.   Based on data in *Bergey's Manual of Systematic Bacteriology*, this manual also includes new genera and species, new combinations, and new taxa published through the January 1992 issue of *International Journal of Systematic Bacteriology*. Contains information on shape and size, gram reaction, morphological features, motility and flagella, relation to oxygen, basic type of metabolism, carbon and energy sources, habitat and ecology. This manual serves as a reference to aid in the identification of unknown bacteria that have already been described and cultured.

Bergey's Manual of Systematic Bacteriology. John G. Holt, ed. Baltimore, MD: Williams & Wilkins, 1989. 4 v. $370.00 (set). ISBN 0683041126 (set).   Definitive reference for classification, nomenclature, and identification of bacteria. Each generic listing includes antigenic structure, pathogenicity, ecology, enrichment and isolation procedures, maintenance procedures, methods for testing special characters, etc. The volumes cover, for the most part: volume 1, the gram-negatives except those in volume 3; volume 2, the gram-positives less actinomycetes; volume 3, the archaeobacteria, cyanobacteria, and the remaining gram-negatives; and volume 4, actinomycotes.

Bergey's Manual of Systematic Bacteriology: The Archaea, Cyanobacteria, Phototrophs and Deeply Branching Bacteria . 2nd ed. George Garrity, ed. New York: Springer-Verlag, 2000. 560 p. $105.00 ISBN 0387987711.   An expanded, revised edition of volume 3.

European Culture Collection Organization. See the Associations section for full annotation. Over 20 countries cooperate in maintaining these collections and serve as an aid in identification.

Euzéby, J. P. *List of Bacterial Names with Standing in Nomenclature*. Toulouse, France: Centre universitaire de calcul de Toulouse, 1998–   . URL: http://www.bacterio.cict.fr/.   This site provides access to alphabetical files of nomenclature of bacteria cited in the *Approved Lists of Bacterial Names* (see previous).

Fraenkel-Conrat, Heinz. *The Viruses: Catalogue, Characterization, and Classification*. New York: Kluwer, 1985. 276 p. $138.00. ISBN 0306417669.   List of well-established and studied viruses, in alphabetical order. Identified in taxonomic terms, illustrated by electron micrographs. Divided into sections for animal and plant viruses, and phages of prokaryotes.

Index to Organism Names. See Chapter 3, "General Sources," for full annotation. This database replaces the BIOSIS Register of Bacterial Nomenclature (BRBN), which contained over 16,400 bacterial names.

Index Virum: Catalogue of ICTV Approved Virus Names. Cornelia Büchen-Osmond, compiler. Canberra, Australia: Bioinformatics Group, Australian National University. URL: http://life.anu.edu.au/viruses/Ictv/fr-index.htm.   The gateway to the descriptions of viruses with links to electron micrographs and genomic sequences, on the Universal Virus Database at the Australian National University in Canberra. Information on more than 4,500 viruses, based on the 6th report of the ICTV (International Committee on Taxonomy of Viruses). For more details about the database, see the Databases section. Also, see International Committee on Taxonomy of Viruses, 6th Report, page 203.

International Code of Nomenclature of Bacteria; *Statutes of the International Committee on Systematic Bacteriology*; and, *Statutes of the Bacteriology and Applied Microbiology Section f the International Union of Microbiological Societies*; *Bacteriological Code*. 1990 revision. P. H. A. Sneath et al., eds. Washington, DC: Published for the International Union of Microbiological Societies by the American Society for Microbiology, 1992. 189 p. $47.00. ISBN 155581039X.   "Approved by the Judicial Commission of the International Committee on Systematic Bacteriology, the International Committee on Systematic Bacteriology, the International Union of Microbiological Societies, and the Plenary Session of the International Congress of Bacteriology and Mycology, Osaka, Japan, September 1990." Contains the latest guidelines for naming newly discovered or engineered bacteria, as approved by the plenary session of the International Congress of Microbiology in Osaka, 1990, the most recent book version since 1975.

International Committee on Taxonomy of Viruses, 6th Report. F. A. Murphy, et al., eds. *Virus Taxonomy: Classification and Nomenclature of Viruses*. New York: Springer-Verlag, 1995. 586 p. $116.00. ISBN 3211825980. A goal of the ICTV is to provide a single universal system for the classification and nomenclature of all viruses. This sixth report adds to the accumulated taxonomic contribution "in progress" since 1966. Contents: Introduction to the Universal System of Virus Taxonomy; the Viruses; the International Committee on the Taxonomy of Viruses; and indexes for author, virus, and taxonomy. Also, see *Index Virum*, page 202.

International Journal of Systematic and Evolutionary Microbiology. v. 47– , 1997– . Spencers Wood, England: Society for General Microbiology. Bimonthly. $395.00 ISSN 1466-5026. Available electronically. The official journal of the International Committee on Systematic Bacteriology and the Bacteriology and Applied Microbiology Division of the International Union of Microbiological Societies. This journal includes articles on the systematics of bacteria, yeasts, and yeastlike organisms, including taxonomy, nomenclature, identification, phylogeny, evolution, biodiversity, characterization, and culture preservation. Formerly: *International Journal of Systematic Bacteriology*.

Japan Collection of Microorganisms (JCM). Saitama, Japan: Japan Collection of Microorganisms. URL: http://www.jcm.riken.go.jp/. This culture collection of microorganisms was founded in 1980 at RIKEN (the Institute of Physical and Chemical Research), a semigovernmental research institute in Japan. JCM supplies authentic microorganisms to researchers in life sciences and biotechnology from over 3,700 strains of bacteria, over 2,300 strains of fungi, and over 130 strains of archaea. In the JCM On-line Catalogue Database, it is possible to search for microorganisms with key words. Strain data is linked to other data, such as history, taxonomic information, references, and cultivation conditions with medium formulations. Also available in a printed catalog (7th ed. in 1999, ISSN 0913-0098, $42.00).

Moore, W. E. C. and Lillian V. H. Moore. *Index of the Bacterial and Yeast Nomenclatural Changes: Published in the International Journal of Systematic Bacteriology since the 1980 Approved Lists of Bacterial Names: (1 January 1980 to 1 January 1989)*. Washington, DC: American Society for Microbiology, 1991. $14.95. ISBN 9993778125.

NCBI Taxonomy Homepage. Bethesda, MD: NCBI, 2000– . http://www.ncbi.nlm.nih.gov/Taxonomy/taxonomyhome.html/. See main annotation in Chapter 3, "General Sources." The taxonomy homepage has direct links to some of the microorganisms commonly used in molecular biology research projects, for example, *E. coli*.

Protoctista Glossary: Vocabulary of the Algae, Apicomplexa, Ciliates, Foraminifera, Microspora, Water Molds, Slime Molds, and Other Protoctists. Lynn Margulis, Heather I. McKhann, and Lorraine Olendzenski, eds. Boston, MA: Jones & Bartlett, 1993. 288 p. $53.75. ISBN 0867200812. Drawings, light and electron micrographs, and photographs illustrate this comprehensive guide to information on the protoctists and their descendants, in the format of term and taxa glossaries. It is an abbreviated version of *Handbook of Protoctista* that is discussed in the Handbooks section.

DATABASES

Databases relevant to the Biochemistry and Biophysics (Chapter 5), Molecular and Cellular Biology (Chapter 6), and Genetics, Biotechnology, and Developmental Biology (Chapter 7), will likely be useful for microbiology and virology.

CGSC: *E. coli* Genetic Stock Center. New Haven, CT: Yale University, 1998– . URL: http://cgsc.biology.yale.edu. The CGSC maintains a database of *E. coli* genetic information, including genotypes and reference information for the strains in the CGSC collections; gene names; properties; and linkage map, gene product information, and information on specific mutations. The public version of the database includes this information and is accessible in three forms: the CGSC DB_WebServer, the CGSC Gopher, and guest logins to CGSC Sybase database. The home page also provides links to other pertinent Web sites.

EcoCyc: Encyclopedia of *E. Coli* Genes and Metabolism. Menlo Park, CA: Pangea Systems. URL: http://ecocyc.pangeasystems.com/ecocyc/ecocyc.html. EcoCyc is a bioinformatics database that describes the genome and the biochemical machinery of *E. coli*. The long-term goal is to describe the molecular catalog of the *E. coli* cell as well as the functions of each of it molecular parts, and to facilitate a system-level understanding of *E. coli*. An account is required to access the database, but noncommercial use by individuals at academic and governmental institutions is free.

Escherichia coli Database Collection (ECDC). URL: http://www.uni-giessen.de/%7Egx1052/ECDC/ecdc.htm. Provides the complete genome map for *E. coli*. (Release June 25, 2001).

DICTIONARIES AND ENCYCLOPEDIAS

Cruse, Julius M. and Robert E. Lewis, Jr. *Illustrated Dictionary of Immunology*. Boca Raton, FL: CRC, 1995. 330 p. $83.95 ISBN 084934557X. Written for students, clinicians, and scientists, this comprehensive dictionary includes hundreds of illustrations and provides a wealth of information and thorough treatment of contemporary immunological definitions. The second edition is expected in 2001.

Dictionary of Immunology. 4th ed. W. John Herbert, Peter C. Wilkinson, and David I. Stott, eds. San Diego, CA: Academic Press, 1995. $53.00. ISBN 0127520252. The aim is to include terms of current immunological usage to satisfy the needs of any biologist, clinician, or biochemist. Over one third of the terms in this fourth edition are new, and the rest have been updated.

Dictionary of Virology. 2nd ed. Brian W. Mahy, ed. San Diego, CA: Academic Press, 1997. 368 p. $58.00. ISBN 0124653251. Completely revised and updated, this reference presents a complete and comprehensive description of every virus affecting vertebrate species from human to fish. Entries provide classification based on the sixth ICTV report, virus structure, replication and role in disease, control and prevention measures. The almost 3,500 alphabetically arranged entries include commonly used cell lines and explanations of terms applicable to molecular biology as it is related to viruses. There are references to journal articles or reviews provided for further reading.

Encyclopedia of Food Microbiology. Richard K Robinson, Carl A Batt, and Pradip Patel, eds. San Diego, CA: Academic Press, 1999. 3 v. $925.00. ISBN 0122270703. The largest comprehensive reference source of current knowledge in the field of food microbiology, this encyclopedia is relevant, up-to-date, and written by authorities in the field. Valuable for the food industry and professionals in the area, and for academic and large public libraries. Web access is available to buyers of the print edition.

Encyclopedia of Immunology. 2nd ed. Peter J. Delves and Ivan M. Roitt, eds. San Diego, CA: Academic Press, 1998. 4 v. $925.00. ISBN 0122267656. Largest comprehensive reference source of current immunological knowledge available. Written by distinguished leaders in the field, the encyclopedia's 639 entries are arranged alphabetically. Web access is available with purchase of the print volume.

Encyclopedia of Microbiology. 2nd ed. Joshua Lederberg, ed. San Diego, CA: Academic Press, 2000. 4 v. $795.00 (set). ISBN 0122268008 (set). Written by some of the world's leading scientists, this comprehensive encyclopedia covers traditional fields as well as the latest microbiological research, applied microbiology, careers, ethics, history, systematics, techniques, etc. Each article provides a table of contents, a glossary of terms, an in-depth presentation of the topic, and a bibliography. Available online from the publisher with purchase of the print encyclopedia.

Encyclopedia of Virology. 2nd ed. Allan Granoff and Robert G. Webster, eds. San Diego, CA: Academic Press, 1999. 3 v. $925.00 (set). ISBN 0122270304 (set). The format is similar to that of the *Encyclopedia of Microbiology* by the same publisher, and is the largest single reference source of current virological knowledge. It includes over 300 articles by leading researchers appropriate for both general and specialist readers. Appendix in volume 3 lists the updated ICTV virus name index published in the 1999 ICTV report. Web access, advanced search tools, and 3D visualizations of viruses are available from the publisher with purchase of the print encyclopedia.

Singleton, Paul and Diana Sainsbury. *Dictionary of Microbiology and Molecular Biology.* 2nd ed. NY: Wiley, 1993. 1,032 p. $84.95 (paper). ISBN 0471940526 (paper). Comprehensive and easy to use with 14,735 entries. This dictionary covers classical descriptive microbiology as well as current developments in related areas such as bioenergetics and molecular biology. The definitions range between very brief to half a page long and include synonyms, cross references, and references to the literature. Appendices provide diagrams of metabolic pathways, acid cycles, fermentation, and biosynthesis.

Vorobjeva, Lena I. *Propionibacteria.* Dordrecht, Netherlands: Kluwer, 1999. $150.00 ISBN 0792358848. This is a practical encyclopedia for information on the unique characteristics and applications of a very useful group of bacteria. Topics include historical background, information about the genus *Propionibacterium*, genetic studies, transformations of energy, biosynthetic processes, immobilized cells, and economic and medical applications.

DIRECTORIES

Linscott's Directory of Immunological and Biological Reagents. 11th ed. Santa Rosa, CA: Linscott's Directory, 2000. 394 p. $100.00. ISBN 1892153009. Catalog for more than 47,000 biological products, reagents, and immune serums. The directory is also available online and on CD-ROM. Access to the online version is free with purchase of the print version, or can be purchased separately.

Microbial Strain Data Network (MSDN). 63 Wostenholm Road, Sheffield, England. Phone: +44 114 258 3397. Fax: +44 114 258 3402. E-mail: msdn@ sheffield.ac.uk. URL: http://panizzi.shef.ac.uk/msdn/msdninfo.html. This nonprofit organization provides specialized information and communications services for life scientists worldwide. There is an international Committee of Management and a Secretariat based in Sheffield, England. MSDN is sponsored by the United Nations Environment Programme (UNEP) and other organizations. MSDN provides a unique package of databases and bulletin boards covering microbiology, biotechnology, and biodiversity. There is information on microbial strains, culture collections from several nations (Russia, Slovenia, Czech Republic, India, Bulgaria, Argentina, and the UK), biotechnology publications and meetings, and environmental matters. The scope includes cell lines, hybridomas, molecular probes and recombinant materials as well as microorganisms. Access to MSDN is free through public data networks and the Web. *The MSDN Directory of Information Resources* is a database indexing microbial cultures of about 60 laboratories.

World Data Centre for Microorganisms (WDCM). URL: http://wdcm. nig.ac.jp. This site provides a comprehensive, worldwide directory of culture collections, databases on microbes and cell lines, and the gateway to biodiversity, molecular biology, and genome projects.

GUIDES TO INTERNET RESOURCES

All the Virology on the WWW. Society for Applied Microbiology, 1995– . URL: http://www.virology.net/garryfavweb.html. "All the Virology on the WWW seeks to be the best single site for Virology information on the Internet. We have collected all the virology related Web sites that might be of interest to our fellow virologists, and others interested in learning more about viruses." While no Web directory can be truly comprehensive, this one comes close. There are links to plant viruses, HIV and AIDS sites, biological warfare, and all the usual taxonomic information plus much more.

Büchen-Osmond, Cornelia and M. J. Dallwitz. ICTVdB: Universal Virus Database. Canberra, Australia: Bioinformatics Group, Australian National University. URL: http://life.anu.edu.au/viruses/Ictv/fr-index.htm. This database was developed under the auspices of the International Committee on Taxonomy of Viruses (ICTV) and is based on the sixth report of the ICTV. *Index Virum*, in the following text, is one of its components, along with projects for Plant Viruses Online, a picture gallery, and a virus-identification data exchange.

Deutsche Sammlung von Mikroorganismenund Zellkulturen GmbH (DSMZ), German Collection of Microorganisms and Cell. URL: http://www.dsmz.de/ dsmzhome.htm. The DSMZ "is an independent, non-profit organization dedicated to the acquisition, characterization and identification, preservation and distribution of Bacteria, Archaea, fungi, plasmids, phages, human and animal cell lines, plant cell cultures and plant viruses."

E. coli Index. URL: http://web.bham.ac.uk/bcm4ght6/. "These pages contain a comprehensive guide to information relating to the model organism *Escherichia coli.*'' The site contains information on *E. coli* databases, researchers, societies, news, protocols, and much more. The site was created by Dr. Gavin H. Thomas at the Department of Molecular Biology and Biotechnology, University of Sheffield, Sheffield, England.

HardinMD. URL: http://www.lib.uiowa.edu/hardin/md/micro.html. Billed as listing ''the best sites that list the sites.'' This ''Microbiology & Infectious Diseases'' page lists primarily medical sites.

MedWebplus. Decatur, GA: y-DNA, Inc., 1998– . URL: http://med webplus.com/subject/Escherichia_coli.html. Provides links to focused information about *E.coli*: encyclopedias, genetics, microbiology, and links to the Genetic Stock Center (CGSC) at Yale University; an organism index; an organism database collection (ECDC); EcoCyc, an encyclopedia of *E. coli* Genes and Metabolism; and the *E. coli* Genome Center at the University of Wisconsin-Madison.

Molecular Microbiology Jump Station. Highveld.com, 1996– . URL: http://www.highveld.com/micro.html. A comprehensive collection of links for microbiologists, covering all areas of basic and applied microbiology. The site is sponsored by several corporations.

ProMEDmail. URL: http://www.promedmail.org/pls/promed/promed.home. The global electronic reporting system for outbreaks of emerging infectious diseases and toxins, open to all sources; a program of the International Society for Infectious Diseases.

Stanford Genomic Resources. URL: http://genome-www.stanford.edu/. The genomic collections contains links to other Stanford databases, for example, the *Saccharomyces* Genome Database Project (SGC); genome centers, published datasets, software resources, research departments, and mirrored sites.

WFCC-MIRCEN, World Data Centre for Microorganisms. URL: http://wdcm.nig.ac.jp/. ''Provides a comprehensive directory of culture collections, databases on microbes and cell lines, and the gateway to biodiversity, molecular biology and genome projects.''

HANDBOOKS

Two publishers that should be especially acknowledged are the American Society for Microbiology in Washington, DC (URL: http://www.asmusa.org/asm.htm) and the Cold Spring Harbor Laboratory Press in Cold Spring Harbor, New York (URL: http://www.cshl.org/books/new-hmpg.htm). Both of these publishers issue authoritative laboratory methods manuals and handbooks of importance to microbiologists, immunologists, and molecular biologists.

Consult the biochemistry, genetics, and molecular biology chapters (Chapters 5, 6, and 7) for other handbooks relevant to microbiology and immunology.

ASM Style Manual for Journals and Books. Washington, DC: American Society for Microbiology, 1991. 199 p. $28.00. No ISBN available. "The new manual supersedes the 1985 edition and all ASM handbooks published previously." Authorized by the American Society of Microbiology (ASM), this style manual covers report writing, dissertation and manuscript preparation, technical writing, and printing for microbiologists.

Atlas of Invertebrate Viruses. Jean R. Adams and Jean R. Bonami, eds. Boca Raton, FL: CRC Press, 1991. 684 p. $375.95. ISBN 0849368065. Useful reference for invertebrate pathologists, virologists, and electron microscopists. Illustrated with black and white photographs; each chapter has a lengthy bibliography. Appendices include information on techniques for light and electron microscopy, staining techniques, morphological guide, fixation and embedding protocols.

Atlas, Ronald M. *Handbook of Microbiological Media.* 2nd ed. Lawrence C. Parks, ed. Boca Raton, FL: CRC Press, 1997. 1,706 p. $135.00. ISBN 0849326389. A comprehensive reference to the formulations and applications of over 2,000 microbiological media used for isolation, cultivation, identification, and maintenance. Includes instruction for preparation and use; accepted name of media; and synonyms, from commercial manufacturers and the literature.

Biosafety in Microbiological and Biomedical Laboratories: Working with Infectious Agents in Laboratory Settings. 4th ed. Jonathan Y. Richmond and Robert W. McKinney, eds. Upland, PA: Diane Publishing, 2000. $45.00. ISBN 0788185136. Standards and safety measures for microbiological and medical laboratories, originally published under the auspices of U.S. Department of Health and Human Services, Public Health Service, Centers for Disease Control, and National Institutes of Health.

Biotechnology Handbooks. 1987– . These handbooks contain data useful for the practice of microorganisms in the service of biotechnology. See Chapter 7, "Genetics, Biotechnology, and Developmental Biology" for the complete citation.

Brock's Biology of Microorganisms. 9th ed. Michael T. Madigan, John M. Martinko, and Jack Parker, eds. NY: Prentice Hall, 1999. 1,046 p. $103.50. ISBN 013819220. Previously called the *Biology of Microorganisms*, this text can serve as a reference with in-depth information in a convenient, well-designed, and organized format.

Cellular Immunology LABFAX. P. J. Delves, ed. San Diego, CA: Academic Press, 1994. 250 p. $50.00. ISBN 0122088859. Another volume in the *LABFAX* series that lists information on cells of the immune system, including data on the development, structure, function, preparation, and assay of immune system tissues, cells, and molecules.

Color Atlas and Textbook of Diagnostic Microbiology. 5th ed. Elmer W. Koneman et al., eds. Philadelphia, PA: Lippincott Williams & Wilkins, 1997. $71.95. ISBN 0397515294. Revised and updated laboratory manual for current rapid techniques and emerging technologies in the laboratory diagnosis of infectious diseases.

CRC Handbook of Microbiology. 2nd ed. Allen I. Laskin and Hubert A. Lechevalier, eds. Boca Raton, FL: CRC Press, 1977–1987. 9 v. $1,700 (set). ISBN 0849372003. Data on properties of microorganisms, their composition, products, and activities. Volume 1: *Bacteria*; Volume 2: *Fungi, Algae, Protozoa, and Viruses*; Volumes 3 and 4: *Microbial Composition*; Volume 5: *Microbial Products*; Volume 6: *Growth and Metabolism*; Volume 7: *Microbial Transformation*; Volume 8: *Toxins and Enzymes*; and Volume 9: *Antibiotics* and *Antimicrobial Inhibitors*.

Cullimore, D. Roy. *Practical Atlas for Bacterial Identification.* Boca Raton, FL: Lewis, 2000. 209 p. $79.95. ISBN 1566703921. This atlas presents a pictorial approach to bacterial identification, focusing on shared characteristics of various families of bacteria rather than on chemical constituents. For microbial ecologists.

DIFCO Manual: Dehydrated Culture Media and Reagents for Microbiology. 11th ed. Detroit, MI: DIFCO Laboratories, 1998. 862 p. $79.95. ISBN 9994853708. Provides comprehensive information about products used in microbiology from a respected pioneer in bacteriological culture media.

Handbook of Human Immunology. Mary S. Leffell, ed. Boca Raton, FL: CRC Press, 1997. 640 p. $119.95. ISBN 0849301343. Provides basic explanations of laboratory tests with 115 tables of reference data and applications.

Handbook of Protoctista: The Structure, Cultivation, Habitats, and Life Histories of the Eukaryotic Microorganisms and Their Descendants Exclusive of Animals, Plants, and Fungi: A Guide to the Algae, Ciliates, Foraminifera, Sporozoa, Water Molds, Slime Molds, and the Other Protoctists. Lynn Margulis et al., eds. Boston, MA: Jones and Bartlett, 1990. 914 p. ISBN 0867200529. Indispensable for anyone dealing with protoctists. This authoritative handbook provides information on protoctist classification, nomenclature, distribution, evolutionary history, life cycles, maintenance, cultivation, identification, and references to the literature.

Hsiung, Gueh-Djen, Caroline K. Y. Fong, and Marie L. Landry. *Hsiung's Diagnostic Virology: As Illustrated by Light and Electron Microscopy.* 4th ed. New Haven, CT: Yale University Press, 1994. 382 p. $70.00. ISBN

0300058454. Concise, easy-to-use reference for the lab covering all aspects of the subject, including specimen collection, laboratory safety, virus isolation and identification, and cell culture. Thoroughly illustrated.

IMI Descriptions of Fungi and Bacteria. 1964– . Kew, Surrey, England: CAB International Mycological Institute. 4 sets/yr. ISSN 0009-9716. Title varies, *Commonwealth Mycological Institute Descriptions of Fungi and Bacteria*; continuation of *CMI Descriptions of Pathogenic Fungi and Bacteria*. Provides standardized, illustrated descriptions of organisms including disease caused, geographical distribution, physiological specialization, transmission, and references to key literature. There is an electronic catalog of the bacteria and fungi available through PESTCABweb by subscription only.

Immunochemistry LABFAX. M. A. Kerr and R. Thorpe, eds. San Diego, CA: Academic, 1994. 256 p. $63.00. ISBN 0124049400. Detailed compendium of essential information on plasma proteins, immumoglobulin properties and purification, antibody products, labeling and derivatization, and data on techniques such as ELISA, blotting, and immunolocalization.

Laboratory Safety: Principles and Practices. 2nd ed. Diane O. Fleming et al., eds. Washington, DC: American Society for Microbiology, 1994. 400 p. $49.00. ISBN 1555810470. Authoritative compilation produced under the auspices of the largest microbiological society in the United States Sections cover hazard assessment in the laboratory, hazard control in the laboratory, safety program management, and appendices including the CDC/NIH *Biosafety in Microbiological and Biomedical Laboratories*, the latest OSHA guidelines on blood-borne pathogens and chemical handling in labs, and a brief guide to first aid.

Leucocyte Antigen Factsbook. 2nd ed. A. Neil Barclay et al., eds. San Diego, CA: Academic, 1997. (Factsbook Series). 660 p. $53.00. ISBN 01207-81859. One-step reference contains overview chapters and entries on leucocyte antigens, provides information on molecular weights, human gene location and size, tissue distribution, structure, ligands and associated molecules, function, amino acid sequences, and database accession numbers.

Manual of Industrial Microbiology and Biotechnology. 2nd ed. Valuable how-to resource annotated in Chapter 7.

Mazzone, Horace M. *CRC Handbook of Viruses: Mass-Molecular Weight Values and Related Properties.* Boca Raton, FL: CRC Press, 1998. 206 p. $149.95. ISBN 0849326257. This very useful compilation provides data in one place, for all classes of viruses: molecular weight, size, shape, sedimentation, and diffusion coefficients. The author also explains and gives examples of the methods for obtaining the mass-molecular weight value of viruses.

Miller, Jeffrey H. *A Short Course in Bacterial Genetics: A Laboratory Manual and Handbook for Escherichia coli and Related Bacteria.* Cold Spring Harbor, NY: Cold Spring Harbor Laboratory Press, 1992. 2 v. Manual and handbook: $80.00. ISBN 0879693495. Contents include physical and genetic maps of various bacteria, clone banks and libraries, databases, sequences, genetic codes and codon usage in selected organisms, properties of amino acids, atomic weights, formulas, procedures, commercial suppliers, etc. A kit of 44 bacterial strains and phage lysates is available for the set of experiments described in *A Short Course* . . . Also, see a related manual, Stanley R. Maloy's *Experimental Techniques in Bacterial Genetics* in the methods section.

The Prokaryotes. 2nd ed. Albert Balows, et al., eds. Secaucus, NJ: Springer-Verlag, 1992. 4 v. $2,635.00 (set). ISBN 0387972587 (set)   "A Handbook on the Biology of Bacteria: Ecophysiology, Isolation, Identification, Applications." Provides a comprehensive survey of all established and proposed bacterial genera for which adequate data are available. Also see the electronic version (next entry).

The Prokaryotes; An Evolving Electronic Resource for the Microbiological Community. Martin Dworkin. Editor-in-Chief. New York: Springer-Verlag, 1999– . ISBN 0387142541. Variously priced; check with the publisher. URL: http://link.springer-ny.com/link/service/books/10125/. "The electronic version of *The Prokaryotes* is an online implementation of the content currently found in the printed reference work, 2nd ed, 1992. About 25 percent of the content will be fully updated each year over a four year period until the work is completely revised. Thereafter, material will be continuously added to reflect developments in Prokaryotic microbiology. It is the editor's hope that the electronic *Prokaryotes* will continue as a comprehensive resource for the bacteria and the Archaea."

Virology LABFAX. D. Harper, ed. San Diego, CA: Academic Press, 1994. 345 p. $78.00 (spiral casebound). ISBN 0123263204. Key data reference book in the *LABFAX* series for virologists. Includes information on virus taxonomy, electron microscopy, viral diseases, cell culture, immunology, monoclonal antibodies, sequence data, safety, vaccines, journals, etc. For other relevant LABFAX titles, consult the biochemistry, and molecular and cell biology chapters.

HISTORIES

Authoritative historical material and reference sources may be found, also, in the *Encyclopedia of Microbiology*, the *Encyclopedia of Immunology*, and the *Encyclopedia of Virology*. Although many of the following histories are out of print, they are included here because of their continuing value and their probable availability in large library systems.

Beck, Raymond W. *A Chronology of Microbiology in Historical Context.* Washington, DC: American Society for Microbiology, 2000. 400 p. $43.95. ISBN 1555811930.   Events in microbiology, from the 3rd millennium B.C. to the late twentieth century, are presented in the light of their historical context, by identifying those individuals who made these events happen.

Brent, Leslie. *A History of Transplantation Immunology*. San Diego, CA: Academic, 1996. 450 p. $65.00. ISBN 0121317706.   An excellent account of the history of transplantation immunology.

Brock, Thomas D. *The Emergence of Bacterial Genetics*. Cold Spring Harbor, NY: Cold Spring Harbor Laboratory Press, 1990. $20.00. ISBN 08796-93509.   The author highlights and analyzes the experimental work that shaped and drove the field of bacterial genetics by concentrating on the science, and discussing key data from the original sources.

Brock, Thomas D. *Milestones in Microbiology*. 2nd ed. Washington, DC: American Society for Microbiology, 1968. 275 p. $29.95 (paper). ISBN 1555811426 (paper).   Historically important papers selected to demonstrate the development of microbiology. The editor comments on each article putting the experiments and the scientists into historical and scientific perspective.

Brock, Thomas D. *Robert Koch: A Life in Medicine and Bacteriology*. Washington, DC: American Society for Microbiology, 2000. 364 p. $39.95. ISBN 1555811434.   The account of a true scientific revolutionary and winner of the Nobel Prize for Physiology or Medicine for his work on tuberculosis in 1905.

Bulloch, William. *The History of Bacteriology*. New York: Oxford University Press, 1938. 422 p.   This authoritative, classic history of medical bacteriology includes "bibliographical notices of some of the early workers in bacteriology."

Burnet, F. M. and D. O. White. *Natural History of Infectious Disease*. 4th ed. New York: Cambridge University Press, 1972. 278 p. ISBN 0521083893, 052109688X (paper).   Out of print, but still a classic.

Clark, Paul Franklin. *Pioneer Microbiologists of America*. Madison, WI: University of Wisconsin Press, 1961. 369 p.   History of early American microbiology.

Collard, Patrick. *The Development of Microbiology*. New York: Cambridge University Press, 1976. 201 p. ISBN 0521211778.   This book presents "the development of certain ideas in microbiology, relating the views held at different times to the contemporaneous state of knowledge in other fields and showing how successive models grew out of the internal contradictions of their predecessors."

Dawes, E. A. The Federation of European Microbiological Societies—An Historical Review. *FEMS Microbiological Letters* 100: 15–23, 1992.

De Kruif, Paul. *Microbe Hunters*. New York: Harcourt Brace, 1996. 347 p.

$13.00 (paper). ISBN 0156002620 (paper).   Fascinating history that has seen many reprints. There is also a series of audiocassettes that contains a complete and unabridged reading of de Kruif's account of the early microbe hunters (New London, CT: Sound Writings, 1992, 8 audiocassettes, running time 12 hours, $39.00).

Grafe, Alfred. *A History of Experimental Virology*. Translated by Elvira Reckendorf. New York: Springer-Verlag, 1991. 343 p. ISBN 387519254.   Comprehensive, compact survey of virology and the knowledge achieved during the past century.

Grainger, Thomas H. *A Guide to the History of Bacteriology*. (Chronica Botanica, no. 18). New York: Ronald Press, 1958. 210 p.   Citations and annotations are provided to the reference tools for the literature of bacteriology, to the history of bacteriology, and to biographical references and biographies of bacteriologists.

Hughes, Sally Smith. *The Virus: A History of the Concept*. New York: Science History Publications, 1977. 140 p. ISBN 0882021680.   Written in nontechnical language for people with a general interest in the history of science.

Immunology 1930–1980: Essays on the History of Immunology. Pauline M. H. Mazumdar, ed. Toronto: Wall & Thompson, 1989. 307 p. $39.95. ISBN 092133219X.   ''Most of the chapters in this volume are based on papers that were originally presented as part of the Sixth International Congress of Immunology, held at the University of Toronto in July 1986.''

Karlen, Arno. *Man and Microbes: Disease and Plagues in History and Modern Times*. New York: Touchstone Books, 1996. 266 p. $15.00 (paper). ISBN 0684822709 (paper).   A historical look at the coevolution of humans and microorganisms.

Kolata, Gina Bari. *Flu: The Story of the Great Influenza Pandemic of 1918 and the Search for the Virus that Caused It*. Farrar Straus & Giroux, 1999. 330 p. $25.00. ISBN 0374157065.   A fascinating look at the 1918 epidemic that killed 40 million people in less than a year.

Lechevalier, Hubert A. *Three Centuries of Microbiology*. New York: Dover Publications, 1974. 536 p. ISBN 048623035X.   Although out of print, this history is useful for quotations from classical papers stressing the main lines of historical development.

Many Faces, Many Microbes: Personal Reflections in Microbiology. Ronald M. Atlas, ed. Washington, DC: American Society for Microbiology, 2000. 328 p. $39.95 (paper). ISBN 1555811906 (paper).   A continuation of the story of the beginnings of microbiology as told by Paul de Kruif in *Microbe Hunters*. This book uses personal essays from leading, contemporary microbiologists to illustrate and update the continuing saga of the field.

Microbe Hunters—Then and Now. Hilary Koprowski and Michael B. A. Oldstone, eds. Bloomington, IL: Medi-Ed Press, 1996. 456 p. $49. 00. ISBN 0936741112. Well-known scientists portray remarkable discoveries, from the past to the present, in the study and control of infectious diseases.

Microbiology: A Centenary Perspective. Wolfgang K. Joklik et al., eds. Washington, DC: American Society for Microbiology, 1999. 576 p. $79.95. ISBN 1555811620. A collection of landmark papers in microbiology from the twentieth century, focusing on the importance of each contribution.

Milestones in Immunology. Debra Jan Bibel, ed. New York: Springer-Verlag, 1988. 330 p. ISBN 0910239150. Consists of reprints of articles from various sources.

Phage and the Origins of Molecular Biology, expanded edition. J. Cairns, G. S. Stent, and J. D. Watson, eds. Cold Spring Harbor, NY: Cold Spring Harbor Press, 1992. 366 p. $29.00 (paper). ISBN 0879695951 (paper). A new, expanded edition of the landmark collection of autobiographical essays honoring Max Delbruck's 60th birthday, originally published in 1966.

Portraits of Viruses: A History of Virology. F. Fenner and A. Gibbs, eds. New York: Karger, 1988. 344 p. $128.00. ISBN 3805548192. Articles originally published in *Intervirology* between 1979 and 1986.

Silverstein, Arthur M. *A History of Immunology.* San Diego, CA: Academic Press, 1989. 422 p. $73.00. ISBN 012643770X. About half of the chapters were published in abbreviated form in the journal *Cellular Immunology.*

Tauber, Alfred I. and Leon Chernyak. *Metchnikoff and the Origins of Immunology: From Metaphor to Theory.* New York: Oxford University Press, 1991. (Monographs on the History and Philosophy of Biology). 247 p. $60.00. ISBN 019506447X. A critical study of the work of Elie Metchnikoff, the founding father of modern immunology.

Waterson, A. P. and Lise Wilkinson. *An Introduction to the History of Virology.* New York: Cambridge University Press, 1978. 237 p. ISBN 0521219175. The underlying theme of the book is the evolution of the present concept of a virus. A very useful 30-page section gives brief biographies of scientists including their dates, memberships, important discoveries, and references to additional information.

Wills, Christopher. *Yellow Fever, Black Goddess: The Coevolution of People*

and Plagues. Reading, MA: Addison-Wesley, 1996. 336 p. $13.00 (paper). ISBN
0201328186 (paper).   Microorganisms that cause human suffering.

Woese, Carl R. "Prokaryote Systematics: The Evolution of a Science." In *The
Prokaryotes*, 2nd ed. p. 3–18. New York: Springer-Verlag, 1992.   A history of
bacterial systematics.

METHODS AND TECHNIQUES

Techniques useful for microbiology may be found, also, in the "Handbooks"
section, or in the biochemistry, genetics, and molecular biology chapters. (Chapters 5, 6, and 7).

Adenovirus Methods and Protocols. William S. M. Wold, ed. Totowa, NJ: Humana Press, 1998. (Methods in Molecular Medicine v. 21). 52 p. $99.50.ISBN
0896035514.   Adenovirus is a premier tool and model for studying molecular
biology. This book is designed to help new researchers conduct studies, and assist
established researchers to branch into new lines of work. The book includes
proven adenovirus research protocols from experts, site-directed methods to ge-
netically manipulate different portions of the adenovirus genome, step-by-step
methods for constricting adenovirus vectors, and methods to study and measure
apoptosis induced by immune cells and intrinsic cellular mechanisms.

Bacteriological Analytical Manual. 8th ed. Division of Microbiology, Center for
Food Safety and Applied Nutrition, U.S. Food and Drug Administration. Gaith-
ersburg, MD: Association of Official Analytical Chemists International, 1998.
$139.00 ISBN 0935584595 (ring bound). The eighth edition of the *Manual* re-
ports methods used by the Food and Drug field laboratories effective for microorganisms in foods. The manual is loose-leaf so that it can be updated easily between editions. It is also available in computer laser disc plus the booklet
Foodborne Pathogenic Microorganisms and Natural Toxins Handbook, commonly known as *The Bad Book*, at http://vm.cfsan.fda.gov/mow/intro.html. The
Handbook provides basic facts regarding foodborne pathogenic microorganisms
and natural toxins. It brings together in one place information from the Food and
Drug Administration, the Centers for Disease Control and Prevention, the USDA
Food Safety Inspection Service, and the National Institutes of Health. At the end
of selected chapters there are hypertext links to relevant Entrez abstracts and
GenBank genetic loci (see annotations in Chapter 7, "Genetics, Biotechnology,
and Develomental Biology").

Bacterial Toxins: Methods and Protocols. Otto Holst, ed. Totowa, NJ: Humana
Press, 2000. (Methods in Molecular Biology, 145). 380 p. $89.50. ISBN
0896036049.   An international group of authorities provide a collection of
readily reproducible methods designed to help researchers interested in bacterial

toxin investigations. Step-by-step instructions are included for purification and detection protocols, methods of conformational analysis, and use of phage antibody libraries.

Bryant, Neville J. *Laboratory Immunology & Serology*. 3rd ed. Philadelphia, PA: Saunders, 1992. 387 p. $51.00. ISBN 0721642128.   Example of a useful bench manual that successfully introduces the student to techniques for diagnostic immunology. For an award-winning textbook in clinical laboratory immunology, see Turgeon, in the Textbooks and Treatises section.

Chemical Methods in Prokaryotic Systematics. Michael Goodfellow and Anthony G. O'Donnell, eds. New York: Wiley, 1994. (Modern Microbiological Methods). 576 p. $319.00. ISBN 0471941913.   Written by leading specialists, this laboratory manual offers comprehensive and up-to-date, reliable techniques for the classification and identification of prokaryotes, both archaea and bacteria. Protocols, difficulties, limitations, and interpretations are discussed.

Clinical Virology Manual, 3rd ed. Steven C. Specter et al., eds. Washington, DC: American Society for Microbiology, 2000. 800 p. $124.95. ISBN 1555811736.   This comprehensive manual is a source of basic and clinical information regarding viruses and viral diseases and a reference source for laboratories to aid in the diagnosis of virus infection. It provides detailed information on individual techniques.

Collins and Lyne's Microbiological Methods. 7th ed. C. H. Collins et al., eds. Boston, MA: Butterworth-Heinemann Medical, 1995. ISBN 0750606533.   Standard guide to bacteriological and microbiological methods and techniques.

Cowan and Steel's Manual for the Identification of Medical Bacteria. 3rd ed. G. I Barrow and R. K. A. Feltham, eds. New York: Cambridge University Press, 1993. 331 p. $90.00. ISBN 0521326117.   Essential for the clinical microbiology laboratory for the rarely encountered or unusual organism.

Current Protocols in Immunology. John E. Coligan, ed. New York: Wiley Interscience, 1991– . 3 v. $695.00 (looseleaf), $635.00 (CD-ROM). ISBN 0471522767, 0471306606 (CD-ROM).   Indispensable to immunology research labs. Core manual published in three volumes with quarterly updates; can be renewed annually.

Diagnostic Molecular Microbiology; Principles and Applications. David H. Persing et al., eds. Herndon, VA: American Society for Microbiology Press, 1993. 660 p. $79.95. ISBN 155581056X.   Covers both principles and applications of molecular diagnostic methods pertaining to infectious diseases. Provides theoretical and practical framework for understanding the powerful uses of nucleic acid amplification technologies for the rapid detection and characterization of bacterial, viral, fungal, and parasitic pathogens in the clinical laboratory. Part I summarizes the basic scientific theory underlying molecular diagnostics. Part II provides 66 protocols, or molecular recipes, from leading labs around the world. The supplement provides a technological update for clinical microbiologists with practical and current applications; reviews application of methods for microbial identification; and presents 12 PCR protocols for detection and characterization of emerging pathogens.

Diagnostic Virology Protocols. John R. Stephenson and Alan Warnes, eds. Totowa, NJ: Humana Press, 1998. (Methods in Molelcular Medicine, v. 12). 370 p. $89.50 (spiral bound). ISBN 0896034011 (spiral bound). Experts present cutting-edge techniques for detecting many of the major viruses that cause human disease. Major features of the volume: human viral diseases, review of technologies and instrumentation, tested molecular techniques, step-by-step instructions, and hints for easy reproducibility.

Enzyme and Microbial Technology. v. 1– , 1979– . New York: Elsevier Science. Irregular. $1,832.00. ISSN 0141-0229. An international biotechnology journal relevant to basic and applied aspects of the use of enzymes and microorganisms. Contributions may be in the form of research papers, rapid communications, or reviews. Patent reports are a regular section for each issue.

Flow Cytometry: A Practical Approach. 2nd ed. M. G. Ormerod, ed. New York: Oxford University Press, 1994. 282 p. $55.00 (paper). ISBN 0199634610 (paper). This laboratory handbook provides an introduction and guide to those new to the field. It also serves as a reference for new applications.

Handbook of Methods in Aquatic Microbial Ecology. Paul F. Kemp et al., eds. Boca Raton, FL: Lewis, 1993. 777 p. $169.95. ISBN 0873715640. Eighty-six chapters and 95 authors provide a compilation of 85 fundamental methods for modern aquatic microbial ecology.

Harlow, Edward and David Lane. *Using Antibodies: A Laboratory Manual: Portable Protocol No. 1.* Cold Spring Harbor, NY: Cold Spring Harbor Laboratory Press, 1998. 512 p. $130.00 (spiral bound). ISBN 0879695447. Although there are introductory chapters summarizing the immune response, the functions of antibodies, and their mechanisms of action, most of the book presents protocols for raising, purifying, and labeling monoclonal and polyclonal antibodies. Techniques to use antibodies to study antigens, tagging proteins, epitope mapping, and instructions for shortened procedures for major methods arc also included.

Hoppert, Michael and Andreas Holzenburg. *Electron Microscopy in Microbiology.* New York: Springer-Verlag, 1998. (Microscopy Handbooks, no. 43). 112 p. $34.95 (paper). ISBN 0387915648 (paper). This is a practical guide for people with little or no experience with electron microscopy preparation techniques.

The authors provide concise descriptions of protocols including procedures for the structural characteristics of whole microorganisms and their subcellular and macromolecular components. The contents cover a wide range of topics from the traditional (rapid freezing methods) to recent developments (*in situ* localization).

Immunoassays: A Practical Approach. James P. Gosling, ed. New York: Oxford University Press, 2000. (The Practical Approach Series, 228). 304 p. $55.00 (paper). ISBN 0199637105 (paper).   Practical manual designed to aid in developing an immunoassay; includes step-by-step protocols.

Immunochemical Protocols. John D. Pound, ed. Totowa, NJ: Humana, 1998. (Methods in Molecular Biology, v. 80). 508 p. $89.50. ISBN 0896034933.   This is an excellent, user-friendly, up-to-date handbook of reliable immunochemical techniques for use by molecular biologists. The book covers the breadth of relevant established methods including the latest refinements, trouble-shooting tips, and time-saving techniques.

Immunocytochemical Methods and Protocols, 2nd ed. Lorette C. Javois, ed. Totowa, NJ: Humana Press, 1999. 465 p. $89.50 (spiral bound). ISBN 0896035700 (spiral bound).   This collection of 52 immunocytochemical method instructions presents valuable protocols for preparing antibodies for staining procedures, light microscopic analysis, electron microscopy, fluorescence-activated cell-sorter analyses, and confocal microscopy.

Immunology Methods Manual: The Comprehensive Sourcebook of Techniques. Ivan Lefkovits, ed. San Diego, CA: Academic Press, 1996. 4 v. $174.00 (paper), $169.95 (CD-ROM). ISBN 0124427103 (paper), 0124427154 (CD-ROM). This comprehensive lab reference of interest to immunologists provides methods and techniques from 369 international contributors.

Koneman, Elmer W, Stephen D. Allen, and William M. Janda. *Color Atlas and Textbook of Diagnostic Microbiology.* 5th ed. Baltimore, MD: Lippincott Williams and Wilkins, 1997. 1,395 p. $71.95. ISBN 0397515294.   This is an excellent diagnostic guide for students or researchers involved in clinical microbiology and the standard in the field for laboratory personnel and educators. It provides a solid overview of microbiology including taxonomy, classification, identification, and the role of microbes in disease. There are charts outlining theory, procedures, and interpretations of tests as well as easy access to information on signs and symptoms of disease.

Johnson, Ted R. and Christine L. Case. *Laboratory Experiments in Microbiology.* 6th ed. Redwood City, CA: Benjamin/Cummings, 2000. 418 p. $52.00 (paper). ISBN 0805375899 (paper).   Laboratory manual for beginning students; companion to Tortora, 6th ed.

Journal of Immunological Methods. v. 1– , 1971/72– . Amsterdam: Elsevier. Monthly. $3,909.00. ISSN 0022-1759. Available electronically. Covers techniques, and articles on novel methods for all aspects of immunology.

Journal of Microbiological Methods. v. 1– , 1983– . Amsterdam: Elsevier Science. Monthly. $1,530.00. ISSN 0167-7012. Available electronically. Original articles, short communications, and review articles on novel methods, or significant improvements to an existing method, in all aspects of microbiology excluding virology.

Journal of Virological Methods, v. 1– , 1980– . Amsterdam: Elsevier. Monthly. $2,777.00 ISSN 0166-0934. Available electronically. Publishes original papers and invited reviews covering techniques on all aspects of virology.

MacFaddin, Jean F. *Biochemical Tests for Identification of Medical Bacteria.* 3rd ed. Baltimore, MD: Lippincott Williams and Wilkins, 2000. 912 p. $56.00 (spiral bound). ISBN 0683053183 (spiral bound). This instructional manual presents biochemical tests for identifying bacteria in the laboratory and includes new nomenclature resulting from the significant advancements since the last (1980) edition.

Maloy, Stanley R. *Experimental Techniques in Bacterial Genetics.* Boston, MA: Jones and Bartlett, 1990. (Jones and Bartlett Series in Biology). 180 p. $42.95. ISBN 0867201185. Designed for a beginning university course in bacterial genetics, this manual provides practical information for the novice.

Manual of Clinical Microbiology. 7th ed. Patrick R. Murray and Ellen Jo Baron, eds. Washington, DC: American Society for Microbiology, 1999. 1,773 p. $129.95. ISBN 1555811264. This reference work is aimed at clinical microbiologists, pathologists, clinicians, and students concerned with the clinical lab, and control and prevention of infection. Diagnostic techniques for clinical microbiology, bacteriology, virology, mycology, parasitology, antimicrobial agents, reagents, stains, and media are included.

Manual of Immunological Methods (Pharmacology and Toxicology). P. Rousseau et al., eds. Boca Raton, FL: CRC Press, 1998. 152p. $64.95. ISBN 084938558X. This book is a collaboration of the Canadian Network of Toxicology centers, a nonprofit network of university-based scientists. The manual provides detailed immunological methods and tools for complying with good laboratory practice, including sample collection, preparation of cells, assay conditions, and data evaluation.

Methods in Enzymology. See Chapter 6, ''Molecular and Cellular Biology,'' for full annotation.

Methods for General and Molecular Bacteriology, 2nd ed. Philip Gerhardt, ed.

Washington, DC: American Society for Microbiology, 1994. 803 p. $89.95. ISBN 1555810489. Revision of *Manual of Methods for General Bacteriology* (1981), retitled to reflect the impact that molecular biology has had on bacteriology. As in the earlier edition, it complements the systematics treatise *Bergey's Manual of Systematic Bacteriology*. It presents reliable, basic methods for practicing general bacteriology in the laboratory. It covers all kinds of bacteria, archaeobacteria as well as eubacteria, complementing general textbooks and systematics treatises. Nine new chapters cover molecular biology as well as antigen-antibody reactions, photography, and records and reports. A classic from the American Society for Microbiology.

Methods in Microbiology., v. 1– , 1969– . San Diego, CA: Academic Press. Irregular. Price varies. ISSN 0580-9517. Reviews devoted to a single topic in each volume. Recent volumes include *Automation* and *Genetic Methods for Diverse Prokaryotes*.

Molecular Bacteriology: Protocols and Clinical Applications. Neil Woodford and Alan Johnson, eds. Totowa, NY: Humana Press, 1998. (Methods in molecular medicine, v. 15). 682 p. $99.50. ISBN 0896034984. State-of-the art collection of detailed molecular methods for the diagnosis and clinical investigation of bacterial infections. Notes at the end of most chapters provide practical advice and tricks of the trade from specialists.

Molecular Microbial Ecology Manual. Antoon D. L. Akkermans, ed. Dordrecht, Netherlands: Kluwer Academic, 1996. $130.00. ISBN 0792339436. This lab manual introduces microbial ecologists to a number of current molecular techniques for detecting and identifying microbes at DNA and RNA levels in the natural environment.

Mycobacteria Protocols. Tanya Parish and Neil G. Stoker, eds. Totowa, NJ: Humana Press, 1998. (Methods in molecular biology, v. 101). 472 p. $89.50. ISBN 0896034712. The contributors present state-of-the-art molecular biology techniques for studying the mycobacteria. Methods included are basic culture techniques, fractionation, nucleic acid isolation, the use of reporter genes, the expression of foreign genes, mutagenesis, genome analysis, speciation, and information on using the Integrated Mycobacterial Database on the Web at http://www.pasteur.fr/recherche/banques/mycdb/.

Mycoplasma Protocols. Roger Miles and Robin A. J. Nicholas, eds. Totowa, NJ: Humana Press, 1998. (Methods in molecular biology, v. 104). 330 p. $89.50. ISBN 0896035255. This lab manual provides methods for the detection, isolation, identification, and characterization of mycoplasmas, utilizing biochemical, genetic, and molecular techniques.

Nucleic Acid Techniques in Bacterial Systematics. Erko Stackebrandt and Michael Goodfellow, eds. New York: Wiley, 1991. (Modern Microbiological Methods). 329 p. $360.00. ISBN 0471929069.   Comprehensive laboratory manual of revolutionary nucleic acid - based techniques for characterizing, classifying, and identifying bacteria.

PCR Protocols for Emerging Infectious Diseases, A Supplement to Diagnostic Molecular Microbiology: Principles and Applications. Washington, DC: ASM, 1996. 180 p. $39.95. ISBN 1555811086 (spiral bound).   The manual will "provide all the theoretical and practical information needed to operate a state-of-the-art facility for doing molecular diagnosis of infectious diseases." Supplement *to Diagnostic Molecular Microbiology.*

Plasmids; A Practical Approach. 2nd ed. Kimber G. Hardy, ed. Oxford, England: IRL Press, 1993. (Practical Approach Series no. 138). 272 p. $50.00. ISBN 0199634459.   Provides protocols for studying bacterial plasmids, and for using both plasmids and phagemids as vectors. Techniques are included, as well as methods for using plasmid vectors in important groups of bacteria.

TEXTBOOKS AND TREATISES

Abbas, Abul K., Andrew H. Lichtman, and Jordan S. Pober. *Cellular and Molecular Immunology.* 4th ed. Philadelphia, PA: Saunders, 2000. 553 p. $47.00 (paper). ISBN 0721682332 (paper).   An excellent up-to-date text for understanding modern immunology.

Alcamo, I. Edward. *Fundamentals of Microbiology.* 6th ed. Sudbury, MA: Jones and Bartlett, 2001. 1 v. $84.95. ISBN 0763710679.   An introductory textbook.

Atlas, Ronald M. and Richard Bartha. *Microbial Ecology: Fundamentals and Applications.* 4th ed. Menlo Park, CA: Benjamin/Cummings, 1998. 306 p. $85.00 (paper). ISBN 0805306552 (paper).   Comprehensive text.

Bacterial Stress Responses. Gisela Storz and Regine Hengge-Aronis, eds. Washington, DC: American Society for Microbiology, 2000. 485 p. $109.95. ISBN 1555811922.   A summary of current research on bacterial stress responses.

Bacteria as Multicellular Organisms. James A. Shapiro and Martin Dworkin, eds. New York: Oxford University Press, 1997. $100.00.   ISBN 0195091590.

Biofilms II: Analysis, Process and Applications. James D. Bryers, ed. New York: John Wiley, 2000. 496 p. $139.95. ISBN 0471296562.   Biofilms are collections of microorganisms that have numerous positive applications for the modern biotechnology and waste and water treatment industry.

Biology of the Prokaryotes. Joseph W. Lengeler, G. Drews, and Hans G. Schlegel, eds. Oxford, England: Blackwell Science, 1999. $89.95. ISBN 0632053577. Also, see *The Prokaryotes* in the Handbooks section.

Birge, Edward A. *Bacterial and Bacteriophage Genetics.* 4th ed. New York: Springer-Verlag, 2000. 554 p. $69.95. ISBN 0387987304. For students of microbiology, bacteriology, and genetics.

Brock's Biology of Microorganisms. 9th ed. Michael T. Madigan, John M. Martinko, and Jack Parker, eds. See the Handbooks section for full annotation.

Cann, Alan J. *Principles of Molecular Virology.* 2nd ed. San Diego, CA: Academic Press, 1997. 310 p. $32.00. ISBN 0121585328. A general text suitable for undergraduates.

The Clostridia: Molecular Biology and Pathogenesis. Julian I. Rood, et al., eds. San Diego, CA: Academic Press, 1997. 533 p. $151.00. ISBN 0125950209. State-of-the-art research for students and researchers.

Collier, L. H., John Oxford and Jim Pipkin. *Human Virology: A Text for Students of Medicine, Dentistry and Microbiology.* New York: Oxford University Press, 2000. 284 p. $38.50 (paper). ISBN 0192628208 (paper). Text on the basics.

Comprehensive Virology. Heinz Fraenkel-Conrat and Robert R. Wagner, eds. New York: Plenum, 1974–1984. 19 v. A classic compendium of information on the viruses. Volume 1 is a catalogue of viruses, while other volumes cover reproduction, structure, genetics, virus-host interactions, viral cytopathology, and other topics.

DNA Replication in Eukaryotic Cells. Melvin L. DePamphilis, ed. Cold Spring Harbor, NY: Cold Spring Harbor Lab Press, 1996. (Cold Spring Harbor Monograph Series, v. 31). 1,058 p. $125.00. ISBN 0879694599; ISSN 0270-1847. Current survey of the concepts aimed at teachers, scientists from allied fields, and others involved with biological problems of eukaryotes.

Environmental Microbiology. Raina M. Maier, Ian L. Pepper, and Charles P. Gerba, eds. San Diego, CA: Academic Press, 2000. 608 p. $99.95. ISBN 0124975704.

Escherichia coli: Mechanisms of Virulence. Max Sussman, ed. New York: Cambridge University Press, 1997. 639p. $100.00. ISBN 0521453615. Description of the variety of diseases caused by *E. coli*.

Extremophiles in Deep-Sea Environments. Koki Horikoshi and Kaoru Tsujii, eds. New York: Springer-Verlag, 1999. 322 p. $139.00. ISBN 4431702636.

Extremophiles: Microbial Life in Extreme Environments. Koki Harikoshi and William D. Grant, eds. New York: Wiley-Liss, 1998. (Wiley Series in Ecological and Applied Microbiology). 322 p. $150.00. ISBN 0471026182. Overview of the current state of knowledge about microorganisms that live in extreme environments.

Field's Virology. 3rd ed. B. N. Fields et al., eds. Baltimore, MD: Lippincott Williams & Wilkins, 1996. 2 v. $339.00 ISBN 0781702534. Comprehensive, encyclopedic text.

Fundamental Immunology, 4th ed. William E. Paul, ed. Philadelphia, PA: Lippincott-Raven, 1999. 1,589 p. $145.00. ISBN 0781714125, 0781716896 (CD-ROM). Standard text and reference in immunology.

Genetics of Bacterial Polysaccharides. Johanna B. Goldberg, ed. Boca Raton, FL: CRC Press, 1999. 400 p. $129.95. ISBN 0849300215.

HIV and the New Viruses. Angus G. Dalgleish and Robin A. Weiss, eds. San Diego, CA: Academic Press, 1999. 576 p. $125.00. ISBN 0122007417. Review of persistent human virus infections with emphasis on epidemiology, pathogenicity, molecular virology, host responses, and management of conditions.

Howland, John L. *The Surprising Archaea: Discovering Another Domain of Life.* New York: Oxford University Press, 2000. 204 p. $29.95. ISBN 0195111834. Records the rise of the *Archaea* from obscurity to their current prominent place in molecular and evolutionary biology.

Lactic Acid Bacteria: Genetics, Metabolism and Applications. Proceedings of the 6th Symposium on Lactic Acid Bacteria: Genetics, Metabolism and Applications, 19–23, September, 1999, Veldhoven, The Netherlands. W. N. Konings, O. P. Kuipers, and J. H. J. Huis, eds. Dordrecht, Netherlands: Kluwer, 1999. 411 p. $201.50. ISBN 0792359534. This volume presents the first report of the complete genome of a lactic acid bacterium, including additional research and applications. Reprinted from *Antonie van Leeuwenhoek*, v. 76 (1–4), 1999.

Molecular Genetics of Mycobacteria. Graham F. Hatfull and Willam R. Jacobs, Jr. eds. Washington, DC: American Society for Microbiology, 2000. 363 p. $99.95. ISBN 1555811914. Reviews all aspects of mycobacterial genetics.

Needham, Cynthia, et al. *Intimate Strangers: Unseen Life on Earth.* Washington, DC: ASM Press, 2000. 191 p. $39.95. ISBN 1555811639.. A lavishly illustrated guide to the microscopic life on earth. The book is based on the PBS television series "Intimate Strangers: Unseen Life on Earth" and provides an excellent overview of microbiology for the general public.

Playfair, J. H. L. and B. M. Chain. *Immunology at a Glance.* 7th ed. Oxford, England: Blackwell Science, 2000. $19.95. ISBN 0632054069. Widely praised quick reference, complete with an illustrative overview of the immunological process.

Postgate, John. *Microbes and Man*, 4th ed. New York: Cambridge University Press, 2000. 373 p. $19.95. ISBN 0521665795. An excellent book discussing the impact of microorganisms, especially bacteria, on humans and the environment.

Priest, F. and B. Austin. *Modern Bacterial Taxonomy*, 2nd ed. London: Chapman & Hall, 1994. 240 p. $65.95 (paper). ISBN 041246120X (paper). This text covers molecular systematics, the construction of phylogenetic trees, typing of bacteria, DNA probes, and the use of the polymerase chain reaction in bacterial systematics.

Principles of Virology: Molecular Biology, Pathogenesis, and Control. S. J. Flint et al., eds. Washington, DC: American Society for Microbiology, 1999. 804 p. $89.95. ISBN 1555811272. Introductory text on the study of animal viruses. See *Field's Virology*, previous, for the best all-inclusive review of specific virus families.

Prokaryotic Development. Yves Brun and Lawrence J. Shimkets, eds. Washington, DC: American Society for Microbiology, 2000. 475 p. $89.95. ISBN 1555811582. Focuses on molecular analysis; aimed at undergraduate and graduate students.

The Ribosome: Structure, Function, Antibiotics, and Cellular Interactions. Roger Garrett et al., eds. Washington, DC: American Society for Microbiology, 2000. 565 p. $125.95. ISBN 1555811841. Summarizes the major advances that have occurred over the past five years in the study of ribosome and protein synthesis.

Schlegel, Hans G. *General Microbiology*, 7th ed. New York: Cambridge University Press, 1993. 655 p. $49.95 (paper). ISBN 0521439809 (paper). Established text with strength in providing a comprehensive description of the physiology and biochemistry of microorganisms.

Sagan, Dorion and Lynn Margulis. *Garden of Microbial Delights: A Practical Guide to the Subvisible World*. Dubuque, IA: Kendall/Hunt, 1995. 232 p. $48.95. ISBN 0840385293. A very readable exploration of the microbial world using drawings and photographs.

Salyers, Abigail A. *Bacterial Pathogenesis: A Molecular Approach*, 2nd ed. Washington, DC: ASM, 2001. 1 v. $44.95 (paper). ISBN 155581171X (paper). This successful text, with its second edition forthcoming in 2000, discusses the application of molecular techniques to the study of bacteria-host interaction, and the molecular basis of infectious diseases.

Singleton, Paul. *Bacteria in Biology, Biotechnology and Medicine*. 5th ed. New York: John Wiley, 1999. 489 p. $44.95 (paper). ISBN 0471988804 (paper). Text for university courses in biotechnology, food science, general biology, and microbiology.

Snyder, Larry and Wendy Champness. *Molecular Genetics of Bacteria*. Washington, DC: ASM Press, 1997. 504 p. $79.95. ISBN 1555811027.   Emphasizes the genetics of *E. coli*, but also includes other organisms. Covers chromosome structure, gene expression, genes and genetic elements, genes in action, genetic analysis, and applications. Each chapter includes problems and suggested readings.

Sompayrac, Lauren M. *How the Immune System Works*. Oxford, England: Blackwell Science, 1999. 111 p. $21.95 (paper). ISBN 0632044136 (paper).

Streptococci and the Host. Thea Horaud, Anne Bouvet and Roland Leclercq, eds. (Advances in Experimental Medicine and Biology, v. 418). New York: Plenum, 1997. 1,064 p. $257.50. ISBN 0306456036.   Proceedings of the September, 1996, 13th Lancefield International Symposium on Streptococci and Streptococcal Diseases.

Turgeon, Mary Louise. *Immunology and Serology in Laboratory Medicine*. 2nd ed. St. Louis, MO: Mosby Year Book, 1996. 496p. $48.00. ISBN 0815187874. This text was awarded the American Medical Writers Excellence in Medical Communication Award in 1997.

Virulence Mechanisms of Bacterial Pathogens. 3rd ed. Kim A. Brogden, James A. Roth, and Thaddeus B. Stanton, eds. Washington, DC: American Society for Microbiology, 2000. 294 p. $84.95. ISBN 1555811744.   This best-selling book provides an overview of the variety of mechanisms used by bacterial pathogens in establishing infection, producing disease, and persisting in the host.

The Viruses. 1982–   . Dordrecht, Netherlands: Kluwer. Irregular. Price varies. "This series is designed to provide a comprehensive review of significant current areas of research in virology. Individual volumes or groups of volumes deal with a single virus family or group and cover all aspects of these viruses ranging from physiochemistry to pathogenicity and ecology." Subseries include *The Retroviridae*, *The Plant Viruses*, *The Herpesviruses*, and others.

Wagner, Edward K. and Martin Hewlett. *Basic Virology*. Oxford, England: Blackwell Science, 1999. 320 p. $54.95. ISBN 0632042990.

White, David. *The Physiology and Biochemistry of Prokaryotes*. 2nd ed. New York: Oxford University Press, 1999. 565 p. $62.95. ISBN 0195125797.   Useful as a course supplement at the undergraduate level.

PERIODICALS

Applied and Environmental Microbiology. v. 1– , 1953– . Birmingham, AL: American Society for Microbiology. Monthly. $863.52. ISSN 0099-2240. Available electronically. Significant current research in industrial microbiology and biotechnology, food microbiology, and microbial ecology.

Archives of Microbiology, v. 1– , 1939– . Berlin: Springer-Verlag. Monthly. $2,539.00. ISSN 0302-8933. Available electronically. Covers basic results on molecular aspects of structure, function, cellular organization and ecophysiological behavior of prokaryotic and eukaryotic microorganisms. Papers should be submitted in English. Formerly: *Archiv fuer Mikrobiologie.*

Cellular Immunology. v. 1– , 1970– . San Diego, CA: Academic Press. Monthly. $2.695.00. ISSN 0008-8749. Available electronically. Original investigations on immunological activities of cells in experimental or clinical situations for *in vivo* and/or *in vitro* studies.

European Journal of Immunology. v. 1– , 1971– . Weinheim, Germany: VCH. Monthly. $1,018.00. ISSN 0014-2980. Available electronically. Associated with the European Federation of Immunological Societies. Publishes papers on various aspects of immunological research from the fields of experimental and human immunology, molecular immunology, immunobiology, immunopathology, immunogenetics, and clinical immunology.

FEMS Immunology and Medical Microbiology. v. 6– , 1993– . Amsterdam: Elsevier. $1,037.00. Monthly. ISSN 0928-8244. Available electronically. Publishes articles and mini-reviews dealing with viruses, bacteria, fungi and protozoa in both human and veterinary medicine. The areas of immunology and medical microbiology, especially the cross-talk between the two, fall within the broad scope of the journal.

FEMS Microbiology Ecology. v. 1– , 1985– . Amsterdam: Elsevier. Monthly. $1,037.00. ISSN 0168-6496. Available electronically. Published on behalf of the Federation of European Microbiological Societies (FEMS). Original articles on fundamental aspects of the ecology of microorganisms in natural soil, air, or aquatic environments, or in artificial or managed environments.

FEMS Microbiology Letters. v. 1– , 1977– . Amsterdam: Elsevier. Bimonthly. $3,599.00. ISSN 0378-1097. Available electronically. Publishes concise papers that are of urgent interest because of their originality and topicality. Areas of special interest include molecular biology and genetics; microbial biochemistry and physiology; structure and development; pathogenicity, medical, and veterinary microbiology; plant microbial interactions; applied microbiology and microbial biotechnology; and systematics.

Immunity. v. 1– , 1994– . Cambridge, MA: Cell Press. Monthly. $535.00. ISSN 1074-7613. Available electronically. Publishes reports of novel results, of unusual significance, in any area of immunology and allied fields.

Immunobiology, v. 156– , 1979- . New York: Fischer. Semiquarterly. $845.59. ISSN 0171-2985. Publishes papers in clinical immunology, immuno-chemistry, tumor and immunopathology, leucocyte physiology, viral and bacte-rial immunology, cell-mediated immunity, and immunogenetics and transplanta-tion. Continues *Zeitschrift für Immunitätsforschung,* founded in 1909 by Paul Ehrlich.

Immunogenetics. v. 1– , 1974– . Berlin: Springer-Verlag. Monthly. $1,579.00. ISSN 0093-7711. Available electronically. Publishes articles, brief communications, and reviews in the following areas: immunogenetics of cell in-teraction; immunogenetics of tissue differentiation and development; phylogeny of alloantigens and of immune response; genetic control of immune response and disease susceptibility; and genetics and biochemistry of alloantigens.

Immunology. v. 1– , 1958– . Oxford, England: Blackwell Scientific. Monthly. $889.00. ISSN 0019-2805. Available electronically. Official journal of the Brit-ish Society for Immunology. Original work in all areas of immunology including cellular immunology, immunochemistry, immunogenetics, allergy, transplanta-tion immunology, cancer immunology, and clinical immunology. Review articles are published occasionally.

Immunology and Cell Biology. v. 65– , 1987– . Carlton, Australia: Blackwell. Bimonthly. $445.00. ISSN 0818-9641. Available electronically. Official Jour-nal of the Australian Society for Immunology. This journal accepts full papers and brief communications describing original research, methods, or concepts in the broad fields of immunology and cell biology. Theoretical papers are encour-aged.

Infection and Immunity. v. 1– , 1970– . Birmingham, AL: American Society for Microbiology. Monthly. $575.00. ISSN 0019-9567. Available electronical-ly. Articles of interest to microbiologists, immunologists, epidemiologists, pa-thologists, and clinicians.

International Immunology. v. 1– , 1989– . Oxford, England: Oxford Univer-sity Press. Monthly. $876.95. ISSN 0953-8178. Available electronically. Ac-cepts a broad range of experimental and theoretical studies in molecular and cell immunology conducted in labs throughout the world.

International Journal of Systematic and Evolutionary Microbiology. See the Classification, Nomenclature, and Systematics section for full annotation.

Journal of Bacteriology, v. 1– , 1916- . Birmingham, AL: American Society for Microbiology. Semimonthly. $1,374.52. ISSN 0021-9193. Available electronically. Articles include new information on genetics and molecular biology, structure and function, plant microbiology, plasmids and transposons, eukaryotic cells, cell surfaces, physiology and metabolism, enzymes and proteins, and bacteriophages. Each issue also contains a mini-review on a selected topic.

Journal of General Virology, v. 1– , 1967– . Reading, UK: Society for General Microbiology. Monthly. $995.00. ISSN 0022-1317. Available electronically. Publishes papers describing original, fundamental research in virology. Full-length papers, short communications, and review articles are included.

Journal of Immunology. v. 1– , 1916. Baltimore, MD: American Association of Immunologists. Bimonthly. $470.00. ISSN 0022-1767. Available electronically. Official journal of the American Association of Immunologists. Publishes original articles on immunochemistry, transplantation and tumor immunology, molecular biology, molecular genetics, cellular immunology, clinical immunology, immunopathology, and microbial and viral immunology.

Journal of Virology, v. 1– , 1967– . Birmingham, AL: American Society for Microbiology. Monthly. $771.00. ISSN 0022-538X. Available electronically. This journal deals with broad-based concepts concerning viruses of plants, animals, bacteria, protozoa, fungi, and yeasts.

Microbial Ecology; An International Journal. v. 1– , 1974– . New York: Springer-Verlag. Bimonthly. $629.00. ISSN 0095-3628. Available electronically. Features articles of original research and mini-review articles on those areas of ecology involving microorganisms, including prokaryotes, eukaryotes, and viruses.

Microbiology. v. 140– , 1994– . Reading, UK: Society for General Microbiology. Monthly. $995.00. ISSN 1350-0872. Available electronically. Includes quality research papers across the whole spectrum of microbiology. The journal also features short reviews on rapidly expanding or especially significant areas. Formerly: *Journal of General Microbiology*.

Molecular Immunology. v. 16– , 1979– . Oxford, England: Elsevier Science. 18/yr. $2,320.00. ISSN 0161-5890. Available electronically. A leading journal for immunologists, molecular biologists, and molecular geneticists publishing immunological knowledge delineated at the molecular level. It reports research reports, short communications, structural data reports, review articles, as well as summaries of meetings, announcements, and letters to the editor. Supplements accompany some volumes beginning with volume 30, 1993. Formerly: *Immunochemistry*.

Molecular Microbiology, v. 1– , 1987– . Oxford, England: Blackwell Scien-

tific. Biweekly. $2.396.00. ISSN 0950-382X. Available electronically.   One of
the most highly cited primary research journals in microbiology. It publishes
original research articles addressing any microbiological question at a molecular
level. *MicroReviews* and *MicroCorrespondence* are regular sections of the journal. Absorbed *Microbiological Sciences*.

Nature Immunology. v. 1– , 2000– . New York: Nature America. Monthly.
$710.00. ISSN 1529-2916. Available electronically.   This multidisciplinary
journal publishes papers of the highest quality and significance in all areas of
immunology.

Virology, v. 1– , 1955– . San Diego, CA: Academic Press. Semimonthly.
$3,295.00. ISSN 0042-6822. Available electronically.   Publishes basic research
in all branches of virology, including viruses of vertebrates and invertebrates,
plants, bacteria, and yeasts/fungi. In particular, articles on the nature of viruses,
on the molecular biology of virus multiplication, on molecular pathogenesis, and
the molecular aspects of the control and prevention of viral infections are invited.

REVIEWS OF THE LITERATURE

Advances in Immunology. v. 1– , 1961– . San Diego, CA: Academic Press.
Irregular. Price varies. ISSN 0065-2776.   A scholarly review of research and
valuable reference work covering current work in immunology.

Advances in Microbial Ecology, v. 1– , 1977– . New York: Kluwer. Irregular.
Price varies. ISSN 0147-4863.   Up-to-date research on the roles of microorganisms in natural and artificial ecosystems, emphasizing microbial processes and
interactions, the effects of environmental factors on microbial populations, and
the economic impact of these organisms.

Advances in Microbial Physiology, v. 1– , 1967– . San Diego, CA: Academic
Press. Irregular. Price varies. ISSN 0065-2911.   This series aims to include articles from the wide range of "specialized interests that constitute microbial physiology." Author and subject indexes.

Advances in Virus Research. v. 1– , 1953– . San Diego: Academic Press.
Irregular. Price varies. ISSN 0065-3527.   Critical review articles are selected to
cover all types of viruses from many different aspects, focusing on the virus not
the disease.

Annual Review of Immunology. v. 1– , 1983– . Palo Alto, CA: Annual Reviews, Inc. Annual. $128.00. ISSN 0732-0582. Available electronically.   Ana-
lytical articles reviewing significant developments within the discipline.

Annual Review of Microbiology. v. 1– , 1947– . Palo Alto, CA: Annual Reviews, Inc. Annual. $120.00. ISSN 0066-4227. Available electronically. Similar to other Annual Review publications reviewing topics of current and enduring interest in microbiology.

Critical Reviews in Immunology. v. 1– , 1979– . New York: Begell House. Bimonthly. $515.00. ISSN 1040-8401. The journal publishes timely and critical review articles in various aspects of contemporary immunology, opinions/ hypotheses, letters to the editor, news and comments, book reviews, and a calendar of events.

Critical Reviews in Microbiology. v. 1– , 1971– . Boca Raton, FL: CRC Press. Quarterly. $461.00. ISSN 1040-841X. Available electronically. Reviews in all areas of microbiology, including bacteriology, virology, phycology, mycology, and protozoology.

Current Opinion in Immunology, v. 1– , 1988- . Kidlington, UK: Elsevier. Monthly. $884.00. ISSN 0952-7915. Available electronically. Each issue contains an editorial overview, short review articles, paper alert and Web alert sections highlighting interesting new papers or sites, and commentaries. Each issue covers one or more broad topics such as autoimmunity and cancer or autoimmunity and atopic allergy.

Current Opinion in Microbiology. v. 1– , 1998– . Kidlington, UK: Elsevier. Bimonthly. $944.00. ISSN 1369-5274. Available electronically. Similar in format to *Current Opinion in Immunology*.

Current Topics in Microbiology and Immunology, v. 1– , 1914– . Berlin: Springer-Verlag. Irregular. Price varies. ISSN 0070-217X. Each volume presents current knowledge on a particular topic. Volume 235 (1999): *Marburg and Ebola Viruses*, Hans-Dieter Klenk, ed.

FEMS Microbiology Reviews. v. 1– , 1985– . Amsterdam: Elsevier. Quarterly. $401.00. ISSN 0168-6445. Available electronically. Published on behalf of the Federation of European Microbiological Societies (FEMS). Includes comprehensive reviews and current interest mini-reviews of the entire field of microbiology.

Immunological Reviews, v. 1– , 1977– . Copenhagen: Munksgaard. Bimonthly. $520.00. ISSN 0105-2896. Available electronically. Comprehensive and analytical reviews within the fields of clinical and experimental immunology.

Microbiology and Molecular Biology Reviews: MMBR. v. 61– , 1997– . Birmingham, AL: American Society for Microbiology. Quarterly. $320.00. ISSN 1092-2172. Available electronically. One of the most prestigious review journals in the field, this authoritative publication reports fundamental knowledge and new developments in all aspects of the molecular biology of microbes, higher organisms, and viral systems, with emphasis on the cell. Continues *Bacteriological Reviews* and *Microbiological Reviews*.

Seminars in Immunology. v. 1– , 1989– . London: Academic Press. Bimonthly. $346.00. ISSN 1044-5323. Available electronically. A review journal dedicated to keeping scientists informed of developments in the field of immunology on a topic-by-topic basis. Each issue is thematic in approach.

Seminars in Virology. v. 1– , 1990– . San Diego, CA: Academic Press. Bimonthly. $180.00. ISSN 1044-5773. Available electronically. This publication presents authoritative topical reviews edited by internationally acknowledged experts.

Trends in Immunology. v. 22– , 2001– . London: Elsevier Science. Monthly. $969.00. ISSN 1471-4906. Available electronically. Similar in format to *Trends in Microbiology*. Formerly: *Immunology Today*.

Trends in Microbiology. v. 1– , 1993– . London: Elsevier Science. Monthly. $969.00. ISSN 0966-842X. Available electronically. This multidisciplinary journal publishes commentary, correspondence, and review articles discussing all aspects of microbiology, virology, bacteriology, protozoology, and mycology, with the focus on molecular microbiology and virology.

9

Ecology, Evolution, and Animal Behavior

This chapter covers materials for the allied fields of ecology, evolution, and animal behavior. Ecology is "the study of the interrelationships between organisms and their natural environment, both living and nonliving" (*Oxford Dictionary of Biology*, 4th ed., 2000). Conservation biology and environmentalism are closely related, but not extensively covered in this chapter. Evolution is "the gradual process by which the present diversity of plant and animal life arose from the earliest and most primitive organisms." See also Chapter 7, "Genetics, Biotechnology, and Developmental Biology," for related materials. Animal behavior, "the activities that constitute an animal's response to its external environment," here encompasses all biological subdisciplines including ethology, sociobiology, and behavioral ecology. Human behavior and comparative psychology are largely excluded from consideration, and neurobiology is covered in Chapter 11, Anatomy and Physiology.

ABSTRACTS AND INDEXES

Animal Behavior Abstracts. v. 1– , 1972– . Bethesda, MD: Cambridge Scientific Abstracts. Quarterly. $515.00. ISSN 0301-8695. Covers all aspects of animal behavior, including psychological as well as biological studies. Also available as part of the Biological Sciences Collection online and on CD-ROM.

Current Advances in Ecological and Environmental Sciences. v. 1– , 1975– . Tarrytown, NY: Elsevier. Monthly. $1,984.00. ISSN 0955-6648. Covers over 2,000 periodicals of interest to ecologists, arranged by subject. Also has cross-references and author index. Available online as part of CABS. Formerly: *Current Advances in Ecological Sciences*.

Ecological Abstracts. v. 1– , 1974- . Norwich, UK: Elsevier. Monthly.

$1,730.00. ISSN 0305-196X. Covers all aspects of ecology, including aquatic, terrestrial, and applied, in about 3,000 journals, as well as material from books, proceedings, and other sources. Includes annual subject, organism, regional, and author indexes. Available online and on CD-ROM as part of Geobase.

Ecology Abstracts. v. 1– , 1975– . Bethesda, MD: Cambridge Scientific Abstracts. Monthly. $985.00. ISSN 0143-3296. Covers all aspects of ecology. Available online and on CD-ROM as part of the Biological Sciences Collection. Formerly: *Applied Ecology Abstracts.*

Environment Abstracts. v. 1– , 1970– . Bethesda, MD: Congressional Information Service, Inc. Monthly. $1,070. ISSN 0093-3287. Covers 650 journals, plus proceedings, select government and other reports, monographs, newsletters, and other sources in areas including management, technology, biology, and law relating to the environment. Available on magnetic tape, online as ENVIRO-LINE, and on CD-ROM as Environment Abstracts. The majority of the documents indexed in *Environment Abstracts* are available in the full-text *Envirofiche* collection.

Environmental Periodicals Bibliography. v. 1– , 1972– . Santa Barbara, CA: Environmental Studies Institute. Monthly. Price varies. ISSN 0145-3815. Indexes over 400 periodicals in the fields of human ecology, water resources, and others. Available online as Environmental Bibliography.

Pollution Abstracts. v. 1– , 1970– . Bethesda, MD: Cambridge Scientific Abstracts. Monthly. $885.00 (with annual index, $745.00 without). ISSN 0032-3624. Covers both scientific research and government policies. Also available online and on CD-ROM as part of PolTox I (1981 to the present).

ASSOCIATIONS

American Society of Naturalists. c/o Dr. Barbara Bentley, State University of New York, Dept. of Ecology and Evolution, Stony Brook, NY 11794. URL: http://www.amnat.org/. Founded 1883. 700 members. Professional naturalists. Affiliated with the American Association for the Advancement of Science. Sponsors *The American Naturalist.* Web site primarily for membership information; includes online directory. Offers Young Investigator's Prizes, Sewall Wright Award, and E.O. Wilson Naturalist Award.

Animal Behavior Society. c/o Susan A. Foster, 2611 E. 10th. St., Office 170, Bloomington, IN 47408-2603. Phone: (812) 856-5541. Fax: (812) 856-5542. E-mail: aboffice@indiana.edu. URL: www.animalbehavior.org. Founded in 1964. 3,000 members. Professional society for the study of animal behavior. Closely associated with the Division of Animal Behavior of the American Society of Zoologists. Affiliated with the Association for the Study of Animal Behaviour (see following text). Publishes *Graduate Programs in Animal Behavior* and the *Newsletter*, and copublishes *Animal Behaviour*.

Association for the Study of Animal Behaviour (ASAB). ASAB Membership Office, 82A High St., Sawston Cambridge CB2 4HJ, England. URL: http:// www.societies.ncl.ac.uk/asab/. Founded in 1936, 1,000 members. A multinational association for the study of animal behavior. Affiliated with the Animal Behavior Society. Publishes the *Newsletter* and copublishes *Animal Behaviour*. Web site primarily for membership information.

British Ecological Society. 26, Blades Ct., Deodar Rd., Putney, London SW15 2NU, England. E-mail: general@ecology.demon.co.uk. URL: http://www. demon.co.uk/bes. Founded in 1913, 5,000 members. Publishes *Functional Ecology*, *Journal of Animal Ecology*, *Journal of Applied Ecology*, and *Journal of Ecology*. Web site primarily for members, but does include international list of ecological societies.

Ecological Society of America. 1707 H St., NW, Suite 400, Washington, DC 20006. Phone: (202) 833-8773. Fax: (202) 833-8775. E-mail: esahq@esa.org. URL: http://www.sdsc.edu/projects/ESA/esa.htm. Founded in 1915. 7,400 members. The largest ecological association in the United States. Affiliated with the American Institute of Biological Sciences. Publishes the *Bulletin*, *Ecological Applications*, *Ecological Monographs*, and *Ecology*. The latter three journals are available full text from volume 1 on JSTOR. Web site includes educational resources created by the society, links to ecological resources on the Web (mostly other associations), and fact sheets.

International Society of Behavioral Ecology. c/o H.C. Gerhardt, Division of Biological Science, Tucker 215, University of Missouri, Columbia, MO 65211-0001. Founded in 1986 to promote the field of behavioral ecology. Publishes *Behavioral Ecology*.

International Society of Chemical Ecology (ISCE). c/o Dr. Jocelyn Millar, Dept. of Entomology, Univ. of California, Riverside, CA 92521. Phone: (909) 787-5821. Fax: (909) 787-3086. E-mail: jocelyn.miller@ucr.edu. URL: http:// www.isce.ucr.edu/society. Founded in 1983. 750 members. Promotes understanding of the origin, function, and importance of natural chemicals that mediate interactions within and among organisms. Publishes *Journal of Chemical Ecology*.

International Society for the Study of the Origins of Life. c/o Dr. Gerda Horneck, DLR Inst for Aerospace Medicine, Radiation Biology Section, Porz-Wahnheide,

Linder Hohe, D-51147 Köln, Germany. URL: http://www.chemistry.ucsc.edu/
~issol/. For scientists of all disciplines interested in studying the origin of life.
Bestows the A. I. Oparin medal. Publishes *Origins of Life and Evolution of the
Biosphere*, and a membership directory. The Web site primarily provides an online version of the society's newsletter.

Society for the Study of Evolution. Business Office, P.O. Box 1897, Lawrence,
KS 66044-1897. URL: http://lsvl.la.asu.edu/evolution/. Founded in 1946.
3,000 members. Biologists working in the area of organic evolution. Publishes
Evolution and a membership directory. Web site primarily for the journal.

The Wildlife Society. 5410 Grosvenor L., Bethesda, MD 20814-2197. Phone:
(301) 897-9770. Fax: (301) 530-2471. E-mail: tws@wildlife.org. URL: http://
www.wildlife.org/index.html. Founded 1937. 9,600 members. Society for
wildlife biologists and conservationists. Publishes *Journal of Wildlife Management*, *Wildlife Monographs*, *Wildlife Society Bulletin*, and the newsletter *Wild-
lifer*. Also publishes annual *Membership Directory and Certification Registry*.
Web site primarily for membership information.

DICTIONARIES AND ENCYCLOPEDIAS

Allaby, Michael. *Dictionary of the Environment*. 3rd ed. New York: New York
University Press, 1991. 423 p. $80.00. ISBN 081470591X. There are brief
definitions of terms dealing with ecology, the environment, and pollution in this
dictionary. One nice feature is a list of 22 environmental disasters that occurred
since the mid-1950s, such as Chernobyl, the Torrey Canyon oil spill, and Love
Canal.

Ashworth, William. *Encyclopedia of Environmental Studies*. New York: Facts
on File, 1991. 480 p. $65.00. ISBN 0816015317. Intended for environmental
activists and other nonscientists, this encyclopedia has entries on environmental
groups and policy-making entities as well as definitions of terms from geology,
ecology, meteorology, environmental engineering, and other scientific disciplines.

Barrows, Edward M. *Animal Behavior Desk Reference: A Dictionary of Animal
Behavior, Ecology, and Evolution*. 2nd ed. Boca Raton, FL: CRC Press, 2000.
936 p. $129.95. ISBN 0849320054. Terms are grouped by broad concept, with
cross references leading from the alphabetic entry to the concept listing.

Beacham's Guide to Endangered Species of North America. Farmington Hills,
MI: Gale Group, 2000. 6-7 v. $595.00 (set). ISBN 0787650285 (set). Covers
more than 800 endangered species of plants and animals. Entries include descrip-

tion, behavior, habitat, distribution, and threats. Updates *The Official World Wildlife Fund Guide to Endangered Species of North America.*

Beacham's Guide to International Endangered Species. Walton Beacham and Kirk H. Beetz, eds. Osprey, FL: Beacham, 1998–2000. 3 v. $290.00. ISBN 0787651710. Covers species living outside of the United States that are listed as threatened or endangered by the U.S. Fish and Wildlife Service, plus a few species from the IUCN and CITES lists. Volumes 1 and 2 cover 351 species, primarily mammals, while volume 3 includes 297 other animal and plant species. Each species is illustrated by a color photograph and has about three pages worth of information on status, description, natural history, distribution, threats, and conservation efforts. The *Encyclopedia of Endangered Species*, see following text, covers species from the same lists, but lacks color photographs and has briefer entries on each species.

Beaver, Bonnie V. G. *The Veterinarian's Encyclopedia of Animal Behavior.* Ames, IA: Iowa State University Press, 1994. 307 p. $34.95. ISBN 0813821142. Covers behavior of interest to veterinarians such as fear of noise or the establishment of dominance. Useful for anyone interested in domestic animal behavior.

Blackwell's Concise Encyclopedia of Ecology. Peter Calow, ed. Osney Mead, Oxford, England: Blackwell Science, 1999. 152 p. $24.95 (paper). ISBN 0632048727 (paper). About 1,500 entries have been extracted and abridged from *The Encyclopedia of Ecology and Environmental Management* (see following text). Terms include topics in both applied and basic ecology, plus a number of statistical terms and tests. While there is some overlap with the *Concise Oxford Dictionary of Ecology* (see below), each dictionary covers a number of terms that the other lacks.

Cambridge Encyclopedia of Human Evolution. Steve Jones, Robert Martin, and David Pilbeam, eds. New York: Cambridge University Press, 1992. 506 p. $110.00. ISBN 0521323703. The entries in this work are not alphabetical, but are arranged by subject in several broad categories. The emphasis here is as much on nonhuman primate evolution, behavior, language, and ecology as on humans, though there are discussions of early human behavior and ecology and human populations past and present, in addition to the human fossil record and other evolutionary topics. Appendices include a who's who in human evolution, a geological timescale, and a world map of important fossil sites.

Concise Oxford Dictionary of Ecology, 2nd ed. Michael Allaby, ed. New York: Oxford University Press, 1999. 448 p. $15.95 (paper). ISBN 0192800787 (paper). Another of Oxford University Press's excellent concise dictionaries. Covers over 5,000 terms in ecology and conservation, as well as relevant terms from fields such as animal behavior, physiology, climatology, and glaciology. Includes figures and biographical notes on eminent ecologists.

Dictionary of Ecology and the Environment. 3rd ed. Peter H. Collins, ed. Chicago, IL: Fitzroy Dearborn, 1998. 288 p. $45.00, $15.95 (paper). ISBN 1579580750, 1901659615 (paper).   Unlike most scientific dictionaries, this one includes phonetic pronunciations. While most definitions are brief and straightforward, many also include paragraph-long commentaries covering the topic in more detail. There are several appendices, one of which lists recent environmental disasters.

Dictionary of Ecology and Environmental Science. Henry W. Art, ed. New York: Holt, 1993. 632 p. $19.95 (paper). ISBN 0805038485 (paper).   Designed for a wide range of specialized and nonspecialized users. There are over 8,000 entries with brief definitions. A number of appendices are also included, though not listed in a table of contents. They include subjects such as the periodic table of elements, a USDA hardiness zone map, leaf-description terms used to identify plants, and the Beaufort wind scale.

Dictionary of Environmental Science and Technology. 3rd ed. Andrew Porteous, ed. New York: Wiley, 2000. 704 p. $115.00, $29.95 (paper). ISBN 0471633763, 0471634700 (paper).   Written for the general reader to introduce a working knowledge of the scientific and technical language associated with current environmental issues and areas of study. Many of the entries deal with environmental technologies and the effects and causes of toxic chemicals. Although emphasis is on the United Kingdom, it includes information on major international and U.S. organizations as well.

Dictionary of Substances and Their Effects (DOSE), 2nd ed. Sharat Gangolli, ed. Cambridge, England: Royal Society of Chemistry, 1999. 7 v. $2,600.00. 0854048030 (set).   This set provides a guide to the effects of over 5,000 substances, including identifiers (registry numbers, molecular formula, etc.), physical properties, occupational exposure, ecotoxicity, environmental fate, mammalian and avian toxicity, legislation, and comments. There are also references where applicable. Also available on CD-ROM and as an online database. Purchasers of the print second edition also have free access to a searchable Web database at http://www.rsc.org/is/database/dosehome.htm.

Encyclopedia of Animal Behavior. Peter J.B. Slater, ed. New York: Facts on File Publications, 1987. 144 p. $29.95. ISBN 0816018162.   This attractive book, like the other Facts on File encyclopedias listed in the following text, is suitable for undergraduate students or the general public. It consists of discussions of animal behavior, including ethology, the behavior of individual animals, and social behaviors.

Encyclopedia of Biodiversity. Simon A. Levin, ed. San Diego, CA: Academic, 2000. 5 v. $795.00 (set). ISBN 0122268652 (set). Contains 313 articles on a wide range of topics relating to diversity. Broad categories of entries include agriculture, biogeography, extinction, public policies, systematics, and techniques. Each article has a glossary at the beginning of the entry, a bibliography at the end, and cross-references. There are numerous tables and illustrations. A comprehensive and valuable resource.

Encyclopedia of the Biosphere. Ramon Folch i Guillén, Ramon and Josep Maria Camarasa, eds. Detroit, MI: Gale, 1999. 11 v. $1,000.00. ISBN 0787645060 (set). Each volume covers a particular type of ecosystem and discusses environmental factors, plant and animal ecology, and human influences. Published under the auspices of UNESCO's Man and the Biosphere Programme.

The Encyclopedia of Ecology and Environmental Management. Peter Calow, ed. Malden, MA: Blackwell Science, 1998. 805 p. $199.95. ISBN 0865428387. Contains 3,000 entries, most of them brief definitions. Most of the terms covered are ecological, and there are about 250 long encyclopedia-type entries. For both students and professionals.

Encyclopedia of Endangered Species. Detroit, MI: Gale, 1994– . 2 v. (Gale environmental library). $152.00 (v. 1), $152.00 (v. 2). ISBN 081038857X (v. 1), 0810393158 (v. 2). While quite similar to *Beacham's Guide to International Endangered Species* (previous), this guide uses black-and-white photographs to illustrate each species. The descriptions are very similar, though this encyclopedia includes more nonmammalian species. Updates *The Official World Wildlife Fund Guide to Endangered Species*.

Encyclopedia of Environmental Biology. William A. Nierenberg, ed. San Diego, CA: Academic, 1995. 3 v. $695.00 (set). ISBN 012267303 (set). Designed for the use of students and professionals. Articles cover basic research, and topics of interest to the general public and environmental lawyers. Each article has an outline, glossary, cross-references, and a brief bibliography. There are numerous illustrations. The articles emphasize research results or present the range of present practice without advocacy.

Encyclopedia of Environmental Science. David E. Alexander and Rhodes W. Fairbridge, eds. Boston, MA: Kluwer, 1999. (Encyclopedia of Earth Sciences Series). 741 p. ISBN 0412740508. Contains approximately 325 articles by 200 authors. About 25 of the articles are long essays, and the rest are evenly split between short entries of about 500 words and longer entries of about 2,000 words. Topics were selected from the geosciences, ecology, meteorology, and other sciences. According to the preface, it is an update of the *Encyclopedia of Geochemistry and Environmental Sciences*, published in 1972.

Environmental Dictionary and Regulatory Cross Reference. 3rd ed. James J. King, compiler. New York: Wiley, 1995. 977 p. $135.00. ISBN 0471119954. This dictionary covers environmental/regulatory terminology taken from the *Code of Federal Regulations, Title 40, Protection of the Environment* and its updates from the *Federal Register*. There are also acronyms used by the Environmental Protection Agency (EPA) and a cross-reference list of the sections of the *Code* that provided the definitions.

Environmental Encyclopedia. 2nd ed. William P. Cunningham, et al., eds. Detroit, MI: Gale, 1998. 1196 p. $225.00. ISBN 081039314X. Includes biographies, environmental societies, and descriptions of environmental disasters among the entries. There are short bibliographies for further reading in most of the over 1,300 articles and definitions. Written in nontechnical language.

Glossary of Environmental Terms and Acronym List. Environmental Protection Agency, Office of Communications and Public Affairs. Washington, DC: U.S. Environmental Protection Agency, 1989. 29 p. This glossary is designed to help the general public define the most common terms found in EPA documents. There is also an extensive list of acronyms.

Heymer, Armin. *Ethologisches Wörterbuch. Ethological Dictionary. Vocabulaire Éthologique.* Hamburg, Germany: Verlag Paul Parey, 1977. 237 p. ISBN 3489663365. This trilingual German/English/French dictionary has short definitions of ethological terms in order of the German term, followed by the English and French terms and their definitions. There are also English and French indices.

Immelman, Klaus and Colin Beer. *A Dictionary of Ethology.* Cambridge, MA: Harvard University Press, 1989. 336 p. $54.00, $23.50 (paper). ISBN 0674205065, 0674205073 (paper). This is a translation of *Wörterbuch der Verhaltensforschung.* Has mostly paragraph-long definitions of terms used in ethology and animal behavior.

Lincoln, Roger J., Geoffrey Allan Boxshall, and Paul Clark. *A Dictionary of Ecology, Evolution, and Systematics.* 2nd ed. New York: Cambridge University Press, 1998. 361 p. $74.95, $29.95 (paper). ISBN 0521591392, 052143842X (paper). As well as brief definitions of 11,000 terms used in the general area of natural history, this dictionary includes 29 appendices covering a range of topics including the geological time scale, zoogeographic areas, transliterations for the Greek and Russian alphabets, and proof correction marks. Special attention has been given in the second edition to including terms dealing with biodiversity and new techniques in molecular biology.

Milner, Richard. *The Encyclopedia of Evolution: Humanity's Search for its Origins.* New York: Facts on File, 1990. 481 p. ISBN 0816014728. Most of the entries in this encyclopedia relate to either modern evolutionary concepts or the history of evolutionary theory. There are also many entries relating to what might be called Darwinian trivia, such as articles about Jemmy Buttons (a Fuegan Indian taken to England on the *Beagle*) and Darwin's Sandwalk path at his home in Sussex.

Stevenson, L. Harold and Bruce Wyman. *The Facts on File Dictionary of Environmental Science*. New ed. New York: Facts on File, 2000. 236 p. $40.00, $17.95 (paper). ISBN 0816042330, 0816042349 (paper). Covers over 3,000 entries from the environmental sciences, as well as legal and governmental terms. Written for both researchers and nonspecialists.

DIRECTORIES

Also see entries under the Associations section.

Conservation Directory. 1956– . Washington, DC: National Wildlife Federation. Annual. $56.00. ISSN 0069-911X. Lists environmental departments, agencies, and offices for about 3,000 entities, including U.S. government agencies, universities with environmental programs and regional, national, and international conservation organizations. The directory includes lists of informational resources, federally protected areas, and indexes by organization name, subject, staff members, and geographical region.

Naturalists' Directory and Almanac (International). v. 43– , 1980– . Kinderhook, NY: World Natural History Publications. Irregular. $32.50. ISSN 0277-609X. This directory is based on the PIFON (Permanent International File of Naturalists) database and provides the address and subject interests of naturalists who wished to be included in the directory. There are geographical and subject indices.

World Directory of Environmental Organizations. 5th ed. Sacramento, CA: California Institute of Public Affairs, 1996. 184 p. $50.00. ISBN 1880028077. This useful directory is a comprehensive guide to 3,200 organizations in over 200 countries that are concerned with problems of the environment and natural resources. The directory groups the organizations in several ways: by subject, type of organization (NGO, government agency, etc.), and by region.

GUIDES TO INTERNET RESOURCES

The Web has a nearly infinite number of pages dealing with ecology, evolution, and animal behavior, but most of the information on the Web is not research-level material. Most ecology pages are actually about the environment, for instance, and most of the evolution pages deal with the creation/evolution controversy. Pet behavior is well covered, but not boring, old insects. However, a growing trend is to put data on long-range ecological studies on the Web, and other major resources are also available.

Biology Links: Evolution. URL: http://mcb.harvard.edu/BioLinks/Evolution. html.Particularly good list of departments, societies, and museums dealing with evolution; also includes general links and information on molecular evolution.

Ecology WWW page. URL: http://www.people.fas.harvard.edu/~brach/ Ecology-WWW.html.   This site provides an extensive list of links, most of them for researchers. It is an alphabetical list with no subject directory, though there is a search function.

Murphy, Toni and Carol Briggs-Erickson. *Environmental Guide to the Internet*. 4th ed. Rockville, MD: Government Institutes, 1998. 407 p. $75.00 (paper). ISBN 0865876436 (paper).   Covers discussion groups, Web sites, and electronic journals.   Both basic ecology and conservation topics groups and sites are listed. Includes a history of environmentalism on the Internet. Updated annually from 1995–1998.

GUIDES TO THE LITERATURE

Beacham's Guide to Environmental Issues and Sources. Walton Beacham, ed. Washington, DC: Beacham, 1993. 5 v. $240.00 (set). ISBN 0933833318 (set).   Has more than 40,000 citations, many with annotations, to books, articles, reports, videos, and a number of other sources dealing with environmental issues. The set is divided into chapters, then subdivided into narrower topics. There are extensive references to topics such as ecology, biodiversity, wildlife conservation, and various ecosystems such as rainforests and deserts in addition to environmental topics such as recycling. A very useful and useable set.

Bibliographic Guide to the Environment. Boston, MA: G. K. Hall, 1992. Annual. ISSN 1063-6153. $165.00.   Updated annually, this guide includes books and related materials covering law, urban planning, public health, the sciences, economics, and industry as they relate to environmental issues. Subject, author, and title access are provided for conservation, pollution, atmospheric trends, alternative and renewable energy, waste management, public policy issues, endangered species, and environmental laws and legislation.

Encyclopedia of Environmental Information Sources. Detroit, MI: Gale, 1993. 1,813 p. $171.75. ISBN 0810385686.   This guide covers a wide variety of information sources, including abstracting and indexing services, almanacs, yearbooks, dirctories, encyclopedias, periodicals, research centers, and societies in the areas of the environment and ecology. Broken down into narrow topics such as bogs, nicotine, or New Mexico environmental agencies. Has 3,400 citations and over 1,100 topics. Also available on magnetic tape or diskette. Covers a wider range of types of information sources than *Beacham's*, above, but has fewer citations.

HANDBOOKS

The Historical Ecology Handbook: A Restorationist's Guide to Reference Ecosystems. Dave Egan and Evelyn Howell, eds. Washington, DC: Island Press, 2001. 469 p. $55.00, $30.00 (paper). ISBN 1559637455, 1559637463 (paper). A guide to determining the historical condition of a landscape in order to restore it.

Jorgensen, Sven Erik. *Handbook of Ecological Parameters and Ecotoxicology*. New York: Elsevier, 1991. 1,263 p. $508.00. ISBN 0444886044. Contains data and parameters for the ecological and toxicological fields, including data on the composition and ecological parameters of organisms, the ecosphere and chemical compounds, equations for environmental processes, biological effects, equilibria and rate constants for environmentally important processes, and the effects of pesticides.

McFarland, David. *The Oxford Companion to Animal Behaviour*. New York: Oxford University Press, 1987. 685 p. ISBN 0198661207, 0192819909 (paper). This handbook has short essays covering a variety of topics in animal behavior, and is intended as a reference work for nonspecialists. The authors also provide indexes of scientific names and common names of the species mentioned in the handbook, with cross-references to the essay in which the species was mentioned.

The Rivers Handbook: *Hydrological and Ecological Principles*. Peter Calow and Geoffrey E. Petts, eds. Boston, MA: Blackwell Scientific Publishers, 1992–4. 2 v. $295.00. ISBN 0632028327. This two-volume set provides information on river management. The first volume discusses the basic scientific principles, including hydrology and geology, the flora and fauna of rivers, and nutrient and energy cycles. There are also five case studies, ranging from the highly managed Rhone River to the largely untouched Orinoco. According to the preface of volume 1, volume 2 will develop "the principles and philosophy presented in volume 1 into the management sphere, organizing the approach around *problems*, *diagnosis*, and *treatment*."

GENERAL WORKS

Bell, Graham. *Selection: The Mechanism of Evolution*. New York: Chapman and Hall, 1997. 699 p. $138.00. ISBN 041205521X. The author feels that selection is often neglected in courses on evolution, and has written a review of the concept and its evidence to help overcome that lack. The intended audience is both professional biologists and students.

Berrill, Michael and Debodrah Berrill. *A Sierra Club Naturalist's Guide to the North Atlantic Coast: Cape Cod to Newfoundland*. San Franciso, CA: Sierra Club Books, 1981. 464 p. ISBN 0871562421, 087156243X (paper).   An example of a series of several guides to the ecology of a region of North America. Rather than identifying plants or animals of the area, these guides cover the natural history of the area and explain the interrelationships between the organisms. See Kricher, in the following text, for a similar series.

The Book of Life. Stephen Jay Gould, ed. New York: W.W. Norton, 2001. 256 p. $45.00. ISBN 0393050033.   A fascinating, beautifully illustrated and well-written book covering the history of life and of evolutionary thought. A coffee-table book sure to please dinosaur lovers and other amateurs, but with lots of meat for the student.

Brooks, Daniel R. and Deborah A. McLennan. *Phylogeny, Ecology, and Behavior: A Research Program in Comparative Biology*. Chicago, IL: University of Chicago Press, 1991. 434 p. $60.00, $25.00 (paper). ISBN 0226075710, 0226075729 (paper).   The authors wrote this volume to encourage the re-integration of the evolutionary perspective with the study of ecology and animal behavior.

Conceptual Issues in Evolutionary Biology, 2nd ed. Elliott Sober, ed. Cambridge, MA: MIT Press, 1994. 506 p. $34.95 (paper). ISBN 0262193361, 0262691620 (paper).   An anthology of essays written by scientists and philosophers on issues in evolutionary biology, such as teleology, fitness, units of selection, and ethics. A very useful supplement for courses in evolution.

Dawkins, Richard. *The Selfish Gene*. New ed. New York: Oxford University Press, 1989. 352 p. $27.95, $13.95 (paper). ISBN 0192177737, 0192860925 (paper).   The author argues that the basic unit of selection is the gene, not the individual, as most other authorities believe. This is a classic, and very important (though controversial) book.

Environmental Evolution: Effects of Life on Planet Earth. 2nd ed. Lynn Margulis, Clifford Matthews, and Aaron Haselton, eds. Cambridge, MA: MIT Press, 2000. 338 p. $27.95 (paper). ISBN 0262161970 (paper), 0262133660.   This volume was developed out of a class given at Boston University and Amherst. The text discusses the evolutionary interactions between organisms and the environment, from the very earliest life to modern organisms. The authors also include discussion of the influence of living organisms on the environment, including the Gaia hypothesis.

Ereshefsky, Marc, ed. *The Units of Evolution: Essays on the Nature of Species.* Cambridge, MA: MIT Press, 1992. 405 p. $65.00. ISBN 0262050447. An anthology of previously published papers discussing the biological concept of species, a particularly thorny problem in evolutionary biology. The authors are all recognized experts, and the topics discussed range from biological concepts to philosophical problems.

Foundations of Animal Behavior: Classic Papers with Commentaries. Lynne D. Houck and Lee C. Drickamer, eds. Chicago, IL: University of Chicago Press, 1996. 843 p. $105.00, $37.50 (paper). ISBN 0226354563, 0226354571 (paper). Includes 44 classic papers in animal behavior by well-known authors from Charles Darwin to John Maynard Smith. The papers are arranged in four broad categories, and each section has a commentary by modern researchers. A companion to *Foundations of Ecology* in the following text.

Grant, Verne. *The Evolutionary Process: A Critical Study of Evolutionary Theory.* 2nd ed. New York: Columbia University Press, 1991. 487 p. ISBN 0231073240. The main objective of the author, a well-known evolutionary biologist, was to "provide a comprehensive and critical review of modern evolutionary theory." He covers topics in genetics and mutation, natural selection, acquired characters, speciation, macroevolution, and human evolution.

Griffin, Donald R. *Animal Minds.* Chicago, IL: University of Chicago Press, 1992. 310 p. $16.00 (paper). ISBN 0226308634, 0226308642 (paper). An accessible volume that takes the stance that animals do have consciousness (maybe even insects); an interesting contrast is with Kennedy's *New Anthropomorphism* (see following text).

Hauser, Marc D. *Wild Minds: What Animals Really Think.* New York: Henry Holt, 2000. 315 p. $25.00, $15.00 (paper). ISBN 0805056696, 080505670X (paper). The author, a behavioral neuroscientist, has written a nontechnical book about animal thought. While he believes that animals do have emotions and communicate among themselves, he also feels that we need to be careful about imputing human emotions or consciousness to animals. The book features a wealth of anecdotes and engaging stories.

Kennedy, J.S. *The New Anthropomorphism.* New York: Cambridge University Press, 1992. 194 p. $59.95, $19.95 (paper). ISBN 0521410649, 0521422671 (paper). The author discusses the dangers of the modern version of anthropomorphism (the attribution of human emotions and thinking processes to animals).

Keywords in Evolutionary Biology. Evelyn Fox Keller and Elisabeth A. Lloyd, eds. Cambridge, MA: Harvard University Press, 1992. 414 p. $57.00. ISBN 0674503120. These short essays cover a range of topics in evolutionary biology, including topics such as adaptation, eugenics, fitness, natural selection, the niche, and units of selection. The essays are written by recognized experts in the field and are designed to provide general readers with an introduction to the concepts discussed.

Kricher, John C. *A Field Guide to California and Pacific Northwest Forests*. Boston, MA: Houghton Mifflin, 1998. 378 p. (Peterson field guide series, no. 50). $19.00 (paper). ISBN 0395928966 (paper).   A combination field guide and natural history guide. Unlike most field guides, in which identifying plants or animals is the main purpose of the book, this guide discusses the ecology of several regions in the forests west of the Rockies. The most common plants and animals are illustrated and identified as well. Other similar Peterson guides include *Field Guide to Eastern Forests* and *Field Guide to Rocky Mountain and Southwest Forests*, all by the same author. The Sierra Club guides, such as Berill and Berrill's *The North Atlantic Coast* (see page 244), discuss regional ecology more extensively and do not identify plants or animals.

Margulis, Lynn. *Symbiosis in Cell Evolution: Microbial Communities in the Archean and Proterzoic Eons*. 2nd ed. New York: Freedman, 1993. 452 p. $66.50. ISBN 0716770288, 0716770296 (paper).   The author presents the thesis that eukaryotic organisms (having cells with nuclei) evolved from the symbiotic relationship between some prokaryotic cells (those without nuclei). While still controversial, the theory is gaining support.

Michod, Richard E. and Bruce R. Levin. *The Evolution of Sex: An Examination of Current Ideas*. Sunderland, MA: Sinauer, 1988. 342 p. ISBN 0878934596. The 17 essays in this book discuss various questions dealing with the evolution of sex as a form of genetic recombination. There is an extensive bibliography. It can be used as a text or a general resource.

North American Terrestrial Vegetation. 2nd ed. Michael G. Barbour and William Dwight Billings, eds. New York: Cambridge University Press, 2000. 708 p. $120.00, $49.95 (paper). ISBN 0521550270, 0521559863 (paper).   Describes 18 major plant formations of North America from the Arctic to Central America, such as grasslands, chaparral, and Alpine areas. Each chapter also includes information on habitat loss and conservation efforts in each biome. There are extensive bibliographies for each chapter.

Peters, Robert Henry. *A Critique for Ecology*. New York: Cambridge University Press, 1991. 366 p. $95.00, $39.95 (paper). ISBN 0521400171, 0521395887 (paper).   The author feels that ecology as a discipline is a weak science riddled with tautologies and weak predictions. He also presents eight classes of model theories in predictive ecology that he feels can be used to develop a stronger science of ecology.

Pickett, Steward T.A., Jurek Kolasa, and Clive G. Jones. *Ecological Understanding*. San Diego, CA: Academic, 1994. 206 p. $77.95. ISBN 012554720X. A philosophical discussion of theory in ecology and evolution and the need for integrating ideas from other fields and subdisciplines. Intended for the use of practicing scientists.

Real, Leslie A. and James H. Brown. *Foundations of Ecology: Classic Papers with Commentaries*. Chicago, IL: University of Chicago Press, 1991. 905 p. $32.00 (paper). ISBN 0226705935, 0226705943 (paper). An anthology of 40 important ecology papers published before 1977, each with an explanatory essay.

Sigmund, Karl. *Games of Life: Models in Evolutionary Biology*. New York: Oxford University Press, 1993. 240 p. $49.95, $17.95 (paper). ISBN 0198546653, 0198547838 (paper). The author discusses mathematical models used in genetics, evolution, population biology, and animal behavior in a very clear and understandable, yet light-hearted manner. Very readable.

Wilson, Edward O. *The Diversity of Life*. Cambridge, MA: Harvard University Press, 1992. 424 p. $29.95. ISBN 0674212983. Wilson discusses a variety of topics dealing with biodiversity on a level suitable for the general public as well as for more advanced readers. One especially useful chapter (Chapter 8, "The Unexplored Biosphere") discusses the estimation of the total number of known species, which Wilson places at 1.4 million, give or take a hundred thousand or so. Other chapters include essays on mass extinctions, the species concept, evolution, and several chapters on the human impact on extinction, and the environmental ethic.

Wilson, Edward O. *Sociobiology: The New Synthesis*. 25th anniversary ed. Cambridge, MA: Belknap Press of Harvard University Press, 2000. 697 p. $78.00, 29.95 (paper). ISBN 0674000897; 0674002350 (paper). This massive compilation helped to launch the field of sociobiology, and is probably one of the best known works in the field.

HISTORIES

Axelrod, Alan and Charles Phillips. *The Environmentalists: A Biographical Dictionary from the 17th Century to the Present*. New York: Facts on File, 1993. 258 p. $45.00. ISBN 0816027153. Covers both individuals and organizations, with about 600 entries ranging in length from a paragraph to a couple of pages. Some surprising individuals appear, such as Saddam Hussein (for his role in the destruction of Kuwait). Most of the entries are for friends of the environmental movement, however, and include the Animal Liberation Front, Alexander von Humboldt, and John Muir.

Biographical Dictionary of American and Canadian Naturalists and Environmentalists. Keir B. Sterling, et al., eds. Westport, CT: Greenwood, 1997. 937 p. $185.00. ISBN 0313230471. Includes 445 individuals from pre-colonial times to 1997. The subjects were chosen using a broad definition, so they include scientists, explorers, politicians, artists, activists, and much more. Entries are from two-to-four pages long and provide information on the subject's family, positions held, career, and major contributions, plus a brief bibliography. A companion volume covering Mexican naturalists is planned.

Bocking, Stephen. *Ecologists and Environmental Politics: A History of Contemporary Ecology.* New Haven, CT: Yale University Press, 1997. $35.00. ISBN 0300067631. The author asks the question, "What is the impact on a scientific discipline when it becomes a focus of society's concerns and values?" He discusses four case studies, the growth of the Nature Conservancy of Great Britain, ecological research at the Oak Ridge National Laboratory in Tennessee, the Hubbard Brook Ecological Study in New Hampshire, and the University of Toronto's research into fish populations.

Bowlby, John. *Charles Darwin: A New Life.* New York: W.W. Norton, 1991. 511 p. $14.95 (paper). ISBN 0393309304 (paper). One of many recent biographies of Darwin; see also Darwin and Desmond and Moore in the following text. Bowlby's main interest is in Darwin's lifelong illness, which he attributes to hyperventilation syndrome, a psychosomatic illness.

Bowler, Peter J. *The Earth Encompassed: A History of the Environmental Sciences.* New York: W. W. Norton and Co., 1993. 672 p. $18.95 (paper). ISBN 0393320804 (paper). This is a history of geography, geology, oceanography, meteorology, natural history, paleontology, evolution, and ecology, written by a well-known scholar of the history of evolutionary theory. The coverage ranges from the ancient world to the modern, with perhaps most emphasis on the eighteenth and nineteenth centuries, and is arranged by concepts such as the tree of life or plate tectonics. Originally published as *The Norton History of the Environmental Sciences.*

Bowler, Peter J. *Evolution: The History of an Idea.* Rev. ed. Berkeley, CA: University of California Press, 1989. 432 p. $19.95 (paper). ISBN 0520063856, 0520063864 (paper). Covers the history of evolutionary theories, including pre-Darwinian, Darwinian, and post-Darwinian thought. Includes controversies, both within and outside of the main scientific line. Considered the standard history of evolutionary thought.

Bramwell, Anna. *Ecology in the 20th Century: A History.* New Haven, CT: Yale University Press, 1989. 292 p. ISBN 0300043430. The "ecology" of the title refers to the political or social environmental movement, not the scientific discipline. The author concentrates on England, Germany, and the United States and covers the time from Ernst Haeckel's coining of the word *ecology* in the 1860s to the modern Green, ecosocialist, neo pagan, and back-to-the-land movements.

Browne, Janet. *Charles Darwin: Voyaging*. New York: Alfred A. Knopf, 1995. 605 p. $21.05 (paper). ISBN 0395579429, 0691026068 (paper). This is the first volume of a projected two volume biography of Darwin that covers his life up to the time he decided to begin writing *On the Origin of Species*. This is a biography rather than a history of Darwin's conversion to evolutionary thought, and events in his life are covered in great detail.

The Darwin CD-ROM. Created by Pete Goldie and Michael T. Ghiselin. 2nd ed. San Francisco, CA: Lightbinders, Inc., 1996. $49.95. ISBN 1889175013 (PC, Mac, and Unix). This multimedia CD-ROM includes the full text, plus illustrations, from Darwin's major works, including *The Origin of Species*, *The Descent of Man*, and *The Voyage of the* Beagle. Darwin and Alfred Russel Wallace's jointly written article, "On the Tendency of Species to Form Varieties," is also included, along with the third edition of Ghiselin's *Triumph of the Darwinian Method* (a guide to the study of Darwin), a Darwin bibliography, and a Darwin timeline. Audio is also included for a number of the organisms (birds and mammals) pictured in *The Voyage of the* Beagle.

Darwin, Charles. *The Autobiography of Charles Darwin*. Edited by Francis Darwin, ed. New York: Prometheus Books, 2000. 365 p. (Great Minds Series). $15.00 (paper). ISBN 1573928348 (paper). Darwin's own version of his life. First published in 1893.

Darwin, Charles. *On the Origin of Species by Means of Natural Selection, Or, The Preservation of Favoured Races in the Struggle for Life*. London: John Murray, 1859. 502 p. *On the Origin of Species* was first published in 1859, and hasn't been out of print since. There are several versions available to modern readers, including multiple electronic versions. The first edition is available from the Talk.Origins Web site at http://www.talkorigins.org/faqs/origin.html.

Desmond, Adrian and James Moore. *Darwin*. New York: Warner Books, 1991. 808 p. $23.95. ISBN 0446515892, 0393311503 (paper). The alternate title of this biography about sums up the authors' premise: *Darwin: The Life of a Tormented Evolutionist*. The focus is on Darwin's personal, rather than his scientific, life. Less emphasis on Darwin's health than Bowlby, previous.

Golley, Frank B. *History of the Ecosystem Concept in Ecology: More than the Sum of the Parts*. New Haven, CT: Yale University Press, 1993. 254 p. $17.00 (paper). ISBN 0300055463, 0300066422 (paper). Eminent ecologist explains the ecosystem concept tracing its evolution and contributions from Americans and Europeans. Discusses the explosive growth of ecosystem studies.

Hagen, Joel B. *An Entangled Bank: The Origins of Ecosystem Ecology*. New Brunswick, NJ: Rutgers University Press, 1992. 245 p. $49.00, $19.00 (paper). ISBN 0813518237, 0813518245 (paper).   Covers the history of ecosystem ecology (as opposed to evolutionary ecology and other specialties) from the early days of ecology to the modern "spaceship Earth" and Gaia viewpoints. The emphasis is on the American schools of thought.

Hull, David L. *Darwin and His Critics: The Reception of Darwin's Theory of Evolution by the Scientific Community*. Chicago, IL: University of Chicago Press, 1983. 473 p. ISBN 0226360466 (paper).   In this book, Hull has collected the major reviews of the *Origin of Species* that were written shortly after its publication, offering a good source of information on what contemporary critics thought of the theory of evolution by natural selection. Originally published in 1973 by Harvard University Press.

Leaders in the Study of Animal Behavior: Autobiographical Perspectives. Donald A. Dewsbury, ed. Lewisburg, PA: Bucknell University Press, 1985. 512 p. $65.00. ISBN 0838750524.   This is a collection of autobiographical essays written by the major figures in the study of animal behavior, including luminaries such as Konrad Lorenz, John Maynard Smith, Edward O. Wilson, Niko Tinbergen, and Irenaus Eibl-Eibesfeldt.

Lorenz, Konrad Z. *The Foundations of Ethology*. New York: Springer-Verlag, 1981. 380 p. $98.00. ISBN 0387816232.   This volume presents Lorenz's personal view of the history and development of ethology.

Mayr, Ernst. *One Long Argument: Charles Darwin and the Genesis of Modern Evolutionary Thought*. Cambridge, MA: Harvard University Press, 1991. 195 p. $15.95 (paper). ISBN 0674639057, 0674639065 (paper).   This well-written and favorably reviewed history, written by a well-known evolutionary biologist, covers the acceptance of Darwin's theory, from the first publication of the *Origin of Species*, through the Evolutionary Synthesis of the 1930s and 1940s. The book consists of both new and previously published essays and is intended for students and the general public, although evolutionary biologists will certainly also find material of interest.

The Philosophy of Ecology: From Science to Synthesis. David R. Keller and Frank B. Golley, eds. Athen, GA: University of Georgia Press, 2000. 366 p. $30.00 (paper). ISBN 0820322199, 0820322202 (paper).   An anthology of 33 readings on the philosophy of ecology.

Reid, Robert G. B. *Evolutionary Theory: The Unfinished Synthesis*. Ithaca, NY: Cornell University Press, 1985. 405 p. $42.50. ISBN 0801418313.   The author discusses the history of neo-Darwinism, the branch of evolutionary theory that holds that natural selection by itself is an insufficient force to explain evolution.

Ruse, Michael. *The Evolution Wars: A Guide to the Debates*. Santa Barbara, CA: ABC-CLIO, 2000. 428 p. $75.00. ISBN 1576071855. A very personal discussion of the controversies over evolution, both within the scientific community and between scientists and creationists. The time period is from 1830 to the present. The book is aimed at an undergraduate or general audience, and the personalities and religious backgrounds of the participants are frequently discussed. The author is proevolution and isn't shy about displaying his own opinions, but the intent of the book is to allow readers to make up their own minds. Each chapter includes an annotated list of further readings, and the book also includes excerpts from important original works about evolution.

Ruse, Michael. *Monad to Man: The Concept of Progress in Evolutionary Biology*. Cambridge, MA: Harvard University Press, 1996. 628 p. $55.00. ISBN 0674582209. The concept of progress is a problem for evolution, because it assumes directionality (i.e., moving from simple to complex, from dumb to smart). The author, a philosopher, discusses the history of the concept, from its origins in pre-Darwinian days to modern controversies. The personalities of evolutionists are highlighted.

Worster, Donald. *Nature's Economy: A History of Ecological Ideas*. 2nd ed. New York: Cambridge University Press, 1994. 505 p. $18.95 (paper). ISBN 0521468345 (paper). Covers the changes in the general and scientific understanding of the natural world, from the Arcadian romance of Gilbert White's *Natural History of Selbourne*, through Thoreau, Darwin, American scientific ecology and its relationship to policy making, and the modern environmentalism. Emphasis is on the American scene, and includes discussion of the development of the science as well as the ecological world view.

METHODS AND TECHNIQUES

Brown, Luther and Jerry F. Downhower. *Analyses in Behavioral Ecology: A Manual for Lab and Field*. Sunderland, MA: Sinauer Associates, 1988. 194 p. $18.95. ISBN 0878931228 (paper). This manual provides examples of experiments to elucidate animal behavior in four broad categories: sensory capabilities, feeding patterns, spacing patterns, and reproduction. They also provide discussions of the most commonly used statistical tests.

Buckland, S. T., D. R. Anderson, K. P. Burnham, and J. L. Laake. *Distance Sampling: Estimating Abundance of Biological Populations*. New York: Chapman and Hall, 1993. 446 p. ISBN 0412426609, 0412426706 (paper). Covers the use of distance sampling for estimating population density. Distance sampling is usually used for vertebrate species or inanimate objects such as burrows and consists of surveying lines or points in the field, recording the distance between objects of interest. This is the only book available that concentrates on this important method.

Design and Analysis of Ecological Experiments. Samuel M. Scheiner and Jessica Gurevitch, eds. New York: Oxford University Press, 2001. 415 p. $80.00, $35.00 (paper). ISBN 0195131878, 0195131886 (paper). The editors have selected methods for use in designing and analyzing experiments that may not be well known to ecologists and students. The authors offer many examples, and computer code where applicable.

Ecological Census Techniques: A Handbook. William J. Sutherland, ed. New York: Cambridge University Press, 1996. 336 p. $80.00, $31.95 (paper). ISBN 052147244X, 0521478154 (paper). Covers census techniques for a range of organisms from plants to mammals. Also includes techniques for sampling environmental variables. The emphasis is on techniques such as trapping rather than statistical analysis.

Ecological Time Series. Thomas M. Powell and John H. Steele, eds. New York: Chapman and Hall, 1994. 496 p. $193.00, $83.50 (paper). ISBN 0412051915, 0412052016 (paper). Covers time series for population processes, community structure, and other subjects.

Haccou, Patsy and Evert Meelis. *Statistical Analysis of Behavioural Data: An Approach based on Time-Structured Models.* New York: Oxford University Press, 1992. 396 p. $45.00. ISBN 0198548508. The analysis of continuous time records of behavior is discussed in this manual. The authors provide a number of different statistical methods, ranging from the relatively simple (different methods of graphing results, for instance) to the statistically sophisticated (such as continuous-time Markov chain modeling). Tables for the most important statistical tests used in the book are also included.

Hairston, Nelson G. *Ecological Experiments: Purpose, Design, and Execution.* New York: Cambridge University Press, 1989. 370 p. (Cambridge studies in ecology). $29.95 (paper). ISBN 0521345960, 0521346924 (paper). Emphasizes proper experimental design in preparing and conducting field studies. Includes chapters on conducting experiments in various environments.

Handbook of Ecotoxicology. Peter Calow, ed. Cambridge, MA: Blackwell Scientific Publishers, 1993– . 2 v. $175.00 (v. 1), $99.95 (v. 2). ISBN 0632035730 (v. 1), 0632049332 (v. 2). Volume one of this handbook provides information on tests for ecotoxicological effects, both field and laboratory, for all types of ecological systems. Volume 2 focuses on the toxicity of synthetic chemicals themselves. The handbook is intended for practitioners and provides extensive references.

Handbook of Environmental and Ecological Modeling. S.E. Jørgensen, B. Halling-Sørensen, and S.N. Nielsen, eds. Boca Raton, FL: Lewis, 1996. 672 p. $114.95. ISBN 156670202X. Provides information on about 400 ecological models created in the last 15 to 20 years. The handbook lists information such as model type, purpose, description, applications, software and hardware requirements, availability, and documentation. The intent is to show other modelers what types of models are available, so that they do not have to reinvent them.

Handbook of Methods in Aquatic Microbial Ecology. Paul F. Kemp et al., eds. Boca Raton, FL: Lewis Publishers, 1993. 777 p. $169.95. ISBN 0873715640. Includes 85 methods for studying aquatic microbial ecology. Most chapters were written by the original developer of the method.

Hayek, Lee-Ann C. and Martin A. Buzas. *Surveying Natural Populations.* New York: Columbia University Press, 1997. 563 p. $66.50, $27.00 (paper). ISBN 0231102402, 0231102410 (paper). Covers statistical methods for studying populations of organisms. Each chapter includes study problems. There are several statistical tables for various tests.

Jørgensen, Sven Erik. *Fundamentals of Ecological Modelling.* 2nd ed. New York: Elsevier, 1994. (Developments in Environmental Modelling, 19) 628 p. $273.50, $160.00 (paper). ISBN 0444815724, 0444815783 (paper). The author offers a discussion of the use of modelling in ecology for both ecologists and engineers. Topics covered include basic concepts, general models, conceptual and static models, and models for modelling population dynamics, biogeochemical processes, and ecosystems, as well as the application of models in environmental management. The second edition also includes a computer disk.

Krebs, Charles J. *Ecological Methodology.* 2nd ed. Menlo Park, CA: Benjamin/ Cummings, 1999. 620 p. $99.00. ISBN 0321021738. Provides statistical methods for ecological studies, such as estimating abundance and determining the optimal sample size.

Lehner, Philip N. *Handbook of Ethological Methods.* 2nd ed. New York: Cambridge University Press, 1996. 672 p. $29.95 (paper). ISBN 0521554055, 0521637503 (paper). Provides general information on designing research, collecting data, and analyzing results for a range of topics in animal behavior.

Martin, Paul and Patrick Bateson. *Measuring Behaviour: An Introductory Guide.* 2nd ed. New York: Cambridge University Press, 1993. 238 p. $16.95. ISBN 0521446147. This edition adds material on new technologies, as well as information on quantitative studies of behavior.

Methods in Ecology Series. Cambridge, MA: Blackwell Scientific Publications. Irregular. Price varies. ''The aim of this series is to provide ecologists with concise and authoritative books that will guide them in choosing and applying an appropriate methodology to their problem. New technologies are a feature of the series.'' A recent example is *Molecular Methods in Ecology*, published in 2000.

Methods in Ecosystem Science. Osvaldo E. Sala, et al., eds. New York: Springer-Verlag, 2000. 421 p. $129.00, $69.95 (paper). ISBN 0387987347, 0387987436 (paper). Reviews methods for studying both aquatic and terrestrial ecosystems, in four broad categories: energetics, nutrient and water cycling, experimental approaches, and modeling.

Skalski, J.R. and D.S. Robson. *Techniques for Wildlife Investigations: Design and Analysis of Capture Data*. San Diego, CA: Academic Press, 1992. 237 p. $62.00. ISBN 0126476756. Includes criteria for designing effective experiments, statistical methods for analyzing mark-recapture data, and many examples.

Spellerberg, Ian F. *Monitoring Ecological Change*. New York: Cambridge University Press, 1991. 334 p. $33.95 (paper). ISBN 0521366623, 0521424070 (paper). Covers techniques for studying changes in ecosystems and the status of species, caused by both man-made and natural effects. After opening chapters covering the scientific basis and the present status of long-term monitoring programs, the author goes on to discuss monitoring in practical terms, with examples for birds, freshwater organisms and ecosystems, and others. Useful for both students and practicing ecologists.

Studying Temperate Marine Environments: A Handbook for Ecologists. Michael Kingsford and Christopher Battershill, eds. Boca Raton, FL: CRC Press, 2000. 335 p. $109.95 (paper). ISBN 0849308836 (paper). Provides methods for studying the ecology of temperate marine environments. Chapters cover both basic procedures such as sampling and how to establish a study, and how to study particular marine environments such as rocky reefs or intertidal areas.

Video Techniques in Animal Ecology and Behaviour, 1st ed. Stephen D. Wratten, ed. New York: Chapman and Hall, 1994. 211 p. $147.00. ISBN 0412466406. Lists techniques for studying the behavior of various animals using video cameras. Examples given include flying insects, parasites, wild birds, farm animals and companion animals, and microscopic organisms.

Young, Linda J. and Jerry H. Young. *Statistical Ecology: A Population Perspective*. Boston, MA: Kluwer Academic, 1998. 565 p. $115.00. ISBN 041204711X. ''This book is a collection of formulae, techniques, and methods developed for use in field ecology.'' It is designed as a reference or textbook for both ecologists and statisticians working in the area of statistical ecology. The emphasis is on data for single species populations. The ECOSTAT software is discussed, which can be downloaded for free from http://www.ianr.unl.edu/ianr/biometry/faculty/linda/lyoung.html.

TEXTBOOKS AND TREATISES

Aber, John D. and Jerry M. Melillo. *Terrestrial Ecosystems*. Philadelphia, PA: Saunders College Publishing, 1991. 429 p. $28.00 (paper). ISBN 0030474434 (paper). Advanced undergraduate text covering basic ecosystem theory topics, including human effects.

Alcock, John. *Animal Behavior: An Evolutionary Approach*. 6th ed. Sunderland, MA: Sinauer, 1998. 640 p. $68.00. ISBN 0878930094.

Bailey, Robert G. *Ecoregions: The Ecosystem Geography of the Oceans and Continents*. New York: Springer, 1998. 176 p. $82.95, $42.95 (paper). ISBN 0387983058, 0387983112 (paper). Covers biomes from around the world. There are numerous color and black-and-white illustrations, but little detail. Bolen's *Ecology of North America* (see following text) covers North American biomes in more detail.

Begon, Michael, John Harper, and Colin Townsend. *Ecology: Individuals, Populations, and Communities*. 3rd ed. Cambridge, MA: Blackwell Scientific Publications, 1998. 1,086 p. $69.95. ISBN 0632043938.

Begon, Michael, David J. Thompson, and M. Mortimer. *Population Ecology: A Unified Study of Animals and Plants*. 3rd ed. Cambridge, MA: Blackwell Scientific Publications, 1996. 256 p. $36.95 (paper). ISBN 0632034785 (paper).

Behavior of Marine Animals: Current Perspectives in Research. Howard E. Winn and Bori L. Olla, eds. New York: Plenum, 1972–84. 6 v. V. 1: Invertebrates; v. 2: Vertebrates; v. 3: Cetaceans; v. 4: Marine birds; v. 5: Shorebirds, breeding behavior and populations; and v. 6: Shorebirds, migration and foraging behavior.

Bolen, Eric G. *Ecology of North America*. New York: John Wiley, 1998. 448 p. $99.00. ISBN 0471131563. Covers each of the major biomes of North America, from Canada to northern Mexico. An undergraduate text, with lists of references at the end of each chapter.

Bulmer, Michael G. *Theoretical Evolutionary Ecology*. Sunderland, MA: Sinauer Associates, 1994. 416 p. $65.00, $35.95 (paper). ISBN 0878930795, 0878930787 (paper).

Cockburn, Andrew. *An Introduction to Evolutionary Ecology*. Boston, MA: Blackwell Scientific, 1991. 370 p. ISBN 0632027290. Advanced undergraduate or graduate students.

Colinvaux, Paul. *Ecology 2*, 2nd ed. New York: John Wiley and Sons, 1993. 688 p. $86.95. ISBN 0471558605.   Undergraduate.

Cook, L. M. *Genetic and Ecological Diversity: The Sport of Nature*. 2nd ed. New York: Stanley Thornes, 1999. 192 p. $47.50. ISBN 074843367.   This slim volume is an introduction to population genetics; it attempts to bring together the work of ecologists and population geneticists on intra- and interspecies diversity.

Cowen, Richard. *History of Life*, 3rd ed. Boston, MA: Blackwell Scientific, 2000. 432 p. $49.95 (paper). ISBN 0632044446 (paper).

Ecosystems of the World. David W. Goodall, series ed. New York: Elsevier, 1977– . v. ISBN 0444417028 (series).   This multivolume set covers the major ecosystems of the world, both terrestrial and aquatic, natural and managed. The set is planned with 29 titles, some titles with 2 volumes. Some examples of the ecosystems covered are *Mires: Swamp, Bog, Fen, and Moor* (2 volumes), *Managed Grasslands*, and *Tropical Savannahs*. Each title contains contributions from a number of individuals and includes discussions both of general topics and descriptions of particular biogeographical regions. The volumes are published out of sequence, and each costs about $200.

Futuyma, Douglas J. *Evolutionary Biology*. 3rd ed. Sunderland, MA: Sinauer, 1997. 763 p. $83.95. ISBN 0878931899.   Gerhart, John and Marc Kirschner. *Cells, Embryos, and Evolution: Toward a Cellular and Developmental Understanding of Phenotypic Variation and Evolutionary Adaptability*. Oxford, England: Blackwell Science, 1997. 642 p. $66.95 (paper). ISBN 0865425744 (paper).   Examines cellular and developmental mechanisms at work in the evolution of the diversity of life in the animal kingdom. With 16 color plates of illustrations.

Goodenough, Judith, Betty McGuire, and Robert A. Wallace. *Perspectives on Animal Behavior*. 2nd ed. New York: John Wiley and Sons, 2001. 542 p. $95.15. ISBN 0471295027.   Upper-level undergraduates, both in biology and psychology.

Gould, James L. *Ethology: The Mechanisms and Evolution of Behavior*. New York: Norton, 1982. 544 p. $50.75. ISBN 0393014886.

Graur, Dan and Wen-Hsiung Li. *Fundamentals of Molecular Evolution*. 2nd ed. Sunderland, MA: Sinauer, 2000. 481 p. $52.95 (paper). ISBN: 0878932666 (paper).   Introductory text for the study of evolution at the molecular level.

Hall, Brian K. *Evolutionary Developmental Biology*, 2nd ed. New York: Chapman & Hall. 512 p. $75.00 (paper). ISBN 0412785803, 0412785900 (paper).   A text for one of the fast-growing fields in biology. It "forges a unification of genomic, developmental, organismal, population and natural selection approaches to evolutionary change.''

Handbook of Ecosystem Theories and Management. S. E. Jørgensen and F. Muller, eds. Boca Raton, FL: Lewis, 2000. 584 p. $99.95. ISBN 1566702534. A broad survey of ecosystem theory and its applications.

Handbook of Functional Plant Ecology. Francisco I. Pugnaire and Fernanco Valladares, eds. New York: Marcel Dekker, 1999. 901 p. $250.00. ISBN 0824719506. Provides reviews of major topics in plant ecology, such as physiological ecology and population ecology. Also includes chapters on several major habitats and suggestions for new approaches. Each chapter includes a general introduction to the topic plus an indication of the author's opinion on future directions for research. A good source for broad overviews of the selected topics.

Huggett, Richard J. *Fundamentals of Biogeography.* New York: Routledge, 1998. 261 p. (Routledge Fundamentals of Physical Geography Series). $75.00, $27.99 (paper). ISBN 0415154987, 0415154995 (paper). An undergraduate text linking biogeography and environmental issues. Each chapter includes essay questions and sources.

Hutchinson, G. Evelyn. *A Treatise on Limnology.* New York: Wiley, 1957–3. 4 v. $275.00. ISBN 0471542946 (v. 4). The classical treatise on limnology. The author died before completing the fourth volume, leaving a proposed fifth volume not begun. The existing volumes are *Geography, Physics and Chemistry*; *Introduction to Lake Biology and the Limnoplankton*; *Limnological Botany*; and *The Zoobenthos*. The final volume would have covered productivity and various ecological topics. Only volume 4 is in print.

Krebs, Charles J. *Ecology: The Experimental Analysis of Distribution and Abundance.* 4th ed. New York: HarperCollins, 1994. 801 p. $83.00. ISBN 0065004108. Advanced undergraduate and graduate.

Krebs, J. R. and N. B. Davies. *Behavioural Ecology: An Evolutionary Approach*, 4th ed. Cambridge, MA: Blackwell Scientific Publications, 1997. 464 p. $54.95 (paper). ISBN 0865427313 (paper). Advanced undergraduate and graduate students.

Krebs, J. R. and N. B. Davies. *An Introduction to Behavioural Ecology.* 3rd ed. Cambridge, MA: Blackwell Scientific, 1993. 432 p. $51.95 (paper). ISBN 0632035463 (paper). Undergraduate text.

Li, Wen-Hsiung. *Molecular Evolution.* Sunderland, MA: Sinauer, 1997. $64.95. ISBN 0878934634. An advanced text on molecular evolution including statistical analysis methodology, useful for graduate students and researchers.

Longhurst, Alan R. *Ecological Geography of the Sea*. San Diego, CA: Academic Press, 1998. 398 p. $79.95. ISBN 0124555586.   The first major synthesis of local studies showing the biogeographical regions of the world's oceans.

Louw, Gideon N. *Physiological Animal Ecology*. London: Longman Scientific and Technical, 1993. 288 p. $68.00 (paper). ISBN 0582059224 (paper).   This text was designed to "bridge the gap between physiology and ecology." For undergraduates.

Manning, Aubrey and Marian Stamp Dawkins. *An Introduction to Animal Behaviour*. 5th ed. New York: Cambridge University Press, 1998. 420 p. $80.00, $29.95 (paper). ISBN 0521570247, 0521578914 (paper).

Maynard Smith, John. *Evolutionary Genetics*. 2nd ed. New York: Oxford University Press, 1998. 330 p. $39.95 (paper). ISBN 0198502311 (paper).   For advanced undergraduate and graduate students.

Maynard Smith, John. *The Theory of Evolution*. 3rd ed. New York: Cambridge University Press, 1993. 375 p. $15.95. ISBN 0521451280.   Describes the theory of evolution and the changes in our understanding of the theory over time. For the third edition, the author added a chapter on the use of molecular data for constructing phylogenetic trees.

McFarland, David. *Animal Behavior: Psychobiology, Ethology, and Evolution*. 3rd ed. London: Longman Scientific and Technical, 1998. 600 p. $55.00. ISBN 0582327326.   Undergraduates, both biology and psychology. More psychological than Alcock or Goodenough.

McKinney, Michael L. *Evolution of Life: Processes, Patterns, and Prospects*. Englewood Cliffs, NJ: Prentice Hall, 1993. $49.00 (paper). ISBN 0132929392 (paper).   For nonmajors.

Meffe, Gary K. and C. Ronald Carroll. *Principles of Conservation Biology*. 2nd ed. Sunderland, MA: Sinauer, 1997. 729 p. $71.95. ISBN 0878935215.

Mitsch, William J. and James G. Gosselink. *Wetlands*. 3rd ed. New York: John Wiley, 2000. 920 p. $85.00. ISBN 047129232X.

Page, Roderic D. M. and Edward C. Holmes. *Molecular Evolution: A Phylogenetic Approach*. Malden, MA: Blackwell Science, 1998. 346 p. $63.95 (paper). ISBN 0865428891 (paper).   Treats molecular phylogenetic trees as a navigational and analytical tool for many kinds of research; chapters cover basic genetics, population genetics, and measuring genetic change, as well as developing and using phylogenies.

Pianka, Eric R. *Evolutionary Ecology*. 6th ed. New York: Addison-Wesley, 1999. 512 p. $73.00. ISBN 0321042883.

Primack, Richard B. *Essentials of Conservation Biology*. 2nd ed. Sunderland, MA: Sinauer Associates, 1998. 660 p. $59.95. ISBN 0878937218.

Putman, R.J. *Community Ecology*. New York: Chapman and Hall, 1994. 178 p. $46.50 (paper). ISBN 0412544903, 0412545004 (paper).

Readings in Ecology. New York: Oxford University Press, 1999. 461 p. $35.00 (paper). ISBN 0195133099 (paper). Includes 28 articles selected as supplementary readings for courses using *Ecology* by Stanley L. Dodson as a textbook. The articles were selected as examples of excellent research and cover all of the major areas in ecology. Can be used with other texts as well.

Ricklefs, Robert E. *The Economy of Nature: A Textbook in Basic Ecology*. 5th ed. New York: W.H. Freeman, 2000. 700 p. $77.95 (paper). ISBN 071673883X (paper). Undergraduate.

Ricklefs, Robert E. and Gary L. Miller. *Ecology*. 4th ed. New York: W.H. Freeman, 2000. 822 p. $95.15. ISBN 071672829X. Advanced undergraduates and graduates.

Ridley, Mark. *Evolution*. 2nd ed. Cambridge, MA: Blackwell Science, 1996. 719 p. $67.95 (paper). ISBN 0865424950 (paper). Undergraduate.

Strickberger, Monroe W. *Evolution*. 3rd ed. Sudbury, MA: Jones and Bartlett, 2000. 722 p. $71.95. ISBN 0763710660.

Tivy, Joy. *Biogeography: A Study of Plants in the Ecosphere*. 3rd ed. New York: John Wiley, 1993. 452 p. $25.00 (paper). ISBN 0470220783.

Trivers, Robert. *Social Behavior*. Menlo Park, CA: Benjamin/Cummings, 1985. 462 p. ISBN 080538507X.

Wilson, Edward O. and William H. Bossert. *Primer of Population Biology*. Stamford, CT: Sinauer Associates, 1971. 192 p. $19.95. ISBN 0978939261.

PERIODICALS

Aggressive Behavior. v. 1– , 1975– . New York: Wiley and Sons. Bimonthly. $1,250.00. ISSN 0096-140X. Available electronically. "Aggressive Behavior will consider manuscripts in the English language concerning the fields of Animal Behavior, Anthropology, Ethology, Psychiatry, Psychobiology, Psychology, and Sociology which relate to either overt or implied conflict behaviors." The official journal of the International Society for Research on Aggression.

American Midland Naturalist. v. 1– , 1909– . Notre Dame, IN: University of Notre Dame. Quarterly. $85.00. ISSN 0003-0031. Publishes "articles reporting original research in any field of biological science and review articles of a critical nature on topics of current interest in biology."

American Naturalist. v. 1– , 1867– . Chicago, IL: University of Chicago Press. Monthly. $278.00. ISSN 0003-0147. Available electronically.   The official journal of the American Society of Naturalists. "While addressing topics in community and ecosystem dynamics, evolution of sex and mating systems, organismal adaptation, and genetic aspects of evolution, AN emphasizes sophisticated methodologies and innovative theoretical syntheses."

Animal Behaviour. v. 1– , 1952– . London: Academic Press. Monthly. $736.00. ISSN 0003-3472.   Published for the Association for the Study of Animal Behaviour (UK) and the Animal Behavior Society (United States and Canada). Publishes "critical reviews, original papers, and research articles on all aspects of animal behaviour."

Animal Learning and Behavior. v. 1– , 1973– . Austin, TX: Psychonomic Society. Quarterly. $109.00. ISSN 0090-4996.   "Publishes experimental and theoretical contributions and critical reviews that cover the broad categories of animal learning, cognition, motivation, emotion, and comparative animal behavior." A journal of the Psychonomic Society.

Aquatic Microbial Ecology: International Journal (AME). v. 9– , 1995– . Oldendorf/Luhe, Germany: Inter-Research. 3/yr. $840.00. ISSN 0948-3055.   "AME serves as a worldwide forum for scientific communications on all aspects of aquatic microbial dynamics." Formerly: *Marine Microbial Food Webs*.

Austral Ecology. v. 25– , 2000–   Carleton, Australia: Blackwell Science Asia. Bimonthly. $695.00. ISSN 0307-692X. Available electronically.   "*Austral Ecology* publishes original papers describing experimental, observational or theoretical studies on terrestrial, marine or freshwater systems, which are considered without taxonomic bias. Special thematic issues are published regularly, including symposia on the ecology of estuaries and soft sediment habitats, freshwater systems and coral reef fish." The official journal of the Ecological Society of Australia (ESA). Formerly: *Australian Journal of Ecology*.

Behavioral Ecology. v. 1– , 1990– . New York: Oxford University Press. Bimonthly. $370.00. ISSN 1045-2249. Available electronically.   "*Behavioral Ecology* is broad-based and covers both empirical and theoretical approaches. Studies on the whole range of behaving organisms, including plants, invertebrates, vertebrates, and humans, are included." The official journal of the International Society for Behavioral Ecology.

Behavioral Ecology and Sociobiology. v. 1– , 1976– . Heidelberg, Germany: Springer-Verlag. Monthly. $2,136.00. ISSN 0340-5443. Available electronically. "The journal publishes original contributions dealing with quantitative empirical and theoretical studies in the field of the analysis of animal behavior on the level of the individual, population and community."

Behaviour: An International Journal of Behavioural Biology. v. 1– , 1947– . Leiden, Netherlands: E.J. Brill. Monthly. $554.00. ISSN 0005-7959. Available electronically. "*Behaviour* aims to publish substantial contributions to the biological analysis of the causation, ontogeny, function, and evolution of behaviour of all animal species, including humans."

Behavioural Processes. v. 1– , 1976– . Amsterdam: Elsevier. Monthly. $1,473.00. ISSN 0376-6357. Available electronically. "The journal publishes experimental, theoretical and review papers dealing with fundamental behavioural processes through the methods of natural science. Experimental papers may deal with any species, from unicellular organisms to human beings. Sample topics are cognition in man and animals, the phylogeny, ontogeny and mechanisms of learning, animal suffering and the neuroscientific bases of behaviour."

Biochemical Systematics and Ecology. v. 1– , 1973– . New York: Pergamon/ Elsevier. Semiquarterly. $1,240.00. ISSN 0305-1978. Available electronically. "Devoted to the publication of original papers and reviews, both submitted and invited, in two subject areas: (i) the application of biochemistry to problems relating to systematic biology of organisms (biochemical systematics); (ii) the role of biochemistry in interactions between organisms or between an organism and its environment (biochemical ecology)."

Biological Conservation. v. 1– , 1969– . Barking, UK: Elsevier Applied Science. 18/yr. $1,942.00. ISSN 0006-3207. Available electronically. Publishes "original papers dealing with the preservation of wildlife and the conservation or wise use of biological and allied natural resources."

Brain, Behaviour and Evolution. v. 1– , 19– . Basel: Karger. Monthly. $781.00. ISSN 0006-8977. Available electronically. "The journal publishes comparative neurobiological studies that focus on the morphology, physiology, and histochemistry of various neural structures, as well as aspects of psychology, ecology, and ethology in both vertebrates and invertebrates as they relate to nervous system structure, function, and evolution." Official organ of the J. B. Johnston Club.

Bulletin of the Ecological Society of America. v. 1– , 1917– . Tempe, AZ: Ecological Society of America. Quarterly. $35.00. ISSN 0012-9623. "The Bulletin publishes letters, longer commentaries, and philosophical and methodological items related to the science of ecology."

Canadian Field-Naturalist. v. 33– , 1919– . Ottawa, Canada: Ottawa Field-Naturalists' Club. Quarterly. $45.00. ISSN 0008-3550. "Features both articles and notes on original research and observations on the natural history of northern North America." The official publication of the Ottawa Field-Naturalists' Club. Formerly: *The Ottawa Naturalist.*

Chemoecology: An International Journal Emphasizing Evolutionary Approaches To Chemical Ecology. v. 1– , 1990– . Stuttgart, Germany: Thieme. Quarterly. $361.00. ISSN 0937-7409. Available electronically. Publishes "research papers that integrate ecology and chemistry in an attempt to increase our understanding of the biological significance of natural products. Its scope is the evolutionary biology of chemically-mediated biotic interactions, including mechanistic approaches as well as environmental aspects."

Conservation Biology. v. 1– , 1987– . Cambridge, MA: Blackwell Scientific. Bimonthly. $360.00. ISSN 0888-8892. Available electronically. "Provides a forum for the discussion and dissemination of the critical ideas in conservation theory and management." The official journal of the Society for Conservation Biology.

Diversity and Distributions. v. 4– , 1998– . Oxford, England: Blackwell Science. Bimonthly. $518.00. ISSN 1366-9516. Available electronically. "*Diversity and Distributions* publishes reviews and primary research papers on a very wide range of subjects relating to biodiversity." Formerly: *Biodiversity Letters.*

Ecography: Ecology in the Holarctic Region. v. 1– , 1978– . Copenhagen: Munksgaard International Publishers. Quarterly. $150.00. ISSN 0906-7590. Publishes "papers in the areas of descriptive ecology as well as on ecological patterns." Formerly: *Holarctic Ecology.*

Ecological Applications. v. 1– , 1991– . Tempe, AZ: Ecological Society of America. Bimonthly. $190.00. ISSN 1051-0761. Available electronically. "Open to research and discussion papers that integrate ecological science and concepts with their applications and implications. Of special interest are papers that develop the basic scientific principles on which environmental decision-making should rest, and those that describe the applications of ecological concerns to environmental problem-solving, policies, and management." An official publication of the Ecological Society of America.

Ecological Modelling. v. 1– , 1975– . Amsterdam: Elsevier. Biweekly. $2,774.00. ISSN 0304-3800. Available electronically. "This journal is concerned with the use of mathematical models and systems analysis for the description of ecosystems and for the control of environmental pollution and resource development." A journal of the International Society for Ecological Modelling (ISEM).

Ecological Monographs. v. 1– , 1931– . Tempe, AZ: Ecological Society of America. Quarterly. $110.00. ISSN 0012-9615. Available electronically. Provides "an outlet for longer papers similar to articles otherwise published in *Ecology*." An official publication of the Ecological Society of America.

Ecological Research. v. 1– , 1986– . Melbourne: Blackwell Scientific Publications. 3/yr. $330.00. ISSN 0912-3814. Available electronically. "The Journal publishes original research papers, critical reviews, technical reports, and notes and comments covering all aspects of ecology." Published for the Ecological Society of Japan.

Ecology. v. 1– , 1920– . Tempe, AZ: Ecological Society of America. Monthly. $470.00. ISSN 0012-9658. Available electronically. "Publishes research and synthesis papers on all aspects of ecology, with particular emphasis on papers that develop new concepts in ecology, that test ecological theory, or that lead to an increased appreciation for the diversity of ecological phenomena." Longer papers are covered in *Ecological Monographs*, previous. An official publication of the Ecological Society of America.

Ecology Letters. v. 1– , 1998– . Oxford, England: Blackwell Science. Bimonthly. $552.00. ISSN 1461-023X. Available electronically. "*Ecology Letters* is a new forum for the very rapid publication of original research in ecology. Manuscripts relating to the ecology of all taxa, in any biome and geographic area will be considered, and priority will be given to those papers exploring or testing clearly stated hypotheses. The journal publishes concise papers that merit urgent publication by virtue of their originality, general interest and contribution to new developments in ecology."

Ecosystems. v. 1– , 1998– . New York: Springer-Verlag. 8/yr. $267.00. ISSN 1432-9840. Available electronically. "*Ecosystems* invites original research papers in the following areas: structure and process in ecosystems, ecosystem concepts and theory, integrated analysis of natural, social and management systems, ecosystems services and management, and new tools and methods of broad interest to ecosystem scientists."

Ecotoxicology. v. 1– , 1992– . London: Chapman & Hall. Quarterly. $545.00. ISSN 0963-9292. Available electronically. The journal is "devoted to the publication of fundamental research on the effects of toxic chemicals on populations, communities and terrestrial, freshwater and marine ecosystems. It aims to elucidate mechanisms and processes whereby chemicals exert their effects on ecosystems and the impact caused at the population or community level."

Ecotoxicology and Environmental Safety. v. 1– , 1977– . Orlando, FL: Academic Press. Bimonthly. $750.00. ISSN 0147-6513. "Publishes studies that examine the biologic and toxic effects of natural or synthetic chemical pollutants on animal, plant, or microbial ecosystems and their routes into the affected organisms. Reports that discuss the entry and fate of chemicals through the biosphere are emphasized." Section B of *Environmental Research*.

Ethology. v. 1– , 1937– . Berlin: Blackwell Science. Monthly. $696.00. ISSN 0179-1613. Available electronically. The journal "welcomes original contributions from all branches of behaviour research on all species of animals, both in the field and in the laboratory, as well as theoretical investigations." Formerly *Zeitschrift für Tierpsychologie*.

Ethology, Ecology, and Evolution. v. 1– , 1989– . Firenze, Italy: Universita di Firenze. Quarterly. $180.00. ISSN 0269-7653. Provides "publication of research and review articles on all aspects of animal behaviour. Articles should emphasize the significance of the research for understanding the function, ecology, or evolution of behaviour." Formerly: *Monitore Zoologico Italiano*.

Ethology and Sociobiology. v. 1– , 1979– . New York: Elsevier. Bimonthly. $324.00. ISSN 0162-3095. Publishes articles "primarily concerned with the publication of ethological and sociobiological data and theories . . . the primary focus of the journal is the human species."

Evolution. v. 1– , 1947– . Lawrence, KS: Allen Press. Monthly. $250.00. ISSN 0014-3820. Published for the Society for the Study of Evolution. Publishes "significant and original results that extend our understanding of evolutionary phenomena and processes."

Evolution and Development. v. 1– , 1999– . Malden, MA: Blackwell Science. Bimonthly. $210.00. ISSN 1520-541X. Available electronically. "Evolution & Development will serve as a conduit for the rapid growth in research at the interface of evolutionary and developmental biology." Sponsored by the Society for Integrative and Comparative Biology.

Evolutionary Ecology Research. v. 1– , 1999– . Tucson, AZ: Evolutionary Ecology. 8 issues per year. $272.00. ISSN: 1522-0613. Available electronically. "A professional scientific journal focusing on the overlap between ecology and evolution."

Evolutionary Trends in Plants. v. 1– , 1987– . Leamington Spa, UK: ETP. Biannual. $300.00. ISSN 1011-3258. "Contains features, research reports and reviews charting major advances across the spectrum of plant evolution, genetics, and ecology."

Functional Ecology. v. 1– , 1987– . Oxford, England: Blackwell Science. Bimonthly. $550.00. ISSN 0269-8463. Available electronically. "Publishes short, original papers in a wide range of ecological topics, but particularly emphasizing the fields of physiological, biophysical and evolutionary ecology.'' An official journal of the British Ecological Society.

Global Change Biology. v. 1– , 1995– . Oxford, England: Blackwell Science. 8 issues per year. $784.00. ISSN 1354-1013. Available electronically. *"Global Change Biology*'s mission is to promote the science of biology in the global change debate. It aims to provide a multi-disciplinary forum for work that contributes to our understanding of responses and feedbacks in global change.''

Global Ecology and Biogeography. v. 8– , 1999– . Oxford, England: Blackwell Science. Bimonthly. $1,518.50. ISSN 1466-822X. Available electronically. *"Global Ecology and Biogeography* welcomes succinct, scientific material relating to historical, spatial, ecological and applied biogeography for rapid publication.'' Published as part of a single subscription package with *Journal of Biogeography* and *Diversity and Distributions*. Formerly: *Global Ecology and Biogeography Letters*.

Journal of Animal Ecology. v. 1– , 1932– . Oxford, England: Blackwell Science. Bimonthly. $550.00. ISSN 0021-8790. Available electronically. Publishes ''original research papers on any aspect of animal ecology.'' Published for the British Ecological Society.

Journal of Applied Ecology. v. 1– , 1964– . Oxford, England: Blackwell Science. Bimonthly. $550.00. ISSN 0021-8901. Available electronically. Publishes ''original papers that apply ecological concepts, theories, models and methods to the management of biological resources in their widest sense.'' Published for the British Ecological Society.

Journal of Arid Environments. v. 1– , 1978– . London: Academic Press. Monthly. $1,045.00. ISSN 0140-1963. Available electronically. ''Publishes original scientific and technical research articles and reviews on climate, geomorphology, geology, geography, botany, zoology, anthropology, sociology, and technical development in arid, semi-arid, and desert environments.''

Journal of Biological Rhythms. v. 1– , 1986– . New York: SAGE Science. Bimonthly. $480.00. ISSN 0748-7304. ''Publishes original, full-length reports in English of empirical investigations into all aspects of biological rhythmicity, particularly rhythms related to the major environmental cycles, including daily (circadian) rhythms, tidal rhythms, annual rhythms (including photoperiodism), as well as other biological rhythms that interact with those rhythms influenced by the environment.'' Published in association with the Society for Research on Biological Rhythms.

Journal of Chemical Ecology. v. 1– , 1975– . New York: Kluwer. Monthly. $1,165.00. ISSN 0098-0331. Available electronically. The official journal of the International Society of Chemical Ecology. "Devoted to promoting an ecological understanding of the origin, function, and significance of natural chemicals that mediate interactions within and between organisms."

Journal of Comparative Psychology. v. 97– , 1983– . Washington, DC: American Psychological Association. Quarterly. $144.00. ISSN 0735-7036. "Publishes original empirical and theoretical research from a comparative perspective on the behavior, cognition, perception, and social relationships of diverse species." Continues, in part, *Journal of Comparative and Physiological Psychology.*

Journal of Ecology. v. 1– , 1913– . Oxford, England: Blackwell Scientific. Bimonthly. $550.00. ISSN 0022-0477. Available electronically. Publishes "original research papers on all aspects of the ecology of plants (including algae) in both aquatic and terrestrial ecosystems." Published for the British Ecological Society.

Journal of Ethology. v. 1– , 1983– . Tokyo: Springer-Verlag Tokyo. Biannual. $156.50. ISSN 0289-0771. Available electronically. "Features reviews and original papers relating to all aspects of animal behavior, including traditional ethology." Published for the Japan Ethological Society.

Journal of Evolutionary Biology. v. 1– , 1988– . Basel: Birkhäuser. Bimonthly. $988.00. ISSN 1010-061X. Available electronically. The journal "covers both micro- and macro-evolution of all types of organisms. The aim of the Journal is to integrate perspectives across molecular and microbial evolution, behaviour, genetics, ecology, life histories, development, palaeontology, systematics and morphology." Official journal of the European Society for Evolutionary Biology.

Journal of the Experimental Analysis of Behavior. v. 1– , 1958– . Bloomington, IN: Indiana University. Bimonthly. $122.00. ISSN 0022-5002. Published for the Society for Experimental Analysis of Behavior. "Primarily for the publication of experiments relevant to the behavior of individual organisms."

Journal of Experimental Marine Biology and Ecology. v. 1– , 1967– . Amsterdam: Elsevier. Biweekly. $3,501.00. ISSN 0022-0981. Available electronically. "This journal provides a forum for work in the biochemistry, physiology, behaviour, and genetics of marine plants and animals in relation to their ecology; all levels of biological organization will be considered."

Journal of Experimental Psychology: Animal Behavior Processes. v. 1– , 1975– . Washington, DC: American Psychological Association. Quarterly. $170.00. ISSN 0097-7403. Continues, in part, *Journal of Experimental Psychology.* "Publishes experimental and theoretical studies concerning all aspects of animal behavior processes. Studies of associative, nonassociative, cognitive, perceptual, and motivational processes are welcome.''

Journal of Freshwater Ecology. v. 1– , 1981– . La Crosse, WI: Oikos Publishers. Quarterly. $70.00. ISSN 0270-5060. ''Intended to be a vehicle for the reasonably rapid dissemination of current limnological information.''

Journal of Molecular Evolution. v. 1– , 1971– . New York: Springer. Monthly. $1,299.00. ISSN 0022-2844. Available electronically. ''The Journal covers experimental and theoretical work aimed at deciphering features of molecular evolution and the processes bearing on these features, from the initial formation of macromolecular systems onward.''

Journal of Tropical Ecology. v. 1– , 1985– . New York: Cambridge University Press. Bimonthly. $256.00. ISSN 0266-4674. ''Publishes articles arising from original research, or reviews, in the field of tropical ecology.'' Published in association with INTECOL.

Journal of Wildlife Management. v. 1– , 1937– . Bethesda, MD: The Wildlife Society. Quarterly. $130.00. ISSN 0022-541X. An official publication of the Wildlife Society. ''Research papers dealing with population dynamics, natural history, ecology, habitat use, genetics, physiology, nutrition, systematics, modeling, research techniques, and reviews that develop theory are published in *The Journal*.'' Subscription price includes subscription to *Wildlife Monographs*, see the following.

Marine Ecology Progress Series (MEPS). v. 1– , 1979– . Halstenbek, Germany: Inter-Research. 8/yr. $2,968.00. ISSN 0171-8630. Available electronically. ''MEPS serves as a worldwide forum for all aspects of marine ecology, fundamental and applied.''

Microbial Ecology: An International Journal. v. 1– , 1974– . New York: Springer International. 8/yr. $650.00. ISSN 0095-3628. ''*Microbial Ecology* is an international journal whose aim is the advancement and dissemination of information describing the interactions between microorganisms and the biotic and abiotic components of their environments.'' The official journal of the International Society for Microbial Ecology.

Molecular Biology and Evolution. v. 1– , 1983– . Lawrence, KS: Society for Molecular Biology and Evolution. Monthly. $425.00. ISSN 0737-4038. Available electronically. Publishes ''research at the interface between molecular and evolutionary biology.'' Sponsored by the Society for Molecular Biology and Evolution.

Molecular Ecology. v. 1– , 1992– . Oxford, England: Blackwell Scientific Publications. Monthly. $2,118.00. ISSN 0962-1083. Available electronically. *"Molecular Ecology* is directed at the interface of molecular biology with ecology, evolution, and population biology.''

Oecologia. v. 1– , 1968– . New York: Springer Verlag. Monthly. $3,500.00. ISSN 0029-8549. Available electronically. Publishes "original contributions and short communications dealing with the ecology of all organisms.'' Published in cooperation with the International Association for Ecology (Intecol).

Oikos. v. 1– , 1948– . Copenhagen: Munksgaard. Monthly. $573.00. ISSN 0030-1299. Available electronically. "Theoretical as well as empirical work is welcome; however, theoretical papers should more than elaborate on previously published analyses, and empirical papers should test explicit hypotheses and/or theoretical predictions. . . . There is no bias as regards taxon, biome, or geographical region.'' Issued by the Nordic Society Oikos.

Origins of Life and Evolution of the Biosphere. v. 1– , 1968– . Dordrecht, Netherlands: Kluwer Academic. Bimonthly. $424.00. ISSN 0169-6149. Available electronically. "While any scientific study related to the origin of life has its place in this journal, the main interests revolve around theoretical and experimental studies dealing with planetary atmospheres, interstellar chemistry, precambrian studies, prebiotic chemistry, and early evolution.'' The journal of the International Society for the Study of the Origin of Life.

Plant Ecology. v. 128– , 1997– . Dordrecht, Netherlands: Kluwer Academic. Monthly. $2,187.00. ISSN: 1385-0237. Available electronically. Publishes "original scientific papers dealing with the ecology of vascular plants and bryophytes in terrestrial, aquatic and wetland ecosystems. Papers reporting on descriptive, historical, and experimental studies of any aspect of plant population, physiological, community, ecosystem and landscape ecology as well as on theoretical ecology are within the scope of the journal.'' Formerly: *Vegetatio.*

Population Ecology. v. 42– , 2000– . Tokyo: Springer-Verlag Tokyo. Semiannual. $210.00. ISSN 1438-3896. Available electronically. Publishes "original research articles and reviews on various aspects of population ecology, from the individual to the community level.'' The official journal of the Society of Population Ecology. Formerly: *Researches on Population Ecology.*

Sociobiology. v. 1– , 1976– . Chico, CA: California State University, Chico. Irregular. $96.00. ISSN 0361-6525. "The serial is devoted to papers giving research results, review articles, or translations of classic papers on any aspect of the biology of social animals.''

Wetlands. v. 1– , 1981– . Lawrence, KS: Society of Wetland Scientists. Quarterly. $125.00. ISSN 0277-5212. The journal is "concerned with all aspects of wetlands biology, ecology, hydrology, water chemistry, soil and sediment characteristics, management, and laws and regulations.'' The journal of the Society of Wetland Scientists. Also included in the membership are the *SWS Newsletter* and a membership directory.

Wildlife Monographs. v. 1– , 1957– . Bethesda, MD: The Wildlife Society. Irregular. $130.00. ISSN 0084-0173. A publication of The Wildlife Society. ''*Wildlife Monographs* was begun in 1957 to provide for longer papers than those normally accepted for *The Journal of Wildlife Management*.'' Subscription price include subscription to *The Journal of Wildlife Management*, see previous.

Wildlife Society Bulletin. v. 1– , 1973– . Bethesda, MD: The Wildlife Society. Quarterly. $80.00. ISSN 0091-7648. ''Manuscripts concerning all phases of management, law enforcement, economics, education, administration, philosophy, and contemporary problems related to wildlife are considered.'' Includes features listing recent publications of interest to Wildlife Society members.

REVIEWS OF THE LITERATURE

Advances in Ecological Research. v. 1– , 1962– . New York: Academic Press. Irregular. Price varies. ISSN 0065-2504. The series aim is ''to allow ecologists in general to remain aware not only of the advances that are made, but of the lacunae that remain in a subject that grows every [sic] more diverse.''

Annual Review of Ecology and Systematics. v. 1– , 1970– . Palo Alto, CA: Annual Reviews. Annual. $135.00. ISSN 0066-4162. The editors ''invite qualified authors to contribute critical articles reviewing significant developments within each major discipline.''

Ecological Studies: Analysis and Synthesis. v. 1– , 1970– . New York: Springer-Verlag. Irregular. Price varies. ISSN 0070-8356. Each volume reviews an ecological topic in depth. Recent volumes include *Responses of Northern US Forests to Environmental Change* and *Activity Patterns of Small Mammals*.

Evolutionary Biology. v. 1– , 1967– . Dordrecht, Netherlands: Kluwer. Irregular. Price varies. ISSN 0071-3260. Focuses on ''critical reviews, commentaries, original papers, and controversies in evolutionary biology. The topics of the reviews range from anthropology to molecular evolution and from population biology to paleobiology.''

Oxford Surveys in Evolutionary Biology. v. 1– , 1984– . New York: Oxford University Press. Annual. Price varies. ISSN 0265-072X. ''The goal of this series, which reviews new theoretical ideas and frameworks, is to stimulate discussion and outline progress in evolutionary studies. It covers the entire field, and presents special features, such as reviews of books in areas of particular interest, essays in response to the publication of major works, and comments on previously published articles.''

Perspectives in Ethology. v. 1– , 1973– . Dordrecht, Netherlands: Kluwer. Irregular. Price varies. ISSN 0738-4394.   Each volume contains articles organized around a general topic relating to animal behavior, such as animal awareness or the future of ethology.

Trends in Ecology and Evolution. v. 1– , 1986– . Barking, UK: Elsevier. Monthly. $969.00. ISSN 0169-5347. Available electronically.   A journal of ''news, reviews and comments on current developments in ecology and evolutionary biology. It is not a vehicle for the publication of original research, hypotheses, synthesis or meta analyses.''

10

Plant Biology

Botany is "the scientific study of plants, including their anatomy, morphology, physiology, biochemistry, taxonomy, cytology, genetics, evolution, and geographical distribution" (*Oxford Dictionary of Biology*, 4th ed., 2000). In this chapter, the terms *botany* and *plant biology* will be used interchangeably. In practice, *botany* may carry the connotation of taxonomic studies, while *plant biology* is often the preferred "modern" term for the entire field.

The study of botany has a long and distinguished history. This fact, coupled with the complexity of the subject as it has grown from descriptive botany to the molecular plant sciences, is reflected in its literature, producing a complicated and often confusing array of resources. In addition, some more traditional botanical fields such as the study of herbal medicine and ethnobotany are currently enjoying resurgence in interest. For the purposes of this book, plant biology encompasses the literature of botany and the plant kingdom, including fungi. This chapter does not include agriculture, forestry, horticulture, or any of the applied areas of plant science, except biotechnology and medicinal plants. The sources mentioned here are not comprehensive, but they are recommended as starting points appropriate for the informed layperson, the student, teacher, or librarian.

Because divisions in the study of plant biology are often, necessarily, arbitrary it is important to consult other chapters in this book for relevant materials that are annotated in the general sources, biochemistry, genetics, and microbiology chapters.

ABSTRACTS AND INDEXES

Current Awareness

Bibliography of Systematic Mycology. v. 1– , 1943– . Wallingford, Oxon, UK: CAB International. Semi-annual. $205.00. ISSN 0006-1573. Lists papers and books on all aspects of the taxonomy of fungi compiled from world literature. Each issue has an author and classified index, and book reviews of interests to botanists. In print, online, and CD-ROM.

Current Advances in Plant Science (CAPS). v. 1–   , 1972–   . Oxford, England: Elsevier. Monthly. $1,900.00. ISSN 0306-4484.   Competitor to *Biological Abstracts* but not as comprehensive. Entries are organized by broad subject categories. Available in print, online, and CD-ROM separately and as part of the Current Advances in Biological Sciences database (see Chapter 4, "Abstracts and Indexes").

Index of Fungi. v. 1–   , 1940–   . Wallingford, Oxon, UK: CAB International. Semi-annual. $205.00. ISSN 0019-3895.   Lists of names of new genera, species and varieties of fungi, new combinations, and new names, compiled from world literature. Supersedes Petrak's *Lists*.

Index of Mosses: A Catalog of the Names and Citations for New Taxa, Combinations, and Names for Mosses, v. 1992–   . Compiled by Marshal R. Crosby, et al. St. Louis: Missouri Botanical Garden. Price varies.   The title provides a good description of the importance and convenience of this source. Four volumes have been published so far covering the literature to 1998. The Index of Mosses Database, listed in the Classification and Nomeclature section, was taken from the *Index*.

Kew Record of Taxonomic Literature. 1971–   . London: Her Majesty's Stationery Office. Quarterly. $235.00. ISSN 0307-2835.   Comprehensive publication of worldwide taxonomic literature of flowering plants, gymnosperms, and ferns. Systematic arrangement; also includes citations to phytogeography, floristics, nomenclature, chromosome surveys, chemotaxonomy, anatomy, reproductive biology, personnalia, etc. Cumulative indexes. Also available on the Web at http://www.rbgkew.org.uk/kr/KRHomeExt.html. There is no charge for simple searches.

Review of Plant Pathology. v. 1–   , 1922–   . Wallingford, Oxon, UK: CAB International. Monthly. $1,185.00. ISSN 0034-6438.   Although somewhat out of scope, this abstracting service is useful for journal articles, reports, conferences, and books dealing with diseases of crop plants and ornamental plants caused by fungi, bacteria, viruses and mycoplasma-like organisms. Information on taxonomy, morphology, genetics, fungicides and antibiotics, physiology, and molecular biology. Includes books and occasional review articles. Also available on the Web.

Retrospective Sources

Bay, J. C. "Bibliographies of Botany. A Contribution Toward a Bibliotheca Bibliographia." *Progressus Rei Botanicae* 3(2): 331–456, 1910.   A valuable source. Arranged by topic: methodology, periodicals and reviews, collective indexes to periodicals, general and comprehensive bibliographies, national bibliographies, morphology and anatomy, plant geography, libraries of institutions, booksellers' catalogs, etc. Many entries are annotated.

Botanical Abstracts, v. 1. 1–15, 1918–1926. Baltimore, MD: Williams and Wilkins. Monthly abstracting serial, international in scope. Continued by *Biological Abstracts*.

Botanisches Zentralblatt, Referiendes Organ für das Gesamtgebiet der Botanik. Im Auftrage der Deutschen Botanischen Gesellschaft, v. 1–179, 1880–1945. Jena, Germany: Fischer. Abstracting publication in German.

The Cleveland Herbal, Botanical and Horticultural Collections: A Descriptive Bibliography of pre-1830 Works from the libraries of the Holden Arboretum, the Cleveland Medical Library Association, and the Garden Center of Greater Cleveland. Compiled by Stanley H. Johnston, Jr. Kent, OH: Kent State University Press, 1992. 1216 p. $60.00. ISBN 0873384334. Describes the holdings of these three collections in great detail. Works are listed chronologically from the fifteenth to the nineteenth centuries.

Flowering Plant Index of Illustration and Information. Garden Center of Greater Cleveland Staff. Boston, MA: G.K. Hall, 1979. 3 v. ISBN 0816103011. Updates *Index Londinensis*. Provides source for colored illustrations of flowering plants. Cross-references for common and botanical names. *First Supplement*, 1982. 2 vols. ISBN 0816104034. $260.00.

Fungorum Libri Bibliothecae Joachim Schliemann. W. Uellner, ed. (Books and Prints of Four Centuries Series.) Forestburgh, NY: Lubrecht & Cramer, 1976 reprint. ISBN 3768210758. Complete bibliographic information with reference to descriptions in other bibliographies, arranged by author. Citations to biographical information are included when available.

Guide to the Literature of Botany: Being a Classified Selection of Botanical Works, Including Nearly 600 Titles Not Given in Pritzel's Thesaurus. Benjamin D. Jackson, ed. Mansfield Center, CT: Martino Fine Books, 1999. 626 p. $65.00. ISBN 3874290697. Reprint of the 1881 edition. An essential companion to Pritzel (see following text), arranged by subject.

Hawksworth, D. L., and M. R. D. Seaward. *Lichenology in the British Isles, 1568–1975: An Historical and Bibliographic Survey.* Surrey, England: Richmond, 1977. 240 p. ISBN 0916422321. Comprehensive survey of lichenology in the British Isles, including 2,695 entries. Books, journal articles, thesis manuscripts, exsiccatae that were published through 1975 are included with some titles added during 1976. Collectors and the particular herbaria with which they are/ were associated are listed, and a biographical index is included.

Henrey, B. *British Botanical and Horticultural Literature before 1800; Comprising a History and Bibliography of Botanical and Horticultural Books Printed in England, Scotland and Ireland from the Earliest Times until 1800.* 3 vols. New York: Oxford University Press, 1975. Comprehensive source; includes location of materials within the British Isles.

Index Kewensis Plantarum Phanerogamarum Nomina et Synonyma Omnium Generum et Specierum a Lennaeo usque ad Annum MDCCCLXXXV Complectens Nomine Recepto Auctore Patria Unicuique Plantae Subjectis. Sumptibus beati Caroli Roberti Darwin ductu et consilio Josephi D. Hooker confecit B. Dayton Jackson. . . . Oxford, England: Clarendon, 1893–95. v. 1–2, *Supplementum* v. 1– , 1886– . Continued by *Kew Index for . . .* compiled by R.A. Davies and K. M. Lloyd. New York: Oxford University Press, 1987– . This indispensable index is an alphabetical listing of plant names with bibliographic references to the place of first publication. All volumes, including supplements, are available from Koeltz Books at present. Also available on CD-ROM from Oxford University Press. Version 2.0 was published in 1997 and is available for $1,950.00 (ISBN 0192684507). It contains all the data from the original volumes and supplements 1–20.

Index Londinensis to Illustrations of Flowering Plants, Ferns and Fern Allies; Being an Amended and Enlarged Edition Continued up to the end of the Year 1920 of Pritzel's Alphabetical Register of Representations of Flowering Plants and Ferns Compiled from Botanical and Horticultural Publications of the 18th and 19th Centuries. Six vols. plus two supplements. 1979 reprint by Lubrecht & Cramer. ISBN 3874291510. Updated by *Index Kewensis* supplements and the *Flowering Plant Index . . . .* Originally published for the Royal Horticultural Society of London, 1929–31.

Index Muscorum. v. 1–5, 1959–1969 reprint. Konigstein, Germany: Koeltz. (Regnum Vegetabile, v. 17, 26, 33, 48, 65). $442.00 (set). Alphabetical lists of the genera and subdivisions of genera of the Musci. Information includes name of genus, its author, place and date of publication.

Index to American Botanical Literature, 1886–1966. Compiled by the Torrey Botanical Club. 4 v. Boston, MA: G. K. Hall, 1969. Invaluable card index in book form arranged by author. Continued as a section in the *Bulletin of the Torrey Botanical Club* compiled by the staff of the New York Botanical Garden.

Index to Botanical Monographs: A Guide to Monographs and Taxonomic Papers Relating to Phanerogams and Vascular Cryptogams Found Growing Wild in the British Isles. Compiled by Douglas H. Kent. London: Academic Press, 1967.

163 p.   Systematic arrangement for publications since 1800. Includes a list of abbreviations of the titles of periodicals.

Index to Plant Chromosome Numbers. 1956– . St. Louis, MO: Missouri Botanical Garden. (Monographs in Systematic Biology). Biannual. Price varies. ISSN 0161-1542.   The index is arranged alphabetically by family within broad groupings of algae, fungi, bryophytes, pteridophytes, and spermatophytes. Variously published by the California Botanical Society, the North Carolina Press, and Koeltz as part of the *Regnum Vegetabile* series. Since 1975 it has been published by the Missouri Botanical Garden.

Index to Plant Distribution Maps in North American Periodicals through 1972. Compiled by W. Louis Phillips. Boston, MA: G. K. Hall, 1978. $110.00. ISBN 0816100098.   This index contains 28,500 entries arranged alphabetically by taxa, representing 268 periodicals published by societies, universities, museums, herbaria, botanical gardens, and arboreta.

International Bibliography of Vegetation Maps. 2nd ed. A. W. Kuchler, ed. Lawrence, KS: University of Kansas Libraries, 1980. 324 p. (Library series, no. 45, University of Kansas.)   Contains vegetation maps of North and South America, Europe, USSR, Asia, Australia, Africa, and the world. Arrangement is geographic and then chronological. Data includes map title, date of preparation, color, scale, legend, author, publication information.

International Catalogue of Scientific Literature, 1901–1914. Section M: Botany. 3 vols. Johnson reprint of the 1902 edition.   Lists botanical literature for the dates covered. See Chapter 4, ''Abstracts and Indexes,'' for full annotation.

Junk, W. *Bibliographia Botanica*, including supplement (1916). Berlin: Junk, 1909.   Bibliography of 6,891 botanical papers and books arranged by subject and then by author. There is a list of periodical of importance.

Lindau, Gustav and P. Sydow. *Thesaurus Litteraturae Mycologicae et Lichenologicae.* . . 5 vols. Johnson reprint of the earlier edition, 1964. (Originally published 1908–1917.)   Mycological books and papers to 1930.

Nissen, Claus. *Die Botanische Buchillustration, Ihre Geschichte und Bibliographie.* v. 1–2. Stuttgart, Germany: Hierseman, 1951. Supplement, 1966.   Vol. 1: History. Vol. 2: Bibliography with indexes for titles, artists, plants, countries, and authors.

Petrak, F. *List of New Species and Varieties of Fungi, New Combinations and New Names Published, 1920–39.* Kew, England: Commonwealth Mycological Institute, 1950–57.   Mycological literature from 1922 to 1935. *Index of Fungi* supplements Petrak's *List.*

Pfister, Donald H., Jean R. Boise, and Maria A. Eifler. *A Bibliography of Taxonomic Mycological Literature, 1753–1821*. Berlin: J. Cramer, 1990. 161 p. (Mycological Memoir, no. 17.) $55.00. ISBN 3443760074.   Fills in some gaps in the mycological taxonomic literature.

Pritzel, G. A. *Thesaurus Literature Botanicae Omnium Gentium*. Mansfield Centre, CT: Martino Publishing, 1999. 576 p. $90.00. ISBN 1888262605.   A facsimile of the original 1872 edition. This is the most important retrospective source indexing early botanical works to 1870.

Rehder, A. *The Bradley Bibliography*. v. 1–5. Cambridge, MA: Riverside Press, Arnold Arboretum, 1983 (originally published around 1900?)   "A guide to the literature of the woody plants of the world published before the beginning of the twentieth century."

Repertorium Commentationum a Societatibus Litterariis Editarum. T. 2: *Botanica et Mineralogia*. J. D. Reuss, ed. Gottingen, Germany: Dieterich, 1803. (Burt Franklin reprint 1961.)   Index to the publications of learned societies to 1800.

Saccardo, Pier A. *Sylloge Fungorum Omnium Hucusque Cognitorum*, v. 1–25. New York: Johnson Reprint. $2,070.00 (set). ISBN 0384528309 (set).   Genera and species to 1921.

Stafleu, Frans Antonie and Richard S. Cowan. *Taxonomic Literature: A Selective Guide to Botanical Publications and Collections with Dates, Commentaries and Types*. 2nd ed. (Regnum Vegetabile, 94, 98, 105, 110, 112, 115, 116, 125, 130, 132, 134, 135, 137). Konigstein, Germany: Koeltz, 1976– . Seven volumes (1976–98) and six supplements (1992–2000) to date.   Excellent resource with comprehensive information given for each entry. There are indexes to titles and names.

ASSOCIATIONS

American Association of Botanical Gardens and Arboreta (AABGA). 351 Longwood Rd, Kennett Square, PA 19348–1807. Phone: (610) 925-2500. E-mail: aagba @voicenet.com. URL: http://www.aabga.org.   Founded 1940. 3,000 members. Directors and staffs of botanical gardens, arboreta, institutions maintaining or conducting horticultural courses, and others. Publishes *American Association of Botanical Gardens and Arboreta-Newsletter*, *Public Garden*, internship directory, technical information papers, etc.

American Botanical Council (ABC). P.O. Box 144345, Austin, TX 78714–4345. Phone: (512) 926-4900. E-mail: abc@herbalgram.org. URL: http://www. herbalgram.org.   Founded 1988. Nonmembership. Seeks to gather and disseminate information on herbs, medicinal plants, and herbal research; increase public awareness and professional knowledge of the historical role and current potential of plants in medicine; promote understanding regarding the importance of preserving native plant populations in temperate and tropical zones. Publishes *HerbalGram*.

American Bryological and Lichenological Society (ABLS), c/o James Lawrey, George Madison University, 4400 University, Fairfax, VA 22030–4444. Phone: (703) 993-1059. E-mail: jlawrey@gmu.edu. URL: http://www.unomaha. edu/~abls/. Founded 1898. 500 members. Professional botanists, botany teachers, and hobbyists interested in the study of mosses, liverworts, and lichens. Publishes *Bryologist, Evansia*, and a membership directory.

American Herb Association (AHA). P.O. Box 1673, Nevada City, CA 95959. Phone: (530) 265-9552. URL: http://www.jps.net/ahaherb. Founded 1981. 1,000 members. Enthusiasts of herbs and herbal products. Publishes *American Herb Association Quarterly Newsletter*; also publishes list of herb books.

American Phytopathological Society (APS). 3340 Pilot Knob Rd., St. Paul, MN 55121–2097. Phone: (651) 454-7250. E-mail: aps@scisoc.org. URL: http:// www.apsnet.org. Founded 1908. 5,000 members. Professional educators, researchers, and other interested in the study and control of plant diseases. Publishes *Molecular Plant-Microbe Interactions, Phytopathology, and Plant Disease: An International Journal of Applied Plant Pathology*.

American Society of Plant Physiologists (ASPP). 15501 Monona Dr., Rockville, MD 20855–2768. Phone: (301) 251-0560. E-mail: aspp@aspp.org. URL: http:// www.aspp.org. Founded 1924. 5,200 members. Professional international society of plant physiologists, plant biochemists, plant molecular and cellular biologists and other plant scientists engaged in research and teaching. Publishes *ASPP Newsletter, Plant Cell, and Plant Physiology*.

American Society of Plant Taxonomists (ASPT). University of Wyoming, Laramie, WY 82071–3165. Phone: (307) 766-2556. E-mail: aspt@uwyo.edu. URL: http://www.sysbot.org. Founded 1935. 1,300 members. Botanists and others interested in all phases of plant taxonomy. Publications: *American Society of Plant Taxonomists-Directory, Systematic Botany Monographs*, and a newsletter.

Botanical Society of America (BSA). c/o Kimberly E. Hiser, Business Manager, Botanical Society of America, 1735 Neil Ave, Columbus OH 43210–1293. Phone: (614) 292-3519. URL: http://www.botany.org/bsa. Founded 1906. 3,000 members. Professional society of botanists. Publishes *American Journal of Botany, Membership Directory, Career Bulletin, Guide to Graduate Study in Botany for the U.S. and Canada, and Plant Science Bulletin*.

Council on Botanical and Horticultural Libraries (CBHL). c/o Charlotte Tancin, Secretary, CBHL Hunt Institute for Botanical Documentation, Carnegie Mellon University, Pittsburgh, PA, 15213–3890. Phone: (412) 268-7301. E-mail: ct0u@andrew.cmu.edu. URL: http://huntbot.andrew.cmu.edu/cbhl/. Founded 1970. 250 members. Libraries and collections in botanical or horticultural materials; librarians, bibliographers, booksellers, publishers, researchers, and administrators. Publishes a newsletter, *Plant Bibliography Series* (discontinued 1999), and an online directory of member libraries.

Herb Research Foundation. 1007 Pearl St. Suite 200, Boulder, CO 80302. Phone: (303) 449-2265. E-mail: info@herbs.org. URL: http://www.herbs.org. Nonprofit research and educational organization that focuses on herbs and medicinal plants. Publishes *HerbalGram, Herbs for Health*, and a newsletter.

Herb Society of America (HSA). 9019 Kirtland-Chardon Rd., Kirtland, OH 44094. Phone: (440) 256-0514. E-mail: herbs@herbsociety.org. URL: http://www.herbsociety.org/. Founded 1933. 3,000 members. Scientists, educators and others interested in botanical and horticultural research on herbs and culinary, economic, decorative, fragrant, and historic use of herbs. Publishes *Herbalist*, a membership directory, and a newsletter.

International Association for Plant Physiology (IAPP). CSIRO Div. of Food Processing, P.O. Box 52 North Ryde, NSW 2113, Australia. Founded 1964. National and regional societies of plant physiologists representing 10,000 individual members in 40 countries. Publishes *International Directory of Plant Physiologists,* and a newsletter.

International Association for Plant Taxonomy (IAPT). c/o Institute of Botany, University of Vienna Rennweg 14, A-1030, Vienna, Austria. Phone: 43 1 4277-54098. E-mail: iapt@s1.botanik.univie.ac.at. URL: http://www.botanik.univie.ac.at/iapt/. Founded 1950. 2,900 members. Coordinates work related to plant taxonomy and international codification of plant names. Formerly Commission on the Nomenclature of Plants. Publishes *Regnum Vegetabile* and *Taxon*.

International Association for Vegetation Science (IAVS). Alterra, Green World Research (formerly IBN-DLO), Postbus 47, NL-6700 AA Wageningen, The Netherlands. Phone: 31 317 47 79 13. E-mail: j.h.j.schaminee@alterra.wag-ur.nl. URL: http://www.iavs.org/. Founded 1930. 1,568 members. Vegetation scientists in 83 countries including botanists and ecologists. Formerly: International Society for Vegetation Science. Publishes Proceedings of the International Symposium, *Applied Vegetation Science, Journal of Vegetation Science*, and a newsletter.

International Association of Botanic Gardens (IABG). c/o Dr J.E. Hernández Bermejo, Jardín Botánico de Córdoba, Apdo 3048, 14071 Córdoba, Spain. Phone:

34 (9)57 200 355. E-mail: jardinbotcord@cod.servicom.es.   Founded 1954. 798 members. Botanic gardens, arboreta, and similar institutions maintaining scientific collections of plants; members of their staffs. Publishes *International Directory of Botanical Gardens*.

International Mycological Association (IMA). c/o Dr. M. Blackwell, Dept. of Biology Sciences, 508 Life Sciences Bldg., Louisiana State University, Baton Rouge, LA 70803. Phone: (225) 388-8485 E-mail: btblac@unix1.sncc.lsu.edu. URL: http://lsb380.plbio.lsu.edu/ima.   Founded 1971. 2,500 members. International society representing 20,000 mycologists from 80 countries. Promotes the study of mycology in all its aspects. Publishes *IMA News* and the *International Mycological Directory*.

International Phycological Society (IPS). c/o Gerald T. Boalch, The Laboratory, Citadel Hill, Plymouth, Devon PL1 2PB, England URL: http://seaweed.ucg.ie/phycologia/IPS.html.   Founded 1960. 900 members. Scientists working to develop phycology. Publishes *Phycologia*.

International Plant Genetic Resources Institute (IPGRI). Headquarters, Via delle Sette Chiese, 142, Rome 00145, Italy. Phone: 39-06 518921. E-mail: ipgri@cgiar.org. URL: http://www.ipgri.cgiar.org/.   Founded 1974. An international research institute with a mandate to advance the conservation and use of genetic diversity for the well-being of present and future generations. Publishes *Annual Report, Geneflow, Plant Genetic Resources Abstracts,* and a newsletter.

International Society for Plant Molecular Biology (ISPMB). University of Georgia, Biochemistry Dept. Athens, GA 30602-7229. Phone: (706) 542-3239. E-mail: ldure@arches.uga.edu. URL: http://www.uga.edu/~ispmb.   Founded 1983. 1,850 members. Scientists whose research involves the molecular biology of plants. Publishes *Directory of Members, Plant Molecular Biology,* and *Plant Molecular Biology Reporter*.

International Society of Plant Morphologists (ISPM). Dept. of Botany, University of Delhi, Delhi 110 007, India.   Founded 1950. 805 members. Individuals in 26 countries interested in plant morphology and its allied sciences. Purpose is to promote international cooperation among botanists. Publishes *Phytomorphology* and *Yearbook*.

Mycological Society of America (MSA). c/o Maren A. Klich, USDA/ARS/SRRC, 1100 Robert E. Lee Blvd. New Orleans, LA 70124. Phone: (504) 286-4361. E-mail: mklich@nola.srrc.usda.gov. URL: http://www.erin.utoronto.ca/w3msa/.   Founded 1931. 1,300 members. Researchers, industrial and medical mycologists, plant pathologists, students, and others interested in the study of fungi through research, teaching, and industrial applications. Annual meeting.

Publishes *MSA Directory, Mycologia, Mycologia Memoirs, Mycology Guidebook*, career brochure, and a newsletter.

North American Mycological Association (NAMA). 10 Lynn Brooke Place, Charleston, WV 25312–9521 Phone: (304) 744-1654. URL: http://www.namyco. org. Founded 1959. 2,200 members consisting of regional, state, and local groups. Amateur and professional mycologists, students, and botanists. Publishes *McIlvainea*, a newsletter, and *Directory*.

Phycological Society of America (PSA). Dept. Biological Science, 800 N. State College Blvd., California State University, Fullerton, CA 92384. Phone: (714) 228-7291. URL: http://www.psaalgae.org. Founded 1946. 1,100 members. Educators, researchers, and others interested in the pure, applied, or avocational study and utilization of algae. Publishes *Journal of Phycology, Phycological Newsletter*, and a membership directory.

Phytochemical Society of Europe (PSE). Div. of Biosphere Sciences, King's College London, University of London, Campden Hill Rd., London W8 7AH, England. URL: http://www.dmu.ac.uk/ln/pse/. Founded 1957. 500 members. Scientists in 17 countries working in the field of plant chemistry. Publishes *Proceedings of the Phytochemical Society of Europe* and *Phytochemistry*.

Phytochemical Society of North America (PSNA). c/o Dr. Cecilia A. McIntosh, Treasurer, Treasurer Dept. of Biology, Box 70703, East Tennessee State University, Johnson City, TN 37614–0703. Phone: (423) 929-5838. Fax: (423) 929–5958. E-mail: mcintosc@etsu.edu. URL: http://www.ucalgary.ca/~dabird/psna/. Founded 1960. 405 members. Membership comprises primarily research scientists interested in all aspects of the chemistry of plants. Publishes *Directory*, a newsletter, and *Recent Advances in Phytochemistry*.

Plant Growth Regulator Society of America (PGRSA). P.O. Box 2945, LaGrange, GA 30241. Phone: (706) 845-9085. URL: http://www.griffin.peachnet. edu/pgrsa. Founded 1973. 850 members. Scientists concerned with plant growth regulation. Publishes *PGRSA Quarterly*, a newsletter, *Membership Directory*, and books on techniques, etc.

Society for Economic Botany (SEB). New York Botanical Garden, Bronx, NY 10458. Phone: (718) 817-8171. E-mail: dlentz@nybg.org. URL: http://www. econbot.org. Founded 1959. 1,200 members. Botanists, anthropologists, pharmacologists, and others interested in scientific studies of useful plants. Publishes *Economic Botany, Membership Directory*, and a newsletter.

Society for Medicinal Plant Research (Gesellschaft für Arzneipflanzenforschung-GA). c/o Dr. B. Frank, Gesellschaft für Arzneipflanzenforschung, Am Grundbach 5, D-97271 Kleinrinderfeld. Fax: 49 931 8002–275. E-mail: GA-Secretary@

t-online.de. URL: http://www.uni-duesseldorf.de/WWW/GA/. Founded 1953. 1,300 members. Scientists in 70 countries who promote medicinal plant research. Publishes *Newsletter* and *Planta Medica*.

The Torrey Botanical Society. c/o Dr. H. D. Hammond, New York Botanical Garden Bronx, NY 10458. Phone: (212) 220-8987. URL: http://www. torreybotanical. com/. Founded 1860. Botanists and others interested in botany and in collecting and disseminating information on all phases of plant science. Publishes *Journal of the Torrey Botanical Society* and *Memoirs of the Torrey Botanical Club*. Formerly: The Torrey Botanical Club.

ATLASES, CHECKLISTS, AND IDENTIFICATION MANUALS

There are many excellent field guides for the identification of plants, and this section includes some of the best. For more information, investigate the well-known field guide series that are annotated in Chapter 3, "General Sources.".

Angier, Bradford. *Field Guide to Edible Wild Plants*. Harrisburg, PA: Stackpole, 1974. 255 p. $12.00. ISBN 0811720187. "A quick all in color identifier of more than 100 edible wild foods growing free in the United States and Canada." Updated by Duke and Elias.

Barnett, James Arthur, et al. *Yeasts: Characteristics and Identification*. 2nd ed. New York: Cambridge University Press, 1990. 1,002 p. $250.00. ISBN 0521350565. Commonly used procedures for yeast identification, including detailed descriptions for all known yeast species. This book is also an important source for yeast taxonomy.

Baumgardt, John Philip. *How to Identify Flowering Plant Families: A Practical Guide for Horticulturists and Plant Lovers*. Portland, OR: Timber Press, 1982. 269 p. $22.95 (paper). ISBN 0917304217 (paper). Identifies over 100 plant genera of North America. Useful in classroom or field.

Common Weeds of the United States. Prepared by the Agricultural Research Service of the U. S. Dept. of Agriculture. New York: Dover, 1971. 463 p. $7.50. ISBN 0486205045. This valuable source, including 224 of the most important U.S. weeds, assists in weed identification for establishing control measures. A republication of *Selected Weeds of the United States*, Washington, DC: USDA, 1970.

Duke, James A. *CRC Handbook of Medicinal Herbs*. Boca Raton, FL: CRC Press, 1985. 696 p. $275.00. ISBN 0849336309. This manual discusses over 365 species of folk medicinal herbs whose safety is, or has been, questioned by various federal agencies. Information includes common and scientific name, description of use, medicinal applications, chemical content, and toxicity. This is a nice companion to Duke's *Handbook of Edible Weeds*, also published by CRC Press in 1992, 232 p. $19.95. ISBN 0849342252. Also, see Angier and Elias.

Elias, Thomas S. *The Complete Trees of North America: Field Guide and Natural History*. New York: Gramercy Pub. Co; distributed by Crown Publishers, 1987. (Reprint of the 1980 edition) 948 p. ISBN 0517641046. This book assists in identifying over 750 North American trees.

Elias, Thomas S. and Peter A. Dykeman. *Field Guide to North American Edible Wild Plants*. New York: Outdoor Life, 1982. 286 p. ISBN 0442222009. An alternative to Angier and Duke.

Farrar, John L. *Trees of the Northern United States and Canada*. Ames, IA: Iowa State University Press, 1995. 502 p. $39.95. ISBN 081382740X. Covers 300 species of trees. Includes keys, color photos, line drawings and maps. Published in Canada as *Trees in Canada*.

Flora of North America, North of Mexico. Flora of North America Editorial Committee and Nancy R. Morin, eds. New York: Oxford University Press, 1993– . Irregular. Price varies. This projected 30-volume monumental work aims to survey and classify all the more than 20,000 plant species known to grow spontaneously from the Florida Keys to the Aleutian Islands. This authoritative set provides identification keys; distribution maps; summaries of habitat and geographical ranges; precise descriptions for families, genera, and species; chromosome numbers; pertinent synonymies; line drawings; endangered and threatened plants; selected references. The set will be updated by a computer database for taxonomic information housed at the Missouri Botanical Garden in St. Louis, MO. See their Web site at http://hua.huh.harvard.edu/FNA/.

Flowering Plants of the World. V. H. Heywood, ed. New York: Oxford University Press, 1993. 336 p. $65.00. ISBN 0195210379. This beautiful book contains over 200 color illustrations and provides comprehensive coverage of the world's dominant plant group.

Gleason, Henry A. and Arthur Cronquist. *Manual of Vascular Plants of Northeastern United States and Canada*. 2nd ed. Bronx, NY: New York Botanical Garden, 1991. 910 p. $69.00. ISBN 0893273651. "This second edition of the Manual has been completely revised by Cronquist, the taxa rearranged according to his phylogenetic system, and the nomenclature updated. The general keys—long known for their ease of use—have been revised, new synoptic keys added, the glossary expanded, and ample place for notes provided."

Gray, Asa. *Gray's Manual of Botany: A Handbook of the Flowering Plants and Ferns of the Central and Northeastern United States and Canada*. 8th (Centennial) ed. Portland, OR: Dioscorides Press, 1987. (Reprint of the 1950 ed.) 1,632

p. $57.95. ISBN 0931146097. The standard descriptive manual for flowering plants and ferns.

Grieve, Maud. *A Modern Herbal: The Medicinal, Culinary, Cosmetic and Economic Properties, Cultivation and Folk-Lore of Herbs, Grasses, Fungi, Shrubs and Trees, with All Their Modern Scientific Uses, with a New Service Index.* New York: Dover, 1971. 2 v. $8.95 each. ISBN 0486227987 (v. 1); 0486227995 (v. 2). This encyclopedic treatment presents synonyms, common and scientific names, part used, habitat, descriptions, medicinal actions and uses, constituents, dose, poisons, history, and recipes.

Hitchcock, Albert Spear. *Manual of the Grasses of the United States.* 2nd ed. New York: Dover, 1971 reprint. 2 v. (USDA Miscellaneous Publication No. 200). $9.95 each. ISBN 0486227170 (v. 1); 0486227189 (v. 2). The classic manual and definitive encyclopedia of all grasses known to grow in the continental United States, excluding Alaska.

Lampe, Kenneth F. and Mary Ann McCann. *AMA Handbook of Poisonous and Injurious Plants.* Chicago, IL: American Medical Association distributed by the Chicago Review Press, 1985. 432 p. $18.95 (paper). ISBN 0899701833 (paper). This authoritative reference book is designed for health care professionals as a convenient field guide to the identification, diagnosis, and management of human intoxications from plants and mushrooms of the United States and Canada. Information includes botanical nomenclature, scientific and common name indexes, and sections on systemic plant poisoning, plant dermatitis, and mushroom poisoning. Each plant is completely described including distribution, toxic part, toxin, symptoms, management, and reference to the literature.

Mitchell, Alan. *The Trees of North America.* New York: Facts on File, Inc., 1987. 208 p. $35.00. ISBN 0816018065. All the common and frequently seen trees plus a wide selection of rare trees. Five hundred species are accurately illustrated together with 250 varieties with information on origin, history, distribution, and growth.

Rickett, Harold W. and W. Niles. *Wild Flowers of the United States.* New York: New York Botanical Garden and McGraw-Hill, 1966–1975. Six volumes plus complete index. A superior, comprehensive work that is beautifully done and scientifically accurate.

Smith, Alexander H. and Nancy S. Weber. *The Mushroom Hunter's Field Guide: All Color and Enlarged.* 2nd ed. Holt, MI: Thunder Bay Press, 1996. 316 p. $24.95. ISBN 1882376242. A standard, accurate, and dependable beginner's field guide to mushrooms.

GUIDES TO FLORAS

Rather than enumerate all the floras that are available, flora will be identified by
guides to location. Although some of these guides are dated, they still contain
very important sources of information.

Blake, Sidney Fay. *Guide to Popular Floras of the United States and Alaska:
An Annotated, Selected List of Nontechnical Works for the Identification of Flowers, Ferns and Trees.* Washington, DC: Government Printing Office, 1954. 56
p. (U.S. Dept. of Agriculture Bibliographical Bulletin 23.)   A useful, short history of popular botanical works.

Blake, Sidney Fay. *Geographical Guide to Floras of the World. Pt. 2: Western
Europe: Finland, Sweden, Norway, Denmark, Iceland, Great Britain with Ire-
land, Netherlands, Belgium, Luxembourg, France, Spain, Portugal, Andorra,
Monaco, Italy, San Marino, Switzerland.* Monticello, NY: Lubrecht and Cramer,
1974. (Reprint of the 1961 ed.) 742 p. $84.00. ISBN 3874290603.   Updated by
Frodin (see following text).

Blake, Sidney Fay and Alice Cary Atwood. *Geographic Guide to Floras of the
World. Pt. 1: Africa, Australia, North American, South America and Islands of
the Atlantic, Pacific, and Indian Oceans.* New York: Hafner, 1967. (Reprint of
the 1942 ed.) 336 p.   Updated by Frodin (see following text).

Frodin, D. G. *Guide to Standard Floras of the World.* New York: Cambridge
University Press, 1985. 580 p. ISBN 0521236886.   "An annotated, geographi-
cally arranged systematic bibliography of the principal floras, enumerations,
checklists, and horological atlases of different areas."

Takhtajan, Armen. *Floristic Regions of the World.* Translated by Theodore J.
Crovello, under the editorship of Arthur Cronquist. Berkeley, CA: University of
California Press, 1986. 522 p. $75.00. ISBN 0520040279.   Geographic distribu-
tion of the plant world.

CLASSIFICATION, NOMENCLATURE, AND SYSTEMATICS

This section lists books concerning classification, nomenclature, and taxonomy
as well as periodical sources for updating this kind of information. See the abstracts and indexes section for taxonomic indexes.

Brako, Lois, Amy Y. Rossman, David F. Farr, *Scientific and Common Names of
7,000 Vascular Plants in the United States.* St. Paul, MN: American Phytopathological Society Press, 1995. 301p. (Contributions from the U.S. National Fungal
Collections, no. 7.) $34.00. ISBN 089054171X.   A useful index that includes
"a majority of the plants of interest to plant pathologists and other agricultural

scientists.'' In four sections: scientific names in alphabetical order by genus; common names followed by the scientific name; major synonyms of the scientific name cross-referenced to the accepted scientific name; and genera of vascular plants arranged by plant family.

Brittonia, v. 1–   , 1931–   . Bronx, NY: New York Botanical Garden. Quarterly. $88.00. ISSN 0007-196X.   Publishes "original research articles on anatomy, botanical history, chemotaxonomy, morphology, paleobotany, phylogenetic systematics, taxonomy, and phytogeography.'' Full text of back issues is available on JSTOR.

Brummitt, R. K. *Vascular Plant Families and Genera: A Listing of the Genera of Vascular Plants of the World According to Their Families . . . with an Analysis of Relationships of the Flowering Plant Families According to Eight Systems of Classification*. Kew, UK: Royal Botanic Gardens, 1992. 804 p. $100.00. ISBN 0947643435.   The standard reference for generic names. In three parts: an alphabetic list of 14,000 accepted generic names, a list of genera by family, and an analysis of plant families following the eight systems of classification mentioned in the title. Also freely available on the Web at http://www.rbgkew.org.uk/data/vascplnt.html.

Chemical Fungal Taxonomy. Jens C. Frisvad, Paul D. Bridge and Dilip K. Arora, eds. New York: Dekker, 1998. 398 p. $175.00. ISBN 0824700694.   A survey of chemical techniques used in fungal systematics.

Crawford, Daniel J. *Plant Molecular Systematics: Macromolecular Approaches*. New York: Wiley, 1990. 388 p. $120.00. ISBN 0471807605.   This book discusses, and evaluates, the use of macromolecular (protein and DNA) data in plant systematics.

Cronquist, Arthur. *The Evolution and Classification of Flowering Plants*. 2nd ed. Bronx, NY: New York Botanical Garden, 1988. 555 p. ISBN 0893273325. Based on Cronquist's *Integrated System* (see following text), this text provides a more compact of version of his system of classification including general information on taxonomy, species and speciation, the origin and evolution of flowering plants.

Cronquist, Arthur. *An Integrated System of Classification of Flowering Plants*. Corrected edition. New York: Columbia University Press, 1993. 1,262 p. $237.00. ISBN 0231038801.   Indispensable for plant classification. There is information on the division, class, order, family, and basic features of almost 400 families of flowering plants.

Dictionary of Generic Names of Seed Plants. Tatiana Wielgorskaya, ed. New York: Columbia University Press, 1994. 472 p. $133.00. ISBN 023107892.

This dictionary follows the system devised by Armen Tahktajan to provide a comprehensive listing of all currently accepted generic names of seed plants, including synonyms.

Elsevier's Dictionary of Plant Names in Latin, English, French, German and Italian. Murray Wrobel and Geoffrey Creber, eds. Amsterdam: Elsevier, 1996. 925 p. $247.00, $245.00 (CD-ROM). ISBN 0444821821, 0444504494 (CD-ROM). Includes over 12,500 Latin terms used as botanical names for over 9,000 species of plants, plus multiple common names.

Harris, James G., and Melinda Woolf Harris. *Plant Identification Terminology: An Illustrated Glossary.* 2nd ed. Spring Lake, UT: Spring Lake Publishing, 2001. 216 p. $18.95. ISBN 0964022168. Illustrated glossary of over 2,400 terms used in plant description. An excellent visual aid for new students of plant taxonomy.

Hyam, R., and R. Pankhurst. *Plants and Their Names: A Concise Dictionary.* New York: Oxford University Press, 1995. 558 p. $35.00. ISBN 0198661894. Provides the "non-specialist with a reference source to some 16,000 of the more commonly occurring vernacular and Latin names."

Index Nominum Genericorum (Plantarum) (ING). Ellen Farr and Gea Zijlstra, eds. URL: http://rathbun.si.edu/botany/ing/. The ING is a collaborative project of the International Association for Plant Taxonomy (IAPT) and the Smithsonian Institution. This is a compilation of the generic names published for all organisms covered by the *International Code of Botanical Nomenclature (ICBN).*

Index of Mosses Database. St. Louis, MO: Missouri Botanical Garden. URL: http://www.mobot.org/MOBOT/tropicos/most/iom.html. "This database of moss names was prepared as part of the Index of Mosses project at the Missouri Botanical Garden." It simply lists moss names, and does not attempt to determine their validity.

International Code of Botanical Nomenclature. Adopted by the Sixteenth International Botanical Congress, St. Louis, MO, 1999. W. Greuter et al., eds. Konigstein, Germany: Koeltz Scientific Books, 2000. (Regnum Vegetabile, v. 138.) 474 p. $44.44. ISBN 3904144227. Updated by *Taxon* or *Mycotaxon.*

The International Plant Names Index. Plant Names Project, 1999– . URL: http://www.ipni.org. This index combines data from *Index Kewensis*, the *Gray Card Index*, and the *Australian Plant Names Index*. It is the most comprehensive listing of plant names to date, with 1.3 million species listed in 2000.

Jeffrey, Charles. *An Introduction to Plant Taxonomy.* 2nd ed. Cambridge, England: Cambridge University Press, 1982. 154 p. ISBN 0521287758. Fundamentals and process of classification, taxonomic hierarchy, naming of plants, systems of classification, and an outline of plant classification.

Judd, Walter S., Christopher S. Campbell, Elizabeth A. Kellogg, and Peter E. Stevens. *Plant Systematics: A Phylogenetic Approach*. Sunderland, MA: Sinauer, 1999. 464 p. $75.95. ISBN 0878934049 (text plus CD-ROM). Includes CD-ROM with over 650 color photographs.

Kartesz, John T. *A Synonymized Checklist of the Vascular Flora of the United States, Canada, and Greenland*. 2nd ed. Portland, OR: Timber Press, 1994. 2 v. ISBN 0881922048 (set). Names and synonyms in current use of native or naturalized plants found in North America. This is one of the best sources for verifying names and locating synonyms. Vol. 1: Checklist; Vol. 2: Thesaurus.

Kartesz, John T., et al. *A Synonymized Checklist of the Vascular Flora of the United States, Puerto Rico, and the Virgin Islands*. 1998– . URL: http://www.csdl.tamu.edu/FLORA/b98/check98.htm. An updated Web version of Kartesz, previous.

Molecular Systematics of Plants. Pamela S. Soltis et al., eds. New York: Chapman and Hall, 1992. 434 p. $90.00 (paper). ISBN 0412022311, 0412022419 (paper). The aim of this is to summarize the achievements of plant molecular systematics; to illustrate the potential of molecular characters in addressing phylogenetic and evolutionary questions; and to suggest the appropriate techniques for systematic inquiries.

Molecular Systematics of Plants II: DNA Sequencing. Douglas E. Soltis, Pamela S. Soltis, and Jeff J. Doyle, eds. Dordrecht: Kluwer, 1998. 574 p. $79.00 (paper). ISBN 0412111314 (paper). ''This completely revised work illustrates the potential of DNA markers for addressing a wide variety of phylogenetic and evolutionary questions.''

NCU-1. Family Names in Current Use for Vascular Plants, Bryophytes, and Fungi. Werner Greuter, ed. Champaign, IL: Koeltz Scientific Books, 1993. 95 p. (Regnum Vegetabile, v. 126.) $24.00 (paper). ISBN 1878762427 (paper). This booklet lists family names found to be currently used for organisms treated as plants under the *International Code of Botanical Nomenclature*.

NCU-2. Names in Current Use in the Families Trichocomaceae, Cladoniaceae, Pinaceae, and Lemnaceae. Edited by Werner Greuter on behalf of the Special Committee on Names in Current Use. Konigstein, Germany: Koeltz Scientific Books, 1993. 150 p. (Regnum Vegetabile, v. 128.) $26.00. ISBN 1878762443. Lists of names currently used covered by the *International Code of Botanical Nomenclature*.

NCU-3. Names in Current Use for Extant Plant Genera. Compiled and edited by Werner Greuter, et al. on behalf of the Special Committee on Names in Current Use. Konigstein, Germany: Koeltz Scientific Books, 1993. 1,464 p. (Regnum

Vegetabile, v. 129.) $209.00. ISBN 1878762486. A list of 28,041 generic names currently in use for extant algae, bryophytes, ferns, flowering plants, and fungi.

The New York Botanical Garden Vascular Plant Type Catalog. Bronx, NY: New York Botanical Garden. URL: http://www.nybg.org/bsci/hcol/vasc/. An online catalog of more than 67,000 vascular plant type specimens. Each entry contains the name of the specimen, where and by whom it was collected, a description of its habitat and a photograph.

Pearson, Lorentz C. *The Diversity and Evolution of Plants*. Boca Raton, FL: CRC Press, 1994. 646 p. $84.95. ISBN 0849324831. This book addresses plant diversity, and evolution as the ultimate cause of diversity. Encyclopedic in scope, it is rich with tables and illustrations, a glossary, and an extensive bibliography.

Quattrocchi, Umberto. *World Dictionary of Plant Names: Common Names, Scientific Names, Eponyms, Synonyms, and Etymology*. Boca Raton, FL: CRC Press, 2000. 4 v. $600.00 (set). ISBN 0849326737. This four-volume set contains a wealth of information on botanical history. A unique reference which covers over 200,000 plant species.

Radcliffe-Smith, A. *Three-language List of Botanical Name Components*. Kew, UK: Royal Botanic Gardens, 1998. 143 p. $20.00 (paper). ISBN 1900347504 (paper). A useful compilation of ''Greek and Latin roots or elements used in botanical names and epithets.'' Components are listed alphabetically in each of the three languages: English, Latin and Greek. Includes a plant name supplement and a numerical supplement in addition to the main list.

Sivarajan, V. V. *Introduction to the Principles of Plant Taxonomy*. 2nd ed. New York: Cambridge University Press, 1991. 292 p. $31.95 (paper). ISBN 0521355877, 0521356792 (paper). A readable exploration of current empirical and theoretical problems in plant taxonomy, phylogenetics and evolutionary systematics, concepts of taxa, characters employed in plant systematics, nomenclature, and history.

Takhtajan, Armen. *Diversity and Classification of Flowering Plants*. New York: Columbia University Press, 1997. 620 p. $100.00. ISBN 0231100981. Includes descriptive keys to the families of flowering plants as well as bibliographic references.

The Yeasts: A Taxonomic Study. 4th ed. Cletus P. Kurtzman and Jack W. Fell, eds. Amsterdam: Elsevier Science, 1998. 1,055 p. $460.00. ISBN 0444813128. Classic treatise on yeast taxonomy. Also, refer to Barnett in the Identification section of this chapter.

Zomlefer, Wendy B. *Guide to Flowering Plant Families*. Chapel Hill, NC: University of North Carolina Press, 1994. 430 p. $55.00, $27.50 (paper). ISBN 0807821608, 0807844705 (paper). Covers 130 flowering-plant families. Beautifully illustrated with over 150 line drawings. Includes glossary and references.

DATABASES

The Arabidopsis Information Resources (TAIR). URL: http://www.arabidopsis. org/home.html. TAIR replaces the *Arabidopsis thaliana* Database Project (AtDB) that ended in 1999. It is a collaborative effort between the Carnegie Institution of Washington Department of Plant Biology and the National Center for Genome Resources.

Brunt, A. A., K. Crabtree, M. J. Dallwitz, A. J. Gibbs, L. Watson, and E. J. Zurcher, eds. 1996– . Plant Viruses Online: Descriptions and Lists from the VIDE Database. Version: 16th January 1997. URL: http://biology.anu.edu.au/ Groups/MES/vide/. ''These pages contain information on most species of virus known to infect plants, not only those whose virions have been described, but also those like umbraviruses that have no virion protein genes of their own, and use the virion proteins of their symbiotic helper viruses instead. We include data on host range; transmission and control; geographical distribution; physical, chemical and genomic properties; taxonomy and relationships; and selected literature references.'' Data from this resource have also been published in 1996 as *Viruses of Plants: Descriptions and Lists from the VIDE Database*.

Carnivorous Plant Database. URL: http://www2.labs.agilent.com/bot/cp_home. Database of over 3,000 carnivorous plants. Each entry consists of the scientific name, date and place of discovery, and name of discoverer. International in coverage. Includes photographs and illustrations. Links to companion listserv CP-L.

Harvard University Herbaria Databases. URL: http://www.herbaria.harvard.edu/ Data/data.html. Includes the Gray Herbarium Index of New World Plants, Harvard University Herbaria Type Specimen Database, Treebase: A database of phylogenetic knowledge, Botanical Collectors database, Botanical Authors database, Botanical Publications database, and much more.

IOPI Database of Plant Databases (DPD). International Organization for Plant Information, 1995– . URL: http://iopi.csu.edu.au/iopi/iopidpd1.html. The DPD is a ''a global list of plant databases, to tell you who is putting together what data and where.'' It includes taxonomic databases, collection catalogues, and DELTA (Description Language for Taxonomy) datasets.

Moerman, Daniel E. Native American Ethnobotany Database—Foods, Drugs, Dyes, and Fibers of Native North American Peoples. URL: http://www.umd.

umich.edu/cgi-bin/herb. Database of plant uses "by 291 Native American groups of 4,029 species from 243 different plant families." This is the third version of the database. It supercedes the 1977 publication, *American Medical Ethnobotany* and the 1986 database, Medicinal Plants of Native America.

PLANTS Database, USDA. URL: http://plants.usda.gov/plants/home_page. html. "The PLANTS Database is a single source of standardized information about plants. This database focuses on vascular plants, mosses, liverworts, hornworts, and lichens of the U.S. and its territories. The PLANTS Database includes names, checklists, automated tools, identification information, species abstracts, distributional data, crop information, plant symbols, plant growth data, plant materials information, plant links, references, and other plant information."

Type Register of the U. S. National Herbarium. URL: http://www.nmnh.si.edu/gopher-menus/TypeSpecimenRegisterU.S.National Herbarium,US.html. A searchable database of over 90,000 type specimens.

DICTIONARIES AND ENCYCLOPEDIAS

Ainsworth and Bisby's Dictionary of the Fungi. 8th ed. D. L. Hawksworth, P. M. Kirk, B. C. Sutton, and D. N. Pegler, eds. New York: CAB International, 1995. 616 p. $70.00. ISBN 0785992618. Over 20,000 entries for fungi and lichens identifying status, systematics, number of species, distribution, and references to key publications. Includes entries for major fungal reference and genetic resource collections.

Brown, Deni. *Encyclopedia of Herbs and Their Uses: The Definitive Guide to the Identification, Cultivation and Uses of 1,000 Herbs.* New York: Dorling Kindersley, 1995. 424 p. $39.95. ISBN 0789401843. Sponsored by the Herb Society of America. Includes over 1500 color photographs and describes medicinal, economic, culinary and aromatic uses. Lacks bibliography.

Coombes, Allen J. *Dictionary of Plant Names*. Portland, OR: Timber Press, 1987. 210 p. $12.95. ISBN 0881922943. Pronunciation, derivation, and meaning of botanical names, and their common name equivalents. A very complete dictionary at a bargain price.

A Dictionary of Plant Sciences. 2nd ed. Michael Allaby, ed. New York: Oxford University Press, 1998. 508 p. $15.95 (paper). ISBN 0192800779 (paper). Contains over 5,500 entries in all areas of botany. Revised edition of *The Concise Oxford Dictionary of Botany.*

Dictionary of Plant Toxins. Jeffrey B. Harborne and Herbert Baxter, eds. New York: Wiley, 1996. 540 p. $455.00. ISBN 0471951072. The "first and only complete reference devoted specifically to phytotoxins." Provides chemical information including common name, chemical structure, classification, CAS Registry Number, etc. for each of approximately 2,000 entries.

Dictionary of Plant Virology in Five Languages, English, Russian, German, French, and Spanish. Compiled by V. Bojnansky and A. Fargasova. New York: Elsevier, 1991. 472 p. $141.00. ISBN 0444987401. This dictionary consists of two parts: a polyglot dictionary of general plant virology terms and a separate listing of common names of virus and virus diseases of higher plants.

Hickey, Michael and C. J. King. *The Cambridge Illustrated Glossary of Botanical Terms.* Cambridge, England: Cambridge University Press, 2000. 200 p. $85.00, $29.95 (paper). ISBN 0521790808, 0521794013 (paper). Not yet seen.

Elsevier's Dictionary of Botany. Paul Macura, ed. New York: Elsevier, 1979–1982. 2 v. Vol. 1: Plant names in English, French, German, Latin, and Russian (1979) $169. 25. ISBN 0444417877. Vol. 2: General terms in English, French, German, and Russian (1982) $169.25. ISBN 0444419772. A multilingual dictionary of over 16,000 terms for botany and related disciplines.

Elsevier's Dictionary of Wild and Cultivated Plants in Latin, English, French, Spanish, Dutch, and German. W. E. Clason, ed. Amsterdam: Elsevier, 1989. 1,016 p. $498.00. ISBN 0444429778. Latin and vernacular names of wild and cultivated European plants.

Flowering Plants of the World. Vernon H. Heywood, ed. New York: Oxford University Press, 1993. 336 p. $84.00. ISBN 0195210379. Introductory material discusses forms, structure, ecology, uses, and classification of the flowering plants of the world. Over 300 angiosperm families are described and illustrated, many in color, with information on distribution, significant features, classification, economic uses, number of species and genera.

Gledhill, David. *The Names of Plants*, 2nd ed. New York: Cambridge University Press, 1989. 202 p. $49.95. ISBN 0521366682. This book is arranged in two parts: a brief description of botanical nomenclature suitable for students and amateurs, and a glossary that translates the more descriptive scientific names into English.

Hortus III: A Concise Dictionary of Plants Cultivated in the United States and Canada. Initially compiled by Liberty H. Bailey and Ethel Z. Bailey, revised and expanded by the staff of the Liberty Hyde Bailey Hortorium. New York: Macmillan, 1976. 1,290 p. $150.00. ISBN 0025054708. ''Inventory of accurately described and named plants of ornamental economic importance.'' Updated by the *New York Botanical Garden Illustrated Encyclopedia of Horticulture.*

Jackson, Benjamin Dayton. *A Glossary of Botanic Terms with Their Derivation and Accent*, 4th ed. (Revised and enlarged.) Forestburg, NY: Lubrecht and

Cramer, 1986. 481 p. $35.00. ISBN 8121100054.   This unique glossary includes 25,000 entries providing derivation and author of terms, accent, and definitions. Especially of historical value.

Mabberley, D. J. *The Plant Book: A Portable Dictionary of the Vascular Plants* . . . . 2ⁿᵈ ed. New York: Cambridge University Press, 1987. 858 p. $52.95. ISBN 0521414210.   This updates Willis's *A Dictionary of the Flowering Plants and Ferns* to include all accepted generic and family names of lowering plants and ferns, with selected common names. There are over 20,000 entries containing information on number of species in each genus and the number of genera in each family, distribution, botanical details, and use.

Malcolm, Bill and Nancy Malcolm. *Mosses and Other Bryophytes: An Illustrated Glossary*. Nelson, New Zealand: Micro-Optics Press, 2000. 220 p. $39.95. ISBN 0473067307.   This colorful glossary contains nearly 1,000 color photographs of bryophytes and their anatomy. Not yet seeen.

Miglani, Gurbachan S. *Dictionary of Plant Genetics and Molecular Biology*. New York: Food Products Press, 1998. 348 p. $89.95. ISBN 1560228717.   Covers 3,500 terms and concepts in plant genetics and molecular biology. Has extensive bibliography.

Moerman, Daniel E. *Native American Ethnobotany*. Portland, OR: Timber Press, 1998. 927 p. $79.95. ISBN 0881924539.   A guide to Native American medicinal uses of plants and the supporting literature. See also the *Native American Ethnobotany Database* under the Handbooks section.

New York Botanical Garden Illustrated Encyclopedia of Horticulture. Compiled by Thomas H. Everett. New York: Garland, 1980–1982. 10 v. $1,070.00. ISBN 0824072227.   This beautifully illustrated set supplements *Hortus III* and is comprehensive, authoritative, and contains major botanical articles. Descriptions are provided for 20,000 species and varieties of plants including 10,000 photographs. Also, see *Dictionary of Gardening* described previously.

The New Royal Horticultural Society Dictionary of Gardening, Anthony Huxley, ed. New York: Stockton Press, 1992. 4 v. $795.00 ISBN 1561590010.   This award-winning dictionary is useful, comprehensive, and includes over 50,000 plant entries with brief description, distribution, cultivation, and important species. Biographies of famous botanists and over 180 articles on aspects of plant biology are a major attraction of this important set. Also called *The New Royal Horticultural Society Dictionary of Gardening*. There is an index to this *Dictionary* that supplies over 60,000 names for ornamental and economic plants: *Index of Garden Plants* published by Timber Press in 1994. (1,200 p, $59.95, ISBN 0881922463)

Plant Sciences for Students. Richard Robinson, ed. 4 v. New York: Macmillan Reference, 2000. $325.00. ISBN 002865434X (set). Presents an overview of current knowledge of plants. This encyclopedia is designed for high school students and undergraduates, so it also covers topics such as careers in plant sciences and includes biographies of famous botanists.

Rodale's Illustrated Encyclopedia of Herbs. Claire Kowalchik and William H. Hylton, eds. Emmaus, PA: Rodale Press, 1998. 545 p. $17.95 (paper). ISBN 087596964X (paper). More detailed that *Encyclopedia of Herbs and Herbalism*, but with fewer examples, this encyclopedia provides articles on lotions, teas, dyes, crafts, and some spices.

Ross, Ivan A. *Medicinal Plants of the World: Chemical Constituents, Traditional and Modern Medicinal Uses.* Totowa, NJ: Humana Press, 1999. 415 p. $99.50. ISBN 0896035425. In-depth coverage of 26 medicinal plants. Includes common names, botanical descriptions, origin and distribution, traditional medicinal uses, chemical constituents, and pharmacological activities and clinical trials.

Stearn, William T. *Stearn's Dictionary of Plant Names for Gardeners: A Handbook on the Origin and Meaning of the Botanical Names of Some Cultivated Plants.* London: Cassell Publishers, 1992. 363 p. $19.95. ISBN 0304341495, 0304347825 (paper). This book provides a reliable source of information on the significance of botanical names attached to cultivated plants. A revised edition of A. W. Smith's *A Gardener's Dictionary of Plant Names* (1972), this is a valuable tool for both gardeners and botanists.

Stearn, William T. *Botanical Latin: History, Grammar, Syntax, Terminology & Vocabulary.* 4th ed. Portland, OR: Timber Press, 1995. 546 p. $45.00. ISBN 0881923214. Authoritative, scholarly discussion of Latin used for the botanical description and naming of plants. Also see Jackson on p. 291.

Turner, Nancy J. and Adam F. Szczawinski. *Common Poisonous Plants and Mushrooms of North America.* Portland, OR: Timber Press, 1991. 324 p. $55.00, $24.95 (paper). ISBN 0881921793, 0881923125 (paper). This is an important reference source for poisonous plants found in homes, buildings, gardens, urban areas, and the wild. There are full descriptions of each plant with information on occurrence, toxicity, and treatment.

Ulloa, Miguel and Richard T. Hanlin. *Illustrated Dictionary of Mycology.* St. Paul, MN: APS Press, 2000. 448 p. $99.00. ISBN 0890542570. Translation of *Diccionario ilustrado de micología.*

DIRECTORIES

Compendium of Bryology: A World Listing of Herbaria, Collectors, Bryologists, and Current Research. Compiled by Dale H. Vitt, et al. (Bryophytorum Bibliotheca, no. 30.) Forestburgh, NY: J. Cramer for the International Association of Bryologists, 1985. 355 p. ISBN 3768214336.   Useful for its world listing of 471 herbaria, over 2,000 collectors, and 535 current researchers in bryology.

International Directory of Botanical Gardens V. 5th ed. Compiled by Christine A Heywood, et al. Champaign, IL: Koeltz Scientific, 1990. 1,021 p. $127.00. ISBN 187876201X.   Arranged by country, this directory lists gardens with address, status, area, latitude and longitude, altitude, rainfall, taxa included, specialties, greenhouses, publications, accessibility, and names of the director and other staff.

Index Herbariorum. Part I: The Herbaria of the World. 8th ed. Patricia K Holmgren, et al., eds. Bronx, NY: New York Botanical Garden, published and distributed for the International Association for Plant Taxonomy, 1990. 693 p. (Regnum Vegetabile, v. 120.) $70.00. ISBN 0893273589.   Directory of the public herbaria of the world. For *Part II: Collectors*, see annotation in the Biography and History section. Also available on the Web at http://www.nybg.org/bsci/ih/ih.html.

The Plant Collections Directory. Richard V. Piacentini, ed. Kennet Square, PA: AABGA, American Association of Botanical Gardens and Arboreta, 1998. 154 p. ISBN 0934843015.   Complete information for important documented collections of living plants in Canada and the United States.

Plant Conservation Directory. Compiled by the Center for Plant Conservation, Missouri Botanical Garden. St. Louis, MO: Missouri Botanical Garden Press, 1997. 137 p. $18.00.   Contact information for botanical, conservation, governmental, and scientific people and organizations in the United States. Includes state rare-plant laws.

Plant Specialists Index: Index to Specialists in the Systematics of Plants and Fungi, Based on Data from Index Herbariorum (Herbaria), Edition 8. Patricia K. Holmgren and Noel H. Holmgren, eds. Königstein, Germany: Koeltz Scientific Books, 1992. 394 p. (Regnum vegetabile, v. 124.) $69.00. ISBN 187876232X. Also available at http://www.nybg.org/bsci/ih/ih.html.

Plant Taxonomists Online (PTO). Albuquerque, NM: University of New Mexico. URL: http://www.unm.edu/jmygatt/waissrch2.html.   This version will be updated as names are added. Also see the *American Society of Plant Taxonomists Membership Directory*.

GUIDES TO THE INTERNET

A great deal of botanical information is available on the Internet. Most notably, large collections of data are being cooperatively collected and stored. This data ranges from taxonomic in nature such as the International Plant Names Index (see Classification and Nomenclature section) to molecular data such as that provided by the National Library of Medicine's GenBank database (see Chapter 6, "Molecular and Cellular Biology").

Botany WWW Virtual Library. Scott Russell, University of Oklahoma. URL: http://www.ou.edu/cas/botany-micro/www-vl/. This venerable site provides a very extensive list of Web links, everything from discussion groups to plant biology departments and associations.

Internet Directory for Botany. Compiled by Anthony R. Brach, Raino Lampinen, Shunguo Liu, and Keith McCree. URL: http://www.botany.net/IDB. An index to botanical information found on the Internet. Divided into an alphabetical directory and a subject directory.

Mycology WWW Sites of Interest. Botanische Staatssammlung München. URL: http://www.botanik.biologie.uni-muenchen.de/botsamml/mycology/mycology. html. An excellent starting point for mycologists, this site contains links arranged by type, such as floras, picture collections, and herbaria collections.

Plant Biology Internet Resources. Diane Rhodes, Arizona State University Libraries. URL: http://www.asu.edu/lib/noble/biology/is_bot-i.htm#. An extensive, annotated list of Internet resources.

Plant Pathology Internet Guide Book. Thorsten Kraska. Institute for Plant Diseases, University of Bonn, Germany. URL: http://www.ifgb.uni-hannover.de/extern/ppigb/ppigb.htm. This site covers plant pathology, applied entomology, and related fields.

Sengbusch, Peter von. Botany Online: The Internet Hypertextbook, International Edition. University of Hamburg. URL: http://www.rrz.uni-hamburg.de/biologie/b_online/e00/contents.htm. This highly regarded site was originally written in German, but is being translated into English. It contains a vast array of textbook-style information on botany, from taxonomy to plant physiology. Over 50 authors have contributed material.

WWW Virtual Library: Mycology. Kathie Hodge, Cornell University. URL: http://www.biodiversity.uno.edu/fungi/. Another good starting point for mycologists. This site is also arranged by subject, but also contains an alphabetical index for browsers.

GUIDES TO THE LITERATURE

B-P-H (Botanico Periodicum Huntianum). Pittsburgh, PA: Hunt Botanical Library, 1968. 1,063 p. $20.00. ISBN 091319610X. *B-P-H/S (Botanico Periodicum Huntianum/Supplementum)*, Gavin D. R. Bridson, ed. Pittsburgh, PA: Hunt Institute for Botanical Documentation, Carnegie Mellon University, 1991. 1,068 p. $95.00. ISBN 0913196541. One of the most important guides to the botanical literature, this serials list and compendium of information for periodicals is extraordinarily useful. It provides titles, abbreviations, subtitles, places of publication, volumes, date of publication, location information, synonymous abbreviations, and abbreviations for synonymous titles.

Davis, Elisabeth B. and Diane Schmidt. *Guide to Information Sources in the Botanical Sciences*, 2nd ed. Littleton, CO: Libraries Unlimited, 1995. 275 p. (Reference sources in science and technology.) $59.00. ISBN 1563080753. Comprehensive guide to the botanical literature.

HANDBOOKS

Handbooks of specific botanical relevance are included in this section. For materials applicable to general biology, biochemistry, genetics and biotechnology, and molecular biology, consult those chapters.

American Type Culture Collection Catalogues. See Chapter 8, ''Microbiology and Immunology,'' for full annotation. Their online catalog for mycology and botany is divided into three subdivisions: fungi and yeasts, plant tissue cultures, and plant seeds.

Arabidopsis: An Atlas of Morphology and Development. John Bowman, ed. New York: Springer-Verlag, 1993. 350 p. $69.00. ISBN 0387940899. This atlas provides documentation for *Arabidopsis thaliana*, the primary model for research in plant genetics, by covering embryogenesis, vegetative growth, root growth, reproductive structures, and host-pathogen interactions.

Bracegirdle, Brian and Philip H. Miles. *An Atlas of Plant Structure*. New York: Heinemann Educational Books, 1971. 2 v. ISBN 0435603124 (v. 1), 0435603140 (v. 2). This unique set assists students in interpreting lab specimens by providing an extensive array of photomicrographs and line drawings for bacteria, algae, fungi, lichens, hepaticae, musci, and other plant issues.

CRC Handbook of Flowering. A. H. Halevy, ed. Boca Raton, FL: CRC, 1985. 6 v. Vol. VI: 776 p. $420.00. ISBN 0849339162. Comprehensive for specific data for control and regulation of flowering for over 5,000 species of plants.

Duke, James A. *Handbook of Biologically Active Phytochemicals and Their Activities*. Boca Raton, FL: CRC Press, 1992. 183 p. $156.05. ISBN 08493367708. Compilation of data, including references, for 3,000 compounds. Reported activities are listed for each chemical, with effective or inhibitory concentrations or doses reported when available.

Herbal Drugs and Phytopharmaceuticals. Max Wichtl, ed. Boca Raton, FL: CRC Press, 1994. ISBN 0849371929. This book contains information on 181 common medicinal herbs. Each entry contains references to sources, synonyms, constituents (often with chemical structures), indications, side effects, preparation, regulatory status, and more. Many of the herbs are illustrated.

The Herbarium Handbook. 3rd ed. Leonard Forman and Diane Bridson, eds. Kew, England: Royal Botanic Gardens, 1998. 334 p. $22.00. ISBN 1900347431. A definitive and authoritative source for curation and management of herbaria.

Johnson, Timothy. *CRC Ethnobotany Desk Reference.* Boca Raton, FL: CRC Press, 1999. $149.95. ISBN 084931187X. Provides data on range, medicinal action, use, chemical properties, habitat, indigenous use and more. Covers over 28,000 plant species. Data has been incorporated from several U.S. government plant databases among other sources. Not recommended.

The Maize Handbook. Michael Freeling and Virginia Walbot, eds. New York: Springer-Verlag, 1994. 759 p. $79.00. ISBN 0387978267. This very useful laboratory guide covers development and morphology, cell biology, genetics, molecular biology, and cell culture, with detailed protocols.

Mycology Guidebook. Russell B. Stevens. Seattle, WA: University of Washington Press, 1981. 712 p. $50.00. ISBN 0295958413. This indispensable handbook assembles information on field collecting, isolation techniques, culture maintenance, taxonomic groups, ecological groups, and fungi as biological tools.

Perry, James W. and David Morton. *Photo Atlas for Botany.* Belmont, CA: Wadsworth, 1998. 141 p. $35.95 (paper). ISBN 0534529380 (paper). An excellent source of photographs of plant structures and representative species from various taxa. Contains over 600 photographs and is aimed at a college-level audience. See also *The Visual Dictionary of Plants,* in the following text, for more plant illustrations.

Physician's Desk Reference (PDR) for Herbal Medicines. 2st ed., revised. Montvale, NJ: Medical Economics Company, 2000. 900 p. $59.95. ISBN 1563633612. Draws on the findings of the German Regulatory Authority's herbal watchdog agency "commission E," as well as the peer-reviewed literature. Covers over 600 botanicals, providing descriptions, indications and usage, contraindications, dosage and more. Well indexed. Includes over 500 color photographs.

Phytochemical Dictionary: A Handbook of Bioactive Compounds from Plants 2nd ed. Jeffrey B. Harborne, Gerard P. Moss, and Herbert Baxter, eds. New York: Taylor and Francis, 1998. 976 p. $450.00. ISBN 0748406204. This dictionary covers over 3,000 substances that are found in plants, including insect antifeedants, carcinogens, phytoalexins, etc. Information is provided for synonyms, structure, molecular weight and formula, natural occurrence, biological activity, and uses. The second edition adds Chemical Abstract Service Registry Numbers. See also *Phytochemical Dictionary of the Leguminosae*, in the following text.

Phytochemical Dictionary of the Leguminosae. Compiled by I. W. Southon using the International Legume Database and Information Service and the Chapman & Hall Chemical Database. New York: Chapman & Hall, 1993. 1,200 p. $795.00. ISBN 0412397706. Divided into two sections: 1. The plant section lists all legume species from which chemical substances have been reported. Entries include accepted species name/common names/synonyms, distribution, life form, botanical source, economic uses, type of compound, organs isolated from, and chemical citations; 2. The chemical section gives chemical data on all identified phytochemicals occurring in the Leguminosae, including accepted and other chemical names, structure diagram, CAS registry number, molecular formula/ weight, use and biological activities. Extensively indexed. Also, see *Phytochemical Dictionary*, previous.

Plant Molecular Biology LABFAX. Oxford, England: BIOS Scientific Publisher/ Blackwell Scientific, 1993. 382 p. $45.00. ISBN 1872748155 (spiralbound). A compendium of essential information and accurate data for plant anatomy, nucleic acids, genetic index, transformation and expression vectors, PCR techniques, and the like.

The Visual Dictionary of Plants. New York: Dorling Kindersley, 1992. 64 p. (Eyewitness visual dictionaries,) $18.95. ISBN 1564580164. While this slim volume is aimed at a young audience, the excellent photographs provide a good source of illustrations of many kinds of plants and plant parts. Perry's *Photo Atlas for Botany*, previous, is intended for a more advanced audience.

Wiersma, John H. and Blanca Leon. *World Economic Plants: A Standard Reference*. Boca Raton, FL: CRC Press, 1999. 749 p. $129.95. ISBN 0849321190. ''. . . a comprehensive reference containing a synopsis of taxonomic information for nearly 10,000 species . . . accompanying each scientific name are multilingual common names, synonymous scientific names, geographical distributions, and economic uses.''

HISTORIES

Ambrosoli, Mauro. *The Wild and the Sown: Botany and Agriculture in Western Europe: 1350–1850*. New York: Cambridge University Press, 1997. 460 p. $83.00. ISBN 0521465095. Describes ''the spread of new agricultural practice in the half millennium after 1350, and reconstructs a neglected part of Europe's agricultural past.''

Arber, Agnes. *Herbals: Their Origin and Evolution; a Chapter in the History of Botany 1470–1670.* 3rd ed. Cambridge: Cambridge University Press, 1987. 358 p. $44.95. ISBN 0521338794. The classic history of herbals with appendixes including a chronological list of the principal herbals, bibliography of references, and a subject index.

Authors of Plant Names: A List of Authors of Scientific Names of Plants, with Recommended Standard Forms of Their Names, Including Abbreviations. R. K. Brummitt and C. E. Powell, eds. London: Royal Botanic Gardens, Kew, 1992. 732 p. $35.00. ISBN 0947643443. A standard index of the authors of plant names, including birth and death dates, recommended abbreviations, and notes on the plant taxa authored for each individual. The index can be searched as part of the International Plant Names Index (see ''Classification and Nomenclature''), at http://www.ipni.org/searches/query_author.shtml.

Biographical Notes upon Botanists. The New York Botanical Garden, compiled by J. H. Barnhart. Boston, MA: G. K. Hall, 1982. 3 v. $430.00 (set). ISBN 0816113424 (set). Information on the life, academic history, obituary notices, location of portraits, travels, and collections of botanists from the earliest times through the 1940s.

Blunt, Wilfrid with the assistance of William T. Stearn. *The Art of Botanical Illustration.* (New edition revised and enlarged.) Forestburgh, NY: Lubrecht and Cramer, 1994. 369 p. $59.00, $11.95 (paper). ISBN 1851491775, 0486272656 (paper). A scholarly historical survey of botanical illustration from prehistoric to modern times. Beautifully illustrated.

Dictionary of British and Irish Botanists and Horticulturists (including Plant Collectors, Flower Painters, and Garden Designers). (Revised and completely updated edition.) Ray Desmond, ed. London: Taylor & Francis, 1994. 825 p. $286.00. ISBN 0850668433. Over 13,000 detailed entries make this biographical dictionary indispensable for anyone who wants to learn about the lives and achievements of past and present horticulturalists working in the United Kingdom and around the world. A key reference.

The Early Days of Yeast Genetics and Molecular Biology. Michael N. Hall and Patrick Linder, eds. Plainview, NY: Cold Spring Harbor Laboratory Press, 1993. 477 p. $29.00. ISBN 0879693789. Reminiscences of early investigators whose pioneering studies before 1975 brought yeast biology to its current maturity. Identification methods for yeasts and other fungi.

Green, J. R. *A History of Botany, 1860 to 1900, Being a Continuation of Sachs 'History of Botany,' 1530–1860.* New York: Russell & Russell, 1909, reissued in 1967. 543 p.   A classic history of botany and a continuation of von Sachs monumental work. To update Green, see Morton or Weevers, in the following text.

Greene, Edward L. *Landmarks of Botanical History; A Study of Certain Epochs in the Development of the Science of Botany.* Frank N. Egerton, ed. Stanford, CA: Stanford University Press, 1983. 2 v. ISBN 0804710759 (set).   In part a reprint of Greene's 1909 work. Part 1 comprises reprint of 1909 edition; Part 2 contains text never before published.

Harshberger, John William. *Phytogeographic Survey of North America: A Consideration of the Phytogeography of the North American Continent, including Mexico, Central America and the West Indies, together with the Evolution of North American Plant Distribution.* New York: G. E. Stechert, 1911. 790 p.   Part I: History and literature of the botanic works and explorations of the North American continent; Part II: Geographic, climatic and floristic survey; Part III: Geologic evolution, theoretic considerations, and statistics of North American plants; and Part IV: North American phytogeographic regions and formations associations.

Huntia: A Journal of Botanical History. v. 1– , 1964– . Pittsburgh, PA: Hunt Institute for Botanical Documentation. Irregular. $50.00. ISSN 0073-4071.   Publishes on all aspects of the history of botany.

Index Herbariorum. Part 2. Index of Collectors. Utrecht, Netherlands: Bohn, Scheltema & Holkema, 1983–8. (Regnum Vegetabile series, v. 2, 9, 86, 93, 109, 114, 117.)   A list of plant collectors including dates active, collection specialty, location of voucher specimens, and sources.

Isely, Duane. *One Hundred and One Botanists.* Ames, IA: Iowa State University Press, 1994. 351 p. $39.95. ISBN 0813824982.   This collection of essays is arranged chronologically featuring such important botanists as Aristotle, Winona Hazel Welch, Henry Gleason, Asa Gray, and Konrad Gesner.

Keeney, Elisabeth B. *The Botanizers: Amateur Scientists in Nineteenth-Century America.* Chapel Hill, NC: University of North Carolina Press, 1992. 206 p. $45.00. ISBN 0807820466.   Engrossing history of amateur botanists active in the 1800s.

Morton, A. G. *History of Botanical Science: An Account of the Development of Botany from Ancient Times to the Present Day.* New York: Academic, 1981. 474 p. ISBN 0125083823.   A "modern" history of botany that traces the emergence of philosophical concepts.

Pistorius, Robin. *Scientists, Plants and Politics—A History of the Plant Genetic Resources Movement.* Rome: International Plant Genetic Resources Institute, 1997. 134 p. ISBN 9290433086. "Presents a description and analysis of the historical background of today's efforts to conserve and use plant genetic resources."

Shteir, Ann B. *Cultivating Women, Cultivating Science: Flora's Daughters and Botany in England, 1760–1860.* Baltimore, MD: Johns Hopkins University Press, 1996. 301 p. $18.95 (paper). ISBN 0801851416, 0801861756 (paper). Award-winning book describes the contribution of women to the history of botany in England.

Turner, William. *A New Herball: Part I.* George T. Chapman and Marilyn N. Tweddle, eds. New York: Cambridge University Press, 1996. $105.00. ISBN 0521445485. Facsimile of the original 1551 publication by Turner (including woodcuts) in addition to a modern transcription of the text with explanatory notes. Also includes a biography of Turner.

Turner, William. *A New Herball: Parts II & III.* George T. Chapman and Marilyn N. Tweddle, eds. New York: Cambridge University Press, 1996. $200.00. ISBN 0521445485. Companion volume to the book described previously.

Von Sachs, Julius. *History of Botany (1530–1860).* Rev. ed. I. B. Balfour, ed. New York: Russell and Russell, 1967 reprint of the 1890 ed. 568 p. ISBN 084621797X. Classic history of botany.

Weevers, Theodorus. *Fifty Years of Plant Physiology.* Netherlands: Scheltema & Holkema, 1949. 308 p. Continuation of botanical history, begun by Von Sachs and Green, with emphasis on the European botanical literature.

METHODS AND TECHNIQUES

Alexiades, Miguel N. *Selected Guidelines for Ethnobotanical Research: A Field Manual.* Bronx, NY: New York Botanical Garden, 1996. 306 p. (Advances in Economic Botany, No. 10.) $22.95. ISBN 0893274046.

Biotechnological Applications of Plant Cultures. Peter D. Shargool and That T. Ngo, eds. Boca Raton, FL: CRC, 1994. 214 p. (CRC Series of Current Topics in Plant Molecular Biology.) $115.95. ISBN 0849382629. State-of-the-art reviews on current techniques in plant culture work, covering four broad areas: production of secondary metabolites by plant cells; plant cell transformation techniques; breeding and micropropagation techniques; and plant cell and tissue bioreactor design.

Burke, Dan, Dean Dawson, and Tim Stearns. *Methods in Yeast Genetics.* Plainview, NY: Cold Spring Harbor Laboratory Press, 2000. 205 p. $75.00 (paper). ISBN 0879695889 (paper).   Developed from the Cold Spring Harbor Yeast Genetics course. Essential techniques and methods for working with this genetic model organism.

Cell Culture and Somatic Cell Genetics of Plants. v. 1– , 1984– . New York: Academic. Irregular. Price varies.   This continuing treatise provides key reference works, descriptions, and discussions of all aspects of modern plant cell and tissue culture techniques.

Collin, H. *Plant Cell Culture*. London: Chapman & Hall, 1994. 160 p. (Introduction to Biotechniques). $30.00. ISBN 182748473.   Overview of all the basic tissue culture techniques.

Cook, Frances E. M. *Economic Botany Data Collection Standard*. Kew: Royal Botanic Gardens, 1995. 146 p. $30.00. ISBN 0947643710.   Provides ''a system whereby uses of plants (in their cultural context) can be described, using standardised descriptors and terms, and attached to taxonomic data sets.''

Endress, R. *Plant Cell Biotechnology*. New York: Springer-Verlag, 1994. 353 p. $136.00. ISBN 0387569472.   ''This book describes methods and techniques for gaining highly productive cells and plants to produce secondary metabolites, enabling the production of plant products on an industrial scale independent of environmental influences and natural resources.''

Holmgren, N. H. and B. Angell. *Botanical Illustration: Preparation for Publication*. Bronx, NY: New York Botanical Garden, 1986. 74 p. $10.00 (paper). ISBN 0893272728 (paper).   An authoritative ''how to.'' Also, see West in the following text.

Houghton, Peter J. and Amala Raman. *Laboratory Handbook for Fractionation of Natural Extracts*. London: Chapman & Hall, 1998. 208 p. $86.50. ISBN 0412749106.   A practical guide to the isolation of bioactive compounds.

Kearns, Carol Ann and David William Inouye. *Techniques for Pollination Biologists*. Niwot, CO: University Press of Colorado, 1993. 583 p. $37.50. ISBN 0870812793.   Practical information for experimental field studies with recipes of how to deal with whole plants, flowers, gynoecia, pollen, nectar, bees, birds, bats, butterflies, beetles, etc. Appendices provide equipment and chemical vendors.

Maintenance of Microorganisms and Cultured Cells: A Manual of Laboratory Methods. 2nd ed. B. Kirsop and A. Doyle, eds. San Diego, CA: Academic Press, 1991. 308 p. ISBN 0124103510.   Preservation methodology for bacterial, yeasts and other fungi, algae, protozoa, and animal and plant cell cultures.

Managing the Modern Herbarium: An Interdisciplinary Approach. Deborah A.

Metsger and Sheila C. Byers, eds. Vancouver: Elton Wolf Publishing, 1999. 384 p. $29.95. ISBN 0963547623. A joint project by the Society for the Preservation of Natural History Collections and the Royal Ontario Museum, this book provides practical guidelines for the proper care of plant and fungal collections as well as recommendations for their use in systematic research.

Martin, Gary J. *Ethnobotany: A Methods Manual*. London: Chapman & Hall, 1995. 268 p. (People and Plants Conservation Manuals, Volume 1.) $74.95. ISBN 041248370X. Produced as part of the ''People and Plants'' initiative of the World Wildlife Fund, the United Nations Educational, Scientific, and Cultural Organization (UNESCO); and the Royal Botanic Gardens, Kew. This manual covers a broad scope with chapters on data collection, botany, ethnopharmacology, anthropology, ecology, linguistics, and conservation and community development.

Methods in Comparative Plant Ecology: A Laboratory Manual. G. A. F. Henfry and J. P. Grime, eds. London: Chapman & Hall, 1993. 252 p. $128.00. ISBN 041246662303 (spiralbound). Ninety diagnostic techniques for investigating the effects on plants of contrasting ecology. This book is a companion to the text *Comparative Plant Ecology: A Functional Approach to Common British Species*, J. P. Grime et al., ed. Chapman & Hall, 1988.

Methods in Plant Biochemistry. v. 1– , 1989– . San Diego, CA: Academic Press. Irregular. Price varies. Highly acclaimed series providing comprehensive, practical information on analytical techniques for a particular family of plant compounds. Vol. 9: *Enzymes of Secondary Metabolism* (1993).

Methods in Plant Molecular Biology: A Laboratory Course Manual. Paul Maliga, et al., eds. Cold Spring Harbor, NY: Cold Spring Harbor Laboratory Press, 1995. 446 p. $75.00. ISBN 087969386X (spiralbound). A course for molecular biologists on the latest in plant gene technology.

Methods in Plant Molecular Biology and Biotechnology. Bernard R. Blick and John E. Thompson, eds. Boca Raton, FL: CRC Press, 1993. 360 p. $70.00. ISBN 0849351642. Comprehensive handbook covering recombinant DNA technology, methods for the production and analysis of plant mutants, relevant computer software, DNA mapping and analysis of DNA polymorphism, and detection and characterization of plant pathogens.

Modern Methods of Plant Analysis. v. 1– , 1985– . New York: Springer-Verlag. Irregular. Price varies. This is a highly regarded, valuable series that devotes an entire volume to one topic. Vol. 13: *Plant Toxin Analysis*, 1992.

Plant Cell Biology: A Practical Approach. N. Harris and K. J. Oparka, eds. New York: IRL at Oxford University Press, 1994. 329 p. $45.00. ISBN

0199633983. Both established techniques and new advances provide a comprehensive guide to methods for studying characterization of growth and differentiation through structural, biochemical, and molecular analysis. This is a natural companion to *Plant Molecular Biology: A Practical Approach*.

Plant Cell Culture Protocols. Robert D. Hall, ed. Totowa, NJ: Humana Press, 1999. 421 p. (Methods in Molecular Biology, v. 111) $89.50. ISBN 0896035492. A step-by-step manual covering the most frequently used techniques for culturing plant cells.

Plant Genomes: Methods for Genetic and Physical Mapping. Jacques S. Beckmann and Thomas C. Osborn, eds. Dordrecht, Netherlands: Kluwer Academic, 1992. 250 p. $205.50. ISBN 0792316304. Introduction to methods written for new investigators in this area.

Ruzin, Steven E. *Plant Microtechnique and Microscopy*. Oxford, England: Oxford University Press, 1999. 322 p. $45.00. ISBN 0195089561. Practical guide book to a broad range of microtechniques. Suitable for both novice and established researchers.

Selected Guidelines for Ethnobotanical Research: A Field Manual. Miguel N. Alexiades and Jennie Wood Sheldon, eds. Bronx, NY: New York Botanical Garden, 1996. 306 p. $22.95. ISBN 0893274046. An interdisciplinary guide that covers protocols and ethics, collecting plant materials and quantitative methods of analysis.

West, Keith. *How to Draw Plants: The Techniques of Botanical Illustration*. Portland, OR: Timber Press, 1996. $19.95. ISBN 0881923508. Other useful books by West are *How to Draw and Paint Wild Flowers* (1993) and *Painting Plant Portraits: A Step-by-Step Guide* (1991). Also, check out Holmgren and Angell, previous.

TEXTBOOKS AND TREATISES

Taxonomic textbooks are listed and annotated in the Classification and Nomenclature section of this chapter.

Alexopoulos, Constantine et al. *Introductory Mycology*. 4th ed. New York: Wiley, 1995. 868 p. $106.95. ISBN 0471522295.

Arabidopsis. Elliot M. Meyerowitz and Chris R. Somerville, eds. Cold Spring Harbor, NY: Cold Spring Harbor Laboratory Press, 1994. 1270 p. $130.00. ISBN 0879694289. Comprehensive volume on this model organism for plant biology covers genetics, development, biochemistry, physiology, etc.

Bell, Adrian D. *Plant Form. An Illustrated Guide to Flowering Plant Morphology.* New York: Oxford University Press, 1991. 341 p. $75.00. ISBN 0198542798.

Bell, Peter R. and Alan R. Helmsley. *Green Plants: Their Origin and Diversity.* 2nd ed. New York: Cambridge University Press, 2000. 349 p. $31.95 (paper). ISBN 0521641098, 0521646731 (paper). Designed to provide a basic knowledge of the diversity of plants as a prerequisite for productive research into other areas of plant biology such as plant growth or molecular biology.

The Biochemistry of Plants: A Comprehensive Treatise. P. K. Stumpf and E. E. Conn, eds. New York: Academic Press, 1980–91. 16 v. Later volumes of this treatise update some of the earlier volumes. All areas of plant biochemistry are covered.

Bold, Harold C. et al. *Morphology of Plants and Fungi.* 5th ed. New York: Harper & Row, 1987. 912 p. ISBN 0060408391.

Capon, Brian. *Botany for Gardeners: An Introduction and Guide.* Portland, OR: Timber Press, 1990. 220 p. $29.95, $17.95 (paper). ISBN 0881921637, 0881922587 (paper). A nontechnical guide to botany, intended to help gardeners understand plants "from the plant's point of view".

Cotton, C.M. *Ethnobotany: Principles and Applications.* New York: Wiley, 1996. 424 p. $69.95. ISBN 047195537X.

Cox, Paul A. and Michael J. Balick. *Plants People and Culture: The Science of Ethnobotany.* New York: Scientific American Library, 1996. 228 p. $32.95. ISBN 0716750619.

Encyclopedia of Plant Physiology. new series. v. 1– , 1975– . New York: Springer-Verlag. Irregular. Price varies. This important monographic review series surveys all aspects of the botanical sciences, devoting several volumes, as needed, to cover any particular topic. The new series is in English, and continues the older series, in German, *Handbuch der Pflanzenphysiologie.* v. 1–18, 1955–67. The *General Index* was published in 1993.

Esau, Katherine. *Anatomy of Seed Plants.* 2nd ed. New York: Wiley, 1977. 550 p. $92.95. ISBN 0471245208.

Fahn, A. *Plant Anatomy.* 4th ed. New York: Pergamon, 1990. 588 p. $99.00. ISBN 0080374905.

Fosket, Donald E. *Plant Growth and Development: A Molecular Approach.* San Diego, CA: Academic Press, 1994. 580 p. $49.95. ISBN 0122624300.

Galston, Arthur W. *Life Processes of Plants: Mechanisms for Survival*. New York: Freeman, 1993. (Scientific American Library) 246 p. $32.95. 0716750449.

Goodwin, Trevor Walworth and E. I. Mercer. *Introduction to Plant Biochemistry*. 2nd ed. New York: Pergamon, 1988 corrected reprint. 677 p. ISBN 0080249221.

Grierson, D and S. N. Covey. *Plant Molecular Biology*. 2nd ed. New York: Chapman & Hall, 1994. 320 p. $75.00. ISBN 0412043416.

Griffin, David H. *Fungal Physiology*. 2nd ed. New York: Wiley-Liss, 1994. $69.95. ISBN 0471595861.

Hall, D. O. and K. K. Rao. *Photosynthesis*. 6th ed. New York: Cambridge University Press, 1999. 214 p. $54.95. ISBN 0521642574.

Handbook of Vegetation Science. Reinhold Tuxen, ed., continued by H. Lieth. v. 1– . The Hague: Junk, 1974- . Price varies. Later volumes published by Kluwer Academic. This multivolume reference work reviews vegetation science in all its many aspects.

Heldt, Hans-Walter and Fiona Heldt. *Plant Biochemistry and Molecular Biology*. New York: Oxford University Press, 1997. 522 p. $54.95 (paper). ISBN 0198501803, 019850179X (paper).

Howell, Stephen H. *Molecular Genetics of Plant Development*. Cambridge, England: Cambridge University Press, 1998. 300 p. $90.00, $42.95 (paper). ISBN 0521582555, 0521587840 (paper).

Ingold, Cecil Terrence and H. J. Hudson. *The Biology of Fungi*. 6th ed. New York: Chapman & Hall, 1993. 224 p. $84.00. ISBN 0412490404.

Johri, B. M. et al. *Comparative Embryology of Angiosperms*. New York: Springer-Verlag, 1992. 1,120 p. $300.00. ISBN 3540536337.

Kendrick, Bryce. *The Fifth Kingdom: A New Look at Mycology*. 2nd ed. Sydney, BC: Mycologue Publications, 1992. $35.00. ISBN 0941051285. New CD-ROM version also available.

Lawlor, David W. *Photosynthesis: Molecular, Physiological, and Environmental Processes*. 3rd ed. New York: Springer-Verlag, 2001. 340 p. $44.95. ISBN: 0387916075.

Long, P. E. *Fungi: A New Synthesis*. Oxford, England: Blackwell Scientific, 1993. 400 p. $55.00. ISBN 0632018011.

Lyndon, R. F. *Plant Development: The Cellular Basis*. (Topics in Plant Physiology Series 3.) New York: Chapman & Hall, 1990. 320 p. $27.50. ISBN 0045810338.

Molecular Biology of Photosynthesis. Govindjee, ed. Dordrecht, Netherlands: Kluwer, 1989. Reprinted from *Photosynthesis Research*. v. 16–19, 1988–9. 815 p. ISBN 0792300971.

The Mycota: A Comprehensive Treatise on Fungi as Experimental Systems for Basic and Applied Research. K. Esser and P. A. Lemke, eds. New York: Springer-Verlag, 1994– . Projected 7 v. set. $200.00 (v.1). ISBN 0387577815 (v.1) Leading research specialists have contributed to this treatise on the fungi covering. Vol. 1: Growth, Differentiation and Sexuality; Vol. 2: Genetics and Biotechnology; Vol. 3: Biochemistry and Molecular Biology; Vol. 4: Environmental and Microbial Relationships; Vol. 5: Plant Relationships; Vol. 6: Animal and Human Relationships; Vol. 7: Systematics and Cell Structure.

North American Terrestrial Vegetation. 2nd ed., rev. Michael G. Barbour and William Dwight Billings, eds. New York: Cambridge University Press, 1999. 530 p. $49.95 (paper). ISBN 0521559863 (paper).

Photosynthesis: Photoreactions to Plant Productivity. Yash Pal Abrol et al., eds. Dordrecht, Netherlands: Kluwer, 1993. 607 p. $308.00. ISBN 0792319435.

Plant Biochemistry. P. M. Dey and J. B. Harborne, eds. San Diego, CA: Academic Press, 1997. 554 p. $79.00. ISBN: 0122146743.

Plant Biochemistry and Molecular Biology. 2nd ed. Peter J. Lea and Richard C. Leegood, eds. New York: Wiley, 1999. 364 p. $54.95 (paper). ISBN 0471976830 (paper).

Plant Physiology: A Treatise. F. C. Steward, ed. New York: Academic Press, 1959–91. Ten volumes in 15 volumes. This multivolume treatise covers all facets of plant physiology.

The Plant Viruses. A subseries within *The Viruses*. See Chapter 8, ''Microbiology and Immunology,'' for full annotation.

Raghavan, V. *Developmental Biology of Flowering Plants*. New York: Springer-Verlag, 2000. 408 p. $79.95. ISBN 0387987819. Discussion of all stages of flowering plant development with special emphasis on molecular genetics.

Raven, Peter H., Ray F. Evert, et al. *Biology of Plants*. 6th ed. New York: W. H. Freeman, 1998. 791 p. $65.00. ISBN 1572590416. One of the most frequently used undergraduate texts.

Romberger, J. A., et al. *Plant Structure: Function and Development: A Treatise on Anatomy and Vegetative Development, with Special Reference to Woody Plants*. Berlin: Springer, 1993. 550 p. $100.00. ISBN 3540563059.

Rose, Anthony. H. and J. Stuart Harrison. *The Yeasts.* 2nd ed. San Diego, CA: Academic Press, 1987–95. 6 v. "We have endeavoured in this mulitvolume treatise to provide as wide a coverage as possible of the different areas of investigation that comprise the science of zymology, the study of yeasts."

Rudall, Paula. *Anatomy of Flowering Plants: An Introduction to Structure and Development.* 2nd ed. New York: Cambridge University Press, 1992. 110 p. $19.95 (paper). ISBN 0521421543 (paper).

Schofield, W. B. *Introduction to Bryology.* New York: Macmillan, 1985. 431 p. $68.00. ISBN 002949660.

Silvertown, Jonathan W. and Jonathan Lovett Doust. *Introduction to Plant Population Biology.* 3rd ed. Boston, MA: Blackwell Scientific, 1993. 210 p. $39.95. ISBN 0632029730.

Stern, Kingsley Rowland. *Introductory Plant Biology.* 8th ed. Boston, MA: McGraw-Hill, 2000. 589 p. ISBN 0070122059.

Taiz, Lincoln and Eduardo Zeiger. *Plant Physiology.* 2nd ed. Sunderland, MA: Sinauer Associates, 1998. 792 p. $94.95. ISBN 0878938311.

Takhtajan, Armen. *Evolutionary Trends in Flowering Plants.* New York: Columbia University Press, 1991. 241 p. $57.50. ISBN 0231073283

Wainwright, M. *An Introduction to Fungal Biotechnology.* New York: Wiley, 1992. (Wiley Biotechnology Series). 202 p. $34.95 (paper). ISBN 047193528X.

Wheals, Alan. *Yeast Genetics and Genomics.* New York: Wiley, 2001. $120.00, $55.00 (paper). ISBN 0471899283, 0471899291 (paper).

PERIODICALS

American Journal of Botany. v. 1– . 1914– . Ames, IA: Botanical Society of America, 1914. Monthly. $205.00. ISSN 0002-9122. Available electronically. "Devoted to all branches of plant sciences." This is a leading botanical journal and an official publication of the Botanical Society of America. Abstracts of the annual meeting, poster sessions, and symposium talks are published as a supplement to the journal. Includes *Plant Science Bulletin.*

Annals of Botany (London). v. 1– . 1887– . London: Academic Press. Monthly. $578.00. ISSN 0305-7364. Available electronically. International journal publishes papers covering "observational, experimental, or theoretical aspects of pure and applied plant science."

Annals of the Missouri Botanical Garden. v. 1– . 1914– . St. Louis, MO: Missouri Botanical Garden. Quarterly. $130.00. ISSN 0026-6493. This journal publishes original papers in systematic botany, primarily from authors connected with the Missouri Botanical Garden.

Botanical Journal of the Linnean Society. v. 1– . 1855– . New York: Academic. Monthly. $896.00. ISSN 0024-4074. Available electronically. Published for the Linnean Society of London, the main focus of this journal is systematics as it relates to all areas of botany.

Brittonia. v. 1– . 1931– . New York: New York Botanical Garden. Quarterly. $88.00. ISSN 0007-196X. Publishes original research papers on systematic botany. Includes the "Index to American Botanical Literature" prepared by the New York Botanical Garden. Full text of back issues is available from JSTOR.

Bryologist. v. 1– . 1898– . Fairfax, VA: American Bryological and Lichenological Society (ABLS). Quarterly. $70.00. ISSN 0007-2745. "Devoted to the study of bryophytes and lichens." Includes book reviews, literature lists, and ABLS news and events. Authors must be members of the society.

Economic Botany. v. 1– . 1947– . New York: New York Botanical Garden. Quarterly. $95.00. ISSN 0013-0001. Published for the Society for Economic Botany, this journal "bridges the gap between pure and applied botany by focusing on the uses of plants by people." Includes research articles, reviews, book reviews and notes.

Environmental and Experimental Botany. v. 1– . 1961– . New York: Elsevier Science. Quarterly. $730.00. ISSN 0098-8472. Available electronically. Publishes "research papers on the physical, chemical and biological mechanisms and processes that relate the performance of plants to their abiotic and biotic environment."

Fungal Genetics and Biology. v. 21– , 1996– . New York: Academic Press. 9 issues per year. $399.00. ISSN 1087-1845. Available electronically. Publishes "original research articles, major and minor reviews and short communications on all aspects of *Saccharomyces* and other yeast genera." Formerly: *Experimental Mycology.*

International Journal of Plant Sciences. v. 153– , 1992– . Chicago, IL: University of Chicago Press. Bimonthly. $135.00. ISSN 1058-5893. Available electronically. "One of the major outlets for botanical research." Full text of back volumes is also available on JSTOR. Formerly: *Botanical Gazette.*

Journal of Bryology. v. 7– , 1972–. Leeds, England: W. S. Maney & Son. Quarterly. $298.00. ISSN 0373-6687. Includes original research articles, notes, book reviews and literature lists. Formerly: *Transactions of the British Bryological Society.*

Journal of Experimental Botany. v. 1– . 1950– . Oxford, England: Oxford University Press. Monthly. $935.00. ISSN 0022-0957. Available electronically. "Covers a range of disciplines from molecular and cellular physiology and biochemistry through whole plant physiology to community physiology." Published for the Society for Experimental Botany and designated as an official journal of the Federation of European Societies of Plant Physiology.

Journal of Natural Products. v. 42– , 1979– . Washington, DC: American Chemical Society and American Society of Pharmacognosy. Monthly. $550.00. ISSN 0163-3864. Available electronically. Comprises "natural product research relating to the chemistry and/or biochemistry of naturally occurring compounds or the biology of living systems from which they are obtained." Includes full papers, rapid communications, notes and reviews. Formerly: *Lloydia.*

Journal of Phycology. v. 1– . 1965– . Malden, MA: Blackwell Science. Bimonthly. $350.00. ISSN 0022-3646. Available electronically. "All aspects of basic and applied research on algae are included to provide a common medium for the ecologist, physiologist, cell biologist, molecular biologist, morphologist, oceanographer, taxonomist, geneticist, and biochemist." A journal of the Phycological Society of America.

Journal of Plant Physiology. v. 115– , 1984– . New York: G. Fischer. Monthly. $1,224.00. ISSN 0176-1617. This international journal publishes English language research articles, reviews and rapid communications in plant physiology, biochemistry, molecular biology and basic aspects of plant biotechnology. Formerly: *Zeitschrift für Pflanzenphysiologie.* Incorporates *Biochemie und Physiologie der Pflanzen (BPP).*

Journal of the Torrey Botanical Society. v. 124– , 1997– . Lawrence, KS: Torrey Botanical Society. Quarterly. $55.00. ISSN 0040-9618. The "oldest botanical journal in the western hemisphere." An important journal of long-standing. Each issue contains original research in all areas of plant biology, excluding horticulture. Emphasis is on plants of the western hemisphere. Full text of back volumes is available from JSTOR. Formerly: *Bulletin of the Torrey Botanical Club.*

Journal of Vegetation Science. v. 1– . 1990– . Uppsala, Sweden: Opulus Press AB. Bimonthly. $375.00. ISSN 1100-9233. Available electronically. Official organ of the International Association for Vegetation Science. Includes original articles, short notes, and reviews.

Molecular Breeding: New Strategies in Plant Improvement. v. 1– . 1995– . Dordrecht, Netherland: Kluwer. Bimonthly. $394.00. ISSN 1380-3743. Available electronically.   Focuses on the applications of plant molecular biology including agricultural biotechnology, genomics, field testing, and intellectual property.

Mycologia. v. 1– . 1909– . New York: New York Botanical Garden. Bimonthly. $140.00. ISSN 0027-5514.   Official publication of the Mycological Society of America, issuing original research articles on all aspects of the fungi, including lichens.

Mycological Research. v. 92- , 1989- . Cambridge, England: Cambridge University Press. Monthly. $875.00. ISSN 0953-7562. Available electronically.   Publishes original research articles, reviews, and short papers in many areas of mycology. Formerly: *Transactions of the British Mycological Society.*

Mycotaxon. v. 1– . 1974– . Ithaca, NY: Mycotaxon. Quarterly. $201.00. ISSN 0093-4666.   "An international journal designed to expedite publication of research on taxonomy and nomenclature of fungi and lichens." Papers may be in French or English with summaries in any language.

New Phytologist. v. 1– . 1902– . New York: Cambridge University Press. Monthly. $898.00. ISSN 0028-646X. Available electronically.   "An International Journal of the Plant Sciences." Articles include commissioned and submitted reviews, research papers, and book reviews on all aspects of the plant sciences.

Perspectives in Plant Ecology, Evolution, and Systematics. v. 1- , 1998– . Jena, Germany: G. Fischer Verlag. Semi-Annual. $71.00. ISSN 1433-8319.   New international journal focuses on the ecology, evolution, and systematics of plants. Includes specialized to interdisciplinary reviews and monographs. Supersedes *Veröffentlichungen des Geobotanischen Instituts der ETH, Stiftung Rübel, Zürich.*

Photosynthesis Research. v. 1– . 1980– . Dordrecht, Netherlands: Kluwer. Monthly. $1,164.00. ISSN 0166-8595. Available electronically.   Official journal of the International Society of Photosynthesis Research. An international journal publishing papers dealing with both basic and applied aspects of photosynthesis.

Phycologia. v. 1– . 1961– . Lawrence, KS: Allen Press. Bimonthly. $350.00. ISSN 0031-8884.   Dedicated to the promotion of phycology and to the encouragement of international cooperation among phycologists and phycological institutes.

Physiologia Plantarum. v. 1– . 1948– . Copenhagen: Munksgaard. Monthly. $675.00. ISSN 0031-9317. Available electronically.   Official journal of the Federation of European Societies of Plant Physiology, published by the Scandinavian

Society for Plant Physiology. The journal publishes papers in English on all aspects of experimental plant biology. Also includes minireviews, rapid communications and opinion articles.

Phytochemical Analysis: An International Journal of Plant Biochemical Techniques. v. 1– . 1990– . Chichester, UK: Wiley. Bimonthly. $955.00. ISSN 0958-0344. Available electronically. "Devoted to the publication of original articles on the utilization of analytical methodology in the plant sciences."

Phytochemistry. v. 1– . 1962– . New York: Elsevier. Bimonthly. $3421.00. ISSN 0031-9422. Available electronically. An international journal of plant biochemistry and molecular biology, and an official organ of both the Phytochemical Society of Europe and the Phytochemical Society of North America. Includes research articles, reviews, and book reviews.

Phytopathology. v. 1– . 1911–. St. Paul, MN: American Phytopathological Society. Monthly. $385.00. ISSN 0031-949X. Available electronically. The official journal of the American Phytopathological Society. Includes research articles, mini-reviews and letters to the editor.

Plant and Cell Physiology. v. 1– . 1960– . Oxford, England: Oxford University Press. Monthly. $500.00. ISSN 0032-0781. Available electronically. An "international journal devoted to the publication of original papers in the biological sciences including: physiology, biochemistry, biophysics, chemistry, molecular biology, cell biology and gene engineering of plants and micro-organisms." A journal of the Japanese Society of Plant Physiologists.

Plant and Soil. v. 1– . 1948- . Dordrecht, Netherlands: Kluwer. 20 issues per year. $2,890.00. ISSN 0032-079X. Available electronically. An international journal on plant-soil relationships issued under the auspices of the Royal Netherlands Society of Agricultural Science.

Plant Cell. v. 1– . 1989– . Rockville, MD: American Society of Plant Physiologists. Monthly. $1,690.00. ISSN 1040-4651. Available electronically. This journal features original research articles specializing in plant cell biology and plant tissue culture.

Plant, Cell & Environment. v. 1– . 1978– . London: Blackwell. Monthly. $1,746.00. ISSN 0140-7791. Available electronically. Original papers in any field of the physiology of green plants, including plant biochemistry, molecular biology, biophysics, cell physiology, whole plant physiology, crop physiology, and physiological ecology, together with structural, genetic, pathological and micrometeorological aspects as related to plant function.

Plant Cell Reports. v. 1– . 1981– . New York: Springer-Verlag. Monthly. $1,440.00. ISSN 0721-7714. Available electronically. This journal presents original research results dealing with new advances concerning all aspects of research and technology in plant cell science, plant cell culture and molecular biology including biochemistry, genetics, cytology, physiology, phytopathology, plant regeneration, genetic manipulations and nucleic acid research.

Plant Ecology. v. 127- , 1997- . Dordrecht, Netherlands: Kluwer. Monthly. $2183.00. ISSN 1385-0237. Available electronically. Publishes "original scientific papers dealing with the ecology of vascular plants and bryophytes in terrestrial, aquatic and wetland ecosystems." Includes review articles, book reviews, comments, and symposium proceedings. Formerly: *Vegetatio.*

Plant Journal. v. 1- . 1991- . Oxford, England: Blackwell Scientific. Bimonthly. $1,836.00. ISSN 0960-7412. Available electronically. Rapid publication of original work on plant molecular sciences. Features include review articles, research papers, short communications, technical advances, and gene and mutant directories.

Plant Molecular Biology. v. 1- . 1981- . Dordrecht, Netherlands: Kluwer. 18 issues per year. $1,999.00. ISSN 0167-4412. Available electronically. "An international journal of fundamental plant research providing a rapid publication of research in molecular biology, biochemistry and molecular genetics of higher and lower plants, including cyanobacteria and algae."

Plant Physiology. v. 1- . 1926- . Rockville, MD: American Society of Plant Physiologists. Monthly. $1,580.00. ISSN 0032-0889. Available electronically. Devoted to physiology, biochemistry, cellular and molecular biology, biophysics, and environmental biology of plants. Supplements to the journal record abstracts of papers presented at the annual meeting of the society.

Plant Science. v. 38- , 1985- . Limerick, Ireland: Elsevier. Semimonthly. $3,112.00. ISSN 0168-9452. Available electronically. Publishes in "all areas of experimental plant biology, under the four major section headings of Physiology and Biochemistry, Genetics and Molecular Biology, Cell Biology, and General." Formerly: *Plant Science Letters.*

Plant Systematics and Evolution/Entwicklungsgeschichte und Systematik der Pflanzen. v. 123- , 1974- . New York: Springer-Verlag. Semimonthly. $2,389.00. ISSN 03782697. Original papers on the morphology and systematics of plants in the widest sense. Formerly: *Österreichische Botanische Zeitschrift.*

Planta. v. 1- . 1925- . New York: Springer-Verlag. Monthly. $3,091.00. ISSN 0032-0935. Available electronically. This international journal publishes original articles in all aspects of plant biology, particularly in molecular and cell biology, ultrastructure, biochemistry, metabolism, growth, development and morphogenesis, ecological and environmental physiology, biotechnology, and plant-microorganism interactions.

Planta Medica. v. 1– . 1953– . Stuttgart, Germany: Thieme. 8 issues per year. $303.00. ISSN 0032-0943.   The official organ of the Society for Medicinal Plant Research. An "international journal of medicinal plants and natural products with original research papers, short reviews, letters, and reports from researchers worldwide."

Studies in Mycology. v. 1– . 1972– . Baarn, Netherlands: Centraalbureau voor Schimmelcultures. Irregular. ISSN 0166-0616.   Publishes articles on "fungal biodiversity through the study of taxonomic and phylogenetic relationships."

Systematic Botany. v. 1– . 1976– . Kent, OH: American Society of Plant Taxonomists (ASTP). Quarterly. $115.00. ISSN 0363-6445.   This journal accepts original articles pertinent to modern and traditional aspects of systematic botany, including theory as well as applications. Papers longer than 50 printed pages and dealing with plant systematics, especially taxonomic monographs and revisions, appear in *Systematic Botany Monographs* published by ASPT. Full text of back issues is available from JSTOR.

Taxon. v. 1– . Utrecht, Netherlands: International Bureau for Plant Taxonomy and Nomenclature, 1951– . Quarterly. $160.00. ISSN 0040-0262.   Journal of the International Association for Plant Taxonomy. "Devoted to systematic and evolutionary biology with emphasis on botany." Issues contain original articles, points of view, methods and techniques, nomenclature, proposals to conserve or reject, news, "Index Herbariorum," book reviews, and announcements.

Theoretical and Applied Genetics (TAG). v. 38– , 1968– . Berlin: Springer-Verlag. Monthly. $3,927.00. ISSN 0040-5752. Available electronically.   "TAG will publish original articles in the following areas: genetic and physiological fundamentals of plant breeding, applications of plant biotechnology, and theoretical considerations in combination with experimental data." Formerly: *Der Züchter.*

Yeast. v. 1– . 1985– . New York: Wiley. 20/yr. $1,500.00. ISSN 0749-503X. Available electronically.   Publishes "original research articles, major and minor reviews and short communications on all aspects of *Saccharomyces* and other yeast genera."

REVIEWS OF THE LITERATURE

Advances in Botanical Research. v. 1– . 1963– . New York: Academic Press. Irregular. Price varies. ISSN 0065-2296.   A "multi-volume publication that brings together reviews by recognized experts on subjects of importance to those involved in botanical research.''

Advances in Bryology. v. 1– , 1981– . Forestburgh, NY: Lubrecht & Cramer. Biennial. Price varies.   The official publication of the International Association of Bryologists. This series aims to present authoritative and current reviews, essays, and summary syntheses of the different fields of bryology written by leaders in the area.

Advances in Economic Botany. v. 1– , 1984– . Bronx, NY: New York Botanical Garden. Irregular. Price varies. ISSN 0741-8280.   This series was established to provide an outlet for monographs and symposia on all subjects in the field of economic botany.

Advances in Photosynthesis. 1994– . Dordrecht, Netherlands: Kluwer Academic. Irregular. Price varies.   Each volume in this series covers a different subject, such as *Biophysical Techniques in Photosynthesis* and *The Photochemistry of Carotenoids*.

Annual Review of Phytopathology. v. 1– . 1963– . Palo Alto, CA: Annual Reviews. Annual. $155.00. ISSN 0066-4286. Available electronically.   This is a highly respected series devoted to review articles, by individual authors, dealing with plant pests and diseases, their history, nature, effects, ecology, and control.

Annual Review of Plant Physiology and Plant Molecular Biology. v. 1– . 1950– . Palo Alto, CA: Annual Reviews. Annual. $155.00. ISSN 1040-2519. Available electronically.   This series is addressed to the advanced student doing research in plant physiology and plant biochemistry. Formerly: *Annual Review of Plant Physiology*.

Botanical Review. v. 1– . 1935– . New York: New York Botanical Garden. Quarterly. $89.00.00. ISSN 0006-8101.   This journal ''draws together outstanding scientists in the field, synthesizes the current knowledge about a specific subject, and promotes the advancement of botany by indicating the gaps in our knowledge and providing new outlooks on the topic.''

Critical Reviews in Plant Sciences. v. 1– . 1983– . Boca Raton, FL: CRC Press. Bimonthly. $630.00. ISSN 0735-2689. Available electronically.   Provides critic reviews on a wide range of topics in the plant sciences, including molecular biology, biochemistry, cell biology, plant physiology, genetics, classical botany, ecology, and agricultural applications.

Current Opinion in Plant Biology. v. 1– . 1998– . Oxford, England: Elsevier. Bimonthly. $884.00. ISSN 0959-4388. Available electronically.   Reviews of current advances in plant biology.

Oxford Surveys of Plant Molecular and Cell Biology. v. 1– . 1984– . New York: Oxford University Press. Annual. Price varies. ISSN 0264-861X. This series contains review articles delineating current progress, news, and views in the field of plant molecular and cell biology.

Progress in Botany. v. 36- , 1974- . New York: Springer-Verlag. Irregular. Price varies. ISSN 0340-4773. The basic mission of this series is to report on all areas of botany, rotating subjects every two to three years. The 2000 volume includes reviews on genetics, cell biology, physiology, comparative morphology, systematics, ecology, and vegetation science. Formerly: *Fortschritte der Botanik.*

Progress in Phycological Research. v 1– , 1982. New York: Elsevier. Irregular. Price varies. ISSN 0167-8574. Excellent contribution to the algal literature relevant to physiologists, plant scientists, and ecologists.

Recent Advances in Phytochemistry. v. 1– . 1968– . New York: Plenum. Irregular. Price varies. ISSN 0079-9920. Contains papers presented at the annual meetings of the Phytochemical Society of North America. Each volume has a different subject, such as phytochemicals in human health protection or functionality of food phytochemicals.

Trends in Plant Science. v. 1– . 1996– . Oxford, England: Elsevier. $907.00. ISSN 1360-1385. Available electronically. This is a "current-awareness journal, publishing news, reviews and comments on research activity at the forefront of plant science."

11

Anatomy and Physiology

The subjects of anatomy and physiology make such convenient and logical associates that they are combined as a package in this chapter, along with the currently hot topics of neurobiology and endocrinology. Anatomy is a ''the study of the structure of living organisms, especially of their internal parts by means of dissection and microscopical examination.'' The same source interprets ''physiology'' as the ''branch of biology concerned with the vital functions of plants and animals, such as nutrition, respiration, reproduction and excretion.'' (*Oxford Dictionary of Biology*, 4th ed., 2000). Neurobiology is the study of the nervous system. This chapter includes primarily human anatomy and physiology: plants and animals are discussed in Chapter 10, ''Plant Biology'' and Chapter 13, ''Zoology.'' Although a few medical titles are included, emphasis in this chapter is on the biological sciences rather than the behavioral or clinical.

There is overlap between this chapter and Chapter 5, ''Biochemistry and Biophysics'' and Chapter 6, ''Molecular and Cellular Biology,'' so don't neglect to broaden the search to these other chapters if the molecular aspects, for example, of a particular discipline are important.

ABSTRACTS AND INDEXES

Current Awareness

Calcium and Calcified Tissue Abstracts. v. 1– , 1969– . Bethesda, MD: Cambridge Scientific Abstracts. Quarterly. $550.00. ISSN 1069-5540. Available electronically. Covers all areas of anatomy and metabolism dealing with calcium, including bone metabolism, tooth development, nerve transmission, and others. Also available as part of the Biological Sciences Collection (see ''Abstracts and Indexes,'' Chapter 4).

Chemoreception Abstracts. v. 1, 1972–   . Bethesda, MD: Cambridge Scientific Abstracts. Quarterly. $585.00. ISSN 0300-1261.   Covers articles in the areas of chemical senses, including chemotaxis, smell, taste, perfumery, and more. Available online, on CD-ROM, and on the Web as part of the Biological Sciences Collection (see "Abstracts and Indexes," Chapter 4).

Neuroscience Abstracts. v. 1–   , 1982–   . Bethesda, MD: Cambridge Scientific Abstracts. Monthly. ISSN 0141-7711. Available electronically.   Provides abstracts for articles in all areas of the neurosciences, both basic and applied. A special topics section features a two-year bibliography covering a different hot topic each issue. Also available as part of the Biological Sciences Collection (see "Abstracts and Indexes," Chapter 4).

Retrospective Sources

Berichte über die gesamte Physiologie und experimentelle Pharmakologie. (Berichte über die gesamte Biologie. Abt. B). Berlin, Germany: Julius Springer, 1920–1969. ISSN 0366-0214. References to articles and books, usually with abstracts. Not as comprehensive as *Biological Abstracts.*

Bibliographia Physiologica. Zurich: Concilium Bibliographicum, 1893/94–1926.   Includes books and reports.

Depth Studies: Illustrated Anatomies from Vesalius to Vicq d'Azyr. Exhibition held at the Smart Museum of Art, March 17 to June 7, 1992. Chicago, IL: Smart Museum of Art, 1992. 23 leaves.   This exhibition catalog is listed as a point of information for history of science scholars. The catalog was issued in conjunction with the Centennial Conference Imaging the Body: Art and Science in Modern Culture, April 1–4. It is further noted in the catalog that "All books on display were loaned by the Department of Special Collections, University of Chicago Library."

Haller, Albrecht von. *Bibliotheca Anatomica.* New York: Olms, 1969. 2 v. Reprint of the edition originally published in Zurich by Orell, Gessner, Fuessli, et Socc., 1774–7. One of the most important works ever published for the history and bibliography of anatomy.

Krogman, Wilton Marion. *A Bibliography of Human Morphology, 1914–1939.* Chicago, IL: University of Chicago Press, 1941. (The University of Chicago Publications in Anthropology. Physical Anthropology Series.) 385 p.   Although somewhat out of scope, this bibliography may be useful for anatomists searching for journal articles in the period covered. Arrangement is by broad subject.

Medical Reference Works, 1679–1966; A Selected Bibliography. John B. Blake and Charles Roos, eds. Chicago, IL: Medical Library Association, 1967. (Medical

Library Association. Publication no. 3.) 343 p. *Supplements 1–3*. Chicago, IL: Medical Library Association, 1970–5. This is an extremely valuable bibliography, especially useful for retrospective materials. Complete bibliographic information is arranged by subject, and then by form, with indexes.

Physiological Abstracts. v. 1–22. London: Physiological Society (Great Britain and Ireland), 1916–37. References with abstracts to articles and books; prepared through v. 9 (1924/25) in cooperation with the American Physiological Society.

Russell, Kenneth Fitzpatrick. *British Anatomy, 1525–1800: A Bibliography of Works Published in Britain, America, and on the Continent*. 2nd ed. Winchester, Hampshire, UK: St. Paul's Bibliographies, 1987. 245 p. $95.00 ISBN 0906795338. Annotated bibliography covering human anatomy books by British authors published in Britain, America, and on the Continent in all languages and editions. It also includes the works of Continental authors translated into English or published in Britain in their original language.

Zentralblatt für Physiologie. v. 1–34. Leipzig: Organ der Deutschen physiologischen Gesellschaft (from v. 19), 1887–1921. Abstracts of articles, although some books, theses, and proceedings of societies are included.

ASSOCIATIONS

American Association of Anatomists (AAA). 9650 Rockville Pike, Bethesda, MD 20814–3998. Phone: (301) 571-8314. Fax: (301) 571-0619. E-mail: exec@ anatomy.org. URL: http://www.anatomy.org/anatomy. Founded in 1888. Now with over 2,500 members. Professional society of anatomists and scientists in related fields. Publishes *Anatomical News, Anatomical Record* (plus the *New Anatomist*), *Directory* (Departments of Anatomy in the United States and Canada), *Developmental Dynamics*. Their Web site includes extensive links and membership information.

American Physiological Society (APS). 9650 Rockville Pike, Bethesda, MD 20814–3991. Phone: (301) 530-7164. Fax: (301) 571-8305. E-mail: info@aps. faseb.org. URL: http://www.the-aps.org/. Founded 1887. 9,100 members. Professional society of physiologists. Publishes: *Advances in Physiology Education, American Journal of Physiology* and all of the sections, *FASEB Directory, Handbooks, Journal of Neurophysiology, News in Physiological Sciences, Physiological Reviews*, and *The Physiologist*. Web site primarily for membership information.

American Society for Neurochemistry (ASN). P.O. Box 143060, Gainesville, FL 32614–3060; Phone: (352) 271-3383. Fax: (352) 271-3060. E-mail: lindahou@ aol.com. URL: http://www.ASNeurochem.org. Founded 1969. Over 1,000 members. Investigators in the field of neurochemistry and scientists who are qualified specialists in other disciplines and are interested in the activities of the society. Publishes *American Society for Neurochemistry Membership Directory*, *Newsletter*, and *Transactions* books. The Web site is primarily for membership information, though it does include links to other societies.

Anatomical Society of Great Britain and Ireland. c/o Prof. G. M. Morriss-Kay, Department of Human Anatomy, University of Oxford, South Parks Rd., Oxford OX1 3QX, England. Phone: 44 1865 272165; Fax: 44 1865 272420; E-mail: gillian.morriss-kay@human-anatomy.oxford.ac.uk. URL: http://www.anatsoc. org.uk. Founded 1887. 650 members. Individuals involved in anatomical science. Promotes development and advancement in anatomy and related science through research and education. Offers program for graduate students. Publishes *Journal of Anatomy*. The Web site provides extensive links to general interest sites, plus educational sites in anatomy, neurobiology, embryology, and other related areas.

Endocrine Society (ES). 4350 East West Highway, Ste. 50, Bethesda, MD 20814, Phone: (301) 941-0200. Fax: (301) 941-0259. E-mail: endostaff@endo-society.org. URL: http://www.endo-society.org. Founded 1918. 8,000 members. Promotes excellence in research, education, and clinical practice in endocrinology and related disciplines. Publishes *Endocrine News*, *Endocrine Reviews*, *Endocrinology*, *Journal of Clinical Endocrinology and Metabolism*, and *Molecular Endocrinology*. Formerly: Association for Study of Internal Secretions. Web site provides news bulletins, information for patients, and links to other societies as well as membership information.

International Brain Research Organization (IBRO). The IBRO Secretariat, Blvd. de Montmorency, F-75016 Paris, France. Phone: 33 1 46479292. Fax: 33 1 45206006. E-mail: admin@ibro.org. URL: http://www.ibro.org. Founded 1960. 55,000 members. Scientists working in neuroanatomy, neuroendocrinology, the behavioral sciences, neurocommunications and biophysics, brain pathology, and clinical and health-related sciences. Works to promote international cooperation in research on the nervous system. Publishes *Directory of Members*, *Neuroscience*, annual *News*. Web site primarily for membership information; also has world and local news of interest to neuroscientists.

International Society of Endocrinology (ISE). c/o Prof. Lesley H. Rees, 51–53 St. Bartholomew's Hospital, Bartholomew Close, London EC1A 7BE, England. Phone: 44 171 6064012. Fax: 44 171 7964676. E-mail: mail@ice.co.uk. URL: http://www.jingo.com/ise. Founded 1966. 53 members. Federation of national endocrinology societies with 15,000 individual members. Disseminates information on endocrinology and facilitates collaboration between national endocrinological societies and persons interested in the field. Publishes *Abstracts of Con-*

gresses and *Symposia Abstracts*. Web site primarily for meeting and membership information.

International Society for Developmental Neuroscience (ISDN). c/o Regino Perez-Polo, Ph.D, Univ. of Texas Medical Branch, 301 University Blvd, Galveston, TX 77550–0652. Phone: (409) 7723667. Fax: (409) 772–8028. E-mail: regino.perez-polo@Utmb.edu. URL: http://www.hbcg.utmb.edu/isdn/. Founded 1978. 850 members. Aims to advance research and knowledge concerning the development of the nervous system and to support the effective application of this information for the improvement of human health. Publishes *International Journal of Developmental Neurosciences, ISDN Newsletter*. Web site provides membership information and newsletter.

Physiological Society-England. P.O. Box 11319, London WC1E 7JF, England. Phone: 44 171 6311457. Fax: 44 171 6311462. E-mail: admin@physoc.org. URL: http://www.physoc.org/. Founded 1876. 1,775 members. Multinational physiologists at senior levels in universities, research institutions, hospitals, and relevant industries and government departments, about a third of whom are resident overseas. Promotes the advancement of physiology in all areas. Publishes *Experimental Physiology, The Journal of Physiology*, study guides, and monographs. Web site provides extensive membership information, educational resources, software archives, and extensive links to programs and societies.

Society for Endocrinology. 17/18 North Court, The Courtyard, Woodlands, Bradley Stole, Bristol BS32 4NQ, England. Phone: 44 1454619347. Fax: 44 1454 616071. E-mail: info@endocrinology.org. URL: http://www.endocrinology.org. Founded 1939. 1,700 members. Clinicians and scientists working within the field of hormones and hormone-related disease. Publishes *Endocrine-Related Cancer, European Journal of Endocrinology, Journal of Endocrinology*, and *Journal of Molecular Endocrinology*. The Web site provides membership information, links to freely accessible articles from *Journal of Endocrinology* and *Journal of Molecular Endocrinology*, and extensive links to other Web pages.

Society for Neuroscience. 11 Dupont Circle, Ste. 500, Washington, DC 20036. Phone: (202) 462-6688. E-mail: info@sfn.org. URL: http://www.sfn.org. Founded 1969. 28,000 members. Scientists engaged in research relating to the nervous system. Seeks to advance understanding of nervous systems, including their relation to behavior, by bringing together scientists of various backgrounds and by facilitating integration of research at all levels of biological organizations. Produces nontechnical reports on the results and implications of current research. Publishes *Abstracts, Journal of Neuroscience, Membership Directory, Neuroscience Newsletter*, and *Neuroscience Training Programs in North America*. The Web site includes a membership directory and links to related sites.

Society of General Physiologists (SGP). P.O. Box 257, Woods Hole, MA 02543. Phone: (508) 540-6719. Fax: (508) 540-0155. E-mail: sgp@mbl.edu. URL: http://www.cc.emory.edu/CELLBIO/SGP/sgp.htm. Founded 1946. 1,000 members. Biologists interested in fundamental physiological principles and phenomena. Publishes *Journal of General Physiology*, *Proceedings of Annual Symposium*, and *SGP Constitution and Membership List*. Web site limited to membership information.

ATLASES

A wide variety of atlases are listed, from the classic to the recently trendy, in an effort to provide examples of illustrations of the human body geared to a wide group of student, medical, or layperson audiences.

Anderson, Paul D. *Human Anatomy and Physiology Coloring Workbook*. 2nd ed. Boston, MA: Jones and Bartlett, 1997. (Health Science Series.) 304 p. $27.50 (paper). ISBN 0763704997 (paper). A good example of the popular "coloring book" type of study guides that are appropriate at the undergraduate, or uninitiated, level.

Clinical Gross Anatomy: A Guide to Dissection, Study, and Review. Gene L. Colborn and John E. Skandalakis, eds. Pearl River, NY: Parthenon, 1993. 581 p. $28.00 (paper). ISBN 1850705224 (paper). A dissection handbook.

Despopoulos, Agamemnon and Stefan Silbernagl. *Color Atlas of Physiology*. 4th ed. New York: Thieme, 1991. 369 p. $29.90 (paper). ISBN 0865773823 (paper). Beautifully reproduced color plates.

Eder, Douglas J., Shari Lewis Kaminsky, and John W. Bertram. *Laboratory Atlas of Anatomy and Physiology*. 3rd ed. New York: McGraw-Hill, 2001. 169 p. $31.95 (spiralbound). ISBN 007290755X (spiralbound). Numerous illustrations answer "what" and "where" in terms of the cat, rat, fetal pig, and human anatomy and physiology. This atlas includes chapters on histology, skeletal and muscular anatomy, dissections, and an index.

Feneis, Heinz. *Pocket Atlas of Human Anatomy*. 3rd ed. New York: Thieme, 1994. 480 p. $29.50. ISBN 086577479X. Update of the well-known atlas.

Grant's Atlas of Anatomy. 10th ed. Anne M. R. Agur and Ming J. Lee, eds. Baltimore, MD: Williams & Wilkins, 1999. 704 p. $59.95. ISBN 0683302647. Revision of the work by John Charles Boileau Grant. A classic atlas worthy of its reputation.

Grant's Dissector. 12th ed. Eberhardt K. Sauerland, ed. Baltimore, MD: Williams and Wilkins, 1999. $35.00 (spiralbound). ISBN 0683307398. Revision of the work by John Charles Boileau Grant. Detailed instructions for performing dissections. Fully illustrated with about 400 color images.

Gray, Henry. *Anatomy of the Human Body.* 30th ed. Carmine D. Clemente, ed. Philadelphia, PA: Lea & Febiger, 1985. 1,676 p. $95.00. ISBN 081210644X. Probably the most famous of all the anatomies, and justifiably so. The first edition of this standard atlas was published in 1858. Title on spine: *Gray's Anatomy.*

Hirsch, Martin C. and Thomas Kramer. *Neuroanatomy: 3D-Stereoscopic Atlas of the Human Brain.* Berlin: Springer-Verlag, 1999. 360 p. $49.95. ISBN 3540659986. This book and CD-ROM edition covers external views and internal structures of the brain, truncus cerebri, diencephalon, telencephalon, ventricular system and main arteries, and functional systems.

Human Body on File: Anatomy. New York: Facts on File, 1996. 1 v. $185.00 (binder), $165.00 (CD-ROM). ISBN 0816035288 (binder), 0816042136 (CD-ROM). Contains easily reproduced diagrams of human anatomy, suitable for use in the classroom.

Human Body on File: Physiology. New York: Facts on File, 1996. 1 v. $185.00 (binder), $165.00 (CD-ROM). ISBN 081603415X (binder), 0816042144 (CD-ROM). Another in the On File series, this volume contains diagrams explicating physiological processes.

The Johns Hopkins Atlas of Human Functional Anatomy. 4th ed. George D. Zuidema, ed. Baltimore, MD: Johns Hopkins University Press, 1997. 184 p. $42.50. ISBN 0801856513. An excellent presentation for general readers and students at all levels. This edition features 226 color illustrations of the organs and systems of the human body.

Krstic, Radivoj V. *Human Microscopic Anatomy: An Atlas for Students of Medicine and Biology.* New York: Springer-Verlag, 1994. 616 p. $96.95. ISBN 0387536663. Detailed line drawings of organ systems based on standard histological sections with associated descriptive text that concisely summarizes the structure and function of each system.

Lillie, John H. *Sectional Anatomy of the Head and Neck: A Detailed Atlas.* New York: Oxford University Press, 1994. 213 p. ISBN 0195042972. Black-and-white illustrations and radiographs. The goal is to present an accurate, detailed series of illustrations, with commentary, depicting the structural relationships of the head and neck.

Mackenna, B. R. and R. Callander. *Illustrated Physiology.* 6th ed. Edinburgh; New York: Churchill Livingstone, 1996. 325 p. $38.95 (paper). ISBN 0443050600 (paper).   This is an illustrated atlas of human physiology, useful, also, as a course outline or syllabus.

Mai, Jurgen K, Joseph K. Assheuer, and George Paxinos. *Atlas of the Human Brain*. San Diego, CA: Academic Press, 1997. 336 p. $99.00. ISBN 0124653618. A series of black-and-white photographs featuring different aspects of brain morphology and topography.

Netter, Frank H. *The Ciba Collection of Medical Illustrations: A Compilation of Pathological and Anatomical Paintings*. East Hanover, NJ: Novartis Medical Edition, reissue ed., 1986. Vol. 1–8, in 12 volumes, including revised editions in some volumes. $510.00. ISBN 0914168002.   The standard collection of medical illustrations by one the best medical illustrator/artist of all time.

Netter, Frank H. *Atlas of Human Anatomy*. 2nd ed. East Hanover, NJ: Novartis Medical Edition, 1998. 525 p. of plates. $89.95, $64.95 (paper). ISBN 0914168800, 0914168819 (paper).   This famous author/illustrator provides an outstanding atlas of gross anatomy that follows the nomenclature adapted by the Eleventh International Congress of Anatomists in 1980. References and an index are included.

Morton, David and James W. Perry. *Photo Atlas for Anatomy and Physiology*. Belmont, CA: Wadsworth, 1998. 150 p. $34.95 (paper). ISBN 0534517161 (paper).   Provides labeled color photographs of human anatomy and physiology, from cells to muscles. Also includes illustrations for cat and fetal pig dissections.

Rohen, Johannes W., Chihiro Yokochi, Lynn J. Romrell, and Elke Lutjen-Drecoll. *Color Atlas of Anatomy: A Photographic Study of the Human Body*. 4th ed. Baltimore, MD: Williams and Wilkins, 1998. 486 p. $64.95. ISBN 0683304925.   Photographs of actual anatomic specimens add a spacial dimension, an effect that is so often lacking, thus assisting students in the dissection course, and surgeons in the operating room to see anatomical relationships exactly as they appear. The volume is arranged by body region of macroscopic anatomy, and includes schematic drawings, CT-scans, and MR-images of main tributaries of nerves and vessels, muscles, and nomenclature.

Takahashi, Takeo. *Atlas of the Human Body; the Complete Human Anatomy in More than 500 Color Illustrations*. New York: HarperCollins, 1994. 140 p. $23.95 (paper) ISBN 0062732978 (paper).   This is a detailed atlas, with clear and concise text and color illustrations throughout. There are separate sections for each organ, the nervous and circulatory systems, and the structure and functions of muscle and bone.

Thiel, Walter. *Photographic Atlas of Practical Anatomy*. Berlin: Springer-Verlag, 1997–1998. 2 v. $325.00. (v. 1) $299.00 (v. 2) ISBN 3540611959.   Companion volume 2 includes *Nomina Anatomica* and an index.

Twietmeyer, Alan and Thomas McCracken. *Coloring Guide to Regional Human Anatomy*. 2ⁿᵈ ed. Baltimore, MD: Williams and Wilkins, 1993. 205 p. $24.95 (paper). ISBN 0812115260 (paper). Atlas for regional anatomy.

Weston, Trevor. *Know Your Body: The Atlas of Anatomy*. Berkeley, CA: Ulysses Press, 1999. 156 p. $14.95 (paper) 1569751668 (paper). Well-received atlas with over 250 color illustrations.

Wolf-Heidegger's Atlas of Human Anatomy. 5ᵗʰ ed. Petra Koepf-Maier, ed. Farmington, CT: Karger, 1999. 2 v. $130.50. ISBN 3805554427. Designed especially for the medical student, these volumes document the macroscopic anatomy of the human body, and can be used in conjunction with any anatomy textbook.

DICTIONARIES AND ENCYCLOPEDIAS

Encyclopedia of Human Biology. 2ⁿᵈ ed. See Chapter 3, "General Sources," for full annotation. Contains many articles dealing with anatomy, neurobiology, and physiology.

Encyclopedia of Neuroscience. 2ⁿᵈ enlarged and rev. ed. George Adelman and Barry H. Smith, eds. New York: Elsevier, 1999. 2 v. $385.00 (set), $1,800.00 (CD-ROM). ISBN 0444816127 (set), 0444826157 (CD-ROM). This standard encyclopedia contains over 800 articles on everything from Acetylcholine to Phrenology. The CD-ROM version is animated and includes atlases, direct links to Web sites, and much more.

Encyclopedia of Reproduction. Ernst Knobil and Jimmy D. Neill, eds. San Diego, CA: Academic Press, 1998. 4 vols. $599.95 (set). ISBN 0122270207 (set). Nearly 550 articles encompass every aspect of the biology of reproduction throughout the entire animal kingdom, covering invertebrates to humans. Each article includes a glossary, illustrations, and a bibliography. There are detailed indexes.

Hirsch, Martin C. *Dictionary of Human Neuroanatomy*. Berlin: Springer-Verlag, 1999. 270 p. $29.95 (paper). ISBN 3540665234 (paper). Written by an authority in this specialized field.

Martin, Constance R. *Dictionary of Endocrinology and Related Biomedical Sciences*. New York: Oxford University Press, 1995. $85.00. ISBN 0195060334. This dictionary provides detailed definitions of terms used in endocrinology and related sciences; acronyms are included.

Nomina Anatomica. Authorized by the Twelfth International Congress of Anatomists in London, 1985. Together with *Nomina Histologica*, 3rd ed. and *Nomina Embryologica*, 3rd ed. Revised and prepared by Subcommittees of the International Anatomical Nomenclature Committee, 6th ed. Edinburgh; New York: Churchill Livingstone, 1989. 1 v. ISBN 0443040850. The authoritative, standard nomenclature for anatomy, embryology, and histology is apparently out of print. Portions of the *Nomina Anatomica* are available at http://www.anat. mu-luebeck.de/na.htm at the Medizinische Universitat Luebeck.

Stedman's Medical Dictionary. Authoritative source for anatomy and physiology. See Chapter 3, "General Sources" for full annotation.

Terminologia Anatomica: International Anatomical Terminology. New York: Thieme, 1998. 292 p. $59.00 (book and CD-ROM), $35.00 (book). ISBN 0865778094 (book and CD-ROM), 0865778086 (book). Translates over 150,000 entries from Latin to English. The only terminology guide approved by the International Federation of Associations of Anatomists.

Turkington, Carol. *The Brain Encyclopedia.* New York: Facts on File, 1996. 320 p. $40.00. ISBN 081603169X. Aimed at nontechnical readers, this encyclopedia covers a broad range of topics concerning the brain. There are appendices of self-help, professional and governmental organizations dealing with brain diseases, research, and education. There is an extensive glossary.

GUIDES TO INTERNET RESOURCES

Busis, Neil A. Neurosciences on the Internet. Pittsburgh, PA: Busis, 1995– . URL: http://www.Neuroguide.com. "A searchable and browsable index of neuroscience resources available on the Internet: Neurobiology, neurology, neurosurgery, psychiatry, psychology, cognitive science sites, and information on human neurological diseases." This site is privately produced by an M.D. and includes links to a wide array of sources: centers/lab, clinical departments, databases, diseases, exams, guides, images, journals, newsgroups and forums, organizations, software, biology, etc.

MIT CogNet. Massachusetts Institute of Technology, 2000– . URL: http:// cognet.mit.edu. By subscription only. This site "provides a unique electronic community for researchers in cognitive and brain sciences, with in-depth current and classic text resources, and a dynamic interactive forum for today's scholars, students, and professionals." For an annual fee of between $30.00–$240.00, individuals can subscribe to the service and gain access to neuroscience materials published by MIT, job listings, virtual poster sessions, and other resources. A library or institutional subscription is also available.

Resources and Hotlinks. American Association of Anatomists. URL: http:// www.anatomy.org/anatomy/nresource.htm. The association provides a particularly good listing of anatomy resources on the Web.

Visible Human Project. Bethesda, MD: National Library of Medicine. URL: http://www.nlm.nih.gov/research/visible/visible_human.html. Excellent access to anatomy is provided by the Visible Human Project and the related Visible Embryo Project with the goal of creating complete, anatomically detailed, 3D representations of the normal male and female human bodies.

HANDBOOKS

Blood and Other Body Fluids. Philip L. Altman and Dorothy S. Dittmer, eds. Washington, DC: Federation of American Societies for Experimental Biology, 1961. 540 p. (Biological Handbooks.) While long out of print, this entry in the Biological Handbooks series is still a useful source of data on blood volumes, constituents, and other data as well as data on lymph, cerebrospinal fluid, body cavity fluids, urine, and other secretions in humans and animals.

Cell Physiology Source Book. 2nd. ed. Nicholas Sperelakis, ed. San Diego, CA: Academic Press, 1998. 1,095 p. $105.00, $59.95 (paper). ISBN 012656972X, 0126569738 (paper). Authoritative text and core sourcebook in the field of cell physiology.

The Chemokine Factsbook. Krishna Vaddi, Margaret Keller, Kris Vaddi, and Robert Newton, eds. (Factsbook series.) San Diego, CA: Academic, 1997. 192 p. $50.00. ISBN 0127099050. Over 40 entries on chemokines and chemokine receptors from human or other origins provide information on tissue sources, target cells, physicochemical properties, transcription factors, regulation of expression, expression in disease, receptor-binding characteristics, gene structure and location, amino acid sequences, database accession numbers, and references.

The Cytokine Handbook. 3rd ed. See Chapter 6, "Molecular and Cellular Biology," for full annotation.

Cytokine Reference: A Compendium of Cytokines and Other Mediators of Host Defense. Joost J. Oppenheim and Marc Feldmann, eds. See Chapter 6, "Molecular and Cellular Biology," for full annotation.

Growth: Including Reproduction and Morphological Development. Philip L. Altman and Dorothy S. Dittmer, eds. Washington, DC: Federation of American Societies for Experimental Biology, 1962. 608 p. (Biological Handbooks.) This handbook covers vertebrate, invertebrate, and plant reproduction; prenatal and postnatal vertebrate reproduction, plant development, animal morphology, environmental factors, and growth regulators.

Handbook of Chemical Neuroanatomy. A. Bjorklund and T. Hokfelt, series eds. v. 1– , 1983– . Amsterdam: Elsevier. Irregular. Price varies. ISBN 0444903402 (series). Major objective of this series as stated in the preface of volume one is to "assemble present-day knowledge on the organization of the chemically identified systems and provide an authoritative and comprehensive reference source for a broad spectrum of neuroscientists."

Handbook of Endocrinology. 2nd ed. George H. Gass and Harold M. Kaplan, eds. Boca Raton, FL: CRC Press, 1996. 2 v. $139.00 (each volume). ISBN 0849394295. This review of selected topics is written by 36 authors for endocrinologists, researchers, and grad students. Descriptions provide data and references in the fields of anatomy, history, physiology, and pathophysiology. There is a comprehensive survey of the chemical nature of hormones, their synthesis, secretion and transport, their actions and mechanisms of action, their degradation and excretion, in mammals and man. Revised edition of the *CRC Handbook of Endocrinology.*

Handbook of Olfaction and Gustation. Richard L. Doty, ed. New York: Marcel Dekker, 1994. 906 p. $225.00. ISBN 0824792521. This handbook includes over 4,400 citations to the literature, more than 275 tables, equations, drawings, and photographs useful for both the researcher and the clinician.

Handbook of Physiology. 1977– . Bethesda, MD: American Physiological Society (APS). Irregular. Price varies. Several volumes/section. Comprehensive and authoritative, the APS organizes this review series with contributions from scientists all over the world. Billed as "a critical, comprehensive presentation of physiological knowledge and concepts," this series presents significant research results, extensive bibliographic references, and detailed indexes, making these volumes indispensable. The series is divided into eleven sections that are updated frequently: Section 1: *Nervous System*; Section 2: *Cardiovascular System*; Section 3: *Respiratory System*; Section 4: *Adaptation to the Environment* (out of print); Section 5: *Adipose Tissue*; Section 6: *Gastrointestinal System*; Section 7: *Endocrinology*; Section 8: *Renal Physiology*; Section 9: *Reactions to Environmental Agents*; Section 10: *Skeletal Muscle*; and Section 11: *Cell and General Physiology.*

Kirkpatrick, C. T. *Illustrated Handbook of Medical Physiology.* New York: Wiley, 1993. (A Wiley Phoenix Publication.) 556 p. $176.95. ISBN 047191455X. Numerous line drawings help explain the mechanisms of the human body, each chapter describing a separate organ or system and providing an account of the relevant functional anatomy and histology.

Metabolism. Philip L. Altman and Dorothy S. Dittmer, eds. Bethesda, MD: Federation of American Societies for Experimental Biology, 1968. 737 p. (Biological Handbooks.) Another out-of-print but useful volume in the Biological Handbooks series, this one covering human and animal nutrition, digestion, nutrient function, metabolic pathways, plant metabolism, and metabolic end products.

Neural Networks in QSAR and Drug Design. (Principles of QSAR and Drug Design.) James Devillers, ed. London: Academic Press, 1996. 284 p. ISBN 0122138155. The editor calls this volume "the first book on the practical use of artificial networks in molecular modeling." It provides descriptions of the main neural network paradigms, access to more than 10,000 bibliographic references to neural networks, case studies showing how neural networks can be used to solve problems, practical information on using neural networks, and on their strengths and weaknesses.

Nonlinear Analysis of Physiological Data. Holger Kantz, J. Kurths, and G. Mayer-Kress, eds. Berlin: Springer Verlag, 1998. $59.95. ISBN 3540634819. Basically a how-to book; some of the procedures discussed are processing of physiological data, problems in the reconstruction of high-dimensional deterministic dynamics from time series, chaotic measures and real-world systems, analyzing spatio-temporal patterns of complex systems, nonlinear algorithms for analysis of heart rate variability, etc.

Patton, Kevin T. and Gary A. Thibodeau. *Handbook for Anatomy and Physiology.* St. Louis, MO: Mosby, 2000. 624 p. $29.95. ISBN 0323010962. An excellent illustrated review of important anatomy and related physiological principles, including summary tables of physiological concepts. A useful handbook designed for quick reference.

Pimentel, Enrique. *Handbook of Growth Factors.* Boca Raton, FL: CRC Press. 3 v. 1994. Price varies. ISBN 0849325056 (v. 1). An expanded version of earlier volumes by the renowned endocrinological expert, this authoritative review covers general basic aspects (v. 1); peptide growth factors (v. 2); hematopoietic growth factors and cytokines (v. 3).

Respiration and Circulation. Philip Altman and Dorothy S. Dittmer. Bethesda, MD: Federation of American Societies for Experimental Biology, 1971. 930 p. (Biological Handbooks.) This handbook covers basic physical data dealing with respiration and circulation, the thorax and ventilation, airways and gas movement, blood gases, the heart and pumping action, the vascular system, capillaries, invertebrate respiration and circulation, and plant respiration.

HISTORIES

The American Association of Anatomists, 1888–1987: Essays on the History of Anatomy in America and a Report on the Membership—Past and Present. John E. Pauly, ed. Baltimore, MD: Williams & Wilkins, 1987. 292 p. ISBN 0683068008 (paper).

The Body in Parts: Fantasies of Corporeality in Early Modern Europe. Carla Mazzio and David Hillman, eds. New York: Routledge, 1997. 376 p. $20.99 (paper). ISBN 0415916941 (paper).   This well-received book examines how the body (its organs, limbs, and viscera) was represented in the literature and culture of early modern Europe.

Choulant, Johann Ludwig. *Geschichte und Bibliographie der Anatomischen Abbildung. History and Bibliography of Anatomic Illustrations.* Translated and annotated by Mortimer Frank. Further essays by Fielding H. Garrison, Mortimer Frank, and Edward C. Streeter, with a new historical essay by Charles Singer and bibliography of Mortimer Frank by J. Christian Bay. New York: Hafner, 1962. 435 p.   Originally published in German in Leipzig, 1852. Contributions and essays by major historians of science.

Circulation of the Blood: Men and Ideas. 2nd ed. Alfred P. Fishman and Dickinson W. Richards, eds. Reprint of the 1964 edition published by Oxford University Press. Bethesda, MD: Oxford University Press, 1988. $56.00. ISBN 0195206991. A study of the origins, discovery, and progress of great ideas in this branch of science.

Clarke, Edwin, Kenneth Dewhurst, and Michael J. Aminoff. *An Illustrated History of Brain Function: Imaging the Brain from Antiquity to the Present.* 2nd rev. and enl. ed. San Francisco, CA: Norman Publishing, 1996. 188 p. $150.00. ISBN 093040565X.   This chronological survey of attempts to localize brain function from antiquity to the present, and provides a valuable guide to the history of the neurosciences and to many of the most-spectacular pictorial sources in the history of neuroanatomy and neurophysiology. Includes 161 illustrations, 11 color plates, and a new bibliography of the neuroscientific literature.

Corner, George Washington. *Anatomical Texts of the Earlier Middle Ages: A Study in the Transmission of Culture, with a revised Latin Text of Anatomia Cophonis and Translations of Four Texts.* New York: AMS Press, 1977. 112 p. ISBN 0404132502.   Reprint of the 1927 edition published by the Carnegie Institution of Washington, which was issued as number 364 of its publication.

Cunningham, Andrew. *The Anatomical Renaissance: The Resurrection of the Anatomical Projects of the Ancients.* Brookfield, VT: Ashgate Publishing Co., 1997. $76.95. ISBN 1859283381.   The history introduces the ancients of anatomy in context with the anatomical Reformation and Renaissance.

Discoveries in the Human Brain: Neuroscience Prehistory, Brain Structure, and Function. Louise H. Marshall and Horace W. Magoun, eds. Totowa, NJ: Humana Press, 1998. 336 p. $69.50. ISBN 0896034356.   This very visual history surveys the progress of brain science from its beginnings through the 1970s.

Dobson, Jessie. *Anatomical Eponyms; Being a Biographical Dictionary of Those Anatomists Whose Names Have Become Incorporated into Anatomical Nomenclature, with Definitions of the Structures to Which Their Names Have Been Attached and References to the Works in Which They Are Described.* 2nd ed. Edinburgh: Livingstone, 1962. 235 p.   The title says it all; unfortunately, this book is out of print.

Endocrinology: People and Ideas. S. M.McCann, ed. Bethesda, MD: American Physiology Society, 1988. 484 p. $75.00. ISBN 0195207181.   Principal ideas and developments in endocrinology from Aristotle to the most recent discoveries.

Essays in the History of the Physiological Sciences. Claud Debru, ed. (Wellcome Institute series in the history of medicine Clio Medica, 33.) Atlanta, GA: Rodopi, 1995. 239 p. $73.50. ISBN 9051836465.   This history focuses on defined disciplines such as neurophysiology and endocrinology in an international approach to the history of the physiological sciences. Proceedings of a network symposium of the European Association for the History of Medicine and Health held at the University Louis Pasteur, Strasbourg, on March 26–27, 1993.

Finger, Stanley. *Origins of Neuroscience; A History of Explorations into Brain Function.* New York: Oxford University Press, 1994. 462 p. $75.00 ISBN 0195065034.   Over 350 illustrations help to trace the development of the history of science relevant to brain function.

Finger, Stanley. *Minds Behind the Brain: A History of the Pioneers and Their Discoveries.* New York: Oxford University Press, 1999. 416 p. $35.00. ISBN 019508571X.   Thousands of years of brain science are illustrated by the biographies of nineteen great scientists.

Foster, Michael. *Lectures on the History of Physiology During the 16th, 17th, and 18th Centuries.* (Cambridge Biological Series.) Cambridge, England: Cambridge University Press, 1901. 310 p.   A classic history by one of the founders of modern physiology.

Geison, Gerald L. *Physiology in the American Context, 1850–1940.* Philadelphia, PA: Lippincott, Williams & Wilkins, 1987. 403 p. $55.00. ISBN 0195206983. Originally published under the auspices of the American Physiological Society.

Gross, Charles G. *Brain Vision Memory: Takes in the History of Neuroscience.* Cambridge, MA: MIT Press, 1999. 255 p. $16.50 (paper). ISBN 0262571358. Gross describes the growth of knowledge about the brain from the Egyptians and Greeks through the Dark Ages and the Renaissance to the present time.

History of Neuroscience in Autobiography. Larry R. Squire, ed. San Diego, CA: Academic Press, 1996– . v. $49.95 (v. 2), $89.95 (v. 3). ISBN 0916110516 (v. 1), 0126603022 (v. 2), and 0126603057 (v. 3).   This most recent book was prepared under the auspices of the Society for Neuroscience. The series presents a collection of autobiographical personal narratives by pioneers of modern neuroscience. Currently, 3 volumes have been published, each with about 15 essays.

History of the American Physiological Society: The First Century, 1887–1987. John R. Brobeck, Orr E. Reynolds, and Toby A. Appel, eds. Baltimore, MD: Williams and Wilkins, 1987. 533 p. $45.00. ISBN 0195206975. History of the beginnings of a major scientific and medical society.

History of the American Physiological Society Semicentennial, 1887–1937. Baltimore, MD: American Physiological Society, 1938. 228 p. Includes portraits and biographical sketches of the original members and of the presidents of the society.

Hunter, William. *Hunter's Lectures of Anatomy.* New York: Elsevier, 1972. 1 v. ISBN 0444409106. Facsimile of two notebooks containing lecture notes from a course given by W. Hunter in Manchester, England, beginning Jan. 20, 1752. The lecture notes were taken by C. White of Manchester, and the notebooks have been prepared for publication by N. Dowd. Hunter was one of the most-famous anatomy teachers of his time, and his lectures are an important source of information on the state of the art in the mid-eighteenth century.

Hunterian Museum. *Catalogue of the Anatomical and Pathological Preparations of Dr. William Hunter.* In the Hunterian Museum, University of Glasgow, catalogue prepared by John H. Teacher. Glasgow: James MacLehose, 1900. 2 v. Catalogs of anatomical and pathological biological specimens prepared by Dr. Hunter.

Membrane Transport: People and Ideas. Daniel C. Tosteson, ed. Bethesda, MD: American Physiological Society, 1989. 420 p. $65.00. ISBN 0195207734. A collection of personal accounts by investigators who have been at the forefront of research in membrane transport.

Neural Science: A Century of Progress and the Mysteries that Remain. Thomas D. Albright, et al. Cambridge, MA: Cell Press, 2000. 55p. $30.00. No ISBN. Leading scholars in the field deliver this comprehensive review outlining the accomplishments and limitations of the reductionist and holistic approaches to the complex problems of neural science. Published as review supplement to *Cell*, vol. 100, Feb. 18, 2000.

O'Connor, W. J. *Founders of British Physiology: A Biographical Dictionary 1820–1885.* Manchester: Manchester University Press, 1988. 278 p. $25.00. ISBN 0719025370. Dictionary of nineteenth-century British human physiologists, arranged by name.

Persaud, T. V. N. *Early History of Human Anatomy: From Antiquity to the Beginning of the Modern Era.* Springfield, IL: Charles C. Thomas, 1984. 200 p. ISBN 0398050384. The author portrays the early history of anatomy in relation to the practice of medicine by charting the achievements and changing concepts from ancient times to the beginning of the scientific era, symbolized by Vesalius and his masterpiece, *De Humani Corporis Fabrica.*

Persaud, T. V. N. *A History of Anatomy: The Post-Vesalian Era.* Springfield, IL: Charles C. Thomas, 1997. 357 p. $92.95. ISBN 0398067724. Written for a general readership, this history continues the author's earlier volume, from Vesalius to the early nineteenth century.

Punt, H. *Bernard Siegfried Albinus (1697–1770), On "Human Nature:" Anatomical and Physiological Ideas in Eighteenth Century Leiden.* Amsterdam: B. M. Israel, 1983. 223 p. ISBN 9060780884. "Addendum: transcriptions and translations of the lecture notes on Albinus' physiology." p. 135–83. Text in English and Latin with a summary in Dutch.

Renal Physiology: People and Ideas. Carl W. Gottschalk, Robert W. Berliner, and Gerhard H. Giebisch, eds. Bethesda, MD: American Physiological Society, 1988. 520 p. $87.50. ISBN 0195207025. Written by well-known physiologists, each chapter offers a unique, inside perspective on the historical record of the historical record of the discipline.

Rothschuh, Karl Ed. *History of Physiology.* Huntington, NY: Krieger, 1973. 379 p. $43.50. ISBN 0882750690. Revised translation, and first English edition, of *Geschlichte der Physiologie,* published in 1953 by the respected scientist; includes bibliographical references. And, it's still in print!

Stevens, Leonard A. *Explorers of the Brain.* New York: Knopf, 1971. 348 p. ISBN 0394429680. History of anatomy including a substantial seventeen-page bibliography.

Tenney, S. Marsh. "The Father of American Physiology," *News in Physiological Sciences* 9: 43–4, Feb. 1994. The life and work of Robley Dunglison, the first professor of anatomy and medicine at the University of Virginia and Thomas Jefferson's personal physician.

Todd, Edwin M. *The Neuroanatomy of Leonardo da Vinci.* Park Ridge, IL: American Association of Neurological Surgeons, 1991. Reprint of the 1983 ed. 192 p. $75.00. ISBN 1879284057. Focused history of one of the greatest scientists and artists of all times.

Wade, Nicholas J. *A Natural History of Vision.* Cambridge, MA: MIT Press, 1998. 486 p. $58.00. ISBN 0262231948. This illustrated anthology represents the principle thinkers on optical science, from antiquity to the present.

Women Physiologists; An Anniversary Celebration of Their Contributions to British Physiology. Lynn Bindman, Alison Brading, and Tilli Tansey, eds. Brookfield, VT: Ashgate Publishing Co., 1993. 164 p. $15.00 (paper). ISBN 1855780496 (paper). This book focuses on a group of women who have made significant contributions to physiology.

METHODS AND TECHNIQUES

Brain Mapping: The Methods. Arthur W. Toga and John C. Mazziotta, eds. San Diego, CA: Academic, 1996. 471 p. $178.00. ISBN 0126925402. Suitable for both novices and experts in the field, this reference provides a comprehensive discussion of all methods used to map the brain. The methodological information spans the range from the molecular to the whole brain, including anatomy, physiology, and pathology.

Brain Research Protocols. v. 1– , 1997– . New York: Elsevier. Bimonthly. $689.00. ISSN 1385–299X. This is a section of *Brain Research* that publishes current and updated protocols in neuromorphology, cellular and molecular neurobiology, neurophysiology, developmental nuerobiology, neuropharmacology, quantitative and computational neurobiology, and behavioural neurobiology. The overriding criteria for publication are significant methodololgical and experimental relevance to a multidisciplinary audience.

Culturing Nerve Cells. 2nd ed. Gary Banker and Kimberly Goslin, eds. (Cellular and Molecular Neuroscience.) Cambridge, MA: MIT Press, 1998. 666 p. $75.00. ISBN 0262024381. A do-it-yourself manual with hands-on advice, complete with recipes and protocols for growing neurons in culture.

Current Protocols in Neuroscience. Jacqueline Crawley et al., eds. New York: Wiley, 1997. Unbound, variously paged. $395.00 (loose-leaf), $450.00 (CD-ROM). ISBN 0471163597, 0471163619 (CD-ROM). These techniques cover the needs of researchers in molecular neurobiology, neurophysiology, neuroanatomy, neuropharmacology, and behavioral neuroscience with a wide range of selected, carefully edited, methods. The initial purchase price includes one year of quarterly updates (can be renewed annually).

Electrical Manipulation of Cells. Paul T. Lynch and Michael R. Davey, eds. New York: Chapman & Hall, 1995. $167.00. ISBN 0412030012. An authoritative, up-to-date review of the field, covering all the major techniques in one source. Information is featured for those involved in the manipulation of cells, specifically, biotechnologists, cell biologists, microbiologists, biophysicists, and plant scientists.

Handbook of Endocrine Research Techniques. Flora de Pablo, Colin G. Scanes, and Bruce D. Weintraub, eds. San Diego, CA: Academic Press, 1997. 599 p. $121.00. ISBN 0122099206. Written by experts in the field, this volume synthesizes in a single source up-to-date methods and strategies useful in endocrinological research. General concepts, detailed protocols, and extensive references to the original literature are provided.

Hockfield, Susan, et al. *Molecular Probes of the Nervous System: Selected Methods for Antibody and Nucleic Acid Probes.* Cold Spring Harbor, NY: Cold Spring Harbor Laboratory Press, 1993. $21.25 (paper). ISBN 0879693517 (paper). Although somewhat dated, this is a basic manual for students and researchers using antibody or nucleic acid probes, with special emphasis on techniques of importance to neuroscientists. It follows the format and exercises for the Molecular Probes of the Nervous System course, taught at the Cold Spring Harbor summer neurobiology program.

Imaging Neurons: A Laboratory Manual. Rafael Yuste, Frederick Lawnni, and Arthur Konnerth, eds. Cold Spring Harbor, NY: Cold Spring Harbor Laboratory Press, 1999. $120.00 (spiralbound). ISBN 0879695412. This manual presents a comprehensive description of imaging methods applicable to living cells, and other cell types. The material was taught at a laboratory course at the Cold Spring Harbor Laboratory and covers established practices as well as cutting-edge techniques.

Journal of Neuroscience Methods. v. 1– , 1979– . Amsterdam: Elsevier. Semimonthly. $3,094.00. ISSN 0165-0270. Available electronically. Publishes research papers and a limited number of broad and critical reviews dealing with new methods or significant developments of recognized methods, used to investigate the organization and fine structure, biochemistry, molecular biology, histo- and cytochemistry, physiology, biophysics and pharmacology of receptors, neurones, synapses, and glial cells in the nervous systems of man, vertebrates, and invertebrates, or applicable to the clinical and behavioral sciences, tissue culture, neurocommunications, biocybernetics, or computer software.

Neuromethods. v. 1– , 1985– . Clifton, NJ: Humana Press. Irregular. Price varies. ISSN 0893-2336. This series encompasses neurochemistry, neuroethology, neural psychiatry, neurology, neurogenetics, molecular neurobiology, etc. There is usually a short introductory review of methods, comparisons with other techniques, and the relationship of substances being analyzed to neural conditions. Methodology details are included along with protocols.

Martin, Rosemary. *Neuroscience Methods.* Harwood, 1997. 272 p. $23.00 (paper). ISBN 9057022451 (paper). This volume presents a convenient and excellent overeiw of 34 specific methods of brain study, covering preparations, electrophysiological techniques, application of drugs, ion concentration measurements, histochemical and biochemical techniques, antibody production, blotting and hybridization techniques, neural grafting, etc.

Martin, Terry R., David Shier, Jackie Butler, and Ricki Lewis. *Hole's Human Anatomy & Physiology: Laboratory Manual.* 8th ed. McGraw-Hill, 1999. ISBN 0697342174. Thoroughly revised and designed to accompany Hole's *Human Anatomy and Physiology* text. Also, see Tortora, in the following text.

Methods in Neuroendocrinology. Louis D. Van De Kar, ed. Boca Raton, FL: CRC Press, 1998. (CRC Press Methods in the Life Sciences Series. Cellular Molecular Neuropharmacology Series) 236 p. $94.95 (paper). ISBN 0849333636 (paper). Intended for students, post docs, and medical residents. Covers the major methods in neuroendocrinology, providing both background information on the method and detailed instructions.

Methods in Neuronal Modeling: From Ions to Networks. 2nd ed. Christof Koch and Idan Segev, eds. Cambridge, MA: MIT Press, 1998. 671 p. $65.00. ISBN 0262112310. Expertise concentrated on state-of-the-art neuronal modeling and techniques useful for computational neuroscientists and theoretical neurobiologists.

Methods in Neurosciences. This series has been incorporated into the review journal *International Review of Neurobiology* listed in the Reviews of the Literature, Neurobiology section in the following text.

Methods in Physiology Series. v. 1– , 1994– . Bethesda, MD: American Physiological Society. Irregular. Price varies. This series describes experimental techniques in cellular, molecular, and general physiology. Each book is edited by experts in the field, and cover theory and history behind the methods, critical commentary, major applications with examples, limitations and extensions of each technique. Vol. 1: *Membrane Protein Structure; Experimental Approaches*, 1994. 395 p. $65.00. ISBN 0196071123. Vol. 2: *Fractal Physiology*, 1994. 400 p. $55.00. ISBN 0195080130.

Modeling in the Neurosciences: From Ionic Channels to Neural Networks. Rosnan R. Poznanski, ed. Amsterdam: Harwood, 1999. 536 p. $95.00. ISBN 9057022842. This monograph provides a comprehensive review of biophysical, cellular, and network aspects of the neurosciences and is useful for the beginner or advanced modeler.

Neuroscience Labfax. M. A. Lynch and S. M. O'Mara, eds. San Diego, CA: Academic Press, 1997. (Labfax Series) 312 p. $66.00. ISBN 0124604900. A comprehensive compilation of up-to-date methods, techniques, and data. The range is interdisciplinary, using methods and data from molecular and cellular neuroscience, biophysics, and behavior.

Neuroscience Protocols. F. G. Wouterlood, ed. Amsterdam: Elsevier, 1993. Modules 1–2, ring binder set: $317.25. ISBN 0444895396 (module 1). A neuroscience laboratory manual; an electronic version is in preparation. This manual provides protocols of new and established techniques in collaboration with *Brain Research.* It covers behavioral neurobiology, cell and molecular neurobiology, developmental neurobiology, neurochemistry, neurophysiology, and quantitative aspects of these disciplines. It is supplied in loose-leaf format with ring binders, compiled of modules, each with 10–12 new or updated protocols covering several subjects. Also available on a subscription basis.

Protocols for Neural Cell Culture. 2nd ed. Sergey Fedoroff and Arleen Richardson, eds. Totowa, NJ: Humana, 1997. 278 p. $69.50 (spiralbound). ISBN 0896034542 (spiralbound). Practical laboratory manual of routine neural tissue culture protocols for researchers.

Quantitative Methods in Neuroanatomy. Michael G. Steward, ed. New York: Wiley, 1992. 349 p. ISBN 0335093248. Techniques for autoradiography, imaging, and neuroanatomical histology of the nervous system.

Sharif, N. A. *Molecular Imaging in Neuroscience.* Oxford, England: IRL Press, 1993. (The Practical Approach Series.) 245 p. $45.00 (paper). ISBN 0199633800 (paper). As the series promises, this book provides practical aspects for detailed protocols and powerful new techniques for neuropharmacology, neuroanatomy, neurogenetics, and neuropathology.

Stamford, J. A. *Monitoring Neuronal Activity.* Oxford, England: IRL Press, 1992. (The Practical Approach Series.) 294 p. $45.00 (paper). ISBN 019963243X (paper). This volume draws together many different methods of monitoring activity of nerve cells. Detailed protocols are available, along with monitoring tips.

Tortora, Gerard J. and Robert J. Amitrano. *Anatomy and Physiology Laboratory Manual.* 6th ed. Upper Saddle River, NJ: Prentice-Hall, 2001. 574 p. $57.00 (paper). ISBN 0139203230 (paper). Top-selling, very successful laboratory manual for anatomy and physiology appropriate at the undergraduate level. It follows a body systems approach and is compatible with any introductory anatomy and physiology text.

TEXTBOOKS AND TREATISES

Bagshaw, C. L. R. *Muscle Contraction.* 2nd ed. Chapman & Hall, 1993. 168 p. $27.50. ISBN 0412403706.

Barr's the Human Nervous System: An Anatomical Viewpoint. 7th ed. J.A. Kiernan and Murray Llewellyn, eds. Philadelphia, PA: Lippincott Williams & Wilkins, 1998. $37.00. ISBN 0397584318.

Basic Neurochemistry: Molecular, Cellular, and Medical Aspects. 6th ed. George J. Siegel, ed. Philadelphia, PA: Lippincott Williams & Wilkins, 1998. 1,250 p. $69.95. ISBN 039751820X.   Also CD-ROM for Windows and Macintosh.

Bolander, Franklyn F. *Molecular Endocrinology.* 2nd ed. San Diego, CA: Academic Press, 1994. 569 p. $69.95. ISBN 0121112314.

Burton, Richard F. *Physiology by Numbers; An Encouragement to Quantitative Thinking.* 2nd ed. New York: Cambridge University Press, 2000. $64.95. ISBN 0521772001.

Delcomyn, Fred. *Foundations of Neurobiology.* New York: Freeman, 1998. 648 p. $71.00. ISBN 0716726270.

Endocrinology. Leslie J. DeGroot et al., eds. 3rd ed. Philadelphia, PA: Saunders, 1994. 3 v. $510.00 (set). ISBN 0721642624 (set).

Fain, Gordon L. *Molecular and Cellular Physiology of Neurons.* New York: Harvard University Press, 1999. 720 p. $65.00. ISBN 0674581555.

Fundamental Neuroscience. Michael J. Zigmond, et al., eds. Orlando, FL: Academic, 1998. 1,000 p. $89.95. ISBN 0127808701.

Hadley, Mac E. *Endocrinology.* 5th ed. Upper Saddle River, NJ: Prentice Hall, 2000. 585 p. ISBN 0130803561.

Hall, Zach W. *An Introduction to Molecular Neurobiology.* Sunderland, MA: Sinauer, 1992. 555 p. $62.95. ISBN 0878933077.

Hole's Human Anatomy and Physiology. 8th ed. Jackie Butler and Ricki Lewis, eds. New York: McGraw-Hill, 1999. 1,047 p. $94.06. ISBN 0697341933.

Huguenard, John and David A. McCormick. *Electrophysiology of the Neuron; An Interactive Tutorial.* New York: Oxford University Press, 1994. 80 p. $24.95 (book and disk). ISBN: 0195091116 (book and disk).   A companion to *Neurobiology* by Gordon Shepherd.

Jacobson, Marcus. *Foundations of Neuroscience.* New York: Plenum, 1995. 400 p. $44.50 (paper). ISBN 0306451654 (paper).

Johnson, Daniel, and Samuel Miao-Sin Wu. *Foundations of Cellular Neurophysiology.* Cambridge, MA: MIT Press, 1995. 904 p. $74.95. ISBN 0262100533.

Koch, Christof. *Biophysics of Computation: Information Processing in Single Neurons.* See annotation in the Text section of Chapter 5, "Biochemistry and Biophysics."

Lecture Notes on Human Physiology, 4th ed. John J. Bray et al., eds. Oxford, England: Blackwell, 1999. 400 p. $34.95. ISBN 0865427755.

Levitan, Irwin B. and Leonard K. Kaczmarek. *The Neuron: Cell and Molecular Biology.* 2nd ed. New York: Oxford University Press, 1996. $49.95 (paper). ISBN 0195100212 (paper).

Martin, R., Bruce Martin, David B. Burr, and Neil A. Sharkey. *Skeletal Tissue Mechanics.* New York: Springer Verlag, 1998. 3384 p. $64.95. ISBN 0387984747.

Matthews, Gary G. *Neurobiology: Molecules, Cells, and Systems.* Oxford, England: Blackwell Science, 1997. 600 p. $54.95. ISBN 0865424047.

Mazumdar, J. *An Introduction to Mathematical Physiology and Biology.* 2nd ed. (Cambridge Studies in Mathematical Biology, 15.) New York: Cambridge University Press, 1999. 256 p. $29.95 (paper). ISBN 0521646758 (paper).

McIlwain, James T. *An Introduction to the Biology of Vision.* New York: Cambridge University Press, 1996. 222 p. ISBN 0521498902 (paper).

Molecular Biology of the Brain. S. J. Higgins, ed. (Essays in Biochemistry, 33.) Rutgers, NJ: Princeton University Press, 1999. 198 p. $32.50 (paper). ISBN 069100952X (paper).

Molecular Physiology of Growth. P. T. Loughna and M. M. Pell, eds. New York: Cambridge University Press, 1997. 170 p. (Society for Experimental Biology Seminar Series, no. 60.) $59.95. ISBN 0521471109.

Neuroendocrinology in Physiology and Medicine. P. Michael Conn and Marc E. Freeman, eds. Totowa, NJ: Humana Press, 1999. 552 p. $125.00. ISBN 0896037258. Leading experts integrate the latest findings from basic and clinical science to create a comprehensive reference work on the processes by which the brain acts as an endocrine organ to control hormonal functions and to maintain homeostasis and regulate behavior.

Neurons, Networks, and Motor Behavior. Paul S. G. Stein, Douglas G. Stuart, and Allen I. Selverston, eds. (Computational Neuroscience.) Cambridge, MA: MIT Press, 1997. 320 p. $60.00. ISBN 0262193906.

Nolte, John. *The Human Brain: An Introduction to Its Functional Anatomy.* 4th ed. St. Louis, MO: Mosby Year Book, 1998. 500 p. $45.00. ISBN 0815189117.

Principles of Neural Science, 4th ed. Eric R. Kandel, James H. Schwartz, and Thomas M. Jessell, eds. New York: McGraw-Hill, 2000. 1,414 p. $85.00. ISBN 0838577016.

Rafinetti, Roberto. *Circadian Physiology*. Boca Raton, FL: CRC Press, 2000. 184 p. $49.95. ISBN 0849322995.

Revest, P and A. Longstaff. *Molecular Neuroscience*. New York: Springer-Verlag, 1998. 240 p. $34.95 (paper). ISBN 0387915192 (paper).

Sandra, Alexander. *Core Concepts in Embryology*. Philadelphia, PA: Lippincott Williams & Wilkins, 1997. 162 p. ISBN 0316018848.

Shepherd, Gordon M. *Neurobiology*. 3rd ed. New York: Oxford University Press, 1997. 784 p. $49.95 (paper). ISBN 0195088433 (paper). See Huguenard for a companion manual, previous.

Shepherd, Gordon M. *The Synaptic Organization of the Brain*. 4th ed. New York: Oxford University Press, 1997. 656 p. $45.00. ISBN 0195118243.

Thibodeau, Gary A. *Anatomy and Physiology*. 4th ed. St. Louis, MO: Mosby, 1999. $117.00 ISBN 0323001912. Book with study guide, lab manual, and quick reference package.

Tortora, Gerard J., Sandra Reynolds, and Bonnie Roesch. *Introduction to the Human Body; The Essentials of Anatomy and Physiology*. 4th ed. New York: Wiley, 1997. 656 p. $85.00 ISBN 0471367915.

Vander, Arthur J., James Sherman, and Dorothy Luciano. *Human Physiology: The Mechanisms of Body Function*. 7th ed. Boston, MA: McGraw-Hill, 1998. 818 p. $75.00. ISBN 007067065X.

Williams' Textbook of Endocrinology. 9th ed. Jean D. Wilson and Daniel W. Foster, eds. Philadelphia, PA: Saunders, 1998. $159.00. ISBN 0721661521.

PERIODICALS

For convenience, journals are divided into subject sections for anatomy, endocrinology, neurobiology, and physiology. These divisions are, in some sense, arbitrary and because titles are not duplicated between divisions, it may be necessary to consult several subject divisions when tracking down a particular journal. Because there are so many current journals in these areas, only the most prominent were selected for inclusion, chosen for their relative importance and high impact.

Anatomy

Anatomical Record. v. 1– , 1906– . New York: Wiley/Liss. Monthly. $3,595.00. ISSN 0003-276X. Available electronically. Official publication of the American Association of Anatomists, issuing research reports, review articles, trends, special communications, and commentaries/letters to the editor concerning broad research interests in anatomy. The journal also publishes Abstracts and Proceedings of the Association's annual meeting.

Anatomy and Embryology. v. 1– , 1892– . Berlin: Springer-Verlag. Monthly. $3,248.00. ISSN 0340-2061. Available electronically. A leading European anatomy journal. Former titles: *Journal of Anatomy and Embryology* and *Zeitschrift fuer Anatomie und Entwicklungsgeschichte.*

Annals of Anatomy. v. 174– , 1992– . Jena, Germany: Urban & Fischer. Irregular. $500.00. ISSN 0940-9602. This continuation of *Anatomischer Anzeiger* is a general anatomical journal. The official organ of the Anatomische Gesellschaft.

Cells, Tissues, Organs. v. 164– , 1999– . Basel, Switzerland: Karger. Monthly. $1,152.00. ISSN 0001-5180. Available electronically. This international forum for experimental and theoretical work presents information on morphology at all levels of organization, from subcellular to macroscopy, with emphasis on humans and higher vertebrates. Formerly: *Acta Anatomica.*

Developmental Dynamics. v. 193– , 1992– . New York: Wiley/Liss. Monthly. $2,395.00. ISSN 1058-8388. Available electronically. An official publication of the American Association of Anatomists, this journal provides a focus for communication among developmental biologists studying the emergence of form during human and animal development. Formerly: *American Journal of Anatomy.*

Journal of Anatomy. v. 1– , 1866– . New York: Cambridge University Press for the Anatomical Society of Great Britain and Ireland. Bimonthly. $896.00. ISSN 0021-8782. Available electronically. Presents articles and reviews covering normal human and comparative anatomy, including applied anatomy, physical anthropology, neurology, endocrinology, and embryology.

Journal of Morphology. v. 1– , 1887– . New York: Wiley/Liss. Monthly. $2,625.00. ISSN 0362-2525. Available electronically. Publishes original papers in cytology, protozoology, embryology, and general morphology.

Endocrinology and Metabolism

Endocrinology. v. 1– , 1917– . Bethesda, MD: Endocrine Society. Monthly. $515.00. ISSN 0013-7227. Available electronically. Includes papers describing results of original research in the fields of endocrinology and metabolism for nonprimate biochemical and physiological studies. Work on material of primate origin is not excluded.

General and Comparative Endocrinology. v. 1– , 1961– . San Diego, CA: Academic Press. Monthly. $1,595.00. ISSN 0016-6480. Available electronically. Published under the auspices of the Division of Comparative Endocrinology of the American Society of Zoologists, and the European Society for Comparative Endocrinology. Includes articles based on studies on cellular mechanisms of hormone action, and on functional, developmental, and evolutionary aspects of vertebrate and invertebrate endocrine systems.

Hormones and Behavior. v. 1– , 1969– . San Diego, CA: Academic. Quarterly. $595.00. ISSN 0018–506X. Available electronically. Publishes a broad range of original articles dealing with behavioral systems known to be hormonally influenced. Scope extends from evolutionary significance of hormone/behavior relations to those dealing with cellular and molecular mechanisms of hormonal actions on neural tissues and other tissues relevant to behavior.

Journal of Endocrinology. v. 1– , 1939– . Bristol, England: Society for Endocrinology. Bimonthly. $685.00. ISSN 0022-0795. Available electronically. Original research on all aspects of the nature and functions of endocrine systems.

Journal of Molecular Endocrinology. v. 1– , 1988– . Bristol, England: Society for Endocrinology Ltd. Bimonthly. $413.00. ISSN 0952-5041. Available electronically. Original research papers, rapid communications, short reviews, and commentaries are accepted on molecular and cellular aspects of endocrine and related systems.

Journal of Neuroendocrinology, v. 1– , 1989– . Oxford, England: Blackwell Scientific. Monthly. $1,220.00. ISSN 0953-8194. Available electronically. Official journal of the European Neuroendocrine Association and the British Neuroendocrine Group, this international journal acts as a focus for the newest ideas, knowledge, and technology in a variety of endocrine, behavioural, electrophysiological, and clinical studies. Deals with manuscripts for vertebrate, invertebrate, and clinical systems.

Journal of Steroid Biochemistry and Molecular Biology. v. 37– , 1990– . New York: Elsevier. Semimonthly. $3,315.00. ISSN 0960-0760. Available electronically. The journal is devoted to new experimental or theoretical developments in areas related to steroids. Original papers, mini-reviews, proceedings of selected meetings, and rapid communications are included. Formerly: *Journal of Steroid Biochemistry.*

Molecular and Cellular Endocrinology. v. 1– , 1974– . New York: Elsevier. Semimonthly. $3,4344.00. ISSN 0303-7207. Available electronically.

Publishes on all aspects related to the biochemical effects, synthesis, and secretions of extracellular signals (hormones, neurotransmitters, etc.), and cellular regulatory mechanisms involved in hormonal control.

Molecular Endocrinology. v. 1– , 1987– . Bethesda, MD: Endocrine Society. Monthly. $368.00. ISSN 0888-8809. Available electronically. Describes results of original research on the mechanistic studies of the effects of hormones and related substances on molecular biology and genetic regulation of nonprimate and primate cells.

Neuropeptides. v. 1– , 1980– . Edinburgh, Scotland: Churchill Livingstone/ Longman Group. Bimonthly. $1,180.00. ISSN 0143-4179. Available electronically. The aim of this journal is the rapid publication of original research and review articles dealing with the structure, distribution, actions and functions of peptides in the central and peripheral nervous systems.

Regulatory Peptides. v. 1– , 1980– . New York: Elsevier. Semimonthly. $2,284.00. ISSN 0167-0115. Available electronically. Provides a medium for the rapid publication of interdisciplinary studies on the physiology and pathology of peptides of the gut, endocrine, and nervous systems that regulate cell or tissue function.

Steroids. v. 1– , 1963– . New York: Elsevier. Monthly. $940.00. ISSN 0039-128X. Available electronically. Accepts papers on basic endocrinology and on the organic, biochemical, physiological, pharmacological, and clinical phases of steroids.

Neurobiology

Biological Cybernetics: Communication and Control in Organisms and Automata. v. 1– , 1975– . New York: Springer-Verlag. Monthly. $2,521.00. ISSN 0340-1200. Available electronically. Foremost in computational neuroscience, this journal provides an interdisciplinary medium for the exchange of experimental and theoretical information in quantitative analysis of behavior; quantitative physiological studies of information processing; computational studies of perceptual and motor information; biologically relevant studies in artificial intelligence, robotics, and information theory; and mathematical models of information processing, control, and communication in organisms, including mechanisms of genetic expression and development. Also, see *Neural Computation.* Formerly: *Kybernetik.*

Brain. v. 1– , 1878/79– . New York: Oxford University Press. Bimonthly. $510.00. ISSN 0006-8950. Available electronically.   Publishes papers on neurology and related clinical disciplines, and on basic neuroscience, including molecular and cellular biology, and neuropsychology when they have a neurological orientation and are relevant to the understanding of human disease.

Brain Research. v. 1– , 1966– . Amsterdam: Elsevier. Frequency varies. $17,440.00 for all sections. ISSN 0006-8993. Available electronically.   "International multidisciplinary journal devoted to fundamental research in the brain sciences." One of the leaders in the field and worth the expense. Comes with *Brain Research Protocols, Brain Research Reviews, Cognitive Brain Research, Developmental Brain Research, Gene Expression Patterns,* and *Molecular Brain Research.* The individual sections are also available as separate subscriptions, but the main title can only be purchased as part of the package. Many articles are published first on the Brain Research Interactive Web site, http://www.bres-interactive.com/. At the time of writing, the site was free but in the future access will be by subscription only.

Brain Research Bulletin. v. 1– , 1976– . Oxford, England: Elsevier. Monthly. $2,563.00. ISSN 0361-9230. Available electronically.   Incorporated *Journal of Electrophysiological Techniques.* Publishes papers on all aspects of the nervous system including brief communications with describe a new method, techniques, or apparatus, and results of experiments.

Cellular and Molecular Neurobiology v. 1– , 1981– . New York: Kluwer. Bimonthly. $550.00. ISSN 0272-4340. Available electronically.   Original research articles are accepted that are concerned with the analysis of neuronal and brain function at the cellular or subcellular levels.

Cerebral Cortex. v. 1– , 1991– . New York: Oxford University Press. 8/yr. $595.00. ISSN 1047-3211. Available electronically.   This journal is multidisciplinary and covers development, organization, plasticity, and function of the cerebral cortex. A large variety of modern neurobiological and neuropsychological techniques are also covered.

Cognitive Brain Research. v. 1– , 1992– . Amsterdam: Elsevier Science. Quarterly. $689.00. ISSN 0926-6410. Available electronically.   "Publishes original experimental studies of neural processes underlying intelligent mental activity and its disturbances. Areas of higher nervous functions of particular interest are perception, learning, memory, judgement, reasoning, language and emotion."

Developmental Brain Research. v. 44– , 1988– . Amsterdam: Elsevier Science. Monthly. $2,329.00. ISSN 0165-3806. Available electronically.   "A special section of *Brain Research* which provides a medium for prompt publication of in vitro and in vivo developmental studies concerned with the mechanism of neurogenesis, neuron migration, cell death, neuronal differentiation, synaptogenesis, myelination, the establishment of neuron-glia relations and the development of various brain barrier mechanisms.''

European Journal of Neuroscience. v. 1– , 1989– . Oxford, England: Blackwell Scientific. Monthly. $1,795.00. ISSN 0953-816X. Available electronically. Published on behalf of the European Neuroscience Association, this multidisciplinary journal of experimental and theoretical studies has a broad scope ranging from the behavioral to the molecular, with European focus but with a worldwide orientation.

Experimental Brain Research. v. 1– , 1966– . Berlin: Springer-Verlag. Semimonthly. $5,259.00. ISSN 0014-4819. Available electronically. Accepts contributions on aspects of experimental research of the central and peripheral nervous system in the fields of molecular, physiology, behaviour, neurochemistry, developmental, cellular and molecular neurobiology, and experimental pathology relevant to general problems of cerebral function.

Glia. v. 1– , 1988– . New York: Wiley/Liss. Monthly. $1,855.00. ISSN 0894-1491. Available electronically. Articles dealing with all aspects of glial structure and function including anatomy, physiology, biochemistry, pharmacology, immunology, and pathology of glial cells.

Journal of Chemical Neuroanatomy. v. 1– , 1988– . New York: Elsevier. Bimonthly. $869.00. ISSN 0891-0618. Available electronically. Presents scientific reports relating to functional and biochemical aspects of the nervous system with its microanatomical organization. The scope covers microanatomical, biochemical, pharmacological, and behavioral approaches.

Journal of Comparative Neurology. v. 1– , 1891– . New York: Wiley/Liss. Weekly. $14,995.00. ISSN 0021-9967. Available electronically. Publishes papers on the anatomy and physiology of the nervous system, not including clinical neurology, neuropathology, psychiatry, and introspective psychology unless these bear on the anatomy and physiology of the nervous system. Preference is given to papers which deal descriptively or experimentally with the nervous system, its structure, growth, and function.

Journal of Computational Neuroscience. v. 1– , 1994– . Boston: Kluwer. Bimonthly. $471.00. ISSN 0929-5313. Available electronically. ''From neurons to behavior. A journal at the interface between experimental and theoretical neuroscience.'' Covers neural networks, mathematical models, and computer simulation of the nervous system.

Journal of Neurobiology. v. 1– , 1969– . New York: Wiley. Monthly. $2,735.00. ISSN 0022-3034. Available electronically. High-quality contributions in all areas of neurobiology are solicited, but there is emphasis on cellular, genetic, and molecular analyses of neurodevelopment and the ontogeny of behavior.

Journal of Neurochemistry. v. 1– , 1956– . Philadelphia, PA: Lippincott Williams & Wilkins. Monthly. $1,774.00. ISSN 0022-3042. Available electronically. Official journal of the International Society for Neurochemistry, devoted to the molecular, chemical, and cellular biology of the nervous system.

Journal of Neuroimmunology. v. 1– , 1981– . New York: Elsevier. Monthly. $3,476.00. ISSN 0165-5728 (print). Available electronically. Official Journal of the International Society for Neuroimmunology, publisher of works applying immunologic methodology to the furtherance of the neurological sciences. Studies on all branches of the neurosciences are accepted.

Journal of Neurophysiology. v. 1– , 1938– . Bethesda, MD: American Physiological Society. Monthly. $856.00. ISSN 0022-3077. Available electronically. Highest-quality science on the function of the nervous system. Includes theoretical studies and rapid communications.

Journal of Neuroscience. v. 1– , 1981– . Washington, DC: Society for Neuroscience. Semimonthly. $1,219.50. ISSN 0270-6474. Available electronically. Official journal of the Society for Neuroscience. A leader in the field, this journal publishes broad, multidisciplinary science articles for effective coverage from molecular and cellular neurobiology to behavioral and system neuroscience.

Journal of Neuroscience Research. v. 1– , 1975– . New York: Wiley/Liss. Semimonthly. $5,595.00. ISSN 0360-4012. Available electronically. Basic reports in molecular, cellular, and subcellular areas of the neurosciences, including clinical studies that emphasize fundamental and molecular aspects of nervous system dysfunction. The journal features full-length papers, rapid communications, and mini-reviews on selected areas.

Molecular and Cellular Neurosciences. v. 1– , 1990– . San Diego, CA. Monthly. $550.00. ISSN 1074-7431. Available electronically. Reports of novel research in any area of the molecular neurosciences.

Molecular Brain Research. v. 5– , 1989– . New York: Elsevier Science. Semimonthly. $ 3,769.00. ISSN 0169-328X. Available electronically. A special section of *Brain Research* that provides a medium for the prompt publication of studies of molecular mechanisms of neuronal synaptic and related processes that underlie the structure and function of the brain.

Molecular Neurobiology. v. 1– , 1987– . Totowa, NJ: Humana Press. Bimonthly. $490.00. ISSN 0893-7648.

Nature Neuroscience. v. 1– , 1998– . New York: Nature America. Monthly. $650.00. ISSN 1097-6256. Available electronically. This offshoot of *Nature* presents papers of high quality and significance in all area of neuroscience. It promises rapid review and publication.

Neural Computation. v. 1– , 1989– . Cambridge, MA: MIT Press. Monthly. $430.00. ISSN 0899-7667. Available electronically. Disseminates multidisciplinary research results and reviews of neural computation, highlights problems and techniques in modeling the brain and in the design and construction of neurally inspired processing systems.

Neurobiology of Learning and Memory. v. 63– , 1996– . San Diego, CA: Academic Press. Bimonthly. $660.00. ISSN 1074-7427. Available electronically. Publishes original research articles dealing with neural and behavioral plasticity, at all levels from the molecular to behavioral. Also includes short communications, mini-reviews, and commentaries. Formerly: *Behavioral and Neural Biology.*

Neurochemistry International. v. 1– , 1980– . Oxford, England: Pergamon (Elsevier). Monthly. $1,232.00. ISSN 0197-0186. Available electronically. Publishes articles on the cellular and molecular aspects of neurochemistry in the form of original and rapid research communications; critical reviews and commentaries are included.

NeuroImage. v. 1– , 1992– . Orlando, FL: Academic. 12/yr. $425.00. ISSN 1053-8119. Available electronically. Provides a vehicle for communication of the most important and best papers, using imaging and mapping strategies to study the brain's structure, function, and the relationship between the two, from the whole brain to the tissue level.

Neuron. v. 1– , 1988– . Cambridge, MA: Cell Press. Monthly. $591.00. ISSN 0896-6273. Available electronically. Publishes reports of novel results in any area of experimental neuroscience, in the form of research articles and mini-reviews. Some issues are accompanied by supplements titled *Cell Neuron.*

Neuroreport. v. 1– , 1990– . Philadelphia, PA: Lippincott Williams & Wilkins. 18/yr. $2,694.00. ISSN 0959-4965. Available electronically. International journal for the rapid communication of research in all aspects of neuroscience.

Neuroscience. v. 1– , 1976– . New York: Elsevier. Semimonthly. $3,305.00. ISSN 0306-4522. Available electronically. ''An International Journal under the editorial direction of the International Brain Research Organization.'' The journal publishes papers describing the results of original research on any aspect of the scientific study of the nervous system.

Neuroscience Letters. v. 1– , 1975– . New York: Elsevier. Fortnightly. $5,011.00. ISSN 0304-3940. Available electronically. Rapid publication of short, complete reports, but not preliminary communications, in all areas in the fields of neuroanatomy, neurochemistry, neuroendocrinology, neuropharmacology, neurophysiology, neurotoxicology, molecular neurobiology, behavioral sciences, biocybernetics, and clinical neurobiology. The overriding criteria for publication are novelty and interest to a multidisciplinary audience.

Synapse. v. 1– , 1987– . New York: Wiley/Liss. Monthly. $2,185.00. ISSN 0887-4476. Available electronically. Accepts articles on all aspects of synaptic structure and function, including neurotransmitters, neuropeptides, neuromodulators, receptors, gap junctions, metabolism, plasticity, circuitry, mathematical modeling, ion channels, patch recording, single unite recording, development, behavior, pathology, toxicology, and so forth.

Physiology

American Journal of Physiology. v. 1– , 1898– . Bethesda, MD: American Physiological Association. Monthly. All seven sections: $2,371.00. All APS journals are available via High Wire Press, the Internet imprint of the Stanford University Libraries. The consolidated *American Journal of Physiology* is billed as "the most comprehensive body of research covering the full spectrum of physiology." Its sections are *Cell Physiology*, ISSN 0363-6143, the cutting edge of cell physiology research; *Endocrinology and Metabolism*, ISSN 0193-1849, original investigation on endocrine and metabolic systems on levels of organization, human and animal; *Gastrointestinal and Liver Physiology*, ISSN 0193-1857, papers on digestion, secretion absorption, metabolism, motility, microbiology and colonization, growth and development, and neurobiology; *Heart and Circulatory Physiology*, ISSN 0363-6135, original research on the heart, blood vessels, and lymphatics; *Lung Cellular and Molecular Physiology*, ISSN 1040-0605, deals with molecular, cellular, and morphological aspects of normal and abnormal function and response of cells and components of the respiratory system; *Regulatory, Integrative and Comparative Physiology*, ISSN 0363-6119, innovative articles illuminating physiological processes at all levels of biological organization; and *Renal Physiology*, ISSN 0363-6127, information on kidney and urinary tract physiology, epithelial cell biology, and control of body fluid volume and composition.

Chemical Senses. v. 5– , 1980– . New York: Oxford University Press. Bimonthly. $460.00. ISSN 0379-864X. Available electronically. Providing an international forum for original and review papers on chemoreception research at morphological, biochemical, physiological, and psychophysical levels. Covers development and specific application of new methods. Formerly: *Chemical Senses and Flavour.*

European Journal of Applied Physiology. v. 1– , 1928– . Berlin: Springer. Monthly. $2,819.00. ISSN 1439-6327. Available electronically. Emphasis is on publishing original research on human integrative physiology utilizing a wide range of techniques and approaches on the function of the intact healthy human body under a variety of environmental and exercise conditions.

European Journal of Physiology. See *Pflueger's Archiv*, in the following text.

Experimental Physiology. v. 75– , 1990– . New York: Cambridge University Press, for the Physiological Society. Bimonthly. $398.00. ISSN 0958-0670. Available electronically. Includes research papers on all aspect of experimental physiology from molecular to animal studies. Formerly: *Quarterly Journal of Experimental Physiology and Cognate Medical Sciences.*

Journal of Applied Physiology. v. 1– , 1948– . Bethesda, MD: American Physiological Society. Monthly. $528.00. ISSN 8750-7587. Available electronically. A leader in its field, this journal publishes original papers dealing with diverse areas of research in applied physiology, especially those emphasizing adaptive (development, aging, pathophysiological conditions, and external environment) and integrative mechanisms (horizontal integration across organ systems and vertical integration from molecule to cell to organ).

Journal of Cellular Physiology. v. 1– , 1932– . New York: Wiley/Liss. Monthly. $4,375.00. ISSN 0021-9541. Available electronically. Devoted to the publication of research papers of high biological significance in all areas of eukaryotic cell biology and physiology, focusing on those articles that adopt a molecular, mechanistic approach to investigate cell biology. In particular, the journal encourages papers investigating the regulation of growth and differentiation by growth factors and cytokines, signal transduction by growth factors, and the conditions that influence the expression and function of these molecules.

Journal of General Physiology. v. 1– , 1918– . New York: Rockefeller University Press for the Society of General Physiologists. Monthly. $510.00. ISSN 0022-1295. Available electronically. Publishes articles concerned with the mechanisms of broad physiological significance covering research of prime importance for cellular and molecular physiology.

Journal of Physiology, v. 1– , 1878– . Cambridge, England: Cambridge University Press for the Physiological Society, London. Semimonthly. $2,298.00. ISSN 0022-3751. Available electronically. Covers physiological research in all areas of physiology illustrating new physiological principles or mechanisms, with emphasis on human and mammalian physiology. Some issues report the proceedings of the scientific meetings of the Society.

Pfluegers Archiv; European Journal of Physiology. v. 1– , 1968– . New York: Springer-Verlag. Semimonthly. $2,949.00. ISSN 0031-6768. Available electronically.　Results of original research considered likely to further the physiological sciences in their broadest sense. Purely clinical papers will be excluded.

The Physiologist. v. 1– , 1957– . Bethesda, MD. American Physiological Society. Bimonthly. $62.00. ISSN 0031-9376. Available electronically.　The newsletter of the American Physiological Society features articles on society affairs, announcements, and articles of interest to physiologists, in general. Supplements appear irregularly.

Respiration Physiology. v. 1– , 1965– . Amsterdam: Elsevier. Monthly. $1,593.00. ISSN 0034-5687. Available electronically.　Original research articles concerning the field of respiration in its broadest sense.

REVIEWS OF THE LITERATURE

Anatomy

Advances in Anatomy, Embryology, and Cell Biology. v. 1– , 1891– . Heidelberg, Germany: Springer-Verlag. Price varies. ISSN 0301-5556.　Reviews and critical articles covering the entire field of normal anatomy (cytology, histology, cyto-and histochemistry, electron microscopy, macroscopy, experimental morphology and embryology, and comparative anatomy.

Endocrinology and Metabolism

Endocrine Reviews. v. 1– , 1980– . Bethesda, MD: Endocrine Society. Bimonthly. $325.00. ISSN 0163-769X. Available electronically.　Features in-depth review articles on both experimental and clinical endocrinology and metabolism.

Frontiers of Hormone Research. v. 1– , 1972– . Basel, Switzerland: Karger. Irregular. Price varies.　Focuses on areas of endocrinology undergoing active investigation by consolidating findings from both experimental and clinical work.

Frontiers in Neuroendocrinology. v. 1– , 1969– . Orlando, FL: Academic Press. Quarterly. $295.00. ISSN 0091-3022.　Review articles for the broad field of brain-endocrine interactions.

Recent Progress in Hormone Research. v. 1– , 1947– . San Diego, CA: Academic Press. Annual. Price varies. ISSN 0079-9963.　Proceedings of the Laurentian Hormone Conference.

Trends in Endocrinology and Metabolism. v. 1– , 1989– . New York: Elsevier. Monthly. $795.00. ISSN 1043-2760. Available electronically.   Review journal providing reviews of the literature, meeting reports, techniques, viewpoints, book reviews, job trends, and calendar.

Vitamins and Hormones; Advances in Research and Applications. v. 1– , 1943– . Orlando, FL: Academic Press. Irregular. Price varies. ISSN 0083-6729.   Quality reviews of the literature of interest to endocrinologists and biochemists.

Neurobiology

Annual Review of Neuroscience. v. 1– , 1978– . Palo Alto, CA: Annual Reviews. Annual. $130.00. ISSN 0147-006X. Available electronically.   A leader in review literature, this well-known and respected review annual provides systematic, periodic examination of scholarly advances in the selected field through critical, authoritative reviews.

Brain Research Reviews. v. 14– , 1989– . Amsterdam: Elsevier Science. Bimonthly. $1,020.00. ISSN 0165-0173. Available electronically.   ''A special section of *Brain Research* which provides a medium for prompt publication of review articles and, occasionally, long research papers with extensive review components, which give analytical surveys that define heuristic hypotheses and provide new insights into brain mechanisms.''

Computational Neuroscience: Trends in Research 2000. James M. Bower, ed. Amsterdam: Elsevier, 2000. 1,134 p. $248.50. ISBN 0444505490.   Recent fundamental contributions in the field of neurocomputing, reprinted from *Neurocomputing*, vols. 32 and 33, 2000; Proceedings of the 8th Annual Computational Neuroscience Meeting held in July, 1999 in Pittsburgh, PA.

Critical Reviews in Neurobiology. v. 1– , 1985– . New York: Begell House. Quarterly. $379.00. ISSN 0892-0915.   Presents comprehensive reviews, analyses, and integration of recently developed substantive observations and information of processes involving the nervous system.

Current Opinion in Neurobiology, v. 1– , 1991– . London: Current Biology. Bimonthly. $884.00. ISSN 0959-4388. Available electronically.   Provides views from experts on current advances in neurobiology; selections annotated by experts of the most interesting papers; and comprehensive bibliographic listings of papers. For the purposes of this journal, neurobiology is divided into several sections, each one reviewed annually.

International Review of Neurobiology. v. 1– , 1959– . Orlando, FL: Academic Press. Irregular. Price varies. ISSN 0074-7742.   This review covers the whole field of neurobiology to include work within a basic science as well as in neurology and psychiatry. The aim is to enable active researchers in neurobiology, neurochemistry, neuroanatomy, neuropharmacology, neurophysiology, psychopharmacology, etc., to give an account of the latest advances in their field. Incorporates *Methods in Neurosciences* and *Neuroscience Perspectives*.

Molecular Neurobiology, v. 1– , 1987– . Totowa, NJ: Humana Press. Bimonthly. $490.00. ISSN 0893-7648.   A review journal recording developments and progress at the forefront of molecular brain research.

Neuroscience and Biobehavioral Reviews. v. 1– , 1977– . Oxford, England: Elsevier. Quarterly. $1,309.00. ISSN 0149-7634. Available electronically.   Publishes original, major reviews of the literature in anatomy, biochemistry, embryology, endocrinology, genetics, pharmacology, physiology, and all aspects of biological sciences with relevant to the nervous system or the investigation of behavior.

Perspectives on Developmental Neurobiology. v. 1– , 1992– . Reading, England: Gordon and Breach. Irregular. Price varies. ISSN 1064-0517.   This review journal presents concise critical reviews of recent progress in developmental neurobiology. Each issue focuses on a single topic from the full range of development from embryogenesis to aging.

Progress in Brain Research. v. 1– , 1963– . Amsterdam: Elsevier. Irregular. Price varies. ISSN 0079-6123.   Each volume reviews a particular topic.

Progress in Neurobiology, v. 1– , 1973– . Oxford, England: Elsevier. Monthly. $2,264.00. ISSN 0301-0082. Available electronically.   Reviews advances in the field of neurobiology with coverage of all relevant disciplines.

Reviews in the Neurosciences. v. 1– , 1986– . London: Freund Publishing House. Quarterly. $310.00. ISSN 0334-1763.   A reference and forum for those working in neurobiology looking for critical evaluations of selected topics.

Trends in Neurosciences. v. 1– . 1978– . New York: Elsevier. Monthly. $907.00. ISSN 0166-2236. Available electronically.   Follows the established *Trends* format; refer to *Trends in Endocrinology*, previous.

Physiology

Annual Review of Physiology. v. 1– , 1939– . Palo Alto, CA: Annual Reviews. Annual. $133.00. ISSN 0066-4278. Available electronically.   Follows the established format of other *Annual Review* series; refer to *Annual Review of Neurosciences*.

Monographs of the Physiological Society. v. 1– , 1953– . New York: Oxford University Press. Price varies. ISSN 0079-2020 (series). Each volume deals with a particular topic in depth; a recent example is the 1999 publication, volume 48 of the series: *Mechanisms of Cortical Development* by David Price and David Willshaw. $59.95. ISBN 019262427X.

News in Physiological Sciences (NIPS), v. 1– , 1986– . Bethesda, MD: American Physiological Society. Bimonthly. $151.00. ISSN 0886-1714. Available electronically. "An international journal of physiology produced jointly by the International Union of Physiological Sciences and the American Physiological Society." Brief review articles on major physiological developments; all primary data reported should have been previously published in peer-reviewed journals.

Nobel Lectures in Physiology and Medicine, 1901–1970. New York: Elsevier, 1964–1973. *Nobel Lectures in Physiology and Medicine 1971–1980*; *Nobel Lectures in Physiology and Medicine 1981–1990.* River Edge, NJ: World Scientific Publishing, 1992–3. Although these volumes appear to be out of print, the Nobel lectures provide fascinating accounts of research of Nobel laureates since the turn of the century.

Physiological Reviews, v. 1– , 1921– . Bethesda, MD: American Physiological Society. Quarterly. $295.00. ISSN 0031-9333. Available electronically. State-of-the-art coverage of issues in physiological and biomedical sciences, including about 25 review articles each year.

Reviews of Physiology, Biochemistry, and Pharmacology. v. 70– , 1974– . New York: Springer-Verlag. Irregular. Price varies. ISSN 0303-4240. Review articles for researchers and scientists. Continues *Ergebnisse der Physiologie Biologischen Chemie und Experimentellen Pharmakologie.*

12

Entomology

Entomology is "the study of insects," according to the *Oxford Dictionary of Biology*, 4th edition, 2000. Strictly speaking, the true insects are only those belonging to the class Insecta, which does not include the spiders and other animals often thought of as insects such as millipedes or ticks. However, this chapter includes material on both insects and their close relatives because many resources treat these related groups together. Applied entomology is largely excluded, although some basic tools are mentioned.

ABSTRACTS AND INDEXES

Current Awareness

Abstracts of Entomology. v. 1– . 1970– . Philadelphia, PA: BIOSIS. Monthly. $550.00. ISSN 0001-3579.   Indexes all areas of entomology, with 20,000 references added each year. Has author, organism, and subject indexes. Data taken from BIOSIS Previews (see Chapter 4 "Abstracts and Indexes").

Apicultural Abstracts. v. 1– . 1950– . Cardiff, Wales: International Bee Research Association. Quarterly. $240.00. ISSN 0003-648X.   Covers the world literature on bees, including their biology and pollination activities. Also available on floppy disks and as part of BeeSearch, a service offered by the International Bee Research Association (IBRA) library (see the Associations section in the following text).

Entomology Abstracts. v. 1– . 1969– . Bethesda, MD: Cambridge Scientific Abstracts. Monthly. $1,190.00. ISSN 0013-8924.   Covers all areas of entomology, including systematics, paleontology, behavior, genetics, physiology, and so on. Author and subject indexes. Available online and on CD-ROM as part of the CSA Biological Sciences database.

Helminthological Abstracts. v. 1– . 1932– . Wallingford, UK: CAB International. Monthly. $860.00. ISSN 0957-6789. Includes journal articles, reports, conferences, and books on all aspects of parasitic helminths. Also available on DIALOG as part of CAB Abstracts (1972 to present). 4,000 abstracts added per year. Includes monthly and annual author and subject indexes. Also available online as part of Vet CABWeb (URL: http://vet.cabweb.org). Formerly: *Helminthological Abstracts, Series A (Animal Helminthology).*

Index-Catalogue of Medical and Veterinary Zoology. v. 1– . 1932– . Animal Parasitology Institute, USDA. Index to the literature of animal parasites of humans and animals. Issued as series of supplements.

Nematological Abstracts. v. 1– . 1932– . Wallingford, UK: CAB International. Quarterly. $370. ISSN 0957-6797. Covers parasitic and free-living nematodes. 2,000 references added each year. Also available online as part of Pest CABWeb (URL: http://pest.cabweb.org). Formerly: *Helminthological Abstracts, Series B (Plant Nematology).*

Odonatological Abstracts. v. 1– . 1972– . Bilthoven, Netherlands: Societas Internationalis Odonatologica. Indexes the literature of dragonflies. Published as part of *Odonatologica* (see the Journals section in the following text).

Review of Agricultural Entomology. v. 1– . 1913– . Wallingford, UK: CAB International. Monthly. $1,110. ISSN 0957-6762. Covers arthropod pests of cultivated plants, trees, and stored products. Most citations also have abstracts. Monthly and annual author and subject indexes. 1,200 records added each year. Available online as part of Pest CABWeb (URL: http://pest.cabweb.org). Formerly: *Review of Applied Entomology, Series A (Agricultural).*

Review of Medical and Veterinary Entomology. v. 1– . 1913– . Wallingford, UK: CAB International. Monthly. $645.00. ISSN 0957-6770. Covers disease-transmitting insects of importance to humans and animals. Includes journal articles, books, reports, and conferences. Monthly and annual author and subject indexes are included. 6,000 records added each year. Available online as part of Pest CABWeb (URL: http://pest.cabweb.org). Formerly: *Review of Applied Entomology, Series B (Medical and Veterinary).*

Tropical Diseases Bulletin. v. 1– . 1912– . London: Bureau of Hygiene & Tropical Diseases. Monthly. $270.00. ISSN 0041-3240. Includes section on medical entomology.

Zoological Record, Section 12: Arachnida. v. 1– . 1864– . Philadelphia. PA: BIOSIS. Annual. $200.00. Covers arachnids and the smaller arthropod groups such as tardigrades and centipedes. Has author, subject, geographical, paleontological, and systematic indexes. Also available on CD-ROM and online as part of the *Zoological Record* database.

Zoological Record, Section 13: Insecta. v. 1– . 1864– . Philadelphia, PA: BIOSIS. Annual. $1,350.00 (6 sections). ISSN 0144-3607. Covers all insects in six sections (General Insecta and Smaller Orders, Coleoptera, Diptera, Lepidoptera, Hymenoptera, and Hemiptera). Has author, subject, geographical, paleontological, and systematic indexes. Also available on CD-ROM and online as part of the *Zoological Record* database.

See also *Bibliography of Agriculture, Biological Abstracts, Biological Abstracts/ RRM, Current Contents/Agriculture,* and *Biology and Environmental Sciences.*

RETROSPECTIVE SEARCHES

Derksen, W. and U. Scheiding. 1963–75. *Index Litteraturae Entomologicae.* Ser. 2, *Die Welt-Literatur über die gesamte Entomologie von 1864 bis 1900.* 5 v. Berlin: Akademie der Landwirtschaftswissenschaften der Deutschen Demokratischen Republik. Continues the entomological literature from Horn and Schenkling, in the following text. Volume 5 contains a list of journal titles.

Experiment Station Record. v. 1–95, 1889–1946. Washington, DC: Government Printing Office, Department of Agriculture Office of Experiment Stations. Important source for retrospective applied entomological literature. Abstracts are arranged by topic with name and subject indexes.

Horn, W. and S. Schenkling. *Index Litteraturae Entomologicae. Die Welt-Literatur über die gesamte Entomologie bis inklusive 1863.* 4 v. Berlin: Dahlem, 1928–29. Revision of Hagen, *Bibliotheca Entomologica* (1862–3), containing 8,000 additional titles. Covers the literature of entomology from its beginning to 1862.

Index to the Literature of American Economic Entomology. v. 1–18, 1905/14– 1959. College Park, MD: Entomological Society of America (Special Publication 1–18 of Entomological Society of America). "Presents articles on economic entomology selected from pamphlets, periodicals, and books received in the National Agriculture Library." The index provides citations arranged by scientific and common names of insects of economic importance.

Royal Entomological Society of London. *Catalogue of the Library of the Royal Entomological Society of London.* Boston, MA: G.K. Hall, 1980. 5 v. ISBN 0816103151. Contains copies of the card catalog of the Royal Society, which holds many rare works.

U.S. Bureau of Entomology. *Bibliography of the More Important Contributions to American Economic Entomology*. Washington, DC: Government Printing Office, 1889–1905. Part 1–3: The more important writings of B.D. Walsh and C.V. Riley. Part 4–5: The more important writings of government and state entomologists and of other contributors to the literature of American economic entomology. Part 6–8: The more important writing published between June 30, 1888 and January 1, 1905. Continued by *Index to the Literature of American Economic Entomology* (see previous).

ASSOCIATIONS

American Mosquito Control Association. c/o Pamela Toups, 2200 E. Prien Lake Road, Lake Charles, LA 70601. URL: http://www.mosquito.org/. Founded in 1935. 2,000 members. Web site includes membership information, "Mosquito Links" (primarily links to mosquito control districts and other technical resources), and a nice page with general information on mosquitos and their control. Publishes *Journal of the American Mosquito Control Association*, *AMCA Newsletter* (available online free from 1998 to date), *Wing Beats* (some issues available for free online), and *AMCA Bulletins*.

American Entomological Society. Academy of Natural Sciences of Philadelphia, 1900 Race St., Philadelphia, PA 19103. E-mail: aes@say.acnatsci.org. URL: http://www.acnatsci.org/aes/. Founded in 1859. 430 members. For professionals and amateurs. Publishes *Entomological News*, *Memoirs of the American Entomological Society*, and *Transactions of the American Entomological Society*. The Web site is primarily for membership information.

Coleopterist's Society. c/o Terry Seero at COFA-PPO, 3294 Meadowview Road, Sacramento, CA 95832–1448. URL: http://www.coleopsoc.org/. Founded in 1969, 775 members. "An international organization devoted to the study of all aspects of systematics and biology of beetles of the world." Publishes *The Coleopterists Bulletin*. Web site includes "Beetle Links," "Beetle Conservation," and "Beetle Newsletters" (PDF files of newsletters published by the society).

Dragonfly Society of the Americas. c/o T. Donnelly 2091 Partridge Lane, Binghamton, NY 13903. E-mail: tdonnel@binghampton.edu. URL: http://www.afn.org/iori/dsaintro.html. Founded 1989. 200 members. Publishes *Argaia* and *Bulletin of American Odonatology*. Formerly: Dragonfly Society of Amcrica.

Entomological Society of America. 9301 Annapolis Rd, Lanham, MD 20706–3115. E-mail: info@entsoc.org. URL: http://www.entsoc.org/. Founded 1953. 8,500 members. The largest U.S. entomological society. Publishes *American En-*

tomologist, Annals of the Entomological Society of America, Arthropod Management Tests, Entomological Society of America-Newsletter, Environmental Entomology, ESA Newsletter, Insecticide and Acaricide Tests, Journal of Economic Entomology, Journal of Medical Entomology, and *Discover Entomology (Careers).* Also publishes many monographic works. Formed by the merger of the American Association of Economic Entomologists and the former Entomological Society of America. Absorbed the American Registry of Professional Entomologists. Site includes membership information, publications, job information, educational information for children, links to other entomological sites, and free e-postcards with insect images. A good site for general information on entomology.

Entomological Society of Canada/Société d'Entomologie du Canada. 393 Winston Ave., Ottawa, ON K2A 1Y8 CANADA. E-mail: entsoc.can@sympatico.ca. URL: http://www.biology.ualberta.ca/esc.hp/homepage.htm. Founded 1868. 550 members. Publishes *The Canadian Entomologist, Bulletin of the Entomological Society of Canada, Memoirs of the Entomological Society of Canada, Occasional Publications.* Web site includes downloadable version of *Common Names of Insects in Canada* (zip file), information on entomology in Canada, and entomological links as well as membership information.

International Bee Research Association (IBRA). 18 North Road, Cardiff, S. Glam, CF1 3DY UK. E-mail: ibra@cardiff.ac.uk. URL: http://www.cf.ac.uk/ibra/index.html. Founded 1949. 800 members. Publishes *Apicultural Abstracts, Bee World,* and *Journal of Apicultural Research.* The extensive Web site lists publications, library services, and bee links in addition to membership information.

International Centre for Insect Physiology and Ecology (ICIPE). P.O. Box 30772, Nairobi, Kenya. E-mail: directorgeneral@icipe.org. URL: http://www.icipe.org. Founded 1970. 310 members. Publishes *Annual Report, Current Themes in Tropical Science* series, *Dudu, ICIPE Profile,* and *Insect Science and its Applications.* Web site has extensive information on ICIPE's programs and services.

The International Society of Hymenopterists. c/o John Huber, Biological Resources Program/ECORC, Agriculture Canada-Research Branch, KW Neatby Building. CEF. Ottawa, ON KIA 0C6 CANADA. E-mail: huberj@ncccot.agr.ca. URL: http://IRIS.biosci.ohio-state.edu/ish/ishhome.html. Founded in 1982. Publishes *Journal of Hymenoptera Research.* Web site primarily for membership information.

International Union for the Study of Social Insects. c/o Dr. M. D. Breed, EPO Biology, University of Colorado, Campus Box 334, Boulder, CO 80309. URL: http://lsvl.la.asu.edu/iussi. Founded in 1952. 800 members. There are several country-specific chapters. Publishes *Insectes Sociaux/Social Insects*. Web site includes links to information about social insects and links to various chapters.

Lepidopterists' Society. c/o Ernest H. Williams, Department of Biology, Hamilton College, Clinton, NY 13323. URL: http://www.furman.edu/snyder/snyder/lep/. Founded 1947. 1,600 members. "Open to all persons interested in any aspect of Lepidopterology." Publishes *Journal of the Lepidopterists' Society*, *News of the Lepidopterists' Society*, a biennial membership directory, and *Memoirs of the Lepidopterists' Society*. Also makes available *Catalogue/Checklist of the Butterflies of America North of Mexico*. Web site includes extensive list of lepidoptera and other entomology links and a statement on collecting butterflies and moths.

Royal Entomological Society. 41 Queen's Gate, London SW7 5HR UK. URL: http://www.royensoc.demon.co.uk/. Founded 1833. 2,000 members. Publishes *Ecological Entomology*, *Physiological Entomology*, *Systematic Entomology*, *Medical and Veterinary Entomology*, *Insect Molecular Entomology*, *Agricultural and Forest Entomology*, *and Antenna*. Web site has entomological links listed under "Places of Interest to Visit" but otherwise is mostly for membership information.

ATLASES, CHECKLISTS, AND IDENTIFICATION MANUALS

There are innumerable excellent field guides for identifying insects. Only a very few are listed, along with more technical manuals and other identification aids. See Chapter 3 for a more detailed description of the major field guide series, all of which cover common insect species. More field guides can be found in Schmidt's *A Guide to Field Guides* (see Chapter 3, "General Sources") and the associated International Field Guide Web site.

Arnett, Ross H., Jr. *American Insects: A Handbook of the Insects of America North of Mexico*. Gainesville, FL: Sandhill Crane Press, 1993. 850 p. $90.00. ISBN 1877743194. Reprint of the 1985 edition. A synopsis of the insects of North America, with keys to the generic level, and descriptions of orders, families, and some subfamilies, as well as a number of representative species. Also includes introductory material on insect biology, systematics, and preparation of specimens. Over 22,000 species are described. An authoritative work; there is nothing else quite as comprehensive for North American insects.

Borror, Donald J. and Richard E. White. *A Field Guide to Insects of America North of Mexico*. Boston, MA: Houghton Mifflin, 1970. (Peterson Field Guide Series, 19.) 404 p. $27.00, $18.00 (paper), ISBN 0395074363, 0395185238 (paper). 579 families including all of the insect orders; black-and-white and color illustrations. Large and conspicuous insects are identified to species, but most inconspicuous or difficult insects are just identified to family (e.g., flies). The standard insect field guide for North America.

Burgess, N. R. H. and G. O. Cowan. *A Colour Atlas of Medical Entomology*. New York: Chapman and Hall, 1993. 152 p. $185.00. ISBN 0412323400. An identification guide to insects of medical importance, mainly of the tropics. The atlas includes many photographs of the insects, their habitats, and the diseases caused by them. Also includes information on the life cycle, habits, and medical problems caused by each species.

CABIKEY Series. 1996– . Wallingford, UK: CAB International. $195-$320 each (single user price, network licenses also available). A series of electronic identification keys to insects and other arthropods, available on floppies or CD-ROMs for Windows. Pictures of insects are included. Six keys have been produced to date, including "Major Beetle Families" and "Aphids on the World's Crops."

Chu, Hung-fu. *How to Know the Immature Insects*. 2nd ed. Dubuque, IA: William C. Brown, 1992. (Pictured Key Series). $25.80 (paper). ISBN 0697048063 (paper). Keys to about 400 families worldwide. The Pictured Key series of guides are intended for students and researchers and cover more specialized or less glamorous groups of organisms than other field guide series. The series is also unique in that each volume consists of an extended and annotated key to the organisms covered, with line drawings of most species or groups.

Covell, Charles V., Jr. *A Field Guide to the Moths of Eastern North America*. Boston, MA: Houghton Mifflin, 1984. (Peterson Field Guide Series, 30.) 496 p. ISBN 0395361001. A classic field guide to 1,300 species of eastern moths.

D'Abrera, Bernard. *Butterflies of the World*. Melbourne: Lansdowne Editions in association with E.W. Classey, 1980– . v.–Price varies. This oversized (33 cm.) set is intended as an aid to identification of the world's butterflies. It is divided into several subsections: *Butterflies of the Afrotropical Region*, *Butterflies of the Australian Region*, *Butterflies of the Holarctic Region*, *Butterflies of the Neotropical Region*, and *Butterflies of the Oriental Region*. The volumes consist of plates of color photographs of butterflies of the various regions, with accepted names, citation to the original description, geographical range, and notes for each species. About 15 volumes have been published to date.

Goddard, Jerome. *Physician's Guide to Arthropods of Medical Importance*. 3rd ed. Boca Raton, FL: CRC Press, 1999. 440 p. $149.00. ISBN 0849311861. Covers the identification of insects, mites, scorpions, and spiders of public health importance. Intended to assist doctors and other medical entomologists in identifying and diagnosing arthropods and the injuries they cause.

Immature Insects. Frederick W. Stehr, ed. Dubuque, IA: Kendall/Hunt, 1987–91. 2 v. $136.00 (v. 1), $241.00 (v. 2). ISBN 0840337027 (v. 1), 0840346395 (v. 2).   Designed to serve as identification guide and textbook, this set includes keys, tables of features, and extended literature references. Covers mainly North American insects. Chu, see previous, offers a less expensive and more portable alternative.

The Insects and Arachnids of Canada. Part 1– , 1977– . Ottawa, Canada: Agriculture Canada. Irregular. ISSN 0706-7313.   A complete listing of all insects and arachnids of Canada and the adjacent states. Part 1 consists of a guide to collecting and preserving insects. The remaining volumes feature keys to species. Part 22, "Aphids," was published in 1993.

Kaston, Benjamin J. *How to Know the Spiders.* 3rd ed. Dubuque, IA: William C. Brown, 1978. 272 p. (Pictured Key Series.) $25.80 (paper). ISBN 0697048985 (paper).   Keys for 271 species of spiders from North America. Identification to species may require microscope and/or hand lens.

Lehmkuhl, Dennis M. *How to Know the Aquatic Insects.* Dubuque, IA: William C. Brown, 1979. 168 p. (Pictured Key Series.) $29.95 (paper). ISBN 0697047679 (paper).   Keys to families and distinctive genera of aquatic insects of North America north of Mexico. Also includes extensive introductory information on aquatic insect ecology and morphology, their role as indicator organisms, and how to collect aquatic insects.

McDaniel, Burruss. *How to Know the Mites and Ticks.* Dubuque, IA: William C. Brown, 1979. 335 p. (Pictured Key Series.) ISBN 0697047563, 0697047571 (paper).   Covers about 400 species of North American mites and ticks, but because many species are widely distributed the key is useful elsewhere.

Medical Insects and Arachnids. Line, Richard P. and Roger W. Crosskey, eds., New York: Chapman and Hall, 1993. 744 p. $199.95. ISBN 0412400006.   An identification guide for medically important insects and arachnids. There are two extensive introductions with extensive references. Each chapter covers a major group and includes information not only on identification, but also control, biology, medical importance, and collecting specimens. Designed for students and field workers as well as researchers.

Michener, Charles D. *The Bees of the World.* Baltimore, MD: Johns Hopkins University Press, 2000. 913 p. $135.00. ISBN 0801861330.   A comprehensive treatment of all bees worldwide, including 1,200 genera and 16,000 species; the author cites nearly 2,500 items. There is an extensive introduction covering the evolution, systematics, anatomy, and behavior of bees. There are a number of black-and-white illustrations and photographs, plus a few color photos.

Michener, Charles D., Ronald J. McGinley, and Bryan N. Danforth. *The Bee Genera of North and Central America*. Washington, DC: Smithsonian Institution Press, 1994. 209 p. $45.00. ISBN 156098256X.   An excellent key to the 169 species of bees found north of the Columbia-Panama border. The key has parallel text in English and Spanish. There are numerous line drawings and photographs, and the introduction includes information on collecting and preserving specimens as well as terminology used in the keys.

Milne, Lorus and Margery Milne. *The Audubon Society Field Guide to North American Insects and Spiders*. New York: Knopf, 1980. (Audubon Society Field Guide Series.) 959 p. $18.00. ISBN 0394507630.   600 species from the major orders, including some caterpillars. Illustrated with color photos. The only major insect field guide to include a few arachnids. See Kaston, previous, for more spider species and McDaniel for more ticks and mites.

Opler, Paul A. *A Field Guide to Eastern Butterflies*. 2nd ed. Boston, MA: Houghton Mifflin, 1998. (Peterson Field Guide Series, 4.) 486 p. $20.00 (paper). ISBN 0395364523 (paper).   524 species, color illustrations. First edition by Alexander Klots, *A Field Guide to Butterflies East of the Great Plains*, 1951.

Opler, Paul A. *A Field Guide to Western Butterflies*. 2nd ed. Boston, MA: Houghton Mifflin, 1998. (Peterson Field Guide Series, 33.) 528 p. $32.00, $24.00 (paper) ISBN 0395791529, 0395791510 (paper).   Revised edition of Tilden and Smith's *A Field Guide to Western Butterflies*. 590 species.

Pyle, Robert Michael. *The Audubon Society Field Guide to North American Butterflies*. New York: Knopf, 1981. (Audubon Society Field Guide Series.) 916 p. $19.00. ISBN 0394519140.   600 species; color photos.

Slater, James A. and Richard M. Baranowski. *How to Know the True Bugs (Hemiptera-Homoptera)*. Dubuque, IA: William C. Brown, 1978. 256 p. (Pictured Key Series.) ISBN 0697048934, 0697048942 (paper).   Keys to 750 common species of North American bugs. The true bugs include most (but not all) of the insects that have ''bug'' as part of their common names, including common insects such as stink bugs, assassin bugs, and water bugs.

Termites of the World. Toronto: Urban Entomology Program, University of Toronto, 1998. URL:http://www.utoronto.ca/forest/termite/dist%5Fspc.htm (viewed November 5, 2000).   This site is part of the University of Toronto's Urban Entomology Program's Web site and features color photographs of 161 termite genera out of the 285 genera found worldwide. There are no descriptions or detailed distribution information.

White, Richard E. *A Field Guide to the Beetles of North America*. Boston, MA: Houghton Mifflin, 1983. (Peterson Field Guide Series, 29.) 368 p. $21.45, $18.00

(paper). ISBN 0395318084, 0395339537 (paper).   600 species, black-and-white and color illustrations. The only popular field guide to the beetles of North America.

CLASSIFICATION, NOMENCLATURE, AND SYSTEMATICS

American Beetles. Ross H. Arnett and M. C. Thomas, eds. Boca Raton, FL: CRC Press, 2001–   . v. $125.00 (v. 1), $125.00 (v. 2). ISBN 0849319250 (v. 1), 0849309549 (v. 2).   This ambitious set covers all of the beetles of North America. Volume 1 includes Archostemata, Myxophaga, Adephaga, and Polyphaga: Staphyliniformia. Volume 2 covers the remainder of the Polyphaga and includes keys to families.

ANI-CD (Arthropod Name Index on CD-ROM). Wallingford, UK: CAB International, 19?–   . Annual. $899.00. ISSN 1359-5415.   "ANI-CD contains approximately 110,000 records, and will be updated annually with over 1,000 new items. This essential tool will enable you to find preferred terms, synonyms, common names, taxonomic positions and important bibliographic references dating back to 1913, for economically important arthropods." Based on CAB's internal authority file for insect names. Both Pittaway and Wood, see following text, are excerpted from the ANI.

Benoit, Paul. *Nomenclatura Insectorum Canadensium/Noms d'Insectes au Canada/Insect Names in Canada*. 5th ed. Sainte-Foy, Quebec: Laurentian Forest Research Center, Canadian Forestry Service, 1985. 299 p. ISBN 0662533747. Supplement, 1986.   Since 1993, the list has been updated in electronic format only. It is currently available on the Entomological Society of Canada's Web site at http://www.biology.ualberta.ca/esc.hp/menu.htm. A DOS zip file is also available for downloading at this site. English and French common names are included for each species, as well as scientific names and order and family names.

Bolton, Barry. *A New General Catalogue of the Ants of the World*. Cambridge, MA: Harvard University Press, 1995. 504 p. $145.00. ISBN 067461514X.   A mammoth work listing all taxonomic names, valid and invalid, applied to ants worldwide. It is in four parts, Checklist of Fossil Taxa, Catalogue of Family-Group Taxa, Catalogue of Genus-Group Taxa, and Catalogue of Species-Group Taxa. There are also extensive references. This is the first attempt at cataloging ant species worldwide since the publication of *Genera Insectorum* (see the following text).

Common Names of Insects and Related Organisms. Committee on Common Names of Insects. 4th ed. Lanham, MD: Entomological Society of America, 1997. 232 p. $45.00. ISBN 0938522647.   This list of standardized common names of insects provides names for 2,046 insects from the United States. Official common names are needed when communicating with the general public, and even with other scientists, and this is the official list for the United States. There are four sections: insects listed by common name, insects listed by scientific name, a hierarchical listing of names, and a final section listing vernacular equivalents for higher taxonomic groups (e.g., Aleyrodidae = whiteflies). Updated on the ESA's Web page at http://www.entsoc.org/pubs/publish/commname.html.

Common Names of North American Butterflies. Jacqueline Y. Miller, ed. Washington, DC: Smithsonian Institution Press, 1992. 177 p. ISBN 1560981229. Provides preferred and alternate common names for butterflies north of Mexico, including Hawaii.

Genera Insectorum. Philogene Wytsman, ed. Brussels: Chez M.P. Wytsman, 1902–71. 218 fascicles.   An important source for insect systematic studies. Each fascicle covers one group of insects worldwide. Each genus is described and ususually illustrated with line drawings, followed by a list of known species with references to the original description. There are also separate plates illustrating selected species. Language varies depending on the author's native tongue. Indexes were prepared by L.H. Townsend in 1937 (*Revista de Entomologica*, 7 [2–3]: 217–230) and Amy L. Paster in 1987.

Grizmek's Animal Life Encyclopedia. Volume 2, *Insects*.   See Chapter 13, "Zoology," for full annotation. Has common names in English, German, French, and Russian (Cyrillic alphabet) in the Animal Dictionary section (p. 565–618).

Harp, Chuck E., Paul A. Opler, Richard S. Peigler, Michael Pogue, Jerry A. Powell, and Michael J. Smith. *Moths of North America*. Jamestown, ND: Northern Prairie Wildlife Research Center, 1999. (Version 17FEB2000). URL: http:// www.npwrc.usgs.gov/resource/distr/lepid/moths/mothsusa. (Viewed February 25, 2000.)   A massive effort, containing distribution maps, species accounts, and photos for the moths of the United States and northern Mexico. Canadian moths will be added in the future. There are also checklists for counties in the United States and states in Mexico, and an Identification of Butterflies and Moths FAQ.

Miller, Lee D. and F. Martin Brown. *A Catalogue/Checklist of the Butterflies of America, North of Mexico*. Los Angeles, CA: Lepidopterist's Society, 1981. 280 p. ISBN 0930282035.   Supplement published 1993.

Opler, Paul A., Harry Pavulaan, and Ray E. Stanford (coordinators). *Butterflies of North America*. Jamestown, ND: Northern Prairie Wildlife Research Center Home Page, 1995. (Version 17FEB2000). URL: http://www.npwrc.usgs.gov/ resource/distr/lepid/bflyusa/bflyusa.htm. (Viewed February 25, 2000).   A companion to Harp's Moths of North America Web page, previous, containing the same types of information.

Pittaway, A. R. *Arthropods of Medical and Veterinary Importance: A Checklist of Preferred Names and Allied Terms*. Wallingford, UK: CAB International, 1991. 178 p. $45.00 (paper). ISBN 0851987419 (paper). A list of the preferred scientific names of arthropods of importance in human and veterinary medicine. Scientific names are listed by genus, with higher taxa listed for each genus and approved name for each species. Based on the card file used by CAB in preparing the *Review of Medical and Veterinary Entomology*, now available as ANI-CD (previous).

Wood, A. M. *Insects of Economic Importance: A Checklist of Preferred Names*. Wallingford, UK: CAB International, 1992. 149 p. $40.00 (paper). ISBN 0851986528 (paper). A checklist to the preferred scientific names of insects of importance in agriculture, forestry, horticulture, and human and veterinary medicine. It is based on the 100,000 species Arthropod Name Index created by CAB and used in its publications. Only the most popular species are listed in this checklist. The insects are listed alphabetically by genus, with indications of preferred scientific names.

Wrobel, M. *Elsevier's Dictionary of Entomology*. New York: Elsevier Science, 2000. Approx. 500 p. ISBN 04444503927. Contains 5,500 orders, families, genera, and species of insects, spiders, and other invertebrates found in Europe, North America, South Africa, New Zealand, and Australia. Names used in French-speaking Canada are also included.

Wrobel, M. *Elsevier's Dictionary of Butterflies and Moths, in Latin, English, German, French, and Italian*. New York: Elsevier Science, 2000. 278 p. $131.00. ISBN 0444504338. Contains 4,000 super- and subfamilies, families, genera, and species of Lepidoptera found in Europe, North America, South Africa, New Zealand, and Australia. Names used in French-speaking Canada are also included.

DICTIONARIES AND ENCYCLOPEDIAS

The Encyclopedia of Insects. Christopher O'Toole, ed. New York: Facts on File, 1987. 151 p. $29.95. ISBN 0816013586. This one-volume encyclopedia provides an excellent introduction to the arthropods of the world, including myriapods (millipedes and centipedes), insects, and arachnids. The entries are by taxonomic groups, and include information on systematics and behavior. There are numerous excellent photographs and line drawings.

Foote, Richard H. *Thesaurus of Entomology*. College Park, MD: Entomological Society of America, 1977. 188 p. Rather than being a true dictionary, this is a thesaurus of indexing terms. About 9,000 terms are included, both by hierarchical classification and in an alphabetical list. While dated, it is still a good source for related terminology.

Gordh, G. and D. H. Headrick. *A Dictionary of Entomology*. Wallingford, UK: CAB International, 2000. c. 900 p. $75.00. ISBN 0851992919. 35,000 terms used in entomology, including origin, etymology, and definition. Deceased entomologists are included, plus citations to biographies. Insect names are also listed.

Harbach, Ralph E. and Kenneth L. Knight. *Taxonomists' Glossary of Mosquito Anatomy*. Marlton, NJ: Plexus, 1980. 415 p. $24.95. ISBN 0937548006. This glossary includes many figures in addition to definitions of terms. It is divided by life cycle stage (adult, egg, larva, and pupa), with a final section on vestiture (the surface of the mosquito and its structures).

Torre-Bueno, J.R. de la, et al. *The Torre-Bueno Glossary of Entomology*. Rev. ed. New York: New York Entomological Society in cooperation with the American Museum of Natural History, 1989. 840 p. $60.00. ISBN 0913424137. This is a revised and expanded edition of Torre-Bueno's 1937 *Glossary of Entomology*, and includes the 1960 *Supplement A* by George S. Tulloch. The terms covered include systematic, descriptive, and general terms. The editors have also included an extensive list of sources and other references. The portion of the glossary dealing with social insects is available at the American Museum of Natural History's Social Insects Web site, at http://research.amnh.org/entomology/social%5Finsects/siglossary.html.

DIRECTORIES

Arnett, Ross H., Jr., G. Allan Samuelson, and Gordon M. Nishida. *The Insect and Spider Collections of the World*. 2nd ed. Gainesville, FL: Sandhill Crane Press, 1993. (Flora and Fauna Handbook, 11.) 310 p. $30.00. ISBN 1877743151. ''The main purposes of this compilation are to inform those doing systematic research of the availability of stored data in the form of specimens and associated information.'' It is arranged by country, with general information on each country (population, size, biogeographical region) as well as detailed information on each major insect collection in the country. An updated version is available at Bernice Pauahi Bishop Museum Web site at http://www.bishop.hawaii.org/bishop/ento/codens-r-us.html. All collections that have a Web site are linked.

Directory of Entomology Departments and Institutes (DEDI). Davis, CA: Scientific Reference Resources, 1999. URL: http://www.sciref.org/links/EntDept/index.htm. Intended to provide a single source of information on entomological research centers around the world. As of 1999, the site listed over 1,500 departments, institutes, and other organizations from 150 countries. A printed version of the directory is also available.

Edwards, Dennis R., Norman C. Leppla, and Willard A. Dickerson. *Arthropod Species in Culture*. College Park, MD: Entomological Society of America, 1987. 49 p. $3.50. ISBN 0938522132.   Lists 680 species of arthropods maintained in 263 facilities in North America. In four sections, the first three listing insects by scientific name, common name, and higher taxonomic group respectively, followed by a final section listing contact information. The information is made available so that researchers can have access to insects without rearing them in their own colonies. Update and revision of the 1980 directory.

Resources in Entomology. College Park, MD: Entomological Society of America, 1987. 269 p. $20.00 (paper). ISBN 0938522329 (paper).   A listing by state and country of academic, private, and governmental institutions dealing with entomology. Each institution is described, with information on museum collections, interests, history, function, faculty or staff names, and degrees or employment opportunities. There is no index, and foreign institutions have addresses only.

GENERAL WORKS

Berenbaum, May R. *Bugs in the System: Insects and Their Impact on Human Affairs*. Reading, MA: Addison-Wesley, 1995. 377 p. $25.00, $17.00 (paper). ISBN 0201624990, 0201408244 (paper).   A popular overview of the human-insect interface. Berenbaum covers basic entomology (classification, insect ecology, and behavior, etc.) and insects and humans (e.g., insects as parasites, dining on insects, insects and the law). An astonishingly broad range of topics are covered.

Evans, Howard Ensign. *The Pleasures of Entomology: Portraits of Insects and the People Who Study Them*. Washington, DC: Smithsonian Institute Press, 1985. 238 p. $16.95 (paper). ISBN 0874744210 (paper).   The author has written about interesting insects and the people who study them. Also has a brief discussion of the history of entomology and the lives of American entomologists. Well written for the general public.

Hogue, Charles L. *Latin American Insects and Entomology*. Berkeley, CA: University of California Press, 1993. 536 p. $90.00. ISBN 0520078497.   This work could be included among the identification materials as well. It consists of an extensive introductory section covering the history and present state of entomology in Central and South America, and a discussion of general entomology followed by accounts of selected families and orders. There is an extensive section listing sources for further information such as Latin American journals, institutions, insect collections, and other resources. The intended audience is anyone from a tourist interested in insects to a professional entomologist. In English.

Hubbell, Sue. *Broadsides from the Other Orders: A Book of Bugs*. New York: Random House, 1993. 276 p. $13.00 (paper). ISBN 0395803261 (paper). Hubbell (a former librarian and professional beekeeper) writes elegantly and eloquently about the fascinating world of insects. Each chapter covers a different order of insects, with Hubbell painlessly imparting a great deal of information about the insects in between describing personal encounters with one or two species in that order. Hubbell has written other books for entomophiles, including *A Book of Bees* and *Waiting for Aphrodite*.

Johnson, Kurt and Steve Coates. *Nabokov's Blues: The Scientific Odyssey of a Literary Genius*. Cambridge, MA: Zoland Books, 1999. 372 p. $27.00, $16.95 (paper). ISBN 1581950098, 0071373306 (paper). Vladimir Nabokov was not only the author of such literary works as *Lolita* and *The Gift*; he was also an expert on the taxonomy of a group of butterflies known as Blues. This book presents the first examination of Nabokov's expertise by an entomologist, so readers find out a great deal about lepidoptera and taxonomy. The book's thesis might be summed up as "taxonomy is fun!"—which makes it a good book for taxonomists of all stripes to recommend to friends and relatives who ask what they do and why.

Preston-Mafham, Rod and Ken Preston-Mafham. *Encyclopedia of Land Invertebrate Behavior*. Cambridge, MA: MIT Press, 1993. 320 p. $55.00. ISBN 0262161370. While this well-illustrated encyclopedia covers more than just insects and arachnids, the majority of the entries relate to those two groups. The authors provide an excellent, authoritative introduction to primarily sexual, egg-laying, parental care, feeding, and defensive behaviors.

Waldbauer, Gilbert. *Insects through the Seasons*. Cambridge, MA: Harvard University Press, 1996. 289 p. $24.95, $14.95 (paper). ISBN 067445488X, 0674454898 (paper). Another fascinating, well-written insect book for the general public. Waldbauer takes a look at the reasons for the success of insects, so his book is more ecological than systematic. He keeps returning to his favorite insect, the handsome cecropia moth. Also by the author: *The Birder's Bug Book* and *The Handy Bug Answer Book*.

Wootton, Anthony. *Insects of the World*. New York: Facts on File, 1984. 224 p. $29.95, $19.95 (paper). ISBN 0871969912, 0713723661 (paper). A colorful general survey of insect biology covering classification, anatomy, life history, behavior, and other entomology topics. Examples are taken from insects around the world. Other volumes in this series include *Bees of the World, Bugs of the World, Butterflies of the World, Grasshoppers and Mantids of the World*, and *Spiders of the World*.

GUIDES TO INTERNET RESOURCES

Entomology is well supplied with electronic resources, ranging from very technical checklists of obscure insect families to cute bug pages for children. Most of the resources are specialized classification or identification tools, and most major insect collections have an Internet presence. There are a few freely accessible Internet glossaries, bibliographies, and other reference tools but these are scattered and incomplete. Most of the major entomological societies listed previously also have useful collections of links.

Best of the Bugs. Gainesville, FL: University of Florida Entomology and Nematology Department. URL: http://www.ifas.ufl.edu/entweb/UF-BOB/. "The sites listed here are judged to be in the top 5% of insect- or nematode-related WWW sites by a committee of professional entomologists and nematologists." This site lists about 10 high-quality Web sites.

The Entomology Index of Internet Resources. John Van Dyke. Ames, IA: Iowa State University. URL: http://www.ent.iastate.edu/list/. This directory covers a wide range of subjects, from beekeeping to pesticides, and an equally wide range of resource types, from bibliographies to newsgroups.

Systematic Entomology Laboratory World Wide Web Page. Beltsville, MD: Systematic Entomology Laboratory (USDA). URL: http://www.sel.barc.usda.gov/. This Web site contains information about the Systematic Entomology Laboratory, plus a great deal of general information on insects such as "BUGS: Good, Bad & Ugly!", several searchable databases on specific insect orders, and a collection of entomology links.

GUIDES TO THE LITERATURE

British Museum (Natural History). *List of Serial Publications in the Libraries of the Departments of Zoology and Entomology*. London: Trustees of the British Museum (Natural History), 1967. Includes reports and publications of organizations.

Chamberlain, W. J. *Entomological Nomenclature and Literature*. 3rd ed., rev. and enl. Westport, CT: Greenwood Press, 1970. 141 p. $65.00. ISBN 0837138108. Excellent guide for its time; still useful for retrospective work.

Gilbert, Pamela and Chris J. Hamilton. *Entomology: A Guide to Information Sources*. 2nd ed. London: Mansell, 1990. 259 p. $110.00. ISBN 0720120527. This guide has extensive coverage of the literature of entomology, including information on entomological collections, suppliers, and sources of illustrations, as well as standard primary and secondary literature. Has a European emphasis.

Hammack, Gloria M. *The Serial Literature of Entomology: A Descriptive Guide*. College Park, MD: Entomological Society of America, 1970. 85 p. A list of the journals publishing the majority of entomological studies, including complete bibliographic information. There are language and geographic indexes.

Hogue, Charles L. *Latin American Insects and Entomology*. See General Works section, page 378, for full annotation: Has extensive information on locating information about Latin American entomology.

Liste de Periodiques d'Entomologie/Lijst van entomologische periodieken. Paulette Dovell and Jan L.J. Hulselmans, eds. Brussels: Institute Royal des Sciences Naturelles de Belgique, 1966. Unpaged. Introduction in French and Flemish. Provides bibliographic information on entomological journals.

HANDBOOKS

Distribution Maps of Plant Pests. 1997– . Wallingford, UK: CAB International. Biannual. $330.00. ISSN 1369-104X. "A series of maps giving the world distribution of arthropod pests of agriculture and forestry, and their products." Supporting references are included. Eighteen maps are issued each year in two batches of nine each. By the end of 1998, over 580 species had been mapped. Formerly: *Distribution Maps of Pests, Series A (Agricultural)*.

Mayer, Marion S. and John R. McLaughlin. *Handbook of Insect Pheromones and Sex Attractants*. Boca Raton, FL: CRC Press, 1990. 1,083 p. $355.00. ISBN 0849329345. Provides a "guide to the literature published before 1988 on chemicals that effect aggregation for mating and/or elicit sexual behavior in insects, mites, and ticks." The bulk of the handbook consists of references to the sex pheromones of insects, in order of genera. There are also indexes to footnoted species, common names, and chemicals. The second part consists of entries dealing with the chemistry of the pheromones, including synthesis and analytical methods.

Poinar, George O. and Gerard M. Thomas. *Laboratory Guide to Insect Pathogens and Parasites*. New York: Plenum, 1984. 392 p. $110.00. ISBN 0306416808. According to the preface, this is "unique in covering all types of biotic agents which are found inside insects and cause them injury or disease." Has pictorial identification and information on the availability of insect pathogens as well as techniques for identification of pathogens such as agars and staining.

HISTORIES

Barnes, Jeffrey K. "Insects in the New Nation: A Cultural Context for the Emergence of American Entomology." *Bulletin of the Entomological Society of*

America 31(1): 21–30. Spring 1985.   Discusses the history of entomology and natural history in America, with emphasis on America's early inferiority complex in matters zoological and on the importance of the expansion of American agriculture.

Carpenter, M. M. "Bibliography of Biographies of Entomologists." *American Midland Naturalist*, 33:1–116, 1945. Supplement 50:257–348, 1953.   Bibliographic information includes obituaries, birthdays, portraits, anniversaries, biographies, and disposition of collections.

"Entomology Serving Society." *Bulletin of the Entomological Society of America* 35(3). Fall 1989.   This special issue was published for the centennial of the Entomological Society of America (ESA), and has articles covering the history of the society, biographies of its past presidents, histories of each of the branches and sections of the society, as well as discussion of the services and publications of the society. There are also several articles on the role of the ESA in several areas, such as establishing official common names of insects and developing insecticides.

Gilbert, P. *A Compendium of the Biographical Literature on Deceased Entomologists*. London: British Museum (Natural History), 1977.   Includes and enhances Carpenter's "Bibliography of Biographies of Entomologists," previous. The bibliography attempts to be complete through 1975, listing the names of 7,500 entomologists.

History of Entomology. Ray F. Smith, Thomas E. Mittler, and Carroll N. Smith, eds. Palo Alto, CA: Annual Reviews, 1973. 517 p. ISBN 0824321017.   A supplement volume to *Annual Review of Entomology*, this volume covers the worldwide history of entomology, with emphasis on "the personalities of past scientists who contributed to the development of entomological ideas and principles." Various volumes of the *Annual Review of Entomology* include chapters on the history of entomology.

Mallis, Arnold. *American Entomologists*. New Brunswick, NJ: Rutgers University Press, 1971. 549 p. ISBN 0813506867.   Consists of biographies of over 200 deceased American entomologists. Nearly all of the entries include portraits, and the emphasis in the biographies is on the lives of the entomologists, not their scientific accomplishments. After initial chapters featuring early entomologists from the United States and Canada, the remaining chapters are arranged by the order of insect studied, that is, butterflies or beetles.

Palladino, Paolo. *Entomology, Ecology and Agriculture: The Making of Scientific Careers in North America, 1885–1985*. Amsterdam: Harwood Academic, 1996. 201 p. $58.00. ISBN 3718659077.   Discusses the history of entomology in the United States and Canada, with heavy emphasis on economic entomology and the role of agricultural experiment stations and government entomologists in the protection of agricultural plants and their encouragement of the use of pesticides. The effects of Rachel Carson's *Silent Spring* and the subsequent age of environmentalism are also examined closely.

Sorensen, W. Conner. *Brethren of the Net: American Entomology, 1840–1880.* Tuscaloosa, AL: University of Alabama Press, 1995. (History of American Science and Technology Series). 357 p. $59.95. ISBN 0817307559. The forty-year period covered in this history is a particularly interesting one during which North American entomology moved from amateur to professional status, from a basis in natural theology to acceptance of evolution, and from inferiority to equality with European science. The entomological activities of the time are covered in detail, both in the "pure" science and applied agricultural aspects. The author also provides appendices listing the 108 entomological authors cited in the *Record of American Entomology* alphabetically and in order of priority. The bibliography is extensive.

METHODS AND TECHNIQUES

Gullan, Penny J. and Peter S. Cranston. *The Insects: An Outline of Entomology.* 2nd ed. See the Textbooks and Treatises section for full annotation. The second edition includes a chapter on methods of collecting, preserving, and identifying insects.

Handbook of Insect Rearing. Pritam Singh and R.F. Moore, eds. New York: Elsevier, 1985. 2 v. ISBN 0444424679 (set). Handbook offering step-by-step instructions for rearing insects. Arranged by insect order.

Imes, Rick. *The Practical Entomologist.* New York: Simon and Schuster, 1992. 160 p. $27.95, $16.00 (paper). ISBN 0671746960, 06170746952 (paper). For the amateur. Includes information on capturing and keeping live insects, making an insect collection, tips on insect photography, as well as chapters on each major order of insects.

Kearns, Carol Ann and David William Inouye. *Techniques for Pollination Biologists.* See Chapter 10, "Plant Biology", for full annotation. Includes chapter on collecting, preparing, and identifying pollinators, as well as methods of study.

Laboratory Training Manual on the Use of Nuclear Techniques in Insect Research and Control: A Joint Undertaking. Food and Agriculture Organization of the United Nations and the International Atomic Energy Agency. 3rd ed. Vienna: International Atomic Energy Agency, 1992. 183 p. (Technical Reports Series, 336.) "The purpose of this manual is to help entomologists . . . in developing countries become familiar with the potential use of isotopes and radiation in solving some of their research and insect control problems.'' After opening sessions discussing safety and the use of radiation in research, the manual goes on to offer applications relating to entomological research, in particular the use of sterile insects in controlling populations.

Leppla, N. C. and Thomas E. Anderson. *Advances in Insect Rearing for Research and Pest Management.* Boulder, CO: Westview Press, 1992. (Westview's Studies in Insect Biology.) 519 p. ISBN 0813378354. Covers rearing insects for research in genetics, molecular biology, and nutrition, as well as pest management and commercial purposes.

Methods in Ecological and Agricultural Entomology. D. R. Dent and M. P. Walton, eds. Wallingford, UK: CAB International, 1997. 387 p. $100.00, $45.00 (paper). ISBN 0851991319, 0851991327 (paper). Covers experimental and analytical methods used to study insects. Topics covered include sampling and rearing insects, methods for studying population, migration, pollination, natural enemies, and other topics, and molecular and biochemical methods.

Methven, Kathleen R. et al. *How to Collect and Preserve Insects.* Champaign, IL: Illinois Natural History Survey, 1995. 76 p. $6.00 (paper). (Illinois Natural History Survey Special Publication, 17.) A spiralbound paperback designed for dedicated amateur entomologists. It provides detailed information on making an insect collection, including capturing and preserving insects, keeping proper records, and identifying species. A bibliography and list of supply companies are also included.

Service, M. W. *Mosquito Ecology: Field Sampling Methods.* 2nd ed. New York: Elsevier Applied Science, 1993. 988 p. $221.95. ISBN 1851667989. A manual for field workers, covering various methods for sampling eggs, larvae, and adults. Has author, mosquito species, and subject index.

TEXTBOOKS AND TREATISES

Borror, Donald J, Charles A. Triplehorn, and Norman F. Johnson. *An Introduction to the Study of Insects.* 6th ed. Philadelphia, PA: Saunders College, 1989. 875 p. $86.00. ISBN 0030253977. Includes keys for all families of insects in North America and some subfamilies. Also has information on collecting and preserving insects. Includes chapter on noninsect arthropods (crustaceans, arachnids, etc.).

Burrows, Malcolm. *The Neurobiology of an Insect Brain.* New York: Oxford University Press, 1996. 682 p. $125.00. ISBN 0198523440. Focuses on the neurobiology of the locust brain. Insects are important study organisms for neurobiologists, because they have simple brains with relatively few neurons. Locusts are studied not only for their economic importance but because they are easily kept in the lab. Burrows covers all aspects of locust neurobiology, including anatomy, development, neurotransmitters, and control of movements. The glossary and list of references are extensive. A major synthesis of insect neurobiology.

Comprehensive Insect Physiology, Biochemistry, and Pharmacology. Gerald A. Kerkut and Lawrence I. Gilbert, eds. New York: Pergamon Press, 1985. 13 v. $3,803.00. ISBN 0080268501 (set).   This massive set contains 200 articles written by 220 researchers, and refers to 5,000 species of insects. It is designed for both practitioners and students. Topics covered include all areas of insect physiology, behavior, biochemistry, pharmacology, and control. Each article contains extensive references and numerous illustrations. The final volume contains species, author, and subject indexes.

Daly, Howell V., John T. Doyen, and Alexander H. Purcell, III. *Introduction to Insect Biology and Diversity.* 2nd ed. New York: Oxford University Press, 1998. 680 p. $76.00. ISBN 0195100336.   Written for general entomology courses. In three sections covering insect biology, ecology, and diversity. About half the book is taxonomy, with keys to over 400 families scattered throughout. Includes about 50 color photos illustrating insects in nature, along with numerous black-and-white illustrations and photos.

Davies, R.G. *Outlines of Entomology.* 7th ed. New York: Chapman and Hall, 1988. 408 p. $99.95, $46.95 (paper). ISBN 0412266709, 0412266806 (paper).   An enlarged edition of Imms' *Outlines of Entomology.* Covers insect biology, ecology, and classification as well as a section on injurious insects. A classic textbook.

Ecological Entomology. Carl B. Huffaker and Andrew P. Gutierrez, eds. 2nd ed. New York: John Wiley and Sons, 1999. 756 p. $98.00. ISBN 047124483X. This multiauthored volume is intended as a reference for researchers and a text for upper-level classes. It covers insect ecology at a more advanced level than Gullan and Cranston, in the following text, and has less taxonomic information. Insect population control is covered extensively, both natural control and pest management. Each chapter concludes with extensive references.

Foelix, Rainer F. *Biology of Spiders.* 2nd ed. New York: Oxford University Press, 1996. 330 p. $35.00, $29.95 (paper). ISBN 0195095936, 0195095944 (paper). A general overview of spider biology, covering everything from anatomy and metabolism to web-spinning and prey capture; also includes phylogeny of spiders.

The Genetics and Biology of Drosophila. M. Ashburner and E. Novitski, eds. New York: Academic Press, 1976–   . v. 1a–   .   This series contains review articles from a variety of experts covering numerous aspects of *Drosophila* genetics and biology, including taxonomy, ecology, parasites, population genetics, molecular genetics, and behavior. Currently up to volume 3e.

Gullan, Penny J. and Peter S. Cranston. *The Insects: An Outline of Entomology.* 2nd ed. Osney Mead, UK: Blackwell Science, 1999. 496 p. $43.00 (paper). ISBN 0632053437 (paper). A general survey of insects and their biology designed for undergraduates. Rather than following an order-by-order taxonomic arrangement, the authors emphasize insect ecology and behavior, with each order discussed in appropriate places throughout the text (e.g., bees and termites in the chapter on social behavior). Black-and-white illustrations.

Heinrich, Bernd. *The Hot-Blooded Insects: Strategies and Mechanisms of Thermoregulation.* Cambridge, MA: Harvard University Press, 1993. 601 p. $83.00. ISBN 0674408381. Provides a review and critique of the literature on insect thermoregulation, designed for researchers and advanced students.

Hinton, H. E. *Biology of Insect Eggs.* New York: Pergamon Press, 1981. 3 v. $494.00. ISBN 0080215394 (set). Covers all areas relating to insect eggs. Volume 1 offers general topics (parental care, oviposition, etc), while volume 2 covers each insect order. The final volume provides references; species, author, and subject indexes; and a bibliography of the author's works.

Insect Learning: Ecological and Evolutionary Perspectives. Daniel R. Papaj and Alcinda C. Lewis, eds. New York: Chapman and Hall, 1993. 412 p. $140.50. ISBN 0412025612. A multiauthored review of learning in both social and nonsocial insects. Includes applications for pest control.

Insect Ultrastructure. Robert C. King and Hiromu Akai, eds. New York: Plenum Press, 1982–4. 2 v. $80.00 (v. 1), $174.00 (v. 2). ISBN 0306409232 (v. 1), 0306415453 (v. 2). "The purpose of the following volume is to provide the interested reader with a series of up-to-date, well illustrated reviews of selected aspects of insect ultrastructure by authorities in the field."

Metcalf, Robert L. and Robert A. Metcalf. *Destructive and Useful Insects: Their Habits and Control.* New York: McGraw-Hill, 1993. Var. pagings. ISBN 0070416923. Designed for undergraduates and nonscientists. Provides keys, life histories, and further references to over 600 species of North American pests. Arranged by type of problem (i.e., pests of cotton, stored grains, etc.). Also useful as a general reference.

Parasites and Pathogens of Insects. Beckage, N. E., S. N. Thompson, and B. A. Federici, eds.. San Diego, CA: Academic Press, 1993. 2 v. $116 (v. 1), $122 (v. 2), $229 (set). ISBN 0120844419 (v. 1), 0120844427 (v. 2), 01208444400 (set). "The focus of this two-volume set is the interface between insects and their associated parasites and pathogens, with particular emphasis placed on the basic biology, biochemistry, and molecular biology of these intimate and intriguing relationships.'' Volume 1 deals with parasites, and volume 2 with pathogens.

Pedigo, Larry P. *Entomology and Pest Management*. 3rd ed. New York: Macmillan, 1998. 720 p. $96.00. ISBN 013780024X. An introduction to applied entomology for undergraduates and beginning graduate students. Also includes list of common insecticides and insect common names.

Price, Peter W. *Insect Ecology*. 3rd ed. New York: John Wiley and Sons, 1997. 874 p. $125.00. ISBN 0471161845. A comprehensive treatise on all areas of insect ecology, with extensive references to the original literature. Intended for the use of advanced undergraduates, graduates, and researchers.

Romoser, William S. and John G. Stoffolano, Jr. *The Science of Entomology*. Boston, MA: WCB McGraw-Hill, 1998. 605 p. $62.50. ISBN 0697228487. A broad survey of entomology, appropriate for general undergraduate courses and a reference text for professionals. After an initial chapter offering a good introduction to the literature of entomology, the book is divided into five broad sections: Structure and Function, Insects and Their Environment, Unity and Diversity, Applied Entomology, and The Modern Interface. Also includes keys to major orders of insects.

Social Insects. Henry R. Hermann, ed. New York: Academic Press, 1978–82. 4 v. A treatise providing extensive coverage of the sociobiology of social insects, including bees, wasps, ants, termites, and arachnids.

PERIODICALS

Acarologia. v. 1– . 1959– . Paris: Acarologia. Quarterly. $163.00. ISSN 0044-086X. ''An International Journal of Acarology.'' Covers agricultural, aquatic, general, medical, and veterinary aspects of Acarina. Primarily taxonomic studies.

Acta Entomologica Sinica. v. 1– . 1954– . Beijing: Science Press. Quarterly. $10.00 per number. ISSN 0454-6296. Also known as *K'un Ch'ung Hsueh Pao* or *Kunchong Xuebao*. The leading Chinese entomological journal, covering all aspects of basic and applied entomology. An English translation is available for v. 16 (1973) to date. Formerly: *Annales Entomologici Sinici*.

African Entomology: Journal of the Entomological Society of Southern Africa. v. 1– . 1993– . Pretoria: Entomological Society of Southern Africa. Semiannual. $110.00. ISSN 1021-3589. Publishes primarily systematics papers, which must be authored or sponsored by a member of the Entomological Society of Southern Africa.

Annals of the Entomological Society of America. v. 1– . 1908– . Lanham, MD: Entomological Society of America. Bimonthly. $156.00. ISSN 0013-8746. Published by the Entomological Society of America. "Contributions report on the basic aspects of the biology of arthropods and are divided into categories by subject matter."

Apidologie. v. 1– . 1970– . Paris: Elsevier. Bimonthly. $308.00. ISSN 0044-8435.

Applied Entomology and Zoology. v. 1– . 1966– . Tokyo: Japanese Society of Applied Entomology and Zoology. Quarterly. $88.00. ISSN 0003-6892. "The journal publishes articles concerned with applied zoology, applied entomology, agricultural chemistry and pest control equipments in English."

Aquatic Insects: An International Journal of Freshwater Entomology. v. 1– . 1979– . Lisse, Netherlands: Swets and Zeitlinger. Quarterly. $412.00. ISSN 0165-0424. "The journal publishes original research on taxonomy and ecology of aquatic insects. Purely faunistic studies and other papers of only regional interest are not considered."

Archives of Insect Biochemistry and Physiology. v. 1– . 1983– . New York: Wiley. Monthly. $1,880.00. ISSN 0739-4462. Available electronically. Published in collaboration with the Entomological Society of America. "An international journal that publishes articles in English that are of interest to insect biochemists and physiologists."

Australian Journal of Entomology. v. 1– . 19– . Carleton, Australia: Blackwell Science. Quarterly. $200.00. ISSN 1326-6756. "Promotes the study of the biology, ecology, taxonomy, and control of insects and arachnids in an Australasian setting." Publishes original research articles, reviews, notes, theses, and book reviews. Formerly: *Journal of the Australian Entomological Society.*

Bee World. v. 1– . 1919– . Gerrards Cross, UK: International Bee Research Association. Quarterly. $84.00. ISSN 0005-772X. "Containing original articles and features which are peer-reviewed and comprises the official organ of the International Commission for Plant-Bee Relationships."

Bulletin of Entomological Research. v. 1– . 1910– . Wallingford, UK: CAB International. Quarterly. $560.00. ISSN 007-4853. Edited by the International Institute of Entomology. "Publishes original research papers concerning insects, mites, ticks or other arthropods of economic importance . . . . The geographical scope of the *Bulletin* is worldwide but with emphasis on the tropics." Some taxonomic papers are accepted.

Bulletin of the Natural History Museum, Entomology Series. v. 1– , 1949– . London: Natural History Museum. Semiannual. $132.00. ISSN 0968-

0454. "Papers in the *Bulletin* are primarily the results of research carried out on the unique and ever-growing collections of the Museum, both by the scientific staff and by specialists from elsewhere who make use of the Museum's resources." Formerly: *Bulletin of the British Museum (Natural History, Entomology Series)*.

Canadian Entomologist. v. 1– . 1868– . Ottawa, Canada: Entomological Society of Canada. Bimonthly. $180.00. ISSN 0008-347X. Published by the Entomological Society of Canada (which also publishes *Memoirs* and *Bulletin*). "Will publish results of original observations and research on all aspects of entomology. Manuscripts from all disciplines of entomology will be considered for publication."

Coleopterists Bulletin. v. 1– . 1947– . Natchez, MS: Coleopterists Society. Quarterly. $50.00. ISSN 0010-065X. "Manuscripts in English, treating systematics and natural history, both broadly defined, of the Coleoptera are accepted for publication as regular papers or as 'Scientific Notes.'"

Ecological Entomology. v. 1– . 1976– . Osney Mead, UK: Blackwell Science. Quarterly. $430.00. ISSN 0307-6946. Published for the Royal Entomological Society. "Publishes only top quality original research papers on the ecology of insects." Formerly: *Transactions of the Royal Entomological Society of London*.

Entomologia Experimentalis et Applicata. v. 1– . 1958– . Dordrecht, Netherlands: Kluwer Academic Publishers. Monthly. $1,220.00. ISSN 0013-8703. Published for the Nederlandse Entomologische Vereniging. Publishes "results in the areas of the physiological, ecological and morphological relations of arthropods to their host plant, as well as the several disciplines in entomology which have grown to prominence as the result of new findings on insect control."

Entomologia Generalis. v. 1– . 1974– . Stuttgart, Germany: E. Schweizerbartsche Verlagsbuchhandlung. Quarterly. ISSN 0171-8177. "An International Journal of General and Applied Entomology, concerned with comparative and descriptive problems in all fields of research in insects and other terrestrial arthropods."

Entomological News. v. 1– . 1889– . Philadelphia: American Entomological Society. Bimonthly. $20.00. ISSN 0013-872X. "Manuscripts on taxonomy, systematics, morphology, physiology, ecology, behavior and similar aspects of insect life and related terrestrial arthropods are appropriate for submission to *Entomological News*." Manuscripts submitted by members receive the highest priority.

Entomological Review. v. 1–   . 1957–   . New York: Scripta Technica. Quarterly. $1,996.00. ISSN 0013-8738.   Consists of translations of papers from the Russian *Entomologicheskoe Obozrenie*. "*Entomological Review* publishes papers dealing with all aspects of theoretical and applied entomology, and covers systematics, faunistics, zoogeography, evolution, ecology, morphology, physiology of insects, spiders and mites, as well as biological and chemical control of pests."

Environmental Entomology. v. 1–   . 1972–   . Lanham, MD: Entomological Society of America. Bimonthly. $162.00. ISSN 0046-225X.   "Contributors report on the interaction of insects with the biological, chemical, and physical aspects of their environment."

Experimental and Applied Acarology. v. 1–   . 19–   . London: Chapman & Hall. Monthly. $1,011.00. ISSN 0168-8162.   "The journal is concerned with the publication of original scientific papers in the field of experimental and applied acarology. . . . The scope encompasses different aspects of working on agricultural mites, stored-products mites, parasitic mites (ticks, Varroa, etc.), and mites of environmental significance."

Florida Entomologist. v. 1–   . 1920–   . Lutz, FL: Florida Entomological Society. Quarterly. $40.00. ISSN 0015-4040.   Published by the Florida Entomological Society. "Manuscripts from *all* areas of the discipline of entomology are accepted for consideration. At least one author must be a member of the Florida Entomological Society."

Great Lakes Entomologist. v. 1–   . 1966–   . East Lansing, MI: Michigan Entomological Society. Quarterly. $30.00. ISSN 0090-0222.   Continues *Michigan Entomologist*. "Papers dealing with any aspect of entomology will be considered for publication in *The Great Lakes Entomologist*. Appropriate subjects are those of interest to professional and amateur entomologists in the North Central States and Canada, as well as general papers and revisions directed to a larger audience while retaining an interest to readers in our geographical area."

Insect Biochemistry and Molecular Biology. v. 1–   . 1971–   . Kidlington, UK: Elsevier. 8/yr. $1,462.00. ISSN 0965-1748.   "This international journal publishes original contributions and mini-reviews in the fields of insect biochemistry and insect molecular biology." Formerly: *Insect Biochemistry*.

Insect Molecular Biology. v. 1–   . 1992–   . Osney Mead, UK: Blackwell Science. Quarterly. $518.00. ISSN 0962-1075.   Published for the Royal Entomological Society. "The Journal publishes only high-quality original research articles on the structure, function, mapping, organization, expression and evolution of insect genomes. It serves both the fundamental and applied aspects of insect molecular biology, and papers relating to the medical and agricultural sectors are welcome.''

Insectes Sociaux: International Journal for the Study of Social Arthropods. v. 1– . 1954– . Basel, Switzerland: Birkhauser Verlag. Quarterly. $411.00. ISSN 0020-1812. Official journal for the International Union for the Study of Social Insects. Publishes ''original research papers and reviews on all aspects related to the biology and evolution of social insects and other presocial arthropods.''

Insect Science and Its Application: The International Journal of Tropical Insect Science. v. 1– . 1980– . Nairobi: ICIPE Science Press. Quarterly. $280.00. ISSN 0191-9040. Available electronically. Sponsored by the International Centre of Insect Physiology and Ecology (ICIPE) and the African Association of Insect Scientists (AAIS). ''Serves as a forum for original research findings on tropical insects and related arthropods, with special emphasis on their environmentally benign and sustainable management.''

International Journal of Insect Morphology and Embryology. v. 1- , 1971– . Kidlington, UK: Elsevier. Quarterly. $908.00. ISSN 0020-7322. ''The Journal will publish original contributions on all aspects of gross morphology, paleomorphology, macro- and microanatomy, ultrastructure . . . , molecular . . . , functional and experimental morphology, and development. . . .''

Invertebrate Neuroscience. v. 1– . 1995– . Berlin: Springer-Verlag. Quarterly. $441.00. ISSN 1354-2516. Available electronically. ''The journal publishes peer-reviewed research articles on invertebrate neurosciences, including but not limited to: molecular biology, development, neurogenetics, neurotoxicology and neuronal networks.'' Formerly published by Sheffield University.

Invertebrate Reproduction and Development. v. 1– . 1979– . Rehovot, Israel: Balaban. Bimonthly. $410.00. ISSN 0168-8170. Published in collaboration with the International Society of Invertebrate Reproduction. ''The journal publishes original papers and reviews with a wide approach to the sexual, reproductive and developmental (embryonic and postembryonic) biology of the Invertebrata.'' Formerly: *International Journal of Invertebrate Reproduction and Development.*

Journal of Apicultural Research. v. 1– . 1962– . Cardiff, England: International Bee Research Association (IBRA). $185.00. ISSN 0021-8839. ''Publishes descriptions of new findings on the scientific aspects of behavior, ecology, natural history and culture of Apoidea in general and Apis species in particular. The Journal also publishes theoretical papers where these relate to Apis, and letters on Apoidea-related subjects which have recently appeared in the journal or elsewhere. Papers dealing with economics, techniques, or society of beekeeping are more usually suited to IBRA's journal *Bee World* or other technical periodicals.'' (See previous text for *Bee World*.)

Journal of Applied Entomology. v. 1– . 1914– . Berlin: Blackwell Wissenschafts Verlag GmbH. 10/yr. $784.00. ISSN 0931-2048. Available electronically. ''The journal presents original articles on current research in entomology applied to agriculture, forestry, biomedical areas, food, and feed storage. The articles by internationally recognized contributors appear in English, German, and French.'' Formerly: *Zeitschrift für Angewandte Entomologie.*

Journal of Arachnology. v. 1– . 19– . New York: American Arachnological Society. 3 times/year. $80.00. ISSN 0160-8202. ''Official organ of the American Arachnological Society.'' Publishes in English, Spanish, French, and Portuguese. Mostly taxonomic.

Journal of Economic Entomology. v. 1– . 1908– . Lanham, MD: Entomological Society of America. Bimonthly. $194.00. ISSN 0022-0493. Published by the Entomological Society of America. ''Contributions report on the economic significance of insects and are divided into categories by subject matter.''

Journal of Insect Behavior. v. 1– . 1988– . New York: Plenum. Bimonthly. $395.00. ISSN 0892-7553. ''*Journal of Insect Behavior* offers peer-reviewed research articles and short critical reviews on all aspects of the behavior of insects and other terrestrial arthropods.''

Journal of Insect Physiology. v. 1– . 1957– . Kidlington, UK: Elsevier. $1,603.00. ISSN 0022-1910. ''All aspects of insect physiology are published in this journal. The journal will also accept papers on the physiology of other arthropods if the referees consider the work to be of general interest.''

Journal of Medical Entomology. v. 1– . 1964– . Lanham, MD: Entomological Society of America. Bimonthly. $156.00. ISSN 0022-2585. Published by the Entomological Society of America. ''Contributions report on all phases of medical entomology and medical acarology, including the systematics and biology of insects, acarines, and other arthropods of public health and veterinary significance.''

Journal of the American Mosquito Control Association. v. 1– . 1985– . Lake Charles, LA: American Mosquito Control Association. Quarterly. $110.00. ISSN 8756-971X. Published for the American Mosquito Control Association. Publishes ''previously unpublished papers which contribute to the advancement of knowledge of mosquitoes and other vectors, and their control.'' Formerly: *Mosquito News*; absorbed *Mosquito Systematics.*

Journal of the Lepidopterists' Society. v. 1– . 1947– . Los Angeles, CA: Lepidopterists' Society. Quarterly. $50.00. ISSN 0024-0966. "Contributions to the *Journal* may deal with any aspect of Lepidoptera study."

Medical and Veterinary Entomology. v. 1– . 1987– . Osney Mead, UK: Blackwell Science. Quarterly. $376.00. ISSN 0269-283X. "The Journal covers all aspects of the biology and control of insects, ticks, mites and other arthropods of medical and veterinary importance."

Memoirs of the American Entomological Society. v. 1– . 1916– . Gainesville, FL: American Entomological Society. Irregular. price varies. ISSN 0065-8162. "Monographic works on insects are published as Memoirs."

Odonatologica. v. 1– . 1972– . Bilthoven, Netherlands: URSUS Scientific Publishers. Quarterly. $199.00. ISSN 0375-0183. "A publication of original papers in all fields of odonatology." Includes Odonatological Abstracts. The official journal of Societas Internationalis Odonatologica (SIO).

Oriental Insects. v. 1– . 1968– . Gainesville, FL: Association Publishers. Annual. $65.00. ISSN 0030-5316. "An international journal of taxonomy and zoogeography of insects and other land arthropods of the Old World Tropics." "Devoted to publication of original research and reviews on the taxonomy, ecology, zoogeography, and evolution of insects and other land arthropods of the Old World Tropics."

Physiological Entomology. v. 1– . 1976– . Osney Mead, UK: Blackwell Science. Quarterly. $383.00. ISSN 0307-6962. Published for the Royal Entomological Society. "*Physiological Entomology* is designed primarily to serve the interests of experimentalists who work on the behaviour of insects and other arthropods. It thus has a bias towards physiological and experimental approaches, but retains the Royal Entomological Society's traditional interest in the general physiology of arthropods." Formerly: *Journal of Entomology, Series A: Physiological and Behaviour*.

Psyche: A Journal of Entomology. v. 1– . 1874– . Cambridge, MA: Cambridge Entomological Club. Quarterly. $30.00. ISSN 0033-2615. Founded by the Cambridge Entomological Club. Emphasis on neotropical insects, including mites and spiders.

Series Entomologica. v. 1– . 1966– . Dordrecht, Netherlands: Kluwer Academic. Irregular. Price varies. ISSN 0080-8954. A series of monograph-length works, mostly systematics but also including ecology, development, biology, etc. Volume 56, *Insect-Plant Relationships* ($150), was published in 1999.

Systematic Entomology. v. 1– . 1976– . Osney Mead, UK: Blackwell Science. Quarterly. $376.00. ISSN 0307-6970. Published for the Royal Entomological

Society. *"Systematic Entomology* publishes original contributions to insect taxonomy and systematics. . . . Emphasis is placed on the publication of comprehensive or revisionary studies, and on work with a biological or zoogeographical relevance. Occasionally papers on descriptive morphology and other subjects with a bearing on taxonomy are published." Formerly: *Journal of Entomology, Series B: Taxonomy and Systematics*.

REVIEWS OF THE LITERATURE

Advances in Insect Physiology. v. 1– . 1963– . New York: Academic Press. Annual. $93.00. ISSN 0065-2806.   Review articles on any aspect of insect physiology.

Annual Review of Entomology. v. 1– . 1956– . Palo Alto, CA: Annual Reviews Inc. Annual. $127.00 ISSN 0066-4170. Available electronically.   Authoritative reviews on various topics in entomology.

Entomography: An Annual Review for Biosystematics. v. 1– . 1982– . Sacramento, CA: Entomography Publications. Annual. $50.00. ISSN 0734-9874.   Publishes review articles dealing with insect systematics.

13

Zoology

Zoology is "the scientific study of animals," according to the *Oxford Dictionary of Biology*, 4ᵗʰ edition 2000. Entomology is treated separately in its own chapter, because it has traditionally been treated as a separate discipline. The other branches of zoology such as ornithology or nematology are not separated in this chapter; rather, the arrangement is by type of material following the pattern established earlier.

ABSTRACTS AND INDEXES

Current Awareness

Aquatic Sciences and Fisheries Abstracts. Part 1: Biological Sciences and Living Resources. v. 8– , 1978– . Bethesda, MD: CSA. Monthly. $1,045.00. ISSN 0140-5373. Covers all aspects of marine and freshwater organisms, including biology and exploitation. Contains author, subject, taxonomic, and geographic indexes. Part 2: *Ocean Technology, Policy, and Non-Living Resources* and Part 3: *Aquatic Pollution and Environmental Quality* are also available. Available on CD-ROM, online, and on the Web as a standalone database and as part of the Aquatic Sciences and Fisheries Abstracts Database and the Biological Sciences Database.

Fish & Fisheries Worldwide. 1992– . Baltimore, MD: National Information Services Corp. Quarterly. CD-ROM. Contains citations from several databases, including: FISHLIT (1985–present), *Fisheries Review* (1971–present); Fishing Industry Research Institute (FIRI) Database from Cape Town, South Africa, Fish Database (1960–present) from the Fish and Wildlife Reference Service, and *Castell's Nutrition References* (1970–present), among others.

Helminthological Abstracts. v. 59– , 1990– . Wallingford, UK: CABI. Monthly. $945.00. ISSN 0957-6789. Covers journal articles, books, reports, and conferences on all aspects of parasitic helminths. Has author and subject indexes. Available on CD-ROM, online, and on the Web as part of CAB Abstracts. Continues *Helminthological Abstracts Series A: Animal and Human Helminthology.*

Nematological Abstracts. v. 59– , 1990– . Wallingford, UK: CABI. Quarterly. $405.00. ISSN 0957-6797.   Covers journal articles, books, reports, and conferences on all aspects of nematodes. Has author and subject indexes and occasional review articles. Available on CD-ROM, online, and on the Web as part of CAB Abstracts and PEST CABWeb. Continues *Helminthological Abstracts Series B: Plant Nematology.*

Protozoological Abstracts. v. 1– , 1977– . Wallingford, UK: CABI. Monthly. $1,010.00. ISSN 0309-1287.   Covers journal articles, books, reports, and conferences on all aspects of protozoa and protozoan diseases. Has author and subject indexes and occasional review articles. Available on CD-ROM, online, and on the Web as part of CAB Abstracts.

Recent Ornithological Literature. 1986– . Washington, DC: American Ornithologists' Union, British Ornithologists' Union, and Royal Australasian Ornithologists' Union. Quarterly.   This publication is a joint supplement to *The Auk*, *The Emu*, and *Ibis*, and is free with subscription to any of the journals. It attempts to provide comprehensive coverage of the world literature in ornithology, scanning about 900 titles. A "List of Journals Scanned" is published each year in the fourth supplement. The bibliography is divided by broad subject category and includes information on new and renamed journals. Starting in 1999, the bibliography is no longer available in print but can be accessed on the Web at http://www.nmnh.si.edu/BIRDNET/ROL/index.html.

Wildlife Worldwide. 1992– . Baltimore, MD: National Information Services Corp. Quarterly. ISSN 1070-5007. CD-ROM.   Wildlife Worldwide covers the literature of mammals, birds, reptiles, and amphibians around the world. It is a combination full-text database and index and contains the database equivalent of the U.S. Fish and Wildlife print publication *Wildlife Review* (1971–present), Wildlife Database (1960–present), the entire WIS (HERMAN) from the Wildlife Information Service (1935–present), Waterfowl and Wetlands Database (1968–94), the BIODOC file from the National University of Costa Rica (1980–present), Swiss Wildlife Information Service (1974–present), three databases from the IUCN, and others. Formerly: *Wildlife & Fish Worldwide.*

Zoological Record. v. 1– , 1864– . Philadelphia: BIOSIS. Annual.   See Chapter 4, "Abstracts and Indexes," for full annotation. The most comprehensive index to systematic zoology.

RETROSPECTIVE SOURCES

Bibliographie Ornithologique Française; *Travaux publiés en langue française et en latin en France et dans les Colonies françaises de 1473 à 1944*. Ronsil, René, ed. v. 1–2. (Encyclopédie ornithologique, VIII and IX.) Paris: Lechevalier, 1948–49. Vol. 1: Bibliography of ornithological literature published in France or one of the French colonies between 1473–1944. Vol. 2: Indexes of abbreviations of periodical publications; ornithological, geographic terms; and history of ornithology.

British Museum (Natural History). *List of Serial Publications in the Libraries of the Department of Zoology and Entomology*. London: British Museum (Natural History), 1967. 281 p. (Publication 664).

Bronn, H.G. *Dr. H.G. Bronn's Klassen und Ordnungen des Thierreichs, Wissenschaftlich Dargestellt in Wort und Bild*. . . . Leipzig, Germany: Winter, 1866–1964. Bibliography of zoology lists titles in morphology, histology, ontogeny, physiology, ecology, phylogeny, and classification.

Coues, Elliott. "List of Faunal Publications Relating to North American Ornithology." In *Birds of the Colorado Valley*, pp. 567–784. New York: Arno Press, 1974. $54.00. ISBN 040505730X. A reprint of the first installment of Coues' bibliography, covering the period from 1600–1878. Originally published in 1878.

Coues, Elliott. *American Ornithological Bibliography*. New York: Arno Press, 1974. 650 p. $43.00. ISBN 0405057040. A reprint of the second (faunal publications for South and Central America) and third (systematic publications) installments of Coues' bibliography, originally published in *Bulletin of the U.S. Geological and Geographical Survey of the Territories*, v. 5 (1879). Covers the late sixteenth century to the late 1870s.

Dean, B. *A Bibliography of Fishes*. Enlarged and edited by Charles R. Eastman. v. 1–3. New York: American Museum of Natural History, 1916–23. Index to the literature of fishes by author, title, pre-Linnean publications, voyages and expeditions, periodicals and subject from 1758. Continued by the American Museum of Natural History under this title until it was incorporated into *Zoological Record* as part of the Pisces section.

Englemann, W. *Bibliotheca Historieco-Naturalis*. Leipzig, Germany: Englemann, 1846. *Bibliotheca Zoologica I*. Leipzig, Germany: Englemann, 1861. v. 1–2. *Bibliotheca Zoologica II*. Leipzig: Englemann, 1887–1923. v. 1–8. Covers the literature of zoology from 1700–1800.

Harvard University, Museum of Comparative Zoology. *Catalogue of the Library of the Museum of Comparative Zoology, Harvard University*. v. 1–8. Boston, MA: Hall, 1968. $835.00. ISBN 081610767X (set). *Supplement*, v. 1– ,

1976– . $140.00. ISBN 0816108110 (sup. 1). Catalog of the volumes, manuscripts, photographs, and maps in Harvard's Library of the Museum of Comparative Anatomy. Arrangement is alphabetical. This is an important source for verification of particular authors' works in monographs as well as serials.

Index-Catalogue of Medical and Veterinary Zoology. v. 1–18, 1932–52. *Supplement*, v. 1– , 1953– . Washington, DC: Government Printing Office. Indispensable source for parasitologists.

International Catalogue of Scientific Literature: N, Zoology. 1st–14th annual issues. London: Harrison, 1902–1916. See Chapter 4, "Abstracts and Indexes," for full annotation.

Irwin, Raymond. *British Bird Books: An Index to British Ornithology, A.D. 1481 to A.D. 1948.* London: Grafton & Co., 1951. 398 p. Divided into several sections, including subject lists, regional lists, systematic list, and indexes to authors, subjects, species, and places. Also includes a supplement bringing coverage to 1950.

Reuss, J.D. *Repertorium Commentationum a Societatibus Litterariis Editarum . . . T. 1, Historia Naturalis, Generalis et Zoologia.* Gottingen, Germany: Dieterich, 1801. (Reprint: New York: Burt Franklin, 1961.) An index to society publications to 1800.

Ruch, T.C. *Bibliographia Primatologica.* A classified bibliography of primates other than man. (Yale medical library, historical library, publication no. 4.) Springfield, IL: Thomas, 1941. Excellent bibliography, covers to 1939. Over 4,000 entries covering anatomy, embryology, quantitative morphology, physiology, pharmacology, psychobiology, phylogeny, etc.

Sherborn, Charles Davies. *Index Animalium: Sive, Index Nominum quae ab A.D. MDCCLVIII Generibus et Speciebus Animalium Imposita Sunt, Societatibus Eruditorum Adiuvantibus.* Bath, England: Chivers, 1969. 1195 p. Reprint. First published 1902–33, this index provides a list of animals named from 1758 to 1800, with citations to the first description.

Strong, R.M. *A Bibliography of Birds; with special reference to anatomy, behavior, biochemistry, embryology, pathology, physiology, genetics, ecology, aviculture, economic ornithology, poultry culture, evolution, and related subjects.* (Publications of the Field Museum of Natural History, v. 25.) Chicago: Field Museum of Natural History, 1939–59. Comprehensive coverage of world literature until 1926, although there are some references later than that year. Part 1: Author catalog, A–J. part 2: Author catalog, K–Z. part 3: Subject index; and part 4: Finding index.

Walker, Ernest P. *Mammals of the World*. 1st ed. Baltimore, MD: Johns Hopkins Press, 1964. 3 v. Volume 3 of this set consists of "A Classified Bibliography of Literature Regarding Mammals." It contains about 70,000 citations arranged by systematic, geographic, or subject categories. Subsequent editions of this work dropped the bibliography volume.

Wood, Casey A. *An Introduction to the Literature of Vertebrate Zoology*. New York, Arno Press, 1974. 643 p. (Natural sciences in America.) $95.00. ISBN 0405057725. Reprint. Originally published by Oxford University Press in 1931. Invaluable retrospective bibliographic reference. Some chapter headings: "Beginnings of Zoological Records," "Medieval Writers on Zoology," "Travelogues of Explorers," "Oriental Literature," "Literature of Zoogeography," etc.

Important Bibliographic Journals

Bibliographia Zoologica. v. 1–43, 1896–1934. Zurich: Sumptibus Concilii Bibliographici, 1896–1934.

Zentralblatt für Zoologie, allgemeine und experimentelle Biologie. bd. 1–6. Leipzig, Germany: Teubner, 1912–18. 6. v.

Zoologischer Anzeiger, v. 1– , 1878– . Leipzig, Germany: Geest and Portig. Records of current literature that were issued separately (1896–1934) as *Bibliographica Zoologica*, supplement to the journal.

Zoologischer Bericht. Im Auftrage der Deutschen Zoologischen Gesellschaft . . . Bd. 1–55. Jena, Germany: Fischer, 1922–43/44. 55 v.

Zoologischer Jahresbericht. Hrsg. von der zoologischen Station zu Neapel. 1879–1913. Leipzig, Germany: 1880–1924. v. 1–35.

ASSOCIATIONS

American Association for Zoological Nomenclature. c/o National Museum of Natural History, MRC 168, Smithsonian Institution, Washington, DC 20560. E-mail: kensley. brian@nmnh.si.edu. URL: http://www.iczn.org/aazn.htm. Founded 1983, 250 members. For those interested in the systematics of both living and extinct animals. Publishes *AAZN Newsletter*.

American Cetacean Society. P.O. Box 1391, San Pedro, CA 90731. Phone: (310) 548-6279. E-mail: acs@pobox.com. URL: http://www.acsonline.org. Founded in 1967. 1,500 members. Laypeople and professionals interested in whales, dolphins, and porpoises. Publishes *Spyhopper* and *Whalewatcher*. Web site provides information on scientific and legislative issues, whale-watching trips, publications, and has an extensive list of links.

American Fisheries Society. 5410 Grosvenor Lane, Suite 110, Bethesda, MD 20814. Phone: (301) 897-8616. Fax: (301) 897-8096. E-mail: main@fisheries. org. URL: http://www.fisheries.org. Founded in 1870, 9,000 members. International organization for aquatic sciences and fisheries professionals. Publishes *AFS Membership Directory and Handbook, Fisheries: Bulletin of the American Fisheries Society, North American Journal of Fisheries Management, Progressive Fish-Culturist,* and *Transactions of the American Fisheries Society.* The Web site contains membership information, job postings, and links to other fisheries pages.

American Malacological Society. c/o Eugene P. Keferl, Coastal Georgia Community College, 3700 Altama Ave., Brunswick, GA 31520–3644. Phone: (912) 262-3089. E-Mail: kefer@bc9000.bc.peachnet.edu. URL: http://pica.wru.umt. edu/AOU/AOU.html. Founded in 1931. 600 members. For professionals and hobbyists interested in mollusks. Publishes *American Malacological Bulletin* and supplements and *Newsletter.* Formerly: American Malacological Union. Web site includes membership information, brief list of links.

American Ornithologist's Union. National Museum of Natural History, Smithsonian Institution, Washington DC, 20560. Phone: (202) 357-2051. Fax: (202) 633-8084. E-mail: aou@nmnh.si.edu. URL: http://aou.org/. Founded 1883. 4,000 members. Publishes *The Auk, Check-List of North American Birds, Membership List* (triennial), *Handbook of North American Birds, Ornithological Monographs, Ornithological Newsletter.* Web site for membership information.

American Society of Ichthyologists and Herpetologists. Grice Marine Laboratory, University of Charleston, 205 Fort Johnson Rd., Charleston, SC 29412. Phone: (843) 406-4017. E-mail: asih@mail.utexas.edu. URL: http://199.245.200.110/. Founded 1913. 3,600 members. For scientists and students interested in fish, amphibians, and reptiles. Publishes *Copeia.* Web site includes membership information, related links.

American Society of Mammalogists. c/o Duane Smith, 290 MLBM, Brigham Young Univ., Provo, UT 84602. Phone: (801) 378-2492. URL: http://www. mammalsociety.org/. Founded in 1919. 3,600 members. Publishes *Journal of Mammalogy* and *Mammalian Species.* Web site includes membership information and links to mammal information and images.

Association of Field Ornithologists. c/o Charles Duncan, Allen Press, P.O. Box 1897, Lawrence, KS 66044–1897. URL: http://www.afonet.org/. Founded 1924. 2,400 members. Publishes *Journal of Field Ornithology.* Web site primarily for membership information. Formerly: Northeastern Bird-Banding Association.

Cooper Ornithological Society. c/o Martin L. Morton, Occidental College, Biology Department, 1600 Campus Rd., Los Angeles CA 90041. URL: http://www.cooper.org/. Founded 1893. 2,200 members. Professional ornithological society. Publishes *Condor*, *The Flock* (directory), *Studies in Avian Biology*. Web site primarily for publication and membership information.

The Crustacean Society. P.O. Box 1897, Lawrence, KS 66044–8897. Phone: (913) 843-1221. URL: http://www.vims.edu/tcs/. Founded 1980. 850 members. Publishes *The Ecdysiast* and *The Journal of Crustacean Biology*. Web site includes membership information, journal information, and related links.

Herpetologists' League. Biological Sciences Box 4050, Emporia State University, Emporia, KS 66801–4050. Phone: (316) 341-5606. E-mail: sievert1@ esumail.emporia.edu. URL: http://www.inhs.uiuc.edu/cbd/HL/HL.html. Founded 1936. 2,000 members. Publishes *Herpetologica* and *Herpetological Monographs*. Web site includes information on membership and links to other herpetological societies.

Society for Integrative and Comparative Biology. 1313 Dolley Madison Blvd., Ste. 402, McClean, VA 22101–3926. Phone: (703) 790-1745. E-mail: sicb@ burklnc.com. URL: http://www.sicb.org. Founded in 1890. 2,300 members. For professional zoologists. Publishes *American Zoologist*. Web site primarily for membership information, but also includes searchable database of member's interests. Formerly American Society of Zoologists; absorbed American Morphological Society.

Society for the Study of Amphibians and Reptiles. Biology Dept., St. Louis University, 3507 Laclede Ave., St. Louis, MO 63103–2010. Phone: (314) 977-3916. Fax: (314) 977-3658. E-mail: ssar@slu. URL: http://www.ukans.edu/ssar/. Founded 1958. 2,700 members. Publishes *Herpetological Circulars*, *Herpetological Review*, and *Journal of Herpetology*. Web site includes membership information and related links on herpetology and conservation. Formerly: Ohio Herpetological Society.

Society of Nematologists. Nematology Dept., University of California, Riverside, CA 92521. Phone: (909) 787-5819. URL: http://www.ianr.unl.edu/son/. Founded in 1961. 650 members. For people interested in basic and applied nematology. Publishes *Journal of Nematology* and *Nematology Newsletter*. Web site provides membership information, related links, and information on publications and discussion groups.

Society of Protozoologists. P.O. Box 1897, Lawrence, KS 66044–8897. Phone: (914) 365-8542, E-mail: kundell@cb.uga.edu. URL: http://www.uga.edu/protozoa. Founded 1947. 1,125 members. Publishes *The Abstracts*, *Directory of Members*, *Journal of Eukaryotic Microbiology*, *Newsletter*, and *Illustrated Guide to the Protozoa*. Web site includes membership information, related links.

Society of Systematic Biologists. c/o Peggy Pagano, Taylor & Francis, 47 Runway Rd., Ste. G, Levittown, PA 19057–4738. Phone: (800) 821-8312. URL: http://www.utexas.edu/depts/systbiol/. Founded in 1948. 1,550 members. Publishes *Systematic Biology*. Web site includes membership information, related links. Formerly: Society of Systematic Zoology.

Wilson Ornithological Society. University of Michigan, Museum of Zoology, Bird Division, Ann Arbor, MI 48109–1079. Phone: (734) 764-0457. Fax: (734) 763-4080. URL: http:// www.ummz.lsa.umich.edu/birds/wos.html. Founded 1888. 2250 members. For professional ornithologists and hobbyists interested in the scientific study of birds. Publishes *Wilson Bulletin* and *Flock* (triennial membership directory). The Web site is primarily for membership information.

ATLASES, CHECKLISTS, AND IDENTIFICATION MANUALS

There are a large number of identification tools, including atlases, manuals, faunas, and field guides. This section annotates only a select portion of them. See Chapter 3, ''General Sources'' for descriptions of the major field-guide series, for instance. Anatomical atlases are listed under the Handbooks section.

2000 IUCN Red List of Threatened Species. Cambridge, UK: International Union for Conservation of Nature and Natural Resources, 2000. http://www.redlist.org/. The IUCN Red Lists of various plant and animal groups have been standard sources for information on threatened and endangered species for many years. Beginning with the 2000 edition, the lists have been combined and will only be available electronically, both on the Web and on CD-ROM.

Animal Identification: A Reference Guide. R. W. Sims, ed. New York: Wiley, 1980. 3 v. ISBN 0471277657 (v. 1), 0471277665 (v. 2), 0471277673 (v. 3). Principle references useful in identifying animals are chosen for the nonspecialist scientist, student, or research worker. Arrangement for each volume is systematic by animal groups. Within each group there is further subdivision for general, systematic, and geographic sections. A very useful set. Volume 1: *Marine and Brackish Water Animals*; volume 2: *Land and Freshwater Animals (Not Insects)*; volume 3: *Insects*.

Bartholomew, J. G., W. Eagle Clarke, and Percy H. Grimshaw. *Atlas of Zoogeography: A Series of Maps Illustrating the Distribution of over Seven Hundred*

Families, Genera, and Species of Existing Animals. Edinburgh: Published at the Royal Geographical Society by J. Bartholomew, 1911. (Physical atlas, v. 5.)

Boschung, Herbert T., David K. Caldwell, Melba C. Caldwell, Daniel W. Gotshall, and James D. Williams. *The Audubon Society Field Guide to North American Fishes, Whales, and Dolphins*. New York: Knopf, 1983. 848 p. (Audubon Society Field Guide series). $19.00. ISBN 0394534050. A photographic guide to marine vertebrates.

Bull, John L. and John Farrand, Jr. *The National Audubon Society Field Guide to North American Birds, Eastern Region*. Rev. ed. New York: Knopf, 1994. 797 p. $19.00. ISBN 0679428526. A photographic guide to birds east of the Rockies.

Catalogue of American Amphibians and Reptiles. New York: American Museum of Natural History for the Society for the Study of Amphibians and Reptiles, 1971– . $20.00. ''Series of individual accounts, each prepared by a separate author.'' Each entry lists previous references, content, definition, description, illustrations, distribution, fossil record, pertinent literature, remarks, etymology, comments, and literature cited. Published by the American Society of Ichthyologists and Herpetologists from 1963–1970.

Check-List of Birds of the World. Ernst Mayr and G. William Cottrell, eds. Cambridge, MA: Museum of Comparative Zoology, 1979–86. 16 v. ''Revision of the work of James L. Peters.'' This massive work includes the Latin name, first description, and distribution of the birds of the world. A second edition of volume 1 was produced in 1979, but appears to be the only volume in the second edition.

Check-List of North American Birds: Species of Birds of North America from the Arctic through Panama, Including the West Indies and Hawaiian Islands. 7th ed. Washington, DC: American Ornithologists Union Staff, 1998. 829 p. $49.95. ISBN 189127600X. The checklist is prepared by the Committee on Classification and Nomenclature of the American Ornithologists' Union and is updated irregularly. Each species is listed with scientific and English name, original citation, habitat, distribution (summer and winter), and notes. The list of birds included in the checklist is also available on the Web at http://www.aou.org/aou/birdlist.html. Downloadable PDF and DBF versions are available from this site.

Conant, Roger and Joseph T. Collins. *A Field Guide to Reptiles and Amphibians: Eastern and Central North America*. 3rd ed., expanded. Boston, MA: Houghton Mifflin, 1998. 616 p. (Peterson Field Guide series, 12.) $20.00 (paper). ISBN 0395904528 (paper). A standard field guide to reptiles featuring color and black-and-white illustrations. The expanded edition also has some color photographs.

Corbet, G. B. and J. E. Hill. *A World List of Mammalian Species.* 3rd ed. New York: Oxford University Press, 1991. 243 p. $72.00. ISBN 0198540175. This list provides Latin name, English name, and geographical range, with selected line drawings.

Eschmeyer, William N. and Earl S. Herald. *A Field Guide to Pacific Coast Fishes of North America: From the Gulf of Alaska to Baja California.* Boston, MA: Houghton Mifflin, 1983. 336 p. (Peterson Field Guide series, 28.) $19.00 (paper). ISBN 061800212X (paper). Color and black-and-white illustrations of coastal fishes.

Field Guide to the Birds of North America. 3rd ed. Washington, DC: National Geographic, 1999. 480 p. $21.95 (paper). ISBN 0792274512 (paper). One of the most highly regarded advanced field guides for North America. Color illustrations.

Hall, E. Raymond. *Mammals of North America.* New York: John Wiley & Sons, 1981. 2 v. $112.50 (set). ISBN 0471054437 (v. 1), 0471054445 (v. 2), 0471055956 (set). Summarizes taxonomic studies on recent mammals of North America. Includes keys, skulls, and distribution maps for most species and line drawings for some.

Handbook of the Birds of the World. Josep del Hoyo, et al., eds. Barcelona: Lynx Edicions, 1992– . v. Price varies. This set is intended to consist of 10 volumes. The first volume begins with an overview of avian biology, with the remainder consisting of species accounts for 27 families. There are numerous excellent illustrations and maps for each species. Currently up to volume 6, *Mousebirds to Hornbills.*

Hickman, Graham C. National Mammal Guides: A Review of References to Recent Faunas. *Mammal Review* 11(2): 53–85. 1981. This article cites over 400 reference guides to mammalian faunas of over 150 countries. The items referred to include field guides, checklists, atlases, and faunas.

Howard, Richard and Alick Moore. *A Complete Checklist of the Birds of the World.* 2nd ed. San Diego, CA: Academic Press, 1991. 622 p. $63.00. ISBN 0123569109. This checklist follows the taxonomic sequence set forth in Peters' classic (see *Check-List of Birds of the World*, page 393). Fossil and extinct birds are not included. The entries include the Latin name, the English name and geographic distribution. The authors also provide an index of Latin names (arranged by species, not generic, name) and an index of English species names.

Iverson, John B. *A Revised Checklist with Distribution Maps of the Turtles of the World.* Richmond, IN: J. Iverson, 1992. 282 p. ISBN 0961743105, 0961743107 (paper).   Includes distribution maps as well as the usual taxonomic and nomen-clatural information. Also available on the Web at http://bufo.geo.orst.edu/turtle/.

Jones, J. Knox and Richard W. Manning. *Illustrated Key to Skulls of North American Land Mammals.* Lubbock, TX: Texas Tech University Press, 1992. 75 p. $9.95 (paper). ISBN 0896722899 (paper).   Dichotomous key to mammalian skulls, to genus. Includes glossary.

Mammalian Species. no. 1– , 1969– . New York: American Society of Mammalogists. Irregular. $15.00. ISBN 0076–3519.   Each number covers one species, including species name, context and content, diagnosis, general characters, distribution, ecology, etymology, function, reproduction, behavior, genetics, literature cited. Authoritative source.

Mammal Species of the World: A Taxonomic and Geographic Reference, 2nd ed. Don E. Wilson and DeeAnn M. Reeder, eds. Washington, DC: Smithsonian Press, 1993. 1206 p. $80.00. ISBN 1560982179.   A checklist, providing original citation, type locality, distribution, status, synonyms, and comments. Also available on the Web at http://www.nmnh.si.edu/msw/.

Meinkoth, Norman August. *The Audubon Society Field Guide to North American Seashore Creatures.* New York: Knopf, 1981. 799 p. (Audubon Society Field Guide series). $19.00. ISBN 0394519930.   Covers marine invertebrates that are commonly found on beaches in North America.

Monroe, Burt L. and Charles G. Sibley. *A World Checklist of Birds.* New Haven, CT: Yale University Press, 1993. 393 p. $65.00, $27.50 (paper). ISBN 0300055471, 0300070837 (paper).   This checklist is based on the taxonomic system of Sibley and Monroe (see following). As well as the usual Latin and English names and distribution of each species, the checklist provides a column for the dedicated birder to check off which of the 9,702 species he/she has seen. Also available on the Web at http://www.itc.nl/~deby/SM/SMorg/sm.html.

Nowak, Ronald M. *Walker's Mammals of the World.* 6th ed. Baltimore, MD: Johns Hopkins University Press, 1999. 2 v. ISBN 0801857899.   Revision of Ernest P. Walker's work. Includes photographs of representatives of each genera, taxonomic and biological information. A major resource. Entries for some families have been extracted and published in separate volumes, to date including *Walker's Primates of the World* and *Walker's Bats of the World.* Available online, by subscription only.

Page, Lawrence M. and Brooks M. Burr. *A Field Guide to Freshwater Fishes: North America North of Mexico.* Boston, MA: Houghton Mifflin, 1991. 432 p. (Peterson Field Guide series, 42.) $18.00 (paper). ISBN 061800212X (paper).   Color and black-and-white illustrations.

Palmer, Ralph S. *Handbook of North American Birds*. New Haven, CT: Yale University Press, 1962– . v. $45.00 (v. 5, pt. 2). ISBN 0300040601 (v. 5, pt 2). Currently up to volume 5, covering the accipiters.

Pennak, Robert W. *Fresh-Water Invertebrates of the United States: Protozoa to Mollusca*, 3rd ed. New York: John Wiley and Sons, 1989. 628 p. $110.00. ISBN 0471631183. Covers the identification and biology of free-living freshwater invertebrates. Some groups are keyed to species, others to genera. Aquatic insects and parasitic invertebrates are excluded.

Peterson, Roger Tory. *A Field Guide to the Birds: A Completely New Guide to All the Birds of Eastern and Central North America*. 4th ed. (completely revised and enlarged) Boston, MA: Houghton Mifflin, 1980. 384 p. (Peterson Field Guide series, 1.) $18.00 (paper). ISBN 0395911761 (paper). The classic field guide.

Peterson, Roger Tory. *A Field Guide to Western Birds: A Completely New Guide to Field Marks of All Species Found in North America West of the 100th Meridian and North of Mexico*. 3rd ed., (completely revised and enlarged) Boston, MA: Houghton Mifflin, 1990. 432 p. (Peterson Field Guide series, 2.) $27.00, $18.00 (paper). ISBN 0395911745, 0395911737 (paper).

Peterson, Roger Tory and Edward L. Chalif. *A Field Guide to Mexican Birds: Field Marks of All Species Found in Mexico, Guatemala, Belize (British Honduras), El Salvador*. Boston, MA: Houghton Mifflin, 1973. 298 p. (Peterson Field Guide series, 20.) $21.00 (paper). ISBN 039597514X (paper).

Robins, C. Richard and G. Carleton Ray. *A Field Guide to Atlantic Coast Fishes of North America*. Boston, MA: Houghton Mifflin, 1986. 354 p. (Peterson Field Guide series, 32.) $20.95, $14.95 (paper). ISBN 0395318521, 0395391989 (paper).

Schmidt, Gerald D. *CRC Handbook of Tapeworm Identification*. Boca Raton, FL: CRC Press, 1986. 675 p. $265.00. ISBN 084933280X. Keys to the identification of nearly 4,000 species of tapeworms with numerous illustrations of adult tapeworm morphology. The only worldwide key to tapeworm identification in print at the time of writing.

Sibley, Charles G. and John E. Ahlquist. *Phylogeny and Classification of Birds: A Study in Molecular Evolution*. New Haven, CT: Yale University Press, 1990. 976 p. $140.00. ISBN 0300040857. "The goals of our study were the reconstruction of the phylogeny of the groups of living birds and the derivation of a new classification scheme based on the phylogeny." For each family of birds, the authors describe past efforts at classifying the species, the present the evidence from their own DNA hybridization tests.

Sibley, Charles G. and Burt L. Monroe. *Distribution and Taxonomy of Birds of the World*. New Haven, CT: Yale University Press, 1990. 1111 p. $140.00. ISBN 0300049692. The goals of this work are to delineate the present distribution of the birds of the world, list the species in a classification based on DNA (see Sibley and Alquist, previous), and offer a gazetteer and maps for locating regions mentioned in the atlas. The indexes are by scientific and English name. A *Supplement* was published in 1993 with updates and corrections.

Sibley, David. *The Sibley Guide to Birds*. New York: Knopf, 2000. 544 p. $35.00 (paper). ISBN 0679451226 (paper). A major new field guide, with multiple illustrations for most species. Too large to be a truly portable field guide, but a good reference source for libraries or birders.

Udvardy, Miklos D. F. *National Audubon Society Field Guide to North American Birds, Western Region*. Rev. ed. New York: Knopf, 1994. 822 p. $19.00. ISBN 0679428518.

Walters, Michael. *The Complete Birds of the World*. North Pomfret, VT: David & Charles, 1980. 340 p. ISBN 0715376667. This work "attempts to list every bird species known to exist or to have existed in recent (i.e., post-Pleistocene) times." More than just a checklist, it provides in very telegraphic form not only information on Latin name, authority, and English name, but also distribution, habitat, food preferences, nest site, clutch size, incubation share of the sexes, and fledging. The indexes, unfortunately, are only to the family name.

Wells, M. G. *World Bird Species Checklist: With Alternative English and Scientific Names.* Bushey, England: Worldlist, 1998. 671 p. ISBN: 0953242005. Includes over 18,000 alternate scientific names and 27,000 alternate English common names found in field guides and the scientific literature. These names represent 9,941 actual species. The checklist is designed to provide a link between scientific and lay studies and includes information on new taxons. Species are listed by scientific name, with their associated common names and alternate scientific names.

Wilson, Don E. and F. Russell Cole. *Common Names of Mammals of the World*. Washington, DC: Smithsonian Institution Press, 2000. 204 p. $19.95. ISBN 1560983833. Provides an authoritative list of standardized and unique English names for all 4,629 mammal species of the world. Includes order and family names as well as those of genera and species.

CLASSIFICATION, NOMENCLATURE, AND SYSTEMATICS

Amphibiaweb: An Information System for Amphibian Conservation Biology. Berkeley, CA: Museum of Vertebrate Zoology, University of California, Berkeley, 2000. URL: http://elib.cs.berkeley.edu/aw/. This database provides taxonomic information on all species of amphibians taken from Frost's *Amphibian Species of the World* (see following text). The intent is to provide detailed taxonomic and ecological information on all 5,000 species of amphibians of the world. At the time of viewing, pages for common species such as *Rana pipiens* and *Bufo americanus* contained only taxonomic information, photographs, and links to museum collections. Other pages such as *Bufo bufo* were more complete, with description, life history, distribution, and references. The site also includes information on the decline in amphibian populations worldwide.

Bulletin of Zoological Nomenclature. v. 1– , 1943– . London: International Trust for Zoological Nomenclature. Quarterly. $165.00. ISSN 0007-5167. The official organ of the International Commission on Zoological Nomenclature. Contains notices prescribed by the International Congress of Zoology, announcements, opinions, new and revived cases, comments, and proposals.

Collins, Joseph T. *Standard Common and Current Scientific Names for North American Amphibians and Reptiles*. 4th ed. St. Louis, MO: Society for the Study of Amphibians and Reptiles, 1997. 40 p. (Herpetological circular, 25.) Includes publication date and describer, and approved scientific and common names as well as appendices covering Hawaiian and alien species.

Common and Scientific Names of Aquatic Invertebrates from the United States and Canada: Mollusks. 2nd ed. D. D. Trugeon, et al., eds. Bethesda, MD: American Fisheries Society, 1998. 526 p. ISBN 1888569018, 1888569093 (CD-ROM). (American Fisheries Society special publication, 26.) CD-ROM contains full text of book in PDF format.

Common and Scientific Names of Fishes from the United States and Canada. 5th ed. C. Richard Robins, et al., eds. Bethesda, MD: American Fisheries Society, 1991. 183 p. (American Fisheries Society, 20.) $32.00, $24.00 (paper). ISBN 0913235709, 0913235695 (paper). Previous editions published as *A List of Common and Scientific Names of Fishes* . . . Contains scientific and common names, occurrence, references for first description, and appendices on exotics and hybrid fishes.

Crocodilian, Tuatara, and Turtle Species of the World: A Taxonomic and Geographic Reference. F. Wayne King and Russell L. Burke, eds. Washington, DC: Association of Systematics Collections, 1989. 216 p. $29.00. ISBN 0942924150. Contains species, taxonomic problems, type and location, distribution, comments, status, and common name(s).

Eschmeyer, William N. *Catalog of Fishes*. San Francisco, CA: California Academy of Sciences, 1998. 3 v. plus CD-ROM. $150.00. ISBN 0940228475. Lists genera in alphabetical order with name, author, date, type specimen, remarks, and status. Separate sections list names by class and literature cited. Updates the author's *Catalog of the Genera of Recent Fishes*, published in 1990. Available on the Web at http://www.calacademy.org/research/ichthyology/catalog/. The online version includes all species, genera, and references, along with the classification, introduction, and list of museum abbreviations from the print version, but excludes the appendices and other material.

Frank, Norman and Erica Ramus. *A Complete Guide to Scientific and Common Names of Reptiles and Amphibians of the World*. Pottsville, PA: N G Publishers, 1995. 377 p. ISBN 0964103230. Contains standard common names for over 12,000 species. In three parts: index to genera, taxonomic listing, and index to common names. "A desk reference for herpetologists."

Frost, Darrel R. Amphibian Species of the World: An Online Reference. New York: American Museum of Natural History, 2000. Version 2.20 (September 1, 2000). URL: http://research.amnh.org/herpetology/amphibia/index.html. (Viewed December 6, 2000.) Provides scientific name, authority, year of publication, type species, specimen, and location, distribution, and status. Updates the author's *Amphibian Species of the World: A Taxonomic and Geographical Reference*, published in 1985.

International Commission on Zoological Nomenclature. *International Code of Zoological Nomenclature*. 4th ed. London: International Trust for Zoological Nomenclature, 1999. 306 p. ISBN: 0853010064. In English and French.

Liner, Ernest A. *Scientific and Common Names for the Amphibians and Reptiles of Mexico in English and Spanish = Nombres Científicos y Comunes en Inglés y Español de los Anfibios y los Reptiles de México*. St. Louis, MO: Society for the Study of Amphibians and Reptiles, 1994. 113 p. (Herpetological circular, no. 23.) $12.00. ISBN 091698432X. Lists the "best practice" scientific name for Mexican herps, along with common names in English (some made up by the author), and common names used by local people.

Luca, Florenza de. *Taxonomic Authority List: Aquatic Sciences and Fisheries Information System*. Rome: Food and Agriculture Organization of the United Nations, 1988. 465 p. (Casfis Ref. Series, No. 8.) $55.00. ISBN 9251027722. Created by the Aquatic Sciences and Fisheries Information System for use in preparing the *FAO Yearbook of Fishery Statistics* and the *Aquatic Sciences and Fisheries Abstracts*. Contains over 10,000 terms, in systematic and alphabetical lists, with the date and author of the term.

McKenna, Malcolm C. and Susan K. Bell. *Classification of Mammals Above the Species Level*. New York: Columbia University Press, 1997. 631 p. $190.00, $50.00 (paper). ISBN 023111012X, 0231110138 (paper). A revision of George Gaylord Simpson's mammalian classification system of 1945. Lists all names that have been used for mammalian groups above the species level, whether currently accepted or not.

Nomenclator Zoologicus, v. 1–9, 1939–94. London: Zoological Society of London. ''A continuous record of the bibliographical origins of the names of every genus and subgenus in zoology published since the 10th edn of Linnaeus' Systema Naturae in 1758.'' The four volumes of the main work cover the period 1758–1935, with supplements occurring approximately every decade thereafter. The combined volumes include over 300,000 names listed alphabetically with the original citation and an indication of which animal group the name belongs to. Only the supplements are in print.

Official Lists and Indexes of Names and Works in Zoology. R. V. Melville and J. D. D. Smith, eds. London: International Trust for Zoological Nomenclature, 1987. 366 p. $110.00. ISBN 0853010048.   Contains scientific names and titles of works that have been voted on by the International Commission on Zoological Nomenclature and published in the *Bulletin of Zoological Nomenclature* up to the end of 1985. In addition to a systematic index and bibliographic references, it contains 4 main sections: family-group names, generic names, specific names, and titles of works. Contains material from earlier editions of *Official Index of Rejected and Invalid Family Group Names in Zoology*, *Official Index of Rejected and Invalid Works in Zoological Nomenclature*, *Official List of Family Group Names in Zoology*, and *Official List of Works Approved as Available for Zoological Nomenclature*.

Robins, C. Richard and Reeve M. Bailey. *World Fishes Important to North Americans: Exclusive of Species from the Continental Waters of the United States and Canada*. Bethesda, MD: American Fisheries Society, 1991. 243 p. (American Fisheries Society special publication, no. 21.) $38.50 (paper). ISBN: 091323 5547, 0913235539 (paper).   Provides standard common names for important species of fishes. Each entry contains the common and scientific names, alternate common names, reason for considering the species important, range and habitat, and remarks.

Wilson, Don E. and F. Russell Cole. *Common Names of Mammals of the World*. Washington, DC: Smithsonian Institution Press, 2000. 204 p. $19.95 (paper). ISBN 1560983833 (paper).   ''This book provides a complete, authoritative list of standardized and unique English names for all 4,629 of the currently recognized mammal species of the world. It establishes common names for hundreds of mammals that have previously been known only by their Latin names. The book's list includes order and family names as well as those of genera and species.''

DICTIONARIES AND ENCYCLOPEDIAS

Allaby, Michael. *Dictionary of Zoology*. 2nd ed. New York: Oxford University Press, 1999. 508 p. (Oxford Paperback Reference.) $15.95 (paper). ISBN 0192800760 (paper). Based on the 1985 *Oxford Dictionary of Natural History*. For students and the general public. Revised edition of *Concise Oxford Dictionary of Zoology*.

Banister, Keith and Andrew Campbell. *The Encyclopedia of Aquatic Life*. New York: Facts on File, 1985. 349 p. $36.00. ISBN 0816012571. Covers fishes, aquatic invertebrates, and aquatic mammals (whales, dolphins, and manatees only). The editors attempted to "distill their knowledge to give the reader a flavor of the essence of" aquatic animals.

Birds of North America: Life Histories for the 21st Century. Alan F. Poole, Peter Stettenheim, and Frank B. Gill, eds. Washington, DC: American Ornithologist's Union; Philadelphia, PA: Academy of Natural Sciences, 1992– . v. $175 per volume. Life history accounts of over 700 species of birds. Issued as separate self-contained profiles; expected to consist of 18 volumes of 40 accounts each. Each account includes extensive bibliography. Updates A. C. Bent's *Life Histories of North American Birds*.

Cambridge Encyclopedia of Ornithology. Michael Brooke and Tim Birkhead, eds. New York: Cambridge University Press, 1991. 362 p. $49.50. ISBN 0521362059. Contains extensive information on all aspects of ornithology, including anatomy, behavior, distribution, ecology, and the relationship of humans with birds. Also includes a survey of bird orders. Very well illustrated.

Choate, Ernest. *The Dictionary of American Bird Names*. Rev. ed. Boston, MA: Harvard Common Press, 1985. 226 p. $10.95 (paper). ISBN 0876451172 (paper). Discusses common and scientific names for birds and their origins. Includes obscure and archaic terms, and has a biographical appendix listing American ornithologists and people who had birds named after themselves.

Cox, Randall T. *Birder's Dictionary*. Helena, MT: Falcon Press, 1996. 186 p. $8.95 (paper). ISBN 1560444231 (paper). A compact dictionary containing ornithological terms that birders might need to define, including biological, anatomical, physiological, behavioral, and taxonomic terms. Includes anatomical illustrations and a listing of bird orders of North America and the world.

A Dictionary of Birds. Bruce Campbell and Elizabeth Lack, eds. Vermillion, SD: Buteo Books, 1985. 670 p. $89.00. ISBN 0931130123. Contains definitions and extended essays on ornithological terms, including systematics, behavior, and biology.

Elsevier's Dictionary of Invertebrates: in Latin, English, French, German, and Spanish. Ilja Okáli, Miroslava Dulová, and Ing. Pavel Mokrán, eds. New York: Elsevier Science BV, 2000. 496 p. $170.00. ISBN 0444505350. Contains approximately 4,000 names of species and subspecies of invertebrates (excluding insects) worldwide. Standard common names are given in English, French, German, and Spanish, with separate indexes for each language.

Encyclopedia of Birds. 2nd ed. Joseph Forshaw, ed. San Diego, CA: Academic Press, 1998. 240 p. (Natural World Series.) $39.95. ISBN 0122623401.

Encyclopedia of Fishes. 2nd ed. John R. Paxton and William N. Eschmeyer, eds. San Diego, CA: Academic Press, 1998. 240 p. (Natural World Series.) $39.95. ISBN 0125476655.

*Encyclopedia of Mammals.*2nd ed. Edwin Gould and George McKay, eds. San Diego, CA: Academic Press, 1998. 240 p. (Natural World Series.) $39.95. ISBN 0122936701. A beautifully illustrated overview of mammal species.

Encyclopedia of Marine Mammals. William F. Perrin, Bernd Wursig, and J. G. M. Thewissen, eds. San Diego, CA: Academic Press, 2001. 1,200 p. $99.95. ISBN 0125513402. Contains 285 articles on all aspects of marine mammals, from anatomy to human interactions.

Encyclopedia of Reptiles and Amphibians. 2nd ed. Harold G. Cogger and Richard G. Zweifel, eds. San Diego, CA: Academic Press, 1998. 240 p. (Natural World Series.) $39.95. ISBN 0121785602.

Nomenclatural Glossary for Zoology. York, England: BIOSIS UK, 1996– . URL: http://www.biosis.org/free_resources/nomglos.html. Covers terminology dealing with zoological systematics and nomenclature, and includes terms listed in the glossary of the new Fourth Edition of the International Code of Zoological Nomenclature.

Gotch, A. F. *Latin Names Explained: A Guide to the Scientific Classification of Reptiles, Birds, and Mammals.* New York: Facts on File, 1996. 714 p. $55.00. ISBN 0816033773. The author explains the meanings of scientific names for many of the world's best-known reptiles, birds, and mammals. He gives both the reason for choosing a particular Greek or Latin word and its definition.

Grzimek's Animal Life Encyclopedia. Bernhard Grzimek, ed. New York: Van Nostrand Reinhold Co., 1972–75. 13 v. The grand old classic, covering all animals. While rather old, there is still nothing to compare with *Grizmek's* for coverage of the animal world. Translation of *Tierleben.*

Grzimek's Encyclopedia of Mammals. Bernhard Grzimek, ed. New York: McGraw-Hill, 1990. 5 v. ISBN 0079095089 (set). A worthy successor to *Griz-*

mek's Animal Life Encyclopedia, previous. Has beautiful color photographs and extensive discussion of mammalian species. Translation of *Grzimek's Enzyklopadie Saugetiere.*

Hayssen, Virginia, Ari van Tienhoven, and Ans van Tienhoven. *Asdell's Patterns of Mammalian Reproduction: A Compendium of Species-Specific Data.* Ithaca, NY: Comstock Publishing Associates, 1993. 1023 p. $90.00. ISBN 0801417538. This compendium lists information on mammalian reproduction, with the exception of well-known domesticated and laboratory species such as cows and rats. It is organized taxonomically, with a summary of the reproduction of each family and order. This summary is followed by a table listing species-specific data, with citations to over 12,000 original articles. The authors also provide a list of the Mammalian Species Accounts published by the American Society of Mammalogists and a list of core journals. There are indexes to the common names of the most well-known mammals and to scientific names. Revised edition of the 2nd edition of *Patterns of Mammalian Reproduction*, S.A. Asdell, 1964.

Jacobs, George J. *Dictionary of Vertebrate Zoology, English-Russian/Russian-English: Emphasizing Anatomy, Amphibians, and Reptiles.* Washington, DC: Smithsonian Press, 1978. 48 p. $8.50 (paper). ISBN 0874745519 (paper). As the subtitle suggests, this dictionary is intended primarily for the herpetologist. Terms are not defined, but rather are translated between Russian and English. Russian common names for species are translated to the Latin name, not the English common name, for greater clarity.

Jobling, James A. *A Dictionary of Scientific Bird Names.* New York: Oxford University Press, 1991. 272 p. $29.95. ISBN 0198546343. Gives derivation and meaning of all currently accepted scientific bird names.

Leahy, Christopher W. *The Birdwatcher's Companion: An Encyclopedic Handbook of North American Birdlife.* New York: Hill and Wang, 1982. 917 p. ISBN 089030365. A dictionary of birding and ornithological terms, with accounts of the families of birds of North America, birding terms, birding "hot spots," and biographies, as well as a phylogenetic list, list of vagrant bird species, and a birder's calendar. One-stop shopping for the birder, but also useful for libraries.

Lodge, Walter. *Birds: Alternative Names: A World Checklist.* New York: Sterling, 1991. 208 p. $19.95. ISBN 0713722673. Provides a list of birds that have multiple alternate names in English that are in common use. This does not include local or dialect names. The names are arranged by taxon, then alphabetic by scientific name.

Names of North American birds. New York: National Audubon Society, 1997–. URL: http://www.audubon.org/bird/na-bird.html. "The list below is provided for your reference when writing about birds. It includes about 1,975 species occurring in North America, Mexico, and Hawaii. The English, or common, name is in the left-hand column and the corresponding Latin, or scientific, name is on the right.''

Nelson, Joseph S. *Fishes of the World*. 3rd ed. New York: Wiley, 1994. 600 p. $150.00. ISBN 0471547131.   The purpose of this book is ''to present a modern introductory systematic treatment of all major fish groups.'' To the family level. Includes number of species or genera per family, range, and description.

Preston-Mafham, Rod and Ken Preston-Mafham. *The Encyclopedia of Land Invertebrate Behaviour*. See Chapter 12, ''Entomology,'' for full annotation. Includes invertebrates such as crustaceans, millipedes, and platyhelminths.

Preston-Mafham, Rod and Ken Preston-Mafham. *Primates of the World*. New York: Facts on File, 1992. 192 p. $29.95, $19.95 (paper). ISBN 0816027455, 0713727918 (paper).   Provides an overview of primates. For students and the general public. One of the . . . *of the World* series published by Facts on File. Other titles include *Grasshoppers and Mantids of the World*, *Frogs and Toads of the World*, and *Whales of the World*.

Rojo, Alfonso L. *Dictionary of Evolutionary Fish Osteology*. Boca Raton, FL: CRC Press, 1991. 273 p. $79.95. ISBN 0849342147.   In English, French, German, Latin, Russian, and Spanish.

Stachowitsch, Michael. *The Invertebrates: An Illustrated Glossary*. New York: Wiley-Liss, 1992. 676 p. $310.00, $165.00 (paper). ISBN 0471832944, 0471561924 (paper).   Contains over 10,000 entries and 1,100 figures in two sections, the first defining anatomical features in a taxonomical arrangement, and the second with adjectives describing modifications of the features. The German equivalent of each term is also given.

Wheeler, Alwyne C. *The World Encyclopedia of Fishes*. London: Macdonald and Queen Anne Press, 1985. 368 p. ISBN 0356107159.   Numerous color plates in addition to line drawings. The dictionary section lists fish species by scientific name and includes information on distribution, size, habits, etc. Common names are cross-referenced to the scientific name. Nelson, see previous text, only lists families and subfamilies.

GUIDES TO INTERNET RESOURCES

The Web is a treasure trove of taxonomic information for animals of all kinds. Many of the Web pages are very technical in nature, and are often specialized. However, some popular groups such as birds or mammals are featured in many

Web sites aimed at amateurs. The major taxonomic sites such as the Tree of Life that cover both plants and animals are covered in Chapter 3, ''General Sources.''

Animal Diversity Web. URL: http://animaldiversity.ummz.umich.edu/. This site is ''an online database of animal natural history, distribution, classification, and conservation biology at the University of Michigan.'' It consists of species accounts written by zoology students, plus descriptions of higher orders prepared by professional biologists. As with most other projects of this scope, it is not complete. Because the project depends on volunteer assistance from students, some ''sexy'' orders are nearly completely covered (e.g., whales and dolphins), while other less attractive groups such as rodents are more sparsely listed. The student-authored species accounts follow a standard template and are reviewed by professionals.

The Electronic Zoo. URL: http://netvet.wustl.edu/e-zoo.htm. Ken Boschert, author. St. Louis, MO: Washington University. Categorizes and lists many Web sites on animals and veterinary medicine, covering everything from animal taxonomic groups to fictional animals to career information for would-be vets. This popular site began life in 1993 as a Gopher list, and has been updated since by the same person.

The Internet Resource Guide for Zoology. URL: http://www.biosis.org/free_resources/resource_guide.html. An excellent starting point for zoological research on the Web. Contains a number of links to sites from a listing of zoological conferences and nomenclature resources to a ''Guide to the Animal Kingdom for Students and Educators.'' Also provides an extensive listing of Web resources arranged by taxonomic group.

GUIDES TO THE LITERATURE

Bell, George H. and Diane B. Rhoades. *A Guide to the Zoological Literature*. Englewood, CO: Libraries Unlimited, 1994. 504 p. $95.00. ISBN 1563080826. An annotated guide to zoology, with general reference sources and sources for major groups of animals, such as fishes or arthropods. A detailed source, especially useful for the extensive lists of field guides, checklists, and other identification sources.

Miller, Melanie Ann. *Birds: A Guide to the Literature*. New York: Garland, 1986. 887 p. $86.00. (Garland reference library of the humanities.) ISBN 0824087100. An annotated list of books written about birds, both popular and technical.

HANDBOOKS

Blackwelder, Richard E. and George S. Garoian. *CRC Handbook of Animal Diversity*. Boca Raton, FL: CRC Press, 1986. 555 p. $216.95. ISBN 0849329922. This handbook is intended as a reference to aspects of animals that can be studied comparatively, especially aspects such as anatomy, physiology, and classification. Arranged by topic such as life cycles, morphology, and behavior.

Chiasson, Robert B. *Laboratory Anatomy of the White Rat*. 5th ed. Dubuque, IA: W. C. Brown, 1988. 129 p. (Laboratory anatomy series.) $36.25. ISBN 0697051323. A standard laboratory manual for rat dissection. The author has also written dissection manuals for several other species, including cat, fetal pig, frog and toad, mink, and perch.

Dunning, John B. *CRC Handbook of Avian Body Masses*. Boca Raton, FL: CRC Press, 1993. 371 p. $104.95. ISBN 0849342589. Includes all known estimates of bird body mass found in the literature. The information provided for each entry includes Latin name, sex and number of individuals sampled, mean, standard deviation, and range of the estimate, collecting season, and citation to the original publication. A section lists body masses and composition for migrant birds in the eastern United States with their wet mass, dry mass, fat-free mass, and ash-free mass. The index is by genus.

Gilbert, Stephen G. *Pictorial Anatomy of the Cat*. Rev. ed. Seattle, WA: University of Washington Press, 1975. 120 p. $20.00. ISBN 0295978678. One of the standard anatomical atlases for the cat; also available in an abridged version (*Outline of Cat Anatomy*). Gilbert has also written and illustrated other laboratory manuals for the fetal pig, the frog, and the dogfish shark.

Goddard, Jerome. *Physician's Guide to Arthropods of Medical Importance*. Boca Raton, FL: CRC Press, 1993. 332 p. $110.00. ISBN 084935160X.

Handbook of Laboratory Animal Science. Per Svendsen and Jann Hau, eds. Boca Raton, FL: CRC Press, 1994. 2 v. $146.95 (v. 1), $129.95 (v. 2). ISBN 084934378X (v. 1), 0849343909 (v. 2). Volume 1 covers the selection and handling of animals in biomedical research (including experimental methods, alternatives to animal experiments, ethics, and legislation), while volume 2 covers animal models.

Handbook of Protoctista: The Structure, Cultivation, Habitats, and Life Histories of the Eukaryotic Microorganisms and their Descendants. . . . Lynn Margulis, et al., ed. See Chapter 8, "Microbiology and Immunology," for full annotation.

Kardong, Kenneth V. and Edward J. Zalisko. *Comparative Vertebrate Anatomy: A Laboratory Dissection Guide*. Boston, MA: WCB/McGraw-Hill, 1998. 214 p.

$55.31. ISBN 0697378799. Covers cat, shark, salamander, and lamprey dissection.

Silva, Marina and John A. Downing. *CRC Handbook of Mammalian Body Masses*. Boca Raton, FL: CRC Press, 1995. 368 p. $149.95. ISBN 0849327903. Contains data on nearly 2,600 species of mammals, including minimal and maximum body sizes for both males and females. There are extensive references.

HISTORIES

Barrow, Mark V. *A Passion for Birds: American Ornithology after Audubon*. Princeton, NJ: Princeton University Press, 1998. 326 p. $77.50, $19.95 (paper). ISBN 0691044023, 0691049548 (paper). The author tells of the tensions between amateur and professional bird people and the changes in the bird lovers' ethos from killing to conserving birds. A fascinating story, full of interesting characters.

Bridson, Gavin. *The History of Natural History: An Annotated Bibliography*. See Chapter 3, "General Sources" for full annotation. Includes extensive bibliography on the history of zoology.

Collection Building in Ichthyology and Herpetology. Theodore W. Pietsch and William D. Anderson, Jr., eds. Lawrence, KS: American Society of Ichthyologists and Herpetologists, 1997. 593 p. (Special publication, American Society of Ichthyologists and Herpetologists, no. 3.) ISBN 0935868917. Covers the history of several major museum collections in ichthyology and herpetology throughout the world. Includes biographical information on several major figures in the field. The results of a symposium held in 1996.

Farber, Paul Lawrence. *Discovering Birds*: *The Emergence of Ornithology as a Scientific Discipline: 1760–1850*. Baltimore, MD: Johns Hopkins University Press, 1997. 191 p. $15.95 (paper). ISBN 0801855373 (paper). Concentrates on the development of ornithology as a science out of natural history. Originally published in 1982.

International History of Mammalogy. Keir B. Sterling, ed. Bel Air, MD: One World Press, 1987. v. $25.00 (v. 1, paper). ISBN 0910485003 (v. 1), 0910485011 (v. 1, paper). "The plan of this work is simple. It is to publish a series of chapters by authorities from every country of the world on the development of mammalogy in each of these nations during the modern scientific period." So far only volume 1 has been published, covering Eastern Europe and Fennoscandia.

Klopfer, Peter H. *Politics and People in Ethology: Personal Reflections on the Study of Animal Behavior*. Lewisburg, PA: Bucknell University Press, 1999. 161

p. $34.50. ISBN 0838754058.   The author, a well-known behavioral ecologist, tells of his career and the personalities of the ethologists and other animal behaviorists that he has met. This includes famous researchers such as G. Evelyn Hutchinson, Konrad Lorenz, and Robert MacArthur. A final chapter discusses Klopfer's musings about the ethics, philosophy, and future of the field.

Mearns, Barbara and Richard Mearns. *The Bird Collectors*. San Diego, CA: Academic Press, 1998. 472 p. $59.50. ISBN 0124874401.   The authors discuss the purpose and history of bird collecting, discussing the activities of people from professional ornithologists to amateurs and world travelers who provided museums with bird specimens. While these collectors enthusiastically shot birds and raided nests, activities that are now frowned upon, their activities were essential in creating the modern field of ornithology. Provides brief biographies of 600 individuals from the late eighteenth century to date who collected birds, along with numerous photographs.

Montgomery, Sy. *Walking with the Great Apes: Jane Goodall, Dian Fossey, Birute Galdikas*. Boston, MA: Houghton Mifflin, 1991. 280 p. $15.00 (paper). ISBN 0395515971, 0395611563 (paper).   The story of the three most famous primatologists of modern times.

Stresemann, Erwin. *Ornithology from Aristotle to the Present*. Cambridge, MA: Harvard University Press, 1975. 432 p. ISBN 0674644859.   Translation of *Entwicklung der Ornthologie* (1951). Covers the development of ornithology up to the 1950s, with emphasis on European activities. Ernst Mayr provided an appendix, ''Materials for a History of American Ornithology'' for this translation.

Women in Ichthyology: An Anthology in Honour of ET, Ro and Genie. Eugene K. Balon, Michael N. Bruton, and David L. G. Noakes, eds. Boston, MA: Kluwer Academic, 1994. 456 p. (Developments in Environmental Biology of Fishes, no. 15). $415.00. ISBN 0792331656.   Focuses on three well-known women ichthyologists: Ethelwynn Trewavas, Rosemary Lowe-McConnell, and Eugenie Clark, discussing both their personal histories and their research. An introductory article on early women ichthyologists provides information on 16 women, most of whom worked in the first half of the twentieth century. Reprinted from *Developments in Environmental Biology of Fishes*, 41(1–4): 7–125.

Zoo and Aquarium History: Ancient Animal Collections to Zoological Gardens. Vernon N. Kisling, Jr., ed. Boca Raton, FL: CRC Press, 2001. 415 p. $69.95. ISBN 084932100X.   The first major work to cover the history of zoos and aquaria in depth. After covering animal collections and menageries in the ancient world (up to about the Renaissance), the focus switches to geographical locations. While North American and European zoos get the most attention because their historical information is more readily available, all parts of the world are included. The authors tell a number of interesting stories, such as the fate of zoos during the World Wars and the long history of our fascination with giant pandas.

METHODS AND TECHNIQUES

Bibby, Colin J., et al. *Bird Census Techniques.* 2nd ed. San Diego, CA: Academic, 2000. 350 p. $55.00. ISBN 0120958317. "This guide is offered largely to people lacking the time or facilities to read and assess the extensive and often conflicting bird census literature." The authors provide general information about the design of bird censuses and describe many methods for performing them, including line transects, marking, and so on.

Cailliet, Gregor M., Milton S. Love, and Alfred W. Ebeling. *Fishes: A Field and Laboratory Manual on their Structure, Identification, and Natural History.* Belmont, CA: Wadsworth, 1986. 194 p. ISBN 0534055567 (paper). Includes laboratory exercises and methods for studying the various aspects of ichthyology such as dissecting and identifying fish in the lab, and capture methods in the field.

CRC Handbook of Census Methods for Terrestrial Vertebrates. David E. Davis, ed. Boca Raton, FL: CRC Press, 1982. 397 p. $261.95. ISBN 0849329701. Brief descriptions of census methods for about 130 species of vertebrates are included, plus a few non-terrestrial species such as coastal whales and manatees where the census methods are useful for other species. There is a separate chapter on calculations and statistics.

The Experimental Animal in Biomedical Research. Bernard E. Rollin, ed. Boca Raton, FL: CRC Press, 1990–5. 2 v. $294.95 (v. 1), $239.95 (v. 2). ISBN 0849349818 (v. 1), 0849349826 (v. 2). Tries to balance ethical and practical aspects of dealing with laboratory animal experimentation. Written at a fairly basic level for researchers who have not had to deal with the issues before. Volume 1 is subtitled *A Survey of Scientific and Ethical Issues for Investigators* and volume 2 is *Care, Husbandry, and Well-Being; an Overview by Species.*

Fry, Frederic L. *Captive Invertebrates: A Guide to their Biology and Husbandry.* Malabar, FL: Krieger, 1992. 135 p. $29.50. ISBN 0894645552. Covers most invertebrate species used for scientific studies or kept as pets. Each group is described, then housing, water, nutrition, reproduction, and medical disorders are discussed. The author also includes an appendix listing commercial sources for invertebrates.

Measuring and Monitoring Biological Diversity: Standard Methods for Amphibians. Washington, DC: Smithsonian Press, 1994. 364 p. (Biological diversity handbook series.) $49.00, $17.95 (paper). ISBN 1560982705, 1560982845 (pa-

per).   As well as the standard methods for monitoring amphibian diversity, this
handbook includes information on handling live amphibians, recording frog calls,
preparing specimens, and vendors selling equipment for amphibian studies.

Molecular Zoology: Advances, Strategies, and Protocols. Joan D. Ferraris and
Stephen R. Palumbi, eds. New York: Wiley-Liss, 1996. 580 p. $145.00, $64.95.
ISBN 0471144495, 0471144614 (paper).   Presents papers from a 1995 symposium. The book is in two sections, one discussing research strategies incorporat-
ing molecular biology into research on physiological, ecological, and evolutionary studies and the other section presenting 60 protocols.

Nagorsen, D. W. and R.L. Peterson. *Mammal Collector's Manual: A Guide for
Collecting, Documenting, and Preparing Mammal Specimens for Scientific Research.* Toronto: Royal Ontario Museum, 1980. 79 p. $8.85. ISBN
0888542550.   Has methods of collecting mammals in the field, documentation,
preservation, and shipping specimens.

Protocols in Protozoology. J.J. Lee and A.T. Soldo, eds. Lawrence, KS: Society
of Protozoology, 1992. ISBN 0935868577 (v. 1).   This is the first volume of a
projected series of protocols. The present volume provides protocols for isolation,
culture, nutrition, and bioassay; ecological methods; fixation, staining, and microscopic techniques; molecular biological and genetic methods; and educational
experiments. About 140 protocols are described.

Skalski, John R. and Douglas S. Robson. *Techniques for Wildlife Investigations:
Design and Analysis of Capture Data.* San Diego, CA: Academic Press, 1992.
237 p. $59.95. ISBN 0126476756.   Provides information on designing and car-
rying out mark-recapture studies, with special emphasis on proper statistical
methods and randomization.

*Survey Designs and Statistical Methods for the Estimation of Avian Population
Trends.* John R. Sauer and Sam Droege, eds. Washington, DC: U.S. Dept. of the
Interior, Fish and Wildlife Service, 1990. 166 p. (Biological report, 90[1].)   The
proceedings of a workshop on the analysis of avian population trends, held in
1988. The first part discusses various survey methods such as the Audubon
Christmas bird counts, while the second discusses methods of statistical analysis
of trends using these surveys. A final section offers examples using trends in
scissor-tailed flycatcher populations.

Thompson, William L., Gary C. White, and Charles Gowan. *Monitoring Vertebrate Populations.* San Diego, CA: Academic Press, 1998. 365 p. $74.00. ISBN
0126889600.   A ''general reference to biological and resource managers who
have been charged with monitoring vertebrate numbers within some area.'' Provides basic tools for meeting objectives within a budget. In addition to general

survey techniques, the authors also provide information on surveying different types of vertebrates.

The UFAW Handbook on the Care and Management of Laboratory Animals. 7th ed. Trevor Poole, ed. Malden, MA: Blackwell Science, 1999. 2 v. $289.95 (set). ISBN 0632051329 (v. 1), 0632051310 (v. 2), 0632051337 (set). The Universities Federation for Animal Welfare (UFAW), is an international organization that deals with issues related to research on animals. This handbook provides detailed information on caring for the entire range of laboratory animals. Entries provide standard biological data such as temperature requirements and normal concentrations of hormones in the blood as well as housing requirements, proper feeding, and how to handle animals. Volume 1 covers terrestrial vertebrates and volume 2 covers aquatic and amphibian vertebrates and invertebrates.

TEXTBOOKS AND TREATISES

Alexander, R. McNeill. *Animals.* New York: Cambridge University Press, 1990. 509 p. $37.50 (paper). ISBN 0521343917, 052134865X (paper). A survey of the animal kingdom; revised from Alexander's earlier works, *The Invertebrates* and *The Chordates.*

Animal Anatomy on File. Rev. ed. New York: Facts on File, 1999. 1 v. $165.00. ISBN 0816038759. Contains 250 diagrams of the anatomy (internal and external) of over 50 animal species, from sponges to whales.

Avian Biology. Donald S. Farner and James R. King, eds. New York: Academic, 1971–93. 9 v. $135.00 (v. 9). ISBN 0122494091 (v. 9). This treatise is intended to update A. J. Marshall's *Biology and Comparative Physiology of Birds.* It covers all aspects of bird biology.

Barnes, R. S. K., P. Calow, and P. J. W. Olive. *The Invertebrates: A New Synthesis.* 2nd ed. Boston, MA: Blackwell Scientific Publications, 1993. 488 p. $44.95 (paper). ISBN 0632031255, 0632031271 (paper). For undergraduates. Includes both systematic and functional treatment of invertebrates.

Berthold, Peter. *Bird Migration: A General Survey.* New York: Oxford University Press, 1993. 239 p. $35.00 (paper). ISBN 0198546920, 0198546912 (paper). A general overview of current research on the topic of bird migration, intended for students and laypeople, as well as researchers.

Biochemistry and Molecular Biology of Fishes. Peter W. Hochachka and T. P. Mommsen, eds. New York: Elsevier, 1991–5. 5 v. *Environmental and Ecological Biochemistry*, v. 5. $260.50 (v. 5). ISBN 0444821775 (v. 5), 0444891854 (set). This set was designed to gather together the scattered literature on the molecular biology and biochemistry of fishes for both students and researchers.

Biology of Crustacea. Dorothy E. Bliss, ed. New York: Academic Press, 1982–5. 10 v. Price varies. Covers all areas of crustacean biology, including systematics, embryology, neurobiology, anatomy and physiology, ecology, and economic aspects.

Biology of the Reptilia. Carl Gans, ed. New York: Academic Press, 1969– . v. Price varies. This treatise is "addressed to and designed for specialists who need a summary on the status of our knowledge in a particular system or process in the reptilia. It is hence intended for people who have at least some minimal background in the areas covered." Currently up to volume 19G, *Visceral Organs*.

Bird, Alan F. and Jean Bird. *The Structure of Nematodes*. 2nd ed. San Diego, CA: Academic Press, 1991. 316 p. $111.00. ISBN 0120996510. A comprehensive reference on the anatomy and pathology of free-living and parasitic nematodes.

Bone, Q., N. B. Marshall, and J.H.S. Blaxter. *Biology of Fishes*. 2nd ed. Chapman and Hall, 1994. 288 p. $143.95, $59.95 (paper). ISBN 075140022X, 0412741407 (paper).

Brusca, Richard C. and Gary J. Brusca. *Invertebrates*. Sunderland, MA: Sinauer Associates, 1990. 922 p. $81.95. ISBN 0878930981. A compendium of information on the invertebrates, from metazoa to chordata. The text is organized around three themes: body architecture, developmental patterns and life history strategies, and evolution phylogenetic relationships. An undergraduate textbook, but valuable as a general reference.

Ecology and Classification of North American Freshwater Invertebrates. 2nd ed. James H. Thorp and Alan P. Covich, eds. San Diego: Academic, 2001. 950 p. $79.95. ISBN 0126906475. Provides taxonomic keys to the generic level; aquatic insects are largely excluded. Chapters on the remaining groups cover general biology, taxonomy, and ecology.

Feduccia, Alan. *The Origin and Evolution of Birds*. 2nd ed. New Haven, CT: Yale University Press, 1999. 466 p. $65.00, $32.00 (paper). ISBN 0300064608, 0300078617 (paper). A comprehensive review of our present knowledge of the evolution of birds, with many illustrations of bird fossils and reconstructions.

Fish Physiology. W. S. Hoar and D. J. Randall, eds. New York: Academic Press, 1969– . v. Price varies. Each volume covers different aspects of fish physiology, such as the gills, locomotion, reproduction, and so on. There are author, systematic, and subject indexes in each volume. Currently up to volume 16, *Molecular Endocrinology of Fish*.

Gill, Frank B. *Ornithology*. 2nd ed. New York: W.H. Freeman, 1995. 763 p. $87.80. ISBN 0716724154.

Hairston, Nelson G. *Vertebrate Zoology: An Experimental Field Approach*. New York: Cambridge University Press, 1994. 280 p. $49.95 (paper). ISBN 0521417031, 0521427126 (paper).

Handbook of Marine Mammals. Sam H. Ridgway and Richard J. Harrison, eds. New York: Academic Press, 1981– . v. Price varies. Covers the biology and life history of marine mammals, as well as distribution and identification. Vol. 1: walrus, sea lions, fur seals, and sea otter; Vol. 2: seals; Vol. 3: sirenians and baleen whales; Vol. 4: river dolphins and the toothed whales; Vol. 5: first book of dolphins, and Vol. 6: second book of dolphins and porpoises.

Handbuch der Zoologie: Eine Naturgeschichte der Stamme des Tierreiches. 2nd ed. Willy Kükenthal, ed. Berlin, Germany: W. de Gruyter, 1968– . Price varies. Another multivolume treatise covering the animal kingdom, similar to *Traite de Zoologie*, previous. In German. The first edition was completed in 1967. To date, the second contains volumes for the insects and mammals updating the first edition.

Helfman, Gene S., Bruce B. Collette, and Douglas E. Facey. *The Diversity of Fishes*. Malden, MA: Blackwell Science, 1997. 528 p. $69.95. ISBN 0865422567. Ichthyology text for advanced undergraduate and graduate students.

Hickman, Cleveland P., Larry S. Roberts, and Allan Larson. *Integrated Principles of Zoology*. 11th ed. Boston, MA: McGraw-Hill, 2001. 899 p. $94.00. ISBN 0072909617. For undergraduates.

Kardong, Kenneth V. *Vertebrates: Comparative Anatomy, Function, Evolution*. 2nd ed. Boston, MA: WCB/McGraw-Hill, 1998. 747 p. ISBN 0697286541. An advanced undergraduate text.

Martin, Robert Eugene, Ronald H. Pine, and Anthony F. DeBlase. *A Manual of Mammalogy: With Keys to Families of the World*. 3rd ed. Boston, MA: McGraw-Hill, 2001. 333 p. $35.50 (spiralbound). ISBN 0697006433 (spiralbound). As the title suggests, this manual includes keys to mammal families, plus information on studying mammals in the field and in the lab. Also includes lab exercises and information on doing literature searches.

Mayr, Ernst and Peter D. Ashlock. *Principles of Systematic Zoology*. 2nd ed. New York: McGraw-Hill, 1991. 475 p. ISBN 0070411441.

McLelland, John. *A Color Atlas of Avian Anatomy*. Philadelphia, PA: Saunders, 1991. 127 p. $109.00. ISBN 0721635369. Color photographs illustrating bird anatomy, chiefly chicken.

Meglitsch, Paul A. and Frederick R. Schram. *Invertebrate Zoology*. 3rd ed. New York: Oxford University Press, 1991. 623 p. $57.00, $55.00 (paper). ISBN 0195049004, 0195539419 (paper). Undergraduate text; taxonomic treatment of invertebrates.

Microscopic Anatomy of Invertebrates. Frederick W. Harrison, ed. New York: Wiley-Liss. 15 v. 1991– . Price varies. Presents microscopic anatomy of all invertebrate groups, from protozoa to the invertebrate members of the phyla Chordata. The emphasis is on functional morphology.

The Mollusca. Karl M. Wilbur, ed. New York: Academic Press, 1983–1988. 12 v. Price varies. Comprehensive treatise discussing all major aspects of molluscan biology and paleontology.

Moyle, Peter B. and Joseph J. Cech. *Fishes: An Introduction to Ichthyology*, 4th ed. Uppersaddle River, NJ: Prentice Hall, 2000. 612 p. $85. ISBN 0130112828.

Physiology of Fishes. 2nd ed. David H. Evans, ed. Boca Raton, FL: CRC Press, 1998. 519 p. (Marine science series.) $99.95. ISBN 0849384273. For advanced students and practitioners. The second edition has been completely rewritten.

Proctor, Noble S. and Patrick J. Lynch. *Manual of Ornithology: Avian Structure and Function*. New Haven, CT: Yale University Press, 1993. 340 p. $27.50 (paper). ISBN 0300057466, 0300076193 (paper). Designed as a lab manual for course in ornithology. In addition to discussion of avian anatomy, includes chapter on field techniques, including identifying, photographing, and banding birds, as well as how to prepare study skins.

Reproductive Biology of Invertebrates. K. G. Adiyodi and R. G. Adiyodi, eds. New York: Wiley-Liss, 1983– . v. Price varies. Covers all aspects of invertebrate reproduction, currently up to volume 9C, *Progress in Male Gamete Ultrastructure and Phylogeny*.

Ruppert, Edward E. and Robert D. Barnes. *Invertebrate Zoology*. 6th ed. Philadelphia, PA: Saunders College, 1994. 1056 p. $93.50. ISBN 0030266688. For undergraduates. Systematic treatment.

Searfoss, Glen. *Skulls and Bones: A Guide to the Skeletal Structures and Behavior of North American Mammals*. Mechanicsburg, PA: Stackpole Books, 1995. 277 p. $19.95 (paper). ISBN 0811725715 (paper). Contains detailed line drawings of the major bones of common mammals, and also indicates how to identify the bones and infer the habits of animals based on their skeletal anatomy. Also includes information on making a bone collection. Intended for the use of interested laypeople and students.

Simpson, George Gaylord. *Principles of Animal Taxonomy*. New York: Columbia University Press, 1990. (reprint of 1961 ed.). 247 p. $65.00 (paper). ISBN 023109650X (paper).

Traite de Zoologie: Anatomie, Systematique, Biologie. P. P. Grassé, ed. Paris: Masson, 1948– . 17 v. Price varies. Encyclopedic treatise on zoology arranged systematically by taxonomic divisions. In French. Survey of the biology of animals; generous bibliographies. Volumes published out of sequence.

Vaughan, Terry A., James M. Ryan, and Nicholas J. Czaplewski. *Mammalogy*. 4th ed. Fort Worth, TX: Saunders, 2000. 565 p. $92.00. ISBN 003025034X.

Welty, Joel Carl and Luis Baptista. *The Life of Birds*. 4th ed. New York: Saunders, 1988. 581 p. $77.00. ISBN 0030689236.

Wilson, E. O., D. Siegel-Causey, D. R. Brooks, and V. A. Funk. *The Compleat Cladist: A Primer of Phylogenetics Procedures*. Lawrence, KS: Museum of Natural History, 1991. 158 p. (Special Publication, 19.) ISBN 0893380350. A workbook providing a guide to basic phylogenetic techniques.

Vermeij, Geerat J. *A Natural History of Shells*. Princeton, NJ: Princeton University Press, 1993. 207 p. $57.50. ISBN 069108596X. A handy guide to the ecology, evolution, and natural history of the Mollusca, suitable for the general public and students alike.

Zug, George R. *Herpetology: An Introductory Biology of Amphibians and Reptiles*. New York: Academic Press, 1993. 527 p. $59.95. ISBN 0127826203. For advanced undergraduates.

PERIODICALS

Acta Zoologica: An International Journal of Zoomorphology. v. 1– , 1920– . Cambridge, England: Blackwell Science. Quarterly. $518.00. ISSN 0001-7272. Published for the Royal Swedish Academy of Sciences and the Royal Danish Academy of Sciences and Letters. Publishes "original research papers and reviews in the fields of animal organization, development, structure and function, from the cellular level to phylogenetic and ecological levels."

American Journal of Primatology. v. 1– , 1981– . New York: Wiley-Liss. Quarterly. $1,860.00. ISSN 0275-2565. Available electronically. "Reviews scientific articles about primate anatomy, behavior, development, ecology, evolution, genetics, neuroscience, nutrition, physiology, reproduction, systematics, conservation, husbandry, and use in biomedical research."

American Zoologist. v. 1– , 1961– . Lawrence, KS: Allen Press. Bimonthly. $505.00. ISSN 0003-1569. A publication of the American Society of Integrative and Comparative Biology. The journal "publishes invited, original papers derived principally from symposia sponsored by the Society for Integrative and Comparative Biology (formerly the American Society of Zoologists). Papers should be of general interest to comparative biologists."

Annales Zoologici Fennici. v. 1– , 1934– . Helsinki: Finnish Zoological Publishing Board. Quarterly. $30.00. ISSN 0003-455X. In English, French, and German. Publishes original research on ecology, ecological physiology, faunistics and systematics of animals in North European countries, though research from other boreal regions is also considered.

Ardea. v. 1– , 1912– . Groningen, Netherlands: Netherlands Ornithologists' Union. Semi-annual. $45.00. ISSN 0373-2266. The journal of the Netherlands Ornithologists' Union. Publishes "manuscripts reporting significant new findings in ornithology. Emphasis is laid on studies covering ecology, ethology, taxonomy and zoogeography." In English and Dutch.

Auk: A Quarterly Journal of Ornithology. v. 1– , 1884– . Lawrence, KS: American Ornithologists' Union. Quarterly. $70.00. ISSN 0004-8038. The journal of the American Ornithologists' Union. "*The Auk* reports the results of recent research on the ecology, systematics, physiology, behavior and anatomy of birds and includes a world-wide review of current ornithological literature."

Australian Journal of Zoology. v. 1– . Jan. 1953– . Melbourne: CSIRO. Bimonthly. $475.00. ISSN 0004-959X. Available electronically. Publishes "original contributions to all branches of zoology: anatomy, physiology, genetics, reproductive biology, developmental biology, parasitology, morphology, behaviour, ecology, zoogeography, systematics, and evolution. In general, the emphasis is on the fauna of the Australasian region."

Bird Behavior. v. 1– , 1977– . New York: Cognizant Communication. Irregular. $120.00. ISSN 0156-1383. "An international and interdisciplinary journal that publishes original research on descriptive and experimental analyses of species-typical avian behavior, including the areas of ethology, behavioral ecology, comparative psychology, and behavioral neuroscience."

Bird Study. v. 1– , 1954– . Thetford, UK: British Trust for Ornithology. 3/yr. $203.15. ISSN 0006-3657. The official journal of the British Trust for Ornithology. "Original papers on all aspects of field ornithology, especially distribution, status, censusing, migration, habitat and breeding ecology."

Bulletin of the Natural History Museum: Zoology Series. v. 1– , 1949– . London: Intercept. Semiannual. $114.27. ISSN 0968-0470. "Papers in the *Bulletin* are primarily the results of research carried out on the unique and ever-growing collections of the Museum, both by the scientific staff and by specialists from elsewhere who make use of the Museum's resources." Formerly: *Bulletin of the British Museum of Natural History: Zoological Series.*

Bulletin of Zoological Nomenclature. v. 1– , 1943– . London: International Commission on Zoological Nomenclature. Quarterly. $200.00. ISSN 0007-5167. "The Offical Periodical of the International Commission on Zoological Nomenclature." "At present the *Bulletin* comprises mainly applications concerning names of particular animals or groups of animals, resulting comments and the Commission's eventual rulings (Opinions). Proposed amendments to the Code are also published for discussion."

Canadian Journal of Zoology/Revue Canadienne de Zoologie. v. 1– , 1929– . Ottawa: National Research Council of Canada. Monthly. $779.00. ISSN 0008-4301. Available electronically.   Publishes "in English and French, articles, notes, reviews, and comments in the general fields of behaviour, biochemistry, physiology, developmental biology, ecology, genetics, morphology, ultrastructure, parasitology, pathology, systematics, and evolution."

Comparative Biochemistry and Physiology: Part A: Molecular & Integrative Physiology of Comparative Biochemistry and Physiology. v. 1– , 1961– . Tarrytown, NY: Elsevier. Monthly. $ 4,420.00. ISSN 0300-9629.   This section "deals with molecular, cellular, integrative, and ecological physiology." The official journal of the European Society for Comparative Physiology and Biochemistry, the Japanese Society for Comparative Physiology and Biochemistry, Canadian Society of Zoologists (CPB Section), the Society for Experimental Biology, the Society for Integrative and Comparative Biology (Formerly: the American Society for Zoologists), the Australian and New Zealand Society for Comparative Physiology and Biochemistry, the South American Society for Comparative Physiology & Biochemistry (SASCPB), the Russian Physiological Society, and the Chinese Association for Physiological Sciences.

The Condor: An International Journal of Avian Biology. v. 1– , 1899– . Lawrence, KS: Allen Press. Quarterly. $115.00. ISSN 0010–5422.   The journal of the Cooper Ornithological Society. "*The Condor* is an international, scientific journal, publishing outstanding original research in all fields of avian biology."

Copeia. v. 1– , 1913– . Lawrence, KS: Allen Press. Quarterly. $90.00. ISSN 0045-8511.   Published by the American Society of Ichthyologists and Herpetologists. Publishes "results of original research performed by members in which fish, amphibians, or reptiles are utilized as study organisms."

Emu. v. 1– , 1901– . Melbourne: CSIRO. Quarterly. $140.00. ISSN 0158-4197. Available electronically.   The journal of the Royal Australasian Ornithologists Union. Publishes "research in all areas of ornithology. The journal's emphasis is on material relating to the Southern Hemisphere from the Indian Ocean to the mid-Pacific.''

Environmental Biology of Fishes. v. 1– , 19– . Dordrecht, Netherlands: Kluwer Academic. Monthly. $1,375.00. ISSN 0378-1909. Available electronically. ''An international journal which publishes original studies on ecology, life-history, epigenetics, behavior, physiology, morphology, systematics and evolution of marine and freshwater fishes and fishlike organisms.''

Folia Primatologica: International Journal of Primatology. v. 1- , 1963– . Basel, Switzerland: S. Karger. Bimonthly. $441.00. ISSN 0015-5713. Available electronically. In English, French, and German. Publishes in all areas of primatology, including full-length articles and short reports.

Herpetologica. v. 1– , 1936– . Johnson City, TN: Herpetologists League. Quarterly. $95.00. ISSN 0018-0831. Publishes ''original papers dealing largely or exclusively with the biology of amphibians and reptiles; theoretical and primarily quantitative manuscripts are particularly encouraged. Contributors need not be members of the Herpetologists' Union.'' Annual supplements published as *Herpetological Monographs*.

Herpetological Review. v. 1– , 1967– . Hays, KS: Society for the Study of Amphibians and Reptiles. Quarterly. $60.00. ISSN 0018-084X. Published by the Society for the Study of Amphibians and Reptiles. ''A peer-reviewed quarterly that publishes, in English, articles and notes of a semi-technical or non-technical nature.'' An organ for news and opinion.

Ibis. v. 1– , 1859– . Osney Mead, UK: Blackwell Scientific. Quarterly. $295.00. ISSN 0019-0019. The journal of the British Ornithologists' Union. ''*Ibis* publishes original papers and comments in the English language, covering the whole field of ornithology.''

International Journal of Primatology. v. 1– , 1980– . New York: Kluwer. Quarterly. $275.00. ISSN 0164-0291. The official journal of the International Primatological Society. ''A multidisciplinary journal devoted to basic primatology, i.e., to studies in which the primates are featured as such'' including laboratory and field work.

Invertebrate Biology. v. 114– , 1995– . Lawrence, KS: American Microscopical Society. Quarterly. $85.00. ISSN 1077-8306. ''Publishes original research papers and occasional reviews focused on understanding all aspects of the biology of invertebrate animals—metazoans and protozoans, aquatic and terrestrial, free living and symbiotic.'' Formerly: *Transactions of the American Microscopical Society*.

Invertebrate Reproduction and Development. v. 15– , 1989– . Rehovot, Israel: Balaban. Bimonthly. $425.00. ISSN 0792-4259. "The journal publishes original papers and reviews with a wide approach to the sexual, reproductive and developmental (embryonic and postembryonic) biology of the Invertebrata." Formerly: *International Journal of Invertebrate Reproduction and Development.*

Journal für Ornithologie. v. 1– , 1853– . Berlin: Blackwell Wissenschafts-Verlag. Quarterly. Price not available. ISSN 0021–8375. Available electronically. Articles published in German and English, with English summaries. Publishes articles on all aspects of ornithology, especially European birds. The official journal of the Deutschen Ornithologen-Gesellschaft.

Journal of Avian Biology. v. 25– , 1994– . Copenhagen: Munksgaard. Quarterly. $153.00. ISSN 0908-8857. Available electronically. Publishes "the results of empirical and theoretical research within all areas of ornithology, with a certain emphasis on ecology." Formerly: *Ornis Scandinavica.*

Journal of Comparative Physiology A: Sensory, Neural, and Behavioral Physiology. v. 1– , 1924– . Berlin: Springer International. Monthly. $3,189.00. ISSN 0340-7594. Topics covered include "physiological basis of behavior, sensory physiology, neuroethology, neural physiology, orientation, communication, locomotion, hormonal control of behavior."

Journal of Comparative Physiology B: Biochemical, Systemic, and Environmental Physiology. v. 1– , 1924– . Berlin: Springer International. 8/yr. $1,525.00.00. ISSN 0174-1578. Covers "comparative aspects of metabolism and enzymology, metabolic regulation, respiration and gas transport, physiology of body fluids, circulation, temperature relations, endocrine regulation, muscular physiology."

Journal of Crustacean Biology. v. 1– , 1981. Lawrence, KS: Allen Press. Quarterly. $105.00. ISSN 0278-0372. Published by the Crustacean Society. "Provides international exchange of information among persons interested in any aspect of crustacean studies."

Journal of Eukaryotic Microbiology. v. 40– , 1993– . Lawrence, KS: Society of Protozoologists. Bimonthly. $175.00. ISSN 1066-5234. Publishes "original research on protists, including lower algae and fungi, and covering all aspects of such organisms." Formerly: *Journal of Protozoology.*

Journal of Experimental Zoology. v. 1– , 1904– . New York: Wiley-Liss. 18/yr. $4375.00. ISSN 0022-104X. Available electronically. "Published under the auspices of the American Society of Zoologists and the Division of Comparative Physiology and Biochemistry." Publishes "the results of original research of an experimental or analytical nature in zoology, including investigations of all levels of biological organization from the molecular to the organismal.''

Journal of Field Ornithology. v. 51– , 1980– . Lawrence, KS: Association of Field Ornithologists. Quarterly. $45.00. ISSN 0748-4690. The journal ''publishes original empirical and methodological papers dealing with the ecology, behavior, taxonomy, life history, and zoogeography of birds in their natural habitats.'' Also publishes bibliography of current foreign ornithological literature. The abstracts are in English and Spanish. Formerly: *Bird-Banding.*

Journal of Fish Biology. v. 1– , 1969– . London: Academic Press. Monthly. $623.00. ISSN 0022-1112. Available electronically. ''Covers all aspects of fish and fisheries research, both freshwater and marine.''

Journal of Mammalogy. v. 1– , 1919– . Lawrence, KS: Allen Press. Quarterly. $170.00. ISSN 0022-2372. The journal of the American Society of Mammalogists. ''It publishes original research on both terrestrial and marine mammals. All aspects of the biology of mammals, including paleontology, are covered in the worldwide scope of this journal.''

Journal of Molluscan Studies. v. 1– , 1893– . Oxford, England: Oxford University Press. Quarterly. $340.00. ISSN 0260-1230. Available electronically. ''The journal features the newly developing subjects of molecular genetics, cladistic phylogenetics and ecophysiology, but also maintains coverage of ecological, behavioural and systematic malacology.''

Journal of Nematology. v. 1– , 1969– . Lawrence, KS: Allen Press. Quarterly. $110.00. ISSN 0022-300X. The official journal of the Society of Nematologists. Publishes ''original papers dealing with basic, applied, descriptive, or experimental nematology.'' Comes with supplement, *Annals of Applied Nematology.*

Journal of Zoological Systematics and Evolutionary Research. v. 32– , 1994– . Berlin: Blackwell Wissenschaft. Quarterly. Price not available. ISSN 0947-5745. Available electronically. Publishes ''papers on zoological systematics and evolutionary research.'' Articles are published in English, French, and German. Formerly: *Zeitschrift für zoologische Systematik und Evolutionsforschung.*

Journal of Zoology. v. 211– , 1987– . Cambridge, England: Cambridge University Press. Monthly. $795.00. ISSN 0952-8369. Published for the Zoological Society of London. ''The *Journal of Zoology* incorporates the *Proceedings of the Zoological Society of London* (founded in 1830) and the *Transactions of the Zoological Society of London* (founded in 1833). It contains original papers within the general field of experimental and descriptive zoology, and notices of the business transacted at the Scientific Meetings of the Society.''

Malacologia. v. 1– , 1962– . Ann Arbor, MI: Institute of Malacology. Biannual. Price not available. ISSN 0076-2997. ''Nearly all branches of malacology are represented on the pages of MALACOLOGIA.'' Publishes articles in English, French, German, and Spanish.

Mammalia: Journal de Morphologie, Biologie, Systematique des Mammiferes. v. 1– , 1936– . Paris: Museum National d'Histoire Naturelle. Quarterly. $183.00. ISSN 0025-1461. ''*Mammalia* publishes in French and English original notes and research papers dealing with all aspects of mammalian systematics, biology and ecology.''

Marine Mammal Science. v. 1– , 1985– . Lawrence, KS: Society for Marine Mammalogy. Quarterly. $110.00. ISSN 0824-0469. ''Publishes siginificant new information resulting from original research and observations on marine mammals, their form, evolution, systematics, function, husbandry, health, populations, and ecological relationships.'' The official journal of the Society for Marine Mammalogy.

Physiological and Biochemical Zoology: PBZ. v. 72– , 1999– . Chicago, IL: University of Chicago Press. Bimonthly. $377.00. ISSN 0031-935X. Available electronically. ''Original research results represent a variety of areas, including thermoregulation, respiration, circulation, osmotic and ionic regulation, environmental acclimation, evolutionary physiology, and metabolic physiology and biochemistry.'' Sponsored by the Division of Comparative Physiology and Biochemistry of the Society for Integrative and Comparative Biology.

Primates. v. 1– , 1957– . Inuyama, Japan: Japan Monkey Centre. Quarterly. $239.00. ISSN 0032-8332.) ''An international journal of primatology, whose general object is to provide facilities for the elucidation of the entire aspect of primates in common with man.''

Systematic Biology. v. 1– , 1952– . New York: Taylor and Francis. Quarterly. $120.00. ISSN 1063-5157. Available electronically. The journal of the Society of Systematic Biologists. Publishes ''original contributions to the theory, principles, and methods of systematics as well as phylogeny, evolution, morphology, biogeography, paleontology, genetics, and the classification of all living things.'' Formerly: *Systematic Zoology.*

The Wilson Bulletin: A Quarterly Magazine of Ornithology. v. 1- , 1889– . Lawrence, KS: Allen Press. Quarterly. $40.00. ISSN 0043-5643. The journal of the Wilson Ornithological Society. ''The principle focus of the *Bulletin* is the study of living birds, their behavior, ecology, adaptive physiology, and conservation.''

Zoological Journal of the Linnean Society. v. 48– , 1969– . London: Academic Press. Monthly. $643.00. ISSN 0024-4082. Available electronically. Published for the Linnean Society of London. Publishes "original papers on zoology with an emphasis on the diversity, systematics, diversity, interrelationships, and evolution of animals both living and extinct." Formerly: *Journal of the Linnean Society, Zoology.*

Zoological Science: An International Journal. v. 1– , 1984– . Tokyo, Japan: Zoological Society of Japan. Bimonthly. $426.00. ISSN 0289-0003. "Devoted to the publication in English of original and review articles in the broad field of zoology, covering physiology, cell biology, biochemistry, developmental biology, endocrinology, behaviour biology and taxonomy." Formed by the merger of *Annotationes Zoologicae Japonenses* and *Zoological Magazine.* The official journal of the Zoological Society of Japan.

Zoologica Scripta. v. 1– , 1971– . Cambridge, UK: Blackwell Science. Quarterly. $658.00. ISSN 0300-3256. Available electronically. Published for the Norwegian Academy of Science and Letters and the Royal Swedish Academy of Sciences. Publishes "empirical, theoretical, and methodological papers, review articles and debate comments and replies dealing with zoological diversity and systematics."

Zoologischer Anzeiger: A Journal of Comparative Zoology, Morphology, Systematics, and Biogeography. v. 1– , 1978– . Jena, Germany: Gustav Fischer Verlag. Quarterly. $278.00. ISSN 0044-5231. "The journal is devoted to comparative zoology with a special emphasis on morphology, systematics, biogeography and evolutionary ecology."

Zoology: Analysis of Complex Systems. v. 98– , 1994– . Jena, Germany: Gustav Fischer Verlag. Quarterly. $278.00. ISSN 0944–2006. "The journal is open to papers taking an comparative and experimental approache to evolution and development, empirical and theoretical evolutionary biology, evolutionary ecology, physiological ecology, functional morphology, neurobiology, comparative immunology, and to comparative and behavioural physiology (including endocrinology)." Formed by the union of three sections of *Zoologischer Jahrbucher: Abteilung für Allgemeine Zoologie und Physiologie der Tiere, Abteilung für Anatomie und Ontogenie der Tiere,* and *Abteilung für Systematik, Okologie und Geographie der Tiere.*

Zoomorphology: An International Journal of Comparative and Functional Morphology. v. 96– , 1980– . Heidelberg, Germany: Springer International. Quarterly. $1,098.00. ISSN 0720–213X. Available electronically. "The journal will accept original papers based on morphological investigation of invertebrates and vertebrates at the macroscopic, microscopic and ultrastructural levels, including embryologcial studies.''

REVIEWS OF THE LITERATURE

Advances in Parasitology. v. 1– , 1963– . San Diego, CA: Academic Press. Annual. $139.95. ISSN 0065-308X.   ''A series of in-depth reviews on current topics of interest in contemporary parasitology. It includes medical studies on parasites of major influence, such as trypanosomiasis and scabies, and more traditional areas, such as zoology, taxonomy, and life history, which shape current thinking and applications.''

Current Mammalogy. v. 1– , 1987– . New York: Plenum. Irregular. $171.00 (v. 2). ISSN 0899-577X.   Includes review articles on a broad range of subjects dealing with mammalogy. To date, only two volumes have been published, in 1987 and 1990.

Current Ornithology. v. 1– , 1983– . New York: Kluwer. $145.00. Irregular. ISSN 0742-390X.   Publishes ''reviews of topics selected from the full range of current research in avian biology. Topics cover the spectrum from the molecular level of organization to population biology and community ecology.''

Mammal Review. v. 1– , 1970– . Oxford, England: Blackwell Scientific Publications. Quarterly. $316.00. ISSN 0305-1838. Available electronically.   A publication of the Mammal Society. ''It is not intended for the publication of the results of original research but carries reviews of, and reports on, any aspects of mammalogy.''

Reviews in Fish Biology and Fisheries. v. 1– , 1991– . Kluwer. Quarterly. $475.00. ISSN 0960-3166. Available electronically.   Publishes ''review articles on varied aspects of fish and fisheries biology. The subject matters focused on include evolutionary biology, zoogeography, taxonomy, including biochemical taxonomy and stock identification, genetics and genetic manipulation, physiology, functional morphology, behaviour, ecology, fisheries assessment, development, exploitation and conservation.''

Index